BUDDHISM BETWEEN TIBET AND CHINA

Studies in Indian and Tibetan Buddhism

THIS SERIES WAS CONCEIVED to provide a forum for publishing outstanding new contributions to scholarship on Indian and Tibetan Buddhism and also to make accessible seminal research not widely known outside a narrow specialist audience, including translations of appropriate monographs and collections of articles from other languages. The series strives to shed light on the Indic Buddhist traditions by exposing them to historical-critical inquiry, illuminating through contextualization and analysis these traditions' unique heritage and the significance of their contribution to the world's religious and philosophical achievements.

Series Titles Previously Published

Publisher's Acknowledgment

THE PUBLISHER gratefully acknowledges the generous help of the Hershey Family Foundation in sponsoring the publication of this book.

STUDIES IN INDIAN AND TIBETAN BUDDHISM

BUDDHISM BETWEEN TIBET AND CHINA

Edited by Matthew T. Kapstein

WISDOM PUBLICATIONS • BOSTON

Wisdom Publications
199 Elm Street
Somerville MA 02144 USA
www.wisdompubs.org

Library of Congress Cataloging-in-Publication Data

Buddhism between Tibet and China / edited by Matthew T. Kapstein.
   p. cm. — (Studies in Indian and Tibetan Buddhism)
   Includes bibliographical references and index.
   ISBN 0-86171-581-0 (pbk. : alk. paper)
   1. Buddhism—China 2. Buddhism—China—Tibet. 3. Tibet (China—Relations—China. 4. China—Relations—Tibet (China) I. Kapstein, Matthew.
   BQ626.B825 2009
   294.30951–dc22

                                      2008054515

12 12 11 10 09
 5 4 3 2 1

Cover and interior design by Gopa & Ted2. Set in Diacritical Garamond Pro
10.5/13.

Cover photo: The Buddha Dīpaṃkara in a Xi Xia painting (eleventh–twelfth
century). Courtesy of the Thomas J. and Margot Pritzker Foundation.

Wisdom Publications' books are printed on acid-free paper and meet the
guidelines for permanence and durability of the Production Guidelines for
Book Longevity of the Council on Library Resources.

Printed in the United States of America.

This book was produced with environmental mindfulness. We have
elected to print this title on 30% PCW recycled paper. As a result, we
have saved the following resources: 24 trees, 16 million BTUs of energy, 2,078
lbs. of greenhouse gases, 8,623 gallons of water, and 1,107 lbs. of solid waste.
For more information, please visit our website, www.wisdompubs.org. This
paper is also FSC certified. For more information, please visit www.fscus.org.

Contents

Illustrations

Unless otherwise noted, all photographs are by the authors of the chapters in which they appear.

Chapter One

FIG. 1   The bilingual treaty inscription on the border between Tibet and China, flanked by the emblems of the sun and moon. From a series of murals illustrating the Fifth Dalai Lama's *Chronicle* in the Potala Palace. (After *A Mirror of the Murals in the Potala* [Beijing: Jiu zhou tushu chubanshe, 2000]).

FIG. 2   The Tibetan Empire and its neighbors, ca. 820 CE.

FIG. 3   Plan of Anxi Yulin, cave 25. (After *Anxi Yulinku*.)

FIG. 4   The guardian king Virūpākṣa. (Lo Archive, Princeton.)

FIG. 5   The guardian king Virūḍhaka. (Lo Archive, Princeton.)

FIG. 6   At the center of the east wall: Buddha Vairocana. (Lo Archive, Princeton.)

FIG. 7   Tibetan imperial bronze (ca. ninth century) of the Buddha Vairocana. (Bodhicitta Collection, courtesy of Namkha Dorje).

FIG. 8   Four bodhisattvas to Buddha Vairocana's right. (Lo Archive, Princeton.)

FIG. 9   Four bodhisattvas to Buddha Vairocana's left. The panel no longer

Chapter Two

Chapter Three

Chapter Four

Chapter Five

Chapter Six

FIG. 1   Gangkar Rinpoché in Kham. (Courtesy of an anonymous private collection.)

FIG. 2   Gangkar Rinpoché (seated) with an attendant in China. (Courtesy of an anonymous private collection.)

Chapter Seven

FIG. 1   A page of the *Dharma Ocean of the Esoteric Vehicle* (82), with a photograph of Geshé Dorjé Chöpa.

FIG. 2   The diagram of the universe according to Buddhist cosmology, as given in *Secret Scriptures of Tibetan Esoteric Dharma Practices* (1.748).

FIG. 3   The Ngakchen Khutughtu in a photograph published in *Secret Scriptures of Tibetan Esoteric Dharma Practices* (5.99). Notice that the image was printed in reverse.

FIG. 4   The phonetic scheme adopted to transcribe Tibetan in connection with Norlha Khutughtu's teachings. From *Secret Scriptures of Tibetan Esoteric Dharma Practices* (2.385).

FIG. 5   A sheet depicting twelve divinities, from the *Five Hundred Buddha-Images of the Esoteric Tradition*.

FIG. 6   A talisman with *dhāraṇī*s in Sanskrit and Tibetan scripts, together with Chinese transcription. From the works of Sun Jinfeng in *Secret Scriptures* (4.508).

Chapter Nine

FIG. 1   Khangsar Rinpoché and lama Nenghai. (Courtesy of Duobaojiang monastery.)

FIG. 2   The new memorial stūpa dedicated to Nenghai at Wutaishan.

Chapter Ten

Preface

URING THE SPRING of 1996, as I was leaving my apartment in
New York's Morningside Heights to buy bagels one Sunday morning, I came across a group of Chinese university students, all wearing T-shirts emblazoned with the characteristic lotus, book, and sword emblem of the Tibetan Sakyapa order. I stopped to chat with them and learned that they were from many different places in China, Taiwan, and Southeast Asia, but were in the States to pursue graduate studies, mostly in the sciences and engineering. They gathered to meditate together on Sundays in the apartment of a fellow student who was connected with the Sakyapa center in Singapore. In fact, they had no idea that Buddhism was a subject taught at Columbia University, where I was then teaching, or that any member of the faculty would have heard of the Sakyapa, in their terms the "white sect" of Tibetan Buddhism. Their bemused expressions as they answered my questions betrayed evident puzzlement about my interest.

As a frequent visitor to Nepal, where Tibetan monastic development has been much assisted by donors from Singapore and Taipei, Hong Kong and Kuala Lumpur, it had become clear to me during the 1970s and 80s that there was very considerable ethnic Chinese involvement in Tibetan religious activity. I was therefore aware that prosperous Chinese had emerged among the major contemporary patrons of Tibetan Buddhist institutions and teachers, no doubt surpassing in this regard the contributions of either Hollywood heroes or Microsoft moguls. Nevertheless, my chance meeting with the overseas Chinese students that morning underscored for me the degree to which religious relationships between Tibet and China had remained invisible even to those of us who were engaged in the academic study of Tibetan or Chinese Buddhism. Was recent Chinese participation in Tibetan Buddhism, I found myself wondering, the fruit of cultural relations developed over centuries, or the product of uniquely contemporary circumstances?

Certainly, the painful political reality of the modern Tibet-China relation has skewed our perspectives and inhibited inquiry in this area. Though
several pioneering scholars in Chinese and Tibetan studies did contribute
to our knowledge of Chinese Buddhism in Tibet and Tibetan Buddhism in
China—one thinks above all here of Berthold Laufer, Ferdinand Lessing, Paul
Demiéville, Rolf Stein, and Herbert Franke—further research along these lines
has languished until very recently, particularly in the United States. Scholars
involved in East Asian Buddhist studies tended to see Tibet as a world apart,
while those of us working on Tibetan Buddhist materials have often had our
professional homes in departments of South Asian studies and have therefore
encouraged our students to focus on something called "Indo-Tibetan Buddhism." As a result, the sustained religious contact between Tibet and China
throughout the past thirteen hundred years has remained obscure.

Nevertheless, in a few areas Tibeto-Chinese religious relations have
aroused recent scholarly interest. The best example, no doubt, is the story
of Tibet's contact with China's Chan Buddhist traditions during the Tang
dynasty. Following the lead of Paul Demiéville's path-breaking investigations
of documents found at Dunhuang, there has been intensive research on this
topic during the past few decades, above all by Buddhist scholars in Japan.
Mention, too, must be made of recent art historical scholarship, which has
shed new light on the cross-pollination of Chinese and Tibetan Buddhist
styles and techniques. The works that have aroused the greatest attention in
this context were executed in Chinese imperial ateliers during the Ming and
Qing dynasties, or by Tibetan painters during the same epoch, notably in
far eastern Tibet, where the use of diaphanous washes inspired by Chinese
brushwork served to convey the sense of aetherial luminosity cultivated in
Tibetan tantric meditation. As the present book seeks to demonstrate, however, the interrelationship of Tibetan and Chinese Buddhist traditions was
more widely ramified, and has proven more enduring, than even these two
very rich areas of study reflect by themselves.

In the introductory chapter I provide a brief historical overview of the religious connections between Tibet and China, surveying the contents of the
volume as a whole. The eleven chapters that follow offer case-studies span-
ning more than a millennium, beginning with the study of a Sino-Tibetan
cave temple in Gansu created under the Tibetan empire during the early
ninth century and continuing down to H.H. the Dalai Lama's 1997 visit to
Taiwan. In between, pertinent examples of the intersections of Tibetan and
Chinese Buddhism during the Yuan (or Mongol), Ming, Qing (or Manchu),
and Republican periods are considered in depth. These studies are all based

on extensive original research and field work, presented here for the first time. Together they demonstrate that Buddhism not only served to mediate relations between Tibetan ecclesiastical powers and the Chinese imperial court, as has often been assumed to be the overarching concern that defined the relationship, but that it also provided what was in effect a cultural lingua franca, through which Chinese, Tibetans, and frequently others as well might, despite their many differences, interact on common, sanctified ground.

As mentioned above, Tibeto-Chinese religious relations have been in large measure neglected by scholars formed after the Second World War. This reflects in part practical limitations on research due to political restrictions, for, from the foundation of the People's Republic in 1949 to the end of the Cultural Revolution in 1978, it was generally impossible for scholars from abroad to pursue Tibetan studies in China. Those interested in Tibet necessarily turned their attention to the Himalayan regions and to Tibetan refugee communities in South Asia. It was only during the 1980s that renewed prospects for Tibetological research in China gradually began to emerge. Hence, recent advances in the study of Tibeto-Chinese relations have been largely due to researchers who have entered the field during the past quarter century. This generational transition is reflected in the composition of the present volume: whereas a few of the contributors are senior figures in Tibetan studies, most belong to the post–Cultural Revolution generation of Tibetanists. Some in fact completed—and several of them published—their dissertations while this book was in preparation. The gradual opening of China to Tibetological research has been in these cases a fundamental, enabling condition, essential to the development of their scholarship, so that their work reflects a new interrogation of Tibeto-Chinese cultural relations, as well as access to newly available materials and sources.

The present volume had its genesis in the meetings of the Tibetan and Himalayan Religions Group of the American Academy of Religion that I organized in 2000. The contributions of the particpants on that occasion— Karl Debreczeny, Rob Linrothe, Paul Nietupski, Gray Tuttle, Zhihua Yao, Abraham Zablocki, and myself—became the point of departure from which the book grew. I wish to thank Professors Janet Gyatso and Georges Dreyfus, then the chairs of the Tibetan and Himalayan Religions Group of the AAR, and the entire Steering Committee of the Group, for their encouragements, and in particular Professor Robert Gimello, who thoughtfully offered the response to the original presentations. I am grateful, too, to Ester Bianchi, Fabienne Jagou, Carmen Meinert, and Elliot Sperling, who graciously consented to join this project after it was already in progress.

The painting that adorns the cover of this volume, generously made available for reproduction here by the Margot and Thomas J. Pritzker Foundation, depicts the Buddha Dīpaṃkara poised literally between Tibetan and Chinese worlds. Probably of Xi Xia provenance, it reflects the unique station of the Xi Xia kingdom of the eleventh-twelfth centuries as a cultural crossroads, where Indian, Chinese, and Tibetan Buddhists contributed to the protection and edification of the realm. In the cartouche to the Buddha's upper right, we read Dīpaṃkara's name in Tibetan, while the same is inscribed in Chinese in the cartouche to his left. As realised here, the Buddha mediates between opposing worlds, a role that he will assume throughout the pages that follow as well.

For their invaluable assistance at the University of Chicago with the preparation of this work for publication, I am grateful to Rachel Lindner and Susan Zakin for their careful editing of the text, and to You Hong for her help with the Chinese glossary. I acknowledge, too, the contribution that the China Committee of the University's Center for East Asian Studies has made over the years to my ongoing research concerning Tibetan affairs in China. Tim McNeill and MacDuff Stewart at Wisdom Publications, together with the editors of the series Studies in Indian and Tibetan Buddhism, have my profound thanks for the characteristic enthusiasm with which they welcomed this project. And kudos are due to Laura Cunningham and Tony Lulek for the expertise and efficiency with which they shepherded the work through the final stages of its production.

Matthew T. Kapstein
Vaishakh, 2008

Contributors

ESTER BIANCHI (Ph.D., University of Venice and the École Pratique des Hautes Études, Paris) teaches at the University of Florence. She is the author of *The Iron Statue Monastery: "Tiexiangsi," A Buddhist Nunnery of Tibetan Tradition in Contemporary China* (Leo S. Olschki Editore).

KARL DEBRECZENY (Ph.D., The Unversity of Chicago) is curator at the Rubin Museum of Art, New York. His dissertation, on Sino-Tibetan art from late Yuan to early Qing, is being prepared for publication.

FABIENNE JAGOU (Ph.D., École des Hautes Études en Sciences Sociales, Paris) is a member of the École Française d'Extrême-Orient. She has written *Le 9ᵉ Panchen Lama (1883-1937): Enjeu des relations Sino-Tibétaines* (École Française d'Extrême-Orient).

MATTHEW T. KAPSTEIN (Ph.D., Brown University) teaches at the University of Chicago and the École Pratique des Hautes Études (Paris). He is the author and editor of several books, including *The Tibetans* (Blackwell).

ROB LINROTHE (Ph.D., The Unversity of Chicago) teaches at Skidmore College. His many publications include *Ruthless Compassion: Wrathful deities in Early Indo-Tibetan Esoteric Buddhist Art* (Serindia).

CARMEN MEINERT (Ph.D., Bonn University) is research fellow at the University of Hamburg. She has published widely on such topics as the relationship between Chinese Chan and Tibetan Buddhism, most recently in *Contributions to the Cultural History of Early Tibet* (Brill).

PAUL NIETUPSKI (Ph.D., Columbia University) teaches at John Carroll University. He is the author of *Labrang Monastery: A Social and Political History of a Tibetan Buddhist Monastery on the Sino-Tibetan Frontier, 1709–1958* (forthcoming).

ELLIOT SPERLING (Ph.D., Indiana University) teaches at Indiana University. His publications include *The Tibet-China Conflict: History and Polemics* (East-West Center).

GRAY TUTTLE (Ph.D., Harvard University) teaches at Columbia University. He is the author of *Tibetan Buddhists in the Making of Modern China* (Columbia University Press).

ZHIHUA YAO (Ph.D., Boston University) teaches at the Chinese University of Hong Kong. He has written *The Buddhist Theory of Self-Cognition* (Routledge).

ABRAHAM ZABLOCKI (Ph.D., Cornell University) teaches at Agnes Scott College. He is the author of the forthcoming *The Global Mandala: The Transformation of Tibetan Buddhism in Exile* (University of Hawai'i Press).

Transcription Conventions

TIBETAN NAMES and terms are given in the main body of this book using simplified phonetic spellings.[1] In this system, most of the letters used may be pronounced according to their common English values. The exceptions to this rule are:

ö and *ü*, which are pronounced as in German
e and *é*, which are both pronounced like the French *é*, the accent being used here only at the end of words, to remind readers that a final *e* is not silent: e.g., *dorjé*
z and *zh*, which resemble *s* and *sh*; thus, *Zhalu* sounds rather like *Shalu*

In some instances, however, we have retained established conventional spellings for proper names, instead of phonetic transcriptions: for instance, Gyantse instead of phonetic Gyeltsé (for literary Tibetan *rgyal-rtse*), and Derge for Degé (lit. *sde-dge*). The Tibetan spelling list given at the end of the book provides the exact literary orthography for all Tibetan names and terms used herein. The literary orthography has also been employed in the following cases: some names, terms and titles given only parenthetically; transcriptions of inscriptions; and all Tibetan expressions given in the endnotes to each chapter.

For Chinese, we use the standard Pinyin transcriptions throughout, though for a small number of proper names, such as Chiang K'ai-shek, we retain the forms that will be recognized by most anglophone readers. Similarly, for persons and places in Taiwan, we employ the standard spellings accepted in the Republic of China. A Chinese glossary supplies the characters corresponding to the transcriptions used in the text.

1 As described in the article by David Germano and Nicolas Tournadre, "THDL Simplified Phonetic Transcription of Standard Tibetan": (http://www.thdl.org/xml/showEssay.php?xml=/collections/langling/THDL_phonetics.xml).

Introduction: Mediations and Margins

Matthew T. Kapstein

D
URING THE 1980S, Buddhist Studies entered a new and dynamic
phase characterized in part by the abandonment of an earlier dis-
position to think of "Buddhism" as a singular term. Gone was the
emphasis on core beliefs and doctrines, with respect to which local developments had often been regarded as late modifications, wholesale deviations,
or else the simple resurgence of non-Buddhist, indigenous cultural strata.
Against this, local Buddhisms were henceforth to hold pride of place and
Buddhism as such was no more. In many respects, this shift of orientation
proved to be a salutory one, as the standard in the field came to be defined
increasingly by historically and culturally nuanced studies of persons, artifacts, schools of thought, and events in particular places and times. Where
Buddhist Studies may have once seemed a narrowly circumscribed and relatively coherent field, it began to transform rapidly into a cluster of specialized disciplines devoted above all to regional Buddhisms: Indian, Chinese,
Korean, Tibetan, Japanese, Sri Lankan, Thai, and so forth.

That the field did not just dissolve into various subunits, however, is perhaps due to two countervailing research trajectories that in quite different
ways reached beyond national bounds. On the one hand, continuing work
on Buddhist scriptural collections required, in many contexts, taking the
canonical languages, rather than individual nations or ethnicities, as the
meaningful units of analysis, thereby giving due allowance to the transnational character of the major classical Buddhist languages and the literature
preserved in them. At the same time, a variety of collaborative, comparative
studies on such topics as Buddhist hermeneutics, soteriology, mnemonics,
hagiography, and mortuary beliefs, among others, continued to underscore
the importance of key themes linking the varied local traditions, even if the
treatment of those themes appeared at times to be notably diverse.[1]

Despite the very rich veins for reflection that have been tapped through these three predominant research areas—canonical Buddhist Studies, local or national Buddhist Studies, and comparative Buddhist Studies—there are significant issues that have nonetheless tended to be overlooked, given this configuration of the field. With the notable exception of so-called "Silk Road Studies,"[2] the role of Buddhism in the cultural, economic, and political relations among different peoples and nations seems a particularly remarkable area of neglect. Though work in this area has by no means been altogether absent—in particular, recent contributions on Sino-Indian relations by Liu Xinru and Tansen Sen testify to the considerable prospects for such research[3]—it is surprising that it has remained marginal to the orientations that in recent years have been most visible in Buddhist Studies overall. Nevertheless, it is indisputable that Buddhism has historically proven to be a powerful medium whereby political, economic, technological,[4] and artistic ties have been negotiated and forged, besides its role in fostering religious life more narrowly conceived.

In seeking to encourage scholarship that examines Buddhism as a bridge among differing Asian milieux, the present volume offers a collection of original studies of Buddhism in the history of cultural and political relations between Tibet and China. Outside of the special value these contributions may have for students of these two lands in particular, it may be hoped that the work as a whole will be also seen as a stimulus to pursue the investigation of Buddhism in Asian "cross-border" relations more generally.

Part of the interest in examining this history through the Buddhist lens stems from the sheer tenacity of the Tibet-China relationship. From the period of their first serious encounters during the seventh through ninth centuries, when the two nations rivaled one another in their quest for imperial supremacy in large parts of Inner Asia, and down to the present day, when Tibet exists as an independent state no more but maintains nevertheless a unique cultural identity both in China and the world at large, Buddhism has regularly provided a vital connecting medium, whether during times of antagonism or of fraternity. Throughout this long history the role of religion in mediating Tibet-China relations has evolved together with the relationship itself, but, at the same time, we will find in the pages that follow that certain patterns and themes regularly reappear, despite marked overriding trends of change.

In its legendary representation, the Buddhist link between Tibet and China was first forged with an imperial wedding that served as a pretext for Buddhist proselytism. Contemporary historians may continue to debate whether the Tibetan monarch Songtsen Gampo (d. 649/650) did in fact adopt the foreign religion and whether his Chinese bride, the Tang princess Wencheng (d. 680), really played any role in its transmission. But for the Buddhists of Tibet, it is an article of faith that the precious image of the Lord Śākyamuni in Lhasa, the most revered object of Tibetan pilgrimage, was brought to their land from China by a royal emanation of the female buddha Tārā, on the occasion of her wedding to their king, a mortal manifestation of the bodhisattva Avalokiteśvara himself.[5] For the Tibetan religious imagination, therefore, Sino-Tibetan relations had as their first and most valued offspring nothing less than Tibetan Buddhism itself.

Whatever may be eventually decided regarding the true historical record of Buddhism in Tibet during Songtsen Gampo's reign, the story nevertheless contains a symbolic measure of truth; for soon Buddhism did come to enjoy a significant role in the mediation of Chinese and Tibetan affairs, providing a common framework of religious meaning for two powers that were otherwise frequently at war. It was a role that, variously adapted and readapted with the passage of time, remained vital until the early years of the twentieth century, influencing religion, politics, and art among Tibetans, Chinese, and their neighbors, leaving a legacy that is still visible, even now when the forms of religio-political culture characteristic of medieval and early modern Central and East Asia have long since passed from the scene.

After the mid-ninth-century collapse of the old Tibetan kingdom, however, Tibet never regained the political and military dominance it had enjoyed during its two centuries of imperial glory. In effect, the Tibetan presence in Inner Asia came to depend increasingly upon the symbolic power of the Tibetan Buddhist clergy, conceiving of itself (and frequently becoming similarly conceived by others) as the truest heir to the great traditions of Buddhism in India, upholding the intellectual prowess of the major monastic universities, especially Nālandā and Vikramaśīla, and supercharged with the mastery of occult ritual and yoga derived from the teachings of the renowned Indian tantric adepts, the *mahāsiddhas*.[6] It was, and for many remains, a unique and heady blend of rational and charismatic authority, and as such proved compelling to the rulers of the Western Xia, Mongol Khans, Chinese and Manchu emperors, and Republican-era warlords alike.

One important aspect of the Tibet-China tie therefore concerns the formation of what is often termed the patron-priest, or donor-chaplain, relationship (Tib. *mchod yon*). As it is generally understood, this was a form of reciprocity in which the religiously symbolic consecration conferred on China's rulers by Tibetan hierarchs was recompensed by the rulers through material and worldly empowerment—in the form of gifts, grants, titles, and seals of authority. However, the relationship was considerably more nuanced than this short explanation suggests and, when studied with care with respect to particular examples, it is frequently found to turn on the necessity of resolving or at least managing specific political or economic sources of conflict, whether actual or potential. The exchange relationship, moreover, served as a vehicle promoting commercial and cultural interactions extending often far beyond the official inventories of initiations bestowed or gifts received. In short, the patron-priest relationship provided a focal point around which a broad range of issues informing Tibet-China connections were arrayed.[7]

Besides this, as suggested by reference to the Xia and the Mongols above, Tibetans and Chinese were by no means the only parties to the Tibet-China Buddhist relationship. A variety of peoples, and sometimes states, in Inner Asia and throughout the Sino-Tibetan Marches (i.e., the border regions extending from Yunnan in the south to the Qinghai-Gansu frontiers in the north) acted as mediators in the rapports of the Tibetans and Chinese. At one time or another, the actual agents or beneficiaries of Tibet-China exchange may have been Tangut, Naxi, Monguor or Yi, and many others as well. The multi-ethnic character of Tibet-China relations in particular permitted China, whose bureaucracy and court often struck outsiders as impenetrable and monolithic, to greet its Inner Asian others with an exceptionally pluralistic face.

The various forms of religious relations that unfolded between Tibet and China through the centuries found their most concrete embodiments in the many material artifacts—the products of extensive architectural, artistic and publication projects—in which the conjunction of the two realms was physically manifested through various forms of production. These range from mid-Tang-period murals in Dunhuang, to celebrated monuments such as the Yuan-dynasty "White Stūpa" in Beijing, to the Ming Yongle editon of the Tibetan Buddhist canon and the elaborate Tibetan tantric formulae adorning the tomb of the Manchu Qianlong Emperor, together with countless more.[8] Through detailed consideration of three prominent religious edifices, the first part of this book, "Sites of Encounter," examines key issues in China-Tibet relations during the periods in which they were constructed.

In "The Treaty Temple of the Turquoise Grove," I suggest that the famous temple of Dega Yutsel, well-known from the documents discovered by M.A. Stein and P. Pelliot at Dunhuang, can in fact be identified with a still-surviving cave-temple in the complex at Anxi Yulin, not far from Dunhuang in Gansu province. Beyond this, however, the chapter urges a broadening of the investigation of the place of Buddhism in relations between Tibet and Tang China. In recent scholarship one notes a tendency to emphasize the question of "Tibetan Chan" while neglecting other aspects of Chinese Buddhism that were transmitted to Tibet during this time, as well as the role of Buddhism in managing often hostile political relations. Here, it is the presence of Buddhism in Tibet-Tang diplomacy that forms the background for understanding the construction of the Treaty Temple.

The second chapter, "The Commissioner's Commissions," by Rob Linrothe, discusses the puzzling Yuan-period site of Feilaifeng in Hangzhou (in modern Zhejiang province), whose Tibetan tantric icons have frequently been understood as evidence of cultural confrontation on the part of the Mongol administration in their relation to the Chinese. Linrothe argues that the controversial Tangut official Yang Lianzhenjia, the principal patron of the site, was perhaps seeking to act with greater nuance than his detractors have generally recognized, and sought not confrontation, but accommodation between Chinese and Tibetan forms of Buddhism.

"Dabaojigong and the Regional Tradition of Ming Sino-Tibetan Painting in the Kingdom of Lijiang," by Karl Debreczeny, introduces us to the powerful role of Tibetan religious culture among the Naxi of Yunnan. Debreczeny's careful art historical analysis of the sixteenth-century temple of Dabaojigong demonstrates the equal importance of Tibetan patronage to the West and Chinese patronage to the East, as allegiances to both were clearly inscribed in the iconographic program of the temple, as well as in the characteristic style of its paintings, despite the evident Tibetan Buddhist affiliation that determined Dabaojigong's overall religious orientations.

In all three of these studies, spatial intermediacy—the frontier settings of Anxi Yulin and Dabaojigong, and the frontier origins of Yang Lianzhenjia—plays a determining role in the formation of cultural ties. This theme serves, too, to introduce the principal concerns of the following section, "Missions from the Frontiers," which turns to examine the manner in which Tibetan clergy from frontier regions acted to facilitate relations between Chinese and Tibetan civilizational spheres. While our subject matter here is in some respects continuous with that of the previous section—for patronage and the development of specific sites are key themes here as well—the agency of religious professionals in relation to worldly powers is now the chief concern.

In chapter 4, "Tibetan Buddhism, Perceived and Imagined, along the Ming-Era Sino-Tibetan Frontier," Elliot Sperling examines three Tibetan monasteries in the Qinghai and Sichuan borderlands that received the support of the imperial court and whose hierarchs sometimes traveled to the capital. What emerges from his investigation is that these connections served the Ming as a form of cultural diplomacy, helping to secure or stabilize the sometimes unruly regions in which direct Chinese authority could be exercised only at great expense and with much difficulty. This is perhaps most striking in the third of his case-studies, concerning the district of Songpan: the Tibetan clerics honored here as "imperial preceptors" were in fact representatives not of the major Buddhist orders, but of Tibet's autochthonous Bön religion. Together with Karl Debreczeny's contribution, this chapter also underscores the importance of Ming-period trade between China and far eastern Tibet. In both of these chapters, it is clear that the sponsorship of religion, whether by the Chinese court or local rulers, at once reflected the prosperity realized through this trade and was intended to secure conditions favoring its continuation and increase.

The patron-priest relationship may be said to have reached its quintessential form during the Ming dynasty.[9] This was in large measure due to the fact that the Ming had few pretensions to rule Tibetan regions, and much less Tibet itself, which is to say that their concerns stressed ceremonial propriety, trade, and the security of China's frontiers. Their precedent, moreover, was in most respects taken over by the Qing. Unlike their predecessors, however, the Qing eventually did seek to exercise authority in Tibet, but unlike the Yuan-dynasty Mongols they came to this reluctantly; although the Manchus overthrew the Ming in 1644, they asserted their rule in Tibetan regions sporadically throughout the eighteenth century.[10] Moreover, as Paul Nietupski shows in "The 'Reverend Chinese' (*Gyanakpa tshang*) at Labrang Monastery," in many places Qing control of Tibetan areas remained nominal at best. Under these circumstances, the continuing ceremonial relations with Tibetan and Mongol Buddhist hierarchs served as an important means to maintain an imperial presence in places remote from the real centers of Manchu power, while, for the hierarchs involved in such relations, the favor of the court advanced their religious mission, and helped to consolidate the position of the monasteries as the effective administrative centers in Qinghai, Gansu, and elsewhere.

The reciprocal relations that were forged between China's rulers and Tibetan ecclesiastical figures, often themselves from border districts, did not come to an end with the fall of the Qing dynasty in 1911. During the Republican period, Chinese interest in Tibetan Buddhism in fact expanded, and the Tibetans who traveled to China to teach, perform rituals, and raise support continued often to be natives of Amdo (Qinghai/Gansu) or Kham (Sichuan/Xikang).[11] One of the most outstanding examples of such missionaries was Bo Gangkar Rinpoché (1893–1957), the subject of Carmen Meinert's study in chapter 6. Indeed, Gangkar Rinpoché's career, which continued into the early days of the People's Republic, mirrors the changing political

circumstances of his time in which he served different political agendas and
was eventually made part of the communists' "civilizing project" in cultural
Tibet. In his story we may even detect the beginnings of the globalization of
the Tibet-China Buddhist relation that will be discussed in greater detail in
the final chapter. For Gangkar's Chinese disciples included such figures as
Zhang Chengji (C.C. Chang) and Charles Luk, whose English translations
of Tibetan and Chinese Buddhist classics opened new vistas to students of
Asian religions in the West.[12]

Although, from the Yuan-period on, Tibetan clerics often traveled to
China on pilgrimage conferring Buddhist teachings on highly placed persons, up to and including the emperors themselves, and received honors and
riches in return, one is struck that so few Chinese Buddhists appear to have
ventured to visit Tibet. The contrast is all the more striking when we recall
that large numbers of Indian and Nepalese Buddhist scholars and adepts did
journey to Tibet, combining pilgrimage, teaching activity, and fundraising
while there.[13] The Chinese may have been put off in part by the Tibetans' barbaric reputation, fostered in Confucian dynastic historiography. Or they may
equally have been dissuaded by the hardship always associated with travel in
the mountains and deserts to the west. Or they may have been convinced that
theirs was an infinitely superior civilization, so that they had nothing of value
to gain from their rude neighbors on the high plateau.[14] Whatever their reasons, however, one of the striking shifts that occurs after the 1911 fall of the
Manchu dynasty is the arrival of numbers of Chinese pilgrims and travelers
in Tibetan Buddhist milieux. "The Modern Chinese Discovery of Tibetan
Buddhism" considers important facets of this development, together with
the parallel expansion of Tibetan Buddhist teaching and practice in the Chinese heartland itself.

One of the attractions of Tibetan Buddhism for the Chinese was certainly the charismatic allure of esoteric tantric ritual, promising both
worldly and spiritual blessings. Strongly associated with the consecration
bestowed by leading lamas upon the emperors, Tibetan tantrism in China
was inevitably tied to images of imperial power. In a sense, this upsurge of
interest and involvement in this form of religion can be seen to directly correspond to the political change whereby the promise of democracy made
every citizen a potential king. Facets of the Republican-period advancement
of Tibetan esotericism in China may be found in the tracts and practice
manuals published in small editions during the 1930s and 1940s on behalf
of practitioners, and later reissued in several collections. Chapter 7, "Translating Buddhism from Tibetan to Chinese" by Gray Tuttle, examines these

documents, identifying the Tibetan and Chinese figures involved and the settings in which they worked. It is noteworthy that we find evidence here, together with the contributions of well-known religious figures such as Nor-lha Khutughtu (1876–1936), of the activity of Chinese Buddhist laymen and the formation among them of lay Buddhist associations.

A quite different aspect of the early-twentieth-century Chinese turn to Tibetan Buddhism is described in Zhihua Yao's chapter, "Tibetan Learning in the Contemporary Chinese Yogācāra School." For the figures discussed here, chiefly the scholars Lü Cheng (1896–1989), Fazun (1902–1980), and Han Jingqing (1912–2003), Tibetan traditions were of interest primarily for preservation of the Indian Buddhist philosophical legacy. In other words, their concerns lay in the areas of Buddhist philology and doctrinal studies, and not (or at most only secondarily) in the approaches to ritual and esotericism that were often accentuated in Tibetan Buddhist practice. As Yao argues, the representatives of contemporary Chinese Yogācāra—much like the partisans of so-called "Critical Buddhism" in recent Japanese Buddhist intellectual circles—have used Indian and Tibetan sources as the basis for launching a critique of developments in East Asian Buddhisms that, they believe, stray far from the teaching's intent.[15]

Throughout much of its history, Tibetan Buddhism has sought to promote a viable synthesis of philosophical insight and ritual virtuosity, even if the ideal of a perfectly harmonious balance of the two has often been only imperfectly realized. Accordingly, while some Chinese Buddhists found inspiration in Tibetan tantra, and others in scholasticism, still others strove to realize the embracing synthesis that many Tibetans themselves took to be the appropriate goal. Particularly noteworthy in this respect was Neng-hai Lama (1886–1967), whose life and teachings are examined in chapter 9 by Ester Bianchi. Though he was a colleague of Fazun early on, Nenghai was clearly more influenced by the charismatic dimensions of Tibetan Buddhism than was the former. And Nenghai, moreover, proved to be an exceptionally charismatic figure in his own right, launching a monastic movement directly in the line of the Tibetan Gelukpa order that remains a dynamic force in mainland Chinese Buddhism today.

Taken together, therefore, the third section of this collection points to two rather different projects informing contemporary Chinese engagements in Tibetan Buddhism. As seen in Zhihua Yao's study, there has been a scholarly, philological interest in Tibetan Buddhist scriptural sources as offering a repository in which the materials needed to make up lacunae in the Chinese Buddhist tradition may be found. The interest, in this case, is largely in

Tibetan translations of Indian doctrinal and philosophical works, not in contributions that Tibetans themselves may have made to the elaboration of Buddhist teaching and practice. Over and against this tendency, some Chinese seekers have responded primarily to the attractions of Tibetan approaches, involving mastery of tantric ritual and yoga, and culminating in spiritual attainment, rather than intellectual refinement, as the major Buddhist goal. Nevertheless, it would be a mistake to insist on too radical a division. In the cases, for instance, of prominent modern Chinese masters such as Fazun and Nenghai, both interests are indeed represented in their lives and writings; what differs is the relative balance they found between scholastic and ritual engagements. What is perhaps most striking is that throughout the twentieth century Chinese Buddhists were moved, as Zhihua Yao puts it, "to search for a more authentic Buddhism, and so looked to Buddhism's Indian origins and its Tibetan transmissions in order to find this."

It may appear that, taking this and the preceding sections together, we seek to confirm the widespread impression that prior to the fall of the Qing the only real involvement of the Chinese in Tibetan Buddhism was limited to court circles, and that it was not until the Republican era that common Chinese Buddhist believers began to be engaged in Tibetan traditions as well. Without denying that there may be some element of truth to this, it is important to note, nevertheless, that we do find occasional indications of grassroots Chinese participation in Tibetan Buddhism during the Qing, and some suggestions along these lines even before. Evidence of this may be seen in Paul Nietupski's comments on the "Chinese lamas" of Labrang Monastery in Gansu Province. And in the biography of the Qianlong Emperor's renowned preceptor Changkya Rölpé Dorjé (1717–1786), we find it recorded that he attracted masses of the Chinese faithful during his visits to Sichuan and Wutai shan, besides his activities as a teacher of the Chinese Buddhist sangha.[16] All things considered, it seems more prudent to admit that the question of Chinese popular involvement in Tibetan Buddhism during the dynastic period has not yet been adequately examined, and remains a topic of interest for future research.[17]

If Tibetan Buddhism in modern China has evolved into an at once popular and learned movement among Chinese Buddhists, the political dimension of the relationship has by no means diminished with the passage of time. Since the seventeenth century, when the Great Fifth Dalai Lama was received in the court of the Manchu Shunzhi Emperor, no single figure has been more emblematic of this connection than the person of the Dalai Lama. The final section of this book, "China and the Dalai Lama in the Twentieth Century," therefore turns to this center of religio-political gravity in studies of China's troubled rapport with Tibet's chief hierarch at the beginning and end of the last century.

Although the Fifth was the sole Dalai Lama to visit the court before the Thirteenth did so in the early twentieth century, the preeminence of the emperor's patronage of the Dalai Lamas was always upheld. Therefore, following his flight from Lhasa in advance of the arrival of the Younghusband expedition in 1904, and his failure to secure the aid he sought from the Jebtsundampa Khutughtu of Urga, Outer Mongolia, the Thirteenth turned to the traditional relationship with the Qing court in his quest for support and arrived in Beijing for imperial audiences in 1908. These events form the focus for Fabienne Jagou's chapter on "The Thirteenth Dalai Lama's Visit to Beijing in 1908." While it has long been clear that the outcome of his meetings with the Emperor Guangxu and Dowager Cixi was not satisfactory, and that the major result of the meeting was the Dalai Lama's determination not to solicit the Chinese court again, Jagou shows that the actual events were marked by considerable complexity reflecting, as she says, "the difficulty each faced in establishing relationships in an environment of political transition." Part of this complexity stemmed from the Dalai Lama's twin spiritual and temporal roles, and the felt need, on the part of the court, to nuance their response to his separate functions somewhat differently. The overriding impression, nevertheless, as noted by the Chinese monk Guankong in remarks cited by Tuttle, was that "the court had not been courteous to the Dalai Lama." The Dalai Lama's answer was his declaration of independence from China as soon as the dynasty fell.

The fall of the Qing, therefore, marked a complete rupture in the ceremonial religio-political bond linking the Dalai Lama to the Chinese ruler, a break whose legacy has had important and continuous implications for Tibet-China relations ever since. For, on the one hand, Chinese rulers, whether Republican or Communist, have been eager to affirm the continuity of a special connection of some kind, but without being committed to maintaining intact the dynastic-period pattern of the patron-priest relation. At the same time, from the position of the Thirteenth's successor, Tenzin Gyatso, the Fourteenth Dalai Lama, the struggle, following China's assertion of its sway over Tibet in 1951, has been to find a new formula for the Tibet-China relationship, one that guarantees the integrity of Tibet. As in the past, part of the complexity of the issue stems from the Dalai Lama's simultaneous political and spiritual roles.

These matters are brought into clear focus in connection with the present Dalai Lama's visits to the Republic of China, that is, Taiwan, discussed in the closing chapter by Abraham Zablocki. Although both the Dalai Lama and Taiwan authorities have been keen to emphasize the non-political nature of his tours of the island, Beijing has of course regarded them as a poorly disguised pretext for collusion among "splittists." And conflicted political reactions have been expressed in Taiwan itself, precisely owing to disagreements there between those who would opt for Taiwanese independence and those favoring, at least rhetorically, eventual reunification with the Mainland. Moreover, given extraordinary levels of interest in Tibetan Buddhism in recent years, the Dalai Lama was welcomed on Taiwan with all the acclaim and excitement that usually attends visiting pop stars. When we recall, too, that Taiwan is not the only part of the Chinese world in which Tibetan Buddhism is currently in vogue—evidence of this may be found throughout overseas Chinese communities and indeed in the PRC as well—it becomes clear that the ancient religious relationship of Tibet and China has entered the new century still full of vigor, together with the unceasing and profound contestation it has come to entail.

*　*　*　*

While the cases studied in the present volume touch on many significant aspects of the role of Buddhism in Tibet-China relations throughout the span of their history, it cannot be said that all issues of importance are treated here. (The puzzling question of pre-modern Chinese popular involvement in Tibetan Buddhism, for instance, has been already noted above.) Accordingly, in the interest of indicating possible directions for future research, let us note some of the outstanding matters not treated at length in this book.

It will be apparent in these pages that Tibet-China ties exhibited a characteristic asymmetry: what Tibet imparted to China was religious goods, while what China bestowed in return was material. This seems to have been the case when Lama Pakpa was named State Preceptor by Khubilai Khan in the thirteenth century, when the Fifth Karmapa hierarch consecrated the Yongle Emperor in the fifteenth, and it remains so when the present Dalai Lama draws eager devotees to fill sports stadiums in Taiwan today. But, although this general impression reflects a measure of truth, it must be nuanced by taking into account the opposite trends, that is, the material goods Tibet provided to China, and the spiritual goods China bequeathed to Tibet.

The first of these points is indeed touched upon at various points throughout this book, particularly in the first five chapters. Connections with Tibet were essential to China both for reasons of security along the western frontiers and lucrative trade-relations. Following the ninth-century collapse of the old Tibetan empire, and given the frequent absence of a single stable polity in Tibet, major monasteries, with their networks of hierarchs and branch temples, often served as the essential guarantors of the peace in endemically strife-filled regions. Simply put, as E. Sperling shows, it was sometimes more cost-effective to sponsor a lama than to send in an army. But the Tibetans also had wealth that was desirable in China. Besides some rare luxury items, such as musk and medicinal plants, there was an almost insatiable demand, particularly during the Ming, for Tibetan-bred horses. Although the abundant trade in tea and horses that arose was not in itself religious in nature, Tibetan monastic establishments often facilitated and sometimes directed this commerce, above and beyond the purely ceremonial rapports they forged, which nevertheless supported the cordiality and trust through which trade is often best able to thrive.

China, moreover, was rich in spiritual goods of its own, and these were not wholly unknown to Tibetans. Two aspects of the Chinese Buddhist legacy in Tibet that have been relatively well studied are Chan Buddhism and Chinese Buddhist aesthetics, particularly in the art of painting. But these were not the only elements of the Chinese Buddhist tradition to have made their way to Tibet.

Though overshadowed by the gigantic proportions of Tibetan translations of Indian Buddhist texts, a significant body of Buddhist works was nevertheless translated from Chinese, and some of these have had a considerable influence in Tibet. Included among them are major sūtras such as the Mahāyāna version of the *Mahāparinirvāṇasūtra* and the Tang-period esoteric master Yijing's *Suvarṇaprabhāsottamasūtra*. Another translation from the Chinese which left a deep imprint on Tibetan Buddhist thought was the Korean Wŏn-ch'ŭk's massive commentary on the *Sandhinirmocanasūtra*, a work that came to be much discussed in Tibetan scholastic philosophy from the early fourteenth century on. Moreover, the early organization of the Tibetan Buddhist canon, as reflected in the extant imperial-period catalogues, may have been indebted in some respects to the models provided by the Chinese Tripiṭakas.[18]

Part of the Chinese literary legacy to Tibetan Buddhism consisted, too, in apocryphal scriptures, in which peculiarly Sinic iterations of Buddhist thought were often articulated and promoted. Some, like the *Vajrasamādhisūtra*, advanced varieties of Chan teaching, while others, including the Chinese traditions of the arhat Mulian (Maudgalyāyana), sought to achieve a seamless integration of the virtue of filial piety with the renunciation extolled on the Buddhist path.[19] It is possible, too, that one of the Chinese Buddhist apocryphal scriptures translated into Tibetan, the *Datong fangguang jing*, inspired a Tibetan abridgement that in later legend became renowned as the first Buddhist sūtra to appear in Tibet, a tale that may be read, perhaps, as a veiled acknowledgement of the early Tibetan debt to Chinese Buddhism.[20] Though most translations of Chinese scriptures into Tibetan date to the Tang dynasty, some activity along these lines continued long after, and as late as the eighteenth century we find the Qianlong Emperor sponsoring Tibetan translations of Chinese sūtras.[21]

Together with the project of translating Chinese Buddhist works, the Tibetans also, to varying degrees, imported Chinese traditions in branches of learning including historiography, divination, and medicine.[22] Though these generally lie beyond the purview of Buddhism, strictly speaking, among the Tibetans they were nevertheless developed and maintained within a predominantly Buddhist milieu. Thus, for example, as the eponymous fount of *Yijing* lore and its related mantic traditions, Confucius is renowned in Tibet as a Chinese emanation of the bodhisattva Mañjuśrī.[23]

The association of China with the bodhisattva of wisdom points to another important area in which the presence of China was felt in the spiritual life of Tibet: pilgrimage. Tansen Sen has recently summarized the findings of several generations of scholars regarding the processes whereby China was transformed into a Buddhist sacred land, on a par in many respects with India, and the importance of the identification of the Five Terrace Mountain, Wutai shan, as Mañjuśrī's earthly abode, in these developments.[24] Though Tibet, like China, came to be regarded as part of the sacred geography of the Buddhist world, it differed in that its geography was recognized almost exclusively by adherents to Tibetan forms of Buddhism. The major Tibetan holy site to achieve international recognition was Mt. Kailash, in far western Tibet, and this was as Śiva's abode in the cosmography of South Asian Hindus.[25] Chinese Buddhist pilgrims therefore generally felt no need to travel to Tibet in order to fulfill their spiritual aims.[26]

Tibetan Buddhists, however, did honor the sacred places of China, and Wutai shan above all. As early as the eighth century, if we are to believe the extant versions of the *Testament of Ba* (*Sba bzhed*), Tibetan envoys to China journeyed to the holy mountain to meet with the bodhisattva; and a tenth-century Tibetan manuscript from Dunhuang records the pilgrimage of an Indian guru who traveled through Tibet on his way to China, where he visited the mountain. The Tibetan veneration of Wutai shan, once aroused, never lapsed: in the eighteenth century, we find Changkya Rölpé

Dorjé writing a pilgrim's guide to the mountain; in the early twentieth, the Thirteenth Dalai Lama visits and teaches there; and late in the twentieth century, on the heels of the Cultural Revolution, the famed "treasure-revealer" (*gter ston*) Khenpo Jikpün discloses a new *sādhana* of Mañjuśrī in the course of his pilgrimage. Wutai shan and its traditions, in short, became integral to and amplified by the culture of Buddhist pilgrimage in Tibet.[27]

Finally, we may add, that numbers of Chinese divinities were absorbed into Tibetan Buddhist traditions, sometimes as local protectors in the frontier regions of Qinghai and Sichuan. An example that has become well known in the anthropological literature is the divinity of the terrain of Trika (*Khri ka'i yul lha*), in Amdo (Qinghai), who is most frequently identified with the Chinese god of war, Guan Yu.[28] And the Chinese god of longevity, Shouxing, is ubiquitous in the Tibetan Buddhist world under the designation of "Long Life Man" (*Mi tshe ring*).[29]

All this being said, however, it remains evident that Chinese traditions of Buddhist study and practice have had much less of an active presence among Tibetans, at least following the waning of the Tibetan Chan movement of the eighth–ninth centuries, than has Tibetan Buddhism in China. Certainly, we would be astounded today (or at almost any time over the past thousand years!) to find young Tibetans taking up an engagement in Pure Land Buddhism or Huayen with the enthusiasm that many of their Chinese counterparts show for Dzogchen meditation or Tibetan tantric rituals. Despite this, however, those aspects of Chinese religions that became known in Tibet certainly merit continuing and thorough historical study, if we are to fully comprehend the richness and extent of Tibet's and China's mutual engagements.

At the start of this introduction, I proposed that the relations among differing Buddhist societies have been a neglected area of inquiry. The exercise we have begun here needs now to be considered in connection to what is already known, and what we might yet learn, of Buddhism in the relations between any pair, or group, of Buddhist realms. For once we understand more clearly than we do at present the role of the religion not just in the commerce of religious ideas, but in all forms of material and cultural exchange, and political and military connections as well, only then will have begun to grasp the full measure of Buddhism in the history of Asia. In large part, this is a task for the future. The horizons for Buddhist Studies in relation to traditional and contemporary Asian patterns of exchange remain quite wide open.

Notes

1 Of course, despite the "transnational" character of the major canonical collections, important questions may be raised concerning their actual role in the life of particular Buddhist communities. An influential statement of the problem may be found in Steven Collins, "On the Very Idea of the Pali Canon," in *Journal of the Pali Text Society* 15 (1990): 89–126. Examples of the comparative studies I allude to include: Donald Lopez, Jr., ed., *Buddhist Hermeneutics* (Honolulu: University of Hawai'i Press, 1988); Robert Buswell and Robert Gimello, eds., *Paths to Liberation* (Honolulu: University of Hawai'i Press, 1992); Janet Gyatso, ed., *In the Mirror of Memory* (Albany: State University of New York Press, 1992); Juliane Schober, ed., *Sacred Biography in the Buddhist Traditions of South and Southeast Asia* (Honolulu: University of Hawai'i Press, 1997); Bryan J. Cuevas and Jacqueline I. Stone, eds., *The Buddhist Dead: Practices, Discourses, Representations* (University of Hawai'i Press, 2007).

2 Art historical research has been particularly noteworthy here. See, for instance, the magisterial work of Marylin M. Rhie, *Early Buddhist Art of China and Central Asia*, 2 vols., Handbuch der Orientalistik, Vierte Abteilung, China 12 (Leiden/Boston: Brill, 1999–2002). Broad surveys will be found in Deborah E. Klimburg-Salter, ed., *The Silk Route and the Diamond Path: Esoteric Buddhist Art on the Trans-Himalayan Trade Routes* (Los Angeles: UCLA Art Council, 1982); Agnès Takahashi et al., eds., *Sérinde, Terre de Bouddha: dix siècles d'art sur la Route de la Soie* (Paris: Réunion des musées nationaux, 1995); and Susan Whitfield with Ursula Sims-Williams, eds., *The Silk Road: Trade, Travel, War and Faith* (London: British Library, 2004).

3 Xinru Liu, *Ancient India and Ancient China: Trade and Religious Exchanges, AD 1–600* (Delhi: Oxford University Press, 1988); Tansen Sen, *Buddhism, Diplomacy, and Trade: The Realignment of Sino-Indian Relations, 600–1400* (Honolulu: University of Hawai'i Press, 2003).

4 John Kieschnick, *The Impact of Buddhism on Chinese Material Culture* (Princeton: Princeton University Press, 2003), offers a pioneering study in this area.

5 Questions surrounding the actual religious life of the Tibetan court under Songtsen Gampo and his successors have been much debated in recent scholarship. Among the major contributions: Ariane Macdonald, "Une lecture des Pelliot tibétain 1286, 1287, 1038, 1047, et 1290: Essai sur la formation et l'emploi des mythes politiques dans la religion royale de Sroṅ-bcan sgam-po," in Ariane Macdonald, ed., *Études tibétaines dédiées à la mémoire de Marcelle Lalou* (Paris: Adrien Maisonneuve, 1971), pp. 190–391; Rolf A. Stein, "Tibetica Antiqua III: A propos du mot *gcug-lag* et de la religion indigène," *Bulletin de l'École Française d'Extrême-Orient (BEFEO)* 74 (1985): 83–133; idem., "Tibetica Antiqua IV: La tradition relative au début du Bouddhisme au Tibet," *BEFEO* 75 (1986): 169–196. For traditional Tibetan representations of Songtsen Gampo's adoption of Buddhism, see, in particular, Per K. Sørensen, *Tibetan Buddhist Historiography: The Mirror Illuminating the Royal Genealogies* (Wiesbaden: Harrassowitz Verlag, 1994); and my *The Tibetan Assimilation of Buddhism: Conversion, Contestation and Memory* (Oxford University Press, 2000), ch. 8.

6 The formation of Tibetan Buddhism during the first centuries of the second millennium CE is studied in depth, with special reference to the Sa-skya-pa order, in

Ronald M. Davidson, *Tibetan Renaissance* (New York: Columbia University Press, 2005). A more general survey will be found in my *The Tibetans* (Oxford: Blackwell, 2006), ch. 4.

7   See, especially, David Seyfort Ruegg, *Ordre spirituel et ordre temporel dans la pensée bouddhique de l'Inde et du Tibet* (Paris: De Boccard, 1995).

8   Among relevant studies of these and related topics, see chapters one through three below, and Sarah Elizabeth Fraser, *Performing the Visual: The Practice of Buddhist Wall Painting in China and Central Asia, 618–960* (Stanford: Stanford University Press, 2004); Heather Karmay, *Early Sino-Tibetan Art* (Warminster: Aris and Phillips, 1975); Anning Jing, "The Portraits of Khubilai Khan and Chabi by Anige (1245–1306), a Nepali Artist at the Yuan Court," in *Artibus Asiae*, vol. 54, no. 1/2 (1994): 40–86; Marsha Weidner, ed., *Latter Days of the Law: Images of Chinese Buddhism 850–1850* (Honolulu: University of Hawai'i Press, 1994); Patricia Ann Berger, *Empire of Emptiness: Buddhist Art and Political Authority in Qing China* (Honolulu: University of Hawai'i Press, 2003); and Françoise Wang-Toutain, "Les cerceuils du tombeau de l'empereur Qianlong," *Arts Asiatiques* 60 (2005): 62–84.

9   Though the Ming court's patronage of Tibetan Buddhism was much contested in China itself, as may be seen in the recent study by Weirong Shen 沈衞榮, "'Accommodating Barbarians from Afar': Political and Cultural Interactions between Ming China and Tibet," *Ming Studies* 56 (2007): 37–93.

10 The major study remains Luciano Petech, *China and Tibet in the Early XVIIIth Century* (Leiden: Brill, 1972); but see now, too, Peter C. Perdue, *China Marches West: The Qing Conquest of Central Eurasia* (Cambridge: Harvard University Press, 2005), which, though focusing on the region that is today Xinjiang, has much to offer to the study of early-Qing-period Tibet. For an introduction, see my *The Tibetans*, pp. 127–55.

11 These developments are studied in Gray Tuttle, *Faith and Nation: Tibetan Buddhists in the Making of Modern China* (New York: Columbia University Press, 2005).

12 The former has written a short, but fascinating, account of his sojourn in Kham, that has generally escaped the notice of scholars and appeared in Richard A. Gard, ed., *Buddhism* (New York: George Braziller, 1961), pp. 196–202. Though Luk (Lu K'uan Yü) wrote extensively on Chinese, rather than Tibetan, Buddhism, his indebtedness to Gangkar Rinpoché is clearly reflected in the dedication found in his translation of *The Śūraṅgama Sūtra* (*Leng Yen Ching*) (London/New York: Rider & Co., 1966).

13 On the early-first-millennium relation with India and Nepal, see now, in particular, Ronald M. Davidson, *Tibetan Renaissance*.

14 This may be seen in one of the rare memoirs of a Chinese monk, Xu Yun (1840–1959), who visited Tibet as a pilgrim prior to the Republican period. His experiences during the years 1888–1889 are summarized in Upāsaka Lu K'uan Yü (Charles Luk), trans., *Empty Cloud: The Autobiography of the Chinese Zen Master Hsu Yun* (Rochester, NY: Empty Cloud Press, 1974), p. 20: "During my march from Szechwan province to Tibet which took a year, I walked by day and rested at night. Often I did not meet a single man for days when I climbed the mountains or crossed the streams. The birds and beasts differed from those in China and the customs there were also different from ours. The Sangha order did not observe the monastic rules and most of the monks ate beef and mutton. They were divided into sects distinguishable by

their red and yellow robes. I thought of the days of the Jetavana assembly and could not refrain from tears (at the sight of this artificial division)."

15 Of course, the teaching of "buddha-nature" (*buddhatva*, i.e. *tathāgatagarbha*), castigated by the proponents of "Critical Buddhism" as *dhātu-vāda* ("essentialism"), is very well represented in the Tibetan Buddhist traditions, though it was perhaps more contested in traditional circles than were analogous teachings in East Asian Buddhist traditions.

16 Thu'u-bkwan Chos-kyi nyi-ma, *Lcang-skya Rol-pa'i rdo-rje'i rnam-thar* (Lanzhou: Gansu Nationalities Press, 1989), pp. 205–6.

17 A study that begins to undertake this may be found in Gray Tuttle, "An Unknown Tradition of Chinese Conversion to Tibetan Buddhism: Chinese Incarnate Lamas and Parishioners of Tibetan Buddhist Monasteries in Amdo," in Avrum Ehrlich, ed., *Negotiating Identity Amongst the Religious Minorities in Asia* (Leiden: Brill, forthcoming).

18 The major surviving imperial catalogues of the canon are the *Ldan-kar-ma* and the *'Phang-thang-ma*, which have been edited and studied in: Marcelle Lalou, "Les Textes Bouddhiques au Temps du Roi Khri-sroṅ-lde-bcan," *Journal Asiatique* 241/3 (1953): 313–353; Rta-rdo, ed., *Dkar chag 'phang thang ma. Sgra sbyor bam po gnyis pa* (Beijing: Mi rigs dpe skrun khang, 2003); and Georgios Halkias, "Tibetan Buddhism Registered: A Catalogue from the Imperial Court of 'Phang thang," *The Eastern Buddhist* 36, nos. 1–2 (2004): 46–105. Though there has been much speculation about Chinese influence on these inventories, the question has never been systematically examined.

19 For discussions of these materials, with further references to scholarship on Chinese apocrypha as known in Tibet, see my *The Tibetan Assimilation*, ch. 5; and "The Tibetan *Yulanpen jing* 佛說盂蘭盆經," in Matthew T. Kapstein and Brandon Dotson, eds., *Contributions to the Cultural History of Early Tibet* (Leiden: Brill, 2007), pp. 211–237.

20 Rolf A. Stein, "Tibetica Antiqua I: Les deux vocabulaires des traductions Indo-tibétaine et Sino-tibétaine dans les Manuscrits de Touen-houang," *BEFEO* 72 (1983): 149–236, esp. pp. 218–19. The Tibetan version is known as the *Spang skong* (= *fangguang*) *phyag brgya pa* and is said to have fallen from heaven to land on the palace of the ancient king Lha tho tho ri.

21 Refer to Léon Feer, *Le Sûtra en Quarante-deux Articles: Textes Chinois, Tibétain et Mongol* (Paris: Maisonneuve, 1868); and A. von Stael-Holstein, "The emperor Ch'ien-lung and the larger *Śūraṃgamasūtra*," in *Harvard Journal of Asiatic Studies* 1 (1936): 136–146.

22 On transmissions of Chinese historiography, see Yoshiro Imaeda, "L'identification de l'original chinois du Pelliot tibétain 1291—traduction tibétaine du Zhanguoce," *Acta Orientalia (Hungarica)* 34/1–3 (1980): 53–68; and Tsuguhito Takeuchi, "A Passage from the *Shih chi* in the *Old Tibetan Chronicle*," in Barbara Nimri Aziz and Matthew Kapstein, eds., *Soundings in Tibetan Civilization* (New Delhi: Manohar, 1985), pp. 135–146. The Chinese legacy in Tibetan medicine is summarized in Fernand Meyer, *Gso-ba rig-pa: Le système médical tibétain* (Paris: CNRS, 1981), pp. 66–71. A major example of Chinese-inspired divination traditions will be found in Gyurme Dorje, trans., *Tibetan Elemental Divination Paintings: Illuminated*

Manuscripts from The White Beryl of Sangs-rgyas-rgya-mtsho (London: John Eskenazi and Sam Fogg, 2001).

23   Kong-sprul Yon-tan-rgya-mtsho [= Blo-gros-mtha'-yas], *Shes-bya kun-khyab mdzod* (Beijing: Minorities Press, 1981), vol. 1, p. 598.

24   Sen, *op. cit.*, pp. 76–86.

25   Refer to Nathan S. Cutler, "Mt. Kailāsa: Source for the Sacred in Early Indian and Tibetan Tradition" (Ph.D. dissertation, California Institute of Integral Studies, 1997).

26   Though refer to n. 14 above.

27   For the version in the *Sba bzhed*, refer to Sba Gsal snang (attributed), *Sba bzhed ces bya ba las Sba Gsal gnang gi bzhed pa bzhugs* (Beijing: Mi rigs dpe skrun khang, 1980), pp. 7–8. On the Tibetan Dunhuang manuscript, see my "New Light on an Old Friend: PT 849 Revisited," in *Tibetan Buddhist Literature and Praxis: Studies in Its Formative Period, 900–1400*, in Ronald Davidson and Christian Wedemeyer, eds. (Leiden: Brill, 2006), pp. 9–30; on Lcang skya, see Gray Tuttle, "Gazetteers and Golden Roof-tiles: Publicizing Qing Support of Tibetan Buddhism at Wutai Shan" (forthcoming); on the Thirteenth Dalai Lama, refer to Elliott Sperling, "The 13th Dalai Lama at Wutai Shan: Exile and Diplomacy" (forthcoming); and on Mkhan po 'Jigs phun, see David Germano, "Re-membering the Dismembered Body of Tibet," in *Buddhism in Contemporary Tibet: Religious Revival and Cultural Identity*, ed. Melvyn C. Goldstein and Matthew T. Kapstein (Berkeley: University of California Press, 1998).

28   Katia Buffetrille, "Qui est Khri ka'i yul lha? Dieu tibétain du terroir, dieu chinois de la littérature ou de la guerre? Un probleme d'identité divine en A mdo," in Katia Buffetrille and Hildegard Diemberger, eds., *Territory and Identity in Tibet and the Himalayas: PIATS 2000: Tibetan Studies, Proceedings of the Ninth Seminar of the International Association for Tibetan Studies, Leiden 2000* (Leiden/Boston: Brill, 2002).

29   It may be noted in this connection that the Sde dge par khang ("Derge Printery") illustration of Mi tshe ring includes a text based on the discourses of Si tu Paṇ chen Chos kyi 'byung gnas (1699–1774), and derived from his travels in Yunnan, explaining something of the cult of Shouxing in Chinese religion.

Part I
Sites of Encounter

~

1: The Treaty Temple of the Turquoise Grove*

Matthew T. Kapstein

Buddhism Between Tibet and Tang

THE RISE of the Tibetan empire during the first half of the seventh
century corresponded closely to that of the Tang dynasty in China
(618–907). With the expansion of their respective realms, it was not
long before the two powers became rivals, particularly in Gansu and Xinjiang, in which both sought to control the routes and realms linking China to
the West.[1] The opposition of China and Tibet, however, served at the same
time to strengthen cultural relations between them. Tibet, like many other
Inner Asian powers, found resources in Chinese material and spiritual culture that contributed to its own civilization-building project, while China
for its part made strategic use of cultural diplomacy as a means to domesti-
cate the surrounding peoples, who so often threatened China's northern and
western frontiers.[2] Buddhism, due in large measure to its place in the international culture of the time, came to play a distinctive role in the process
of bilateral "confidence-building" such as this was pursued according to the
diplomatic codes of the day.

Tibetan traditional accounts, of course, lay greatest stress in this context
upon the religious activities of the Chinese princesses sent to Tibet.[3] It was
the princess Wencheng (in Tibet from 641, d. 680), the bride of the Tibetan
monarch, or *tsenpo*, Songtsen Gampo (ca. 605–650), who most fascinated
the later Tibetan imagination, and to whom was attributed the Tibetan adoption of Buddhism in large measure. Nevertheless, current scholarship has not
supported the elaborate legends that were built around her and her marriage
to Songtsen Gampo.[4] Though, like other Tang princesses who were sent to wed
foreign rulers, she may be considered as a cultural emissary whose mission was
conceived as a type of soft diplomacy, the extant record does not indicate that
religious affairs, or political developments relating to religion, were strongly

influenced by her. In 648, some years after her arrival in Tibet, the Tibetan military intervened in support of the Tang envoy to India, Wang Xuance, who had come under attack by an usurper to the throne of Magadha. As Wang's mission in India involved visits to the major sites associated with the Buddha's life, this perhaps suggests that Buddhism was not altogether over-looked in Sino-Tibetan relations during Wencheng's lifetime. But she had no discernable role in connection with these events and the Tibetan action is reported without any reference to religion at all.[5] During the last decades of Princess Wencheng's life, when as queen dowager she apparently was still involved in official correspondence with the Tang court,[6] Tibet entered into direct competition with China for the conquest and control of the strategi-cally vital regions that are today Xinjiang and Gansu provinces. It was Tibet's expansion in these territories, where Buddhism had been long established, that intensified its contact with the Indian religion, while simultaneously cre-ating an ongoing pressure on Tang China to come to terms with a neighbor that aggressively threatened its prerogatives to the West.[7]

If Wencheng remains an elusive figure, her "niece," Princess Jincheng (in Tibet from 710, d. 739) left a more clearly defined imprint upon the early reli-gious history of Tibet.[8] Married to the *tsenpo* Tri Detsukten (704–755) when he was a six-year-old child, she is credibly recorded to have energetically pro-moted Buddhism among the Tibetan nobility, inviting monks from Khotan (which by this time was a Tibetan colonial territory) to found the first sangha in Central Tibet. This endured until her death during a plague epidemic, one of the results of which was a reaction against the presence of the foreign reli-gion and the expulsion of the Khotanese monks. During the middle decades of the eighth century, Buddhist activity in Tibet was reduced to the point that it all but vanished.[9]

Buddhism therefore, despite its presence in cultural affairs, played no appreciable role in Tibet-Tang relations during the period preceding the rebellion of An Lushan (755–757), nor did it enter into diplomacy proper, specifically the management of matters of war and peace between the two states. The imperatives that periodically drove Tibet and China to the bar-gaining table to discuss prisoner exchanges, the adjudication of frontiers, and the cessation of hostilities, did not, up to this point, involve the Bud-dhist religion so far as the extant record allows. Though a partial excep-tion might be made for the expedition of 648 on behalf of Wang Xuance, even here it is not at all clear that the Tang emissary's mission to tour the Indian Buddhist sites influenced the Tibetan decision to lend him armed support. Buddhism, in fact, entered into Tibeto-Chinese formal relations

only during the last quarter of the following century, at some point following the *tsenpo* Tri Songdetsen's 762 conversion and subsequent adoption (ca.
779) of it as the Tibetan state religion. As this prima facie suggests, it was
the transformation of the Tibetan religious constitution that drove subsequent changes in diplomatic practice. This, at least, is the conclusion that
may be drawn from the two versions of the *Tang shu* ("Tang Annals"), in
their reports of the treaties negotiated by China with Tibet in 762, 783 and
821/822 respectively.[10] Concerning the first, the *Old Tang Annals* (*Jiu Tang
shu*) offers this account:

> In the first year of the reign of Suzong (756),[11] in the first month,
> on the *jiachen* day, a Tibetan mission arrived at the court to ask for
> peace. The Emperor ordered the ministers of state, Guo Ziyi, Xiao
> Hua, Zhang Zunqing, and others to entertain them at a banquet,
> and to proceed to the Guangzhaisi [a Buddhist temple], to con-
> clude a treaty, to be sworn by sacrificing three victims and smear-
> ing the lips with the blood. As it had never been customary to
> conduct affairs in a Buddhist temple, it was proposed that on the
> morrow, at the Honglusi [the Foreign Affairs Bureau], the rite of
> smearing blood on the lips be accomplished in accordance with
> the rites of the Tibetans. This was allowed.[12]

It is notable here that, while the possibility of swearing to the treaty in a
Buddhist temple is mentioned, it is explicitly refused. And that this incident
occurred in the aftermath of the Tibetan *coup d'état* of 755, in which Tri Detsukten was deposed and assassinated, the succession passing to his thirteen-year-
old son Tri Songdetsen, is significant as well. These events, which unfolded
during the same tumultuous years as did the An Lushan rebellion in China,
marked the culmination in Tibet of a ministerial rejection of the Buddhism
that the former Tibetan ruler had favored. So it is perhaps not surprising,
under the circumstances, that during the period still prior to Tri Songdetsen's
rehabilitation of Buddhism, the Tibetan nobles charged with negotiations
would not have displayed a particular affinity with the foreign faith.[13]

Although Tri Songdetsen may have been personally drawn to Buddhism
as early as 762, it was not until his promotion of it as a state religion during
the late 770s that China seems to have taken notice of its growing role in
Tibet. The first reference to this in Chinese records dates to 781, when the
decision was made to dispatch what was envisioned as a regular embassy of
Buddhist missionaries to Tibet.[14] This corresponds to the apparent upsurge

of interest in Chinese Buddhism shown by the Tibetan court following the conquest of Dunhuang.[15] An oath-taking ceremony that accompanied the treaty of 783 unambiguously included a Buddhist rite, although the program overall remained primarily a sacrificial covenant. As the description that we find in the *Old Tang Annals* provides us with one of the best general accounts of Tang-Tibetan diplomatic usage, it merits citation at length:

> In the first month of the fourth year (February–March 783), the imperial decree was issued that Zhang Yi and Shang Jiezan should make a sworn compact at Qingshui. . . . It had at first been agreed that the Chinese should sacrifice an ox, the Tibetans a horse, but Yi, ashamed of the alliance with the Tibetans, wished to depreciate the rites, and said to Jiezan: "The Chinese cannot cultivate the ground without oxen, the Tibetans cannot travel without horses, I propose therefore to substitute a sheep, pig and dog as the three victims." Jiezan consented. But there were no pigs outside the barrier, and Jiezan determined to take a wild ram, while Yi took a dog and a sheep. These victims were sacrificed on the north of the altar, the blood mingled in two vessels and smeared on the lips. The sworn covenant [in the Chinese text] was: "The Tang possess all under heaven, wherever are the footprints of [Emperor] Yu, and as far as boats and chariots can go there is no one that does not obey them. Under successive sovereigns their fame has increased, and its years have been prolonged, and the great empire of its sovereigns extended, till all within the four seas listen to its commands. With the Tibetan *tsenpo* it has made matrimonial alliances to strengthen the bonds of neighborly friendship and unite the two countries, and the sovereigns have been allied as uncle and nephew for nearly two hundred years. Meanwhile, however, in consequence of minor disagreements, their good relations have been broken off by war, so that the borderland has been troubled and without a quiet year. The Emperor on his recent accession compassionated his black-haired people, and sent back the enslaved captives to their own country, and the Tibetan nation has exhibited good feeling and agreed to a mutual peace. Envoys have gone and returned, carrying in succession sovereign orders, putting a stop to secret plotting or the dispatch of chariots of war. They have, with the view of making the covenant of the two countries lasting, proposed to use the ancient sworn treaty, and the government, resolved to give

rest to the natives on the border, have alienated their ancient territory, preferring good deeds to profit, and have made a solemn treaty in accordance with the agreement. [The text at this point includes a geographical description of the frontiers.] With regard to the places not included in the covenant, wherever the Tibetans have garrisons the Tibetans shall keep, wherever the Chinese have garrisons the Chinese shall keep, each retaining its present possessions, and not seeking to encroach on the other. The places that heretofore have not been garrisoned shall not have troops stationed in them, nor shall walled cities be built, nor land cultivated. Now the generals and ministers of the two countries having been commissioned to meet, and having fasted and purified themselves in preparation for the ceremony, proclaim to the gods of heaven and earth, of the mountains and the rivers, and call the gods to witness that their oath shall not be broken. The text of the covenant shall be preserved in the ancestral temple, with a duplicate in the official archives, and the officers in charge according to the regulations of the two nations shall always keep it."

Jiezan also produced a sworn covenant which he did not put into the pit where only the victims were buried. After the conclusion of the sworn ceremony, Jiezan proposed to Yi to go into a tent of the Buddha at the southwest corner of the altar to burn incense and make oath. When this was finished, they again ascended the altar, when they drank wine and both gave and received ceremonial presents, each offering the products of his country, as a mark of liberal friendship. Finally they returned home.[16]

Significantly, it is the Tibetan Shang Jiezan[17] who in this narrative proposes that the oath be sworn in a "tent of the Buddha" located to the southwest of the altar (a placement that seems intentionally homologous with the geographical position of India relative to China). In all events, as Imaeda suggests, the refusal of the Tibetan to deposit his copy of the covenant in the sacrificial pit may imply a disinclination toward this rite, for which the oath sworn before the Buddha was intended to compensate.[18] In sum, during the final decades of the eighth century, though China may have to some degree supported Buddhist missionary activity in Tibet, in the context of more formal diplomatic practice a distinction was emerging between adherence to a sacrificial covenant, which had been the ancient practice of both the Chinese and the Tibetans, and an oath sworn before the Buddha, the practice to which the Tibetans increasingly adhered. Be this as it may, none of the treaties forged between Tibet and China succeeded in interrupting their hostilities for very long, and only with a treaty forged in the years 821–822 would a lasting peace be realized.

The relevant background can be reconstructed on the basis of the Chinese and Tibetan sources:[19] Tibet, as we have seen above, had begun to seize control of parts of what is today China's Xinjiang province during the mid- and late seventh century, and by stages came to hold sway over several of the important stations of the Silk Road, including the city-state of Khotan. By the late eighth century Dunhuang and neighboring territories in the Gansu Corridor, where the trade routes converged before entering China proper, had fallen to Tibet. The Tibetans were thus planted between China and those western powers with which China might become politically or commercially engaged, whether Arab, Iranian, Turk, or other.[20] Throughout the first decades of the ninth century, events in the region thus came to be punctuated by shifting alliances and warfare among the Tibetans, Uighur Turks, and Chinese. During this period, the Uighur Empire repeatedly petitioned the Tang court for a princess to marry their Khan, and thereby to seal an accord between the two realms. In his study of Tang relations with the Uighurs, Colin Mackerras summarizes the course of events leading up to the marriage-alliance:

> There was one faction at court which advised the emperor to grant the marriage in the interests of the state's security.
> This clique was led by Li Jiang (764–830), chief minister from 811 to 814. Shortly after he resigned, he sent memorial to the emperor setting forth in detail the reasons for his view. He pointed out the inadequate defenses of the borders and believed that it would be inviting trouble under these circumstances to irritate the Uighurs. He also raised the possibility that by refusing their request, the emperor would drive them into the arms of their traditional enemies the Tibetans, which could well result in an alliance between the two states against China. On the other hand, to grant the Uighurs a bride would intensify the Tibetan hostility towards the Uighurs by arousing their jealousy. . . .
> [The Emperor] Xianzong was unmoved by these arguments. . . .
> Early in 820 a third mission arrived to make a further petition for the marriage. This time Xianzong at last gave his consent. The situation had indeed changed since 817. . . . Li Jiang's arguments

about the Tibetans made much better sense now, for in 818 they had broken a lull of over a decade and begun making raids against China's borders. . . .[21]

The emperor's acceptance of the proposal was quickly interpreted by the Tibetans—no doubt correctly—as ratifying a strategic partnership whose aim was primarily to force them out of the Gansu corridor by exerting pressure from both the east and west simultaneously. The response was fast and furious, and the "pacified West" (Hexi) and adjacent areas were soon plunged into intensive warfare. As Mackerras continues:

> Li Jiang's suggestion that the marriage would inflame Uighur-Tibetan hostility proved justified. No sooner had the Princess of Taihe been ordered to marry the khaghan, than the Uighurs announced that they had sent forces to the far western districts of Beiting and Anxi to ward off the attempts the Tibetans were making, or might make, to prevent the Princess of Taihe from reaching Karabalghasun. Although in the first instance China also suffered renewed Tibetan raids on her borders owing to the marriage, a Sino-Tibetan peace agreement was reached soon after and the hostilities were discontinued. From a political point of view, the marital alliance with the Uighurs had definitely worked to China's advantage.[22]

Accordingly, beginning in 821, when the Tibetan *tsenpo* was Tri Tsukdetsen, who is better known to posterity as Relpachen (806–838), a series of treaties between China and Tibet, and between Tibet and the Uighurs, was negotiated, aiming primarily to stabilize and reaffirm the integrity of the frontiers, and to restore harmonious relations between the Tibetan and Tang courts.[23] The treaty of 821/822 is well known through the celebrated bilingual "uncle-nephew pillar inscription" (*dbon zhang rdo ring*) in Lhasa, the contents of which, like those of the treaty of 783, demonstrate the importance to the parties of the adjudication of borders.[24] Despite uncertainties surrounding points of detail, these events would be generally remembered in later Tibetan historiography. The Fifth Dalai Lama, for instance, refers to them in his famous *Chronicle*,[25] and they may be seen accordingly depicted in murals in the Potala Palace, which show how the frontier wars of the early ninth century were rendered by seventeenth-century painters, as well as the dedication of a version of the "uncle-nephew pillar inscription" at Gongbu Maru (fig. 1), said to mark the frontier between the two empires.[26] The latter panel makes a visual allusion to the famous metaphor comparing the Chinese emperor and the Tibetan *tsenpo* to the sun and moon, together holding dominion over all under heaven. The metaphor was employed in the west face of the treaty inscription of 821/822 itself, where it is written that the newly established peace between China and Tibet shall be such that "the report of its fame will embrace all that is touched by sun or moon."[27]

FIG. 1 The bilingual treaty inscription on the border between Tibet and China, flanked by the emblems of the sun and moon. From a series of murals illustrating the Fifth Dalai Lama's *Chronicle* in the Potala Palace. (After *A Mirror of the Murals in the Potala* [Beijing: Jiu zhou tushu chubanshe, 2000].)

The treaty was ratified in separate ceremonies in the Chinese and Tibetan courts, in connection with the first of which the record makes no mention whatsoever of Buddhism, but alludes only to a sacrificial rite such as we have seen earlier.[28] Concerning the oath taken in Tibet in 822, however, the *New Tang Annals* (*Xin Tang shu*) provides a remarkable account, derived certainly from the report of the Chinese ambassador Liu Yuanding:[29]

The valley to the north of the Tsang river is the principal summer camp of the *tsenpo*. It is surrounded by [a fence of] staves attached together. At an average distance of ten paces [one from the other] 100 long lances are arranged. There are three gates, with a great standard planted before each,[30] at 100 paces from one another, with armored soldiers guarding the gates. Sorcerers with head-dresses of bird[-feathers] and belts of tiger[-skin] beat drums. Whoever entered was searched before he was allowed to go in. In the middle [of the camp] there was a raised platform, surrounded by a rich balustrade. The *tsenpo* was seated in his tent. [There, there were] dragons with and without horns, tigers, and panthers, all made of gold. [The *tsenpo*] was clothed in white wool; a red muslin [turban] was tied so as to cover his head.³¹ He wore a gold-inlayed sword. Pelchenpo³² was standing to his right. The ministers of State were stationed at the foot of the platform. Since the arrival of the Tang ambassador, the *jishezhong*,³³ minister Xidaruo, came to deliberate with him regarding [the ceremony of] the oath. There was a great feast to the right of the tent. The serving of the dishes and the circulation of the wine there were roughly of the same order as in China. The band played the air "The Prince of Qin defeated [the enemy] ranged in battle," and other diverse airs . . . all of the musicians being Chinese. The altar for the oath was ten paces wide and two feet high. The ambassador and more than ten great ministers of the Tibetans³⁴ faced it. More than 100 chiefs were seated below the altar. On the altar, they had arranged a great banquet. Pelchenpo ascended upon it and announced the alliance [to the gods]. A man stationed beside him translated [his words] to communicate them to those below. When Pelchenpo had finished, [those assembled] smeared their lips with blood. Pelchenpo did not smear his lips with blood. The oath being completed, one swore once again before the Buddha, and they brought saffronated water that one drank. Congratulations were exchanged with the ambassador and one descended [from the altar].³⁵

The Tibetan ecclesiastical figure named here as Pelchenpo is certainly to be identified with one of the most powerful personages of early-ninth-century Tibet, Trenka Pelgi Yönten.³⁶ He had risen to prominence already during the reign of Relpachen's father, Tri Desongtsen (r. 804–815), dominating ecclesiastical affairs, and he came to assume a legendary status in later Tibetan tradition.³⁷ As Relpachen was perhaps just sixteen years of age at the time that the treaty of 821/822 was enacted, we may assume that Trenka Pelgi Yönten still played a determining role in the affairs of his court. It was the influential position of the Buddhist monk, no doubt, that impelled the intensive religious orientations for which Relpachen's reign would be later remembered.

The insistence upon a key role for Buddhist ritual in the context of Tang-Tibetan diplomacy, a development that was due primarily to the emergence of Buddhism as the Tibetan state religion, was in evidence not only in court ceremonial. It had notable ramifications, too, for the conduct of affairs along the frontiers. The invocation of the Buddha's august presence by the Tibetan colonial administration in order to guarantee the peace in these regions will illustrate something of the extent to which religious change came to penetrate political affairs.

The Temple of the Treaty

Among the early sources of information concerning the issues discussed in the present chapter, some of the most valuable are known thanks to the Taoist priest Wang's revelation at the beginning of the twentieth century of the hidden text chamber in Dunhuang Mogao cave 17. His discovery brought to light roughly 4,000 Tibetan texts and documents dating to the last centuries of the first millennium, of which many stem from the period of the Tibetan occupation of Dunhuang and the surrounding regions. These materials, whose value for historical scholarship was first recognized by M.A. Stein and Paul Pelliot, remain the bedrock for all study of dynastic and early post-dynastic Tibetan culture and history, and, a full century after their discovery, there remain plenty of surprises for us within them. Nevertheless, investigations of these texts have generally lagged behind the study of the larger corpus of Chinese-language manuscripts also revealed in cave 17.[38] One area in which this is quite conspicuous involves the use of Dunhuang manuscript sources in connection with the interpretation of other types of material evidence from Dunhuang and elsewhere: whereas the Chinese documents have sometimes been found to refer to specific, identifiable sites, temples, icons, and so forth, relatively little progress has been made in locating convincing correlations between Tibetan Dunhuang texts and other archeological and art historical remains.[39]

One of the most famous of these Tibetan documents is an incomplete manuscript, roughly the last half of which is preserved in two separate sections, catalogued respectively as PT 16 in the Paris Bibliothèque nationale de France and IOL Tib J 751 in London's British Library.[40] (As the text has come to be known conventionally as the "Prayers of Dega Yutsel," this is the usage that we shall follow here.) The portions available to us provide a highly formalized series of prayers and memorials, celebrating the establishment of a temple, known as the "Temple of the Treaty" (*gtsigs kyi gtsug lag khang*), at a place called Dega Yutsel, the "turquoise grove of Dega." The text was first studied, and parts of it translated, by F.W. Thomas in his pioneering researches, *Tibetan Literary Texts and Documents Concerning Chinese Turkestan*.[41] Since his time, valuable comments on it have been presented in the writings of Ariane Macdonald and Rolf Stein;[42] and additional contributions of geographical importance, to be considered in some detail below, are found in the remarks of Hugh Richardson and Géza Uray, among others.

As the narration of the text itself makes clear, the Temple of the Treaty was founded during the reign of the Tibetan *tsenpo* Tri Tsukdetsen, i.e. Relpachen,[43] famed in later Tibetan historiography for his lavish patronage of Buddhism.[44] Following the traditions codified by his father Tri Desongtsen, he was raised under the tutelage of Buddhist monks, no doubt including Pelgi Yönten.[45] The foundation of the Temple of Treaty was intended to commemorate the council and subsequent treaty concluded between Tibet and the powers of China, the Uighurs, and possibly Nanzhao, during the first years of the 820s.[46] The religious solemnity of the treaty was no doubt underscored by the construction of a temple in its honor, for the very name by which it is designated means literally the "temple of the treaty-edict."[47] The location for the temple's construction, moreover, is described as the "plain of the peace council" (*mjal dum thang*). In the following sections, I shall attempt to offer some suggestions regarding where precisely this is, and to suggest further that the temple in question may in fact still exist.

The "Prayers of Dega Yutsel," as it has been preserved, consists of a series of benedictions honoring the foundation of the temple, beginning on the numbered folio 22 of the manuscript. While we have no evidence as to what may have occupied the missing folios 1–21—further benedictions, selections from appropriate scriptures, or perhaps even a detailed narrative account of the temple's creation and the events surrounding it—given the careful preparation of the work, it is most unlikely that materials not related in some way to Temple of the Treaty would have been included therein.

Of the seven surviving benedictions, the sources of five may be identified and these were all explicitly offered by prominent parties in the Tibetan colonial administration of what is today Gansu. A general outline of the portions of the manuscript that have been preserved runs as follows:

(1) "Offered as a prayer . . ." (PT 16, 22a1–32b4: *smon lam du gsol ba//*). As the title in this case evidently began on the now missing folio 21, we have no way of knowing just who presented this prayer. It is by far the

most elaborate of the group, and, given the apparent arrangement of the collection according to descending hierarchical rank-order, must have emanated from among the highest echelons of Tibetan civil or religious authority.[48] We shall return to this issue in discussing this remarkable text in greater detail.

(2) "Offered as a prayer, and presented as a donation, by the domain of the great military headquarters[49] of Yarmotang, on behalf of the Three Jewels in connection with the edification of the most famous Temple of the Treaty concluded at the great council with China, the Uighur, etc." (PT 16, 33a1 - IOL Tib J 751, 35a3: *rgya drug las stsogs pha mjal dum chen po mdzad pa'i gtsigs gyi gtsug lag khang grags pha chen po bzhengs pa'i dkon mchog gsum la dbyar mo thang khrom chen po khams nas smon lam du gsol ba dang/ yon du dbul ba'//*). The identity of the place called Yarmotang, which is of central importance in the present context, will be the subject of further discussion.

(3) "Offered as a prayer by[50] the Pacification Minister on the occasion of the consecration of the Temple of the Treaty of Dega" (IOL Tib J 751, 35a3–38b2: *de ga gtsigs kyi gtsug lag khang zhal bsro ba'i tshe bde blon gyi smon lam du gsol ba'//*). The "Pacification Minister" (*bde blon*) was among the highest ranked of the Tibetan colonial officers and seems to have been, in effect, the governor of Tibet's conquests in Gansu and adjacent territories.[51]

(4) "Offered as a prayer by the great military headquarters of Khartsen on behalf of the Temple of the Treaty of the Turquoise Grove of Dega" (IOL Tib J 751, 38b2–39b1: *de ga g.yu tshal gtsigs gyi gtsug lag khang du mkhar tsan khrom chen pos smon lam du gsol ba//*). The toponym "Khartsen" may have been applied at various points to several different locations, but in our present context, as will be seen momentarily, it can only refer to Liangzhou, to the northeast of Kokonor in Gansu.[52]

(5) "Offered as a prayer by the great military headquarters of Guazhou on behalf of the Temple of the Treaty of the Turquoise Grove of Dega" (IOL Tib J 751, 39b1–40a2: *de ga g.yu tshal gtsigs kyi gtsug lag khang du kwa cu khrom chen po nas smon lam du gsol ba'//*). The Tibetan transcription of Guazhou (*kwa cu*) is unambiguous and corresponds to the well-known region of Anxi in northwestern Gansu, to the immediate east of Dunhuang.

(6) "Offered as a prayer by the chiliarch of Chuktsam and his servitors" (IOL Tib J 751, 40a2–41a1: *phyug tsams stong pon dpon g.yog gi smon*

lam du gsol ba'//). Though the location of Chuksam is uncertain, references in other Dunhuang texts, to which we shall have occasion to return, suggest that it was also in the vicinity of present day Anxi.[53]

(7) "Offered as a prayer by Drom Pékhongma (?)" (IOL Tib J 751, 41a2–41b4: *'brom ?spe khong ?ma'ï smon lam du gsol ba'//*). The reading of several syllables of the donor's name is in this case uncertain.[54]

In sum, the provenance of the manuscript in Dunhuang comports closely with the geographical frame of reference that is represented within it, that is, far western Gansu. As will emerge, however, though I am in favor of regarding matters from this angle, it is a conclusion that will prove in some respects problematic once the sum of the evidence is reviewed.

The "Prayers of Dega Yutsel" includes, in addition to the formal features of Buddhist dedicatory texts—salutations, praises, aspirations on behalf of living beings, etc.—a considerable amount of historical detail concerning the circumstances under which the temple came to be established by two very prominent ministers, Zhang Trisumjé and Zhang Lhazang. The historical narrative is repeated in longer or shorter form in several of the prayers,[55] which reproduce essentially the same account with the addition or subtraction of some elements of information. In the first and fullest of the surviving prayers, the foundation of the temple is related as follows:

25b3   ... The divine *tsenpo* of Tibet, the lord of men appointed by the gods, Tri Tsukdetsen, like a body magically emanated by his ancestors,

25b4   is inscrutable[56] and revered, like heaven and earth. Upright and equanimous, he commands all creatures. Open and expansive, his religious and political wisdom are refined in accordance with custom.[57] His governance, sagacious and firmly crowned,[58]

26a1   is of great splendor so that [all] under the sun[59]—even the kingdoms of the south, north, east, and west—receive his order with respect, and are gathered under his sway,[60] wherefore all of his undertakings are altogether realized as he intends.

26a2   The great ministers of [his] governance [as it has been just described] are the great minister Zhang Trisumjé and the great Zhang Lhazang, who, owing to the excellence of their intelligence are like precious wish-granting gems. Through their heroic labors[61] the Chinese, Uighurs,

26a3   and others who were inflated with their own pride, having become objects of wrath, due to [their] enmity were defeated, their splendor annulled and the source of their cunning effaced. Their weapons of enmity

26a4 were laid down, and great fidelity then followed.[62] As for the increase of the good, having enthroned the best, nobility and honor may be firmly upheld.[63] Being without conflict, having treated [one another] as dear,[64] the one kingdom of Tibet,

26b1 for both its high and low subjects, both its great and small, enjoys the pervasive grace of happiness, for each at his own door. Having established Great Tibet, China and the Uighurs, etc., in an age of happiness in each of their respective countries, the Chinese and Uighurs, moreover,

26b2 requested that there be a governmental peace council, and, as if among men of a single household, a treaty for a common peace with the powers of China and the Uighurs was made in the auspicious land, Dega Yutsel, the peace-council plain.

26b3 Thereupon, as a sign of [its] truth, so that the limits of government would be perpetually unshaken and firm, and forever trusted by the many, it was inscribed upon a stone pillar. And afterward, this shrine of the Three Jewels was established in accord with the transmission of the

26b4 sūtra—"When someone establishes a temple in the world, as an image of that great merit a gods' mansion arises in the Akaniṣṭha heaven"—

27a1 declared by the Buddha. The great benefactors who have established the Temple of the Treaty-Edict (*gtsigs kyi gtsug lag khang*) are the great minister Zhang Trisumjé and the great Zhang Lhazang.

27a2 Several benefactors, rejoicing in this, joined the effort with faith and devotion.

The expressed motivations of the two ministers, however, extended beyond their urge to celebrate the peace, honor their lord, and make merit. Contrition for the damage wrought by war is a further theme of importance in these prayers, contributing to the exceptional value of their testimony. This is most clearly evident in the prayer of the Pacification Minister, who writes:

38a2 ... Formerly, when we did not convene with China and the Uighurs in governance, and there were hostilities between us, the Divine Son of firm crown, and the heroic and intelligent ministers,

38a3 skilled in the ways of war,[65] assaulted the enemy and with the steady power of many armies brought down the enemy's fortresses, defeated them in battle, conquered the land, cut off their supplies,[66]

38a4   etc. Many of the enemy's men and beasts were deprived of life, and what was not given [to us] was taken [by us]. We pray that all of these sins, by the splendor and brilliance of this great merit [derived from the foundation of the temple], be overcome and purified.[67]

It is perhaps here, above all, that we remark the depth to which Buddhist sentiments and values had penetrated the discourse of these servants of the *tsenpo*, for the rhetoric of earlier Tibetan martial culture seems to have left little place for reflection upon the horrors of war.[68]

Finally, we may note that although the kingdom of Nanzhao is mentioned on four separate occasions in the prayers,[69] it is omitted from all references to the battles preceding the peace-council. One can imagine that, although Nanzhao may not have been a party to the hostilities that necessitated the negotiation of the treaty, it was invited nevertheless to dispatch an emissary. Perhaps it was the case that those responsible for the security of the Tibetan empire along its eastern borders, tired of wars that were proving costly and indecisive, wished to settle its frontiers once and for all. In all events, of the seven treaties that we know Tibet to have negotiated with Tang China, the treaty of 821/822 was the only one that ever held.[70]

Where Is Dega Yutsel?

We are now faced with the question of whether or not it is possible to determine just where the "peace-council plain" may have been located and the Temple of the Treaty established. In order to address this adequately, it will be necessary in the present section to examine some fine points of historical geography and linguistics.

The location at which the Temple of the Treaty was founded is referred to in full as the "peace-council plain of Dega Yutsel" (*de ga g.yu tshal mjal dum thang*). In this expression, the "plain of the peace-council" is a descriptive phrase and not a proper geographical name. Dega, which is repeated several times in conjunction with Yutsel, has not so far been satisfactorily interpreted, though I shall propose an explanation below. The second element, Yutsel, by contrast is unambiguously a toponym meaning the "turquoise wood." Indeed, it would be difficult to imagine a more characteristically Tibetan designation, or one more auspicious from the perspective of a Tibetan cultural framework.[71] As I hope to sufficiently demonstrate later in this chapter, this is no doubt precisely what the authors of PT 16 - IOL Tib J 751 intended. The exact identity of the location of the "turquoise wood," however, has proven deeply problematic. As our texts refer frequently to identifiable places to the far northeast of Tibet, places located mostly in the Gansu corridor, such as Guazhou, Ganzhou, and Liangzhou, it seems reasonable to begin our search in this area. Besides this, we find one further geographical specification, which some have thought might be the key to the exact location of Dega Yutsel: it is said to be situated in Yarmotang.[72] Taking in turn, then, the puzzles surrounding the identities of the three key toponyms that concern us—Yarmotang, Yutsel, and Dega—we shall attempt to establish, at the least, a range of possible interpretations.

Yarmotang

This geographical term, which is encountered many times in Old Tibetan documents, has been discussed by a noted scholar of early Tibetan history, Géza Uray:

> The location of the region dByar- (or g.Yar- or g.Yer-) mo thang (which frequently occurs not only in the ancient records but also in the geographic literature, and, especially, in the religious and heroic epic) was at all times thought to be found in the neighbourhood of Lake Ch'ing-hai; it was, however, only recently that Richardson recognized the importance of the Zhol inscription in Lhasa for a more exact location of dByar-mo-thang in the 8–9th centuries. Since, in the description of the conquest of Chinese territories between 758 and 763 this inscription mentions among others *rGya'i/ kha[ms]-su [gto]gs-pa dByar-mo-thang*, 'the dByar-mo-thang belonging to the Chinese country' (south side, ll. 32–33), there can exist no doubt, even given the incompleteness of the text, that dByar-mo-thang should be located east or northeast of Lake Ch'ing-hai.[73]

By contrast, Helga Uebach has noted an important reference from the thirteenth-century writings of Chögyel Pakpa Rinpoché that supports a location in the Luchu region, that is, in what is today the southwest of modern Gannan prefecture in Gansu Province, not far from the area that includes the famous monastery of Labrang Trashikyi.[74] If we follow, as Uebach proposes, indications that Yarmotang was the "region where the Vihāra De-ga

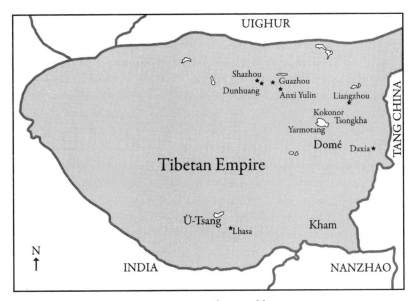

FIG. 2 The Tibetan Empire and its neighbors, ca. 820 CE.

gYu-chal and a stone-pillar had been erected in commemoration of the treaty of 821/823,"[75] then we will seek to locate the temple somewhere in the southern Gansu-Qinghai frontier.

Although, for reasons that will become clear below, I do not believe that this hypothesis can be altogether ruled out, taking Uray's and Uebach's suggestions together, it is at once evident that we must not restrict too narrowly the limits of the area to which the designation Yarmotang may have applied at one time or another. The most we can say with assurance on the basis of their arguments is that it embraced areas beyond Kokonor (from the Central Tibetan perspective), was considered by the Tibetans to have formerly been Chinese territory, and extended into southern Gansu. It may be helpful at this point, then, to ask, just what did "Yarmotang" signify generally in traditional Tibetan geographical literature? Although an answer can only be gleaned from relatively late sources, it will be seen that this will nevertheless help us to clarify earlier references.

The great nineteenth-century history of Amdo, the *Doctrinal History of Domé* (*Mdo smad chos 'byung*) by Könchok Tenpa Rabgyé (b. 1801), lists Yar- or Yermotang among the three *gang* ("highlands") or *kham* ("realms") into which eastern Tibet is divided, and holds the term to be synonymous with Domé itself.[76] This latter designation is however problematic, for some hold it to mean Amdo generally, while others prefer to limit it to the Yellow River basin in southern Amdo, and the regions to the west and southwest of the Kokonor. As the Tsongkha region of Amdo, to the east of the Kokonor, is identified in the *Doctrinal History of Domé* as a separate *gang* or *kham*,[77] it is the latter usage that must be preferred in the present context. The Luchu valley, favored by Uebach as the location of Yarmotang, may thus perhaps be included in that region by extension, but cannot be taken to delimit its full extent.

The identification of Yarmotang with the upper Yellow River basin is confirmed by contemporary geographical nomenclature, for we find a location in the "source area of the Yellow River"—to the south of the Ngoring lake in Qinghai province situated at approximately 34.7°N, 98° E—called in Chinese "Yematang."[78] The suspicion that this is in fact a transcription of a Tibetan toponym is increased by the occurrence of a second, identically named location further to the north, roughly 100 km to the west of the Kokonor at 37.4° N, 98.3° E.[79] The continuing use of these designations suggests that, as traditional Tibetan geography maintains, Yarmotang embraced the regions to the south of the Kokonor, and was extended to the west as well. That this usage is not of very recent vintage is demonstrated by the Yuan-period toponym "Yemotang," found in close proximity to the second modern "Yematang" just noted.[80] It is evident, therefore, that the toponym Yarmotang was applied, at one time or another, to the immense stretch of territory extending from southern Gansu to the northwest of Lake Qinghai.

Additionally, if we continue further to the northwest, adopting a trajectory that runs directly from the Kokonor to Dunhuang, we find that upon crossing the modern border from Qinghai into Gansu we traverse the mountain ranges Yema Nanshan and Yema shan.[81] Given that we have now seen that *yema*, "wild horse," is the modern Chinese transcription of Tibetan *yarmo/yermo*, it is not impossible that these ranges owe their names, too, to the earlier Tibetan designation for the entire region. If the term Yarmotang had been at one time extended to include Chinese territories in Gansu brought under Tibetan rule, then there is no reason to assume, with Uray, that only locations to the northeast of the Kokonor would have been so designated; for, indeed, the regions of Dunhuang and Anxi, to the northwest of the Kokonor, are clearly contiguous with areas included under the traditional designation. I take it that the term was extended to embrace these "new territories" because they fell within the same Tibetan imperial administrative division, namely, the province of the chief colonial officer in the northeast, the governor known as the "pacification minister," or *delön*.[82]

Interestingly, the association of Yarmotang with the eminent Tibetan ministers mentioned in PT16 - IOL Tib J 751, Zhang Trisumjé and Zhang Lhazang, would be recalled in later legends. One of these, illustrated in a mural in the Potala, depicts Zhang Lhazang's meeting there with the armies of the god Kubera. Unfortunately, however, these legends do not appear to convey additional geographical information.[83]

Finally, we should note that the relationship between Yarmotang, as a general geographical designation, and the "great military headquarters of Yarmotang," from which prayer (2) emanated, is not altogether clear. The latter was no doubt somewhere within, or in close proximity to, the former, but it is probably not warranted to identify it with the former *tout court*.

Yulin

Among the prayers offered in honor of the temple's founding, there is one sent from the "great military headquarters" (*khrom chen po*) of Kwa cu. This is one of the places mentioned in the prayers that can be identified with exactitude, for Kwa cu is certainly a transcription of Guazhou, that is to say, the prefecture of the region immediately to the east of Dunhuang and now known as Anxi. If we assume that the place we are seeking might be in the general vicinity of Anxi it becomes plausible to suggest that *yutsel* (*g.yu tshal*), the "turquoise wood," might be none other than one of the most renowned temple complexes in that region, Yulin. Rolf Stein, to be sure, raised this possibility some two decades ago, but did not seem to believe that his hypothesis could be rigorously defended.[84] I think, however, that it is probably correct, though there are some problems that must be addressed.

To begin, Tibetan *tshal* is an exact translation of Chinese *lin*, so that the second syllable poses no difficulty whatsoever. The first syllable of the Chinese, *yu*, however, refers to the elm tree, so that we must explain the first syllable of the Tibetan, *g.yu*, "turquoise," now pronounced *yu*, not as a translation in this case, but as a transcription. In principle, of course, there is no objection to a Tibetan binomial phrase consisting of a transcription of Chinese in compound with a properly Tibetan syllable. An example in Old Tibetan is the term *hen khang*, occurring in the *Testament of Ba* (*Sba bzhed*) and referring to a Buddhist temple.[85]

Nevertheless, *g.yu* is not precisely a transcription of the Chinese in this case either. Even after taking into account the reconstructed Tang-period pronunciation of the Chinese *yu*, we are at a loss to explain the Tibetan pre-initial *g-*, which was no doubt still pronounced when our texts were written.

The suspicion that Tibetan *gyu* cannot be an exact transcription of Chinese *yu* is strengthened by the observation that Tibetan Dunhuang manuscripts (e.g. PT 997 and PT 2122) do exist that refer to temples at a place called *yu lim*.[86] This looks to be a very close transcription of the medieval pronunciation of Yulin. (Middle Chinese final *-m* usually becomes *-n* in modern Mandarin.) If this is correct, then it is virtually certain that the Tibetan word for "turquoise" is *not* being used here to transcribe the Chinese for "elm."

The sole resolution that seems to me plausible, without sacrificing the possible identification of *yutsel* with Yulin, is to regard the Tibetan place-name as inspired by the Chinese, but adjusted so as to suit the religio-political concerns represented in PT 16 - IOL Tib J 751. Given the importance of the site in relation to the negotiation of the treaty, and the later construction of a commemorative temple there, it makes good sense to suppose that the Tibetan imperial administration would have wished to designate the place in Tibetan, and to do so auspiciously. The elm tree, though mentioned in later Tibetan *materia medica*, where it is called *yombokshing*,[87] does not appear to have had very notable cultural connotations; and we know nothing so far of the significance of the elm tree in ninth-century Tibet. (A place called *yomboktang*, "elm plain," is referred to in central Tibet,[88] but in this case the name seems purely descriptive, with no remarkable connotations attached to it.) My supposition, therefore, is that, in seeking to coin a suitable Tibetan name for Yulin, **yu tshal* (which if read as purely Tibetan rather than Chinese + Tibetan would mean the "grove of the handle") and **yo 'bog tshal* would have both been ruled out as unsuitable in the rather exalted context of the commemorative dedication. The Chinese syllable *yu*, however, was phonetically suggestive of one of the most auspicious terms in Tibetan, *gyu*, the talismanic stone *par excellence*, the turquoise. The authors of PT 16 - IOL Tib J 751 (or those who created the designations they employed), sought, in my view, to accentuate at once the importance of the formerly Chinese territory of Yulin as now a true part of Tibetan geography and its auspicious connotations within that geography; but they sought to do this in a manner that did not altogether erase its established identity.

Still, as Stein has pointed out, there were several locations in regions where the Tibetans were active during this period that were all called Yulin.[89] Do we have any further grounds to hold that it is indeed *Anxi Yulin* that was intended? We shall return to this question later, but here we may note one further item that contributes to a response: the chiliarch of Chuktsam, to whom the sixth of the "Prayers of Dega Yutsel" is attributed, is also mentioned in the Dunhuang Tibetan inventory of Yulim (PT 997).[90] Given the organization of the "Prayers" according to the ranks of the donors, it seems most unlikely that an official of this grade would have been included here had the domain of his responsibilities not been closely tied to Dega Yutsel itself. The clearest way to account for his presence in our texts, therefore, is to assume that Yutsel is none other that Yulim. If this is so, however, we are still left with the thorniest geographical and lexical question of all.

Dega

Though varied interpretations of Yarmotang and Yutsel have been discussed in the literature, "Dega" has been generally ignored. Thomas understood there to be some possibility that this is merely a pronominal expression, but that, given the syntax of the phrases in which it occurs, it seems to make better sense if taken as part of a toponym.[91] Noting the frequent occurrence of the suffix -ga/-ka in northeastern Tibetan place-names (e.g., *Khri ga, Tsong k(h)a, Byang ka*, etc.), he suggested that *De ga* might be another example adhering to the same pattern.[92] If this were the case, however, then either we have an odd orthography for a Tibetan place name (which Thomas artfully sought to derive from *bde ga*[93]), or if not, then without prejudice to the form of the suffix, we should see here instead the transcription of a non-Tibetan term. This latter hypothesis is, I think, certainly the more likely, as the manuscript in question was prepared with painstaking attention to Tibetan grammar, orthography, form, and penmanship, as befitting an official document emanating from the upper echelons of the Tibetan imperial administration.[94] And, although many languages were in use among various peoples throughout the Sino-Tibetan marches of Gansu, the most prominent candidate as the source for a borrowed term in this context is certainly Chinese. If Dega transcribes a Chinese toponym, however, it is one that has eluded those who have examined the relevant texts to date.

We have earlier met the Tang envoy Liu Yuanding, who was dispatched to Central Tibet in connection with the treaty of 822. An interesting story is related in the *New Tang Annals* in connection with his return journey to China:

> When [Liu] Yuanding was on his way back, the supreme commander of the slaves, Shang Tazang, received him in the valley of Daxia, offered him a residence, and convened an assembly of the various generals of the administrative commission of the eastern region, numbering more than a hundred. [Shang Tazang] placed the text of the treaty upon a raised platform, and made its contents known to all. Then he advised all [the generals] to protect

their respective territories, without engaging in aggressions and mutual incursions.[95]

Demiéville long ago suggested that the Shang Tazang mentioned here might be identified with Zhang Trisumjé, one of the important figures we have seen referred to in connection with the "Prayers of Dega Yutsel."[96] However, it seems far more plausible to hold him to be the latter's colleague Zhang Lhazang, whose name is in this case the better phonetic match.[97] Curiously, this would correspond closely with the legend concerning his encounter with Kubera that, as we have seen earlier, remained in circulation in Tibet in later times. In the legend, the meeting of the minister with the god took place in Yarmotang, but here the location is said to be Daxia. If my hypothesis is correct, this is none other than Dega. The linguistic arguments for maintaining that the two are equivalent are best summarized in a note at this point.[98] The phonological considerations that are presented there may be supplemented by noting that, as Daxia literally means "great summer" in Chinese, so the Tibetan Yarmotang signifies "summer plain," Chinese *xia* and Tibetan *yar* being precise synonyms.[99]

In the light of Uebach's citation of Chögyel Pakpa's mention of a Yarmotang in southern Gansu, the correspondence of Daxia with that region, and the suggestive convergence of the *New Tang Annals* with Tibetan legend, it may seem that we are entitled to cut to the chase and conclude that the Temple of the Treaty must have been located in or around the area that is now well-known for the great monastic complex of Labrang, itself significantly considered as marking a cultural frontier (as will be examined in chapter 5). Although this conclusion cannot, I think, be altogether excluded, there are nevertheless several difficulties that accompany it.

To begin, given the concentration of references in PT 16 - IOL Tib J 751 to places in and around far northwestern Gansu, and the provenance of the manuscript in Dunhuang, southern Gansu seems somewhat far afield in relation to the geographical frame of reference. The probable equivalence of Yutsel and Yulin, together with the occurrence in both the "Prayers of Dega Yutsel" and the Dunhuang "Inventory of the Yulin Temple" of references to a Chuktsam that can only have been in the vicinity of Anxi Yulin, further argue against a location roughly 1000 km to the southeast. And although the Daxia in southern Gansu mentioned in *New Tang Annals* was the location for a rehearsal of the treaty, it was not, as the "Prayers" affirm that the "peace-council plain" was, the site of its negotiation. The toponym Daxia, finally, has also been used to name many diverse locations to China's west or northwest, including Bactria, parts of northern India, possibly Tokharia, and later the Xi Xia realm, together with numerous more minor localities.[100] It is this last consideration that, when taken together with the synonymity of *xia* and *yar*, "summer," suggests a possible resolution to the difficulty of finding a satisfactory synthesis of the apparently conflicting information that we now have before us. For it is possible that the Tibetans took "Daxia" to be precisely a synonym of "Yarmotang," and thus applicable to all those regions covered by this designation in Tibetan. This would permit all the data we have examined to cohere in a single explanation, though it may appear at this point to be still speculative. Is there, then, any additional evidence that would contribute to our assessment? It is time to return to the text of the "Prayers."

Dega Yutsel Discovered?

The conclusions of the foregoing discussion are less decisive than we may prefer. Nevertheless, a number of points have been clarified and a range of possibilities comes into view:

(1) The designation *yutsel*, "turquoise grove," occurring in the name of the temple possibly is used in our texts for Chinese *yulin*, "elm grove." Though this names several places during the Tang, it applies most plausibly in the present case to Anxi Yulin, the site of the famed cave-temple complex to the southeast of Dunhuang. Indeed, one of the "Prayers of Dega Yutsel" was offered by a local official, the Chuktsam chiliarch, who, on the basis of other Dunhuang documents, is known to have been particularly connected with a temple complex at Yulim (Yulin).

(2) The Tibetan toponym Yarmotang, which properly refers to the upper basin of the Yellow River (Tib. Rma chu) to the south and west of the Kokonor, has been extended at one time or another to include neighboring territories, at least as far east as what is today southern Gansu, and in the northwest to the Gansu-Qinghai frontier. In the context of the "Prayers of Dega Yutsel," taken alone, reference to the northwest seems more plausible, given the frequent mention there of districts that can all be identified as lying within that part of the Gansu corridor that is to the north of Qinghai.

(3) The third term used to situate the temple, Dega, has hitherto proven the most resistant to satisfactory interpretation. Nevertheless, it is quite likely that it can be explained as a straightforward transcription of Chinese Daxia, which, among other places, names a well-known river valley in southern Gansu. This identification seems most plausible in the light of the

description, in the *New Tang Annals*, of a meeting there, following the ratification of the treaty of 821/822, of a Chinese envoy with Zhang Lhazang or Zhang Trisumjé, the figures prominently mentioned in the "Prayers" as the founders of the Treaty Temple.

A solution to the difficulty that these conflicting observations present is possible if we imagine that, because Chinese "Daxia" and Tibetan "Yarmotang" were nearly equivalent place-names, associating the locations to which they referred with the summer (Ch. *xia*, Tib. *dbyar*), the Tibetan authors of the "Prayers" were in fact using them as synonyms. To determine whether or not this is plausible, however, we shall have to take additional evidence into account. We may therefore turn now from the linguistic and geographical data to another important clue as to the identity of the temple given in the text of PT 16 - IOL Tib J 751, for its iconography is described there in some detail. This occurs in the first of the "Prayers." To place the iconographical passage contained here in its proper context, let us begin by reviewing the structure of the text overall.

The prayer begins with an elaborate statement of the services performed at the commencement of Mahāyāna Buddhist rituals in general: salutations (*vandana*, 22a1–23b1), rejoicing in the good done by others (*anumodana*, 23b1–24a1), worship with offerings (*pūjā*, 24a1–24b1), confession of sins (*pāpādeśana*, 24b2–25b1), and going for refuge (*śaraṇagamana*, 25b1–25b2). The first and fourth of these require some comment.

The salutations are extremely ornate, and demonstrate at once that their author has a sophisticated command of both Buddhist doctrine and Tibetan rhetoric. In addition to the salutations to each of the Three Jewels of Buddha, Dharma, and Sangha, we find here a fourth: a salutation to the wrathful embodiments, "who do not rest in the ways of those tamed by the vows of the Vinaya, who by their beauty tame heedless beings inflated with pride, who express the wrath and gladness of their compassionate nature but at the same time put down pride because they are emanated from the body of the Tathāgata, who are skilled in training all beings while neither purposing to enter into careless sin nor transgressing the bounds of sin, who radiate light rays so as to overwhelm the three realms, and who in an instant [throughout] the world-ocean cause all worlds to prosper by the emanations of their body, speech, and mind..." (23a2–b1). It is certain that the cult of the tantric wrathful deities was already associated with the martial ethos of the old Tibetan monarchy during the reign of Tri Songdetsen. The exaltation of the empire's conquering prowess throughout the "Prayers of Dega Yutsel" seems to offer further confirmation of this association.

The violence of worldly power, however, was not rendered unproblematic just by assimilating it to the image of divine wrath. It is in this regard that the confessional passage of the prayer we are considering is of great interest; for here, for the first time in the prayer, the formulae of the service explicitly include reference to the agents of the empire: the confession is performed to expiate the sins of all sentient beings beginning with "the lord of Tibet, his ministers and entourage" (*bod rje blon 'khor dang bcas pa*). The significance of this, as we have seen, is underscored elsewhere in the "Prayers," above all in those offered by the Pacification Minister, wherein the merit of the edifying of the temple is called upon to purify especially the sins of battle during the period preceding the peace. Later Tibetan historical tradition would also recall that a temple was built in connection with the treaty enacted at this time.[101]

Following the conclusion of the opening services, the long prayer we are considering enters into the extended narration concerning the circumstances of the temple's foundation that is translated above. The act of constructing the temple is treated here as a precise analogue to the karmic construction of a divine mansion in heaven. Insomuch as this relates to the person of the *tsenpo* himself, a prayer is later offered that, as a result of this merit, he become a Cakravartin, and eventually a Buddha (28b3). Any doubts that one may have harbored regarding the "ideology of Cakravartin kingship" should be dispelled by this remarkably clear statement. The prayer for the king is followed by prayers specifically dedicated to the two ministers (28b3–30a1), and then, for the remainder of the text, prayers offered collectively on behalf of the *tsenpo* and his court, the two ministers, and sentient beings in general. The entire work is brought to a conclusion with the aspiration to realize the wisdom of Mañjuśrī, the vows of Samantabhadra, the compassion of Avalokiteśvara, the power of Vajrapāṇi, and the skillful means of Vimalakīrti (32b1–32b4). This last recalls in some respect the close contact with Chinese Buddhism during this period, for Vimalakīrti did not enjoy the great popularity in later Tibetan Buddhism that he did in China.[102] Let us recall, too, in this regard, that the celebrated portrait of a Tibetan *tsenpo* in Dunhuang Mogao cave 159 places the monarch in the entourage of the bodhisattva Vimalakīrti.[103]

With this framework in mind, we may turn now to examine the passage describing the construction of the temple itself:

27a2 ... Because it is said, "as for those who give aid, the fruit of merit will be like that of the master of the undertaking,"

27a3   for all those who have given precious aid, [their merit] will not go to waste, but an image of that great merit will arise in the heavens of the gods. The causes and conditions for [the arising of this image] are: the construction of the temple,

27a4   the bodily image of Vairocana installed in its center. His body, achieved through inconceivable accumulations of merit and gnosis, teaches the enjoyment of the doctrine by means of the three secrets to bodhisattvas of the tenth level,

27b1   and thus removes and purifies in an instant the obscuration of the knowable. By means of the emanational body he thoroughly matures sentient beings of the world-realms of the ten directions.

27b2   Installed, too, is the bodily image of buddha Amitābha, whose field is best among those of all buddhas, where even the names of the three evil destinies and eight obstacles are unknown. Dwelling there, adorned with all the ornaments of

27b3   divine enjoyment, so that there cannot even be the name of nirvana, in that field adorned with all perfect, world-transcending happiness,

27b4   he acts on behalf of sentient beings. Because his compassion is especially great, just by calling his name all sins are purified and one is blessed to be born in that buddha-field.

28a1   Installed, too, is the bodily image of Buddha Maitreya, who now, in the Tuṣita heaven, in a jeweled mansion adorned with all divine ornaments, matures all the offspring of the gods (devaputra),

28a2   and so abides, never straying from that single mode of conduct, turning the wheel of the doctrine. Nevertheless, by means of light-rays of great compassion and instantaneous omniscient gnosis

28a3   he abides delighting in the bliss of divine attributes throughout the ocean of world-systems. That Buddha Maitreya, in future time, will encourage the wishes and aspirations of all, and his name will accord with its meaning,

28a4   so that by the power of great compassion all will be embraced by love. Also installed is the retinue of eight great bodhisattvas, the two wrathful [deities, i.e. Acala and Trailokyavijaya],[104] etc.

28b1   Also installed are the shrines that have been established of the lords and protectors of the four directions, of the eight classes of gods and nāgas, etc. Having done so, and having offered donations of mounts and walkways and groves and all pure

28b2   requisites, by the merits of the authority thus determined,[105] we pray that the countenance of the tsenpo Tri Tsukdetsen, enjoy limitless longevity, great power, and the achievement of all his intentions, so that,

28b3 like a Cakravartin emperor, he exercise authority over the four continents and other kingdoms as well, and in the end achieve unsurpassed buddhahood!

Significantly, there is a temple conforming to this description located among the Yulin cave temples, and dating to the period of the Tibetan rule of the Dunhuang region, whose iconography closely matches that which is described in the prayer. I am speaking of Anxi Yulin 25, one of the most famous of the caves owing to the surpassing quality of its murals, its exceptional size, and the geometric precision of its excavation. (It was owing to these remarkable aesthetic qualities that it was chosen as one of the four caves reproduced according to its actual dimensions in the National Historical Museum in Beijing as part of the Dunhuang exposition there in 2000.[106]) The sole statue in the cave, it may be noted, dates to the Qing-period—or at least has a Qing-period head—and so our only concern here will be with the murals.[107] It is possible of course that some of the figures mentioned in our text were once realized sculpturally, but if so they are now altogether lost.

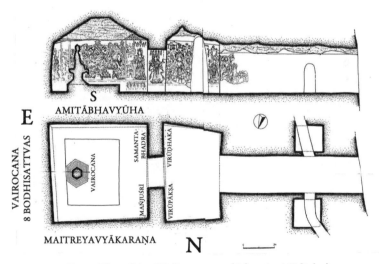

FIG. 3 Plan of Anxi Yulin, cave 25. (After *Anxi Yulinku*.)

We may begin by noting the icons, among those listed above, that are represented in Yulin cave 25:

FIGS. 4–5 The guardian kings Virūpākṣa and Virūḍhaka.
(Lo Archive, Princeton.)

○ Line 28b1: "lords and protectors of the four directions." The kings of the
directions (*tianwang* in Chinese) are represented both in the antechamber, and in the retinues of the Buddhas in the main hall. The refinement
of the draftsmanship and painting is particularly clear in the images of
Virūḍhaka and Virūpākṣa in the antechamber (figs. 4–5).

○ Line 27a4: "the bodily image of Vairocana" (fig. 6), and line 28a4: "the
retinue of the eight great bodhisattvas" occupy the east and central wall
of the main chamber, and hence are preeminent in its composition overall. At the present time only the four bodhisattvas to the left remain (fig.
8), though photographs taken during the 1940s, and preserved in the
Lo Archive in Princeton, show that the right hand portion of the wall,
though already crumbling, was still extant at that time (*fig. 9*). Recent
photographs demonstrate that the right half of the wall has been replas-
tered in recent years.[108]

FIG. 6 (top left) At the center of the east wall: Buddha Vairocana.
(Lo Archive, Princeton.)

FIG. 7 (top right) Tibetan imperial bronze (ca. ninth century) of the Buddha
Vairocana. (Bodhicitta Collection, courtesy Namkha Dorje.)

FIG. 8 (bottom left) Four bodhisattvas to Buddha Vairocana's right.
(Lo Archive, Princeton.)

FIG. 9 (bottom right) Four bodhisattvas to Buddha Vairocana's left. The panel no
longer exists and was clearly already deteriorating at the time the photograph was
taken (c. 1943). (Lo Archive, Princeton.)

FIG. 10 Detail of the *Amitābhavyūha*, south wall.
(Lo Archive, Princeton.)

FIG. 11 The dance of the bodhisattva, miraculously born in Amitābha's realm.
(Lo Archive, Princeton.)

FIG. 12 Detail of the *Prophecy of Maitreya*, north wall.
(Lo Archive, Princeton.)

○ 27b2: "the bodily image of buddha Amitābha" is represented on the south wall (fig. 10), by a mural devoted to the *Amitābhavyūha*, that is, the Sukhāvatī paradise. The wonders of rebirth there are represented in fine detail, in accordance with the descriptions given in the *Sukhāvatīvyūhasūtra*, as seen here in a detail, depicting a heavenly neonate dancing for joy following his miraculous appearance on a lotus before the eyes of Buddha Amitābha (fig. 11).

○ 28a1: "the bodily image of Buddha Maitreya." The north wall is dedicated to the future paradise of Maitreya, as revealed in the *Maitreyavyākaraṇa*, and illustrates the marvelous forms of happiness that, according to this prophecy, beings will enjoy when that Buddha appears (fig. 12). For instance, even in later life, when persons in our era can think only of aging and death, women will still have the vitality to marry.[109] One of the remarkable features of this scene is that it is in fact a *Tibetan* wedding that is illustrated, as proven b y the clothing depicted (fig. 13).[110] The old man before the tomb (fig. 14), a motif encountered elsewhere in Dunhuang painting, is perhaps also a visual reference to the great longevity promised to inhabitants of Maitreya's world. The Maitreya panel also includes the sole Tibetan inscription in cave 25, probably a late graffiti, of which I shall

FIG. 13 (left) A Tibetan wedding in Maitreya's world.
(Lo Archive, Princeton.)

FIG. 14 (right) An old man enters the tomb. (Lo Archive, Princeton.)

have more to say in the appendix below. The delicate illustrations of everyday occupations are among the more critically renowned features of Anxi Yulin cave 25 (fig. 15).

Though other divinities mentioned in our text—for instance, the two wrathful [deities, i.e. Acala and Trailokyavijaya] and the eight classes of gods and nāgas—have not so far been identified in the surviving murals, there is, nevertheless, a strikingly high correspondence, which suggests to me, in conjunction with the geographical arguments reviewed above, that Anxi Yulin 25 is in fact none other than Dega Yutsel. What is initially most remarkable is the distinct presence of two very different iconographic programs, one following the conventions of "sūtra-painting," as is well known from murals executed throughout the Tang-period at Dunhuang,[111] the other, represented by the east wall, clearly adhering to the principles of the esoteric Buddhist maṇḍala. We would be wrong to assume that these two programs can in general be related to distinctively Chinese and Tibetan approaches respectively, but, nevertheless, in this case there may be some reason to consider matters in just this way.

FIG. 15 Harvest scene. (Lo Archive, Princeton.)

The centrality of Vairocana and the eight bodhisattvas, as well as the actual conventions of their representation, relate Anxi Yulin 25 to a widespread group of early-ninth-century Tibetan icons that have been the object of ongoing study by Amy Heller.[112] More broadly speaking, it also relates this temple to the wide-ranging association between Vairocana and the royal cult that we see represented during the ninth century at sites as far afield as Barabudur, Todai-ji (Kyoto), and Famensi (Xi'an).[113] However, the Vairocana and eight bodhisattvas at Anxi Yulin are remarkable for the degree to which these images are consistent with other known Tibetan depictions during this period, including even such details as the draping of the robes and their patterns, the manner in which their hair is arrayed, their ornaments, etc. This may be seen in comparing the Anxi Yulin Vairocana with the stunning Tibetan imperial bronze from a private collection, shown beside it above (fig. 7). And, as I have argued elsewhere, the form of Vairocana in question is intended to represent the imperial presence of the Tibetan monarch whose maṇḍala was none other than the Tibetan empire itself.[114]

Nevertheless, because ninth-century Tibetan icons of Vairocana and the eight bodhisattvas are now known from a number of locations throughout eastern Tibet, their occurrence alone by no means establishes a unique connection between Anxi Yulin and Dega Yutsel. It is, rather, the totality of the iconographic program, especially in light of earlier suggestions regarding the name of the place, that seems to warrant this conclusion. The extraordinarily high quality of the murals in cave 25, certainly on a par with the best of mid-Tang-period painting at Dunhuang, underscores the special care that was lavished on this commission, something that we would expect in the case of an important imperial project like the temple of Dega Yutsel.[115]

We should note, too, that although the east wall, depicting Vairocana and the bodhisattvas, seems stylistically almost altogether distinct from the north and south walls, showing the paradises of Maitreya and Amitābha, there is no reason to suppose that these were executed during different periods or by different ateliers.[116] A close stylistic comparison—focusing upon such details as hair styles, garments, and brush strokes—suggests quite the opposite.[117] It is more plausible to hold that what we see here is the product of one and the same group of artists struggling to execute a commission requiring the representation of a somewhat unfamiliar type of composition, one based upon the organization of the maṇḍala rather than upon that of the Buddha-field. In both iconography and style, Anxi Yulin 25 thus expresses the coexistence of the Tibetan and Chinese Buddhist worlds. On the surface at least, it seems an especially fitting memorial to a peace-accord between the two powers.

These appearances notwithstanding, however, the record as a whole suggests that it was primarily the Tibetan administration, and not the Chinese, that was eager to establish an enduring place for Buddhism in the bilateral diplomacy linking the two powers. Individual Chinese officials, and certainly important constituencies within the local populations of modern Gansu, Sichuan and, in general, the Sino-Tibetan frontiers, no doubt often viewed an explicit allegiance to Buddhism favorably as well. Nevertheless, the relatively restricted role of Buddhism in the Chinese official record of relations with Tibet demands further reflection.

In part, the diminished significance of the foreign religion may be due to the general tendency, underscored by Tansen Sen, for the later Tang court to have backed away from the robust commitment to Buddhism that it had shown during the seventh century. In the course of this shift, moreover, the Tibetans may have appeared as an obstacle to, and not a facilitator of, Tang China's relations with Buddhist India.[118] What is clear is that so long as Buddhism still flourished in India, and while the Tibetans were viewed as dangerous and largely uncivilized rivals, Tibetan interest in Buddhism would not have been felt as more than a minor theme in the Tang court's reflections on its foreign affairs. In the two centuries that followed, however, the picture began to change. Despite a brief and intense revival of Chinese interest in Indian Buddhism under the Song,[119] during the early second millennium Buddhism in India was in sharp decline. At the same time, post-imperial

Tibet, no longer capable of threatening China directly, was beginning to emerge as India's successor in terms of spiritual authority throughout much of the Inner Asian Buddhist world. So it was, therefore, that the subtle seed planted during the time of the Tibetan empire and the Tang, and nurtured too by the Tibetan frontier regime, eventually yielded the stout vine of religio-political order that bound Tibetan-Chinese relations for the greater part of the next thousand years.

Appendix: Some Objections Considered

As a coda to this chapter, I wish to review briefly some of the objections that my hypothesis may evoke, together with the sole alternative to it that seems to me viable, though I think less credible than what I have proposed. In all events, I remind my readers that what I offer here is strictly an hypothesis, and that without further evidence forthcoming it will be difficult to present a case that amounts to certain proof.

Although there is no doubt that the iconographic program described in the "Prayers" does conform with remarkable exactitude to that of Anxi Yulin cave 25, the significance of this observation is diminished if it proves to be the case that the program in question was relatively widespread. As we know that Vairocana with the eight major bodhisattvas became the objects of a long-sustained and very widely distributed cult, that may be traced to western India beginning in about the sixth century, and that inspired the production icons at various places in Tibet, as well as in China and Japan, are there clear reasons to associate the "Prayers" directly with the particular cave under discussion here?

In response, and without returning to the issue of the toponyms, we must stress once again that it is not only the presence of Vairocana and the eight bodhisattvas that is of concern, for this is indeed too common to serve as a sole index. It is rather the presence of Vairocana in direct proximity to the fields of Amitābha and Maitreya that seems a decisive characteristic. The only other contemporary example of these three Buddhas depicted together in a Tibetan-period (mid-Tang) temple of which I am aware is the "Zhai-family Temple," i.e., Dunhuang Mogao cave 220.[120] In this case, however, the eight bodhisattvas are absent, the Vairocana image does not conform to the iconographic specifications of the known Tibetan models, and Amitābha and Maitreya are solitary, without their surrounding retinues and fields. While it is possible that the Zhai family, as important administrators in Dunhuang, were inspired by the example of their Tibetan lords to include in their family shrine the same three Buddhas as those adorning the Temple of the Treaty, there can be no question that anything more than very rough imitation was involved in this case. It therefore in no way refutes my proposals with respect to Anxi Yulin cave 25.

A more delicate problem is posed by the sole Tibetan inscription in the cave, located on the north wall in the mural of Maitreya's earthly paradise. It is not the only inscription in the edifice, but the others—Chinese donor inscriptions relating to later restorations and Uighur graffiti of the tenth century—are generally agreed to post-date the temple's foundation by several decades and more.[121] While the Tibetan inscription, from the perspective of Tibetan paleography, gives the impression that it too dates to the period following the Tibetan occupation of the Dunhuang region, when Tibetan was still in use as a *lingua franca* in the region,[122] it is only thanks to a recent discovery on the part of Yoshiro Imaeda that it has become decisively clear that it cannot date to the period of the temple's construction.[123] For Imaeda has convincingly demonstrated that, under the Tibetan occupation, the cartouches for the inscriptions accompanying murals were characteristically provided in the form of a capital "T": the upper bar in these cases is used for the horizontally written Tibetan script, surmounting a vertical bar for Chinese. In Anxi Yulin cave 25, the central mural of Vairocana and the eight bodhisattvas is thus appropriately accompanied by T-shaped cartouches (figs. 8–9). In the Maitreya panel, however, only vertical cartouches for Chinese are present, one of which was rather awkwardly employed by the author of the Tibetan inscription. To all evidence, therefore, this individual was not familiar with the earlier convention; his words accordingly must be considered to be late graffiti. Despite this, two Tibetanists in China, Xie Jisheng and Huang Weizhong, have recently argued that the Tibetan inscription refers to the original donor.[124] While, on the basis of the foregoing observations, I cannot concur, their arguments do require some further comment.

The inscription in question reads: *// dze'u/ de'i cung gis/ phags pa' khor cig/ bgyis pa'/ 'di shang she'i/ sku yon du/ bsngas pa'/ lags so//.*

This means: "This circle of *ārya*s, which Dze'u De'i cung enacted, is dedicated as a pious donation to Shang she."[125] The meaning of "enacted" (*bgyis pa*), the honorific past stem of "to do," in this context is not entirely clear. It most likely refers to the act of commissioning or sponsoring the paintings or their restoration. The names of the donor and recipient, in any case, are clearly Chinese.

In their reading, Xie and Huang are surely correct to hold that Dze'u is a transcription of the name of the important Dunhuang family Cao, but they implausibly go on to hold that *de'i cung* is to be derived from the Tibetan phrase *de'i gcung*, "his little brother."[126] It is clear, however, that Dze'u De'i cung is to be read as a single Chinese name, of which Dze'u is the *xing* and De'i cung the *ming*. Taken thus as a whole, it partially resembles the name of one of the figures named in the Chinese donor inscriptions, Cao Yuanzhong,[127] though I see no way to reconcile the *de'i* of the Tibetan with *yuan* in Chinese, even taking into consideration the reconstructed Tang-period pronunciations. (Cao Yuanzhong is well known as the "king of Dunhuang," during whose reign [944–974] the oasis was virtually an independent city-state.[128]) More plausible is the possibility that Dze'u De'i cung is a transcription of Cao Yangong (originally Yanjing), Yuanzhong's successor whose brief reign spanned only two years (974–976).[129] In any event, there can be no basis for arguing that the inscription pre-dates the inception of the rise of the Cao to power in the region during the early tenth century.

Regarding the name Shang she, Xie and Huang offer a number of suggestions without arriving at any definite conclusion. While acknowledging that any firm identification is doubtful, they dwell at length on the resemblance between this name and that of a famous personage of mid-eighth-century Tibet, Ba Sangshi.[130] They overlook, however, Tucci's important observation, following Demiéville, that this name, attributed to an individual said to have been a proponent of Chan Buddhism in Tibet, closely resembles the transcription *shan(g)/shen(g) shi* found frequently in Dunhuang Tibetan Chan documents and used to transcribe the Chinese title "dhyāna master" (Ch. *chanshi*).[131] Though no definite conclusion about the interpretation of Shang she seems to be thereby warranted, the arguments of Xie and Huang, to the effect that the inscription refers to the early ninth century and alludes to the original donation, cannot be accepted on the basis of their suggestions regarding either of the names mentioned in it. It is a tenth-century addition, probably dating to the period of the Cao-family restoration of the cave, possibly (though this remains quite uncertain) referring to a grant in favor of one or more local *chan*-practitioners.

We have seen, too, in connection with the toponym Daxia, that we faced some interpretive difficulties, and that, on the basis of Chögyel Pakpa's testimony, Uebach had located Yarmotang close to Daxia in southern Gansu. Would it not be preferable, then, to hold that Dega Yutsel was in fact located in that region, and, while accepting the general drift of the interpretation advanced here, to consider that Anxi Yulin cave 25 was more likely created in imitation of it? This, of course, is the best alternative theory, and, though

I cannot exclude it altogether, it seems unlikely to be true. The geographical frame of reference of PT 16 - IOL Tib J 751 has been already discussed, including the important evidence provided by the Chuksam chiliarch, whose presence points directly to Anxi Yulin. The exceptional quality of the artistry of cave 25, and especially its strict adherence to early-ninth-century Tibetan iconographic codes in its depiction of the central Vairocana and eight bodhisattvas, points to Tibetan involvement of a very high order, such as would accord with a commission from the upper echelons of the colonial administration. The major objections to this thesis that have come to my attention so far have been answered above.

In sum, then, in the "Prayers of Dega Yutsel," and at Anxi Yulin cave 25 which likely corresponds to the Temple of the Treaty described therein, together with the Chinese record of the ceremonies surrounding the ratification of the treaty of 822 in Lhasa, we find clear evidence for the beginnings of the process whereby Buddhism assumed a position of centrality in Sino-Tibetan relations overall. As would continue to be the case down through the centuries, diplomacy, ritual, and icon were interwoven in the tissue of events, places, and texts according to the ideal of a sublime, transcending plan.

NOTES

* I am grateful to many colleagues, students, and friends for their responses to this chapter, on the several occasions when I presented earlier formulations of it to them. In particular, I wish to thank Karl Debreczeny, Brandon Dotson, Yuesan Gao, Robert Gimello, Phyllis Granoff, Amy Heller, Bianca Horlemann, Huo Wei, Yoshiro Imaeda, Kuo Liying, François Martin, Christine Mollier, Ulrich Pagel, Tsuguhito Takeuchi, Katherine R. Tsiang, Helga Uebach, Wang Yudong, Dorothy Wong, Wu Hung, You Hong, and Zhang Changhong for their varied contributions to the development of this research. Above all, I am indebted to Mrs. Lucy Lo and the Lo Archive (Princeton) for generous permission to reproduce here photographs from their invaluable visual record of Anxi Yulin cave 25, made during the course of James and Lucy Lo's documentation of the Dunhuang grottoes during the 1940s.

  A preliminary account of this research appeared in "The Treaty Temple of De ga g.Yu tshal: Iconography and Identification," in *Essays on the International Conference on Tibetan Archeology and Art*, ed. Huo Wei (Chengdu: Sichuan Renmin Chuhanshe, 2004), pp. 98–127. The present chapter may be considered to supercede that version.

1 Christopher I. Beckwith, *The Tibetan Empire in Central Asia* (Princeton: Princeton University Press, 1987), provides the major study to date of Tibet's rivalry with China in regions to China's west. The essentials are summarized in brief by Denis Twitchett, ed., *The Cambridge History of China, Volume 3, Sui and T'ang China, 589–*

906 (Cambridge: Cambridge University Press, 1979), pp. 35–36: "Tibet suddenly grew into a powerful united kingdom and embarked on a career of aggressive expansion. From their original centre in southern Tibet the Tibetans expanded westward toward the Pamirs, eastward toward Yunnan, and northward to impinge upon China's fresh conquests in the Tarim, where they threatened China's trade routes to the west. Then, during Kao-tsung's reign, the Tibetans destroyed the T'u-yü-hun kingdom in modern Ch'ing-hai province, which had previously formed a buffer between them and the Chinese territories in Kansu. From this time onward the Tibetans constantly threatened the Chinese both in the Kansu corridor and in the region around Lan-chou, in which regions the T'ang was forced to maintain huge permanent armies. When, after 755, the An Lu-shan rebellion forced the government to withdraw these garrisons for the defence of the capital, the Tibetans occupied most of modern Kansu province where they remained from 763 until the 840s. The Chinese outposts in the Tarim and Zungharia were cut off from metropolitan China, and they too were later overrun by the Tibetans."

2 For a sustained overview of China's relations with Tibet, the Uighurs, and others during the mid-first millennium, see Pan Yihong, *Son of Heaven and Heavenly Qaghan: Sui-Tang China and its Neighbors* (Bellingham, Washington: Western Washington University, 1997).

3 Hugh E. Richardson, "Two Chinese Princesses in Tibet: Mun-sheng Kong-co and Kim-sheng Kong-co," in *High Peaks, Pure Earth: Collected Writings on Tibetan History and Culture*, ed. Michael Aris (London: Serindia Publications, 1998), pp. 207–215.

4 Per K. Sørensen, *Tibetan Buddhist Historiography: The Mirror Illuminating the Royal Genealogies* (Wiesbaden: Harrassowitz Verlag, 1994), translates one of the fullest elaborations of the legend. Aspects of its development are studied in my *The Tibetan Assimilation of Buddhism: Conversion, Contestation and Memory* (New York: Oxford University Press, 2000), ch. 8.

5 Sylvain Lévi, *The Mission of Wang Hiuen-ts'e in India*, trans. S.P. Chatterjee, ed. B. C. Law (Calcutta: Indian Geographical Society, 1967). The original version of this article appeared in the *Journal Asiatique* in 1900.

6 She appears to have played some sort of ongoing role in correspondence between the powers. In 679, shortly before her death, she is recorded as having solicited the Tang court, requesting that a princess be sent to wed the *btsan-po* 'Dus-srong. Refer to Paul Demiéville, *Le concile de Lhasa: une controverse sur le quiétisme entre bouddhistes de l'Inde et de la Chine au VIIIe siècle de l'ère chrétienne*, Bibliothèque de l'Institut des Hautes Études Chinoises, vol. VII (Paris: Imprimerie Nationale de France, 1952), p. 3.

7 Thus, referring to the situation in 670, Beckwith, *The Tibetan Empire*, p. 37, writes: "The Tibetans had now conquered a fairly large expanse of territory in eastern Central Asia. The region straddled the main East-West transcontinental trade routes, and was then a dynamic, integral part of the highly civilized Buddhist heartland of Eurasia. Thus, the loss of this profitable and most strategic part of their colonial empire was a shock to the T'ang Chinese. . ." See also Pan, *Son of Heaven*, pp. 243–247. It should be recalled that the Tibetans were also exerting pressure at the same time to the southwest of China, in Nanzhao, where Buddhism was also prominent.

8 Richardson, "Two Chinese Princesses," pp. 211–214; Kapstein, *The Tibetan Assimilation*, ch. 2. For her place in the history of Khotan, see Ronald Eric Emmerick, *Tibetan Texts Concerning Khotan* (London: Oxford University Press, 1967).

9 Nevertheless, the traditions of the *Dba'/Sba bzhed* do hold a Chinese Buddhist monk to have still been active in Lhasa: Pasang Wangdu and Hildegard Diemberger, *dBa' bzhed: The Royal Narrative Concerning the Bringing of the Buddha's Doctrine to Tibet* (Vienna: Österreichische Akademie der Wissenschaften, 2000), p. 39; Kapstein, *The Tibetan Assimilation*, p. 39.

10 The *New Tang Annals* and *Old Tang Annals* document altogether seven treaties, or "sworn covenants," between China and Tibet, offering some description of the ceremonial arrangements in three cases. For a thorough survey, see Yihong Pan, "The Sino-Tibetan Treaties in the Tang Dynasty," *T'oung Pao* 78 (1992): 116–161. Earlier, R.A. Stein had examined the oath-taking ceremonies that these involved in "Les serments des traités sino-tibétaines (8e–9e siècles)," *T'oung Pao* 74 (1988): 119–138; and Yoshiro Imaeda has treated the same subject matter, challenging aspects of Stein's findings, in "Rituel des traités de paix sino-tibétaines du VIIIe au IXe siècle," in Jean-Pierre Drège, ed., *La Sérinde, terre d'echanges: Art, religion, commerce du Ier au Xe siècle* (Paris: La Doumentation française, 2000), pp. 87–98.

11 Stein, "Les serments," pp. 134 and 136, argues that the date 756 given in the *Jiu Tang shu* is erroneous and must be corrected on the basis of other sources to 762. Pan and Imaeda have both followed him on this point.

12 After S.W. Bushell, "The Early History of Tibet," *Journal of the Royal Asiatic Society*, new series 12/4 (1880): 479. I have modified Bushell's now dated translation somewhat, taking account of Paul Pelliot, *Histoire ancienne du Tibet* (Paris: Adrien-Maisonneuve, 1961), p. 29, as well as the translation of this passage in Imaeda, "Rituel des traités," p. 92.

13 On the Tibetan rebellion of 755, see Christopher I. Beckwith, "The revolt of 755 in Tibet," in *Contributions on Tibetan Language, History and Culture*, ed. Ernst Steinkellner and Helmut Tauscher, Vol. 1 of the Proceedings of the Csoma de Kőrös Symposium held at Velm-Vienna, Austria (Vienna: Arbeitskreis fur Tibetische und Buddhistische Studien Universität Wien, 1983), pp. 1–16. There has been some disagreement over the interpretation of the 762 treaty between Tibet and China, R.A. Stein seeking to find here the evidence of a double rite—sacrificial and Buddhist—despite the explicit refusal of the Buddhist rite. While Pan Yihong, "The Sino-Tibetan Treaties," follows Stein about this, Imaeda, "Rituel des traités," has rejected this interpretation, and argues for adhering to a more straightforward reading of the text. The anti-Buddhist nature of the 755 Tibetan rebellion has not previously been taken into account, but I think that it does support Imaeda's perspective. Nevertheless, a well-known early Tibetan history, the *Sba bzhed*, does have Tibetan Buddhist ministers traveling to China during this period, in part to escape the reaction against their religion: *The Tibetan Assimilation*, pp. 71–72. In the account found in the *Dba' bzhed*, however, the mission takes place at a later date, when Khri Srong lde'u btsan is already interested in Buddhism: Wangdu and Diemberger, *dBa' bzhed*, pp. 47–52. The Tibetan envoys are not recorded, however, to have participated specifically in treaty negotiations while there. All in all, it seems to me that the reference to Buddhism in the *Tang Annals'* account of the treaty of 762 prob-

ably reflects the vogue that the religion, particularly in its esoteric form, was enjoying in the Tang court during this period. See Twitchett, ed., *The Cambridge History, Volume 3*, pp. 576–580.

14 Demiéville, *Le concile de Lhasa*, pp. 183–184. Though Demiéville speaks here of a permanent Chinese Buddhist mission established by the Tang in Tibet in 781, it is not entirely clear for how long the project was actually continued.

15 For the most recent review of the problem of dating the Tibetan occupation of Dunhuang, arguing that the hitherto accepted dates (781 or 787) are too late, see Bianca Horlemann, "A Re-evaluation of the Tibetan Conquest of Eighth-century Shazhou/ Dunhuang," in Henk Blezer, ed., *Tibet, Past and Present: Tibetan Studies I*, PIATS 2000 (Leiden: Brill, 2002), pp. 49–66. The correspondence of a Tibetan ruler, probably Khri Srong lde'u btsan, with the Dunhuang-based monk Tankuang well illustrates the interest of the Tibetan court in Chinese Buddhism at this time. See W. Pachow, *A Study of the Twenty-two Dialogues on Mahāyāna Buddhism* (Taipei, Taiwan: [s.n.], 1979).

16 Bushell, "The Early History," pp. 487–490. Edited on the basis of Pelliot, *Histoire ancienne*, pp. 43–45.

17 His title and name in Tibetan may perhaps be reconstructed as *Zhang Skyes bzang. Though no person of precisely this appellation is known from Old Tibetan sources, the *Old Tibetan Annals* (PT 1288) does mention several individuals of ministerial rank (*blon*) named Skyes bzang under the years 729, 734, 737, 746 (Skyes bzang ldong tsab); 744, 761 (Skyes bzang); 746, 758, 759 (Skyes bzang stag snang); and 756, 757 (Skyes bzang rgyal kong). Perhaps one of the latter was granted the title of Zhang blon later in his career, although, because the personal name seems rather common, Shang Jiezan may have been another individual altogether. Alternatively, Jiezan may represent *Rgyal btsan/mtshan.

18 Imaeda, "Rituel des traités," pp. 93–94.

19 The history that concerns us here, and the previous research devoted to it, is surveyed in Pan, *Son of Heaven*, ch. 9–10.

20 Beckwith, *The Tibetan Empire*, pp. 151–152, for instance, cites the Chinese minister Li Mi as advising the emperor during the autumn of 787: "I would like His Majesty to make peace with the Uyghurs in the north, come to terms with Nan-chao in the south, and unite with the Arabs and Hindustan in the West. In this way the Tibetans would themselves be in trouble, and horses would be easy [for us] to obtain."

21 Colin Mackerras, *The Uighur Empire According to the T'ang Dynastic Histories: A Study in Sino-Uighur Relations 744–840.* (Columbia, SC: University of South Carolina Press, 1973), pp. 44–46. I have taken the liberty of substituting, here and in the following quotation, Pinyin transcriptions for the Wade-Giles used by Mackerras.

22 Mackerras, *The Uighur Empire*, pp. 46–47.

23 I speak here of a "series of treaties" with some hesitation, for, with the exception of the 821/822 treaty between China and Tibet, our evidence for Tibet's treaties with the Uighurs and, in particular, Nanzhao is rather hazy. For a review of the problem, see J. Szerb, "A Note on the Tibetan-Uigur Treaty of 822/823 A.D.," in *Contributions on Tibetan Language, History and Culture*, pp. 375–387.

24 Editions and studies of the "uncle-nephew pillar inscription" include: Bsod nams skyid, *Bod kyi rdo ring yi ge dang dril bu'i kha byang* (Beijing: Mi rigs dpe skrun khang, 1984), pp. 21–58; Hugh E. Richardson, *A Corpus of Early Tibetan Inscriptions*

(London: Royal Asiatic Society, 1985), pp. 106–143; Dkon mchog tshe brtan, *Dbon zhang rdo ring dang thang bod bar gyi 'brel ba* (Lanzhou: Kan su'u mi rigs dpe skrun khang, 1986); Li Fang Kuei and W. South Coblin, *A Study of the Old Tibetan Inscriptions*, Institute of History and Philology, Special Publications No. 91 (Taipei: Academia Sinica, 1987); Go shul Grags pa 'byung gnas, *Bod btsan po'i skabs kyi gna' rtsom gces bsdus slob deb* (Beijing: Mi rigs dpe skrun khang, 2001), pp. 1–12 (Tibetan text only); and four studies of the text in Kha sgang Bkra shis tshe ring, ed., *Bod kyi yig rnying zhib 'jug* (Beijing: Mi rigs dpe skrun khang, 2003), pp. 8–40. My references to the inscription here will be to Richardson's edition.

25 Rgyal ba Lnga pa chen mo (Dalai Lama V) Ngag dbang blo bzang rgya mtsho, *Bod kyi deb ther dpyid kyi rgyal mo'i glu dbyangs* (Beijing: Mi rigs dpe skrun khang, 1988), p. 73: "At this time, China and Tibet being in disaccord, a great [Tibetan] army, ferocious and awesome, waged war upon the land of China, vanquishing many Chinese fiefs [lit. 'principalities'], and killing numerous lords and heroic warriors, so that they were brought to defeat. Then, the Chinese monk(s) and the Tibetan translators and paṇḍitas interceded and by their verbal admonitions they made the uncle [the Chinese emperor] and nephew [the Tibetan *btsan-po*] come to an accord. At Gung gu rme ru in China a pillar was erected, which was determined to be the China-Tibet boundary, whereupon [they agreed] not to let their armies transgress these frontiers so as to make war upon one another, etc. With the stern gods and nāgas bearing witness, they swore an oath to this, which was inscribed in writing upon three pillars: in Lhasa, the palace of the Chinese emperor, and Gung gu rme ru. At that time, because there was harmony between China and Tibet and their relations were good, it was said that 'in the heavens there is the single pair of sun and moon, while on earth, the *btsan-po*, uncle and nephew.'" (*'di'i dus su rgya bod gnyis ma mthun par/ gtum drag rngam brjid dang ldan pa'i dmag gi dpung tshogs chen po rgya nag po'i yul du gyul bshams te/ tsi na'i rgyal khams du ma bcom zhing/ mi dpon dang/ dpa' bo stag shar mang du bsad de cham la phab/ de nas rgya'i hwa shang dang bod kyi lo paṇ rnams kyis bar du bzhugs te tshig gi sbyang bshad kyis dpon* [read: *dbon*] *zhang mthun par mzdad/ rgya'i gung gu rme rur rdo ring zhig btsugs te rgya bod kyis sa mtshams su bcad nas phan tshun gnyis kas sa mtshams las phyi rol tu bsgral ba'i dmag gi gyul bshams pa sogs mi byed pa'i dpang du lha klu gnyan po bzhag ste bro bor ba'i yi ge lha sa/ rgya rje'i pho brang/ rme ru gsum gyi rdo ring la bris/ dus der rgya bod gnyis mthun zhing 'brel bzang bar byung bas/ gnam la nyi zla zung gcig dang/ sa la btsan po dpon* [read: *dbon*] *zhang zhes gleng skad do//.*)

26 *A Mirror of the Murals in the Potala* (Beijing: Jiu zhou tushu chubanshe, 2000), pp. 80–82.

27 *Dbon zhang rdo ring*, west face, lines 56–58 (Richardson, *A Corpus of Early Tibetan Inscriptions*, pp. 124–125).

28 Pelliot, *Histoire Ancienne*, pp. 72–74. Once again, Stein, "Les serments," p. 128, goes to lengths to find a trace of a Buddhist rite in the ceremony performed in Chang'an, while Imaeda, "Rituel des traités," p. 94, prefers to adhere to the explicit statements of the primary source, the *Jiu Tang shu*.

29 Liu Yuanding is also mentioned as a participant in the *Dbon zhang rdo ring*, south face, lines 39–40 (Richardson, *A Corpus of Early Tibetan Inscriptions*, pp. 142–143).

30 Pelliot translates, "au milieu d'elles [the lances], était planté un grand étendard," but

I prefer to follow in this case the Tibetan translation of Don grub rgyal and Khrin Chin dbyin [Chen Qingying], trans., *Thang yig gsar rnying las byung ba'i bod chen po'i srid lugs* (Xining: Mtsho sngon mi rigs dpe skrun khang, 1983), p. 105, according to which a standard was raised at each of the three gates.

31 Again, Pelliot's translation, "une mousseline rose était nouée pour lui couvrir la tête," seems to me less plausible that that of Don grub rgyal and Chen Qingying, who, quite in accord with the iconographic tradition, represent the Btsan po as wearing a red turban. The description of Khri Gtsug lde btsan's costume given here corresponds with remarkable precision to the depiction that we find of a Tibetan Btsan po in the entourage of Vimalakīrti in the murals of Dunhuang Mogao cave 159, where he is shown with white robes and a red turban. Refer to Heather Karmay, "Tibetan Costume, Seventh to Eleventh Centuries," in Ariane Macdonald and Yoshiro Imaeda, eds., *Essais sur l'art du Tibet* (Paris: Jean Maisonneuve, 1977), pp. 73–75.

32 In his text, Pelliot left this in the transcription *po-tsh'ö-pou*, but in his "Index des noms tibétains," p. 146, gives *po-tch'an-pou*, which he elsewhere (Index général, p. 159) treats as synonymous, as equivalent to Dpal chen po in Tibetan. This suggestion was subsequently adopted by Demiéville, *Le concile*, pp. 228–230, and by Stein, "Les serments," p. 129. The identification is confirmed by the occurrence in the *Dbon zhang rdo ring*, north face, line 9, of the *ban de chen po dpal chen po yon tan*, "the great monk [minister] Dpal chen po yon tan" (Richardson, *A Corpus of Early Tibetan Inscriptions*, pp. 128–129).

33 This title, which is recorded three times in Pelliot's text (pp. 9, 106, 131) has not to my knowledge been satisfactorily explained. Don grub rgyal and Chen Qingying (p. 106) interpret the name of the minister who held it, Xidaruo, as a transcription of the Tibetan Stag bzher, a name that is indeed known from the *Dbon zhang rdo ring*, north face, line 35 (Richardson, *A Corpus of Early Tibetan Inscriptions*, pp. 132–133). As a minister belonging to the same Bran ka clan from which the monk-minister Dpal gyi yon tan hailed, he was no doubt in a position of considerable authority.

34 Pelliot translates "esclaves."

35 Pelliot, *Histoire ancienne*, pp. 130–131. Don-grub-rgyal and Chen Qingying, trans., *Thang yig gsar rnying*, pp. 105–106.

36 Refer to Richardson, "Great Monk Ministers of the Tibetan Kingdom," in *High Peaks, Pure Earth*, pp. 145–148.

37 See my *The Tibetans* (Oxford: Blackwell, 2006), pp. 80–82.

38 The generally useful bibliography by Michela Bussotti and Jean-Pierre Drège, "Essai de bibliographie des travaux sur Dunhuang en langues occidentales," in Jean-Pierre Drège, ed. *De Dunhuang au Japon: Études chinoises et bouddhiques offertes à Michel Soymié*, Hautes Études Orientales 31 (Geneva: Droz, 1996), pp. 411–454, neglects a considerable portion of work on the Tibetan materials, a preliminary bibliography of which may be found in: Yoshiro Imaeda, Tsuguhito Takeuchi, et al., eds., *Tibetan Documents from Dunhuang kept at the Bibliothèque nationale de France and the British Library*, Old Tibetan Documents Online Monograph Series Vol. 1 (Tokyo: Tokyo University of Foreign Studies, 2007), pp. xxi–xxx. This may be supplemented by consulting the bibliographical notes in J. Dalton and S. van Schaik, *Tibetan Tantric Manuscripts from Dunhuang: A Descriptive Catalogue of the Stein Collection at the British Library*, Brill's Tibetan Studies Library 12 (Leiden: Brill,

2006); and M.T. Kapstein and B. Dotson, eds., *Contributions to the Cultural History of Early Tibet*, Brill's Tibetan Studies Library 14 (Leiden : Brill, 2007).

39 For a general survey, see Susan Whitfield, ed. *The Silk Road: Trade, Travel, War and Faith* (London: Serindia, 2004). Among recent studies in which the relation between text and artistic production at Dunhuang figures prominently, note in particular: Sarah E. Fraser, *Performing the Visual: The Practice of Buddhist Wall Painting in China and Central Asia, 618–960* (Stanford: Stanford University Press, 2004); Ning Qiang, *Art, Religion and Politics in Medieval China: The Dunhuang Cave of the Zhai Family* (Honolulu: University of Hawai'i Press, 2004); and Eugene Wang, *Shaping the Lotus Sutra: Buddhist Visual Culture in Medieval China* (Seattle: University of Washington Press, 2005).

40 PT, "Pelliot tibétain," is used to denote Tibetan Dunhuang manuscript holdings of the Bibliothèque nationale de France that were collected by Paul Pelliot, while IOL Tib J is the British Library's designation for the Tibetan documents brought from Dunhuang by Marc Aurel Stein and long kept at the India Office Library (London). The sections of the manuscript preserved separately in Paris and London were reunited in the facsimile reproduction given by Ariane Macdonald and Yoshiro Imaeda in the first volume of *Choix de documents tibétains*, and later edited by Imaeda and Tsughohito Takeuchi in the third volume of the same series: Ariane Macdonald and Yoshiro Imaeda, *Choix de documents tibétains*, vol. I (Paris: Bibliothèque Nationale, 1978); Yoshiro Imaeda and Tsuguhito Takeuchi, *Choix de documents tibétains*, vol. 3 (Paris: Bibliothèque Nationale, 1990). All subsequent references to the text of PT 16 - IOL Tib J 751 will be to the latter edition.

41 F.W. Thomas, *Tibetan Literary Texts and Documents Concerning Chinese Turkestan, Part II: Documents,* (London: Luzac and Company, 1951), pp. 92–109; idem, *Tibetan Literary Texts and Documents Concerning Chinese Turkestan, Part III: Addenda and Corrigenda* (London: Luzac and Company, 1955), pp. 4–5, 42–46.

42 Ariane Macdonald, "Une lecture des Pelliot tibétain 1286, 1287, 1038, 1047, et 1290: Essai sur la formation et l'emploi des mythes politiques dans la religion royale de Sroṅ-bcan sgam-po," in Ariane Macdonald, ed., *Études tibétaines dédiées à la mémoire de Marcelle Lalou* (Paris: Adrien Maisonneuve, 1971), pp. 190–391; Rolf A. Stein, "Tibetica Antiqua I: Les deux vocabulaires des traductions Indo-tibétaine et Sino-tibétaine dans les Manuscrits de Touen-houang," *Bulletin de l'École Française d'Extrême-Orient (BEFEO)* LXXII (1983): 149–236; idem, "Tibetica Antiqua III: A propos du mot *gcug-lag* et de la religion indigène," *BEFEO* LXXIV (1985): 83–133; idem, "Tibetica Antiqua IV: "La tradition relative au début du Bouddhisme au Tibet," *BEFEO* LXXV (1986): 169–196.

43 Thomas mistakenly identified the monarch concerned as Khri Lde gtsug btsan/brtan (r. 710–755) and therefore incorrectly dated the foundation of the temple to the early eighth century. The error was noticed and corrected by Demiéville (*Le concile*, pp. 362–364) and subsequently acknowledged by Thomas.

44 An example may be found in Dudjom Rinpoche, Jikdrel Yeshe Dorje, *The Nyingma School of Tibetan Buddhism: Its Fundamentals and History*, trans. Gyurme Dorje and Matthew Kapstein (Boston: Wisdom Publications, 1991), vol. 1, pp. 521–522.

45 The entrustment of royal education to the Buddhist clergy is specifically ordained in the Skar chung inscription of Khri Sde srong btsan. See my *The Tibetans*, p. 76.

46 Refer to Szerb, "A Note on the Tibetan-Uigur Treaty." Although Nanzhao is cer-
    tainly mentioned in the text of PT 16 - IOL Tib J 751 (*jang* 33b3, 36b2, 38b3, 39b2),
    suggesting that it was a party to the treaty or treaties at issue, it is not quite clear to
    me that it is mentioned as anything more than one of the lands that was in some
    sense a beneficiary of the peace, whose representatives may have participated in
    some ceremonies.

47 The meaning of *gtsigs* in the present document has been discussed at length in Stein,
    "Les serments," pp. 122–123. On his reading, my phrase "treaty-edict" is somewhat
    inexact, at least in relation to the primary and original meaning of the word, which
    referred to an orally sworn oath. The most pertinent passages for an interpretation of
    the term in our text are: PT16, line 34a1: *myi 'gyur ba'i gtsigs kyï rdo rings btsugs*, IOL
    Tib J 751, 39b3: *gtsigs bka' stsald to 'tsal du mnos pa*, and 40b2–3: *mjal dum gyi gtsigs
    bcas nas rdo rings la brïs* (cf. PT16, 26b2–3: *tshigs bcas nas . . .*). There is no question
    but that the *gtsigs* was considered to be a written edict here.

48 Szerb, "A Note on the Tibetan-Uigur Treaty," p. 376, erroneously considers the first
    part of the manuscript preserved in PT 16 to have emanated from Dbyar mo thang,
    though in fact it is only prayer (2) that did. Perhaps prayer (1) was presented by rep-
    resentatives of the court. This, at least, is what may be suggested by a phrase from the
    Bde blon's prayer (3), IOL Tib J 751, 38b2: *smon lam gzhan yang/ bla nas mdzad pa
    dang mthun bar smond to//*, "as for other prayers, I pray in conformity with what was
    done from above," where "from above" (*bla nas*) likely refers to the court. If this is
    so, then it can only refer to the first surviving prayer (1), or perhaps to a lost text that
    occupied part of the missing portion of the manuscript.

49 *khrom*. Though often translated as "market," "city," or even "fortified city," the *khrom*
    of the old Tibetan empire correspond more closely to the administrative center of
    a prefecture in Chinese practice, though, as Uray has shown, with a clearer accent
    on its role as a center for the military administration. It thus resembles a canton-
    ment in Indian English usage. See Géza Uray, "*Khrom*: Administrative units of the
    Tibetan Empire in the 7th–9th centuries," in Michael Aris and Aung San Suu Kyi,
    eds., *Tibetan Studies in Honour of Hugh Richardson* (Warminster: Aris and Phillips,
    1980), pp. 310–318.

50 Here and in (6) and (7) below I have interpreted the genitive *g(y)ï/'ï* as agentive
    g(y)is/'is.

51 Refer to Richardson, "The Province of the *Bde-blon* of the Tibetan Empire, Eighth
    to Ninth Centuries," in *High Peaks, Pure Earth*, pp. 167–176.

52 As Stein notes, "Tibetica Antiqua I," p. 216, the Japanese historian of early Tibet, Z.
    Yamaguchi, believed that Mkhar btsan (= Leng cu) should refer here to Lingzhou
    (Lingwu) in modern Ningxia province, which was the northwestern frontier of the
    Tibetan empire at the beginning of the ninth century (Tan Qixiang 谭其骧, ed., *The
    Historical Atlas of China* 中國歷史地圖集, volume V [Beijing: China Cartographic
    Publishing House, 1996], map 76–77). However, as Beckwith, *The Tibetan Empire*,
    p. 167, shows, Lingwu was likely lost to the Tibetans sometime before our texts were
    produced. (Refer to Pelliot, *Histoire ancienne*, p. 74, which does mention a negotia-
    tion over boundaries immediately following the Tibetan defeat by the commissioner
    of Lingwu.) Given therefore its proximity to the other regions in Gansu mentioned
    in the prayers, and the fact that it had been firmly under Tibetan command since 808

(Beckwith, p. 163), Liangzhou seems the more probable identification. This was also the conclusion of Uray, "*Khrom*," p. 314.

53   Helga Uebach, "An 8th Century List of Thousand-Districts in Ne'i Paṇḍita's History," in B.N. Aziz and M. Kapstein, eds., *Soundings in Tibetan Civilization* (New Delhi: Manohar, 1985), pp. 147–151, records a *phyugs mtshams* in Central Tibet (*dbu ru*), but this seems surely not to be identified with the location mentioned here.

54   Thomas, *Tibetan Texts II*, p. 104, reads "the district ḥBrom khoṅ," but this seems doubtful.

55   Refer to the translations of Thomas, *Tibetan Texts II*, pp. 99–104. Though now dated in terms of many particulars, these still provide an adequate view of the general contents of IOL Tib J 751.

56   *dgab*, lit. "hidden, concealed."

57   *chos gtsug nï/ lugs kyïs bzang/*. With the exception of the grammatical particles *nï* and *kyïs*, all of the terms used in this phrase are dense with meaning, and no translation can hope to achieve its semantic richness while preserving its concision. The term *gtsug*, in particular, which Ariane Macdonald regarded as the ancient name of the Tibetan royal religion, following further contributions by Stein is now generally agreed to refer to the particular wisdom that characterizes just rulership. (See n. 42 above for their principal discussions of this issue.) The etymology of the word is brilliantly analyzed in Michael Hahn, "A propos the term *gtsug lag*," *Tibetan Studies: Proceedings of the Seventh Seminar of the International Association for Tibetan Studies*, ed. Ernst Steinkellner et al. (Vienna: Austrian Academy of Sciences, 1997), vol. 1, pp. 347–354.

58   *thug skam dbu rmog btsan pa'i chab srid*. Again, this is a stock characterization of the merits of the Tibetan Btsan po. Cf. the colophon cited in *The Tibetan Assimilation*, pp. 231–232, n. 64.

59   *nyï 'og*. Like *tianxia*, "under heaven," in Chinese, this probably means here "the whole world." I do not believe that it should be taken in this context as naming a particular country, i.e. Bactria (Skt. Aparāntaka), as it apparently does in the introduction to the *Sgra sbyor bam po gnyis pa*, referring to the homeland of the "Indian" *ācārya*-s at the court of Khri Lde srong btsan: refer to Mie Ishikawa, *A Critical Edition of the Sgra sbyor bam po gnyis pa, An Old and Basic Commentary on the* Mahāvyutpatti, Studia Tibetica 18 (Tokyo: The Toyo Bunko, 1990), p. 1, para. 2. A translation of this passage will be found in my *The Tibetans*, pp. 76–77.

60   *chag 'og tu 'dus phas. . .* The meaning is clear enough, though *chag* perhaps is err. for *chab*.

61   *dpa' ba'i la bor bas*. I have not succeeded in ascertaining the precise significance of *la bor ba*, though it is reminiscent of expressions such as *la zlo ba*, "to ascertain," or of *mna' bor ba*, "to swear an oath." Perhaps it means roughly "commitment, decision." In the absence of a sure interpretation, I have allowed the fortuitous circumstance that the English homonym of the first two syllables yields an intelligible translation to suggest a tentative rendering.

62   *gna'i chos chen po nï bstud*. Here, *gna'* should perhaps be read *mna'*. In any event, the parallelism in the phrases *dgra chos* "enmity" and *gna'i chos* is unmistakable, so that the translation of the latter as "fidelity" seems certain. If interpreted according to the classical Tibetan orthography it would mean roughly "traditions of yore," which, though not impossible, seems not to make good sense here.

63   *rabs khrïr bzhag nas chu gang khrel ltas nï brlïng du btsugs.* My translation of this passage is tentative.

64   *gces par byas nas.* I.e., having made (ourselves) dear (to our former enemies), or having made (our former enemies) dear (to ourselves). Perhaps the lack of specification should be taken to suggest that the new-found cherishing is (or at least is conceived to be) expressly mutual.

65   *dgra thabs mkhas pa'i skyims kyïs.* The precise meaning of *skyims* is unclear to me and my translation omits it.

66   *mnangs bcad pa.* "Plundered" is perhaps what is meant. Refer to the definitions of this and related terms in Rnam rgyal tshe ring, *Bod yig brda rnying tshig mdzod* (Beijing: Krung go'i bod rig pa dpe skrun khang, 2001), p. 289.

67   Cf. Thomas, *Tibetan Texts II*, pp. 101–102.

68   The *Old Tibetan Chronicle* (PT 1287) may be taken as a case in point.

69   See above, n. 46.

70   But consider the comments of Pan, "Sino-Tibetan Treaties," pp. 147–148, who remarks that "peace . . . prevailed most of the time from 822 to 847," while calling into question "whether this period of peace was maintained solely as a result of the 821/822 treaty." While Pan invokes the Tibetan ruler's commitment to Buddhism as an additional factor, I am skeptical of this explanation and believe that the economic decline of the Tibetan empire more likely restrained Tibetan aggression toward its neighbors. See *The Tibetans*, pp. 77–83.

71   On the talismanic role of the turquoise in Tibetan religious culture, see in particular Samten G. Karmay, "The Soul and the Turquoise: A Ritual for Recalling the *bla*," in his *The Arrow and the Spindle: Studies in History, Myths, Rituals and Beliefs in Tibet* (Kathmandu: Mandala Book Point, 1998), pp. 310–338.

72   IOL J Tib 751, folio 41b1–2: *yul bkra shïs dbyar mo thang de ga g.yul * g.yu tsal du/ / blon chen po zhang khrï sum rje dang zhang chen po lha bzang dang/ bka'* [b2] *'khor dang bdag cag las stsogs phas gtsug lag khang brtsïgs . . .*

73   Uray, "*Khrom*," p. 313.

74   Helga Uebach, "Dbyar-mo-thaṅ and Goṅ-bu ma-ru: Tibetan Historiographical Tradition in the Treaty of 821/823," in E. Steinkellner, ed., *Tibetan History and Language: Studies Dedicated to Géza Uray on his Seventieth Birthday* (Vienna: Arbeitskreis fur Tibetische und Buddhistische Studien Universität Wien, 1991), p. 522. Richardson, "The Province of the *Bde-blon*," pp. 174–175, has also suggested that the southern Gansu area may have been of importance in the administration of the Tibetan "Pacification Minister." This would perhaps explain the background for 'Phags pa's use of the designation Dbyar mo thang to refer to the Klu chu region. We shall return to this issue in discussing the toponym Dega below.

75   Uebach, "Dbyar-mo-thaṅ and Goṅ-bu ma-ru," p. 502.

76   Brag dgon pa Dkon mchog bstan pa rab rgyas, *Mdo smad chos 'byung* (Lanzhou: Kan su'u mi rigs dpe skrun khang, 1982), p. 1: *sgang gsum la byed tshe mdo khams la smar khams btags pa khams gcig/ mdo smad la g.yer mo thang btags pa khams gcig/ tsong kha la gyi thang btags pa khams gcig tu byed. . .*

77   There may be some ambiguity about this, however. Despite the apparently clear classification of the three *sgang*, or *khams*, as presented in the preceding note, the same work, p. 53, says: *tsong chu'i gdags srib dang/ tsong la ring mo lho byang gi sa'i*

khams kyi g.yer mo thang ngam/ shar mdo smad tsong kha sprul pa'i zhing zhes yongs su grags. . . This clearly suggests that *g.yer mo thang* designates Mdo smad *including* Tsong kha. In Zhang Yisun 張怡蓀 et al., eds., *Bod rgya tshig mdzod chen mo* (*Zang-han dacidian* 藏漢大辭典; *The Great Tibetan-Chinese Dictionary*) (Beijing: Minzu chubanshe, 1985), p. 2627, *g.yer mo thang* is defined as a former designation for Mdo smad. The uncertainty as to whether the term embraces Tsong kha or not seems to be reflected in the work of R.A. Stein. In his *Les tribus anciennes de marches sino-tibétaines: Légendes, classifications et histoire*, Bibliothèque de l'Institut des Hautes Études Chinoises, vol. XV (Paris: Presses Universitaires de France, 1961), he identified *g.yar mo thang* as Mdo smad and as the "plaine du Kokonor." Accordingly, it is clearly indicated as the vast territory to the southwest of the Kokonor on the accompanying map. And elsewhere (*Recherches su l'épopée et le barde au Tibet* [Paris: Presses Universitaires de France, 1959], p. 207, n. 11) he has written that it refers to "la grande plaine du nord renfermant le lac Kokonor," which on p. 294 he identifies as the location of De ga g.yu tshal (though without mentioning the temple by name). In the map of early Tibet given in his *La civilisation tibétaine*, 2nd ed. (Paris: le Sycomore-l'Asiathèque, 1981), pp. 58–59, however, it has been moved to the east of the Kokonor and runs north-south to include Tsong kha and A myes rma chen.

78   For geological remarks on this location, see Cheng Jie, Zhang Xujiao, Tian Ming-zhong, Yu Wenyang, and Yu Jiangkuan, "Ice-wedge Casts Showing Climatic Change Sine the Late Pleistocene in the Source Area of the Yellow River, Northeast Tibet," *Journal of Mountain Science* 2/3 (2005): 193–201. Although not immediately relevant to our present subject matter, it is not without interest that these China-based scientists refer to the region they are studying in Qinghai as "Northeast Tibet."

79   Refer to the *Zhonghua Renmin Gongheguo Fen Sheng Dituji* (Hanyu Pinyinban) (Beijing: Ditu Chubanshe, 1983 [1977]), map 28 "Qinghai Sheng." Both of the two "Yematang" mentioned here are indicated on this map.

80   I am grateful to Biancha Horelmann for sharing with me the drafts of her forthcoming article "Buddhist Sites in Eastern A mdo/Longyou from the 8th to the 13th Century," through which I learned of the Yuan-period Yemotang. It denotes the valley of the Buh He, which enters the Kokonor from the northwest. See Tan Qixiang 譚其驤, ed., *The Historical Atlas of China* 中國歷史地圖集, volume VII (Beijing: China Cartographic Publishing House, 1996), map 36–37.

81   These ranges are indicated on both the Qinghai and Gansu sheets (27–28) of the *Zhonghua Renmin Gongheguo Fen Sheng Dituji.*

82   Cf. Richardson, "The Province of the *Bde-blon.*"

83   Uebach, "Dbyar-mo-thaṅ and Goṅ-bu ma-ru," surveys these legends and their literary sources in considerable detail. In connection with the tale of Zhang Lha bzang's meeting with Kubera (Vaiśravaṇa, Rnam thos sras) in Dbyar mo thang, we find a seventeenth-century mural illustration of the scene in the Potala: *A Mirror of the Murals in the Potala*, p. 88. Ironically, the English caption in this case falls into unnecessary geographical confusion, owing perhaps to the proximity of the painting with an illustration of Bsam yas Monastery. Whereas the Tibetan caption correctly names Dbyar mo thang as the site of the encounter, the English version reads: "In the time of the Tibetan King Trisong Detsen, at a visit to Samye by God Namse and

entourage, a minister called Lhasang managed to see in front a massive force numbering 440,000 bird-faced, horse-legged, mouse-tailed, and donkey-eared freaks marching towards them."

84 Rolf A. Stein, 1983, "Tibetica Antiqua I: Les deux vocabulaires des traductions Indo-tibétaine et Sino-tibétaine dans les Manuscrits de Touen-houang," *BEFEO* LXXII: 216. Stein's perplexity stemmed from his identification of several locations named Yulin in Tang times, which, besides Anxi Yulin, include two occurrences in the Ordos and one near Turfan.

85 In this case this represents Chinese *fan*, "Brahman, Buddhist" + Tibetan *khang*, "house." The term was no doubt modelled on a Chinese binome such as *fangong*, meaning a Buddhist monastery or temple. Refer to my *The Tibetan Assimilation*, p. p. 221, n. 3.

86 Richardson, "The Inventory of Yu-lim Gtsug-lag-khang," in *High Peaks, Pure Earth*, pp. 279–285.

87 Zhang Yisun et al., *Bod rgya tshig mdzod*, p. 2599, defines *yo 'bog* as equivalent to Ch. *yu*, "elm."

88 Bdud-'joms Rin-po-che 'Jigs-bral-ye-ses-rdo-rje, *Bod kyi rgyal rabs 'dus gsal du bkod pa*, in *The collected writings and revelations of H.H. Bdud-'joms Rin-po-che 'Jigs-bral-ye-ses-rdo-rje* (Kalimpong: Dupjung Lama, 1979–1985), vol. 2, p. 260, line 4.

89 See n. 84 above.

90 Richardson, "The Inventory of Yu-lim," pp. 281–282. The designation as given here, *phyug mtshams btsan la snang dpon g.yog*, differs somewhat from the form we find in the "Prayers of De ga g.yu tshal," *phyug tsams stong pon dpon g.yog*.

91 Thomas, *Tibetan Texts II*, p. 108.

92 Thomas, *Tibetan Texts III*, pp. 5, 46.

93 Thomas, *Tibetan Texts III*, p. 5, suggests that we can account for the pre-initial *b-* of *bde* being dropped by the same principle that applies to the simplification of certain numerals, *gnyis > nyi* (e.g., in *nyi shu*), etc. He offers no clear account, linguistic or otherwise, of this otherwise undocumented transformation, which seems altogether arbitrary.

94 Richardson, *High Peaks, Pure Earth*, p. 78, approvingly cites Thomas's description of the diction of these texts as "magniloquent," suggesting that this may be "the product of a colonial frontier régime," something of which he had, of course, considerable personal experience.

95 Pelliot, *Histoire ancienne*, p. 131. My translation.

96 Demiéville, *Le concile*, pp. 266, 283. In this he was no doubt trying to reconcile the passage from the *Xin Tang shu* with the parallel passage in the *Jiu Tang shu* (Pelliot, *Histoire ancienne*, p. 75) that has Zhang Khri sum rje meeting Liu Yuanding in He Zhou, adjacent to Daxia. However we explain the discrepancy between the two accounts though, for the reasons given in the following note I believe that Shang Tazang is most likely a transcription of Zhang Lha bzang. Demiéville also proposed that Shang Tazang might be Zhang Stag bzang, though this seems unlikely in view of other known Tang-period Chinese transcriptions of *stag*, which are in two syllables so as to conserve both the pre-initial *s-* and the radical *t-*.

97 Because the Tibetan syllable *lha* is often transcribed *luo* in the *Tang shu*, e.g., in Luo-suo (Lha sa), Demiéville and others may have drawn the conclusion that this is a

"standard" transcription. However, the Tibetan initial *lh-*, which does not correspond precisely with any phoneme in modern or medieval Chinese, has not been interpreted uniformly in all contexts. Consider, for instance, the current situation, in which Lha sa is rendered Lasa, but Lha sgang (in Mi nyag lcags la, Sichuan) is Tagong. Assuming that the situation in earlier times was in some respects similar, Shang Tazang appears to be a relatively straightforward rendering of Zhang Lha bzang.

98 Following Bernard Kalgren, *Analytic Dictionary of Chinese and Sino-Japanese* (New York: Dover Publications, 1991 [1923]), Daxia in "ancient Chinese" (ca. sixth century) was *dʾâi/tʾâi-γaʾ* (*dai/tai-ka* in Japanese), which very plausibly would have been transcribed as *de ga* in Tibetan. The refinements of E.G. Pulleyblank, *Middle Chinese: A Study in Historical Phonology* (Vancouver: University of British Columbia Press, 1984) do not seem to me to substantially alter this impression. For *da* he proposes Early Middle Chinese tʾaj^h/daä^h (p. 157), and for *xia* γɛrh in Early Middle Chinese and xɦjaa in Late Middle Chinese (p. 186).

99 Tibetan uses three spellings of this word—*dbyar*, *gyar*, and *gyer*—of which only the first in fact means "summer." In modern pronunciation, however, all three are near homonyms throughout a broad range of dialects. One wonders if the last two, *gyar* and *gyer*, might not have arisen as transcriptions of Chinese *xia*, particularly in the light of Pulleyblank's reconstructions given in the preceding note.

100 See, for instance, the article in Morohashi Tetsuji 諸橋轍次, ed., *Dai Kan-Wa jiten* 大漢和辞典 ("Comprehensive Chinese-Japanese Dictionary"), 13 vols, 1955–1960, Revised and enlarged ed. (Tokyo: Taishukan, 1984–1986).

101 Often two temples, one Chinese and one Tibetan, are referred to. The sources are surveyed in Uebach, "Dbyar-mo-thaṅ and Goṅ-bu ma-ru."

102 Nevertheless, he was not altogether forgotten either. The extant Sanskrit text of the *Vimalakīrtinirdeśasūtra* (Tokyo: Taisho University Press, 2004) was preserved thanks to a copy made on behalf of a certain Śīladhvaja (p. 511), who is no doubt to be identified as the well-known twelfth-century Tibetan visitor to India and translator Tshul khrims rgyal mtshan, a student of the *mahāpaṇḍita* Abhayākaragupta at Vikramaśīla.

103 Refer to n. 31 above.

104 My assumption that "two wrathful" (*khro bo gnyis*) refers to Acala and Trailokyavijaya in this context is based on Khri Srong lde btsan's own homage to these divinities following the eight bodhisattvas, in his *Bka' yang dag pa'i tshad ma* (Toh 4352, P 5839). For translation and discussion of the verses in question, see my *The Tibetan Assimilation*, pp. 61–62.

105 *mnga' ris bcad pa'i bsod nams kyis.*

106 Zhang Wenbin 张文彬, ed., *Dunhuang: jinian Dunhuang zangjingdong faxian yibai zhounian* 敦煌: 紀念敦煌藏经洞发现一百周年 (Beijing: Chaohua Chubanshe, 2000), pp. 31–39.

107 For recent color photographic documentation, see Duan Wenjie 段文傑, ed., *Yulinku di'erwuku fu diyiwuku* (*zhongtang*) 榆林窟第二五窟附 第一五窟(中唐), in the series *Dunhuang shiku yishu* 敦煌石窟藝術 (Jiangsu Meishu Chubanshe, 1993); and Dunhuang Yanjiuyuan 敦煌研究院, comp., *Anxi Yulinku* 安西榆林窟, in the series *Zhongguo shiku* 中国石窟 (Beijing: Wenwu Chubanshe, 1997), plates 12–43. The latter also includes historical commentary, pp. 162–167.

108 For example, *Anxi Yulinku*, plates 37 and 39.

109 *Maitreyavyākaraṇam*, v. 12, in Nalinaksha Dutt, ed. *Gilgit Manuscripts* (Calcutta 1959, rprt. Delhi: Sri Satguru, 1984), vol. IV, p. 190.

110 Refer to H. Karmay, "Tibetan Costume, Seventh to Eleventh Centuries."

111 Refer to the contributions of Fraser, Ning, and Wang in n. 39 above, and to Tan Chung, ed., *Dunhuang Art through the Eyes of Duan Wenjie* (New Delhi: Indira Gandhi National Centre for the Arts, 1994).

112 Amy Heller, "Ninth Century Buddhist Images Carved at Ldan-ma-brag to Commemorate Tibeto-Chinese Negotiations," in Per Kvaerne, ed., *Tibetan Studies*, 2 vols. (Oslo: The Institute for Comparative Research in Human Culture, 1994), vol. 1, pp. 335–349, and appendix to vol. 1, pp. 12–19; and idem, "Early Ninth Century Images of Vairochana from Eastern Tibet," *Orientations* 25/6 (1994): 74–79.

113 Geri H. Malandra, *Unfolding a Maṇḍala: The Buddhist Cave Temples at Ellora* (Albany: State University of New York Press, 1993) examines the sculptural evidence for the emergence of the cult of Vairocana and the eight bodhisattvas in India during the mid-first millennium. The study of its diffusion in much of east, central, and southeast Asia during the following centuries remains a desideratum. An interesting example from Central Asia is studied in Phyllis Granoff, "A Portable Buddhist Shrine from Central Asia," *Archives of Asian Art* (1969): 80–96. On Famensi, in particular, see now Wu Limin 吳立民 and Han Jinke 韩金科, *Famensi Digong Tangmi Manchaluo Zhi Yanjiu* 法门寺地宫唐蜜曼茶罗之研究 (Hong Kong: Zhongguo Fojiao Wenhua Chubanshe, 1998).

114 *The Tibetan Assimilation*, pp. 60–65.

115 This may be seen at once in comparison with some of the clearest iconographical comparisons of the period, e.g., in Dunhuang Mogao cave 220: Ning Qiang, *Art, Religion and Politics in Medieval China: The Dunhuang Cave of the Zhai Family* (Honolulu: University of Hawai'i Press, 2004), p. 73, figure 2.7.

116 This is not to say, however, that the cave was not subject to restorations, with some additions, during the centuries following its original construction.

117 I am indebted here to the observations of Karl Debreczeny, who has been able to study the painting in cave 25 at first hand.

118 Tansen Sen, *Buddhism, Diplomacy, and Trade: The Realignment of Sino-Indian Relations, 600–1400* (Honolulu: University of Hawai'i Press, 2003), p. 25: "Hostilities between China and Tibet, which resurfaced in the late 660s, the Sino-Tibetan war that followed in 670, and the Tibetan incursions into the Gangetic basin of India in the last quarter of the seventh century, reduced the traffic between India and China through the Tibetan route. By the late seventh or early eighth century, as Yijing suggests, the Tibetans seem to have completely blocked the road that passed through their territory linking India and China." Although I rather doubt that "the traffic between India and China through the Tibetan route" was very substantial during the period concerned—Chinese travelers to India certainly preferred the routes that circumvented Tibet—Sen's characterization of the situation seems generally correct. For, from the late seventh century on, though Tibet itself might be avoided, Tibetan-ruled territory could not be so easily bypassed.

119 Sen, *Buddhism, Diplomacy, and Trade*, ch. 3.

120 In the mural mentioned in n. 115 above.

121 The Chinese inscriptions are recorded in Lo Chi-mei 羅寄梅, "The Mural Paintings

of the Yu-Lin Cave at Anshi" 安西榆林窟的壁畫, in *Annual Bulletin of the China Council for East Asian Studies*, no. 3 (June 1964), pp. 21–23.

122 The use of Tibetan among sinophone communities in the Dunhuang area is treated at length by Tokio Takata, "Bouddhisme chinois en écriture tibétain: le Long Rouleau chinois et la communauté sino-tibétaine de Dunhuang," in Fukui Fumimasa and Gérard Fussman, eds., *Bouddhisme et cultures locales: Quelques cas de réciproques adaptations*, Études thématiques 2 (Paris: École française d'Extrême-Orient, 1994), pp. 137–144; idem, "Multilingualism in Tun-huang," *Acta Asiatica* 78 (2000): 49–70.

123 Yoshiro Imaeda, "T-shaped Inscription Frames in Mogao (Dunhuang) and Yulin Caves," *Report of the Japanese Association for Tibetan Studies* 53 (June 2007): 89–99.

124 Xie Jisheng 谢继胜 and Huang Weizhong 黄维忠, "Yulinku di 25 ku bihua zangwen tiji shidu" 榆林窟第25窟壁画藏文题记释读, in *Wenwu* 文物 (2007/4): 70–78. For an excellent reproduction of the inscription, see Imaeda, "T-shaped Inscription Frames," p. 99.

125 Imaeda, "T-shaped Inscription Frames," p. 91, translates: "May the act of Dze'u Dei'-cung joining the holy clergy be transfered to the merit of Shang she," and adds: "It is a graffito which was added later, like all other graffiti inscriptions in Tibetan, Uighur and Chinese in other parts of the cave."

126 Xie and Huang, "Yulinku di 25 ku bihua zangwen tiji shidu," p. 72.

127 Lo Chi-mei, "The Mural Paintings," p. 21.

128 For an introduction to the history of Dunhuang during this period, see Rong Xinjiang, "Official Life at Dunhuang in the Tenth Century: The Case of Cao Yuanzhong," in Whitfield, ed., *The Silk Road*, pp. 57–62.

129 Rong, *op. cit.*, p. 58. Following Kalgren (p. 95), the first syllable of his given name, *yan*, is reconstructed as *iän*, but derived from an archaic form beginning in *d-*. Might this explain the syllable *de'i* in the Tibetan transcription? As *gong* (ancient *ki^{w}ong* according to Kalgren, p. 158) might readily have come to be represented in Tibetan as *cung*, it seems possible that Dze'u De'i cung is indeed Cao Yangong. I concede at once, however, that as one not specialized in the relevant domains in historical linguistics, I offer this only as a layman's guess.

130 Xie and Huang, "Yulinku di 25 ku bihua zangwen tiji shidu," pp. 74–75.

131 Giuseppe Tucci, *Minor Buddhist Texts*, Parts 1 and 2, Serie Orientale Roma IX (Kyoto: Rinsen Book Company, 1978 [1956–1958]), p. 334.

2: The Commissioner's Commissions: Late-Thirteenth-Century Tibetan and Chinese Buddhist Art in Hangzhou under the Mongols[*]

Rob Linrothe

THE "NOTORIOUS" Yang Lianzhenjia (Tib. Rinchenkyap[1]) was a prominent official in the Mongol administration of late thirteenth century Hangzhou (Lin'an).[2] He was of Tangut ethnicity from Hexi in Gansu.[3] Yang was a married lay-monk, as during the Yuan it was not at all uncommon—or illegal—for Daoist and Buddhist monks to marry, and it was commented on at the time as a particularly frequent practice in the area of Gansu where Yang originated.[4] While it is assumed that he was of Sakya affiliation, the lineage favored at Khubilai's court, it is possible that he could have been Kagyü, which was more prominent among the Tanguts. An appointee of Khubilai Khan, Yang held a powerful position as Hangzhou's Branch Commissioner for Tibetan and Buddhist Affairs (Xuanzheng Yuan).[5] His mentor was the "treacherous official" Saṅgha (d. 1291), Khubilai's chief minister during the 1280s. Saṅgha, probably "a border Tibetan belonging to a partly Uighurized family," was originally a disciple of the Tibetan-born Yuan State Preceptor Dampa Kungadrak (1230–1303), before joining the staff of the illustrious Pakpa Lodrö Gyeltsen (1235–1280) as an interpreter.[6] Saṅgha rose through Khubilai's administration to become Chief Minister, and by 1283, during Saṅgha's tenure, Yang Lianzhenjia had become the Commissioner in Hangzhou.[7]

The largest city in the Mongol realm, Hangzhou had been the capital of the Wu Yue kingdom in the tenth century, and later the capital of the Southern Song in the twelfth and thirteenth centuries. Historically, therefore, Hangzhou was the center of an immensely wealthy and cultured region. It was also a thriving center for Chinese Buddhism; through the Northern and Southern Song it had several hundred monasteries and temples of various sizes.[8] It was conquered by Mongols in 1276, but the last remnants of Southern Song loyalists were not eliminated until 1279, just as Yang arrived to begin his position.[9] For at least ten years, Yang acted as Branch Commissioner for Tibetan and Buddhist Affairs, holding a post that was crucial for both political and religious reasons, especially since, as Su Bai has shown, Hangzhou was an important hub of Tibetan Buddhist activities.[10] Yang was responsible for controlling, supporting, and directing all Buddhist activities in Hangzhou, not just Tibetan, though since Khubilai was a consecrated sovereign, and both Saṅgha and Yang were adherents of Esoteric Buddhism, Tibetan Buddhism took public or official precedence over Han-style Buddhism in Hangzhou as it did in the northern capitals. Yang devoted himself to Buddhist activities such as supporting the printing and distribution of Buddhist scriptures, building Tibetan-style stūpas and monasteries, and sponsoring the creation of sculptures in caves and within temples.[11]

But it all came to an end for Yang when Saṅgha was arrested for corruption in March of 1291 and executed that August. Yang was subsequently thoroughly investigated and removed from office, and by the third month of 1292, a long and detailed list of outrageous charges against Yang was submitted to the emperor. He was accused of graft on a vast scale, with amassing a private hoard of cash, gold, jade, pearls, and silver, with illegally confiscating Song imperial palaces, mansions, and Confucian and Daoist temples, converting them into Buddhist monasteries, fraudulently removing commoners from the tax rolls by registering them as tenants of the monasteries, forcefully expropriating land from wealthy landowners to support Buddhist monasteries, killing commoners, and, most egregiously, with pillaging Song aristocratic tombs in order to pay for his Buddhist activities and venality.[12] The details of Yang's actions, in both the historical record and in the sculptural art he commissioned, create a compelling yet contradictory picture of one man's role in the communication of Tibetan Buddhism on the state level.

Our picture of Yang Lianzhenjia and his activities is usually based on two different types of sources, to which I add a third: first, Chinese histories, official and unofficial; second, inscriptions written by or for Yang himself; and third, surviving sculpture associated with him.[13] The first two of these sources are textual, conventional, and have been examined by many scholars who acknowledge that the sources are flawed due to the biased perspectives of their authors. The most important of these sources is the official history of the Yuan, the *Yuan Shi*, compiled at the very beginning of the Ming dynasty.[14] "After 70 years of Mongol rule, the Confucian historians were finally permitted to write their histories,"[15] and one almost senses an atmosphere of revenge. As Huang Chi-chuang has pointed out in relation to the activities of monks at Hangzhou in the preceding Song dynasty, official histories "were often compiled by conservative Confucians for didactic purposes," they "promote a negative image of monks," and "often ignored the positive contributions of Buddhists."[16] In the case of the official Yuan history, to this bias against monks in general is added the deep resentment of foreigners during the Mongol period. For Mongols or Tanguts or Tibetans to be chief administrators in Hangzhou was a reversal of what educated Chinese felt was the proper order of things, and the official histories, written by Confucian historians, can hardly be expected to take a neutral perspective toward the case of someone like Yang. Even official reports compiled during Yang's lifetime and included in the *Yuan Shi* are suspect, as they were composed in the midst of a bitter factional conflict in which Yang was targeted because of his connections to the deposed chief minister Saṅgha. As Chen Gaohua points out, "after Saṅgha lost power and was executed, his clique members were tracked down one by one, and Yang Lianzhenjia was among this number."[17] It was a time of deadly partisan politics encumbered with ethnic resentment, and bias and distortion are to be expected.

Contemporaneous or later Chinese *un*official histories are if anything even more negative toward Yang, dwelling on his arrogance, his violent rampage against "the elderly, the virtuous, and the respected," his lack of sensitivity to Chinese values, his greed and profligacy, and especially, apparently most galling to the Chinese writers, his confiscation of land and property owned by local elites. The stock in trade of unofficial histories is typically colorful details and dramatic anecdote.[18] In Yang's case, they document the rage against his "conduct [which] violated deeply rooted Chinese feelings."[19]

The second type of source needs to be handled with equal caution. It consists of dedication inscriptions which Yang himself wrote and had carved alongside images he commissioned at the site of Feilaifeng. Naturally, they create a very different picture of the man, someone who is formulaically devout, but also very aware and responsive to events at court. For example, in conjunction with a triad of sculptures in the Tibetan style dated by inscription to 1292 (fig. 1), Yang refers to himself as having "solemnly generated a sincere heart, donated pure offerings, and commissioned craftsmen to carve Amitāyus Buddha, Mañjuśrī Bodhisattva, and the Saviouress Prajñāpāramitā, these sacred images of the three deities. [This is for] the benefit of and longevity [of the Emperor] to whom is wished perfect peace. To Consort Kökojin is wished

FIG. 1 Amitāyus Buddha (center), Mañjuśrī Bodhisattva (left), and
Prajñāpāramitā in the Tibeto-Chinese style at Feilaifeng, dated by Yang
Lianzhenjia's inscription to 1292.
(After Zhejiang Sheng Wenwu Kaogu Yenjiu Suo, *Xihu Shiku*, pl. 107.)

continuous, everlasting longevity. As for the Imperial Princes, Kammala and
Temür, may their longevity be calculated at a thousand autumns."[20]

This is actually a very savvy negotiation of delicate court politics. We
know that at the time of its writing, a struggle for designation as heir-apparent
between Kammala and the ultimate victor, his younger half-brother Temür,
was taking place. Temür was officially designated heir in 1293 and eventually succeeded Khubilai after the latter's death in 1294. The Kökojin in Yang's
inscription was Temür's mother and promoter (Khubilai's widowed daughter-
in-law Yusheng, d. 1300). She was a significant force in the late Khubilai-period
court to which Yang apparently had access.[21] Yang finesses the awkwardness
of the fraternal rivalry by calling both contenders Imperial Princes, and con-
spicuously mentions Kökojin.

There are four relatively lengthy if platitudinous inscriptions by Yang at
Feilaifeng, one dated to 1289, three to 1292, and one by his wife the same
year.[22] The self-image that emerges from these inscriptions is naturally at odds
with the sketch drawn by the Chinese histories of Yang as a corrupt terror-
izer of virtuous Chinese. Yang's public face is that of a faithful and devoted

FIG. 2 Triad of Amitāyus Buddha (center), Avalokiteśvara Bodhisattva (left), and Mahāsthamaprāpta Bodhisattva in the Chinese style at Feilaifeng, dated by Yang Lianzhenjia's inscription to 1292. (After Zhejiang Sheng Wenwu Kaogu Yenjiu Suo, *Xihu Shiku*, pl. 108.)

servant of the Mongol rulers, a devout Buddhist who desires to benefit all sentient beings (including his family) and who wishes to contribute to the preservation of a peaceful realm.

So far, there is nothing new in harnessing these textual sources and carefully assessing their utility. All of the modern historians dealing with this subject have been judiciously cautious in analyzing the historical sources or in taking either type—the condemnatory or the pious—at face value. For most of Yang's activities we have only these two kinds of evidence. Material evidence has largely disappeared. But one arena where we can follow his activities further is in the sculptures themselves. They have the virtue of being the products of his actions, not representations of his activities. The onus of interpretive bias is more strictly then on us, not on the sources. We turn to an assessment of them now.

The earliest sculptures at Feilaifeng, just to the west of Hangzhou's West Lake, date to the tenth-century Wu Yue kingdom, while others date from the later

Song period. In the Yuan, dozens of new images were added to the rocky out-crop that is located opposite the gates of the Lingyin monastery. There are a few caves in the rocky ridge, but most of the images are carved onto the exposed sur-face of the rock face. By one count, there are 280 sculptures from all periods at the site, of which 116 or, alternatively, 117 were added in the Yuan period.[23]

The Lingyin si had been an imperially supported Chan monastery under the Song. Its abbots were named by Song emperors, it had been granted tax privi-leges, and it was charged to pray for the Song emperors on their birthdays.[24] The national reputation of the Lingyin si must have made it a key site in Yang's eyes, and he and his contemporaries made sculptural commissions which bear wit-ness to the importance of Tibetan Buddhism under the Mongols.[25]

The insertion of Tibetan-style themes and aesthetic elements into a pre-existing Chinese Buddhist site is later generally credited to—or rather, blamed on—Yang alone.[26] However, members of his administration and the military also identify themselves in donation inscriptions.[27] Nevertheless, given the importance of the site, Yang most likely gave approval to their contributions.

The sculptures give us an opportunity to compare his conflicting profiles with his actions. His negative portrait suggests he was a rabid promoter of Tibetan Esoteric Buddhism, who was not only willing to go along with the suppression of Confucians and Daoists, but also to sacrifice or restrain Han-style Buddhist schools in order to privilege Tibetan Buddhism.[28] This is the picture we are given also by modern scholars who have tended to interpret the sculptures at Feilaifeng as evidence of Yang's blatant sectarianism. The insertion of Tibetan-style themes is termed by Paula Swart a "confrontation" between Tibetan and Chinese Buddhism.[29] Richard Edwards describes the Tibetan-style sculpture at Feilaifeng as intentionally "overwhelming and intrusive."[30] Chen Gaohua also holds that Yang's purpose at Feilaifeng "clearly is still to extend the influence of Lamaism."[31] Yet looked at in the context of the site as a whole, these images belie intentional confrontation. It seems to be quite the opposite.

The majority of the particular themes which Yang and his associates added to Feilaifeng are ones which are shared by the popular cults of the Mahāyāna. There are no wrathful *yidam* like Saṃvara, Mahākāla (Khubilai's *iṣṭadevatā*), or Hevajra, nor any *yabyum* (father-mother) images which have come to be thought of as the signature imagery of Tibetan Buddhism.[32] Such themes are quite prominent in Yuan dynasty Sakya art at the capital, as evidenced, for instance, by the pair of woven maṇḍalas of Vajrabhairava, one of which is now in the Metropolitan Museum of New York, depicting portraits of two Mongol brothers who would become emperors. Another example is the silk *kesi* Acala locally manufactured in Hangzhou for Tibetan and Mongol patrons.[33] Despite

FIG. 3 Vaiśravaṇa in Tibeto-Chinese style at Feilaifeng, dated by Yang Lianzhen-jia's inscription to 1292.

its prominence in Mongol court art, this type of imagery is not in evidence at Feilaifeng. One explanation is the secrecy surrounding such esoteric icons which, according to the strictures of the Sakyapa order, would have been kept from common or casual view. Assuming such scruples restrained Yang's iconographic program, it would appear that he was determined that Felaifeng should represent only the public, universally acceptable face of Tibetan Buddhism.

Considering what *is* there, certainly Vaiśravaṇa is a stern figure (fig. 3), but not necessarily exceptional, as he is attested in paintings and sculptures since Tang times.[34] The four-armed form of Avalokiteśvara known as Chenrézi or Ṣaḍakṣarī (fig. 5) was depicted at Feilaifeng at least three times in Yang's period,[35] and if it was an unfamiliar Indian or Tibetan form of the most common popular Buddhist deity in China (and perhaps in Buddhism generally), Guanyin's oft-noted multiplicity of forms makes this

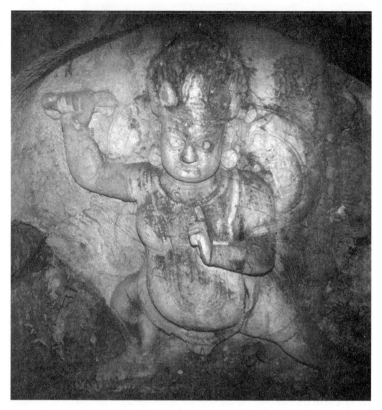

FIG. 4 Vajrapāṇi in Tibeto-Chinese style at Feilaifeng, dated by
Yang Lianzhenjia's consort's inscription to 1292.

figure less than revolutionary or unorthodox. Moreover, there were several two-armed Chinese-style Avalokiteśvara images added during Yang's
tenure (fig. 6).[36] It is difficult to discover anything offensive or controversial in any of these sculptures, nor in an image of Mañjuśrī.[37] Although the
Tibetan-style images are considered to be more "sensuous" in their exposure of the body, even those who see the images as deriving from Tibetan or
even Indian canons of figural sculpture acknowledge that they have "been
subject to Chinese artistic modification."[38] It is not altogether clear, moreover, that the alleged sensuousness would have been so apparent if, as may
have been the case during the Yuan, the images in question were painted or
draped with cloth.

The most likely candidates for interpretation as distinctively "tantric" are
Vajradhara, Vajravidāraṇa, Siṃhanāda Avalokiteśvara, Tārā, Marīcī, and the

FIG. 5 Ṣaḍakṣarī Avalokiteśvara (Tib. Chenrézi) in Tibeto-Chinese
style at Feilaifeng, datable to the late thirteenth century.

two-armed Sitātapatrā.[39] Yet they are actually more unfamiliar than they are
"confrontational" to Chinese Buddhists in the sense that *yabyum* images
would be. Uṣṇīṣavijayā, who appears at least twice at Feilaifeng,[40] was also
prominent in Tangut art, and the *dhāraṇī* which she personifies is very well
attested from Tang times in China (fig. 7). Nevertheless, her image was
admittedly unfamiliar in China outside of Tibetan-inflected contexts.[41] The
wealth-deity Yellow Jambhala was also a distinct import (fig. 8),[42] as was the
Mahasiddha Virūpa (fig. 9),[43] though in the context of the popular Budai
theme of a big-bellied Chan exemplar also at Feilaifeng (fig. 10),[44] the amaz-
ing life-size tableau of Virūpa being served wine by two female wine-shop
attendants, and the similarly scaled Jambhala, are hardly shocking by conservative Chinese standards. So, again, in a sense what is *not* found (i.e. wrathful *yidam* and *yabyum* images) is quite telling about Yang's intentions. It

FIG. 6 Two-armed Avalokiteśvara in Chinese-style at Feilaifeng,
dated by inscription to 1288.

also suggests that those who found the Tibetan themes at Feilaifeng offensive had a predisposition to do so, one not based on the visual or even iconographic features of the sculptures, but on the presumed ethnicity or loyalties
of the patrons.

Yang's own selections are extreme only in their restraint. Iconographically, they are rather conservative: Amitāyus, Mañjuśrī, Prajñāpāramitā,
Avalokiteśvara, Mahāsthāmaprāpta, and Vaiśravaṇa (figs. 1–3). All are well
represented in the Chinese Buddhist visual and textual canon. His wife's
choice of Vajrapāṇi is the most radical of the group (fig. 4),[45] but even Vajrapāṇi
is very familiar in Chinese Buddhism, appearing during the Tang period at
Dunhuang and not always in the context of Esoteric Buddhism.[46] Based on
the general tenor of Yang's selections, it would seem that he sought to affirm
only those aspects of Esoteric Buddhism that were compatible with the cul-

FIG. 7 Uṣṇīṣavijayā in Tibeto-Chinese style at Feilaifeng,
datable to the late thirteenth century.

tic Mahāyāna, with which most Chinese viewers were familiar. In short, the
Tibetan-style Buddhism he championed was not anathema to Chinese-style
Buddhism.[47] If this conclusion is tenable, it would provide evidence for an
attitude diametrically opposite to that of the conventional understanding of
Yang as privileging Tibetan Buddhism at the expense of Chinese values in
general, and Han-style Buddhism in particular.

I would like to propose three other aspects of the sculptures at the site that
undermine the assumption that Yang's intention was to force Tibetan Buddhism onto the Chinese Buddhists at Feilaifeng in a confrontational manner. The evidence supports the conclusion that Yang was more likely trying
to integrate Esoteric Buddhism into the Chinese context. The first example
we have of this is the fact that in 1289, Huyan Jingfu, the Chinese abbot
of the Lingyin si, the adjoining Chan monastery, wrote a long poetic enco-
mium praising Yang's dedication to Buddhism. The poem was inscribed next
to a Tibeto-Chinese style image of Amitābha which Yang commissioned in
1289.[48] Yang was apparently keen to have the abbot endorse his activities, as if
acknowledging the importance of the local Chinese Buddhist clergy. While

Fig. 8 Yellow Jambhala in Tibeto-Chinese style at Feilaifeng,
datable to the late thirteenth century.

one could assume that the abbot was forced, literally or figuratively, to write such a polite poem (Edwards calls it "pedantic but revealing") for his administrative superior, at the very least it must be admitted that if Yang did not have the negative reputation disseminated by his enemies, we would have no *a priori* reason to impugn the abbot's sincerity.

A second point suggesting that Yang's intentions were synthetic and not divisively confrontational is the fact that the Tibetan-style images were dispersed along the entire cliffside. The older Chinese style themes were neither eliminated nor sequestered; indeed they continued to be renewed in Yang's time.[49] The Tibetan themes appear side by side with old and new versions of Chinese themes (figs. 11–12), although in some areas there are obvious small clusters of both. If his intentions were to demonstrate the superiority of Tibetan Buddhism, it would seem reasonable for Yang and his associates to place all of the Tibetan images *above* the level of the Chinese images. That did not happen. The integration of Tibetan and Chinese themes and styles, which is hard to illustrate but quite evident at the site itself, emphasizes for the attentive viewer a certain continuity rather than divergence.[50] It suggests

FIG. 9 Virūpa Mahāsiddha with two wine-servers in Tibeto-Chinese style at
Feilaifeng, datable to the late thirteenth century. (After Zhejiang
Sheng Wenwu Kaogu Yenjiu Suo, *Xihu Shiku*, pl. 194.)

the esoteric themes expand or are imbricated with the themes of Chinese
Mahāyāna Buddhism, which is not to be abrogated or replaced with Tibetan
Buddhism, but only extended.

Finally, we have more evidence of the type proper to art history: the evidence of style. Surely no less than his choice of themes, Yang's choice of artists and styles is meaningful and not random. So it is quite significant that
among Yang's final commissions in the fall of 1292, two triads appear, one
in a Tibetan style, and one in Chinese (figs. 1–2). It is a matter of some
debate whether the two together can be called alternate modes within the
same style (as I would argue), or whether completely different groups of artists with varying backgrounds and aesthetic training worked on each separately.[51] Which view is accepted is not crucial for my argument here. Either
way, Yang's themes were visually ecumenical: his Amitābha, Avalokiteśvara,
and Mahāsthāmaprāpta are in the Chinese style (fig. 2), while his Amitāyus,
Mañjuśrī, and Prajñāpāramitā are in the Tibetan style (fig. 1).

Stylistically, the Yuan-period sculptures can be divided into two broad
groups: the Chinese and the Tibetan or Tibeto-Chinese. However, as a

FIG. 10 Budai in Chinese style at Feilaifeng, datable to ca. the thirteenth century. (After Zhejiang Sheng Wenwu Kaogu Yenjiu Suo, *Xihu Shiku*, pl. 42.)

whole the sculptures could also be thought of as forming a stylistic evolution, for while some sculptures clearly represent the extremes, others convey more conservative imagery. Among the points of comparison that enable us to establish distinctions are the differences in the treatment of garments (which tend to leave one shoulder bare in Tibetan Buddhas while covering both in the Chinese), the lotus thrones (over which garment drapery tends to flow in the Chinese style), the head nimbus (round in the Chinese, oblate in the Tibeto-Chinese), and the body type (massive, rounded, and obscured by drapery in the Chinese mode, slenderer with more articulation of torso sections in Tibeto-Chinese). The *uṣṇīṣa* of Tibeto-Chinese Buddhas are slightly pointed; on the Chinese Buddhas they are rounded. Tibeto-Chinese lotus bases are often supported by *ratha*-like projections.

Yang's two triads of 1292 illustrate the two modes quite well (figs. 1–2). Both triads were completed in the same autumn month of 1292, so the differences cannot be attributed to an evolution of preferences over time. In the propagation of both the Tibetan and the Chinese visual language and taste, there is at least a hint of balance, of recognition of equal validity. Since this is found in what he actually did, and not in what others said he did, the art his-

FIG. 11 Adjacent Buddhas in Chinese and Tibeto-Chinese styles at Feilaifeng, both datable to the late thirteenth century.

torical evidence directly contradicts the flawed portrait of Yang as a wicked, corrupt official bent on viciously trampling Chinese values.

The aesthetic ecumenicism of Yang's commissions meshes well with Yang's Tangut ethnicity. As I have argued elsewhere, the Tanguts were impressively bicameral in their Buddhism and their art, uniting the Chinese and Tibetan worlds by simultaneously participating in them both.[52] In addition, as has been commented about Northern Song Buddhism at Hangzhou, "Part of what made Hang-chou such a thriving center of Buddhism during the Northern Sung was the presence of a variety of Buddhist schools," including Tiantai, Chan, Vinaya (Lu), and Huayan.[53] Assuming this still held in the Southern Song period and into the post-conquest climate which found Yang trying to direct the discourse of Buddhism in Hangzhou, then Yang's efforts to introduce Tibetan Buddhism did not break apart a seamless unity of Han-style Buddhism. He brought in new methods which were both compatible and competitive with existing practice. But what made them unacceptable to contemporary and later Chinese was most likely simply who he was: a Tangut in the employ of the Mongols.

FIG. 12 Adjacent Avalokiteśvara sculptures in Chinese and Tibeto-Chinese styles at Feilaifeng, both datable to the late thirteenth century. (See figs. 5 and 6.)

Both of Yang's triads, his Vaiśravaṇa, and his wife's Vajrapāṇi were finished in the fall of 1292. Yang's superior and mentor Saṅgha had been arrested and executed the previous year. By the time these sculptural compositions were dedicated, the group of officials investigating Yang's crimes had already submitted their damning report. According to the *Yuan Shi*, the local Hangzhou officials and elites clamored to the emperor that Yang's punishment fit his crimes and that he be made a public example—implying that he should be executed. To be sure, he was arrested, his property confiscated, his wife and servants indentured. But Khubilai ultimately commuted the death sentence, and returned all his property and household to him.[54] Unlike most others in the Saṅgha group who were either executed or exiled, Yang was restored to freedom and rank, and his son was appointed Commissioner. Obviously, Khubilai, who is noted even by Confucians for his excellent insight into character and ability,[55] continued to trust and appreciate Yang. This makes us wonder if Yang might have been set up as the convenient target of Chinese resentment of deeply unpopular policies that were actually established by Khubilai but implemented by Yang.[56] Chen Gaohua argues that even the oft-mentioned desecration of the Southern Song imperial tombs was approved by Khubilai.[57] Open opposition to the Sage Emperor was unthinkable, but Yang could be targeted. Probably Khubilai saw through the accusations accumulating against his Commissioner, and so he pardoned and exonerated Yang.

Having come through this trial, in which friends, mentors, and colleagues were exiled or executed, Yang and his wife had much to be grateful for in the fall of 1292 as they donated sums of money to create the sculptures at Feilaifeng. Perhaps they were chastened by the experience, and tried to make amends with the Buddhists of Hangzhou. But if the character of Yang was anything like the outrageous portrait drawn by the anti-Mongol Chinese sources, one would have expected him now, secure in his knowledge of the emperor's backing, to flaunt his Tibetan beliefs as clearly opposed to more mainstream Chinese Buddhist practice and belief. Instead, intensely grateful to the emperor for his clemency, Yang piously offered up prayers for the longevity of the emperor and his relatives, for peace and tranquility in the state, and for the prosperity of his own family.

There seem indeed to be at least two very different portraits of Yang, and the conflict is very much about the fact of Tibet in China, or better, of Buddhism between Tibet and China. Above all, it is this resentment of the foreignness which, for contemporary and later Chinese viewers of the sculptures at Feilaifeng, colored them negatively, at least for those whose views are recorded. The ethnic origins and loyalties of their commissioners created an "external enclosure" or lens through which later Chinese viewed these images.[58] The extrinsic fact that they were the products of the hated Yang Lianzhenjia distorted the sculptures for those Chinese who seem to be looking at different images than we are when they condemn them as "ugly and weird, assaulting the eye," as one Ming viewer wrote.[59] Thus, even granting what the art historical evidence I have marshalled suggests, while Yang's intentions were not confrontational, he ultimately failed in his attempt to integrate Tibetan Esoteric Buddhism with Han-style Buddhism. The sculptures' association with Yang himself seems to have made later viewers find reflections of their own ethnic resentments and historical experience in the Commissioner's commissions.

NOTES

* This essay grows out of a presentation given at the American Academy of Religion national conference in Nashville in November 2000. I have benefited from the comments of a co-presenter, Karl Debreczeny, and those of the chair and editor of this volume, Matthew Kapstein. On-site research in Hangzhou in 1999 and 2000 was supported in part by Faculty Development Grants from Skidmore College.

1 For the reconstruction of the Tibetan name, see H. Franke, "Tibetans in Yuan China," chapter 8 in John D. Langlois, Jr., ed., *China under Mongol Rule* (Princeton: Princeton University Press, 1981), p. 321.

2 In connection with Yang and his associates, the assumption often guiding previous scholarship has been that Tibetan Buddhism in Yuan China was simply following a path of ethnic and political advantage. See for example the remarks of Eugene Yue-jin Wang in an insightful review of Marsha Weidner, ed. *Latter Days of the Law: Images of Chinese Buddhism, 850–1850* (Lawrence, KS: Spencer Museum of Art, 1994), in *Art Bulletin* 78/3 (1996): 556–559. Agreeing with Patricia Berger's point of view expressed in an essay in the Weidner catalog, Wang points out that, "Perpetuated respectively by the Tanguts (probably of Tibetan origin), Tibetans, Mongols, and Manchus, esoteric tantric art in post-Tang China carried strong ethnic overtones. As the art of an ethnic minority, it was foreign to the majority that formed its audience. The choice of such a 'foreign' art was deliberately engineered for political gains, often in a subtle way. Attempts were made to keep the 'foreignness' alive for designated purposes" (p. 557). Cf. also Xiong Wenbin who assumes that "the overtly political nature of the introduction of Tibetan Buddhism to Hangzhou" is a "given": Xiong Wenbin, "A textual study of the Nine Gods of the Usnisavijaya Mandala Statues in niche no. 55 at Felai Peak in Hangzhou (summary)," *China Archaeology and Art Digest* 4/1 (2000): 408.

3 Although H. Franke and M. Rossabi have cautiously stated that Yang's ethnicity was either Tangut or Tibetan, Chen Gaohua convincingly draws on contemporary accounts to show that the Yangs were Tanguts from Hexi. See Chen Gaohua 陳高華, "Luelun Yang Lianzhenjia he Yang Anpu Fuzi 略論楊璉真加和楊暗普父子," *Xibei Minzu Yanjiu* 1 (1986): 55–63; I thank Zaixin Hong for pointing out this article to me, and Ruth Dunnell for tracking it down in Beijing. Patricia Berger is mistaken in referring to Yang as Mongol in "Preserving the Nation: The Political Uses of Tantric Art in China," p. 107, in *Latter Days of the Law*, ed. by Marsha Weidner. For Yang, see the section by Morris Rossabi in Herbert Franke and Denis Twitchett, eds. *The Cambridge History of China, Volume 6: Alien Regimes and Border States, 907–1368* (Cambridge: Cambridge University Press, 1994), pp. 479–480; Morris Rossabi, *Khubilai Khan: His Life and Times* (Berkeley: University of California Press, 1988), pp. 196–199; and Herbert Franke, "Tibetans in Yuan China," pp. 318, 321–325.

4 Chen Gaohua, "Luelun Yang Lianzhenjia," p. 61. See also Jiunn Yih Chang, "A Study of the Relationship Between the Mongol Yuan Dynasty and the Tibetan Sa-skya Sect" (Ph.D. dissertation, Indiana University, 1984), pp. 158–159, on a decree of 1293 against monks marrying, which Chang interprets to be applied to all monks *except* Tibetan monks.

5 The Bureau of Tibetan and Buddhist Affairs and its equivalents (as the name and structure were continually modified) are discussed in H. Franke, "Tibetans in Yuan China," pp. 311–315; David M. Farquhar, *The Government of China Under Mongol Rule: A Reference Guide* (Stuttgart: Franz Steiner Verlag, 1990), pp. 153–157; and Jiunn Yih Chang, "A Study of the Relationship Between the Mongol Yuan Dynasty and the Tibetan Sa-skya Sect," pp. 113–126. A translation of the *Yuan Shi* discussion of this office is provided by Tucci in *Tibetan Painted Scrolls* (Rome, 1949), pp. 31–33.

6 For Saṅgha, see Rossabi, *Khubilai Khan*, pp. 192–196. Later, Saṅgha was estranged from Dam pa. See H. Franke "Tan-pa, A Tibetan lama at the Court of the Great Khans," *Orientalia Venetiana* 1 (1984): 157–180; idem, "Sangha," pp. 558–583, in *In the Service of the Khan: Eminent Personalities of the Early Mongol-Yüan Period (1200–1300)*, edited by Igor de Rachewiltz et al. (Wiesbaden: Harrassowitz, 1993); and Luciano Petech, "Sang-ko, A Tibetan Statesman in Yüan China," *Acta Orientalia Academiae Scientiarum* 34/103 (1980): 193–203; the quote regarding his ethnic origin comes from page 195.

7 H. Franke writes that Yang was appointed Supervisor of the Buddhist Teaching for the Jiangnan region as early as 1277, one year after Hangzhou was conquered by the Mongols. Franke, "Tibetans in Yuan China," p. 322.

8 By the end of the Northern Song, it had as many as 658; Chi-Chiang Huang, "Elite and Clergy in Northern Sung Hangchou: A Convergence of Interest," pp. 295–339, in Peter N. Gregory and Daniel A. Getz, Jr., eds., *Buddhism in the Sung* (Honolulu: University of Hawai'i Press, 1999), p. 299. Gernet gives figures for the thirteenth century which are smaller but still impressive: Jacques Gernet, *Daily Life in China on the Eve of the Mongol Invasion 1250–1276* (Stanford: Stanford University Press, 1962), p. 212.

9 For a recent account of the years of conquest from the perspective of the Song imperial clan, see John W. Chaffee, *Branches of Heaven: A History of the Imperial Clan of Sung China* (Cambridge: Harvard University Press, 1999), pp. 242–259.

10 Su Bai 宿白, "Yuandai Hangzhou de Zangchuan Mijiao ji qi youguan yiji 元代杭州的藏傳密教及其有關遺迹," pp. 365–387, in *Zangchuan Fojiao Siyuan kaogu* 藏傳佛教寺院考古 (Beijing: Wenwu chuban she, 1996).

11 A translation of a diary by a contemporary of Yang's includes mention and brief descriptions of some of the buildings and sculptures attributed to Yang. See R.C. Rudolph, "Kuo Pi, A Yuan Artist and His Diary," *Ars Orientalis* 3 (1959): 183–184.

12 An account of the pillaging of the tombs, encouraged by local Chinese monks and with the approval of Saṅgha, is provided in Paul Demiéville, "Les tombeaux des Song méridionaux," *Bulletin de l'École française d'Extrême-Orient* 25 (1925): 458–467. Also Chang, "A Study of the Relationship," pp. 160–161.

13 A fourth type of potential source is Tibetan historical texts, but, to the best of my knowledge, these have not been mined for insight into Yang. For some of the likely Tibetan historical sources, see Josef Kolmaš, "Tibetan Sources," pp. 129–140, in Donald D. Leslie et al., *Essays on the Sources for Chinese History* (Columbia: University of South Carolina Press, 1973); and Dan Martin, *Tibetan Histories: A Bibliography of Tibetan-Language Historical Works* (London: Serindia, 1997), esp. nos. 70, 77, 94, 96, 115, 140, 165. Martin's no. 115 is Śrībhūtibhadra's *Rgya bod kyi yig tshang* of 1434, which has been translated into Chinese: Chen Qingying 陳慶英, *Hanzang Shiji* 漢藏史記 (Lhasa: Tibetan People's Publishing, 1983, re-issued 1986). I have been unable to locate any mention of Yang in it, even in section 24 which concerns Saṅgha. The Tibetan original has been utilized splendidly by Petech, who critically compares its favorable point of view toward Saṅgha with the negative one presented in Chinese sources. Petech, "Sang-ko." Another example of the complementary use of Tibetan and Chinese sources for events of this time is Wang Yao, "Fragments from Historical Records About the Life of Emperor Gongdi of the Song Dynasty," in Ernst Steinkellner and Helmut Tauscher, eds., *Contributions on Tibetan Language,*

History and Culture, Vol. 1 of the Proceedings of the Csoma de Kőrös Symposium held at Velm-Vienna, Austria (Vienna: Arbeitskreis fur Tibetische und Buddhistische Studien Universität Wien, 1983), pp. 431–447.

14 Wang Gungwu, "Some Comments on the Later Standard Histories," pp. 53–63, in Leslie, *Essays in the Sources for Chinese History*.

15 Wang Gungwu, "Early Ming Relations with Southeast Asia: A Background Essay," pp. 34–62. in John K. Fairbank, ed., *The Chinese World Order* (Cambridge, Mass.: Harvard University Press, 1968), p. 45.

16 Chi-Chiang Huang, "Elite and Clergy in Northern Sung Hangchou," pp. 296–297.

17 Chen Gaohua, "Luelun Yang Lianzhenjia," p. 56.

18 See Colin Mackerras, "Unofficial Regional Records," pp. 75–82, in Leslie, *Essays on the Sources for Chinese History*.

19 H. Franke, "Tibetans in Yuan China," p. 325. For example, see the incident related there concerning the painter Ziwen; note 122.

20 Translation of the inscription is mine, based on the Chinese provided in Zhejiang Sheng Wenwu Kaogu Yenjiu Suo 浙江省文物考古研究所, *Xihu Shiku* 西湖石窟 (Hangzhou, 1985). Chinese inscriptions are correlated where possible with those given in Daijo Tokiwa and T. Sekino, *Buddhist Monuments in China* (Tokyo, 1925), vol. 5., pp. 134–138, pls. V-86–96. I would like to thank Morris Rossabi for generously going over my translations and making helpful suggestions relating to both accuracy and style. Errors that remain are all my responsibility.

21 It was on her behalf that Temür commissioned Anige to build a major Buddhist temple on Wutai shan. See Anning Jing, "The Portraits of Khubilai Khan and Chabi by Anige (1245–1306), A Nepali Artist at the Yuan Court," *Artibus Asiae* 54/1–2 (1994): 55–56.

22 Zhejiang Sheng Wenwu Kaogu Yenjiu Suo, *Xihu Shiku*, inscriptions given in captions for plates 107, 108, 128, 158, 159.

23 See Hong Huizhen 洪惠鎮, "Hangzhou Feilaifeng 'fanshi' zaoxiang chutan 杭州飛來峰 '梵式' 造像初探," *Wenwu* 文物 1 (1986): 50. Lai Tianbing counts 117 Yuan sculptures in "Hangzhou Feilaifeng Yuandai Shike zaoxiang yishu 杭州飛來峰元代石刻造像藝術," *Zhongguo Zangxue* 中國藏學 4 (1998): 96–107. See also the English summary of the article, "The Yuan dynasty stone sculptural art at Feilaifeng, Hangzhou," in *China Archaeology and Art Digest* 4/1 (2000): 402–403.

24 Huang, "Elite and Clergy in Northern Sung Hangchou," pp. 317–318.

25 The national reputation of the Lingyin si continued into the twentieth century. Holmes Welch describes it as "the largest [monastery] in Hangzhou and one of the most famous in China" (Holmes Welch, *Buddhism Under Mao* [Cambridge: Harvard University Press, 1972], p. 69). Government supplies were stored in the caves at the Lingyin si—probably Feilaifeng—"for security against Nationalist air raids," p. 71. Events after Liberation at the Lingyin si are described pp. 69–71, 153, 305–306, 342–344; see also figs. 35a–e.

26 Hong Huizhen credits the creation of the sculptures to the convergence of Khubilai, the Newari artist Anige, and Yang Lianzhenjia. Hong Huizhen, "Hangzhou Feilai Feng 'Fanshi,'" p. 53. There is no direct evidence for Anige's involvement.

27 Nor was he the first commissioner to make donations at Feilaifeng. See Zhejiang Sheng Wenwu Kaogu Yenjiu Suo, *Xihu Shiku*, pl. 106, where the damaged inscrip-

tion mentions a Commissioner Xu of 1282. Marsha Weidner suggests this "indicat[es] government involvement in the project." Marsha Weidner, "Painting and Patronage at the Mongol Court of China, 1260–1368" (Ph.D. dissertation, University of California, Berkeley, 1982), p. 49.

28 The Qianlong Emperor's essay on Tibetan Buddhism, carved into a stele at the Yonghegong, criticizes the high positions and arrogance of "western monks" under the Yuan, who "presumed on their prestige," and were haughty and ostentatious. This seems to be a pointed reference to Yang Lianzhenjia. See Ferdinand D. Lessing, *Yung-ho-kung: An Iconography of the Lamaist Cathedral in Peking* (Stockholm, 1942), p. 59.

29 Paula Swart, "Buddhist Sculptures at Feilai Feng: Confrontation of Two Traditions," *Orientations* 18/12 (1987): 54–61.

30 Richard Edwards, "Pu-tai-Maitreya and a Reintroduction to Hangchou's Fei-lai-feng," *Ars Orientalis* 14 (1984): 5–50; quote on p. 11. On p. 10, Edwards speaks of the creators of the program at Feilaifeng in the Yuan dynasty as "very much aware of their own intrusion," which I interpret to mean consciously or intentionally intrusive. Overall, Edwards' article is exemplary and strives to put Yang's activities in context.

31 Chen Gaohua, "Luelun Yang Lianzhenjia," p. 57–58.

32 I assume that most offensive to Chinese tastes were a) "demonic" imagery cast into the spotlight as Buddhas; and b) *yab yum* imagery. The anomalies depicted at Feilaifeng may be the four two-armed wrathful attendants to Uṣṇīṣavijayā (fig. 7), on whom see below, yet they are clearly subordinate to a pacific form of the main deity. I am also assuming that what currently survives at the site accurately represents the original themes. Certainly with one exception noted here, there are no obviously ruined sculptures at the site today which would support the conclusion that offensive images were destroyed immediately after the Yuan period. However, that possibility must be considered. The exception is a triad of which only the central image remains, a four-armed Tibetan-style Chenrezig bodhisattva; one would expect that two other bodhisattva images accompanied him. They are neatly cut out of the niche as if the victims of art theft rather than vengeful desecration. See Zhejiang Sheng Wenwu Kaogu Yenjiu Suo, *Xihu Shiku*, pl. 188.

33 James C.Y. Watt and Anne E. Wardwell, *When Silk Was Gold: Central Asian and Chinese Textiles* (New York: Metropolitan Museum of Art, 1997), pp. 95–99; for fragments of a closely related *kesi* which might have depicted Hevajra at the center, see Antonia Tozer, *Threads of Imagination: Central Asian and Chinese Silks from the 12th to the 19th century* (London: Spinks, 1999), no. 8. See also the Acala and related woven images on pp. 90–94 of Watt and Wardwell, *When Silk Was Gold*, which the authors argue rather unconvincingly can be connected to the Tangut Xia dynasty instead of the Mongol Yuan. Amy Heller has recently shown that images which have conventionally been identified as Vighnāntaka (like the Cleveland Museum *kesi* referred to above) should actually be recognized as a variant form of Acala. Amy Heller, "On the Development of the Iconography of Acala and Vighnāntaka in Tibet," *Embodying Wisdom: Art, Text and Interpretation in the History of Esoteric Buddhism*, edited by Rob Linrothe and Henrik Sørensen (Copenhagen: Seminar in Buddhist Studies, 2001). Su Bai argues for a Hangzhou provenance of these

weavings with Tibetan themes in "Yuandai Hangzhou de Zangchuan Mijiao," p.
375. These ferocious *yi dam* and *yab yum* deities dominate the painted program at
Dunhuang cave 465, which Wei Yang argues should be dated to Khubilai Khan's
reign: Wei Yang, "A Study of Dunhuang Cave 465" (master's thesis, Smith College,
1998).

34 Zhejiang Sheng Wenwu Kaogu Yenjiu Suo, *Xihu Shiku*, pl. 159.

35 Zhejiang Sheng Wenwu Kaogu Yenjiu Suo, *Xihu Shiku*, pls. 177, 187, 188. They are
in both Chinese and Tibetan styles.

36 Zhejiang Sheng Wenwu Kaogu Yenjiu Suo, *Xihu Shiku*, pls. 126, 156, 168.

37 Zhejiang Sheng Wenwu Kaogu Yenjiu Suo, *Xihu Shiku*, pl. 175, 193; again, both Chinese and Tibetan styles are represented.

38 Lai Tianbing, "The Yuan dynasty stone sculptural art," p. 403. In my opinion Lai
overemphasizes a stylistic connection to Pāla sculpture.

39 Zhejiang Sheng Wenwu Kaogu Yenjiu Suo, *Xihu Shiku*, pls. 160–164, 174, 176, 182.

40 Zhejiang Sheng Wenwu Kaogu Yenjiu Suo, *Xihu Shiku*, pls. 117, 166, both misidentified by the authors. But see Xiong Wenbing, "Textual Research on Usnishavijaya,"
Zhongguo Zangxue 4 (1998): 81–95, which shows that scholars in China are incor-
porating Tibetan and western iconographic studies into Chinese scholarship.

41 Rob Linrothe, "Renzong and the Patronage of Tangut Buddhist Art: The *Stūpa*
and Uṣṇīṣavijayā Cult," *Journal of Sung-Yuan Studies* 28 (1998): 91–121; idem,
"Uṣṇīṣavijayā and the Tangut Cult of the Stūpa at Yu-lin Cave 3," *National Palace
Museum Bulletin* 31/4–5 (1996): 1–24. See also the two Uṣṇīṣavijayā images in cave
3 at Wugemiao, misidentified as Avalokiteśvara in Zhang Baoxi, *Gansu shiku yishu
bihua bian* (Lanzhou, 1997), p. 38.

42 Zhejiang Sheng Wenwu Kaogu Yenjiu Suo, *Xihu Shiku*, pl. 171. He does appear
in similar form in the Tang cave 15 at Yulin. See Dunhuang Yanjiu Suo, *Zhongguo
Shiku: Anxi Yulin Ku* (Beijing: Wenwu, 1997), pl. 4.

43 Zhejiang Sheng Wenwu Kaogu Yenjiu Suo, *Xihu Shiku*, pl. 194; Edwards remarks
that "It is impossible to see this as anything other than a scene of drinking." Edwards,
"Pu-Tai-Maitreya," p. 11.

44 Edwards dates the Budai tableau to the Southern Song and feels it could not be contemporary with Yang; Edwards, "Pu-tai Maitreya and Hangchou's Fei-lai-feng," pp.
14–15.

45 Zhejiang Sheng Wenwu Kaogu Yenjiu Suo, *Xihu Shiku*, pl. 158.

46 H. Franke suggests Vajrapāṇi was later associated with Chinggis Khan; the references
he cites are much later, so it is difficult to consider this as having been the case in the
thirteenth century. Franke, *From Tibetan Chieftain to Universal Emperor and God:
The Legitimation of the Yüan Dynasty* (Munich: Bayerischen Akademie der Wissen-
schafgten, 1978), p. 67. For examples of Chinese images of Vajrapāṇi, see the peaceful bodhisattva form in cave 3 of the Wugemiao caves, published in Zhang Baoxi,
Gansu shiku yishu bihua bian, p. 34. The author dates it to the tenth century though
it looks later to me. The Vajrapāṇi form is found in both murals and scripture illustrations: Dunhuang Wenwu yanjiu suo, *Zhongguo Shiku: Dunhuang Mogao ku* (Beijing:
Wenwu, 1987), 4:60 (Cave 112), and Roderick Whitfield and Anne Farrer, *Caves of the
Thousand Buddhas: Chinese Art from the Silk Route* (New York: G. Braziller, 1990),
p. 96, fig. 76B. See also Henrik Sørensen, "Typology and Iconography in the Esoteric

Buddhist Art of Dunhuang," *Silk Road Art and Archaeology* 2 (1991/1992): 312, where Vajrapāṇi is said to be "found relatively frequently among the paintings from Mogao."

47 Of course, it is generally true that Esoteric Buddhism saw itself as integrated with, and based upon Mahāyāna, so this interpretation of Yang's intention seems compatible with his Tibetan or Tangut Esoteric Buddhist perspective.

48 Zhejiang Sheng Wenwu Kaogu Yenjiu Suo, *Xihu Shiku*, caption to pl. 128, includes the inscription which is translated in Edwards, "Pu-tai-Maitreya and a Reintroduction to Hangchou's Fei-lai-feng," p. 10. However, in the first line of the poem, after the title, "Eulogy for the mountain stone image[s] in the Buddhist realms of Hangchou, the great kingdom of Yüan," Edwards translates Yongfu as "eternally blessed," where Franke points out that it is a place name. Franke, "Tibetans in Yuan China," p. 321. Chen Gaohua still feels it is a title bestowed by Khubilai. See Chen Gaohua, "Luelun Yang Lianzhenjia," p. 55.

49 In fact, it is quite possible he is responsible for several more of those dating to his tenure there, the inscriptions of which are no longer legible. One candidate is an Amitābha sculpture in the Chinese style dated by inscription to the twenty-eighth year of the Zhiyuan reign (1291), though the rest of the inscription is too weathered to be read. Zhejiang Sheng Wenwu Kaogu Yenjiu Suo, *Xihu Shiku*, caption to pl. 129. See also pls. 140, 145.

50 The sense of the layout is most clearly conveyed by the foldout drawing in Huang Yongquan 黄湧泉, *Hangzhou Yuandai Shiku Yishu* 杭州元代石窟藝術 (Beijing, 1958), opposite p. 18. Its numbering system of niches is convenient but other systems are now in use among Chinese scholars, unfortunately without consensus. Huang's incorporates both Yuan and pre-Yuan niches. Hong Huizhen, "Hangzhou Feilai Feng 'Fanshi,'" p. 50, includes a map of numbered niches of Yuan sculpture which does not agree with that in use in Lai Tianbing, "Hangzhou Feilaifeng Yuandai Shike zaoxiang yishu."

51 The abbot's poem mentioned above ends by naming Qian Yongchang from Hangzhou as the artist of the Amitābha sculpture which is in the Tibetan-inflected style. The designs for the Tibetan iconography may have been derived from court-appointed artists such as Anige, as Hong Huizhen believes. On Anige, see Jing, "The Portraits of Khubilai Khan and Chabi by Anige," pp. 40–86. The execution of the Tibetan-style images is still infused with Chinese qualities, so I doubt Tibetan or Newari artists were directly involved in the actual carving. Jing notes that Anige taught Liu Yuan "and probably many other Chinese artists, how to make Himalayan-style Buddhist images" (p. 46). Liu Yuan's career as a sculptor is discussed in Weidner, "Painting and Patronage at the Mongol Court," pp. 46–48.

52 Rob Linrothe, "Peripheral Visions: On Recent Finds of Tangut Buddhist Art," *Monumenta Serica* 42 (1995): 235–262.

53 Chi-Chiang Huang, "Elite and Clergy in Northern Sung Hangchou," pp. 322.

54 Chen Gaohua, "Luelun Yang Lianzhenjia," p. 56.

55 Rossabi, *Khubilai Khan*, p. 229.

56 This is also the interpretation of Chen Gaohua in his article "Luelun Yang Lianzhenjia."

57 Chen Gaohua, "Luelun Yang Lianzhenjia," p. 58. Demiéville and Petech write that the pillaging of the tombs was approved by Saṅgha but not by Khubilai. Demiéville, "Les tombeaux des Song méridionaux," p. 461; Petech, "Sang-ko," p. 201.

58 The term is borrowed from Wu Hung who argues that textual enclosures, consisting of historical anecdotes and interpretations, predispose viewers toward particular readings of works of art, in the process blinding them to the visual elements manifested by the work of art itself. Wu Hung, *The Double Screen: Medium and Representation in Chinese Painting* (Chicago: University of Chicago Press, 1996), pp. 29–48.

59 Chen Gaohua, "Luelun Yang Lianzhenjia," p. 57.

3: Dabaojigong and the Regional Tradition of Ming Sino-Tibetan Painting in the Kingdom of Lijiang*

Karl Debreczeny

Tibetan Buddhism among the Naxi

SOME OF THE most vibrant intersections of Tibetan and Chinese Buddhist artistic culture were made possible by the active interest of third party intermediaries such as the imperial courts of the Tanguts, Mongols, and Manchus. This pattern of patronage can also be found on a smaller scale along the Sino-Tibetan border, where local rulers faced problems similar to those of the emperors, including the difficulty of finding a language of sacral rule that could span the multi-ethnic territories they controlled. Dabaojigong (fig. 1) is a small, late-Ming Buddhist temple located in Baisha village, several miles outside of Lijiang (Tib. 'Jang Sa tham) in northwestern Yunnan, an area official Ming histories recognize as being beyond direct imperial control. The temple was built by the Naxi people, an ethnic group living in areas between Han Chinese and Tibetan regions that drew from both cultural spheres. This confluence resulted in a local painting tradition that was a hybrid of Tibetan and Chinese painting in both style and subject matter. Dabaojigong seems to have played a pivotal role in the development of Naxi wall-painting, as it is the earliest extant temple in Lijiang that evidences a local painting workshop which had fully absorbed and synthesized both Chinese and Tibetan painting traditions. It is true that the Naxi and the Tibetans were often military and political adversaries, but it is equally true that they were also often economic and cultural allies. Their complicated relationship belies the oversimplified Chinese models of conflict and submission that are often presented as the sole pattern of Sino-Tibetan relations. Although such a complex

FIG. 1 The exterior of Dabaojigong

intersection of geopolitical and cultural relations may not be unusual to
Sino-Tibetan relations, it has not generally received sufficient attention.
This chapter will examine how a more nuanced model of this at times contentious relationship can account for the hybrid selection of themes and
modes of painting in Naxi works.

The Naxi are thought to descend from the Qiang, a nomadic "proto-
Tibetan" people who migrated during the Han Dynasty to southern Sichuan
and northern Yunnan.[1] Naxi oral tradition offers a corresponding history,
situating their ancestors in the northwest, and describing them as living in
tents and tending to animals. The Naxi language is classified as belonging
to the Tibeto-Burman family, and the local ethnonym for Tibetans, *guzong*,
means "ancestor," reflecting an indigenous recognition among the Naxi of
their ancient ancestry.[2] However, by the time of the Ming dynasty, the Naxi of
Lijiang had allied themselves to the Chinese, both politically and culturally.
They built ancestral temples, depicted themselves as Chinese officials in official portraiture, and kept official Confucian-style historical records in Chi-

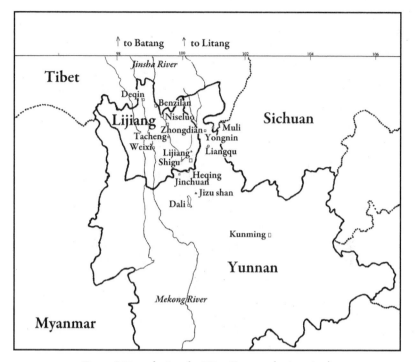

FIG. 2 Lijiang during the Ming Dynasty (1369–1644)

nese. Additionally, the early presence of Chinese Buddhist temples and the recurrent reference in Tibetan sources to the presence of Chinese monks further suggest a strong Han Chinese cultural presence in Lijiang.

The Naxi are mainly found in northwestern Yunnan, in southwestern Sichuan, and in the Tibetan Jinsha River Valley areas (fig. 2).[3] The location of Lijiang is critical to a discussion of Sino-Tibetan interaction because key strategic positions between Yunnan, Sichuan, and Tibet—such as the famous iron bridge (*tieqiao*) at Shimen pass, which served as the primary route of invasion of Yunnan—fell within the Kingdom of Lijiang. While the Naxi were to varying degrees within Chinese and Tibetan spheres of influence from at least the early Tang Dynasty (618–907) onward, it is in the thirteenth century that Lijiang first enters the imperial orbit.[4] In 1253, when Khubilai Khan led his troops against the Dali kingdom, he passed through Lijiang. The Naxi submitted and were incorporated into the Mongol Empire prior to the founding of the Yuan Dynasty. This marks the establishment of the Lijiang *tusi*, or "indigenous office," within the central government. *Tusi* was a title of recognition of local rulers in border regions, especially in south and southwest China, who had submitted to the central government but had not been directly incorporated into the central bureaucracy. The Naxi ruling house held this position until 1723, when Lijiang became directly incorporated under the authority of the Qing central government, via magistrates from outside the region who were sent to govern in rotating shifts.[5] It is during the long period of *tusi* governance that Tibetan Buddhist temples are first recorded as being built in the Sichuan-Yunnan border area.

At the founding of the Ming Dynasty (1369–1644), the Naxi were one of the few border peoples to pledge allegiance immediately. This was a matter of great political importance to the newly founded Chinese court, as the Yuan provincial regime led by Basalawarmi (d. 1382)—the Prince of Liang and a descendent of Khubilai Khan's fifth son—still held power in Yunnan. He led a bitter opposition to the Ming incorporation of Yunnan in the 1360s and 70s, fielding troops against the Ming in Sichuan, and encouraging local tribes to resist Ming authority.[6] According to his official Chinese biography, the Naxi ruler, by contrast, sent his son "to submit a map of their land"[7] as a token of their submission as soon as the Ming Dynasty was established in 1368. In 1381 the Naxi actively aided the Ming southern expedition led by Mu Ying, the future military commander of Yunnan, to pacify Yunnan, and captured key strategic points in the name of the Ming including the aforementioned iron bridge. As a reward for their loyalty, the Ming Emperor granted the hereditary title of "prefect of Lijiang *fu*" and the Chinese surname Mu to the Naxi ruling house. They were made responsible for defending the Sino-Tibetan border at Shimen pass and resisting Tibetan advances. In this way, the Ming court enacted a policy of using the Naxi, a group that was admittedly beyond direct imperial control, to keep the Tibetans in check and secure the empire's southwestern border.

As a result of military campaigns during the Ming Dynasty, the Kingdom of Lijiang, often in the name of the central government, expanded its domain to areas of northwest Yunnan and southwest Sichuan, putting largely Tibetan territories under its jurisdiction. The height of this expansion occurred from the mid-sixteenth to the early seventeenth centuries, and at its apex their kingdom extended west to Weixi ('Ba' lung) and north to Zhongdian (Rgyal thang), Benzilan (Spong tse ra), Deqin (Bde chen), Muli (Smi li), and even to Batang ('Ba' thang) and Litang (Li thang), which are deep in modern western Sichuan (fig. 2).[8] During this period, when the Kingdom of Lijiang controlled large areas of Tibetan territory, the Mu ruling family began to take an active interest in Tibetan Buddhism and there was a corresponding explosion of temple construction during the sixteenth and seventeenth centuries. The push to build temples in Lijiang during the Ming dynasty may have been in part in order to attract major Tibetan hierarchs to the local ruling family's court, and thereby to gain prestige within the region's Tibetan community. The Mu family also collected taxes from these lands, providing an important source of revenue that allowed them to fund such a productive temple building program. Among these temples is the site that will be our focus, Dabaojigong.

During this period of military expansion the three main trade routes between Yunnan and Tibet all passed through Lijiang-controlled territory, giving the Naxi control over the Yunnan-Tibet tea-horse trade as well.[9] The Naxi primarily traded tea from the south and salt mined locally for livestock from Tibetan areas, horses being the single most important commodity. Control of the Yunnan-Tibet tea-horse trade also provided a great deal of revenue which the Naxi ruling family could use to support construction projects such as Dabaojigong throughout their kingdom. In the mid-fourteenth century, the Sino-Tibetan frontier, especially along the Sichuan and Yunnan borders, gained new economic and cultural prominence. With the decline of Buddhism and Muslim invasions in India in the twelfth and thirteenth centuries, the Tibet-India trade became less viable. This may have encouraged some movement of Tibetans east to the Chinese border and a corresponding shift of Chinese to the western borders, to take advantage of economic activities.[10] The first Tibetan Buddhist monastery built in northwest Yunnan was established by the Second Karmapa, Karma Pakshi (1204–1283), in somewhat distant Dechen, and the first temple built in close proximity to Lijiang was Dzebo Dargyeling (Ch. Zhebo Sajiasi), in Yongning in 1353. Both the monastery and the temple came under the control of the Kingdom of Lijiang in the late Ming dynasty. Tibetan Buddhism is not thought to have entered into Lijiang proper until later during the Ming, corresponding to the period when Dabaojigong was built. While Tibetan Buddhism had gained a foothold in northwest Yunnan in the thirteenth and fourteenth centuries, it was the new economic base that developed during the Ming that fostered the founding of new monasteries along the Sino-Tibetan frontier, an area that had not previously seen construction on such a large scale, and enabled the invitation of great lamas into the area. While all orders of Tibetan Buddhism participated in construction, the Karma Kagyü hierarchs were especially vigorous in their endeavors in Eastern Tibet. Thus, the flourishing of Tibetan Buddhism and the concomitant monastic construction in Lijiang during the sixteenth to seventeenth century should be seen in the context of the larger economic and cultural expansion that was taking place along the southern Sino-Tibetan border.

Among the Mu rulers during the Ming, the two primary patrons of Tibetan Buddhism were Mu Wang (r. 1580–1596), founder of the Dabaojigong temple, and his grandson, Mu Zeng (r. 1598–1624 [d. 1646]) (fig. 3) who was likely responsible for Dabaojigong's wall-paintings. The accounts in official Confucian style biographies of the Mu rulers, the *Mushi huanpu*, written in Chinese and begun in the early sixteenth century, are limited to their protagonists' political and military exploits. So it is to Tibetan sources that we must often turn to learn the details of their religious patronage. The Ninth Karmapa's biography states that Mu Wang had a Tibetan Buddhist preceptor named Jangshepa, and that in 1582 Mu Wang expressed his wish to commission a new woodblock edition of the Kanjur (the Tibetan Tripiṭaka), a monumental task that was only completed during the reign of his grandson, Mu Zeng.[11] This was the same year Dabaojigong was founded, and so it is possible that the temple was built expressly to house this new edition of the Tripiṭaka, which would have involved tens of thousands of woodblocks, or that both projects were commissioned to celebrate Mu Wang's recent enthronement. Unfortunately, no evidence directly supports either of these theories.

Mu Wang did not limit his patronage of Buddhism to the Karmapas or to Lijiang, but was also in contact with hierarchs from other major Tibetan Buddhist traditions. In 1580, he sent invitations to the Third Dalai Lama (1543–1588), who was then proselytizing in Mongolia and Amdo (modern Qinghai Provence), and provided for the construction of Jampaling (Litangsi), a Gelukpa monastery in Litang, southwest Sichuan, which by that time had come under Mu rule.[12] As previously noted, Mu's power extended to territories well outside of Lijiang during the period Dabaojigong was constructed, and the Mu rulers also built and supported temples in these areas as well. Additionally, in what may have been part of a larger attempt to project themselves beyond their provincial status as devout Buddhist monarchs, the Mu rulers were also patrons of temples on the four primary mountain pilgrimage sites in China: Wutai shan (Shanxi), Putuo shan (Ningbo, Zhejiang), Emei shan (Sichuan), and Jiuhua shan (Anhui), as well as the more local pilgrimage site of Chicken Foot Mountain (Ch. Jizushan, Tib. Ri bo bya rkang), near Dali in Yunnan. However, as we shall see, despite such wide-ranging patronage, when the Gelukpa later came into conflict with the Kagyüpa in the mid-seventeenth century the Naxi showed themselves to be militant partisans of the Karmapa.

Mu Zeng (fig. 3)—known in Tibetan accounts as Karma Mipam Tsewang

FIG. 3 Mu Zeng (r. 1598–1646), Official Portrait.
(After *Mushi Huanpu*, p. 134.)

Sonam Rabten—as the greatest patron of Tibetan Buddhism in Lijiang, constructing a greater number of temples than any of his predecessors or successors. Early in his career, Mu Zeng expanded Lijiang's territory through military campaigns to the greatest extent it would ever see. But in 1624, at the age of thirty-six, Mu Zeng abdicated the throne to concentrate his efforts on his religious activities, choosing to spend most of his days receiving religious instruction at the Tibetan Buddhist temple Fuguosi, which he had founded.[13] However Mu Zeng still acted as regent for his son, Mu Yi (r. 1624–1669) for the next ten years, a fact spelled out in Mu Yi's official biography. A set of scrolls containing a separate biography detailing Mu Zeng's extensive involvement in Buddhist activities was preserved until the time of Joseph Rock's scholarship in the early twentieth century. Rock noted that the scrolls are purported to have said that while Mu Zeng's predecessors were longtime Buddhist converts, his spiritual attainments far surpassed them all.[14] Furthermore, in keeping with his image as a sacral wheel-turning king (*cakravartirāja*), Mu Zeng was popularly known as Mu Tianwang, "Mu Heavenly King," a reference to

FIG. 4 Portrait of Mu Zeng in monastic robes.
(After Rock [1947], plate 44.)

the royal guardian deities who protect the dharma in the four directions. Several of his larger temples, such as Fuguosi and Xitansi, even contained shrines called "Mu Heavenly King Hall," where statues of Mu Zeng were housed.[15] A portrait in which he is depicted in monastic robes suggests that he eventually became a monk (fig. 4), in contrast to his official portrait seen above (fig. 3), in which he appears as a Chinese official. While his robes are Chinese, the Amitāyus Buddha painted in gold above him is executed in a Tibetan manner, alluding to his Tibetan Buddhist practice. Thus in a single portrait Mu Zeng is identified with both the Chinese and the Tibetan traditions, reflecting in microcosm the pattern of Mu patronage and rulership. Moreover, as we shall see shortly, Mu Zeng was involved in the refurbishment of Dabaojigong, a temple that exemplifies the synthesis of Chinese and Tibetan traditions characteristic of the Mu rulers.

The Painting Program at Dabaojigong

Dabaojigong sits west and faces east. It is located directly behind the early Ming temple Liulidian (1417), which it closely resembles in its Chinese architecture. It is roughly square in appearance, with a face three *jian* wide, and a double-eaved, hip-gabled tile roof. Dabaojigong, Liulidian, and a third hall, Zangjinglou ("Tripiṭaka Pavilion"), share an outer wall[16] with a fourth structure, Hufatang ("Hall of the Protectors"), located directly behind it; however, the relationship between these structures has yet to be established. There is some discrepancy in the dates given for Dabaojigong's construction; most Chinese scholars give the year as 1582, though they seldom cite their sources.[17] A dated Tibetan inscription located on the north wall reads:

> This great inconceivable temple which rivals the divine abode, of excellent Dharma, of the Emperor Dharmarāja called Vajra Saṃvara, was perfectly completed on the third day of the sixth month of the female water-sheep year.[18]

Important internal evidence for the dating of this inscription is the reference to Vajra Saṃvara (Rdo rje bde [m]chog) invoked in the first line of the inscription. This is likely the initiatory name of the Wanli Emperor (r. 1573–1620), who re-established close ties to the Karma Kagyü after the Emperor Shizong's (r. 1522–1567) backlash against the Emperor Zhengde's (r. 1506–1521) excessive enthusiasm for Tibetan Buddhism at the Ming court.[19] If this identification is correct, it would confirm reading the cyclical date, which functions much like a Chinese reign date, as 1583.[20] A set of wooden horizontal name boards (*bian'e*), inscribed in Chinese, records that Dabaojigong was built by the prefect Mu Wang in 1582: "Respectfully written on the Duanyang [festival] (the 5th day of the 5th month) of the *renwu* year (10th year) of the Wanli era (1582), by the 'aboriginal official,' the meritorious donor Mu Wang."[21] Joseph Rock speaks of a "temple tablet," but suggests that it is undated, and states that Mu Wang's title on the tablet is *zhifu*, "prefect," placing the date of the temple within his reign dates of 1580–1598.[22] Both Chinese accounts of the temple's dedication record that Mu Wang was Dabaojigong's founding patron, which would place the date of the construction in the Wanli era (1573–1620) and establish the date of the Tibetan inscription as 1583.

Twelve bays of wall-paintings survive nearly intact, however large portions of the rear (west) wall of Dabaojigong are lost, as are both sides flanking the doors of the east wall.[23] More recent damage was suffered during the Cultural

Revolution (1967–1976) when the building was used as a grammar school. Numerous eyes were gouged out and a revolutionary slogan was scratched into the paint in large characters on the south wall.[24] Already by the time Joseph Rock lived in Lijiang—on and off for twenty-seven years from 1922 to 1949—Dabaojigong was decayed and dilapidated, though it was still inhabited by two "Karmapa lamas" from Fuguosi, one of the five major Karma Kagyü temples in the Lijiang area. Any statuary that was once standing in the temple has been completely lost.

The overall palette of the wall-paintings is extremely dark. There is some degree of over-painting, including an over-layer of an apparent varnish on top of the background landscape which seems to have darkened the overall program. Evidence of this over-painting is most visible where dark pigment overlaps the Tibetan cartouches, partially obscuring them. According to Guo Dalie, analysis of Dabaojigong's wall-paintings indicates that the paint surface did not originally appear so dark, but in areas where the paint has peeled away azurite (*shiqing*) and malachite (*shilu*) are revealed, and these have "oxidized and become dark."[25] According to the local museum staff, the recent cutting of the paintings off the walls has resulted in further darkening. That the wall-paintings' current appearance is considerably darker than when first painted leads us to believe that in all likelihood the palette once resembled the brighter blue-green palettes and stronger color contrasts of late-Ming contemporaries.

The wall-paintings contain Chinese Buddhist, Daoist, and Tibetan Buddhist figures, and an altar screen roughly separates the front and rear of the hall. The paintings at the front of the hall contain a mixture of imagery derived from all three traditions and focuses on themes of worldly concerns, while those at the rear of the hall are entirely Tibetan Buddhist in nature and are devoted to inner practices (fig. 5). The brush work is tight and well knit, characterized by a (now) dark palette and a delicate flowing line. The figures' ornaments are accentuated by being set in relief through the generous use of gold paste. There are also some unusual formal techniques—such as the distinctive wispy flame patterns that appear at both the front and rear of the hall—conforming to neither Chinese nor Tibetan painting traditions, and are likely characteristic of the local painting workshop that produced them. Although many of the wall-paintings in both the front and back contain Tibetan inscriptions and identifying cartouches, Chinese scholarship has strangely made little or no use of them. As a consequence, the subjects of many of the paintings have so far been misidentified, and thus some clarification is required here.

FIG. 5 Diagram of the Dabaojigong painting program

Front

1. Mahāmāyūrī, inscribed *'Phag rma bya chen mo la na mo*, in *shuilu* assemblage (203 x 446 cm)
2. Mārīcī, inscribed *'Od zer can la na mo* (207 x 123 cm)
3. Scenes from the *Guanyin Pumen* 觀音普門 chapter of the *Lotus Sūtra* (with dated inscription) (203 x 446 cm)
4. Three Officials of Heaven, Earth, and Water (*tian di shui sanguan*, 202 x 119 cm)
5. Tathāgata refuge field (367 x 498 cm) ceiling: Kālacakra *mantra* surrounded by the eight Chinese trigrams

Rear

6. Mahākāruṇika Jinasāgara, inscribed *Thug rje chen po rgyal ba [m]tsho la na mo* (203 x 123 cm)
7. Vajravārāhī as Vajrayoginī (203 x 123 cm)
8. Vajrasattva, inscribed *Dpal Rdo rje sems pa la na mo* (208 x 121 cm)
9. Mahāmudrā lineage (208 x 195 cm)
10. lost (Mahākāla?) (76 x 94 cm)
11. Vajradhara surrounded by the Eighty-four Mahāsiddhas (208 x 195 cm)
12. Vajravidāraṇa (?) (208 x 124 cm)

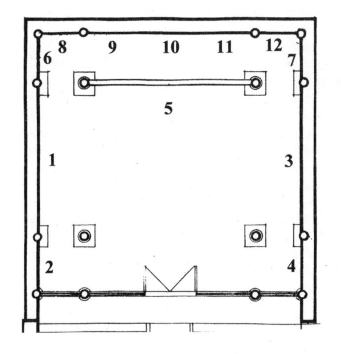

The front hall is dominated by iconographic themes standard to Buddhist temple wall-paintings of the Ming dynasty; nonetheless Tibetan elements permeate these paintings. On the south wall (fig. 5, no. 1; 203 x 446 cm) Mahāmāyūrī (fig. 6), identified by the Tibetan inscription on her throne—"Praise to Mahāmāyūrī" ('Phag (sic) rma bya chen mo la na mo)—is surrounded by one hundred deities who are drawn predominantly from Chinese Buddhist and Daoist pantheons, including twenty-eight Daoist constellation deities, dragon kings, thunder gods, offering goddesses, sixteen arhats, dijun, and fierce heavenly generals. Chinese scholars identify the subject of this painting as the "Mahāmāyūrī Preaching Assembly."[26] However, I would argue that these deities constitute a complete, if abbreviated, shuilu, or "water-land" assemblage, a common theme in the wall-paintings of Chinese Buddhist temples by the late Ming dynasty.

Shuilu zhai is a Chinese Buddhist ritual of universal salvation designed to feed the untended spirits of the dead, a clever co-optation of Confucian concerns into a Buddhist ritual framework. In the water-land rite the deities are conceived hierarchically. Corresponding to this, the painting depicts an "upper hall" forming the center of the composition and devoted to the Three Jewels (Buddha, Dharma, and Sangha) and various enlightened beings such as bodhisattvas, pratyekabuddhas, the sixteen arhats, and Dharma protectors, and a "lower hall" flanking the periphery and devoted to the beings of the six realms, such as (Daoist) rulers, ministers, celestial deities, asuras, dragon kings, local deities, and others. Such a division of space would usually be communicated symbolically, especially in ritual practice, rather than by a literal ·division into different halls. In essence, the arrangement on the south wall of Dabaojigong is similar to that found at Pilusi (in Hebei province), where the entire painting program of one of its halls is devoted to the depiction of a shuilu zhai rite, but is here condensed onto a single wall.[27]

Despite the Chinese origins of shuilu practice, the paintings exhibit a mixture of Chinese and Tibetan imagery. For example, the portrayal of Mahāmāyūrī seems to be drawn from Tibetan iconographic models.[28] The strong iconic emphasis on the central figure, with its sharply delineated arms and strong color contrasts, is also more characteristic of Tibetan Buddhist images than of Chinese Buddhist paintings of the Ming dynasty, which tend to be much more anthropomorphizing in their approach to deities. In addition, a Tibetan style maṇḍala hangs from Mahāmāyūrī's throne, complete with tiny deer flanking the wheels atop the gates, themselves enclosed in vajra prongs, and with double vajras in the corners framing the composition. The maṇḍala is flanked on the right by what appears to be a Tibetan monk, iden-

FIG. 6 Mahāmāyūrī "water-land" assemblage (203 x 446 cm) south wall.
(After Wang Haitao, fig. 98.)

tifiable by his bare right shoulder, and on the left by a sleeved Chinese monk, the pair giving formal visual expression to the Naxi ruling house's embrace of both Buddhist traditions.[29]

Seated on a throne at the center of the north wall (fig. 5, no. 3; 203 x 446 cm), arranged symmetrically across from Mahāmāyūrī, is what appears to be a form of Avalokiteśvara surrounded by scenes from the *Guanyin Pumen* chapter of the *Lotus Sūtra*, which recounts the earthly perils from which Guanyin will save the devoted, a popular theme for Chinese Buddhist wall-paintings of this period.[30] The symmetry between the central figures of the south and north walls, in size, color scheme, thrones, ornamentation, and arrangement of arms is striking and immediately impresses the viewer upon entering the temple.

Near the door on the east side of the south wall (fig. 5, no. 2; 207 x 123 cm) is the figure Mārīcī (fig. 7), identified by the Tibetan inscription "Praise to Goddess Mārīcī!" (*Lha mo 'Od zer can la na mo*). She has two arms and three heads, including a sow's head, her distinguishing attribute. In Chinese esoteric doctrine Mārīcī is a goddess of war and victory, and a protector of warriors. As I have noted, during the late sixteenth century, when Dabaojigong was built, Naxi rulers were promoting constant military campaigns, which may explain her presence in the mural. While Mārīcī appears in many Ming temples such as Fahaisi, Dahuisi, Longqingsi, and Baoningsi, the form seen here is not consistent with Chinese Ming painting. Even more unusual is her retinue: in the top row appear the Daoist supreme deities, the Three Purities (*Sanqing*), and in the lower rank the four gods of Wind, Rain, Snow, and Lightning, beings who seem more related to the Daoist deities depicted on the opposite wall than to this Buddhist deity.[31]

FIG. 7 (left) Mārīcī (207 x 123 cm), south wall.
(After *Lijiang Baisha bihua*, fig. 52.)

FIG. 8 (right) Three Officials of Heaven, Earth, and Water (202 x 119 cm),
north wall. (After *Lijiang Baisha bihua*, fig. 60.)

On the east side of the north wall (fig. 5, no. 4; 202 x 119 cm), directly
across the hall from Mārīcī, are the Daoist deities known as the Three Officials of Heaven, Earth, and Water, *tian di shui sanguan* (fig. 8). The Three
Officials were believed to have kept an equilibrium in the world through
their bureaucratic management of natural forces, and to have played a key
role as intermediaries between the living and the bureaucracy of the under-
world. The devoted would confess sins and address prayers in the form of
written petitions for protection, the curing of illness, and relief from disaster
to the Three Officials and celestial bureaucrats.[32] The painting of these deities
as they appear together at Dabaojigong became commonplace by the time
of the Ming, and can be found in the same arrangement, with the Official of
Heaven at center, the Official of Water to the left, and the Official of Land to
the right, in an illuminated manuscript dated 1470 in the Museum of Fine
Arts in Boston.[33] While the central figures on the east end of the north and

south walls are not similar in any way, the three Daoist figures at the top of each composition (the Three Purities on the south wall and the Three Officials on the north wall) are visually balanced, which reinforces their connection as members of the same Daoist pantheon. These are the only overtly Daoist figural themes found in the wall-painting at Dabaojigong.[34]

Perhaps most interesting in this painting are the two figures dressed in contemporary Ming court attire at the top left and right, who have been identified by Chinese scholars as members of the locally ruling Mu family, the Mushi *tusi*.[35] As I discussed above, the two primary patrons of Buddhism in the Ming were Mu Wang, builder of Dabaojigong, and his grandson, Mu Zeng, who was likely responsible for the wall-paintings as they appear now. It may well be that it is Mu Wang and Mu Zeng who are depicted here. One can compare these figures to their official portraits in the *Mushi huanpu*, as in figure 3. The two figures have also been identified as the Daoist deities Wenchang (left) and Zhenwu (right).[36] Thus it is possible that the Mu rulers are here being conflated with Daoist celestial rulers, a standard iconographic ploy in representations of royal patronage and projections of divine power in both Daoist and Buddhist traditions.

The largest painting at Dabaojigong (fig. 5, no. 5; 367 x 498 cm) is on the altar screen and depicts a Tathāgata refuge field (fig. 9). The central Buddha figure is unusual in that it seems to mix both Chinese and Tibetan aesthetics. At the bottom of the altar screen are three Tibetan Buddhist protectors, which are in poor condition. The surviving figure on the right is the Six-Armed Mahākāla (Mgon po phyag drug pa), identifiable by the characteristic implements he holds—a rosary of human skulls, a *ḍamaru* (hand drum), a chopper, a skull cup, a lasso, and a trident—and he stands on White Gaṇapati (Gaṇeśa, here as lord of obstacles), who holds a skull cup and radish (*la phug*).[37] The other two protectors at the lower center and left are more severely damaged, but appear to be Pañjaranātha Mahākāla, with the right portion of his magical staff (*'phrul gyi gaṇḍi*) still discernable, cradled in the crook of his arm, and Four-Armed Mahākāla with trident and sword.

On the ceiling above the central altar screen, the interlocked syllables of the Kālacakra mantra (*oṃ haṃ kṣa ma la va ra ya svā hā*)—known in Tibetan as "the ten syllables of power" (*spungs yig rnam bcu dbang ldan*)—are surrounded by the eight Chinese trigrams and painted on the leaves of a lotus in the center of a sunken well (fig. 10).[38] Although it was customary to place mantras and/or maṇḍalas on the symbolically important ceiling in Ming temples, this particular mantra is more commonly found as a protective talisman in Tibetan monasteries. Typically in Chinese temples the eight trigrams

FIG. 9 Tathāgata refuge field (367 x 498 cm), altar screen.
(After *Wang Haitao*, fig. 85.)

would surround a *yin-yang* circle, forming a Daoist protective talisman.[39] The
presence of the Kālacakra mantra here combined with the trigrams makes for
a fascinating hybrid of Tibetan and Chinese protective symbols on the ceiling of Dabaojigong. Although Chinese Buddhist themes appear to dominate
the front hall and both Chinese and Tibetan imagery are combined there, it
is important to keep in mind that this temple is said to have housed a now lost
sculpture of Mahākāla, as well as a shrine devoted to him. These might have
served as the temple's primary images, perhaps altering our perception of the
overall iconographic and stylistic program found at Dabaojigong. In this
light, the presence of Tibetan statuary at Xitansi (discussed below), another
Ming temple built by Mu Zeng, which dates to the time Dabaojigong was
being decorated, is very suggestive.

    Each painting behind the altar screen exhibits general Tibetan Buddhist
themes standard for temples of the Karma Kagyü order. They are not part
of a fixed iconographic arrangement, but are representative of teachings
and deities common to the Karma Kagyü order, and thus could have been
selected for display for any number of reasons—perhaps because they correspond to practices favored by the patron or clergy associated with the temple.

FIG. 10 Kālacakra mantra surrounded by the eight Chinese trigrams,
ceiling of Dabaojigong

It is interesting to note that almost all of the deities represented in the rear
of Dabaojigong appear as tutelary deities in the hagiographies of the Sixth
Zhamar (1584–1630) and his student the Tenth Karmapa (1604–1674), the
two Kagyü hierarchs most influential in Lijiang, and in particular both painters in their own right (as will be discussed below).

The rear section of the south wall (fig. 5, no. 6; 203 x 123 cm), divided
from the *shuilu* painting by a half-pillar, depicts a standard Kagyü
Avalokiteśvara lineage (fig. 11), which is identified by the Tibetan inscription on Avalokiteśvara's throne: "Praise to Mahākāruṇika Jinasāgara" (*Thug
rje chen po Rgyal ba tsho* [sic] *la na mo*). Each of the figures surrounding
Avalokiteśvara is also labeled. Above Avalokiteśvara is Tipupa, wearing red
robes and a pointed *paṇḍita* cap, and seated in debate posture, his right hand
pointing up and his left hand holding a bowl in his lap. In the upper left corner is Padampa Gyagar, founder of the Zhijepa order, in white robes, and
in the upper right corner is his student Machik Labdrön dancing in white
robes and a crown.[40] The figure in the upper mid-left is Lotsawa Chenpo, "the
Great Translator," in red robes in a *paṇḍita* hat, and in the upper mid-right
is Milarepa's student Rechungpa [Dorjédrak]. At the middle left is a form of

FIG. 11 (left) Mahākāruṇika Jinasāgara (203 x 123 cm), south wall

FIG. 12 (right) Vajravārāhī (203 x 123 cm), north wall

Hayagrīva (Khro bo'i rgyal po Rta mchog dpal), with his identifying horse head peeking out from his angry waving hair. On the right is a four-armed form of the wrathful female deity Guhyajñānaḍākinī (Gsang ba ye shes ḍā ki ma) wielding a skull-cup, chopper, sword, and *khaṭvāṅga* staff. On the lower left and right are a series of ten mounted warriors who are also labeled.[41] Curiously this series is usually depicted flanking Vaiśravaṇa, who appears at the bottom of the southwest adjoining panel (fig. 5, no. 8). It is unusual for a retinue to be separated from its deity like this, and one wonders whether the sketch/pounce used as a model for this wall-painting might have had the deities arranged in a continuous series on a single sheet or hand scroll that was later divided into individual panels by the painting workshop, while retaining the original order. At the bottom center is a dwarf form of Mahākāla (Yab drang srong legs ldan mgon po), black-cloaked and holding a large club. Flanking Mahākāla on the right is the dharma-protector Śrīdevī (Dpal ldan lha mo) mounted on her mule, the only unlabeled figure in the entire composition. She is also the only deity that breaks the uniformity, as all of the other mounted figures face outward, while she faces inward. Her flaming halo is similar to that of Lhamo and the Blacksmith pictured beneath the painting of the Karmapa (fig. 5, no. 9), but differs from the distinctive wispy flame pattern characteristic of all the other wrathful deities found throughout the temple. All these factors point to the possibility of some repainting.[42]

On the north wall (fig. 5, no. 7; 203 x 123 cm), divided from the *Guanyin Pumen* scenes by a half-pillar is the dancing figure of Vajravārāhī as Vajrayoginī (fig. 12), flanked by her six emanations, with white Amitāyus above her. The bottom of the painting has been destroyed, so it cannot be determined if she was once labeled.

On the south end of the back wall (fig. 5, no. 8; 208 x 121 cm) is an image of Vajrasattva identified by the inscription "Praise to Glorious Vajrasattva! (*Dpal Rdo rje sems pa* [sic] *la na mo*). The majority of the surrounding figures are also accompanied by labels: Vairocana (Rnam par snang mdzad), Bhaiṣajyaguru (Sman lha), Vajrasattva (Rdor rje sems pa [*sic*]), and one figure whose label is lost (though one can still make out *'i ma'i lha* [?]). Below these is an unlabeled Vaiśravaṇa (Rnam thos sras), whose retinue, as mentioned above, appears on the left adjoining wall (fig. 5, no. 6).[43]

The throne of the central figure on the north end of the rear wall (fig. 5, no. 12; 208 x 124 cm) (fig. 13) is badly damaged, and the identifying Tibetan cartouche has been lost. The deity is shown holding a double vajra in his right hand at his chest and a bell with a double vajra handle in his left hand at his lap, iconography consistent with that of Vajravidāraṇa (Rdo rje rnam par 'joms pa).[44]

On the north side of the center of the rear wall (fig. 5, no. 11; 208 x 195 cm) is a painting of Vajradhara surrounded by the Eighty-four Mahāsiddhas (fig. 14). The central figure is not labeled, but the surrounding mahāsiddhas are (see appendix 2, Painting Key 2, below for a list of the Tibetan inscriptions).[45] Vajradhara is the root-guru of the Mahāmudrā teaching lineage, and the mahāsiddhas are the exemplary practitioners of Mahāmudrā, meditators and yogis of great spiritual attainment from all castes and professions. They were often unorthodox in their behavior, and are revered especially by the Kagyü-pas, who strongly emphasize meditation and yoga. The pairing of Vajradhara with the mahāsiddhas is seen frequently in Tibetan painting, especially in Kagyü temples.[46] However, the particular set of mahāsiddhas we find here is not the grouping typical in Kagyü temples, but seems to follow the verse eulogy to them attributed to Vajrāsana (ca. 1100),[47] suggesting the eclectic nature of the sources used as visual models for these wall-paintings.

The painting on the central panel of the rear wall (fig. 5, no. 10; 76 x 94 cm) is the smallest at Dabaojigong, and is almost entirely lost, its original theme now unidentifiable. One Chinese source attests that Mahākāla (Daheitian

FIG. 13 Vajravidāraṇa (?) (208 x 124 cm), west wall.
(After *Lijiang Baisha bihua*, fig. 70.)

shen) was once the subject of the composition, with his different emanations in the four corners.[48] This would be consistent with Joseph Rock's testimony that Dabaojigong once housed a shrine of Mahākāla. Rock also noted that Dabaojigong was also known as Huofatang (i.e., Hufatang) and Hufaqielan, meaning "Hall of the Dvārapāla" likely in reference to Mahākāla.[49]

Of relevance to our discussion of the dating of the wall-paintings at Dabaojigong is the south central section of the rear wall (fig. 5, no. 9; 208 x 195 cm), which depicts the Mahāmudrā lineage (fig. 15), one of the two primary teaching lineages of the Kagyü order. While the figures are not all iconographically distinctive, with the exception of the central figure they are labeled, which makes it possible to trace the transmission of the teachings from master to disciple (see appendix 2, Painting Key 1), starting with the supreme source of the lineage, Buddha Vajradhara (no. 1), through the Ninth Karmapa, Wangchuk Dorjé (1556–1603) (no. 25).

FIG. 14 Vajradhara surrounded by the Eighty-four Mahāsiddhas
(208 x 195 cm), west wall. (After *Wang Haitao*, plate 155.)

Dating the Paintings: Contexts and Conjectures

In order identify the central figure (fig. 16), it is first necessary to briefly discuss the various Tibetan hierarchs who visited Lijiang during this period.
While the kings of Lijiang were in close contact with the Kagyü order since
at least the fifteenth century, when the Mu rulers had a Tibetan preceptor
named "Zhi-mei-ba,"[50] the first hierarch whose impact on Lijiang is recorded
is the Eighth Karmapa Mikyö Dorjé (1507–1554) in 1516, when he was only
ten years old.[51] A brief account of his seven-day visit is found in his Tibetan
biography which notes that the Mu ruler dispatched four generals and 10,000
soldiers as escort, that a huge drum dragged by sixteen people sounded in his
honor,[52] and that he was met at the border by the king with his uncle and
younger brother all riding on elephants. It is interesting to note that Chinese
monks (Tib. *hwa shang*) are specifically mentioned as being in the king's retinue.[53] As a result of his visit, Mu Ding (r. 1503–1526) promised that five hundred boys would be trained as monks at his expense and that he would build
"one hundred temples." A visit from the Karmapa hierarch, even a short one,
was a momentous occasion, making a significant cultural impression on the

FIG. 15 Mahāmudrā lineage (208 x 195 cm), west wall, Dabaojigong.
(Collage based on Wang, *Yunnan lishi bihua yishu*,
plate 124)

region, as his accompanying camp, the Karma Garchen, was essentially a traveling monastery with thousands of monks and retainers as well as its own
painters and artisans in attendance.[54] (In fact, it is from this encampment that
the Tibetan painting tradition that draws most heavily on Chinese professional painting gets its name: Karma Gardri, the "painting school of the Karmapa encampment.") Such a high profile tour on the part of the Karmapa,
whom the Ming Emperor Zhengde (1506–1521) himself could not persuade
to visit,[55] likely signals a significant level of patronage of Tibetan Buddhism
in the kingdom of Lijiang, and seems to have inspired further temple building activity in the sixteenth century, some sixty-four years before the founding of Dabaojigong in 1582–1583. In all events, since Mikyö Dorjé (marked
no. 23 in fig. 15 and appendix 2, Painting Key 1) is listed with the smaller lineage figures in the lower right-hand side of the Mahāmudrā painting, he can
be eliminated as a prospective candidate in respect to the identity of the unlabeled central figure.

The next visit of a Kagyü hierarch did not take place until 1610, when the
Sixth Zhamar, Garwang Chöki Wangchuk (1584–1630), came to Lijiang with
a large retinue.[56] The single most important result of this visit was the com-

FIG. 16 Mahāmudrā lineage, central detail. Possibly the
Tenth Karmapa Chöying Dorjé (1604–1674).

pletion, under the oversight of the Zhamar, of the still extant Jang Satam edition of the Tibetan Kanjur (now known as the "Litang Edition"), produced
at the request of Mu Zeng, who wrote in its Chinese preface that he was fulfilling the will of his father Mu Wang, founder of Dabaojigong.[57] Mu Zeng
built Tsishak Monastery specifically to house the new edition. Furthermore,
the Sixth Zhamar brought six Naxi disciples to Tibet to be educated, and they
later returned to Lijiang and completed construction of a temple.[58] In this way
Fuguosi (Tib. 'Og min rnam gling), said to be the first and most important
Tibetan Buddhist temple built in Lijiang, was founded in 1627.[59] In its heyday
Fuguosi housed two hundred disciples, and served as an educational center for
Naxi monks. The rear hall was called Fayun'ge, within which was kept a part
of the Tripiṭaka bestowed by the Wanli Emperor. The Sixth Zhamar is also
credited with building the three of the main Karmapa temples in the Lijiang-
controlled area of Zhongdian (Rgyal thang): Kongxiasi (Zixiasi), Jiaxiasi, and
Kangsisi, presumably with Mu Zeng's aid.[60]

   Besides this, the Sixth Zhamar was a painter of some note, and his biography records several instances of his painting images in monasteries. In the
"tantric temple" (Gsang sngags lha khang) at Gyaja Monastery, which lies
on the road to Lijiang at Gönkar, he is reported to have painted an image of

Śrīdevī and placed it in the chapel of the protectors (*mgon khang*).[61] Then, just before returning to Lijiang for the completion of the Tripiṭaka in 1621, he fashioned images of the First Karmapa and the recently deceased Ninth Karmapa, produced paintings of the three divinities known as "Ma, Gön, and Gar" (*ma mgon mgar gsum*)—Śrīdevī (Dpal ldan lha mo), the Black-cloaked Mahākāla (Mgon po ber nag chen), and the "Blacksmith" (Dam can mgar ba nag po)—at Gönkar Monastery, and painted illustrations for the *Aṣṭasāhasrikā Prajñāpāramitā* (*Brgyad stong*) in its sanctuary.[62] Images of Ma, Gön, and Gar, the standard set of protectors of the Karmapa lineage, also appear in Dabaojigong at the bottom of the Mahāmudrā lineage painting. While there is no suggestion in Situ Paṇchen's biography of the Sixth Zhamar that he may have been responsible for painting any of the monasteries in Lijiang, it is quite likely that he was consulted on various aspects (from locations to iconographic composition) related to the kingdom's ambitious temple building program, which reached its apex under his patron Mu Zeng. Although the Sixth Zhamar would rightfully be the next figure in the Mahāmudrā lineage, following the Ninth Karmapa, his name does not appear listed among the smaller lineage holders in this painting, making him a possible candidate for the large central figure, yet not the strongest.

The most prominent hierarch to spend time in Lijiang, and the one who had the greatest impact on the area, was the Sixth Zhamar's student, the Tenth Karmapa Chöying Dorjé (1604–1674), who took shelter in Lijiang for some fifteen years beginning in the early 1640s in the wake of Gushri Khan's invasion of Tibet at the behest of the Fifth Dalai Lama.[63] This Mongol onslaught resulted in the slaughter of virtually everyone in the Karmapa's encampment and the almost total eclipse of the Karma Kagyü tradition. The Karmapa and his attendant Küntu Zangpo barely escaped, and eventually fled to Lijiang. Sometime during the period of roughly 1645–1649 the Karmapa was invited to the Baisha (Tib. "Rbo sher" or "Bha she") palace by Mu Zeng's heir, Mu Yi, whose Tibetan name was Chimé Lhawang. Mu Yi took the Karmapa under his protection, and when a Mongol splinter force of 300,000 approached Lijiang they were defeated by Naxi troops. Heartened by this victory, the king mobilized troops against the main Mongol force in Tibet, and offered to establish the Karmapa as supreme ruler.[64] In retaliation for the Fifth Dalai Lama's actions against the Karma Kagyü order, Naxi troops burned down several Gelukpa monasteries in Muli and several others along the way to Litang, including Jampaling (Litangsi), which had been established with the patronage of Mu Yi's own great grandfather, Mu Wang. Mu Yi showed himself to be a staunch supporter of the Karmapa and provided funds to re-establish the Karmapa encampment as it had existed in its grandeur.[65] The Karmapa stayed in the Lijiang area for close to fifteen years, making it his base of operation, while also making secret excursions to Kham and Amdo to bring several young reincarnations of the major Kagyü hierarchs to Lijiang for their educations. Included among them were the Fifth Pawo, Trinlé Gyatso (1649–1699) and the Sixth Situ, Mipam Chögyel Trinlé Rabten (1658–1682).[66] He ordained some one thousand Naxi in Lijiang as monks at the Situ's final ordination, and even went so far as to recognize, in Lijiang, the son of a Naxi woman, who appears to have been his own son, as the reincarnation of the Sixth Gyeltsap, Norbu Zangpo (1659–1698),[67] a move that created even deeper ties between the Naxi of Lijiang and the Karma Kagyü. During his long residency he founded numerous temples, including Gyelwa riknga (Dabaosi), which he named "Potala."[68] His impact on the region was sufficiently strong so as to have warranted a brief account in the local Chinese gazetteer, the Lijiang fuzhi lue, written in 1742, about eighty years after Chos dbying rdo rje's departure.[69]

Returning to the question of the dating of the wall-paintings at Dabao-jigong, the identity of the unlabeled central figure (fig. 16) in the portrayal of the Mahāmudrā lineage would provide important evidence. The single most compelling clue to his identity is that he wears the black hat, the iconographic signature of the Karmapa hierarchs. As all of the Karmapas are accounted for in the painting, from the First through the Ninth Karmapa (1555–1603), it seems most likely that the unidentified figure is the Tenth Karmapa Chöying Dorjé (1604–1674). If this were the case, the intervening hierarch, the Tenth Karmapa's own teacher, the Sixth Zhamar (1584–1630), would be missing from the painting of the lineage. One possible explanation for such a remarkable omission might be that its composition was overseen by the Sixth Zhamar, and that he omitted himself out of modesty. This would place the execution of the painting between 1611 (the date of the Tenth Karmapa's enthronement) and 1630 (the Sixth Zhamar's death). The Sixth Zhamar was known to be in Lijiang several times between his first arrival in 1610 and the consecration of the Kanjur in 1621. Had the painting been executed after his lifetime, however, and overseen by the Tenth Karmapa, it is unlikely that he would have left his teacher out of the lineage. After all, the very function of a lineage painting is to trace the unbroken transmission of teachings and initiations through an accepted series of masters, from their current holder back to the revered Indian masters. By omitting the Sixth Zhamar, the Karmapa would have been severing his own claim as a direct descent of this transmission. A third possible explanation therefore is that the central figure was indeed intended to be the Sixth Zhamar, and that the color of the hat is a mistake or the result of later over-painting. (For *zhwa dmar* literally means "red hat," and this corresponds both to the hierarch's actual crown and to its representation in artwork.) In this case, the painting would likely predate the recognition of the Tenth Karmapa, i.e., closer to 1610, the year that the Sixth Zhamar first visited Lijiang, but prior to the Tenth Karmapa's enthronement in 1611. It has further been suggested that the painting of historical figures with long-life vases such as we see here was meant to signify that the image was created during the lifetime of its subject as a wish for his longevity. This visual evidence demonstrates that these paintings must have been completed well after the temple's founding in 1582–1583, likely between 1610 and 1630, as part of Mu Zeng's ambitious patronage program of temple construction, and the conversion of existing temples to Tibetan Buddhism.[70]

All of the Karma Kagyü temples built in the Lijiang area became branch temples of Pelpung in Dergé (now western Sichuan) after its construction in 1728. Pelpung was founded as the seat of the Situ lineage, and while many of the satellite temples in the Lijiang area predate it, they came under its aegis after its establishment. As we know, the Fifth Dalai Lama's attack on the Karma Kagyü left its leadership in shambles, which resulted in the almost total eclipse of the tradition and the Karmapa's retreat to Lijiang. It was the Dergé Situ lineage that in effect resurrected Kagyü leadership in Eastern Tibet and Western China.[71] Pelpung—which holds a high position within the Kagyü order, second only to the principal temple of Tsurpu outside Lhasa, seat of the Karmapa lineage[72]—had jurisdiction over branch temples constituting seventy to eighty seats distributed in such places as Dergé, Dengke, Kangding (Tib. Dar rtse mdo), Batang, Litang, Muli, Daofu, Danba (in Rgyal mo rong), extending as far as Lijiang in the south, and Qinghai (Amdo) to the north.[73] The Naxi Kagyü monks of Lijiang would therefore travel to Pelpung in Sichuan or Tsurpu in Central Tibet to further their doctrinal studies. At the latter, owing to the prominence of the kingdom of Lijiang in the Karma Kagyü system, a grand monastic residence was created to house three hundred monks, based on Lijiang regional affiliation ('jang pa'i grwa rgyun) and called the "Yellow House of Lijiang" ('Jang khang ser po).[74]

Dabaojigong in the Tibetan Temple System

Dabaojigong can be counted among the minor Kagyü temples in Lijiang, though it is the only one to survive relatively intact from the Ming period. The foremost of the five major Karma Kagyü temples in the region was Fuguosi, built on Zhishan overlooking Baisha village by Mu Zeng in the Tianqi period (1621–1627), at about the same time Dabaojigong was being painted. Sadly, during the Cultural Revolution Fuguosi was damaged more than most temples in the area, suffering nearly total obliteration, making any comparison to Dabaojigong impossible.[75] This was Mu Zeng's largest temple in Lijiang and presumably served as a center of Karma Kagyü activity. Mu Zeng himself retired there and it is said that the Tenth Karmapa resided there during his time in Lijiang.[76] The other four temples were all founded in the eighteenth century: Yufengsi (Tib. Bkra shis chos 'phel gling, ca. 1700), which housed its own local incarnate lama; Zhiyunsi (Tib. Nges don phun tshogs gling, 1727), the first Buddhist temple recorded to have been built in Lijiang by an outside patron; Wenfengsi (Tib. 'Jang ri smag po dgon, 1733), the highest local education center for the Kagyü order of northwest Yunnan; and Pujisi (Tib. Phun tshogs gling, 1771), which functioned as both a Chinese and Tibetan Buddhist temple. A history of Pelpung states that there were thirteen satellite temples in Lijiang and lists nine Tibetan names: Mingyur Gön, Nyen Gön, Trabur Gön, Lhashi Gön, Trashi Chöpel Ling (Yufengsi), Wokmin Ling (Fuguosi), Püntsok Ling (Pujisi), Jangri Makpo Gön (Wenfengsi), and Shaktup Ling. Having not yet ascertained Dabaojigong's Tibetan name, however, it is difficult to determine if it is included in this list.[77] Yang Xuezheng gives a full list of thirteen temples, with both Chinese names and transliterated Tibetan names, but none of them correspond to any known names for Dabaojigong.[78] Despite these complications with respect to Dabaojigong's inclusion in the recognized system of Pelpung satellites, its very name, "Dabaojigong," means "great gem heap," which is a translation of Pelpung, "glorious heap," lending support to the view that it was a branch monastery of Pelpung.[79] Internal iconographic evidence within the painting program at Dabaojigong, such as the presence of the Mahāmudrā lineage, is also consistent with the iconographic programs in temples of the Pelpung system.

A Local Tradition of Wall Painting

Two important questions remain: where does Dabaojigong fit into the local tradition of temple art? And when did the hybrid tradition of wall paintings represented at Dabaojigong begin? In art historical terms, Dabaojigong marks the seamless incorporation of Tibetan visual modes into the previously Chinese-dominated visual culture of the local workshops. Chinese scholars divide the Ming period wall-painting in Lijiang into two phases, which is summarized in appendix 1, no. 1, "Lijiang Wall-paintings": The early phase spans the fourteenth through the mid-sixteenth centuries, when seven generations of Mu rulers from Mu Chu (r. 1383–1426) to Mu Gong (r. 1527–1553) built four temples: Zhenwuci, Liulidian, Guiyitang, and Jushengsi.[80] The later period spans the mid-sixteenth to the mid-seventeenth centuries, when five generations from Mu Gao to Mu Zeng (1597–1646) built seven places of worship: Wandegong, Hufatang, Dadingge, Dabaojigong, Dajuesi, Leiyinsi, and Fuguosi. The early period is characterized by entirely Chinese style and subject-matter, while the later period is marked by the introduction and growing dominance of Tibetan themes and painting techniques. The rate of temple construction and the shift in their content is correlated with the Mu family's power and influence. In the early period when the Mu first established themselves militarily and were beginning to prosper, approximately fifty to sixty years intervene between construction projects, whereas in the later period, when the Mu family extends their territory into Weixi, Zhongdian, Batang, and Litang, the time between construction narrows to only twenty to thirty years. The thirty year period of Mu Zeng's reign, when four or five temples were established in Lijiang, can be called the time of their greatest prosperity.[81] Recent scholarship fails to state this directly, but the obvious implication is that the expansion of Mu power north into Tibetan and Mosuo areas in the later period precipitates the arrival of Tibetan stylistic influences in painting technique, as well as the integration of esoteric imagery in the content.[82]

The two examples we know from the early period in Lijiang seem to be entirely Chinese in content. Liulidian, dedicated to the worship of the Medicine Buddha (Yaowang, i.e. Bhaiṣajyaguru), is located directly in front of Dabaojigong in Baisha village and was built in the fifteenth year of the Yongle reign (1417) by Mu Chu (r. 1383–1426). Liulidian's inscriptions are all in Chinese, and its surviving wall-paintings exhibit no Tibetan influence, depending rather on Tang Chinese esoteric models as preserved in Sichuan and the Bai Kingdom of Dali in Yunnan.[83] Textual evidence for a connection to Dali painting at this time is provided in the *Lijiang fuzhi lue*, which records that a stele, the *Jian Mushi xunci ziji* dated 1528 and issued by Mushi xunci, names an artisan from Dali, Yang De, as its builder and painter.[84] The second example of an early temple is Guiyitang, built in the seventh year of Chenghua (1470) by the patron Mu Qin (1442–1485) in Dayanzhen (the modern town of Lijiang). In 1957 five bays of paintings were still extant; however the building no longer survives. Judging from copies of those bays, their inscriptions were in Chinese, including a list of names and a eulogy, and there was no trace of Tibetan painting style or content.[85]

Beginning in the Wanli period (1573–1620), the introduction of Tibetan esoteric Buddhist imagery in Lijiang wall-paintings becomes clearly visible, a development fully realized at Dabaojigong. A fundamental problem with the Chinese chronologies of Lijiang wall-painting, such as those proposed by Li Weiqing, Yang Zhou, and Li Kunsheng, is that they assume that the extant paintings there date from the time the temple was built, ignoring internal visual evidence.[86] A few Chinese authors take the date of the Tibetan inscription at Dabaojigong, read either as 1523 or 1583, as evidence that the temple was painted a year after its construction. I have already demonstrated this to be unlikely, unless one tries to read the date as one sexagenary cycle (*rab byung*) later, that is, 1643.[87] While it is possible that the paintings in the rear of the hall were produced later than those in the front, identifiable stylistic markers such as wispy flames, throne patterns, and head shapes are uniform in both the front and rear of the temple, suggesting that they were painted at the same time by the same workshop. Close comparisons can be made, for instance, between the throne patterns of Mārīcī in the front of the hall (fig. 7) and the throne of Vajravidāraṇa in the back of the hall (fig. 13) or between the unusual wispy flame patterns that appear in almost every panel in the temple. This homogeneity allows us to extend the dating of the Mahāmudrā lineage painting (ca. 1610 to 1630) to the paintings throughout Dabaojigong, roughly simultaneous to the five other construction projects in Lijiang sponsored by Mu Zeng. Taking into account other epigraphic evidence, it would seem that Wandegong, built in the thirty-ninth year of Jiajing (1560) by Mu Gao in Yangxi, actually provides the earliest evidence for Tibetan painting in Lijiang, as its stele records a Tibetan painter's name "*huagong guzong* Gu Chang," "the Tibetan artisan-painter Gu Chang (Rgod tshang)," *guzong* here signifying "ancestor," the local Naxi ethnonym for Tibetans.[88] It is further said that the artistry of the beautiful wall-paintings in Wandegong's main hall were on par with that of Dabaojigong, and that its remains also showed Tibetan influence.[89] This would alter the chronology slightly, moving the "later period" of Lijiang wall-painting approximately twenty-six years earlier. Li Weiqing's claim that Tibetan script appears to have been painted over at Guiyitang, dated 1470, may force a further reassessment of this chronological division into early and late periods of Mu construction, particularly if evidence of Tibetan paintings is found to survive in the copies of Wandegong's murals executed in 1957.[90] However, Guiyitang, once located just south of the Mu family palace, is no longer extant.

According to Joseph Rock, the wall-paintings of Dabaojigong were made by the same artist who painted the murals at Xuesong'an, which was once covered by beautiful frescoes of which only a small portion remained when he saw them. The temple had recently been dismantled and moved in Rock's time, the murals destroyed, and the building converted into a forestry station. Xuesong'an was once one of twelve homes owned by the Mu family, where the Naxi chieftains spent parts of the year, and was particularly favored by Mu Zeng.[91] Rock says a stele in the courtyard of the temple that contained rules of conduct was dated 1608 (thirty-sixth year of Wanli), though he points out that the founding of the temple itself may have been earlier.[92] This provides us with evidence of at least one other project painted by the workshop that painted Dabaojigong. Moreover, Xuesong'an is also associated with Mu Zeng, who was building temples and converting existing structures like Dabaojigong to Tibetan Buddhism, and was actively recruiting painters to decorate his many construction projects.

The wall-paintings at Dadingge, located northeast of Dabaojigong and also built by Mu Zeng, show similar formalities as well as a dark palette. The main hall is spatially organized much like Dabaojigong, displaying both Chinese themes such as Water Moon Guanyin and Samantabhadra at the front of the hall, and Tibetan themes such as Vajrapāṇi; Kālacakra, Hevajra, and Guhyasamāja; and Saṃvara and Vajravārāhī on the rear (east) wall. A stele at Jingangdian states that Dadingge and Jingangdian, both of which are only a few hundred feet northeast of Dabaojigong, were first built "with exquisite painting" by Mu Zeng. The stele also states that Dadingge was restored or rebuilt in the eighth year of Qianlong (1743).[93] Although we do not know to which period the extant paintings date, I suspect that they date to the Qing despite previous attributions to the Ming period, and were replacements for an earlier set, as the several paintings that survive in the central hall display numerous stylistic differences when compared to Dabaojigong. I would therefore hesitate to say that they were created by the same workshop, but that rather it seems that certain features of the influential Dabaojigong workshop were continued as part of a local tradition into the Qing. Jingangdian is also of structural interest, for while all of the wall-paintings have been lost, the layout of its main hall with eleven panels—four panels on the side walls in front of the altar screen, and seven smaller panels behind the altar screen—is almost identical to the arrangement of panels found at Dabaojigong. Perhaps if the copies of the one hundred thirty panels of paintings made by Chinese artists in 1957 in Lijiang are found,[94] a direct connection between Dabaojigong and Jingangdian will be established.

In addition to Dadingge and Jingangdian, a fourth temple, Hufatang ("Hall of Dharma Protectors"), is said to have sat directly behind Dabaojigong. However, the relationships of these five temples—Dabaojigong, Liulidian, Dadingge, Jingangdian, and Hufatang—built so close together over a span of two centuries from the early fifteenth to the early seventeenth century by successive Mu rulers, have yet to be established.[95] Perhaps they were built around the Baisha palace or pleasure park, often mentioned in Tibetan sources as the *Rbo she(r)* or *Bha she pho drang*—the location of which is now unknown—as part of a larger complex of royal chapels where the kings of Lijiang received Tibetan hierarchs. Baisha was the original capital of the Naxi Kingdom before it was moved to Lijiang in the Yuan dynasty. While Liulidian was built in 1417 and Dabaojigong in 1582, the other three temples were all built in the Wanli era by Mu Zeng, and, as we have seen from examining the internal evidence, Dabaojigong was also (re)painted during his reign. One possible explanation is that Mu Zeng refurbished and expanded the existing palace and temple site, concentrating his patronage on creating a complex in which he could receive Tibetan dignitaries, one that would reflect his stature as a Dharma king. While the small upper panels near the rafters at Liulidian preserve earlier paintings after a Bai model, the main wall-paintings have been lost, and may have undergone a similar renovation. The pre–Cultural Revolution copies of these temples may help provide a link between them that would support conceiving them as part of a larger complex. Suggestive in this context, as yet unidentified ruins have been found in the soccer field that now separates these structures.

Of the surviving wall-paintings in Lijiang, only at Dajuegong (also called Dajuesi) in Shuhe village do we find purely Chinese Buddhist painting preserved into the later period.[96] First built in the Hongwu period (1368–1398), Dajuegong originally served as a Mu family residence, then as an ancestral temple, and was later converted into a Buddhist temple in the Wanli period (1573–1620) by Mu Zeng.[97] It originally contained nine bays of wall-paintings of which only six now survive: the twenty-eight constellation deities, the sixteen arhats, and a pair of crowned deities in Chinese style bodhisattva ornaments, divided into facing panels. This confirms that the Mu rulers continued to build and patronize Chinese Buddhist temples alongside Tibetan Buddhist projects into the seventeenth century. Given this state of affairs, it is interesting to consider the Chinese painters whose services were recruited by Mu Zeng at the height of Lijiang's temple-building activity.

Tradition says that during the Tianqi period (1621–1627), Mu Zeng invited a Han Chinese painter named Ma Xiaoxian from Ningbo to paint wall-paintings, first at the local pilgrimage site of Chicken Foot Mountain, then to participate in the numerous wall-painting projects in Lijiang.[98] Ningbo was at the time an international port city, near Hangzhou in Zhejiang, and was a center of production for Buddhist painting in China, exporting a great deal of Buddhist art to Japan and Korea.[99] Ningbo was also an important religious center, just to the north of which is the popular pilgrimage site Putuo shan, and to the south Tiantai shan, central to the cosmology of the Tiantai sect. The Mu rulers were patrons of temples in Putuo shan, and this patronage was perhaps the source of the Lijiang-Ningbo connection. A relief carving of Guanyin of the South Sea, a form of Avalokiteśvara particularly associated with Putuo shan, survives from Dabaojigong.[100] It is also interesting to note that the rulers of Lijiang worked closely with the Mu family (Mu Sheng),[101] the hereditary military governors of Yunnan, who were themselves prominent patrons of famous professional painters who came from Zhejiang, such as Dai Jin (active in the early fifteenth century) who worked for them.[102] Perhaps their governmental superiors provided a model for the importation of Zhejiang painters to Yunnan. Mu Zeng built the grandest temple on Chicken Foot Mountain, Xitansi, in 1617, which appears to be the same temple as "Shyig shyi'i tan nan"—described in an important early twentieth century Tibetan pilgrimage account by Katok Situ (1880–1925) as the King of Lijiang's temple on Chicken Foot Mountain—and said to have been beautifully decorated with images "drawn by incomparable artists" ('gran zla med pa'i lha bzos bris pa).[103] The Guomindang scholar Li Lincan, who performed research in the area from 1939–1943, described "Tibetan-style esoteric statues" (xizang feng de mizong suxiang) and "tall Tibetan-shaped [gilt] bronze buddhas" (gao zang fang tong fo) within Xitansi, suggesting that this temple, like Dabaojigong, exhibited both Chinese and Tibetan imagery simultaneously.[104] It is probably this temple that Ma Xiaoxian was invited to paint by Mu Zeng.[105] A biographical note on Ma Xiaoxian appears in the gazetteer Lijiang fuzhi lue:

Ma Xiaoxian was a native of Jiangnan. He was skilled at depicting landscapes, which attained the divine class [*shenpin*, the highest classification]. None of his flowers and figure paintings are not refined and marvelous. The *cognoscenti* praised them as "Ma's immortal paintings." He was renowned in the "western regions" [Tibet] and traveled extensively there for several years, later returning to Lijiang. The day he died, people saw that his fingers had signs, or so it is said.[106]

According to traditional accounts, when the Tenth Karmapa went to Lijiang, he saw the wall-paintings that Ma Xiaoxian was making and admired their superb artistry.[107] Afterward Ma Xiaoxian was invited to the Karmapa's court and taken to Tibet to paint wall-paintings at Tsurpu Monastery.[108] Ma is said to have stayed in Tibet for over ten continuous years, where he presumably served as a painter in Chöying Dorjé's court from approximately 1661 to 1674, and even visited India.[109] Later he returned to Lijiang where he lived in Baisha and was buried at the eastern foot of Zhishan Mountain.

Several modern Chinese scholars maintain that the Lijiang Museum has twenty-four of Ma Xiaoxian's paintings, the subjects of which are all described as buddhas and arhats, but within those paintings are a profusion of birds such as peacocks (*kongque*), roosters (*huoji*), white silver pheasants (*bai xian*), and partridges (*zhegu*), as well as distant mountains, rocks, and trees, delicately composed with lively forms.[110] According to some sources, these paintings, all 92 x 63 cm and mounted as *thangka*, were supposed to have been originally made for the Karmapa but later changed hands and were given to the Situ reincarnation at Pelpung Monastery in Dergé, who then presented them as gifts to the "Dongbao fawang" reincarnation of Zhiyunsi in Lijiang.[111] If ever found, these paintings should be compared to wall-paintings associated with Mu sponsorship from the seventeenth century, such as those at Dabaojigong, Wandegong, Xitansi, and Dajuegong, in order to identify his hand. Additional sites requiring artistic work, such as Daoist and ancestral temples, which are named in local sources such as the *Lijiang fuzhi lue* as having been built in the Ming (refer to appendix 1), should also be considered. Some Chinese scholars even go so far as to attribute the bulk of Lijiang's (high quality) wall-paintings, including those discussed here at Dabaojigong, to "the Han Chinese painter Ma Xiaoxian," though the true scale of his involvement has yet to be established.[112]

Because the Tenth Karmapa, while in Lijiang, developed a painting style similar to that found in Chinese scroll paintings, and his work was described

as similar to Ma Xiaoxian's own paintings (the profusion of birds is particularly striking), it is reasonable to surmise that the Karmapa took Ma Xiaoxian's
paintings as a model, or perhaps even studied directly with this professional
Chinese painter as maintained by local tradition. These paintings, if they are
indeed correctly attributed, may also be the source for the Tenth Karmapa's
distinctive new Chinese style of *thangka* painting (*rgya bris thang ka*), which
was quite unlike earlier Tibetan adaptations of Chinese visual idioms.[113] In a
signed and dated set of seven paintings by Chöying Dorjé, kept in the same
museum (and discussed elsewhere),[114] the crown prince of Lijiang Mu Jing,
the named recipient of the paintings, is depicted wearing the same Chinese Ming-dynasty court attire in which the Mu family had themselves been
depicted in their official portraiture.[115] This painting is thus a visual record
of not only the Mu ruling family's patronage of Tibetan Buddhism, but also
more specifically of their close relationship with the Karmapa, who is shown
floating in the clouds above. While there is no specific record affirming that
the Tenth Karmapa was involved in the actual painting of any of the monasteries around Lijiang, there is a strong possibility that he participated in the
greater project in an advisory role. Considering that Chöying Dorjé spent
over fifteen years in exile in Lijiang as the spiritual preceptor of the Naxi
ruling house, and was moreover a famous painter in his own right, it seems
almost certain that he would have been consulted by the kings of Lijiang
regarding the ambitious temple-building program that reached its peak in
the mid-seventeenth century.

Fragmentary evidence from temples built in Lijiang early in the Qing
(1644–1911), after the peak period of Mu rule, which are strictly Tibetan in
style and iconography, suggest that the local workshop that produced the fascinating hybrid wall-paintings found at Dabaojigong had ceased to function
by then.[116] With the decline and fall of the kings of Lijiang and the consequent
disappearance of their patronage, the local workshop could no longer be sustained. One could therefore identify the Sino-Tibetan wall-paintings found
at Dabaojigong as the result of a distinctive local tradition, and endemic to
the specific set of geo-cultural and geo-political relations among Chinese,
Naxi, and Tibetans in northwest Yunnan in the late sixteenth and early seventeenth centuries. These paintings and the connections among the Sixth
Zhamar, the Tenth Karmapa, the Chinese painter Ma Xiaoxian, and their
patron Mu Zeng exemplify the complex meeting of Tibetan and Chinese cultural and artistic traditions, through the medium of Naxi royal patronage, in
the Kingdom of Lijiang during the Ming.

Appendix One: Lijiang Temples and Wall-paintings

1. Lijiang Wall-paintings

EARLY PERIOD

1. Zhenwuci (Mu ancestral temple), probably built in Hongwu (1369–1398)
2. Liulidian, built in Hongwu or Yongle by Mu Chu in Baisha
3. Guiyitang, built seventh year Chenghua (1470) by Mu Qin in Dayanzhen (Lijiang)
4. Mushixunci, built in 1528 by Mu Gong (a stele records the Dali artisan Yang De)
5. Jushengsi, built in ninth year Jiajing (1530) by Mu Gong in Xuesong
6. Leiyinsi, built in Jiajing era (1522–1566) in Shuhe

LATE PERIOD

7. Wandegong, built in thirty-ninth year Jiajing (1560) by Mu Gao in Yangxi (a stele records the Tibetan painter's name "Gu Chang" and remains are said to show Tibetan influence)
8. Dabaojigong, built tenth year Wanli (1582) by Mu Wang in Baisha (remains show Tibetan influence)
9. Xuesong'an, in Baisha, at the foot of Xueshan (same workshop as Dabaojigong)
10. Hufatang, built in Wanli (1573–1620) by Mu Zeng (1597–1646) in Baisha (remains said to show Tibetan influence)
11. Dadingge, built in Wanli (1573–1620) by Mu Zeng (1597–1646) in Baisha (remains show Tibetan influence, restored or rebuilt in eighth year of Qianlong [1783])
12. Jingangdian, built in Wanli (1573–1620) by Mu Zeng (1597–1646) in Baisha (remains said to show Tibetan influence)
13. Dajuegong, first built in Hongwu (1368–1398), in Shuhe (converted to temple in Wanli era [1573–1620] by Mu Zeng [1597–1646], only temple to preserve strictly Chinese imagery)
14. Fuguosi, built in Tianqi (1621–1627) by Mu Zeng (1597–1646) on Zhi shan (remains said to show Tibetan influence)

2. Other Temples Built in Ming
(According to the *Lijiang fuzhi lue* [1743])
Jiuhe shenmiao, southwest of Lijiang in Jiuhe Guanyinge, outside of the south city gate in Dayanzhen (modern Lijiang)

Taiji'an, on Zhi shan
Guiyitang, in Baisha
Hufa qielan, in Baisha
Yingxianlou, in Baisha
Xiyuan'an, in Baisha
Dawangchu shenmiao, south of Lijiang in Qihe
Mu Guanyin shenmiao, in Jiangxi

3. Ancestral Temples and Qunsi Built in Ming

Chenghuang miao, in Dayanzhen (modern Lijiang)
Wuliexian shenci, ten *li* east of Lijiang at Dongshan
Zizhaitan, built in 1610 (by Mu Zeng [1597–1646]?) in Shuhe
Beiyu miao, built by Nanzhao king in 784/5, rebuilt in 1535 by Mu Gong, on
   Xueshan

Appendix Two: Key to Paintings at Dabaojigong

Painting Key 1: Dabaojigong Mahāmudrā Lineage (see fig. 15)

1 Rdo rje 'chang (Vajradhara, root of the lineage)
2 Ti lo pa (988–1069) first in transmission
3 Na ro pa (1016–1100)
4 Mar pa (1012–1097) first Tibetan in transmission lineage
5 Bzhad pa rdo rje [Mi la ras pa] (1052–1135)
6 Dag po Rin po che [Sgam po pa] (1079–1153)
7 Dus gsum [m]hkyen pa [First Karma pa] (1110–1193)
8 'Gro mgon ras pa ['Gro mgon Sangs rgyas ras chen Dpal grags]
9 Sbom grag pa [founder of Sbom grag Monastery]
10 Karma Pag shi [Second Karma pa] (1206–1283)
11 Mkhas khrub (*sic*) O rgyan pa [Grub thob O rgyan pa seng ge dpal]
   (1230–1308/1309)
12 Rang [']byung rdo rje [Third Karma pa] (1284–1339)
13 Rgya[l]ba G.yung ston pa [G.yung ston rdo rje dpal] (1284–1365)
14 'Dzam gling Chos gyis grag pa [Fourth Karma pa Rol pa'i rdo rje] (1340–
   1383)
15 Stog ldan Mga' sbyod (*sic*) dbang po [Second Zhwa dmar] (1350–1405)
16 Chos rje De 'zh[i]n gzheg[s] pa [Fifth Karma pa] (1384–1415)
17 Rad na bhadra [Sog dbon rin chen bzang po]

18 [M]th[o]ng bo don ldan [Sixth Karma pa] (1416–1453)
19 Dpal 'byor don [']grub [First Rgyal tshab] (ca. 1427–1489)
20 [Kun mkhyen] 'Jam dpal bzang po
21 'Dzam gling chos grags rgya mtsho['] [Seventh Karma pa] (1454–1506)
22 Grub chen Bkra 'shi dpal byo[r] [Third Si tu] (1498–1541)
23 Mtsu (sic) med Mi bskyod rdo rje [Eighth Karma pa] (1507–1555)
24 Sprul sku Dkon [m]chog yan lag [Fifth Zhwa dmar] (1525–1583)
25 Rje btsun Dbang phyug rdo rje [Ninth Karma pa] (1556–1603)

PROTECTORS AT BOTTOM:
Left: Dam can mgar ba nag po, the Blacksmith
Middle: [no label] Mgon po ber nag chen (Mahākāla)
Right: Dpal ldan lha mo

**Painting Key 2: Vajradhara and the
Eighty-four Mahāsiddhas (see fig. 14)**

LEFT SIDE
Tier 1: 1 Klu grub snying po (Nāgārjuna), 2 Arya derba (Āryadeva), 3 Tsanaḍa
    go man (Cendra go mi?), 4 'Bir ba pa (Virūpa), 5 Lo he pa (Lūipa);
Tier 2 (left): 6 Na phen tra pa, 7 Ku ku ri pa (Kukkuripa), 8 Byung si (sa?), 9
    Nag po pa (Kāṇhapa), 10 A[ma?] tra bho bhi (Indra bhu ti?);
Tier 3: 11 Ti lo pa, 12 Thog tsa pa, 13 Pad tra pa, 14 Zla wa pa, 15 Shwan ti pa
    (Śāntipa);
Tier 4: 16 Shab ri pa, 17 Dha ri ka pa, 18 Ma dha ha (Mekhala?), 19 Lding ki
    pa (Dengipa), 20 (inscription lost);
Tier 5: 21 Kam ma la (Kambala), 22 Sing bhi pa (Singkhipa);
Tier 6: 23 Nya ma pa ka (Nyi ma sbas pa? Ravigupta), 24 b□ ma ro pa;
Tier 7: 25 Bu ma ra, 26 Tsa pu pa (Tsa pa ri? Carbaripa);
Tier 8: 27 San dha pa, 28 Mi sha za;
Tier 9: 29 Dznyan rom pa, 30 A nan ta, 31 Kun dga['] sang (Kun dga' snying?),
    32 Zla wa grags pa;
Tier 10: 33 dhu ti pa, (A dhū ti? Avadhūtipa?), 34 Ba wang pa (Bha wa pa?),
    38 Sgr[ol]l ma (Tārā);
Tier 11: 35 Nyi ma sbas pa, 36 Ngag gis dbang phyug, 37 Shakya gsheg 'na
    (Shākya bshes gnyen), 39 (no label), 40 □ sa pa, 41 Ga la mang gha (Ka la
    lang ka), 42 [Phang lo?] Bde [m]chog (Saṃvara), 43 (no label—female),
    44 (no label), 45 Bha ga ni (Bha yi ni?), 46 A ghi pa, 47 Ka ma lā (Kam-
    bala), 48 Sgra khen thab (Sgra mkhan), 49 Bha □ □ (Bha wa pa)

Right Side

Tier 1: 50 Pad ma bdzra (Padmavajra), 51 Mtsho skyes rdo rje, 52 □ □ ta rdo rje (Nag po rdo rje?), 53 Ḍom ba he ru ka, 54 Rdo rje Dril bu pa (Vajraghaṇṭa);

Tier 2 (right): 55 'Phag □ □ □ mad ('Phags pa lha?), 56 (no label), 57 Gling bu khen, 58 Sa ra ha pa, 59 '[?] su ta;

Tier 3: 60 Mar me mdzed (Dīpaṃkara), 61 Na ro □ (Naropa?), 62 Nag po spyod pa (Kṛṣṇācārya), 63 Phag tshang pa, 64 Bzang po (Bhadrapa);

Tier 4: 65 Ji ta pa (Dze ta ri?), 66 Sa ba ra, 67 Shan ta pa (Śāntipa), 68 Thag ga pa,

Tier 5: 69 ['Arya pa?] (Āryadeva? Karṇaripa or Ārya Nāgārjuna?), 70 Ki la na? (Kilapa?), 71 Sa ri [pa?];

Tier 6: 72 Bud ta pa (Buddhapa), 73 Karma □ ga rti;

Tier 7: 74 Na la pa (Ni la pa), 75 Pad ma ka ra (Padmākara),

Tier 8: 76 Sprin gyi shug can (Sprin shugs can), 77 Ka ro pa;

Tier 9: 78 Si dha pa, 79 Zla ba bzang po

The lower right corner of this panel, which likely contained the missing siddhas, is entirely lost.

Notes

* This paper was first presented at the 2000 meeting of the American Association of Religions panel "Buddhism Between Tibet and China." Continuing research has been made possible by a University of Chicago Visiting Committee Research Travel Grant 2001, a U.S. Department of Education Fulbright-Hays Doctoral Dissertation Research Abroad Fellowship, 2003–2004, and a National Gallery of Art Center for Advanced Study in the Visual Arts Ittleson Fellowship, 2004–2006. I would like to thank Professors Elliot Sperling, Matthew Kapstein, and Jennifer Purtle, as well as Kristina Dy-Liacco for their helpful suggestions and input.

1 Guo Dalie 郭大烈, *Naxizu wenhua daguan* 納西族文化大觀 (Kunming: Yunnan minzu chubanshe, 1999), pp. 79–106.

2 Some modern Tibetan scholars, such as Sde rong Tshe ring don grub (Derong Zerendengzhu 得荣 · 泽仁邓珠), *Zangzu tongshi, jixiang baoping* 藏族通史 · 吉祥宝瓶 (Lhasa: Xizang renmin chubanshe, 2001), have even gone so far as to assert that the indigenous Naxi Dongba religion is simply derivative of the Tibetan Bön religion, the word "dongba" being a corruption of "Denba", i.e., Ston pa gshen rabs, the founder and central deity in the Bön faith. See also Joseph F. Rock, *The Ancient Na-khi Kingdom of Southwest China*, 2 vols. (Cambridge: Harvard University Press, 1947), p. 267, and Rock, "The Birth and Origin of Dto-mba Shi-lo," in *Artibus Asiae* 7 (1938): 5–85.

3 Michael Oppitz and Elisabeth Hsu, *Naxi and Moso Ethnography: Kin, Rites, Pic-*

tographs (Zürich: Völkerkundemuseum Zürich, 1998). See Map 2, p. 11, for ethnic distributions.

4 The first patriarch of the Naxi ruling house established his rule in 618, the same year as the founding of the Tang Dynasty and roughly the period of the founding of the Tibetan Empire as well. In 703 the Tibetan Emperor Khri 'dus srong (r. 677–704) successfully occupied 'Jang (Lijiang) in the year before his death. A Tibetan presence during the imperial period is attested to by a stele in Old Tibetan (Tufan wenzi bei) currently in the Lijiang Naxi Dongba Cultural Museum (see *Xizang wenxue* 4 [1994]: 136–145). The Naxi Kingdom submitted to the Nanzhao Kingdom, an ally of the Tang Empire, shortly after they had united in 730. In 751 the Nanzhao allied themselves with the Tibetan Empire, and Naxi troops fought alongside Nanzhao and Tibetan troops against the Tang Empire. In 785 Nanzhao submitted again to the Tang, and Naxi troops then fought alongside Tang and Nanzhao troops against Tibet. When Nanzhao turned on the Tang for the second time in 828, the Naxi remained loyal to the Tang, marking the first establishment of independent ties between the Naxi and the Chinese Tang court. With the collapse of the Tang Dynasty and the geographical and cultural retrenchment that characterized the Song dynasty, Lijiang appears to have slipped from official Chinese records.

5 Charles O. Hucker, *A Dictionary of Official Titles in Imperial China* (Stanford: Stanford University Press, 1985), p. 547, entries 7355 and 7352, translates *tusi* as "Aboriginal office." Also see Fang Guoyu, 方國瑜, ed. *Yunnan shiliao mu lu gai shuo. di yi ce, di san ce* 雲南史料目录概說 (Beijing: Zhonghua shuju chuban, 1984), vol. 1, pp. 457–489, for primary sources dealing with the *tuguan* in Sichuan and Yunnan (and, regarding the Mu *tuguan*, pp. 473–476); and Edward L Dreyer, *Early Ming China: A Political History, 1355–1435* (Stanford, Calif: Stanford University Press, 1982), pp. 113–114.

6 See Dreyer, "The Frontier: Yunnan and the Non-Chinese Peoples," in *Early Ming China*, pp. 109–114.

7 Lijiang xianzhi bangongshi, 麗江縣志辦公室, ed., "Mushi Huanpu" 木氏宦譜, in Lijiang Zhiyuan 麗江志苑 2 (August 1988): 22; and, for another published illustrated version from which the images come, Yunnan sheng bowuguan 雲南省博物館, *Mushi huanpu yingyin ben* 木氏宦譜 影印本 (Kunming: Yunnan meishu chubanshe, 2001). See, too, Rock, *The Ancient Na-khi Kingdom*, p. 154.

8 See Yu Qingyuan 余慶遠, *Weixi wenjianlu* 維西聞見錄, in *Yunnan Beizhengzhi* 雲南備徵志 (ca. 1769), ch. 17 folio 84a, ch. 18, folios 1a–2a; Rock, *The Ancient Na-khi Kingdom*, pp 294–295.

9 The first route passed through Heqing, Lijiang, Tacheng, Benzilan (Tib. Spong tse ra), Deqin (Tib. Bde chen), and on to central Tibet. The second started in Lijiang and went through Shigu, Judian, Weixi (Tib. 'Ba' lung), and then up and across the Rdza chu river to Bde chen and to Tibet. An alternative to the second route went via Jianchuan, Weixi, and Bde chen to Tibet. The third trade route started in Zhongdian (Tib. Rgyal thang), passing through Niseluo and Benzilan on the way to Tibet. See Zhuma Yingzhui 珠瑪英追, "Jian shu Ming Qing shiqi Dian xibei de Minzu guanxi" 簡述明清時期滇西北的民族關係, in *Yunnan Zangxue Yanjiu Lunwenji* 2 云南藏学研究论文集, 第二集, ed. Gu Kerong 贾克荣 (Kunming:Yunnan Minzu Chubanshe, 1997), pp. 266–267, and Li Xu 李旭, "Dian Zang cha ma gu dao yu zongjiao wenhua" 滇藏茶马古道與宗教文化, in Gu Kerong, ed., *op. cit.*, pp. 297–311.

10 Elliot Sperling, "The Szechwan-Tibet Frontier in the Fifteenth Century," in *Ming Studies* 26 (Fall 1988): 39. Sperling further suggests that the blossoming of trade along the southern Sino-Tibetan border may have been further accelerated by an influx in southeast Tibet of Tangut (Mi nyag) refugees from the Mongol invasion in the thirteenth century (who had themselves controlled the northwest horse trade though Qinghai and Gansu in the late tenth to the early thirteenth century). By the fifteenth century the tea-horse trade was a regular part of the southwest economy.

11 Si tu Paṇ chen Chos kyi 'byung gnas, *Sgrub brgyud karma kaṃ tshang brgyud pa rin po che'i rnam par thar pa rab 'byams nor bu zla ba chu shel gyi phreng ba* (New Delhi: D. Gyaltsan and Kesang Legshay, 1972), p. 151 (line 5), and p. 180 (lines 1–2). I would like to thank Elliot Sperling and Kristina Dy-Liacco for pointing this out to me.

12 Feng Zhi, 馮智, "Mingdai Lijiang mushi tusi yu Xizang Gamabapai guanxi shulue" 明代麗江木氏土司與西藏噶瑪巴派關係述略, in *Zangzu lishi zongjiao yenjiu*, diyi ji 藏族歷史宗教研究 (Zhongguo Zangxue chubanshe), pp. 57–58; and Yang Xuezheng 楊學政. "Xizang fojiao zai Yunnan de chuanbo he yingxiang" 西藏佛教在雲南的傳播和影響, in *Yunnan zangxue yanjiu lunwen ji* 雲南藏學研究論文集 (Kunming: Yunnan minzu chubanche, 1995), p. 265, who cites the *Mingshilu* as his source.

13 He Zhonghua 和鍾華 and Yang Shiguang 楊世光, et al., *Naxizu wenxue shi* 納西族文學史 (Chengdu: Sichuan minzu chubanshe, 1992), p. 510.

14 Rock, *The Ancient Na-khi Kingdom*, p. 162. These scrolls seemed to have recorded a great deal of information about Mu Zeng's religious activities, including the founding of monasteries, not recorded in his official biography, but I do not know if these scrolls survive today.

15 Rock, *The Ancient Na-khi Kingdom*, p. 162, and Li Lincan 李霖燦, "Xitansi de Mu Zeng suxiang" 悉檀寺的木增塑像 ("Xitansi's Statue of Mu Zeng"), reprinted in *Shen you Yulongshan* 神游玉龍山 (Kunming: Yunnan renmin chubanshe, 1999), pp. 203–207. According to Rock, the chapel devoted to Mu Zeng at Xitansi was called "Chapel of Prefect Mu" (Mu tai shou ci). It would seem that neither of these statues survives.

16 See Jiang Gaochen 蔣高宸, *Yunnan minzu zhuwu wenhua* 雲南民族住屋文化 (Kunming: Yunnan daxue chubanshe, 1997), fig. 3–83.

17 Guo Dalie 郭大烈 and He Zhiwu 和志武, *Naxizu shi* 納西族史 (Chengdu: Sichuan Minzu Chubanshe, 1994), p. 334, give the date 1582. Another date often given for Dabaojigong by Chinese scholars without citation is 1523 (for example, both Feng Zhi 馮智, "Mingdai Lijiang mushi tusi yu Xizang Gamabapai guanxi shulue," 明代麗江木氏土司與西藏噶瑪巴派關係述略, in *Zangzu lishi zongjiao yenjiu*, diyi ji 藏族歷史宗教研究 [Beijing: Zhongguo Zangxue chubanshe, 1996], p. 63, and Li Weiqing 李偉卿 "Lijiang Mushi tufu miaoyu bihua chutan," 麗江木氏土府廟宇壁畫初探 *Wenwu* 6 [1960]: 63, say Dabaojigong was built by Mu Gong in 1523 [second year of the Jiaqing era], and assume that its wall-paintings date from the same period). The source for this claim appears to be the article written in 1960 by Li Weiqing, who is the only one of these scholars to discuss the dating of this temple, and who to his credit is also one of the few to make use of the Tibetan inscription. Li Weiqing's article, does not, however, reproduce the Tibetan, but only provides an abbreviated Chinese translation: "mu shui yang nian liu yue chu san ji xiang ruyi," using the date in the Tibetan cartouche to date the painting of the temple to 1523.

18 *Gong ma chos rgyal Rdo rje bde [m]chog zhes/ chos bzang lha gnas de dang 'gran nus pa'i/ gtsug lag khang chen bsam gyis mi khyab 'di: chu mo lug lo zla [ba] drug pa'i/ tshes pa gsum la bkra shis bde leg[s] grub/* Spelling anomalies throughout the Tibetan inscriptions found at Dabaojigong suggest that they may have been written by non-Tibetans.

19 The first word in the inscription, *gong ma*, was often used to refer to the emperor. *Chos rgyal*, or *dharmarāja*, meaning "dharma-king" is also suggestive of this reading. On the Wanli Emperor see: *Dictionary of Ming Biography*, p. 309; and Timothy Brook, *Praying for Power: Buddhism and the Formation of Gentry Society in Late Ming China* (Cambridge: Harvard University Press, 1993), p. 313. Alternatively this could also be the initiation name of one of the kings of Lijiang, but it does not correspond to any of the Tibetan names of Mu rulers given in the Karma pa *rnam thar*. Mu Zeng (1597–1646) is called Bsod nams rab brtan. The first line of the inscription could also perhaps be read simply as an invocation of the deity Saṃvara.

20 If one takes the date to be 1643, then one could read the second line as a pun. On this reading, the phrase "a temple which rivals Lhasa (literally, the *abode of the gods*)" would be comparing Dabaojigong to the Potala palace, which was under construction at the time, and would constitute a jab at the Fifth Dalai Lama, who destroyed or forcibly converted many Bka' brgyud monasteries at just around this time. Prof. Kapstein suggested this alternate reading, but considers overall that it is unlikely.

21 "Wanli renwu (1582) duanyang yuanman baishu, *tuguan* gongdezhu Mu Wang zhi" 萬曆壬午端陽圓滿拜書, 土官功德主木旺志. This is also recorded in Guo Dalie, ed., *Naxizu wenhua daguan*, p. 486. *Yuanman* can also refer in a Buddhist context to the end of a ritual confession of sin, *chanhui*. Lijiang Naxizu zizhi xian wenhuaju 麗江納西自治縣文化局 and Lijiang Naxi Dongba wenhua bowuguan 李將納西東巴文化博物館, eds., *Lijiang Baisha bihua* 麗江白沙壁畫 (Chengdu: Sichuan renmin chubanshe, 1999), p. 12, only gives the boards' text as "Wanli renwu nian duanyang" 萬曆壬午年端陽 with no reference to Mu Wang, but states that a Qing Dynasty manuscript, *Guanxu Lijiang fu zhi gao* 光緒麗江府志稿 (xylograph, Lijiang City Archive, 清代光绪二十年 [= 1894]), says that Dabaojigong "was built by the Ming Wanli Mu *tusi*." Strangely, it would appear that Li Weiqing, "Lijiang Mushi tufu miaoyu bihua chutan," did not know about this dedication board, which would seem to settle the issue.

22 Rock, *The Ancient Na-khi Kingdom*, p. 210. I did not see this tablet on site. It may have been a stele that did not survive. However Rock routinely copied stele and inscriptions so it is likely that a copy of it survives in one of Rock's archives, which are divided between Seattle, Cambridge, and Washington D.C. Rock (*ibid.*) also states that according to the *Yunnan tongzhi* the temple was built during the Ming Dynasty, but Dabaojigong does not seem to appear in editions of the *Yunnan tongzhi* that are currently available to me.

23 The overall area of the paintings is 61.48 square meters; the largest of the paintings is the "Tathāgata refuge field" on the central altar screen, which measures 3.67 meters tall and 4.98 meters wide. Guo Dalie and He Zhiwu, *Naxizu shi*, p. 335, say that Dabaojigong's wall-paintings were completed over several years.

24 The story of Dabaojigong's desecration is related by one of the participants, a descendant of the Mu ruling family, in a National Geographic video on the Naxi of Lijiang called "Beyond the Clouds." Nevertheless, Dabaojigong is especially valuable for its

relative completeness, as the temples in Lijiang have suffered repeatedly from a variety of adverse events, including the Muslim rebellion of the 1880s which saw the destruction of the five major temples in Lijiang; the "modernization" of the Republican Period (1911–1949); the vandalism of the Cultural Revolution (1966–1976); and most recently a series of devastating earthquakes, the most serious of which occurred in 1996, measured 6.0 on the Richter scale, and brought down as many as 300,000 buildings in the greater Lijiang area.

25 Guo Dalie, *Naxizu wenhua daguan*, p. 491.

26 I.e., Mahāmāyūrī from the *Fomu dajing yao kongque mingwang jing*, translated by Amogha in the Tang Dynasty. Nevertheless, the same scholars referred to admit that the deity appears inconsistent with the textual description. (See *Lijiang Baisha bihua*, pp. 12 and 15; Guo Dalie and He Zhiwu, *Naxizu shi*, p. 335, etc.) Nor do they account for the wide array of Daoist deities.

27 Pilusi 毗盧寺 (Vairocana Monastery), is near Shijiazhuang 石家莊 in southwestern Hebei province, and the walls of the rear hall contain mid-sixteenth century *shuilu* paintings. See: Wang Haihang 王海航 and Chen Yaolin 陈耀林, *Pilusi Bihua* 毗盧寺壁画 (Hebei: Hebei meishu chubanshi, 1984); and Kang Dianfeng 康殿峰, *Pilusi bihua* 毘盧寺壁畫 (Shijiazhuang: Hebei meishu chubanshe, 1998). For an explanation of the water-land rite and its accompanying imagery, see Marsha Weidner, ed., *Latter Days of the Law: Images of Chinese Buddhism 850–1850* (Honolulu: University of Hawai'i Press, 1994), pp. 280–282; *Baoningsi Mingdai Shuiluhua* 寶寧寺明代水陸畫 (Beijing: Wenwu chubanshi, 1995), pp. 212–217; and Caroline Gyss-Vermande, "Démons et merveilles: vision de la nature dans une peinture liturgique du XVe siècle," *Arts Asiatiques* 43 (1988): 106–122. Yet it is Śākyamuni, not Mahāmāyūrī, who is the standard focus of *shuilu* imagery. This discrepancy poses a challenge to my reading of the mural. One possible explanation for Mahāmāyūrī's appearance here is that she represents the protective virtue of all the Buddhas and is a non-wrathful manifestation of Śākyamuni Buddha, invoked to protect against poisons, calamities, and to bring rain and relieve drought (*Buddhism: Flammarion iconographic guides* [Paris/New York: Flammarion, 1995],. pp. 230–231). Perhaps then it is in her role as a manifestation of Śākyamuni, the usual host of the *shuilu* assemblage, that Mahāmāyūrī, the magical reliever of suffering, is a suitable host for the *shuilu* rite depicted, as the rite itself is intended to relieve the suffering of the dead, and ultimately of all sentient beings. It should also be noted that other divine bringers of rain, such as the dragon kings, were popular subjects of wall-paintings in Chinese Buddhist temples during the Ming dynasty. For example, the dragon kings have their own small chapel at Guangshengsi in Hongtong County, Shanxi.

28 For a detail of this figure see: Wang Haitao 王海濤, *Yunnan lishi bihua yishu* 雲南歷史壁畫藝術 (Kunming: Yunnan renmin chubanshe, 2002), fig. 99; and Zhou Qiyu 鄒啟宇, ed., *Yunnan fojiao yishu* 雲南佛教藝術 (Kunming: Yunnan jiaoyu chubanshe, 1991), figs. 284, 289, also reproduced in Karl Debreczeny, "Sino-Tibetan Synthesis in Ming Dynasty Wall Painting at the Core and Periphery," in *The Tibet Journal* 28/1–2 (2003): 49–108, fig. 32. Still, it is not a perfect iconographic match, missing the open vase found in Tibetan works. For a similar Tibetan form, see Sushama Lohia, ed., *Lalitavajra's Manual of Buddhist Iconography* (New Delhi: International Academy of Indian Culture and Aditya Prakashan, 1994), p. 184–185, no. 176.

29 Tibetan monks in Chinese portrayals are often distinguished from Chinese monks—who wear long sleeves—by virtue of their bare shoulders. For instance, in the Chinese "Record (of making) of the Memorial Image of Dpal ldan Bkra shis," the statue of Dpal ldan bkra shis at Fayuansi is described as "a seated image carved from sandalwood, his right shoulder is bare, his hands joined at his chest, bald headed, round and fleshy face, large ears, his physique is full and round and has a rather graceful bearing." Refer to Huang Hao 黄颢, *Zai Beijing de Zangzu wenwu* 在北京的藏族文物 (Beijing: Minzu chubanshe, 1993), pp. 36–37, and Bu Liansheng "Ming Xuande shi nian diaozao Bandanzhashi xiang," *Wenwu* 7 (1979): 82–86. Similar images can be found in other Ming temples; for example, a figure in Tibetan monk's garb appears at Fahaisi, in Beijing, depicted as central among the five Buddhas seated on lotus thrones at the east wall.

30 For images see: *Lijiang Baisha bihua*, fig. 42; Wang Haitao, *Yunnan lishi bihua yishu*, figs. 133–144. Yet, like the Mahāmāyūrī seated across from her, this is not the form of Avalokiteśvara that commonly appears in this context. I have not been able to identify this form of Avalokiteśvara, and in fact it seems to resemble a form of Mañjuśrī, but in the context of the *Guanyin Pumen*, it makes more sense to identify the figure as Avalokiteśvara. Could this be a form of Aṣṭamahābhaya-Tārā, who takes on the role of Protector from the Eight Fears (Sgrol ma 'jigs pa brgyad skyobs) in Tibetan Buddhism? Yunnan sheng wenwu gongzuo dui 云南省文物工作队, "Lijiang bihua diaocha baogao" 丽江壁画调查报告, *Wenwu* 12 (1963): 7–13, says that this scene does not depict the *Guanyin Pumen*, but has a "lama explanation" that identifies the deity as "Wugou jingguang fo," or the "Buddha of Pure Immaculate Light" = *Raśmivimalaviśuddhaprabhā ('Od zer dri ma med pa rnam par dag pa'i 'od).

31 Yunnan sheng wenwu gongzuo dui 云南省文物工作队, "Lijiang bihua diaocha baogao" 丽江壁画调查报告, *Wenwu* 12 (1963): 7–13. Rather it is at Dajuesi (see: *Lijiang Baisha bihua*, fig. 99), a Lijiang temple whose artistic program is purely Chinese, that the depiction of Mārīcī is in keeping with other Ming temples.

32 Stephen Little, *Taoism and the Arts of China* (Chicago: Art Institute, 2000), pp. 234 and 41.

33 See Little, *op. cit.*, fig. 72, pp. 235–236. The text is called the "Marvelous Scripture of the Most High Three Principles Who Protect and Prolong Life, Eliminate Disaster, Abolish Danger, Forgive Sins, and Confer Blessings" *Taishangsanyuan cifu shezui jie'e xiaozai yansheng baoming miao jing.*

34 The Three Officials were incorporated into the Buddhist pantheon as part of the *shuilu* rite; their presence here is indicative of the Daoist-Buddhist syncretism so prevalent by the Ming Dynasty.

35 For a detail, see *Lijiang Baisha bihua*, figs. 62 and 63.

36 See: Yunnan sheng wenwu gongzuo dui 云南省文物工作队, "Lijiang bihua diaocha baogao" 丽江壁画调查报告, *Wenwu* 12 (1963): 7–13. In keeping with this second identification, Susan Shih-shan Huang kindly pointed out to me that the bare feet peeking out from under the robe of the upper right figure in this composition is a distinctive iconographic trait of Zhenwu.

37 See Lohia, *Lalitavajra's Manual of Buddhist Iconography*, pp. 218–219, no. 230. For a good detail of this image, see *Lijiang Baisha bihua*, fig. 18, also reproduced in Debreczeny "Sino-Tibetan Artistic Synthesis," fig. 30.

38 For an image, see Lijiang Naxizu zizhi xianzhi bianzuan weiyuan hui, 麗江納西族自治
    縣志編纂委員會, ed., *Lijiang Naxizu zizhi xianzhi* 麗江納西族自治縣志 (Shenchuan:
    Yunnan renmin chubanshe, 2001), p. 817. For a brief explanation of the Kālacakra
    mantra image, see Robert Beer, *The Encyclopedia of Tibetan Symbols and Motifs* (Bos-
    ton: Shambhala, 1999), pp. 123–127.

39 This very arrangement is found in the sunken well of the ceiling at Jingangdian
    ("Vajra Hall"), another temple of that period built by Mu Zeng, only a few hundred
    yards northwest of Dabaojigong and with a similar layout.

40 Some labels are difficult to read due to some degree of over-painting obscuring the
    gold paint of the lettering. Grub mchog dam pa rgya gar was the Indian founder of
    the Zhi byed pa ("Pacification") order; he traveled widely in Tibet and China dur-
    ing the eleventh-twelfth centuries. See Lohia, *Lalitavajra's Manual of Buddhist Ico-
    nography*, p. 87, no. 34. His disciple, Ma cig lab sgron, is credited with founding the
    ritual tradition of Gcod ("Severance"). See ibid, no. 35.

41 On the left are the god of wealth Phyug lha'i rgyal po Parna shwa ba ri, the god of the
    road Lam lha'i rgyal po dpal Rab chang ba, the lord of trade/merchants Tshong dpon
    Leg ldan nag po, the god of wealth 'Dzom bha la (Jambhala); on the right are the god
    of horses Rta lha'i rgyal po Arya ri man rta, Bdud 'dul grag lha mgon, Mgon po Rnom
    tho sras mounted on a lion (= Rnam thos sras, i.e. Vaiśravaṇa), Btsug rtor ljang khu,
    'Og phyog khro'o rakata gzig 'bar ba, and Sting phyog tsug pung can mounted on a
    dragon.

42 In a published detail, one can discern, under the top layer of pigment that renders
    Lha mo, the raised outline of the armor of a male warrior, mounted on a lion and
    facing right, who looks very similar to "Mgon po rnom thos sras" just to Lha mo's
    right, and much like the series of ten mounted warriors around her, suggesting that
    she was painted over another figure (*Lijiang baisha bihua*, fig. 59). However, another
    more recently published photograph of this figure (Wang Haitao, *op. cit.*, fig. 117)
    shows no such evidence of over-painting. Barriers recently erected along the walls
    have made it difficult to make a closer examination that might decide the matter.
    The first photograph could simply be in error, superimposing another figure like the
    one labeled "Mgon po rnom thos sras" (*sic*) whose composition seems to be identi-
    cal. On the other hand, the lion "Mgon po rnom thos sras" rides has a green mane,
    while the one under Lha mo appears to have a tan or brown mane.

43 See: *Lijiang baisha bihua*, fig. 66. The label *'i ma 'i lha* is written in a cruder hand,
    suggesting that it is not the original label. Perhaps it was written later to restore
    a label that had been covered over by the dark layer of over-painting in the back-
    ground, which is in evidence throughout the temple. The figures in the lowest regis-
    ter flanking Vaiśravaṇa also may have labels, but this was difficult to confirm.

44 Lohia, *Lalitavajra's Manual of Buddhist Iconography*, pp. 180–181, no. 173. Samaya-
    vajra was kindly suggested as an alternative identification by Prof. Kapstein. Chinese
    scholars have mistakenly identified this figure as "Green Tārā" (*Lijiang baisha bihua*,
    p. 67).

45 For images, see Wang Haitao, *op. cit.*, pl. 155–162; Yang Zhou, *op. cit.*, plate 88; and
    Lijiang Baisha bihua, figs. 68 and 69. Chinese scholars typically identify this paint-
    ing as "scenes from Naxi life" or "100 artisan deities" (e.g. Yang Liji 楊禮吉, "Lijiang
    Dajuegong bihua jianjie" 麗江大覺宮壁畫間介, in *Cha ma gu zhen—Lijiang Shuhe*

茶馬古道鎮—麗江東河 [Kunming: Yunnan minzu chubanshe, 2004], p. 193). Many of the labels are damaged and difficult to read. The lower right corner of this panel is entirely lost and likely contained the five missing siddhas.

46 The theme of Vajradhara surrounded by the Eighty-four Mahāsiddhas can be found in a wall-painting attributed to the Ming in the northwest corner of the ruins of the Sūtra Hall of Mkha' lhag dgon (Kadasi) built in 1442 in Lho kha khul, Mtsho sna County, near the Indian border. See Suolang Wangdui [Bsod nams dbang 'dus], ed., *Xizang fojiao siyuan bihua yishu* 西藏佛教寺院壁畫藝術 (*Fresco Art of the Buddhist Monasteries in Tibet*) (Sichuan: Sichuan People's Publishing House, 1994), p. 333, where it is mislabeled as "Green Tārā and Eminent Monks"; see also p. 155, the west wall of Dar rgyas gling Monastery. A set of *thang ka* of Vajradhara and the *mahāsiddhas* can be found in Sonam Topgay, *Tibet House Museum: Catalog of the Inaugural Exhibition* (New Delhi, 1965), plate 5, pp. 23–63, which gives a few lines about each saint's life.

47 I.e., the *Grub thob brgyad cu rtsa bzhi'i gsol 'debs*, sometimes followed in Sa skya pa depictions of the mahāsiddhas, as well as in later Dge lugs pa sets (for instance, the set collected by Sven Hedin and reproduced in Toni Schmid, *The Eighty-five Siddhas* [Stockholm: Statens Etnografiska Museum, 1958]. M. Kapstein notes that these verses, which contain elementary errors of interpretation of basic Indian terms, could not have been composed by an Indian master such as Vajrāsana, and that this in fact was the assessment of them by the renowned Tibetan historian Tāranātha (1575–1634).

48 "Zhong wei Daheitian shen, si zhou wei qi ge jieduan bianhua de xingtai." 中為大黑天神，四周為其各階段變化的形態. Guo Dalie, *Naxizu wenhua daguan*, p. 487, painting no. 6. The only part of the painting at all readable is the image at the bottom of the panel of a Nāga in the water holding up offerings; although unidentified, this image seems to be reproduced in Wang Haitao, *op. cit.*, fig. 163.

49 I suspect that Rock may be conflating Dabaojigong with another temple located directly behind it, which according to local residents of Baisha village was once called Hufatang and is now a private residence. While this temple is now lost, Bai Gengsheng 白庚胜 and Sangji Zhaxi 桑吉扎西, *Naxi Wenhua* 纳西文化 (Shenzhou wenhua ji cheng 神州文化集成) (Beijing: Xinhua chubanshe, 1993), pp. 85–86, says that among the then surviving wall-paintings at Hufatang, built in the Wanli period (that is, during Mu Zeng's reign), was one panel of Mahākāla that "possessed the greatest feeling, heavy [use of] color, robust brushwork, and a truly shocking spirit of artistic power." If this had been the temple's central image, it would suggest that the temple Rock is describing as dedicated to Mahākāla is not Dabaojigong, but in fact Hufatang. Guo Dalie and He Zhiwu, *Naxizu shi*, p. 337, which also treats this as a separate temple, says that "according to scholars" Hufatang was painted in a Tibetan style.

According to Rock, *The Ancient Na-khi Kingdom*, vol. 1, p. 210 and note 26, the shrine was kept closed except for the twentieth day of the first moon when all peasants from the Lijiang plain, as well as those from Axi, would come to worship, at which time a live chicken would be thrown into the box-like shrine as an offering where it was supposed to die instantly. It would seem that, in the period Rock lived there, no lama of any import had resided in Lijiang for some time, and local Dongba devotional practices had reasserted themselves. The sacrifice of animals, or "red sacrifice," is strictly forbidden in Tibetan Buddhist practice, though in remote areas it is not uncommon to find communities that have resumed such practices under the influence of local custom. Abolishing these rituals was a constant struggle and preoccupation of Tibetan Buddhist clergy in both the Eastern and Western border regions. (See, for instance, Stan Mumford, "Repudiation of the Red Sacrifice," in his *Himalayan Dialogue: Tibetan Lamas and Gurung Shamans in Nepal* [Madison: University of Wisconsin Press, 1989], pp. 80–92.) According to scholars in Lijiang, Rock's description closely resembles that of a local Naxi Dongba practice in which a chicken is thrown into a box-like shrine called a *damei*. The whereabouts of this shrine is not currently known, though a purportedly old box-like shrine, said to contain an image of Mahākāla and only opened once a year, is now kept in the main hall of Wenfengsi (about 10 *li* southwest of Lijiang); the shrine is flanked by modern statues of Dpal ldan lha mo and Dam can mgar ba nag po (the Blacksmith), suggesting that the concealed central image is the third in the standard set of Karma Bka' brgyud protectors, Mahākāla as Mgon po ber nag chen.

50 Zhi mei ba might possibly represent Tib. *'chi med pa*. There was at this time a certain 'Chi med dpal bzang (b. fifteenth century), founder of Smon mkhar dgon and a teacher of the famous historian of the Bka' brgyud order Dpa' bo Gtsug lag 'phreng ba (1504–1566), close disciple of the Eighth Karmapa and author of the *Mkhas pa'i dga' ston*. According to Yang Xuezeng 楊學政, *Zangzu, Naxizu, Pumizu de Zangchuan fojiao* 藏族納西族普米族的藏傳佛教 (Kunming: Yunnan renmin chubanshe, 1994), p. 204, Zhi mei ba was a disciple of [the Third Zhwa dmar] Chos dpal ye shes (1406–1452). On the other hand, Zhi mei pa could also be a transliteration of Dri med.

51 It is possible that prior to the founding of the Yuan, the kings of Lijiang were in contact with the Second Karma pa Karma Pakshi in the mid-thirteenth century, as he traveled in Yunnan, founded a monastery in nearby Bde chen, and is said to have given teachings that "reached Lijiang" (Feng Zhi, *op. cit.*, p. 51). During the Ming it is recorded in Si tu Paṇ chen's biographies of the Karma pas that in 1473 the Seventh Karma pa (1454–1506) received gifts from the Lijiang Mu Qin, and that during 1485–1487 the Fifth Mu tusi Mu Qin (1442–1485) and the Sixth Mu tusi Mu Tai (1486–1502) both sent invitations to the Seventh Karma pa to come to Lijiang, but he did not accept. For a detailed historical study of Naxi-Bka' brgyud relations, see Kristina Dy-Liacco, "The Victorious Karma-pa Has Come to 'Jang: An Examination of Naxi Patronage of the Bka'-brgyud-pa in the 15th–17th Centuries" (master's thesis, Indiana University, 2005).

52 Large bronze drums are among the characteristic objects excavated in Yunnan. See: Yunnan sheng bowuguan 云南省博物馆, eds., *Yunnan ren lei qi yuan yu shi qian wenhua* 云南人类起源与史前文化 (Kunming: Yunnan renmin chubanshe, 1991).

53 Si tu Paṇ chen, *Sgrub brgyud karma kaṃ tshang*, p. 17.

54 Included in the Eighth Karma pa's entourage to Lijiang were the Rgyal tshab Bkra shis rnam rgyal, 'Dan ma Grub thob Sangs rgyas, Mnyan pa Bkra shis dpal 'byor, and Dum mo Bkra shis 'od zer. For an outline of the organization of the Karma pa encampment, see Rin chen dpal bzang, *Mtshur phu dgon gyi dkar chag kun gsal me long*.

55 It was the year after the Eighth Karma pa's visit to Lijiang (1517) that the Karma pa received the ill-treated delegate sent by the Ming Emperor Zhengde (1506–

1521), who is often also referred to by his temple name, Wuzong. Zhengde was an
enthusiastic patron of Tibetan Buddhism who took his religious zeal to a level few
emperors had dared: he studied both Tibetan Buddhism and the Tibetan language,
adopted the Tibetan name Rin chen dpal ldan, kept many Tibetan monks around
him, and wore monk's robes at court. He even styled himself an emanation of the
Seventh Karma pa! The emperor's invitation was not received warmly, whereupon
the eunuch-envoy Liu Yun took the gifts back, only to be plundered by bandits on
his return journey to China. The letter of this mission was preserved at the Karma
pa's seat at Mtshur phu (see Hugh E. Richardson, "The Karma-pa Sect: A Historical Note, Part I", in *Journal of the Royal Asiatic Society* [1958]: 151–153, and "Part II,
Appendix A,B,C" [1959]: 6–8). This is one of few Chinese missions for which there
is a detailed record in Tibetan sources; not surprisingly, Confucian historians do not
record these unflattering events. Some Chinese scholars assert that Zhengde's envoys
arrived in Tibet before the Eighth Karma pa actually went to Lijiang, and that he
undertook this journey in order to flee the increasingly hostile armed imperial mission. However, the chronology is clear from Dpa' bo Gtsug lag 'phreng ba, *Dam pa'i
chos kyi 'khor lo bsgyur ba rnams kyi byung pa gsar bar byed pa mkhas pa'i dga ston* (Beijing: Nationalities Publishing House, 1986), p. 1241. This work is especially valuable
as its author, Dpa' bo Gtsug lag phreng ba (1504–1566), was one of the Eighth Karma
pa's own disciples and a personal witness to these events. See Dy-Liacco, "The Victorious Karma-pa," pp. 29–31.

56   In 1561 the Ninth Karma pa Dbang phyug rdo rje (1555–1603) had received presents
from the king of Lijiang (Mu Gao, b. 1515, r. 1554–1568), a devotee of the previous
Karma pa. In 1582 (the year Dabaojigong was built), 1586, and 1593 he received invitations to visit Lijiang and offerings from the ruler of Lijiang, Mu Wang (r. 1580–
1598). In 1600 he received an invitation from Mu Zeng (b. 1587, r. 1598–1646; his
Tibetan name was Karma Mi pham tshe dbang Bsod nams rab brtan) for the purpose of making a new edition of the Kanjur (Si tu Paṇ chen, *Sgrub brgyud karma
kaṃ tshang*, p. 180). While it is not mentioned in Si tu Paṇ chen's account, according to the modern Tibetan scholar Tshe dbang lha mo, "Bod du bka' brgyud pa'i grub
mtha'i srol phyes shing yun nan sa khul du ji lhar dar khyab byung ba," in *Yunnan
zangxue yenjiu lunwen ji* 雲南藏學研究論文集 (Kunming: Yunnan minzu chubanshe, 1995), pp. 98–99, who seems to draw heavily on Karma Nges don's biography of
the Ninth Karma pa, when this last invitation arrived Karma Lhun grub pa and the
Sixth Zhwa dmar were in the Karma pa's retinue, and the Karma pa sent Zhwa dmar
to Lijiang in his stead. (I was not however able to find this statement myself in Karma
Nges don.) This would suggest that the Sixth Zhwa dmar was not personally invited
to Lijiang, but sent as the Ninth Karma pa's representative. Chinese sources on the
other hand say that the Sixth Zhwa dmar was invited by the then Mu ruler, Mu Zeng.
Zhwa dmar stayed at a temple to the east that housed seventy Chinese monks. Here
again it would seem that the Zhwa dmar was traveling with an entire encampment,
as the Mu court received his entire retinue.

57   The catalogue volume is entitled *Bde bar gshegs pa'i bka' gangs can gyi brdas 'dren
pa ji snyed pa'i phyi mo par gyi tshogs su 'khor ba'i byung ba gsal bar brjod pa legs
byas kyi rang gzungs kun nas snang ba nor bu rin po che'i me long*. Preparation was
started in 1608 by Mu Zeng, and the Lijiang Tripiṭaka was completed in 1621. See

Yoshiro Imaeda, "L'édition du Kanjur Tibetain de 'Jang sa-tham," *Journal Asiatique* 270 (1982): 176. Sometime before 1698 the wood blocks of the Lijiang edition were taken to Byams pa gling (Litangsi), a Dge lugs pa monastery in southwest Sichuan, by a Mongolian army led by Dar rgyal bo shog thus, a grandson of Gushri Khan. Later this edition was known by its place of publication in Li thang.

58 Before returning to Tibet the Sixth Zhwa dmar went on pilgrimage to Chicken Foot Mountain, between Lijiang and Dali. The mountain is named for Kukkuṭapādagiri near Gaya (India), the abode of the arhat Kaśyapa. The mountain was a popular pilgrimage site for local Tibetans and Naxi. Mu Zeng built several halls and temples on Chicken Foot Mountain at around this time. See footnote 105.

59 Fuguosi was known as Jietoulin and was renamed Fuguosi by Emperor Ming Xizong (r. 1621–1627). The rear hall was called Fayuange, within which was kept a part of the Tripiṭaka bestowed by Emperor Wanli (1573–1620). Before its founding, the site was an execution ground, and then later a small Chinese Buddhist temple was built there. When the Sixth Zhwa dmar was passing through Lijiang on his way to Jizushan he pointed out to the king that it was an excellent site on which to build a monastery, whereupon the Naxi king presented him with the land. Six Naxi disciples whom the Sixth Zhwa dmar took with him to be educated in Tibet later returned to build Fuguosi. See Yang Xuezheng, *Zangzu, Naxizu, Pumizu de Zangchuan fojiao*, pp. 213 and 228; Qiu Xuanchong 邱宣充, "Lijiang Naxizu zizhixian" 麗江納西族自治縣, *Yunnan Wenwu Guji Daquan* 雲南文物古籍大全 (Kunming: Yunnan Renmin Chubanshe, 1992), p. 672; and Rock, *The Ancient Na-khi Kingdom*, pp. 205–206 and pl. 64; Yunnansheng qunzhong yishu guan 雲南省群眾藝術館, ed., *Yunnan minzu minjian yishu* 雲南民族民間藝術. (Kunming: Yunnan renmin chubanshe, 1994), pl. 581, 583, 584.

60 Feng Zhi, *op. cit.*, p. 62.

61 Si tu Paṇ chen, *Sgrub brgyud karma kaṃ tshang*, p. 237, lines 5–6. I have yet to identify these monasteries, if they still survive, but based on the chronology of this biography I suspect that Dgon dkar refers to a mountain range running north-south to the southwest of Bde chen in Northwest Yunnan near the Tibetan and Burmese borders.

62 Si tu Paṇ chen, *Sgrub brgyud karma kaṃ tshang*, p. 275, line 3.

63 Chos dbyings rdo rje first received gifts and invitations to Lijiang from Mu Zeng almost immediately after his recognition and enthronement. After receiving the second invitation the Tenth Karma pa set out, but was held back by the political tension between his primary patrons, the king of Gtsang (Gtsang Sde pa Karma Phun tshogs rnam rgyal) and his successor Karma Bstan skyong dbang po, and the Dge lugs pa (specifically the monasteries of Se ra and 'Bras spungs). The Fifth Dalai Lama sent three missions to Mongolia seeking military aid, and Gushri Khan (O rod Bstan 'dzin Chos rgyal), chief of the Qoshot Mongols, promised support. As the king of Gtsang gathered a large army, the Karma pa, hoping to diffuse the situation, sent a letter assuring the Fifth Dalai Lama that he did not support the Gtsang king's actions, but this was to no avail. In 1639 Gushri marched into Khams and killed the Beri chief Don yod rdo rje, an ally of Gtsang. After one year of campaigning Gushri brought all of Khams under his control and moved toward Gtsang. The Karma pa fled ahead of the invasion, and in 1642 the Gtsang capital at Shigatse fell to the Mon-

gols. While the Karma pa was encamped at Yam Dur, a letter from the Dalai Lama arrived demanding to know the Karma pa's intentions. Apparently the Dalai Lama found his answer unacceptable, and forces were sent to attack the Karma pa's camp, where thousands of monks were slaughtered.

64 This offer mirrors both Khubilai Khan's offer to 'Phags pa in the thirteenth century and Ming Yongle's offer to the Fifth Karma pa in the fifteenth century, and the Tenth Karma pa's refusal of the offer in favor of religious plurality mirrors his predecessor's response.

65 Gtsang mkhan chen 'Jam dbyangs dpal ldan rgya mtsho, *Poetical Biographies of Dharmakīrti and the Tenth Karma-pa Chos-dbyings-rdo-rje with a Collection of Instructions on Buddhist Practice* (Delhi: Lakshmi Press, 1982), pp. 200 and 204.

66 He also discovered the Seventh Zhwa dmar incarnation (Ye shes snying po, 1631–1694). For more on the large ordination, see Hugh E. Richardson, "Chos-dbyings rdo-rje, the Tenth Black Hat Karma-pa," in *High Peaks, Pure Earth: Collected Writings on Tibetan History and Culture* (London: Serindia Publications, 1998), p. 511. The Karma pa was in Lijiang for the 1660 New Year's celebration, being treated along with the Zhwa dmar, Si tu, Dpa' bo, Phag mo Zhabs drung, Zhwa sgom, and other incarnations to entertainment provided by Mu Yi, suggesting that Lijiang was indeed both a haven and a center of activity for the Karma Bka' brgyud in the seventeenth century. Not until 1661 did the Tenth Karma pa set out for Lhasa and his own seat at Mtshur phu which he had not seen for twenty years.

67 Richardson, "Chos-dbyings rdo-rje," p. 512.

68 His biography by Si tu Paṇ chen also calls it 'Og min gling, the Tibetan name for Fuguosi. However, Chinese sources give the date of the temple's founding as 1627. The imperial bestowal of the name Fuguosi by Emperor Xizong (r. 1621–1627) confirms that it was founded before the arrival of the Tenth Karma pa. This discrepancy could be explained if the Tenth Karma pa oversaw its reconstruction, expansion, or reconsecration, as Fuguosi grew over time into a fairly large temple. See footnote 59.

69 I have translated and discussed this passage elsewhere: Karl Debreczeny, "Ethnicity and Esoteric Power: Negotiating the Sino-Tibetan Synthesis in Ming Buddhist Painting" (Ph.D. dissertation, University of Chicago, 2007), pp. 298–299; and "Tibetan Interest in Chinese Visual Modes: The Foundation of the Tenth Karma-pa's 'Chinese Style Thang ka Painting,'" in Matthew T. Kapstein and Roger Jackson, eds., *Mahāmudrā and the Kagyü Tradition* (forthcoming).

70 This theory is supported by a Tianqi period (1621–1627) plaque which records that "at Baisha [village's] Liulidian [Mu Zeng] increased the painting of wall paintings and repaired the hall and temple." *Tianqi huangdi yuci jin e, zai Liulidian zeng hui bihua xiuqi dian tang* 天启皇帝御赐金额, 在白沙琉璃殿增绘壁画修葺殿堂. Mu Zeng is the subject of the overall passage and Liulidian and Dabaojigong are often conflated. However the Chinese here is not clearly written, so the subject of this sentence is debatable. See Yu Haibo (2002), p. 257. It is also important in this context to keep in mind that Liulidian, Dabaojigong, and the protector chapel behind, are often conflated in Chinese sources as a single site. This would place the date of these paintings in the early 1620s, about the time of, or just after, the Sixth Zhwa dmar's second visit in 1621.

Interestingly Situ Paṇchen (1700–1774), who visited Lijiang three times over a thirty-year period from 1729 to 1759, says in his own diaries that the protector chapel in Baisha was erected by the Ninth Lord Karmapa, who is the last labeled person among the minor figures in the Mahāmudrā lineage painting in this hall: *Tā'i si tur 'bod pa ka.rma bstan pa'i nyin byed kyi rang tshul drangs por brjod pa dri bral shel gyi me long* (The autobiography and diaries of Si-tu Paṇ-chen) (New Delhi: International Academy of Indian Culture, 1968), p. 183. See also Karl Debreczeny, "Bodhisattvas South of the Clouds: Situ Paṇchen's Activities and Artistic Inspiration in Yunnan" in David Jackson, *Patron and Painter: Situ Paṇchen and the Revival of the Encampment Style* (New York: Rubin Museum of Art, 2009). Although the Ninth Karmapa is not recorded to have ever visited Lijiang, it is quite possible that a protector chapel was built in Baisha by order of the Ninth Karmapa to one of his disciples, such as the Sixth Zhwa dmar. (Situ knew the Ninth Karmapa never visited Lijiang, as his official biography is contained in Situ and 'Be lo's *History of the Karma Kagyu*.) This new piece of information from Tibetan sources dovetails nicely with the hypothesis put forward here, that these wall paintings at Dabaojigong were painted after the temple's founding in 1582, during one of the visits of the Sixth Shamar, or shortly afterward, circa 1610–1630.

71   For a short history of Dpal spungs in Chinese, see Sichuan sheng Dege xianzhi bian weiyuanhui 四川省德格縣志編委員會, ed., *Dege xianzhi* 德格縣志 (Chengdu: Sichuan renmin chubanshe, 1995), pp. 498–499. For more comprehensive histories of Dpal spungs in Tibetan, see Karma Rgyal mtshan, *Kaṃ tshang yab sras dang Dpal spungs dgon pa* (Chengdu: Sichuan minzu chubanshe, 1997), and *Khams phyogs Dkar mdzes khul gyi dgon sde so so'i lo rgyus gsal bar bshad pa nang bstan gsal ba'i me long* (Beijing: krung go'i bod kyi shes rig dpe skrun khang, 1995), vol. 1, pp. 555–590. Refer, too, to Carmen Meinert's chapter in the present volume.

72   For a history of Mtshur phu Monastery, see Rin chen dpal bzang, ed., *Mtshur phu dgon gyi dkar chag kun gsal me long* (Lhasa: Bod ljongs mi rigs dpe skrun khang, 1995).

73   Yang Xuezheng, *Zangzu, Naxizu, Pumizu de Zangchuan fojiao*, p. 200; and Feng Zhi, *op. cit.*, p. 51.

74   Rin chen dpal bzang, *op. cit.*, pp. 161–162.

75   The only paintings to survive into the modern period at Fuguosi are said to have been of Mahākāla and to have been located in the north and south Hufatang (Dharma Protector Hall); for instance Guo Dalie and He Zhiwu, *Naxizu shi* (p. 337) mentions Fuguosi's most remarkable surviving painting is of Mahākāla. Fuguosi was destroyed by fire in 1820 (or 1864?), rebuilt in 1873, and then repaired in 1882, but it was a large temple complex with many buildings, so it is unclear how much of the original seventeenth-century artwork would have survived. During the Cultural Revolution most of the buildings were reduced to rubble. In 1976 one of its few surviving halls, Wufenglou, was moved into Lijiang's tourist park, Heilongtan, whereupon all remaining wall-paintings were lost. Wufenglou has three double-eaved roofs, each of the four corners has five flying eaves "fengtou"-shaped, i.e. phoenix-like, from which it gets its name. See Qiu Xuanchong, "Lijiang Naxizu zizhixian," p. 672.

76   Lijiang xian Xianzhibian weihui 麗江縣縣志編委會, ed., *Lijiang fuzhilue* 麗江府志略 (by Guan Xuexuan 管學宣, 8th year Qianlong 1743) (Lijiang Naxizu zizhixian, 1991), p. 180.

77 Karma Rgyal mtshan, *Kaṃ tshang yab sras*, pp. 283–284. It is interesting to note that
in the Tenth Karma pa's poetical biography (Gtsang mkhan chen, *Poetical Biographies*, pp. 197–198) are listed thirteen Tibetan names of temples and monasteries
built by the king of Lijiang; unfortunately the names do not coincide with any other
lists, making firm identifications difficult: "The many monasteries and monastic colleges that the *dharmarāja* of 'Jang (Lijiang) had previously established were thus:
First is the place called Rtsi zhag monastery, that *vihāra* in which resides the blocks
for the full *Bka' 'gyur*, and the writings of the Great [Śākya]muni and so on, which
has a *saṅgha*. Otherwise there are the places called Rgya bya monastery, Khang sar
monastery, A bong monastery, Rtsa monastery, Tus monastery, Bro shong monastery, the *chos sde* called Khrung khrung rtse gang, A 'dod *chos sde*, Ldob spang phus
monastery, the *chos sde* Karma lha ldings, Sga tu *chos sde* and Dga' snang *chos sde*—
those renowned monasteries. In the large monasteries [there were] assemblies of as
many as six to seven hundred [monks], assemblies of three hundred or two hundred
monks. There were those rich in *saṅgha* of tens of thousands" (Dy-Liacco, "The Victorious Karma-pa, p. 47). I would like to thank Kristina Dy-Liacco for sharing her
translation of this text from her master's thesis with me.

78 The following is Yang's list of the thirteen Karma Bka' brgyud temples in Lijiang
with his Chinese transliterations of their Tibetan names, followed by their Tibetan
equivalents: 1) Wenfengsi (Lijiang): Sang ang ga ze lin = Gsang sngags gar tse gling
['Jang ri smag po dgon]; 2) Zhiyunsi (Lijiang): E dun pin cuo lin = Nges don phun
tshogs gling; 3) Pujisi (Lijiang): Ta bai lie zheng lin = Thar pa'i gling khri gling
[Phun tshogs gling]; 4) Fuguosi (Lijiang): E ming nang zhu lin = 'Og min gling; 5)
Yufengsi (Lijiang): Za xi qu pi lin = Bkra shis chos 'phel gling; 6) Linzhaosi (location
unknown): Ge can lin = Rgyal mtshan gling; 7) Xihuasi (location unkown): Teqin
dajia lin = Theg chen dar rgyas gling; 8) Talaisi (Weixi): Dajie lin = Dar rgyas gling;
9) Shouguosi 壽國寺 (Weixi): Zaxi dajie lin = Bkra' shis dar rgyas gling; 10) Laijingsi
(Weixi): Zaxi raodan lin = Bkra shis rab brtan gling; 11) Puhuasi (Gongshan): Sang-
zhu dajie lin = Bsam grub dar rgyas gling; 12) Damasi (Weixi): Danpei lin = Bstan
'phel gling; and 13) Laiyuansi (Weixi): Raojie lin = Rab dga' gling. Yang Xuezheng
was able to identify all but two of the temples; Linzhaosi (Gecan lin = Rgyal mtshan
gling?) and Xihuasi (Teqin dajie lin = Theg chen dar rgyas gling). Refer to Yang Xuezheng (1994), pp. 217–218, and Xi Yuhua and Wang Xiaosong, pp. 191–192. Interestingly the Tibetan names given by Yang do not seem to correspond well with the
list given by the *Kaṃ tshang yab sras dang Dpal spungs dgon pa* or the Tenth Karma
pa's biography. Tshe dbang lha mo, *op. cit.*, pp. 114–115, also gives a list of monastery
names in Tibetan, but does not provide the Chinese equivalents. In her list there is
a Theg chen dar rgyas gling, but no Rgyal mtshan gling.

79 Still, the chronology of Dabaojigong's naming remains unclear, as it could not have
been named after Dpal spungs almost 140 years before Dpal spungs was built. Interestingly, Lijiang's only gazetteer, Lijiang xian Xianzhibian weihui 麗江縣縣志編委
會, ed., *Lijiang fuzhilue* (1743), p. 204, does not list Dabaojigong among its temples,
but does give the name Hufa qielan, an alternate name given for Dabaojigong by
Joseph Rock, *The Ancient Na-khi Kingdom*, p. 210. It is possible that the temple was
originally known as "Hufa qielan" but was renamed "Dabaojigong" after it became
a branch temple of Dpal spungs in the eighteenth century. Again, it is also possible

that Rock is conflating Dabaojigong with another temple named Hufatang located directly behind it, which is no longer extant.

80 Yang Zhou 楊周, ed., "Baizu, Naxizu de simiao bihua" 白族納西族的寺廟壁畫, *Yunnan minzujian wenxue yishu* 雲南民族間文學藝術 (Kunming: Yunnan renmin chubanshe, 1985), pp. 243–249.

81 Yang Zhou, *op. cit.*, p. 247–248.

82 This comparative study is limited to temples built in Lijiang and does not take into account the many monasteries built by the Mu rulers outside their immediate territory, like Byams pa gling built in Litang by Mu Wang, or Xitansi built on Chicken Foot Mountain by Mu Zeng.

83 According to Qiu Xuanchong, "Lijiang Naxizu zizhixian," p. 671, it originally had sixteen bays (Yang Zhou, *op. cit.*, p. 248, says twelve bays from the Ming), painted from Yongle to the late Qing, the early works being "simple and plain" while the later works are characterized by "lines that are unrestrained." Now only copies of three bays survive in the Yunnan Sheng Bowuguan; all the rest were destroyed in the 1996 earthquake. Each bay had three figures, and above each was written the deity's names, while below was written a Mu family member's name, suggesting a direct association between deity and ruler. For example:

above:

Nanwu dawei dehai haihui "homage to Yamāntaka's assembly"	*Nanwu daoshi rulai haihui* "homage to Jina Tathāgata's assembly"	*Nanwu amitafo hui* "homag to Amitābha Buddha's assembly"

below:

Mu Chu	Mu Zhong	Mu Chang

Qiu concludes with the statement that the painting style at Liulidian is simple with no esoteric content. Regarding Chinese esoteric models as preserved in Sichuan and Yunnan, see for instance Angela Howard, "The Dharani Pillar of Kunming, Yunnan: A Legacy of Esoteric Buddhism and Burial Rites of the Bai People in the Kingdom of Dali (937–1253)," *Artibus Asiae*, 77, no. 1/2 (1997): 33–72; and the same author's "The Development of Buddhist Sculpture in Yunnan: Syncretic Art of a Frontier Kingdom," in Janet Baker, ed., *The Flowering of a Foreign Faith: New Studies in Chinese Buddhist Art* (Mumbai: Marg Publications, 1998), pp. 134–145.

84 "Qi tu mu zhuan shi, caihui zhi lei, nai Dali qiaogong Yang De shi cheng de" 其土木磚石, 彩绘之类, 乃大理巧工楊得. 氏成之. Lijiang xian Xianzhibian weihui 麗江縣縣志編委會, ed., *Lijiang fuzhilue*, p. 237.

85 Painted copies were made in 1957 by the Yunnan sheng wenhua ju of 130 *fu* (panels) of wall-paintings in Lijiang for an exhibition, but while a few appear in scattered publications, it is unclear whether the entire set was ever published. The five paintings mentioned here depicted Śākyamuni, four great bodhisattvas, eighteen arhats, Dharmapāla, patrons, and Daoist deities. Yang Zhou reports that the painting quality was very high, and stylistically similar to "Taiziyouyuanyantu" in Xingjiaosi (Jianchuan). Refer to Yang Zhou 楊周, "Lijiang si shi bihua," 麗江寺史壁畫, *Yunnan minzu minjian yishu* 雲南民族民間藝術 (Kunming: Yunnan renmin chubanche, 1985), pp. 49–58; and Guo Dalie 郭大烈 and He Zhiwu 和志武, *Naxizu shi* 納西族史 (Chengdu: Sichuan Minzu Chubanshe), 1994, p. 334.

86 Li Weiqing, "Lijiang Mushi tufu miaoyu bihua chutan," p. 64; Yang Zhou, ed. "Baizu, Naxizu de simiao bihua" 白族納西族的寺廟壁畫, *Yunnan minzujian wenxue yishu* 雲南民族間文學藝術 (Kunming: Yunnan renmin chubanshe, 1985), p. 247; and Li Kunsheng 李昆聲, *Yunnan meishu shi* 雲南美術史 (Kunming: Yunnan jiaoyu chubanshe, 1995), p. 307.

87 *Lijiang Baisha bihua*, p. 16, gives the year as 1583. Feng Zhi, *op. cit.*, p. 63, says Dabaojigong was built by Mu Gong in 1523 (second year Jiaqing), presumably based on the article by Li Weiqing discussed in footnote 17, and assumes the paintings date from the same period. 1643 would be after the Fifth Dalai Lama inspired the Mongol attack on the Karma Bka' brgyud, but a year or so before the arrival of the Tenth Karma pa.

88 Guo Dalie and He Zhiwu, *Naxizu shi*, p. 337; Joseph Rock, *The Ancient Na-khi Kingdom*; Li Weiqing, "Lijiang Mushi tufu miaoyu bihua chutan," p. 63; and Qiu Xuanchong, "Lijiang Naxizu zizhixian," p. 674, say that Wandegong was built in the thirty-fifth year of Jiajing (1556). However, that would be under the reign of a different ruler, Mu Gong (r. 1522–1566). Rgod tshang is also the name of a village in Sger rtse county, Tibet, so perhaps the painter's moniker was taken from his birthplace.

89 Wandegong survived into the 1950s, and some painted copies were made of Wandegong's wall-paintings in 1957, but by 1980 Wandegong was largely destroyed. Wandegong's main hall had housed a colossal [gilt] bronze Buddha. See Yu Haibo 余海波 and Yu Jiahua 余嘉華, *Mushi tusi yu Lijiang* 木氏土司與麗江 (Kunming: Yunnan minzu chubanshe, 2002), p. 217, and Mu Licun 木麗春, Lijiang bihua jiemi 麗江壁畫揭密 (Dehong: Dehong minzu chubanshe, 2000), p. 128.

90 Li Weiqing, "Lijiang Mushi tufu miaoyu bihua chutan," p. 63, observes that although the Guiyitang wall-paintings are without obvious Tibetan painting influence, they are nonetheless finely and skillfully done, and all somewhat similar in technique to Tibetan painting. The inscriptions on the painting surface are done in Chinese and similar to those of Liulidian, but on the large pillars of the main hall under a layer of red lacquer are also passages of Tibetan scripture written in cinnabar (*zhusha zhi zangwen jingdian*). This, he says, is somewhat similar to Dabaojigong, where underneath the plaster ground layer (*mahuiceng*), Tibetan script is written on the *huangtu* layer. I investigated Li Weiqing's observation on a second trip to Dabaojigong in 2001, but did not observe Tibetan writing on any of the exposed under-layers.

91 It contained an image of a Tibetan-style Buddha in the earth-touching *mudrā*, which had been hidden during anti-religious riots in the third year of the Republic (1914) and then restored. The statue was later moved to a different part of the village when the temple was taken over by the Forestry Department.

92 Rock, *The Ancient Na-khi Kingdom*, vol. 1, p. 156, footnote 8, and p. 219.

93 However, Chen Gaochen, ed., *Lijiang meili de Naxi jiayuan* (Beijing: Zhongguo jianzhu gongye chubanshe, 1997), p. 201, dates both of these temples to 1573, about ten years earlier than Dabaojigong.

94 See n. 83.

95 A sixth structure, Canjinglou, which sits just north of Liulidian's entrance, sharing the same courtyard, could also be included in this series of chapels. It is said to be contemporary with Liulidian and Dabaojigong (that is Ming), however there do not appear to be any surviving records of its construction. It is empty of artistic content, having been recently white washed. Both Liulidian and Canjinglou were badly

damaged in the earthquake of 1996 and were only recently re-opened. Another structure, Wenchanggong, sits just across the field.

96 The glaring exception to this is the ceiling in eight carved roundels, the Kālacakra mantra at the center surrounded by seven of the eight auspicious symbols (the canopy is missing). This ceiling appears to be a much later repair. For images of Dajuegong's well-preserved wall-paintings, see *Lijiang Baisha bihua*, figs. 80–113, and Wang Haitao, *Yunnan lishi bihua yishu*, figs. 198–218.

97 Li Kunsheng 李昆聲, *Yunnan meishu shi* 雲南美術史 (Kunming: Yunnan jiaoyu chubanshe, 1995), p. 307; Duan Yuming 段玉明, *Xinan simiao wenhua* 西南寺廟文化 (Kunming: Yunnan jiaoyu chubanshe, 2001), p. 206; and Yang Liji, "Lijiang Dajuegong bihua jianjie," p. 192, attribute the conversion of Dajuegong to Mu Zeng. One source credits the building of Dajuegong to Mu Dong, and hence dating to the early Wanli period, which would thus challenge the chronology I have proposed, though not necessarily the date of the painting.

98 Guo Dalie and He Zhiwu, *Naxizu shi*, p. 337, *Lijiang Baisha bihua*, p. 13, and Mu Lichun 木麗春, *Lijiang bihua jiemi* 麗江壁畫揭密 (Dehong: Dehong minzu chubanshe, 2000), p. 62. One source attributes most of the wall-painting in Baisha to "the work of the Han Chinese Ma Xiaoxian" (Naxizu jianshi bianxie zu 納西族簡史編寫組, eds., *Naxizu jianshi*, 納西族簡史編寫組 [Kunming: Yunnan renmin chubanshe, 1984], p. 155). Guo Dalie, *Naxizu wenhua daguan*, p. 485, claims that Ma Xiaoxian was a Daoist, perhaps due to the word *xian* "immortal" in his name, but no other evidence supports this contention.

99 There does not appear to be a painter named Ma Xiaoxian, or a family of painters surnamed "Ma" in the local gazetteer *Ningbo tongzhi*. There is, however, a painter with the *zi* of Xiaoxian, Wu Shisi, in the index of Chinese artists. See Yu Jianhua 俞 劍華, ed., *Zhongguo meishu jiaren ming zidian* 中國美術家人名字典 (Shanghai: Renmin yishu chubanshe, 1990), p. 280. It is possible that Ma was not actually his surname, but added as an embellishment to connect him stylistically to the famous Ma Yuan family tradition, which was still flourishing in Zhejiang. I would like to thank Huang Shih-shan for suggesting this possible explanation.

100 See: *Lijiang Naxizu zizhi xianzhi*, p. xxiv. While this text only identifies this image as a "Ming dynasty wood carving," Li Kunsheng, *Yunnan meishu shi* (p. 309, fig. V-10) identifies this work as being from Dabaojigong. Sadly the reproduction quality in both publications is quite poor.

101 There are numerous examples given in the *Mushi huanpu* of the Mu governor in Kunming sending orders to Lijiang to suppress this or that uprising or bandit, and sending recommendations to the Ming court to reward the Naxi ruling Mu family for service to the throne.

102 See Mary Ann Rogers, "Visions of Grandeur: The Life and Art of Dai Jin," in Richard Barnhart, *Painters of the Great Ming: The Imperial Court and the Zhe School* (Dallas: Dallas Museum of Art, 1993), pp. 127–158, especially pp. 147–159 for his career in Yunnan.

103 This temple is described in some detail in a short section about Chicken Foot Mountain (Tib. Ri bo bya rkang) in an account of a pilgrimage to Yunnan during the early twentieth century. See Kaḥ thog Si tu Chos kyi rgya mtsho, *Kaḥ thog Si tu'i Dbus Gtsang gnas yig* (Chengdu: Sichuan minzu chubanshe, 2001), p. 515. This text is repro-

duced almost word for word in a 1923 work by Dge 'dun chos 'phel included in a recent anthology of Tibetan guides to temples and places: *Gnas yig phyogs bsgrigs* (*Simiao zhi huibian*) (Chengdu: Sichuan minzu chubanshe, 1998), pp. 581–582. I would like to thank Kristina Dy-Liacco for bringing this text to my attention.

104   Li Lincan, "Xitansi de Mu Zeng suxiang" ("The Statue of Mu Zeng of Xitansi"). Xitansi was badly damaged during the Cultural Revolution, and recent authors such as Li Ruming do not mention Tibetan imagery there at all, so perhaps this material does not survive.

105   Earlier in 1615 Mu Zeng also built a pavilion called Zangjingge in the temple of Hua-yansi on Chicken Foot Mountain in which he deposited a copy of the Tripiṭaka. In 1617 Mu Zeng built a copper temple called Xitansi, and inside it built a hall called Wanshoudian. In 1624 Emperor Tianqi gave him a copy of the Tripiṭaka and bestowed on his temple the name Xitanshensi. In 1628 Mu Zeng solicited the Ming court for a set of the Tripiṭaka for the purpose of depositing it in that hall. In recognition of this, the monks of Xitansi consecrated a chapel to Mu Zeng called the "Chapel of Prefect Mu" (Mu tai shou). In 1629 Mu Zeng built Fayun'ge and in it placed the classics. In 1631 Mu Zeng's son Mu Yi added to it and embellished it so it would seem the finest on the mountain. The gate and pavilion were later rebuilt by Mu Yao. In the Wanli era (1573–1619) Mu Zeng also built Huayan'ge and deposited there the "Tibetan Classics" (the Kanjur?), though it was destroyed by fire in 1597. See Rock, *The Ancient Na-khi Kingdom*, p. 160, note 19, and p. 162, who quotes Gao Wengying 高翁映, *Jizu shan zhi* 鸡足山志 (Kunming: Yunnan renmin chubanshe, 2003 [1692]), ch. 4, folio 4b–5b.

106   "Ma Xiaoxian Jiangnan ren, gongtu hua shanshui, zhen shenpin, huahui renwu, mibu jingmiao, shizhe cheng wei Ma xianhua. Xiyu jian qi ming, yan qu shusui, hou fu hui Li. si zhi er, ren jian qi zhishou you zi yun" 馬肖仙江南人, 工圖畫山水, 臻神品, 花卉人物, 靡不精妙, 識者稱為馬仙畫. 西域聞其名. 延去数載, 後复歸麗. 死之日, 人見其指頭有字云. *Lijiang fuzhilue*, p. 181. Are these signs, "zi," in this case *cakras* implying he was actually a bodhisattva? This reading would be in keeping with the Tibetan hagiographic tradition of finding physical signs or marks as manifestations of spiritual attainment, or divinity after death. For example, see Chokgyur Lingpa, *Karmapa: The Sacred Prophecy* (New York: Kagyu Thubten Choling Publications Committee, 1999), for a photograph of a spontaneously generated image said to be found in the bones among the ashes of the cremated Sixteenth Karma pa.

107   Most Chinese sources (such as Guo Dalie and He Zhiwu, *Naxizu shi* [p. 337] and Mu Licun [2003] p. 62) say it was the "Dabao fawang"—the Karma pa—but *Lijiang Baisha bihua* (p. 13) says that it was the "Erbao fawang"—the Sixth Zhwa dmar. However, as the Zhwa dmar was the Tenth Karma pa's teacher, and both were painters, it is possible that this connection is still valid. Sadly neither publication cites their source for this "tradition."

108   A variant account has them meet when the Karma pa went to worship at Chicken Foot Mountain.

109   These dates are based on the thirteen-year period between the Karma pa's departure from Lijiang for Mtshur phu (1661) and his death (1674).

110   Guo Dalie and He Zhiwu, *Naxizu shi*, p. 337, and Mu Licun, *Lijiang chamagudao shi*

hua 麗江茶馬古道史話 (Dehong: Dehong minzu chubanshe, 2003), p. 62, say there are twenty-four paintings. Guo Dalie, *Naxizu wenhua daguan*, p. 491, says there are twenty paintings, all 92 x 63 cm mounted as *thang ka*. None of these sources say how they identified the paintings as being by Ma Xiaoxian, and Li Xi, the director of the Lijiang museum, although aware of the painter Ma Xiaoxian, claimed no knowledge of the existence of such paintings in the museum's collection. This collection, he explained, was formerly in the Lijiang County Cultural Institute, which was then transferred to the Lijiang Dongba Cultural Museum in 1984, but little information accompanied the pieces, and any attributions there may have been to Ma Xiaoxian have since been lost.

111 Mu Licun, *Lijiang chamagudao shi hua*, p. 62, provides the most detailed account to date of the relationship between Ma Xiaoxian and the [Tenth] Karma pa, however he also says that the Ma Xiaoxian's paintings were supposed to have been given to the Si tu incarnation in Dpal spungs while Ma Xiaoxian was in Tibet, which is impossible as Dpal spungs was not built until 1726.

112 E.g., *Naxizu jianshi*, p. 155; and Yu Haibo 余海波 and Yu Jiahua 余嘉華, *Mushi tusi yu Lijiang* 木氏土司與麗江 (Kunming: Yunnan minzu chubanshe, 2002), p. 283. Others make vague statements such as one "can see his hand in Lijiang's wall-paintings," but provide no specific examples.

113 However, I suspect that the paintings being referred to here are actually two sets of arhat paintings by the tenth Karma pa himself: the inscribed set of seven "Śākyamuni and the Sixteen Arhats," and another set of seventeen, totalling twenty-four paintings. This suspicion has been reinforced by another description of these paintings by Mu Lichun, *Lijiang bihua jiemi*, p. 121, which says that Ma Xiaoxian painted a set of paintings for the Karma pa, and within those, seventeen were mounted in the Tibetan style, and seven mounted in the Chinese style, again for a total of twenty-four paintings, the content of which are images of "esoteric Buddha(s) and the Eighteen arhats."

114 See my "Tibetan Interest in Chinese Visual Modes: The Foundation of the Tenth Karmapa's 'Chinese Style Thang ka Painting,'" forthcoming.

115 The costume of the royal Naxi patron in this set can be compared to Mu Zeng's official portrait in fig. 3. For a brief discussion of the full set, see my "The Buddha's Law Among the 'Jang: The 10th Karma-pa's Development of His 'Chinese Style Thang-ka Painting' in the Kingdom of Lijiang," *Orientations* 34/4 (April 2003): 46–53. Note that images 8e and 8f have been inadvertently switched by the editors, and that the much deserved thanks expressed to Ulrich von Schroeder and Alain Bordier for their generosity in sharing images was deleted, for which I apologize to them.

116 Dadingge may be the exception, depending on what an examination of the paintings reveals about the date of the extant wall-paintings. However, between the ravages of the Cultural Revolution and the earthquakes that plague the region there is precious little of the once bountiful visual material referred to in textual sources *in situ* to work with.

PART II
MISSIONS FROM THE FRONTIERS

4: Tibetan Buddhism, Perceived and Imagined, along the Ming-Era Sino-Tibetan Frontier

Elliot Sperling

TIBETAN BUDDHISM became a potent force in the political relationship that was forged between Tibet and China beginning in the
twelfth century, though its significance has often been ignored or
underestimated. The ritual empowerment it afforded the emperors of several dynasties—the Xi Xia, Yuan, Ming, and Qing—was perceived by those
who were aware of it as a means of placing esoteric power at the disposal of
a worldly sovereign. This allowed that ruler to influence, affect, and govern
events in the mundane world with the assistance of supramundane ability.
We need not exaggerate the significance of Tibetan Buddhism in Chinese
history; while its presence was more often than not peripheral in Chinese
courts, it was felt far more than most historical studies indicate. Though a
predilection for Tibetan Buddhism varied greatly from reign to reign, both
Tibetan and Chinese sources show it to have been a very real element in imperial ideology in the courts of specific emperors. It was an ever-present back-
drop, even during those times when a given court was not actively engaged
with Tibetan Buddhist practice, leading us to see that this relationship was
by no means one-dimensional. Indeed, strategic considerations could also
be, not surprisingly, central to Ming interests in Tibetan Buddhist establishments. But the underlying basis for imperial Ming interest in Tibetan Buddhism—attraction to the authority it could bestow—is secondary here to
our considerations for the relationship from the perspective of three Tibetan
monasteries lying physically between Tibet and China.

The monasteries in question represent three distinct religious traditions
in Tibet. The first is Drotsang lhakhang, or Drotsang Dorjé-chang (Ch.
Qutansi < Tib. Go tam sde),[1] a Karma Kagyü establishment founded in the
area east of Xining. The second is Chöjé Monastery (*dgon*) in Dzamtang, a

still-functioning and vital center of the Jonang tradition, a school for which some Western scholars had long since prepared an obituary. Finally, Kyang-tsang Püntsok Dargyé Ling, or Zhangpa Gön (Ch. Shangbasi), a monastery in the Songpan region of modern Sichuan Province, is an institution of the Bön tradition, which holds itself to be the pre-Buddhist faith of Tibet, a notion that, at least with regard to many of the tradition's present practices and manifestations, is problematic. By examining these frontier monasteries, which came under the purview of the Ming court, we can see different aspects of the way in which Ming political policies along the frontier were enmeshed with the religious environment of ethnic Tibetan areas.

The first monastery, Drotsang Dorjé-chang, is emblematic of Ming involvement with Tibetan Buddhism at the highest levels of the court. The Karma Kagyü had re-emerged, prior to the collapse of the Mongol Yuan Dynasty in 1368, as the primary bearers of the imperial empowerment traditions, and for a short period in the fourteenth and fifteenth centuries, this monastery and its abbots and administrators played very significant roles in the development of Ming policy toward Tibet.[2] Formal recognition of the monastery in 1393 was one of the earliest manifestations of the Ming court's interest in Tibetan Buddhism and awareness of its role in the Amdo frontier area. The earliest mention of the monastery in a Chinese source appears in an entry in the the *Ming shilu* for April 8, 1393, where it is noted that the emperor granted it support, protection, and an imperial name board.[3] Significantly, the first Ming Emperor, Ming Taizu (r. 1368–1398), was thereby establishing a relationship with a prominent Kagyü cleric and founder of the monastery, Hé Lama Sanggyé Trashi.

Available sources tell us that Lama Sanggyé Trashi was originally from Lhodrak Drowolung (whence the name Drotsang) in Central Tibet.[4] Tibetan sources assert that his departure for Amdo had been predicted by deities and by his own lamas, and that he was a lineal descendant of Marpa Lotsawa.[5] In Amdo, Sanggyé Trashi took up residence on the island in the middle of the Tso'ngön lake known as Tsonying ("Heart of the Lake"). As a result he came to be known as Tsonyingba, or as Langkarpa (the latter name said to be derived from his traveling on a white ox).[6] His connection with the Tso'ngön lake gave him the appellation "Hé" (< Ch. *hai* ["sea"]), which is prefixed to his name.[7] In the *Ming shilu* he is known uniquely as Sanla. According to the *History of the Dharma in Domé* (*Mdo smad chos 'byung*), Ming Taizu had divined that it was necessary to bring to his court a lama from the nomadic grasslands far to the west. The officials dispatched to seek a suitable lama were taken with Sanggyé Trashi, and he was invited to court, given an edict granting him the title of *dishi* (Tib. *te'i shri*), and provided with support for his monastery.[8]

FIG. 1 General view of Qutansi (Drotsang Dorjé-chang) in Qinghai.
(After Qinghai sheng wenhua ding 青海省文化丁, eds., *Qutansi* 瞿昙寺
[Chengdu: Sichuan kexue jishu chubanshe and Xinjiang keji weisheng chuban-
she, 2000], p. 80.)

Sanggyé Trashi makes an appearance in Chinese sources due to his role in
the pacification of a certain tribe around Handong, to the north of Amdo.
The incident referred to is a well-known one: he persuaded the followers of
Qi Jessün (> Ch. Zhesun), an actively hostile opponent of the Ming, to ten-
der their submission to the Ming court.[9] It was at about this time that Sanggyé Trashi, having established his monastery, came to court, offering horses
as tribute, and seeking imperial support and an imperial name board. These
were granted and Taizu issued orders stating:

Since the time of the Buddha, there have been none among those
who have seen a Buddha who have not shown him veneration.
Though one be fierce and cruel, ignorant and stupid; still one has
respect for and faith in him. He transforms evil into good: such is
the fundamental power of the Buddha! Now the Tibetan monk
Sanla was born and resides in the Western lands. He follows in the
path of the Buddha. He has great affinities with the people. He has
gathered gold and silk to construct a Buddhist monastery. Lately
he has come to court at the capital. We commend the sincerity of
his exemplary goodness. In particular, We bestow orders for his

protection. All are prohibited from harming him and ordered to
heed his clear practice. All in violation will be punished. Thus this
order.[10]

In addition, Sanggyé Trashi was given a nominal place within the Buddhist
bureaucracy of the Ming as Chief (Ch. *dugang*) of the Xining Prefectural
Buddhist Registry (Ch. Xining Senggangsi), according to a *shilu* entry for
May 2nd, 1393 (less than a month after the imperial name board for Drotsang
Dorjé-chang had been granted).[11]

The monks at Drotsang Dorjé-chang during the time of Sanggyé Trashi are
said to have practiced according to the traditions of both the Sakya and Kagyü
schools (with the main emphasis on those practices related to Cakrasaṃvara,
regardless of their provenance from among the two sects).[12] However, at its
founding the monastery was identified with the Karma Kagyü.[13] Given the
restored prominence of the Karma Kagyü at the end of the Yuan dynasty, as
well as Taizu's own earlier attempt to establish contact with the Karmapa sub-
sect through a missive sent in 1375 to the Fourth Karmapa Rölpé Dorjé, the
emperor's interest in Sanggyé Trashi should be understood against the background of the perceived esoteric powers associated with the Karma Kagyü.
Taizu's message to Rölpé Dorjé, in which he portrayed himself as the guardian of the lama's spiritual practice, suggests that his role in that relationship
was much like the one that court historians present him as playing in his relationship with Sanggyé Trashi.[14] At the same time, the *History of the Dharma
in Domé* gives ample evidence that Sanggyé Trashi, though dependent on the
emperor's power for material support and protection, evinced command of
the esoteric power on which the emperor's authority conversely relied.[15]

By the mid-fifteenth century Drotsang Dorjé-chang had come under the
influence of the Geluk sect; its later inclusion in Desi Sanggyé Gyatso's survey
of Geluk monasteries makes this affiliation clear.[16] The Ming court had established broad relations with a number of Tibetan hierarchs and monasteries
from various schools by this time, and while interactions with Drotsang Dorjé-chang and its leading figures did not cease, they were far less consequential
than they had been during the late fourteenth century. However this ought
not lead us to underestimate the significance of their ties at their inception.[17]

We see a similar relationship being developed between the Ming court and
Chöjé Gön in Dzamtang. During the past decade the publication of works
by the Jonang scholar Ngawang Lodrö Drakpa (1920–1975) on the history
of the Jonang sect and its base at Chöjé Gön has allowed us a glimpse of
Dzamtang in the context of its contacts with China and the Mongols dur-

ing the Ming period. Particularly informative about these affairs is Ngawang Lodrö Drakpa's *Supplement* (Tib. *lhan thabs*) to his history of the Jonang tradition, as it elaborates on critical events and factors in Ming-Tibetan relations that go unmentioned in the standard Chinese sources for the period. Details supplied in this work can now be bolstered by several modern studies produced in China which appear to have made use of the *Supplement* and which draw in part on a few largely unpublished original Ming missives sent to the monastery's hierarchs.[18] Together, the *Supplement* and letters indicate the utility of maintaining relations with Chöjé Gön for a Ming policy aimed at securing stability along the Ming-Tibetan frontier. In the case of Chöjé Gön, it seems that the Chinese court was motivated not by the acquisition of esoteric empowerment but rather by strategic concerns.

Historically, Dzamtang is notable largely for the Jonang presence within its borders; we actually have little information about the area prior to the establishment there of the Jonang monastery, Chöjé Gön, in 1425/1426. Still, there are some indications that Dzamtang, or the surrounding region, was a place of significance at an even earlier time. In addition to the Ming creation of the Dokham Dzamtang Pacification Commission in 1375, we learn from Ngawang Lodrö Drakpa that the Second Chöjé (as the incarnate heads of the monastery are called), Gyelwa Senggé (1509/1510–1580), was a descendant of one Könchok-kyap, who had exercised wide dominion over Kham in the thirteenth century. In his youth, Könchok-kyap is said to have served the Mongols during Khubilai Khan's campaign against Jang[19] and afterward to have traveled to Central Tibet, returning east only decades later to serve the Mongols in Amdo in his old age. Since one of his progeny, the Second Chöjé, was born in Dzamtang, it is reasonable to assume that the area had become the family base. Interestingly, as is the case with several local ruling houses in scattered parts of the Tibetan world, the family claimed descent from the royal lineage of the Tibetan imperial period.[20]

The founding of Dzamtang Chöjé Gön is attributed to Drungpa Rinchenpel (1350/1351–1435), a student of, among others, Sazang Mati Paṇchen, a disciple of Künkhyen Dölpopa. According to the *Supplement*, Dölpopa had predicted that someone born in Tsarong would be the founder Dzamtang's Jonang monastery; this was later taken to refer to Gyelmo Tsawerong, Rinchen-pel's actual birthplace, in the biographical traditions of the monastery's hierarchs.[21] This was not the first instance of the sect turning its gaze to Eastern Tibet; the *Supplement* recounts that Dölpopa had instructed one of his disciples, Jampa khawoche ("Big-mouth Jampa"), to go to Kham and there benefit the doctrine. This eastward shift is reflective of the general

FIG. 2 A recent image of the Jonangpa master Dölpopa (1292–1361) at Chöjé monastery in Dzamtang, Sichuan. (Matthew Kapstein.)

change in the economic circumstances of Eastern Tibet which had, since the decline of Buddhism in north India, made the Sino-Tibetan border Tibet's most economically viable frontier.[22] Jampa khawoche protested his unwillingness to be separated from Dölpopa but in the end went to [Dar]tsedo.[23] Similarly, Rinchen-pel was told by several of Dölpopa's disciples that the late lama had predicted that he too would proceed to Kham to work for the benefit of those adhering to the doctrine. At that, it is said, he set out for Dokham where, in 1425/1426, he founded a monastery at Dzamtang.[24]

The need for material support for the sustenance of the monastery would also appear to have been foreseen by Dölpopa. Before he dispatched Jampa khawoche to [Dar]tsedo, he told him that merchants would gather around his establishment.[25] The founding of Dzamtang's Chöjé Gön was likewise predicated on a good deal of external support. The *Supplement* comments on the elaborate structures and large sangha that the monastery encompassed from its inception, implying that even then it possessed impressive resources. The establishment of a position of stature early on would seem to have been a necessity, given the hostile relations that ensued between the Jonangpa and the local Bönpo. Among the prophecies Dölpopa made when he foretold the birth of the monastery's founder is one that predicted strife between the Jonangpa in Dokham and the Bönpo in Zungchu.[26] In fact, the *Supplement* makes reference to military action undertaken by the Jonangpa in order to drive out the Bönpo in Dzamtang so they could cement their own monastic base there. "Emanated troops" (Tib. *sprul pa'i dmag dpung*) are said to have forced the Bönpo to flee.[27] The Jonangpa presence in the region must have been strong at this time. In addition to Dzamtang Chöjé Gön, a good number of subsidiary monasteries were established in neighboring areas; Ngawang Lodrö Drakpa comments that the monastery was the first of the massive cloisters that were to spring up in Eastern Tibet, predating such well-known institutions as Labrang Trashikyi and others.[28]

Despite the absence of any mention of Dzamtang and Chöjé Gön in the standard sources for Ming history (with the one exception noted earlier), there was a certain degree of Ming awareness of Dzamtang and its significance. Dzamtang was, by dint of its location, economic strength, and influence, a major center of local power along the Ming-era Sino-Tibetan frontier, and Ming interests in Dzamtang were sensitive to its potential for helping maintain a favorable situation in a region that often proved volatile.

Recent studies produced in the People's Republic of China show that the monastery's hierarchs were recognized, through the grants of titles and gifts, by several Ming emperors over the course of the dynasty. All of these studies appear to have made use of the *Supplement*, though they are not consistent in what they take from it or from the original edicts. In any event, they adduce ample evidence that several hierarchs of Chöjé Gön were granted titles during the fifteenth and sixteenth centuries.[29] The first title we know of was given to Rinchen-pel, who was designated *hongjiao chanshi* in 1408. Some modern studies ascribe this grant to the occasion of Rinchen-pel's visit to the court of Ming Chengzu to seek support for his efforts.[30]

The next title we know to have been bestowed on the head of the monastery was that of *shanwu guanding guoshi* ("Virtuously-Awakened Initiating State Preceptor"). It was presented to the First Chöjé, Gyelwa Zangpo (1419/1420–1487), in 1472, but there seems to be a good deal of confusion among the various works describing the event. The *Supplement* is particularly egregious in the matter, placing the bestowal during the lifetime of the Second Chöjé, albeit with the correct Chinese date.[31] One modern study convincingly states that documents relating to this grant were held by the monastery, and seen by a number of people, until the period of the Cultural Revolution, when they were lost.[32] Chöjé Gyelwa Zangpo was clearly someone worthy of this sort of Ming attention. He had been a significant figure at the monastery during the last years of Rinchen-pel's life. In spite of his youth he was designated Regent (*rgyal tshab*) in accord with the instructions of Rinchen-pel and in that capacity governed the monastery,[33] while also effectively establishing patronage relationships with some of the surrounding powers. During his lifetime the prestige of the monastery increased with the establishment of subsidiary centers elsewhere.

Events during the lifetime of the Second Chöjé, Gyelwa Senggé Peljor Zangpo, give us greater insight into the dynamics that made Dzamtang of interest to the Ming. The *Supplement* as well as the Chinese sources all agree that Gyelwa Senggé was the recipient of honors from the Ming court. We know that in 1509, just after his birth (but well before he was recognized as the Second Chöjé), Ming Wuzong (r. 1505–1521) gave permission for the title of *shanwu guanding guoshi*, previously accorded to the First Chöjé, to be inherited at the monastery.[34] One recent study maintains that this action constituted the beginnings of the joint religious and political system at Chöjé Gön.[35]

The *Supplement* conflates matters and tells us that Gyelwa Senggé visited the Ming court and received the title *dashan fawang* ("*Dharmarāja*, Possessed of Great Virtue"; Tib. *tā'i hran hwa wang*) from the emperor on the eighth day of the eighth month of the eighth year of the Chenghua period.[36] The Chenghua period, designating the reign of Ming Xianzong (r. 1464–1487), lasted from 1465–1488 and is a chronologically impossible date for events occurring during the lifetime of Gyelwa Senggé. In actuality, Gyelwa Senggé was honored by Ming Shizong (r. 1521–1567) in 1550 and from him received the title *dashan fawang*.[37] The *Supplement* further states that he was presented with a variety of gifts, including an ivory seal with a crouched tiger and twisted wild yak (Tib. *ba so'i tham ga stag nyal 'brong rgur bcas*), a jade tortoise seal (Tib. *g.yang ṭi'i tham ga rus sbal bcas*), and the clothes commensurate with appointment to an official post (Tib. *cho lo las zhwa gos bcas*). The *Supplement* also quotes from what Ngawang Lodrö Drakpa describes as a document written by the emperor himself in his own hand that states "I, the Heaven-appointed king, hold this precious Chöjé as my most esteemed *mūlaguru*."[38] A recent Tibetan study that also dates the visit to 1550 gives a longer version of this pronouncement (and encloses it within modern quotes, giving the impression that it was copied from an original document): "I, the Heaven-appointed king, hold this precious Chöjé very much as my initiating and esteemed *mūlaguru*. It goes without saying that all under Heaven, the mighty and the humble, must show him respect."[39]

Additionally, the *Supplement* reports that

> He was granted, as presents from the emperor's inner treasury, the great white musical [conch] that could be heard at 500 lengths, the cymbals that make the dragon-roar of the sun, and so forth, strange and marvelous items that are necessities for [unified] religious and political [functions]; and he was appointed the highest *mahādharmarāja*, who exercises rule through the union of religion and politics over the eight great plains in Dokham, in the area of Tibet...[40]

The "eight great plains" given over to the rule of the Second Chöjé encompass territory between Dzamtang and the Zungchu (or Songpan) area, and the author of one of our modern studies, Dzamtang Tsering Samdrub, concludes that this grant further enhanced the status of the Chöjé lamas of Dzamtang as leading political figures.[41] This is a rather ideological reading, meant to emphasize Ming sovereignty over all of the territories concerned. The eight plains mentioned are identified in the official (albeit "restricted" [Ch. *neibu*]) Dzamtang place-name index as well as by Dzamtang Tsering Samdrub. That the geographical location would make them subject to substantive Ming jurisdiction cannot seriously be entertained. In fact, one of the areas named, Dziké Lhamo Dartang, can easily be linked to Dziké Nyinag Shöda, one of two places mentioned by Mugé Samten as having been offered in part, if not in whole (and along with their resident clergy), to the Chöjé of Dzamtang by the Golok chief Naktar, the son of Pemabum of the Achakdri tribe. Mugé Samten holds, moreover, that it was this presentation from the Golok that constituted the beginnings of the joint religious and political authority of the Chöjé incarnations—joint, that is, in the sense of entailing a patronage relationship with the Golok.[42] Indeed, the *Supplement* later mentions Dziké Lhamo Dartang as the site of a "Chöjé" palace.[43] The presentation was said to encompass the territories "down to" (Tib. *man chad*) Dziké Nyinag Shöda; according to an account of the Golok tribes, Naktar's father had earlier become the lord of all of Upper and Lower Dzika.[44]

During the Ming period the Chinese court was often troubled by its inability to maintain tranquility in the frontier area dominated by Songpan. Chinese sources contain numerous accounts of fighting in the area, including raids into Songpan by the neighboring Tibetan tribes. Given that this troublesome region was on the frontier, good relations with the leading figures at Dzamtang Chöjé Gön in the west were strategically useful. Apparent displays of Ming bounty and kindness were meant to facilitate such relations. From the very beginning of the dynasty, the court saw Songpan as essential for securing China's southwest frontier along the Sichuan border. This was the view of Ming Taizu when, on March 22, 1379, he ordered the "Qiang Pacification General" (Ch. *ping Qiang jiangjun*), Ding Yu, to bring order to the state of affairs there: "Songpan lies hidden among 10,000 mountains and touches on the regions of the Western Rong. How can We wish to exhaust troops with punitive campaigns so far away! And yet the barbarian chiefs repeatedly cross over and raid, bringing trouble on our border population."[45] The creation of a Pacification Commission for Songpan and Other Areas (Ch. *Songpan dengchu anfusi*) two years later did not really solve the problem.[46] The institution was meant to bring local figures into peaceful relations with the court by recognizing and co-opting the prominent positions these persons already held in their communities (we ought to view the aforementioned grant of the "eight great plains" to Gyelwa Senggé in the same light). Still, serious attacks against the Ming continued to be made in Songpan during much of the fifteenth and sixteenth centuries, by tribes and individuals who would otherwise have been considered allied with and submissive to the dynasty. These confrontations drew in surrounding tribes who, according to some records, perpetrated great slaughter and looting.[47] The outlay by the Ming, in terms of defensive expenditures, was significant, and it was only natural that the court would have viewed the maintenance of cordial relations with Dzamtang Chöjé Gön as an effective diplomatic tool.

This attitude is reflected in the *Mingshi* in the description of the formation of Ming policies toward Tibet: "At the beginning of the Hongwu period, Taizu took the disorders caused by the Tibetans during the Tang era as a warning and wanted to control them. But because of their prevailing custom of using monks to instruct them and to guide them toward good, he thereupon sent an emissary [i.e., to the monks] to widely proclaim his edict."[48] Of course, we have seen that Chöjé Gön was possessed of more than moral authority in the regions around it. Indeed, at the time the Golok chieftain Naktar bestowed his land grant, we find that the Chöjé hierarch requested and received from him several Bön lands in Dzamtang and elsewhere,[49] perhaps indicating that his influence now stretched into Songpan. But there is an even more obvious reason for the Ming court to have considered links with the leaders of Chöjé Gön advantageous, namely, that the monastery had ties to the Mongols who represented another threat to the Ming frontier. As recounted in the *Supplement*, with regard to Gyelwa Senggé:

In the latter part of the Chöjé's life the Heaven-appointed Wanli Emperor dispatched imperial envoys with presents and edicts, etc., gifts of positions; and through these showed great reverence and respect. Otherwise, the Chöjé was invited by the Mongol king Yüngsiyebü dayičing and respectfully revered as his lama; he was accorded the title "Gyelwa Mipam Gönpo" and given gifts of a seal made from fifty silver *srang* and official documents. The Mongol king Abai and King Čing Batur, etc., respectfully proffered service and the Karma lama from the Karma temple, etc., monks, students, and patrons, were very many. The many Chinese, Mongol, and Tibetan subjects of the lord of the fortress of Xining, etc., bowed respectfully and made offerings of gifts. In the north, the Mongol kings and, in the south, the king of Jang Satam in Yunnan honored him as their royal lama by inviting him and presenting him with edict documents.[50]

This brief passage suggests that Chöjé and his monastery were the ready recipients of Mongol support. Elsewhere, in his shorter Jonangpa history, Ngawang Lodrö Drakpa lists Yüngsiyebü dayičing as one of the prominent patrons of Gyelwa Senggé. Yüngsiyebü dayičing (like the other two Mongol lords mentioned in this passage) was a nephew of Altan Khan and a figure of consequence, particularly in terms Ming border policies, in that he posed a problem vis-à-vis Ming desires for stability along the Tibetan frontier in Amdo.[51] A passage in the *Ming shilu* brings up events in the year 1578/1579, when the court was supporting a monastery linked to Altan Khan and states that "Yüngsiyebü then led his tribe and, stationing himself in the temple, plundered the Tibetans; he gathered a crowd and turning his back on [Qing] hai, proclaimed himself the martial leader."[52]

Leaving aside the matter that this passage represents a Ming interpretation of events, we may minimally conclude that Yüngsiyebü dayičing's relations with important Tibetan monastic centers along the frontier would be seen as threatening to the Ming conception of a stable Sino-Tibetan frontier. This lends substantiation to much of our speculation regarding Ming contacts with Dzamtang Chöjé Gön. The monastery was a powerful center in the eastern portion of the Tibetan Plateau. It exercised its own dominion over certain territories and maintained a commanding presence to the west of the Songpan region, an area of frequent worry for the Ming. In addition, it enjoyed support from powerful and potentially troublesome figures ranging along the border. During the lifetime of the Third Chöjé, Bönri shingpa

Kunga Tupten Gyeltsen Sengé (1588–1615), the broad nature of the base of support for Chöjé Gön was very much in evidence. It was during this period that the patronage of the Tsangpa *desi* Püntsok Namgyal, which had been enjoyed by Tāranātha, passed to Chöjé Gön, and the young Chöjé received a *jasa* from the Tsangpa *desi*, designating him Dokham *dharmarāja* (Tib. *Mdo khams chos kyi rgyal po*).[53] The next Chöjé too was the recipient of a *jasa* from the Tsangpa *desi*, as well as the inheritor of the title of [*shanwu*] *guanding guoshi* from the last Ming Emperor.[54] It was the breadth of support and influence that the monastery enjoyed, more than simple notions of Ming patronage and respect for a cloister within its jurisdiction, that was the dominating factor in the court's relationship with Chöjé Gön.

The story of Kyangtsang Püntsok Dargyé Ling, or Zhangpa Gön, and the clan that supported it during the Ming further nuances this picture, as relations with the monastery were established on the basis of misinformation and misperceptions. The contacts that various Bönpo maintained with the Ming court constitute one of the more interesting elements of Sino-Tibetan relations during the Ming period. This subject has already drawn some welcome attention,[55] but has yet to be dealt with in great detail. This is in part due to the apparent silence of the major Chinese sources for the Ming period about the existence of Bönpo populations. Nevertheless, we do have materials that cast light on the role of Tibetan Bönpo communities in Ming-Tibetan relations. For our purposes, one of the more striking aspects of this story is the Ming assumption that the monastery was a Buddhist center.

One of the most difficult frontier regions for the Ming to manage was the area of Zungchu-kha (= Sharkhog), i.e., Songpan. Sources are replete with accounts of the difficulties in maintaining peace in the area. Ming Taizu's admonition of 1379 about the state of affairs there amply characterizes the problems presented by the region, and I have already alluded to the prediction by Künkhyen Dölpopa that there would be strife between the Jonang and the Bön sects in Zungchu. The powers that so vexed the Ming in that area included some who were associated with Bön, and during the course of the Ming period the court did at times endeavor to maintain good relations with prominent Bön figures in Zungchu. However, so long as such relations persisted, the Ming court often found itself in the position of having to make diplomatic calculations based in part on internecine conflicts in the region, and thus frequently became ensnared in difficulties with various local powers.

The Zhangpa were not simply local chiefs. They also served as important religious figures, receiving titles from the Ming court and presiding over a monastery linked to the clan, Zhangpa Gön, known as Shangbasi in Ming sources. As Toni Huber has pointed out, the Zhangpa monastery referred to in the modern Songpan *xian* place name guide is effectively the Kyangtsang Püntsok Dargyé Ling listed by him among the Bön monasteries reestablished in Zungchu since 1980.[56] The monastery was originally founded in 1290 by Kyangtsang Lama Sönam Zangpo, but it seems to first appear in Chinese sources only in Ming-era records.

The earliest mentions of the Zhangpa clan in Ming sources are not very propitious, but rather they highlight one of the more serious obstacles to Ming efforts to maintain good relations with the region: official incompetence. The first mention of the Zhangpa describes the trouble caused by a figure named Zhangpa Lodrö Gyeltsen.[57] According to a *Ming shilu* entry for January 7, 1440, Zhao De, the Grand Defender for Songpan and Regional Military Commissioner (Ch. *zhenshou Songpan du zhihui shi*), memorialized that

> Zhangpa, a Tibetan brigand of the Trimön [Ch. Qiming] tribe,[58] gathered his group, blocked the roads, and plundered grain. Moreover, he carved a message into wood setting a date for his attack on the town. Troops captured him and held him and others, a total of seventeen people. The bandits scattered. His younger brother, "Little Zhangpa" [Ch. Xiao Shangba] gathered them at the passes of Pujiang and Xintang, occupied strategic points, looted and burned the Guihua relay post, and the forts of Beiding and Pujiang. He fought against and wounded soldiers; his power has grown and spread. I request the raising of a large army to wipe him out.[59]

Zhao De's request was sent to the Ministry of Revenue (Ch. *hubu*) and the Ministry of War (Ch. *bingbu*) for consideration, and was approved. A force of more than 20,000 was put together and sent out, however, a *shilu* entry for January 8, 1440, just one day later, records a stark reversal of the initial evaluation of the situation. According to this entry, imperial orders were sent out to Zhao De stating that

> Earlier you memorialized that the Tibetan brigand Zhangpa had rebelled; recently it has been said that he is not a rebel. However his tribesmen had blocked roads and plundered grain. But you then did not satisfactorily defuse and calm things; you lured him out and took him prisoner. This had the effect of inciting his partisans

to wild abandon and looting. We believe that this explains everything. You and others have committed the offense of provoking a
rebellion. For now it will be recorded. The Regional Commander
and Commissioner-in-Chief (Ch. *zongbing guan dudu*) Li An has
already been ordered to raise a military force to wipe him out. You
and others ought to exert yourselves to the fullest extent in the
acquisition of merit so as to atone for your past transgressions.[60]

The situation had become a veritable mess. A further *shilu* entry for January 31, 1440, details three distinct policy alternatives for dealing with Little Zhangpa, which were presented to the court by Kan Lin, Commander of
the Right Battalion of Songpan (Ch. *Songpan you qianhusuo qianhu*). The
possibilities proposed were (1) forgiveness and reconciliation (Ch. *zhao*), (2)
enticement and entrapment (Ch. *you*), and (3) extirpation (Ch. *jiao*). The
first of these entailed threatening a massive military strike with the aim of
provoking fear and submission. The second involved the dispatch of interpreters along with assimilated local officials and Tibetan monks (Ch. *xianghua tuguan fanseng*) so as to gain Little Zhangpa's confidence, and thereby
set him up to be captured by Ming forces. The third called for a major military advance into the Songpan region, in order to force Little Zhangpa out
of all of his strongholds until he could finally be captured and executed. The
emperor ordered that Kan Lin be sent to meet up with Li An and Wang Ao,
the Right Assistant Censor-in-Chief (Ch. *yu qian duyushi*), who were both
at the head of the force advancing toward Songpan, so that he could discuss
the three options with them. The outcome of these deliberations and of the
affair is recorded in an informative *shilu* entry for May 15, 1440. According
to the entry:

> Once more Zhangpa of the Trimön tribe of Songpan was
> appointed "State Preceptor Who is Pure in Vows and Spreads
> Compassion" (Ch. *jingjie hongci guoshi*). In the beginning
> Zhangpa was at odds with Zhao Liang, the Grand Defender
> and Vice-Regional Military Commissioner for Songpan (Ch.
> *Songpan zhenshou du zhihui tongzhi*). Liang lured him out and
> captured him, raised troops and surrounded his monastery, plun-
> dering his wealth and animals. Because he and Zhao De, Grand
> Defender and Regional Military Commissioner (Ch. *zhenshou
> du zhihui*), had falsely memorialized that Zhangpa had rebelled,
> his younger brother, Little Zhangpa, thereupon led a large num-

ber who attacked and reduced the forts at the passes. The emperor ordered the Commissioner-in-Chief (Ch. *dudu*), Li An, and the Assistant Censor-in-Chief (Ch. *qian duyushi*), Wang Ao, to go and attack him. But then the Regional Inspector (Ch. *xunan yushi*) voiced his grievances. Ao and the others were ordered to weigh both sides. Ao arrived, released Zhangpa from prison and called for his younger brother. He fully memorialized the facts of the matter, that there was no rebellious plot and that it had all been an affair provoked by Liang and others. At that the court ordered An to station his troops nearby and to return to Zhangpa the silver seal he had received. He was to stay at Songzhou to await further orders. Little Zhangpa and others all then accepted the call. And so Zhangpa was restored to the position of national preceptor and his former territories were returned to him. Liang was executed and De was transferred to a garrison in Guangxi. Songpan was thus pacified.[61]

This *shilu* entry illuminates the incompetence and malfeasance of Ming officials in the Zungchu region. This was a recurring issue in the area throughout the Ming period. Also noteworthy is the brief reference to the title *guoshi* ("State Preceptor") held by Zhangpa Lodrö Gyeltsen. The initial presentation of the title to Zhangpa does not pass unremarked in the *shilu*. It is recorded in an entry for February 6, 1438, but there the recipient is named simply as Lodrö Gyeltsen (Ch. Luozhi'er jianzang) and is not linked to the Zhangpa clan. This was not a unique event that day. In addition to Lodrö Gyeltsen's designation as *guoshi*, another monk, Palden Yeshé, from the area to the southwest of Zungchu was likewise designated a *guoshi* (in his case "State Preceptor Who is Possessed of Wondrous Intelligence and Thoroughly Awakened" [Ch. *miaozhi tongwu guoshi*]) We are told that on this occasion both figures received letters patent, silver seals, and clerical robes interwoven with gold thread.[62]

A year after the resolution of the troubles described above, a *shilu* entry for May 28, 1441, briefly notes that Lodrö Gyeltsen and another Tibetan monk, whose name is given as Panbo yan (Bon po g.yung [drung]?), along with others, had come to court, where they offered horses as tribute and in return received, each according to his status, varicolored silks (Ch. *caibi*) and other objects.[63] Given the dearth of further information about this visit, we can not say what religious activities, if any, were performed (although it should be noted that we are dealing with a monk duly recognized as a "state preceptor"). However, a most intriguing *shilu* entry appears for June 30, 1441, just a month later, which implies that the court suddenly felt a need to learn more about Zhangpa Lodrö Gyeltsen. Thus it asked for and received a report about the cleric, which supplied the court with its first indication that the monk from Zungchu was not a Buddhist. The report came from Qi Quan, Translator-Usher (Ch. *tongshi xuban*) in the Court of State Ceremonial (Ch. *Honglusi*), who was dispatched to Songpan to investigate the situation. The *shilu* entry implies both that Lodrö Gyeltsen was visiting the court for the purpose of enlisting its support in an ongoing conflict he was having with a local lama, and that his religious position had rightfully come under scrutiny. Qi Qian's report relates that

> I first received orders to go to Sichuan and investigate the situation. I've seen that the Tibetans among the Qiming and other tribes and fortresses in Songpan and other regions dwell in scattered places. They are divided on the basis of major and minor lineages and in following either the teachings of monks or those of the Dao. For example, the *guoshi* Zhangpa Lodrö Gyeltsen and others are of a minor lineage that follows the Dao, while the *chanshi* ("Meditation Master") *Chörin (? Chuoling) and others follow the teachings of monks and are of a major lineage. Each have their own areas of authority and don't interfere with each other. In recent years Zhangpa has been engaged in a territorial conflict with Liba Lama [Tib. ? + bla ma], gathering groups of Tibetans, mutually engaging in vendetta killings and opportunistically plundering animals belonging to the military and civilian populations; so much so that border regions are not at peace. Stirring up and then calming large groups of soldiers is deeply undesirable. Now Zhangpa and *Chörin are at the capital. I ask that they be given orders to adhere to one and the same principles; and that they be commanded to administer and hold their territories on the basis of clan lineage, control the Tibetans, and not undertake mutual transgressions, so that the uncivilized peoples in the south (Ch. *manyi*) will have stern warning and the border areas will be peaceful and quiet.[64]

This passage clearly indicates that Ming relations with the Zhangpa clan were not based on the most solid of foundations. In addition to the malfeasance and ineffectiveness of Ming officials in the Zungchu area, here it becomes evident that it was only when Zhangpa Lodrö Gyeltsen came to court that he was discovered to be a Bönpo—described here, not surprisingly, as one who "follows the Dao." Even more damaging, at a court that was invested in having a positive relationship with many of the Buddhist hierarchs of Tibet, the report reveals him to the court as a figure of strife in Songpan, locked in struggle with one "Liba Lama," who was doubtlessly a Buddhist. This is made evident by the report's presentation of *chanshi* *Chörin as a Buddhist cleric and a party to the hostilities involving Zhangpa Lodrö Gyeltsen. *Chörin was a figure already known to the court; he appears with the title *chanshi* in a *shilu* entry for April 15, 1438, which recounts that he came to court presenting horses as tribute. He is also described as the *chanshi* of the Trimön and other clans, a circumstance that would make his conflict with Lodrö Gyeltsen rather internecine in character.[65] Moreover, *shilu* entries for April 16 and 27, 1441, note that he again presented tribute while on a visit to the court (a visit no doubt coinciding with that of Lodrö Gyeltsen). Given his status among Tibetan clans, it is not surprising that the Ming court sought to augment *Chörin's prestige. On July 16 the court made him a *guoshi*—the same rank held by Zhangpa Lodrö Gyeltsen—and accorded him the title *qingxiu guanghui guoshi* ("State Preceptor Who is Possessed of Immaculate Cultivation and Vast Wisdom").[66]

Following this, there are several references to the Zhangpa clan, some indicating that the Ming recognized the Zhangpa remained figures of authority in Zungchu, but others indicating that the court considered the clan something of a problem as far as sustaining tranquility in the area was concerned. On occasion, there are entries recording that Zhangpa Lodrö Gyeltsen, together with Ming officials, took part in missions designed to pacify certain unsubmissive figures in the region, described as brigands and robbers.[67] In a *shilu* entry for July 11, 1448, it is noted that garments and cash were granted to him, as well as similar gifts granted to other local officials, as rewards for the capture of some Tibetan brigands.[68] On April 10, 1449, we find Lodrö Gyeltsen using his court access to request that a certain Ming official remain stationed along the border.[69] On December 15, 1451, however, an accusatory memorial was recorded, submitted by a Tibetan official from a neighboring area:

> For some time I have felt that all the local officials within the jurisdictions of the Wei, Bao, Song, and Mao Guards and Battalions and under Zhangpa *guoshi* have been filling in registers on their own with memorials, wildly hoping for promotions and rewards,

having illicit relations with soldiers' wives, harming others in order to rise—all of it contrary to law.[70]

From this point on, the Ming court regarded the Zhangpa clan with increased suspicion. Lodrö Gyeltsen seems to have died in the early 1450s—as will be seen, he was apparently killed. On February 22, 1454, orders were sent to Chöying Gyeltsen (Ch. Chujing zhanzang), the nephew of Lodrö Gyeltsen, insisting that peace be made between the Zhangpa and the Liba clans.[71] Yet, the Zhangpa appear to have become increasingly problematic. Orders sent out from the court on February 5, 1455, to Ming officials in Zungchu reiterated fears that this feud could become a pretext for the Zhangpa to foment an uprising on the border; the officials were advised to be particularly vigilant.[72] It should therefore come as no surprise to find that the ultimate verdict of the *shilu* on Zhangpa Lodrö Gyeltsen and the Zhangpa clan is unambiguously disparaging. In an entry for October 22, 1455, we read:

> The Tibetan Zhangla [= Tib. Zhang bla?] and the *guoshi* Zhangpa were crafty in many different ways and did much damage along the western border. Fortunately Heaven saw that he was killed.[73]

Ming contact with the Zhangpa clan must be examined with the understanding that the Ming and the Jonangpa in Dzamtang had a common problem in Zungchu. For the Jonangpa, the problem was tied to their conflict with the Bönpo. Ngawang Lodrö Drakpa's history of the Jonangpa makes reference to the discord and describes military action undertaken by the Jonangpa to drive the Bönpo out of Dzamtang that they might establish their own monastic base there. We have already seen that the hierarchs of Chöjé Gön Monastery in Dzamtang received titles and gifts from the Ming, and that this munificence was undoubtedly part of the court's strategy to deal with problematic groups and individuals in the area, among whom the Zhangpa must be numbered.

That the Ming court considered itself to be working with a Buddhist monastery when it first entered into relations with Zhangpa Gön can make for an intriguing footnote in the history of Ming-Tibetan affairs. But it is also illustrative of an important aspect of the court's relations with many of the institutions in the Ming-Tibetan frontier regions. The court was an outsider—and particularly so when engaged in developing strategic political connections with religious institutions, a circumstance in which it often found itself on unfamiliar ground. Misunderstandings sometimes ensued, as in the miscalculation whereby the Zhangpa turned out to be part of the very problem the Ming were trying to ameliorate.

In other cases, such as with Drotsang Dorjé-chang, ties were more intimate. There, the hierarch of the monastery had a much closer, religiously based link with the Ming court. This kind of affiliation did not exclude the concurrence of dealings based on political utility, but the nature of the relationship was multifaceted, and unlike that of the other two monasteries discussed, contact between the court and this monastery was more substantial in both personal and material terms. In this relationship we do indeed see the element of esoteric power—the core of imperial Ming interest in Tibetan Buddhism—lurking in the background. However, with regard to Chöjé Gön and ·Zhangpa Gön, it was the more mundane concern to secure the frontier that was the primary motivation for the contacts that ensued.

NOTES

1 See Xie Zuo, *Qutansi* 瞿曇寺 (Xining: Qinghai People's Press, 1982), p. 2, which writes 'Ga'u tam for Go tam < Skt. Gautama.

2 For an expanded discussion of Gro tshang Rdo rje 'chang in the Ming period, see Elliot Sperling, "Notes on the Early History of Gro tshang Rdo-rje-'chang and Its Relations with the Ming Court," *Lungta* 14 (2001): 77–87.

3 Gu Zucheng 顾祖成 et al., *Ming shilu Zangzu shiliao* 明實錄 (Lhasa: Tibet People's Press, 1982), p. 95.

4 Lho brag is the well-known region in the southern part of Central Tibet where Gro bo lung—well known as the residence of Mar pa, Mi la ras pa's teacher—is found. See Alfonsa Ferrari, *Mk'yen Brtse's Guide to the Holy Places of Central Tibet* (Rome: Is.M.E.O., 1958), pp. 57 and 138 ("Lho Gro bo lun").

5 Skya tsa Sgom pa tshe ring, "Gro tshang gi chos srid byung rim mthong gsal me long," *Sbrang char* (1989.4): 54–55.

6 It is as Glang dkar can that he is described by Sum pa mkhan po; see Ho-chin Yang, *The Annals of Kokonor* (Bloomington, 1969), p. 29: "[T]here also appeared the Bla-ma Glang-dkar-can, who traveled by riding a white ox and seemed to be a holy man. This Bla-ma lived in places such as the Mtsho-snying-[ri]. . ." Brag dgon pa Dkon mchog bstan pa rab rgyas, *Mdo smad chos 'byung* (Lanzhou: Gansu Minzu Chubanshe, 1982), p. 170, has Sum pa mkhan po and others asserting that Sangs rgyas bkra shis was an incarnation of Glangs dkar pa, but this is clearly not the case. Cf. the Chinese translation of the *Mdo smad chos 'byung*: Wu Jun 吳均, Mao Jizu 毛继祖, and Ma Shilin 马世林, trans., Zhiguanba Gongquehu danba raoji 智观巴·贡却乎丹巴绕吉, *Anduo zhengjiaoshi* 安多政教史 (Lanzhou: Gansu Nationalities Press, 1989), p. 165, which interprets the passage in question somewhat differently.

7 Brag dgon, *Mdo smad chos 'byung*, p. 170, cites Lcang skya Rol pa'i rdo rje's comment that the surname Hai derives from Qinghai, the Chinese name for the Mtsho sngon lake.

8 Brag dgon, *Mdo smad chos 'byung*, pp. 171–172. Note that the Chinese translation omits reference to the *dishi* edict; see Wu Jun et al., *Anduo zhengjiaoshi*, p. 166. The bestowal of the title *dishi* is certainly an error, as the title, though often encountered during the Yuan, is otherwise not known to have been used by the Ming. We must also note the comments of Sangs rgyas, "Gro tshang Rdo rje 'chang gi bshad pa dri med shel gyi me long," *Sbrang char* (1981.2): p. 43, which date the invitation and visit to the Ming court to 1389; no source is cited for this date.

9 Zhang Tingyu 張廷玉 et al., *Mingshi* 明史 (Beijing: Zhonghua shuju, 1974), 330:8561. This incident is also mentioned by Henry Serruys, "The Mongols of Kansu During the Ming," *Mélanges chinois et bouddhiques* 10 (1952–1955): pp. 244–245. The area of the Handong guard (Ch. *wei*) stretched from the northern shores of the Qinghai lake up to the area of modern Dunhuang. The campaign in Handong is noted in a *shilu* entry for April 23, 1392; see Gu Zucheng, *Ming shilu*, p. 87. The targets of the campaign are described as Tibetans (Ch. Xifan), which may underscore Sangs rgyas bkra shis's influence with them. This incident recalls another situation in late fourteenth-century Hezhou (Tib. Ga chu), where the Tibetan lord "He Suonanpu" (i.e., *Ga Bsod nams) tendered his allegiance to the Ming and in turn was rewarded with recognition and power in his area. See Elliot Sperling, "The Ho Clan of Ho-chou: A Tibetan Family in Service to the Yüan and Ming Dynasties," in Paolo Daffinà, ed., *Indo-Sino-Tibetica: Studi in onore di Luciano Petech* (Rome: Bardi, 1990), pp. 359–377. Ga chu is modern-day Linxia, to the north of Bla brang Bkra shis 'khyil.

10 Gu Zucheng, *Ming shilu*, p. 95.

11 Gu Zucheng, *Ming shilu*, p. 96. Strangely, the establishment of the Xining Prefectural Buddhist Registry and Sangs rgyas bkra shis's appointment as chief are repeated in a *shilu* entry for March 28, 1397 (p. 107). Both entries also mention two similar prefectural Buddhist registries for Hezhou, one for Tibetan monks, and one for Chinese monks. Because these entries do not divide the registry created for Xining along these categories, we can assume that it was essentially concerned with the region's Tibetan Buddhists.

12 Brag dgon, *Mdo smad chos 'byung*, p. 172, citing unspecified writings of Kun mkhyen 'Jigs med (i.e., 'Jam dbyangs bzhad pa 'Jigs med dbang po) and Rje Chos kyi nyi ma (i.e., Thu'u bkwan Blo bzang chos kyi nyi ma).

13 Xie Zuo, *Qutansi*, p. 14. Sum pa mkhan po refers to Sangs rgyas bkra shis as "Karma He bla ma"; see Sum pa mkhan po ye shes dpal 'byor [=Sumpa Khan po Yeçe Pal Jor] *Dpag bsam ljon bzang* [=*Pag Sam Jon Zang*] (Kyoto, 1984), p. 346.

14 See Elliot Sperling, "Two Early Ming Missives To Karma-pa Hierarchs," in a forthcoming volume to be published by the Library of Tibetan Works and Archives in memory of Rai Bahadur Athing T.D. Densapa. In the missive Taizu proclaimed that "the Karma [pa] lama [in] the monastery of Mtshur phu abides there, sitting and cultivating himself in right practice. I believe that cultivating oneself in right practice is a fine enterprise and instruct that he sit there in safety and security; that all of the various peoples, etc., cease the instigation of disturbances; and that this be told to the officials in that area so that each of them may know it."

15 See Sperling, "Notes on the Early History," pp. 79–80.

16 Sde srid Sangs rgyas rgya mtsho, *Dga' ldan chos 'byung baiḍūrya ser po* (Xining: Qinghai People's Press, 1989), p. 339; and Brag dgon, *Mdo smad chos 'byung*, p. 172.

17 And indeed, even Ming Chengzu, the dynasty's third emperor, was in direct contact with the Fifth Karma pa, De bzhin gshegs pa, who had visited the court in 1407–1408. A master of esoteric power, the Karma pa initiated the emperor into various practices, the fruits of which were partly described by Chengzu in a missive of 1415, recounting the results of one particular session of visionary meditation. See Sperling, "Two Early Ming Missives."

18 These studies are: (1) Yu Wanzhi 余万治 and Awang 阿旺, "Rangtang Qu'erjisi jian-shu" 壤塘曲尔基寺简述, *Zhongguo Zangxue* 中国藏学 (1991.3), pp. 98–108. This article has made direct use of original imperial edicts presented by the court and quotes from the Chinese text of some of the relevant ones. (2) Rangtangxian diming lingdao xiaozu 壤塘县地名领导小组, ed., *Sichuansheng Aba Zangzu zizhizhou Rang-tangxian diminglu* 四川省阿坝藏族自治州壤塘县地名录 (hereafter Rangtang Diming-lu; Chengdu [?], 1986). I am grateful to Dr. Karl Ryavec for providing me with a copy of the relevant pages of this item. This source seems to rely at least in part on the *lhan thabs*; the latter's erroneous Sanskrit rendering of Rin chen dpal, "Rarna shri" (i.e., for Ratnaśrī) is likely what appears in Chinese here as "Ranna xiri 然那西日. (3) Yang Boming 杨伯明, "Juenangpai zongtan" 觉囊派综探, in Yangling duoji 杨岭多吉 and He Shengming 何盛明, eds., *Sichuan Zangxue yanjiu* 四川藏学研究 (Beijing: China Tibetology Press, 1993), pp. 216–251. This article draws on another one, presently unavailable to me: Yu Wanzhi 余万治 and Awang 阿旺, "Dashan fawang qu'erji ershi huofo Jiewa sengge" 大善法王曲尔基二世活佛杰瓦僧格, *Xinan minzu xueyuan xuebao* 西南民族学院学报 (1990.2). (4) 'Dzam thang Tshe ring bsam grub, "'Dzam thang du gzhan stong gi lta ba dar rgyas phyin pa'i gnas don skor gyi thog ma'i 'char snang," *Krung go'i Bod kyi shes rig* (1995.1), pp. 67–74. Note that this work, in contrast to the *lhan thabs*, sanskritizes Rin chen dpal more properly as "Ratna shri."

19 This must be a reference to the 1253 campaign against the Dali Kingdom. On this conflict, see Ed. Chavannes, "Inscriptions et pièces de chancellerie chinoises de l'époque mongole," *T'oung pao* 6 (1905), pp. 1–7; and Morris Rossabi, *Khubilai Khan* (Berkeley: University of California Press, 1988), pp. 22–28.

20 Ngag dbang blo gros grags pa, *Jo nang chos 'byung zla ba'i sgron me* (Beijing, 1992), p. 123. This volume actually contains two separate works by the author: *Dpal ldan Jo nang pa'i chos 'byung rgyal ba'i chos tshul gsal byed zla ba'i sgron me* (pp. 1–88) and *Dpal ldan Jo nang pa'i chos 'byung rgyal ba'i chos tshul gsal byed zla ba'i sgron me zhes bya ba'i gzhung gi kha skong lhan thabs brgyud rim dpal ldan bla ma gang dag gi mtshan nyid rab tu gsal ba nyi gzhon 'od snang dad pa'i pad mo rnam par bzhad byed* (pp. 89–591). A Chinese translation of the first work is available: Xu Dezai 许得在, trans., Awang luozhui zhaba 阿旺洛追扎巴, Juenangpai jiaofashi 觉囊派教法史 (Lhasa, 1993). It is the second of these texts, however, the *lhan thabs*, that provides most of our information about the Jo nang pa in 'Dzam thang. The first work was published earlier by itself in reproduced blockprint form (Delhi, 1983). A fuller print of it, accompanied by a *Jo nang pa bstan rtsis* by the same author entitled *Thub bstan snga phyi'i dar tshul la nyer mkho'i legs bshad kyi cha*, was published later as the first

volume in a projected reprinting of the *gsung 'bum* of Ngag dbang blo gros grags pa, *'Dzam thang mkhan po Blo gros grags pa'i zhabs kyi gsung pod dang po Jo nang bstan rtsis dang chos 'byung* (Dharamsala: Library of Tibetan Works and Archives, 1993). Although these are all twentieth century works, it is clear from Ngag dbang blo gros grags pa's comments (pp. 120 and 123) that the biography of the Second Chos rje he provides in the *lhan thabs* was compiled via reference to Rgyal ba seng ge's own auto-biographical writings and the biography composed by his nephew. These works, if still extant, are yet to surface.

21 For Dol po pa's prediction, and the birth of Rin chen dpal, see Ngag dbang blo gros grags pa, *Jo nang chos 'byung*, pp. 104–105. Rin chen dpal's biography is covered on pp. 104–112.

22 See Elliot Sperling, "The Szechwan-Tibet Frontier in the Fifteenth Century," *Ming Studies* 26 (1988), pp. 37–55.

23 Ibid., p. 103.

24 Ibid., pp. 107–108. The name by which we now know the monastery, "'Dzam thang chos rje dgon," seems clearly to derive from its function as the seat of the Chos rje incarnations. Ngag dbang blo gros grags pa, *Jo nang chos 'byung*, p. 112, notes that when the First Chos rje, Rgyal ba bzang po, came to 'Dzam thang in his youth (which must have been just after the monastery's founding), he went to "'Dzam thang Bsam 'grub nor bu'i gling." The name of the monastery's site when rendered literally is "The Plain of Jambhala" (Tib. *'Dzam lha'i thang* [i.e., Dzam bha la>'Dzam lha]), p. 107. Yang Boming, "Juenangpai zongtan," p. 229, links the place name to the founding of the monastery and Rin chen dpal's sense that the sect would materially prosper here (Jambhala being the well-known epithet for the "God of Wealth"). This, however, is clearly an anachronistic interpretation, since we have seen that the name "'Dzam thang" was known to the Ming court by 1375, at least.

25 Ngag dbang blo gros grags pa, *Jo nang chos 'byung*, p. 103.

26 Ngag dbang blo gros grags pa, *Jo nang chos 'byung*, p. 104. Zung chu is, of course, the area of modern Songpan.

27 Ibid, pp. 107–108.

28 Ibid., p. 111.

29 See footnote 18. Yu Wanzhi and Awang, "Rangtang Qu'erjisi jianshu," make use of original imperial edicts presented by the court and quotes from the Chinese text of some of the relevant ones.

30 Yang Boming, "Juenangpai zongtan," p. 229. *Rangtang Diminglu*, p. 81, has Rin chen dpal receiving a "rescript" (Ch. *zhizhao*) from the emperor, but dates the event to 1419. 'Dzam thang Tshe ring bsam grub, "'Dzam thang du gzhan stong," p. 71, mentions the grant of the title but not the trip to court, while the *lhan thabs* is wholly silent about Ming contact with him. The most complete account of the event is given by Yu Wanzhi and Awang, "Rangtang Qu'erjisi jianshu," p. 99. Although they don't mention a visit to court, they quote the Chinese text of the actual document (held at the Southwest Normal University in Chengdu). They further note that the Chinese and Tibetan texts of the document render Rin chen dpal's name as "Snang bzhi Rin chen seng ge" (Ch. Nangri Lingzhan xing). This, they posit, must have been another of his names.

31 Ngag dbang blo gros grags pa, *Jo nang chos 'byung*, p. 126.

32 Yu Wanzhi and Awang, "Rangtang Qu'erjisi jianshu," p. 100. Yang Boming, "Juenangpai zongtan," p. 230, has Rgyal ba bzang po receiving a letter and seal from Ming
Yingzong (r. 1435–1464) in 1445, but *Rangtang Diminglu*, p. 81, is particularly mud-
dled, giving the same year, but dating the bestowal to the eighth year of the Chenghua period, when in fact 1445 was the tenth year of the Zhengtong period. Both
works also mention a later presentation of a seal and a letter (but not in conjunction
with the bestowal of a title), the former dating it to 1472 (i.e., the actual year the title
in question was presented), and the latter to 1475.

33 Ngag dbang blo gros grags pa, *Jo nang chos 'byung*, p. 113.

34 Yang Boming, "Juenangpai zongtan," p. 230; and 'Dzam thang Tshe ring bsam grub,
"'Dzam thang du gzhan stong," p. 71–72.

35 'Dzam thang Tshe ring bsam grub, "'Dzam thang du gzhan stong," pp. 71–72.

36 Ngag dbang blo gros grags pa, *Jo nang chos 'byung*, p. 126.

37 Yu Wanzhi and Awang, "Rangtang Qu'erjisi jianshu," p. 101; and 'Dzam thang Tshe
ring bsam grub, "'Dzam thang du gzhan stong," p. 72.

38 Ngag dbang blo gros grags pa, *Jo nang chos 'byung*, p. 126: *Bdag gnam skos rgyal pos
kyang Chos rje rin po che 'di nyid rtsa ba'i bla ma ches mchog tu 'dzin pa yin.* Yu Wanzhi
and Awang, "Rangtang Qu'erjisi jianshu," p. 101, provides similar wording in Chinese and takes note of the seals and other presents.

39 'Dzam thang Tshe ring bsam grub, "'Dzam thang du gzhan stong," p. 72: *Bdag gnam
bskos rgyal pos kyang Chos rje rin po che 'di nyid spyi bo dbang bskur ba ches rtsa ba'i bla
ma mchog tu 'dzin pa yin/ gnam 'og gi mi drag zhan kun nas gus bkur byed dgos smos
ji dgos/.* Commenting on the sources for this encounter with the emperor, 'Dzam
thang Tshe ring bsam grub states that there are a number of traditions concerning the
date of the Second Chos rje's visit to Beijing, making it difficult to fix. He ultimately
accepts the date of 1550, basing himself on unspecified oral and written sources.

40 Ngag dbang blo gros grags pa, *Jo nang chos 'byung*, p. 126: *gong ma'i nang mdzod nas
rol chen dkar mo'i rgyang grags dang sil snyan nyi ma 'brug grags sogs dngos rdzas khyad
mtshar ba chos srid la nyer mkho'i rigs rgya che ba'i legs skyes dang bcas te Bod phyogs
Mdo khams kyi thang chen brgyad la chos srid zung 'brel gyis mnga' dbang bsgyur ba'i
bla med chos kyi rgyal po chen por mnga' gsol...*

41 'Dzam thang Tshe ring bsam grub, "'Dzam thang du gzhan stong," pp. 72–73.

42 Dmu dge Bsam gtan, *Rje Dmu dge bsam gtan rgya mtsho mi 'jigs dbyangs can dga'
ba'i blo gros dpal bzang po'i gsung 'bum* (Xining: Qinghai People's Press, 1997), vol.
3, p. 304. The "eight great plains" named in the *lhan thabs* are: 1) Rnga ru ru thang,
2) Skong gser zha thang, 3) 'Dzi ka'i lha mo dar thang, 4) Smra se le thang, 5) Mi
nyag gser thang, 6) Gser sgo rgan thang, 7) Pho dre'i bye ma'i thang, and 8) Pā la rje
mo'i thang. They are also so named in *Rangtang Diminglu*, pp. 81–82; Yang Boming,
"Juenangpai zongtan," p. 232, however, gives number 2 as Skong gser zhwa thang, 5 as
[Mi nyag] Gser bye thang, and 7 as Phe dre'i bya ma'i thang; and 'Dzam thang Tshe
ring bsam grub, "'Dzam thang du gzhan stong," p. 72, gives number 2 as Skong gser
zhwa thang, 3 as Dzi ka'i lha mo dar thang, 5 as Mi nyag gser bye thang, 6 as Gser rgod
rgan thang, and 7 as Pho dri'i bye ma'i thang. Their locations are all provided in these
works; they spread over the areas of modern Rnga ba, 'Dzam thang, Mgo log, 'Bar
khams, and Gser rta. The third of these plains, 'Dzi ka'i lha mo dar thang (located in
the 'Dzam thang region), is no doubt the same as or part of 'Dzi ska'i myi nag shos

mda', the area that Dmu dge Bsam gtan says was presented by Nag thar to the Chos rje. The other area mentioned by Dmu dge Bsam gtan is named Bsi mda', the presentation of which was occasioned by the completion of a handwritten sixteen-volume gold *Prajñāpāramitā* (Tib. *gser 'Bum po ti bcu drug ma*). The dates for the presentation by Nag thar are somewhat vague. However, since according to Don grub dbang rgyal and Nor sde, *Mgo log lo rgyus deb ther* (Xining: Qinghai People's Press, 1992), p. 126, Nag thar's son Karma bkra shis became the tutor to the Tenth Karma pa, Chos dbyings rdo rje (1604–1674), we can reliably place Nag thar in the late sixteenth century, in spite of the same text's earlier statement that Karma bkra shis was born in the twelfth *rab byung* cycle; given the dates for the Tenth Karma pa, this is probably an error for the tenth *rab byung*. The same work (p. 128) also records the presentation of 'Dzi ska'i myi nag shos mda' and Bsi mda' to the Chos rje. The works by Dmu dge Bsam gtan and by Don grub dbang rgyal and Nor sde rely on Gyi lung Bkra shis rgya mtsho and Gyi lung Thugs mchog rdo rje, *Bod mi bu gdong drug gi rus mdzod me tog skyed tshal* (Xining: Qinghai People's Press, 1991), p. 58, as their source for Nag thar's presentation (Don grub dbang rgyal and Nor sde [p. 128] give the title *Bod mi bu gdong drug gi rus mdzod padma dkar po'i skyed tshal*, but it seems clearly to be the same text).

43 Ngag dbang blo gros grags pa, *Jo nang chos 'byung*, p. 134. This mention occurs in the biography of the Fourth Chos rje, Grags pa 'od zer. His exact dates are uncertain, but the reference must relate to the events around his recognition, in the early seventeenth century, since the Third Chos rje is assumed to have died in 1615 (see note 53, below, concerning his dates).

44 Gyi lung Bkra shis rgya mtsho and Gyi lung Thugs mchog rdo rje, *Bod mi bu gdong dru*, p. 50. The lineage of the A lcags 'bri tribe is recounted in this work on pp. 26–85.

45 Gu Zucheng, *Ming shilu*, p. 48. Cf. Zhang Tingyu, *Mingshi*, 311:8024.

46 Gu Zucheng, *Ming shilu*, p. 57. The pacification commission was established on February 3, 1381.

47 For a general summary of the problems in the Songpan area, see Zhang Tingyu, *Mingshi*, 311:8025–8031.

48 Zhang Tingyu, *Mingshi*, 331:8572.

49 Gyi lung Bkra shis rgya mtsho and Gyi lung Thugs mchog rdo rje, *Bod mi bu gdong drug*, p. 58.

50 Ngag dbang blo gros grags pa, *Jo nang chos 'byung*, p. 127: *de lta bu'i Chos rje 'di'i sku tshe'i smad tsam la gnam skos gong ma wan li nas kyang gser yig pa btang ste legs skyes 'ja' sa sogs kyi las ka gnang sbyin dang bcas pas brtsi bkur che ba mdzad/ gzhan yang Chos rje 'di nyid Sog po'i rgyal po Yongs shu'i bu dus bying gis gdan 'dren zhus te gus pas bla mar legs bkur mdzad nas Rgyal ba mi pham mgon po zhes pa'i mtshan gsol zhing dngul srang lnga bcus legs bskrun tham ga dang bka' yig sogs kyi gnang sbyin mdzad/ Sog rgyal A sbal dang/ Be thu rgyal po chin rgyal sogs kyis kyang gus bkur bcas kyis zhabs tog legs po byas nas nang so Karma lha khang gi Karma bla ma sogs grwa slob yon bdag kyang cher mang/ Zi ling mkhar bdag sogs Rgya Sog Bod kyi che dgu 'bangs sde mang pos kyang gus 'dud zhus shing skyes 'bul mdzad/ Byang phyogs Hor gyi rgyal po dang/ Lho phyogs Yun nan 'Jang sa dam rgyal po dag gis gdan 'dren gyi sgo nas dbu blar bkur te bka' yig sogs kyi 'ja' sa gnang/.* The identification of the Mongol figures

is slightly problematic but ultimately seems resolvable. Yongs shu'i bu dus bying can only refer to Yüngsiyebü dayičing, the *dayičing* of the Yüngsiyebü tribe and a nephew of Altan Khan. He is described by Henry Serruys, *Genealogical Tables of the Descendants of Dayan Qan* ('S-Gravenhage, 1958), pp. 129–130, wherein his name is given as Engkeder. Be thu rgyal po chin rgyal would seem to be a convoluted rendering of Čing Batur, likewise a nephew of Altan Khan (but the son of a different brother), who is described by Serruys, pp. 122–123. A sbal is most likely Čing Batur's nephew, Abai, discussed by Serruys, p. 123. Though party to tribute relations with the Ming, these figures still remained problematic for China to varying degrees.

51 Henry Serruys, *Genealogical Tables*, p. 84.

52 Gu Zucheng, *Ming shilu*, p. 1187.

53 Ngag dbang blo gros grags pa, *Jo nang chos 'byung*, p. 133; and Yu Wanzhi and Awang, "Rangtang Qu'erjisi jianshu," p. 103. The latter article provides the dates for the Third Chos rje's life; they are not mentioned by Ngag dbang blo gros grags pa.

54 Ngag dbang blo gros grags pa, *Jo nang chos 'byung*, p. 136.

55 See Roger Greatrex, "Bonpo Tribute Missions to the Imperial Court (1400–1665)," in Helmut Krasser et al, *Tibetan Studies*, vol. 1 (Vienna: Verlag der Österreichischen Akademie der Wissenschaften, 1997), pp. 327–335.

56 Toni Huber, "Contributions on the Bon Religion in A-mdo (1): The Monastic Tradition of Bya-dur dGa'-mal in Shar-khog," *Acta Orientalia* 59 (1998), pp. 182–183; and e-mail communication, May, 3, 2001. The Chinese transcription "Shangbasi" is today commonly given as Shanbasi; see Songpanxian diming lingdao xiaozu 松潘县地名领导小组, ed., *Sichuansheng Aba Zangzu zizhizhou Songpanxian diminglu* 四川省阿坝藏族自治州松潘县地名录 (hereafter *Songpan Diminglu*; Chengdu [?], 1983), pp. 112–114. This same place name guide renders Shanba in Tibetan as Bsam pa, parenthetically giving Zhang tshang as another Tibetan form of its name. It is this latter form (transcribed in modern Chinese in the Songpan Diminglu as Xiangzang) that is reflected in the Chinese transcription Shangba (< Tib. Zhang pa) in Ming sources. Indeed, the Songpan Diminglu states that Shangba reflects the original name for the local chiefs. Phonetically, of course, one can see that it is not a great leap to go from Shangba to Shanba.

57 His name is found transcribed into Chinese as Shangba Luozhier jianzang in a *shilu* entry for May 28, 1441. See Gu Zucheng, *Ming shilu*, p. 404.

58 On Khri smon as the Tibetan form for the Qiming of Chinese sources, see *Songpan Diminglu*, p. 118. Today the town of Khri smon is located on the west side of the Zung chu river (Ch. Minjiang), just a short distance from the town of Shanba. See the map attached to *Songpan Diminglu*. The history of the Shangpa and Qiming fortresses (Ch. *zhai*) during the Qing period are described very briefly in Gong Yin 龚荫, *Zhongguo tusi zhidu* 中国土司制度 (Kunming: Yunnan Nationalities Press, 1992), pp. 196–197.

59 Gu Zucheng, *Ming shilu*, pp. 383–384. The Xintang pass lies about two-thirds of the way on the main road that runs south from modern Songpan to the town of Minjiang. The town of Minjiang itself is the former Guihua, mentioned in this passage, to the south of which lies the Beiding pass, no doubt the site of the Beiding fort also mentioned here; see *Songpan Diminglu*, p. 63, and note the Tibetan equivalents Gdong sna and Dong sna given for Minjiang. Pujiang was just south of Beiding; see

Tan Qixiang 谭其骧, *Zhongguo lishi dituji* 中国历史地图集 [=*The Historical Atlas of China*] 7 (Beijing: Cartographic Publishing House, 1982), pp. 62–63.

60 Gu Zucheng, *Ming shilu*, p. 384.

61 Gu Zucheng, *Ming shilu*, p. 391. Cf. Zhang Tingyu, *Mingshi*, 331:8027.

62 Gu Zucheng, *Ming shilu*, p. 372.

63 Ibid., pp. 404–405.

64 Ibid., p. 407.

65 Ibid., p. 373. Here Khri smon is transcribed with a slightly different character.

66 Ibid., p. 408.

67 See the *shilu* entries for February 17, 1442, and May 31, 1444, in Gu Zucheng, *Ming shilu*, pp. 412–413 and 441–442.

68 Ibid., p. 501.

69 Ibid., p. 512.

70 Ibid., pp. 535–536. The areas mentioned in this entry are all in the general vicinity of Zung chu. See Tan Qixiang, *Zhongguo lishi dituji*, pp. 63–64.

71 Gu Zucheng, *Ming shilu*, p. 556. Liba is here transcribed differently than in the previous mentions.

72 Ibid., p. 561.

73 Ibid., p. 567.

5: The "Reverend Chinese" (*Gyanakpa tsang*) at Labrang Monastery

Paul Nietupski

Introduction

URING THE EARLY eighteenth century central Tibet was experiencing political chaos, while, in the region of Amdo, the fortunes of the Mongols were declining, the Manchu imperial vision in China was expanding, and slightly later, Muslim power began to increase. It was at this time that Labrang Monastery, situated in modern Xiahe County in southern Gansu province near Qinghai and northern Sichuan, became an influential Tibetan institution. Over the years it emerged as a bastion of Tibetan politics and culture, as well as a conduit for the circulation of Buddhism between Tibet, China, and Mongolia.

Tibetans from Labrang established a strong presence in major Chinese centers like Beijing and Wutai shan, as well as throughout Mongolia, and they also administered control over a large number of local religious communities in Gansu, Qinghai, and Sichuan. The Manchu imperial government endorsed and made donations to Labrang and other regional monasteries as expressions of political diplomacy and Buddhist piety. Interrelations between Tibetan teacher-diplomats and the Qing emperors and the court served both religious and political purposes, as did Tibetan Buddhist involvement in local communities. The history of Buddhist exchange between Tibet and China during this period of regional instability reveals inter-ethnic cooperation, conflict, and survival.

Interaction and ideological exchange between Tibet and China that originated at Labrang Monastery reflect both its location on the frontier between ethnic Tibet, China, and Mongolia and the period of its establishment during an especially volatile age. Of the many examples of the passage of Buddhist ideas from Labrang to China, one of the most obvious is found in the institution of a lineage of so-called *Gyanakpa* lamas (*bla ma*), ethnic Tibetans from Labrang who taught in China and so were given the title *Gyanakpa*, or "Chinese."[1]

The practice of designating Tibetan lamas "Chinese" began prior to the 1709 founding of Labrang. In 1682, in Lhasa, Lubum Lodrö Gyatso—the first teacher in what became one of the many lineages of incarnate lamas that eventually developed at Labrang—was assigned the post of minister of the Tibetan government, that of the Ganden throne holder (*Dga' ldan khri pa*). As many of his successors in Lhasa and at Labrang Monastery would later do, he soon traveled to Mongolia and Beijing to serve as an emissary of the Tibetans and Tibetan Buddhism. The kinds of activities in which he and later "Chinese" Tibetans were engaged, the content of their teachings, their political involvements, their audiences, and their impact on inter-ethnic relations are the subject of this chapter.

The nature of the ongoing transmission of Buddhism from Labrang to China can be seen both in the history of Labrang's social and political development and in the respective ideological frameworks of Tibetan and Chinese societies. While Chinese civilization exerted a strong influence, the extent to which the Qing had uniform and consistent ideological, political, and military control of the Labrang area and other border lands was minimal, when it existed at all, and their effective infrastructures were intermittent at best. Qing frontier policies varied from place to place, were subject to change, and not necessarily controlled by the central government.[2] Moreover, the vision and rhetoric of empire were sensitive subjects for the Qing emperors and their successors. At the time of Labrang's founding, the Manchu leaders were undergoing a redefinition of their internal politics and foreign policies, reformulating ethnic, political, and social self-identity[3]—from Ming Han to Manchu to Han—in a world that was being increasingly divided into empires by European colonial powers.[4] The Qing were not unaware of, or isolated from, global concerns, and were thus very self-conscious of their position and the standing of their new empire.

The Qing vision of empire, their uneven exercise of dominion, and the turmoil in Tibet and China were significant factors of the political environment in which the careers of the Gyanakpas flourished, and an accurate picture must portray the dynamism of the interactions between the various parties. The roles, motives, and impact of these Tibetan teachers will be better understood if it is kept in mind that "in the early modern Qing empire, neither identities nor territorial boundaries necessarily conformed to twentieth-century conceptions."[5] In this context Buddhism could serve as a vehicle for diplomacy. It is thus problematic that many primary Chinese and Tibetan sources as well as numerous secondary studies are prone to describing the Qing Chinese empire as a homogenous, unitary whole, even when they record details that contradict this notion. In fact, during the Kangxi, Yongzheng, and Qianlong periods, the Labrang Tibetans maintained autonomy and a distinctive ideology.

The founding of Labrang and the functions it served had their basis in the central Tibetan religious imagination. Tibetan sources elaborately detail the prophecies and fortuitous religious circumstances surrounding the founding of the monastery, which coincided with the three-hundred-year anniversary of Tsongkhapa's founding of Ganden Monastery in 1409.[6] Labrang grew in size and reputation and became one of the largest and most important monasteries in Tibetan history.

The Tibetan community surrounding Labrang benefited from both an ideological and tangible frame of reference, in that Labrang localized the hierarchies that defined their relationships, both human and divine. This resonated among the local Chinese, who also functioned in a world populated by deities and spirits of varied description. Although the Chinese religious context was different from the Tibetan, it could easily accommodate components of Tibetan religion, as the Gyanakpas were surely aware. These Tibetan teachers would also have understood that, as was the case in Tibetan politics, Chinese political decisions, no matter how mundane or pragmatic, were fueled or at least influenced by their religious sensibilities.[7] In both China and Tibet, politics and religious ideology could not be disimbricated. The very broad sense of being Chinese was further complicated by the fact that the Qing "Chinese" emperors were in fact not Han Chinese like their Ming predecessors at all, but Manchus, who struggled to retain their Manchu identity and ideology while at the same time gradually adopting Chinese traditions.[8] The presence of Tibetan Buddhists added to this complexity. The extent to which the Chinese and Mongol leaders were genuinely interested in the religious components of Tibetan Buddhism, or were trying to manipulate Tibetan Buddhism for political leverage, cannot be determined definitively. Likewise, the agendas of the Tibetan lamas remain uncertain. Nevertheless, their political effectiveness can be seen in the enduring stability of their relationships with the Chinese court, and their religious effectiveness is shown by the support given to Tibetan institutions by the court and the general public. This support provided a measure of Chinese and local involvement in Tibetan Buddhism, yet was requisite for the religious and political work of the Gyanakpas.

The Origin of Labrang and the Gyanakpa Lamas

One of the first Gyanakpa lamas, the above-mentioned Ganden Throne-Holder Lubum Lodrö Gyatso, who was given the title Gyanakpa in 1682, was a contemporary of the founder of Labrang Monastery, Jamyang Zhepa (1648–1721). Given the contact between these two individuals, it is reasonable to assume that the politically astute Jamyang Zhepa was cognizant of Chinese power while in Lhasa as well as later when he returned to his Amdo homeland, where his support was essential for the success of the Labrang Gyanakpas.

Jamyang Zhepa's education was typical for advanced Tibetan scholars, but his actual role in politics is more elusive.[9] It is clear that during his long career in Lhasa, he gradually rose to political prominence, and in 1697 participated in the ordination ceremony of the Sixth Dalai Lama Tsangyang Gyatso (1683–1706), which was led by the Paṇchen Lama at Trashilhünpo in Shigatse. He soon became abbot of Gomang College at Drepung Monastery in 1700, an important political and religious post.

After the Sixth Dalai Lama rejected his position in 1702, Lhazang Khan, the Khoshot Mongol leader in Lhasa, clashed repeatedly with the Regent Sanggyé Gyatso. The Regent attempted to murder Lhazang Khan in 1703 and again in 1705. Luciano Petech notes that Jamyang Zhepa intervened on both occasions on behalf of Lhazang Khan, who in 1705 had the Regent executed,[10] and later, in 1706, had the Sixth Dalai Lama forcefully removed.[11] When Lhazang Khan subsequently went on a rampage in Lhasa, it was none other than Jamyang Zhepa who restrained him. The result of all of these machinations between the Tibetans, Mongols, and Manchus was that Lhazang Khan managed to alienate everyone—the central Tibetan nobles and monastic authorities, the Mongol chiefs in Kokonor, who had remained loyal to the Sixth Dalai Lama,[12] and the Manchus. He subsequently installed, with the Paṇchen Lama's support, his own choice for the Seventh Dalai Lama, Mönpa Pekar Dzinpa, who may have been Lhazang's own son, Ngawang Yeshé Gyatso (b. 1686).[13] Meanwhile, the Tibetan religious authorities, including Jamyang Zhepa, identified their own Seventh Dalai Lama (b. 1708) in Litang. Having lost his central Tibetan support, Lhazang turned to China for help, forming an alliance with the Kangxi Emperor (1661–1722), who was concerned about the Zunghar Mongols in the Ili valley west of the Kokonor region. Kangxi initially supported the Seventh Dalai Lama chosen by Lhazang, the Paṇchen Lama, and the Regent in the hope of securing an advantage against the Zunghars, and in 1707 he sent a Chinese envoy to Tibet.[14] During this

time, Jamyang Zhepa was beginning to accumulate political power in central Tibet, allying himself with the Mongols in central Tibet, Kokonor, and
Mongolia.

In 1716, the Seventh Dalai Lama Kelzang Gyatso, the Tibetans' candidate,
who by now was also supported by the Emperor Kangxi, was escorted to
Amdo and Lhasa by a retinue that included Cagan Danjin (Erdeni Jinong, d.
1735) of the Kokonor Mongols.[15] Finally, the Kokonor Mongols, with Manchu support, invaded central Tibet in 1717; in 1718 the Kokonor Mongols,
including Cagan Danjin and Lubsangdanjin, were decorated by the Manchus for their efforts, but were not allowed control over the government later
formed in Lhasa in 1720. In 1719 Kelzang Gyatso was officially recognized as
the Seventh Dalai Lama and in 1720 he was enthroned. Jamyang Zhepa had
left the troubles in Lhasa behind him in 1709, but moved into an equally, or
perhaps even more, complicated political environment, which found him in
very close proximity to Chinese and Manchu authorities. Jamyang Zhepa's
motives for returning to Amdo can be interpreted as a political strategy and
a survival tactic. For the next twelve years, from 1709 until his death in 1721,
he worked to build Labrang Monastery with the support of Amdo Mongols
and Tibetans, and with the acquiescence of the Manchus.

Labrang and the Border Politics of Amdo[16]

There are good reasons to consider Tibetan involvement with China during this period as primarily political, with Buddhism applied as a diplomatic
means to facilitate good relations. Similarly, Manchu and Chinese interest
in Tibetan Buddhism may have been mainly a matter of policy designed to
appease the Tibetans and Mongols, and even to divide Mongol loyalties.[17] In
1717 and 1718, the Zunghar Mongols, endorsed by Kangxi, attacked Tibet
and Lhazang. In the aftermath of the bloody defeat of the Lhasa Khoshots by
their Kokonor Zunghar cousins,[18] in 1721 Lubsangdanjin and Cagan Danjin
left Lhasa and returned to Kokonor and Labrang. In 1722, Yongzheng, the
new Qing Emperor, decided not to fulfill the promise made to the Kokonor
Mongols by the previous emperor, namely to allow them to appoint a Mongol *cagan* to replace Lhazang, and instead gave power to Tibetan nobles. In
reaction to this broken promise, Lubsangdanjin and Cagan Danjin decided
to resist the Chinese with force.[19] When Cagan Danjin later decided to
back down, Lubsangdanjin proceeded alone and was defeated by the Qing
forces led by Manchu Generals Nian Gengyao and Yue Zhongqi.[20] In 1725,

he escaped to Ili.[21] Cagan Danjin's decision to dissociate himself from Lub-sangdanjin's resistance undoubtedly helped to ensure Labrang Monastery's survival, and may have also have prompted the Chinese to rebuild two of Labrang's affiliate monasteries in 1729, Serkhog and Tongkhor near Kokonor, which had been destroyed by Manchu forces in 1723.

Welmang Könchok Gyeltsen (1764–1853) and others explain that after the "rebellion" led by Lubsangdanjin, the Manchus asserted control over Tibet, and that during the period that followed the region was "collected at the feet of the Emperor [Qianlong (r. 1735–1795)]."[22] Though Amdo was at the feet of the emperor, both the Yongzheng Emperor (r. 1722–1735) and Qian-long were disciples of Gelukpa lamas, who were said to "adorn the emperors' crowns" (*dbu'i gtsug tu mchod*), and with whom Qianlong had a patron-dis-ciple relationship (*mchod yon gyi bka' drin*).[23] In this sense, the emperors were at the feet of the lamas.

Meanwhile, the Mongols, although gradually losing political and mili-tary power, were still a force to be reckoned with, particularly in the western Zunghar homelands. The Mongols were close allies of the Tibetan reli-gious establishment and in a critical relationship with the Qing court, cre-ating a situation of shifting alliances, tentative assertions of control, cautious diplomacy, and at times bloody warfare. In the late seventeenth and eigh-teenth centuries the Qing empire was not a "homogenous Chinese element [with] . . . cultural penetration westward and south-westward . . . ," nor were Tibet, Xinjiang, and Mongolia "practically and theoretically subject to the Chinese central government."[24] In some places, such as Mongolia, the Qing were clearly a colonial and imperialist force. At Labrang and elsewhere, how-ever, the de facto Chinese policy was not one of annexation, colonization, or even inclusion of the neighboring territories; it was rather one of alliances with neighbors.[25] These alliances were intended to maintain buffers between the traditional Chinese homelands and their neighbors both near and far. The Manchus sought to keep trade routes open, leaving the internal affairs and cultures of the buffer countries to their own devices, intervening only as necessary to promote their own ends. In Joseph Fletcher's words, "Ch'ing authority was an overlay, far above the Emperor's subjects in periods of peace, pressing down on them only in times of rebellion."[26]

Despite such evidence to the contrary, Petech believed that the Kokonor Mongols and Tibetans were under localized Manchu "suzerainty."[27] In sup-port of this, Sumpa Khenpo asserted that beginning with the installation of the Xining *amban* in 1725, after Lubsangdanjin's rebellion of 1723–1724 had been quelled, "[t]he Emperor . . . brought the people of Kokonor under his power and bound the good relationship between the Chinese and Mongols with a golden cord."[28] These sources claim that the Manchus had established a solid presence in the Kokonor region, at least among the Chinese and the Mongols.

However, while there can be no doubt that the Manchus had established a presence in the region, their influence in this period was neither as extensive nor as simple as Petech, Sumpa Khenpo, and others report.[29] Contrary to their explanations, it seems that in general the Qing treated the Amdo Tibetans, Mongols, and Muslims as frontier peoples who were to be manipulated and controlled only insofar as this would further Qing interests.[30] Taxes were not the issue: "no great revenues flowed to Peking from Inner Asian dependencies. Indeed there was nothing that the Ch'ing wanted from them except peace. Strategy rather than profit—a desire to forestall the rise of rival powers—had inspired the Manchus' Inner Asian conquests."[31] This was the case at Labrang, even with Qing military action and political assignments nearby in Qinghai. Moreover, there were central Tibetan officials in Amdo until the nineteenth century, and "at least some people were paying taxes to Lhasa."[32] The Fifth Dalai Lama, well before the founding of Labrang, but influential among Labrang's eventual Mongol sponsors, "could and sometimes did order Mongol troop movements outside Tibet; he could also make peace between warring Mongol tribes, and his influence over the Mongols surpassed the influence of the Qing court."[33] Thus, Qing "control" should be understood as irregular and inconsistent, and often disrupted by the actions of its neighbors.[34] Tibetan lamas often invoked religious power and protection in their dealings with the Chinese, and Tibetan authorities of the time "enjoyed an independent authority that posed an obstacle to Qing control of Tibetan and Mongol affairs,"[35] making the degree to which the Manchus "administered" the region negligible.[36]

Moreover, the proliferation of Tibetan Buddhist monasteries in Mongolia and the Mongol support for monasteries such as Labrang was no accident. While this new support for Tibetan Buddhism may have reflected the degree of Mongol religious piety, it also suggests a desire to use the monastic infrastructure as a political instrument.[37] Thus, at the time of its founding, Labrang's bargaining position was not rendered ineffective by its engagement with the Qing. On the contrary, Labrang's *labrang* (estate) had instead nearly unlimited latitude to determine its internal policies and external alliances.

In the context of the fluctuations in Qing border relations, other groups—Tibetans, Mongols, and later Muslims—in similar fashion attempted to manipulate the Manchus to their respective advantage. All alliances between ethnic groups on this borderland were on the "inner frontier" model, "whereby the weaker party in civil war on the steppe seeks a Chinese [or other] alliance to destroy his rival."[38] This model of alliances extended to agreements between all parties, since it served the interests of the Mongols and Tibetans as much as it did the Qing.[39] The Manchus certainly had a military advantage, but the Mongols and Tibetans were able to form alliances that were causes for Manchu concern.[40] The Labrang estate managed to survive and prosper as an independent enclave in this unique borderland environment, with Gyanakpa lamas acting as diplomats in negotiations between Labrang and the Qing court. Owen Lattimore described Tibet and the Amdo region as a territorially large, inclusive realm, with great distances between population centers and poor communications, wherein "techniques of mobilizing, applying, and administering the manpower of the larger state [are] so imperfectly developed that in fact most social activity, including production, taxation, trade, administration, and war, is carried on within regional divisions of the larger realm."[41] In short, these regions were not part of the centralized Manchu/Chinese state. They lacked clearly defined Manchu/Chinese boundaries, they did not pay regular tax revenues, they did not observe Manchu or Chinese law, and, with the exceptions of temporary assignments, they were not occupied by a standing Manchu or Chinese military. Instead, Labrang and other border regions functioned as independent enclaves with autonomy developed in negotiations with their neighbors. Lattimore and others have noticed and described the Qing policy as a curious kind of diplomacy, one of non-intervention, not conquest. It was a "second-stage feudalism" in which border cultures adopted Chinese feudal lifestyles organically, providing a military buffer and a medium for communication between the imperial court and nomadic tribes and foreign cultures in the process.[42]

In his recent study of Yunnan frontier policies during the Qing, C. Pat Giersch writes that "early modern states such as the Qing, Burmese, and Siamese did not exercise the same degree of sovereignty over frontier regions as do modern nations. Few demarcated political boundaries existed between the Qing and other large states until the 1890s. Instead, at the large states' outer limits were a complex array of smaller polities, that often maintained some degree of autonomy."[43] Labrang offers a case in point; the Tibetans were the dominant ethnic group, they were hardly sinicized, retained their identity and independence, and maintained a significant and distinctive presence locally as well as in the Qing court and later Republican government. Labrang's estate developed its own infrastructure, validated and run by its network of monasteries and supported by its extended community. In

FIG. 1 General view of Labrang Monastery.

sum, at Labrang "Tibetan Buddhist monasteries became 'the de facto centralized state institution' of a decentralized nomadic society."[44] Their political influence was recognized by the Chinese and Mongol courts and local clan chiefs.[45] In this way, Labrang Monastery, along with its support community, was for all practical purposes an independent Tibetan enclave in the eighteenth and nineteenth centuries, representing itself in Beijing, in Lhasa, at the Mongol seats of power, and in neighboring communities.[46] The situation at Labrang, unique in many respects because of its well-established nature among Tibetan institutions, provided for a process of negotiation that took place between peers—the Tibetans, the Chinese, later the Muslims, and though gradually waning, the Mongols—rather than between subordinates and principals. Tibetan ethnic, religious, and political identities were recognized by the Qing and in this context the Gyanakpa lamas acted as Tibetan political and cultural emissaries.[47]

Religion

Labrang was significant as a religious institution in that it was one of the largest Tibetan Buddhist monasteries ever founded. It was the seat of numerous pre-eminent scholars and had a sizeable constituency of local Tibetan and Mongol faithful. It served as a conduit for religious contacts between China and Tibet, and as such was recognized, endorsed, protected, and fought over by the Qing emperors, Tibetan nobles, and local Mongol chieftains.[48] What was the nature of the Buddhist contacts between Tibet and China in which it was implicated? Were the Chinese emperors well-informed converts to Tibetan Buddhism (as has been often argued, concerning Qianlong in particular), or was this tradition's presence in China primarily a matter of diplomacy?

Religious beliefs and practices were key factors in the institutionalized social and political structures surrounding Labrang; and monastic bureaucracies in fact administered the community. At Labrang and elsewhere, the Gyanakpa lamas were among the most privileged of the community's monastic classes. As in central Tibet, Labrang's monastic infrastructure was supported and protected by local nobles and their communities, who in this case included local Tibetans, Mongols, and, to a lesser extent, Chinese. In return for protection and financial support, the monasteries provided pious and not-so-pious lay people with a focal point for community gatherings and marketplaces, with elaborate ritual performances and religious counsel for daily life. The Tibetan faithful, of variable knowledge and ability, went to Labrang's temples and monasteries to make offerings, meditate, pray, invoke, and pay homage, taking advantage of whatever mediums of public discourse the political and religious institutions made available. In the case of Labrang, these included public teachings, festivals, and consultations with lamas, prognosticators, and a wide assortment of monks and religious people. In short, Buddhist discourse clearly penetrated all strata of Labrang society, and the local people, from the highest social classes to the uneducated villagers and pastoral nomads, were thoroughly immersed in a Buddhist ideological orientation.[49]

Religion in China was distinctively Chinese, but as complicated and multifaceted as religion in Tibetan regions. Here one must remember that the Qing court was not ethnically "Chinese," but Manchu, despite the Manchus' great effort to assimilate Chinese beliefs and practices. Although it is unnecessary to provide here an overview of Chinese religions, the complexity of their history, or the extent of their interactions with outside influences (including Tibet and Manchuria), we should note nevertheless that Buddhism in China developed in a cultural environment entirely different from that of Tibet. For even though Tibetan Buddhism was practiced and available in the Chinese-Manchu cultural milieu, it did not penetrate all strata of society and every aspect of cultural life to the degree it did in Tibetan communities. Instead, the Chinese "folk religions" and the full range of Daoist and Confucian ideologies (along with those absorbed through historical contacts with Tibetan Buddhism and other religions over many centuries) provided the context in which Chinese Buddhism grew, as well as the background for Tibetan Buddhism in Qing China.[50] In such a setting, what accounts for the attraction Tibetan Buddhism exerted on Chinese people? It may well be that Chinese interest in Tibetan Buddhism was in fact due to the this-worldly power that both the Chinese and the Tibetans believed was made accessible by Tibetan Buddhist rituals.[51] The Chinese world was populated by a fantastic and extensive array of invisible beings that included ancestors, demons, saints, heroes, and other beings of remarkable description.[52] The Chinese and Manchu religious imagination could thus accommodate the Tibetan tantric Buddhist pantheon and system, with its medical procedures, prognostications, means for protection from and opposing undesirable forces, and other beneficial applications. It is in this light, and not with reference to the transcendent ideal of enlightenment realized over many lifetimes, that we may understand the attraction of Tibetan Buddhism to Chinese communities.

Hence, while acknowledging the diversity of Chinese religions, we may nevertheless note some fundamental differences in the motives, goals, and worldviews of the Tibetans and the Chinese. Unlike the Buddhist goal of release from the cycle of death and rebirth, the fundamental Chinese religious aspiration was focused on "knowledge of practical skills in actions," or on "activity with an immediate practical result." It is true that the Chinese sought to "master a set of practices that restructure one's perceptions and values," but the locus of this mastery and its results were situated in this world.[53] Tu Wei-ming and others have elaborated on this fundamental element of Chinese ideology in great detail. Tu shows that the Confucian tradition was not only concerned with politics but also had an active "anthropocosmic vision,"[54] arguably a vision different from that of Tibetan Buddhists. Like Buddhism, the religious dimension of Confucianism focuses on inner cultivation and social responsibility. There is also a sense of the moral perfectibility of human beings in Confucianism, but the concept of transcendental truth or reality inaccessible to humans was not a core part of Confucian thought.[55] With a primarily humanist perspective, Confucianism addresses the question of the ultimate meaning of human existence on a level that is both philosophical and anthropological, or, more accurately, anthropocosmic in nature.[56] The highest goal of humanity in this view is "in the inner resources of man anthropocosmically defined. . . . To realise humanity as the ultimate value of human existence eventually became the spiritual self-definition of a Confucian." Quoting the *Analects* 15:8, Tu argues that the search for perfectibility is confined to human life, and that "Only with death does his course stop."[57] This view is obviously quite different from that found in the doctrines of Tibetan Buddhism, and therefore held by the Labrang Gyanakpas.

Confucian thinkers were unable to detach themselves from the world; "they had to work through the world because their faith in the perfectibility of human nature through self-effort demanded that they do so."[58] Moreover, in an essay on Qing learning that addresses the subject of the ideology of the Qing court in particular, Tu describes several scholars who were known for their studies of classical texts in their efforts "to be human."[59] The famous scholar and philosopher Dai Zhen (1723–1777) "attempted to reorient the spiritual direction of his age from metaphysical speculations on the ultimate reality [of *li*] to lived experiences of ordinary people."[60] During the Qing period, the classical Confucian goal persisted. The ideal for Chinese religious followers was generally to be engaged in "the quest for self-knowledge as a way of learning to be human . . . and a deepened appreciation of common humanity."[61]

Given this orientation to life in the world and the general objectives and presuppositions of mainstream Chinese thought, Tibetan Buddhist ethical teachings, and especially those on conventional reality and karma, resonate well within Chinese ideologies. However, Tibetan Buddhists, while certainly interested in skillful action in this world, simultaneously sought a related yet transcendent objective that went beyond the dominant Chinese frame of reference. In the Tibetan Buddhist view, "[t]here is a continuity of being between the environmental qualities and inhabitants of the sublime and the gross material dimensions of the three-level world."[62] The ambitions of Tibetan Buddhism reach beyond the human body and the human realm.[63]

This brief description of Chinese religious sensibilities may serve to underscore the staggering complexity of imperial Chinese and Qing ritual and help explain the Qing imperial interest in Tibetan Buddhist tantric ritual. It also accounts for the apparent lack of widespread interest in those Tibetan Buddhist philosophies, precepts, and worldviews that are not anthropocentrically oriented. From this perspective, the Chinese were interested in Tibetan Buddhism insofar as it complemented the extensive Chinese ritual corpus they had accumulated over many centuries, derived from Buddhist, Daoist, and other religious traditions.[64]

At the same time, Buddhist interactions between Tibet and China very often served as an avenue for political diplomacy, as is seen with the Gyanakpa lamas.[65] It is fair to ask, given the nature of religious exchange between the Tibetans and Chinese, to what degree their religious activity was a form of high-level posturing and political expediency. Matthew Kapstein has noted that since the earliest period of Tibet's conversion, Chinese attitudes have exerted an influence on Tibetan Buddhism, and we may assume that Tibetan Buddhist culture has had a reciprocal impact on Chinese religions. It is often difficult to gauge, however, whether Tibetan influence in China was assimilated into Chinese religion generally, or remained restricted to isolated pockets.[66]

In interactions between Labrang and the Qing court, the Tibetan Buddhism that was disseminated from Labrang to China often involved the highest level of Buddhist tantrism, as known and practiced by the Tibetan Gelukpa order. The available sources show that highly educated teachers and especially those who were authenticated rebirths—including the Gyanakpa lamas—went from Labrang to Urga in Mongolia, and often to Beijing and Wutai shan. Manchus and Chinese may have recognized that Tibetan Buddhism was a force that could be used to control lay peoples, including the ferocious Tibetan nomads on the Chinese borders. But they were also interested in what they did not have in their own Buddhist system: a fully developed tantric system and the power it was able to bestow on individual human practitioners. The extensive tantric scholarship and rituals associated with *Anuttarayogatantra* were surely widely known to Tibetan and Mongol monks in China, but these practices had not been well-established in Chinese circles. Furthermore, the institution of reborn lamas was bizarre, foreign, and yet intriguing to both Manchus and Chinese.[67]

In addition to the adoption of Tibetan Buddhism by the court for reasons of political expediency and access to new sources of mystical power, there is evidence that Chinese persons both inside and outside of the imperial court were interested in and practiced Tibetan Buddhism.[68] Although aspects of Tibetan and Chinese religions were known and practiced to varying degrees in each culture, the average Tibetan or Chinese person's formal religious knowledge may well have been minimal. Despite this, elementary religious understandings may have been in some respects similar, notwithstanding the profound philosophical differences found at the highest theoretical levels in the practices of scholars of Tibetan Buddhist and Confucian and Daoist thought.

While it is well known that Tibetan Buddhist teachers, including the Gyanakpas, were present in the extended Qing court and in other communities in China (for instance, Wutai shan),[69] there is also some evidence that ethnic Han Chinese were sometimes recognized as reborn Tibetan Buddhist lamas (*sprul sku*), notably in the Sino-Tibetan borderlands. One of the several

Chinese scholars consulted for this research insisted that this had been the case in the greater Labrang region, though not always in monasteries directly under the jurisdiction of Labrang (i.e. not always in the Labrang estate). In the Qing Dynasty, for instance, in the lineage of reborn lamas at the Bumling (Ch. Bingling) Grottoes Upper Monastery in modern Yongjing County, in proximity to Labrang, at least one Tibetan Buddhist lama appeared in a Han Chinese family. Jamyang Lodrö (1645–1705) was born in the Yang family village of Northeast Peak near Bumling Monastery to Han Chinese parents named Yang Yucheng and Zhou Lianying. He was a remarkable child who purportedly spoke at a very early age and was soon recognized as the rebirth of Jikmé Trinlé Gyatso (1555–1625). He went on to take monastic vows and study at Sera Monastery in Lhasa. Upon returning home, he became an influential local Tibetan Buddhist teacher and political figure with close connections to the Qing court, where he served as one of Kangxi's eighteen imperial resident Tibetan Buddhist lamas. His Tibetan-born successor served as an intermediary between the Sixth Paṇchen Lama and the Qianlong Emperor.[70] Jamyang Lodrö's influence on his birthplace is still felt, as even in the present day Tibetan is the liturgical language of the Bumling Upper Monastery, though Chinese is the main colloquial language in use there. Similarly, with respect to material culture, the architecture and iconography of the region is layered, clearly showing a mixture of Tibetan and Chinese influences over the centuries.

Having illustrated some of the interactions between Tibetan and Chinese cultures on the borderlands, we may turn to the nature and extent of the connections facilitated by a shared Buddhism beyond these frontier regions. In spite of sustained political dealings, the borrowing and sharing of doctrinal materials over many centuries, and the presence of Tibetan Buddhism in some Chinese communities, it is nevertheless apparent that Buddhists in the imperial court were not generally well-informed about views central to Tibetan Buddhism. Still, Qing court officials heard teachings on Buddhist tenets and received *Anuttarayogatantra* initiations. The Manchus built temples in Beijing, Chengde, and elsewhere in China, and there were some eighteen Tibetan Buddhist teachers in Kangxi's and later in Qianlong's court. Nonetheless, it does not appear that outside of the high profile and formal demonstrations of Qing royal piety there was widespread public conversion to Tibetan Buddhism.[71] The acceptance of Tibetan Buddhism in Beijing and elsewhere in China proper occurred as a relatively isolated phenomenon, one of the many different religious manifestations of the period.

Tibetan Buddhism was not institutionalized in Qing China in the manner that it was at Labrang and in other Tibetan Buddhist communities. Alongside the evidence of Tibetan Buddhist presence in China, there is also a demonstrated insensitivity to or ignorance of customary Tibetan Buddhist beliefs, as is shown by the apparent lack of understanding of the status of Tibetan Buddhist incarnate lamas. A reborn lama, or *trülku*, is understood to be an Emanation Body (*nirmāṇakāya*) of a Buddha or bodhisattva.[72] The concept of the three bodies (Tib. *sku gsum*, Skt. *trikāya*) or aspects of an enlightened being is crucial to Tibetan Buddhism, particularly in the context of esoteric, tantric practice, wherein a sound understanding of the three-body theory and of the status of bodhisattvas is considered foundational. While the Qing emperors did acknowledge the authority of the Tibetan lamas as teachers, they seem to have resisted the full implications of the *trülku* system and so could not accept the necessity of, in Welmang's words, "seeing one's lama as a fully enlightened Buddha."[73] The Chinese, in spite of the widespread popularity of Mahāyāna teachings on and worship of bodhisattvas, seemed to have difficulty accepting these ideas. The Qing rejection of Tsangyang Gyatso's status as the Sixth Dalai Lama in 1719, and their corresponding endorsement of Kelzang Gyatso as the Sixth, not the Seventh Dalai Lama, is another indication of both their misunderstanding of Tibetan religious views and their interest in manipulating the Tibetan system.[74] This is further confirmed by the Qing attempt, in 1792, to control the selection and succession of Dalai Lamas by the use of the "golden vase" lottery system.[75] "The Gelukpa sect . . . had to give up autonomy over rebirths, whose selection now required confirmation from Peking."[76] This was a deliberate misconstrual for the sake of manipulating the foreign religion (as recent events confirm). These incongruencies show that the Tibetan adherence to and institutionalization of a system based on the belief in the intentional, verifiable, and inviolable rebirth of bodhisattvas as human beings was not in fact shared at the Chinese court, in spite of the presence there of Tibetan teachers. Whether this constitutes proof that the Manchus were interested in Tibetan Buddhism only as a political tool or simply illustrates pious Buddhists reinterpreting an unfamiliar (or uncomfortable) concept is not always clear, and several factors may well have been involved.

Whatever their motivations or interest in Tibetan Buddhist ethical and philosophical doctrines, several emperors and members of the court nevertheless received tantric initiations. They clearly respected the power of Tibetan Buddhism as a metaphysical instrument and most definitely as a device for securing political authority.[77] Those Chinese with exposure to Tibetan temples, monks, and monasteries could hear teachings, read texts if literate, and take monastic vows. They were perhaps most involved, however, through attendance at public festivals, blessings, and religious events, and through visits to Tibetan temples and monastic shrines, especially those in places such as Beijing and Wutai shan, in order to worship and invoke the blessings of the prodigious pantheon of Tibetan Buddhist deities. On the whole it appears that, while there was some genuine interest on the part of the court, scholars, and laypeople, Tibetan Buddhism was often not well understood in China. Encounters between Labrang Tibetan and Chinese Buddhists, and between military and government officials, were often if not usually precipitated by political and military events, and not by matters particularly characteristic of Buddhist practice.

The discussion of Buddhist exchanges between Labrang and China in this period would be incomplete without refering to the Mongols, often a crucial party in the relationship. Though Mongol power was in decline, in the early eighteenth century the Mongols were still able to launch successful military operations in large parts of inner Asia. At this time the "new Qing empire" had little actual control over the different groups of Khoshot Mongols to the west and east of the Kokonor region, or over Lhazang and his forces in central Tibet, and certainly not over the Zunghars west of Xinjiang in the Oxus region.

On the other hand, during these years the Mongols were not at all unified,[78] and would continue to fragment and lose their once grand empire. The Kokonor Khoshots, the patrons of Labrang, proved to be no exception to this trend toward fragmentation. In response to Qing encroachment and Mongol disintegration, Cagan Danjin, a great grandson of the Fifth Dalai Lama's supporter Gushri Khan, offered tactical sponsorship to Labrang and loyalty to the Gelukpa hierarchy, winning him Tibetan and Manchu support, and security for his followers.[79] This signals the possibility that the Mongols were sometimes exploiting Tibetan Buddhism, often via Labrang, as a means to promote social unity and as a political instrument in negotiations with the Manchus and the Tibetans. A striking difference between the Mongols and the Manchus, however, is that in addition to endorsing Tibetan Buddhism for political reasons, the Mongols were wholehearted converts.[80]

The Gyanakpa Lamas

While several of Gyanakpa lamas inherited the title from their prior incarnations, in some cases the title appears to have been used generically to refer to any Tibetan teacher who taught in Chinese communities in and around the Labrang territories or in the Chinese court, even those who were not recognized as reborn lamas.[81] There were many such local teachers, coming not only from Labrang but also from Lhamo Monastery, Zamtsa Monastery, and other monasteries in Qinghai and elsewhere. The local Chinese communities (for example, at Binglingsi/Bumling) were clearly receptive to the presence of these Tibetan Buddhist teachers and their teachings. A number of prominent Labrang lamas who served as high level tutors in the Chinese court were also given the title Gyanakpa. While the missionary activities of the local Gyanakpas is interesting in many respects, the work of the prominent emissaries to China and Mongolia was of greater political significance. Lineages of high-level Gyanakpa incarnations began several decades prior to the founding of Labrang Monastery, and I will now turn to outlining the major ones.

The first important lama to be given the title Gyanakpa was Lubum Ngawang Lodrö Gyatso (1635–1688), the forty-fourth throne-holder (*khri pa*) of Ganden Monastery, the great Gelukpa center near Lhasa. Like his successors, he was from Amdo, born near Kumbum in Tsongkha, at Minyak Tsowa Rading, and there he first entered monastic life. He soon went on to Lhasa where he completed his education and was ordained in 1661. He had considerable interaction with the Fifth Dalai Lama, became the abbot of the Gomang college at Drepung in 1665, and of both the Gyümé and Ganden Jangtsé colleges in 1673. In later years, he became famous for his interactions with the Mongols and Chinese, particularly during his tenure as the Ganden throne holder from 1682–1685.[82] At the same time, he maintained his monastic seat at the Mongol-sponsored Lamo Dechen monastery in Qinghai. In 1685, at the request of the Manchu Emperor, he first went to Mongolia, where in 1686 he brokered an agreement between two rival Mongol groups.[83] His success in Mongolia was rewarded with a title and endorsement from the Emperor Kangxi. He then went on to Beijing in 1687 as an emissary of the Fifth Dalai Lama at Kangxi's court. There he served as a Buddhist teacher to the emperor until he returned to his homeland, renewed his contacts with the Mongol nobility, and died in 1688.

His reincarnation, Lozang Tenpé Nyima, was born in 1689 near the Yellow River in Trika (Khu khe nor yul), Qinghai, to a royal Mongol family.[84] This birth had been prophecied by his predecessor, and his status was confirmed using traditional methods by Changkya Ngawang Chöden—the Monguor lama who was the first embodiment of what later became a lineage at Gönlung Monastery in Qinghai that had close ties to the Qing court—who was

then the leading figure at Lamo Dechen Monastery, and by the Nechung ora-
cle of central Tibet. In 1693, he went to Lamo Dechen, where he was given
novice vows and the name Jamyang Gyatso, and was formally recognized as
the rebirth of Lubum Lodrö Gyatso. He entered the monastery in 1696 at the
age of seven and spent the next four years there, leaving in 1701. He began
his studies of the major Buddhist philosophical and ethical works in 1701
and was reportedly an extremely gifted student, taking up the study of the
Buddhist tantras at age twelve. In 1710, the year after Labrang Monastery's
founding, he met the First Jamyang Zhepa and received a number of initiations and teachings from him. The next year, 1711, he went to Gönlung Monastery, where he studied with Changkya and others, including a number of
Mongols, eventually completing his education in the major Buddhist curriculum. He later went to nearby Serkhog, and then Kumbum Monastery,
where he engaged in further studies. These details are significant given the
strong relationship between Gönlung Monastery and the Qing court, as well
as the prominence of the Mongols in the region.

In 1714, at the age of twenty-five, in the company of a group of scholars, Lozang Tenpé Nyima went to Labrang and again met with the First
Jamyang Zhepa, a further indication connecting Labrang, the Qinghai
Mongols and Monguors, and the Qing court. After that he returned to
Qinghai with a number of prominent Mongol scholars, where he formed a
religious connection with the young Seventh Dalai Lama, Kelzang Gyatso,
who at that point was still residing in Amdo (not until 1720 did the Seventh
go to Lhasa). In 1722, the year after the death of the First Jamyang Zhepa
and one year before the death of Kangxi and the accession of Yongzheng
(r. 1722–1735), Lozang Tenpé Nyima went to Lhasa. There, he visited the
major monasteries, and went on to Trashilhünpo, the seat of the Paṇchen
lamas, where he received full ordination from the Paṇchen Lozang Yeshé,
returning home to Qinghai in 1723. These were turbulent years in Amdo
and Lhasa, the years of "Lubsangdanjin's rebellion" of 1722–1723 and the
subsequent Qing reprisals in Amdo.[85] The Gyanakpa became the throne-
holder of Chuzang Monastery in 1726, at the age of thirty-eight, a position
he held for eight years.

In 1734, at the request of the Qing court, Lozang Tenpé Nyima went to
Beijing, where he became an active member of the Tibetan Buddhist community installed there, earning the title Gyanakpa. He gave teachings on
some difficult points of Madhyamaka philosophy to the Yongzheng Emperor
and held discussions with him. He also worked closely with the second Monguor Changkya, the famous Rölpé Dorjé (1717–1786), and was given the

title *Hui wu chan shi Ganden khri pa Hutuktu* by the emperor, and was decorated along with the Tuken Rinpoché in 1735.[86] In the years between 1736 and 1740, during the reign of Qianlong (r. 1736–1795), the lamas spent summers in Chengde and winters at the Beijing palace. Beginning in 1742, together with Changkya, the Gyanakpa oversaw the translation of the Buddhist canon from Tibetan into Mongolian. He was reportedly a key figure in the 1744 construction of Ganden Jinling at the Yonghegong in Beijing and, in the following year, the establishment of its main monastic colleges (*mtshan nyid, rgyud pa, sman pa,* etc.). Over the course of his career, Lozang Tenpé Nyima also wrote texts on philosophy, monastic discipline, and tantra.[87] In 1762 he left Beijing for Dechen Monastery, where he died in the same year at age seventy-four.[88] Lozang Tenpé Nyima's long and intimate contacts, as the second Labrang Gyanakpa, with the Qing, the Monguor lamas, and the Labrang authorities provides further evidence of religio-political exchange between Labrang and the Qing court.[89]

The next Gyanakpa, and third in the lineage of the Labrang "Chinese" estate was Jamyang Tendzin Trinlé Gyatso. He was from a prominent Mongol clan in the Right Group in Qinghai, and was related to Mergan Ta'i Ching. Born in 1763, he was recognized as a rebirth of the previous Gyanakpa and enthroned at Lamo Dechen. He went to China in 1771, but died in Beijing the following year.[90]

His successor, the fourth in this lineage, was Ngawang Tupten Wangchuk Pelden Trinlé Gyatso, who was born in 1773. He was invited to the Mongol-sponsored Chuzang Monastery in Qinghai in 1777, at which time he was recognized as the *trülku* of the Labrang Gyanakpa. In 1779, he took novice vows at Chuzang and in 1780 received the preliminary ordination (*dge tshul*) at Kumbum; in the following years he stayed at Lamo Dechen and Chuzang Monasteries. In 1784 he had an audience with the Qianlong Emperor and in 1787 re-entered Chuzang Monastery, after which he went to Lhasa, returning home to Chuzang in 1789. While en route to Lhasa, he stopped at Kumbum Monastery, where he met the Jamyang Zhepa and Tuken incarnations, and affirmed the connections between Labrang, the Mongols, the Monguors, and the Manchus.[91] He was fully ordained in 1796, the year after Qianlong died. He was endorsed (*pho brang gi tham ka bla ma*) by the Jiaqing Emperor (1760–1820).

The Fifth to be recognized as a Labrang Gyanakpa was Ngawang Tupten Tenpé Nyima. He was born near Kumbum in 1816 into a family from Minyak, and soon entered Lamo Dechen Monastery. He studied at both Kumbum and Lamo Dechen. He was in China from 1826 to 1830, and then returned to Kumbum, Lamo Dechen, and Labrang. He went to China again in 1840 and died there in 1846.

He was followed by Lozang Tupten Gyatso, the Sixth Labrang Gyanakpa. Born in 1847 into a family with ties to the local religious establishment, he developed a reputation for excellent behavior and intelligence. He was recognized and enthroned at Lamo Dechen in 1851. In 1858 he went to Beijing and met the emperor, who gave him the symbols of authority: a blue crystal and a peacock feather. He returned to Lamo Dechen in 1861, was ordained in 1866 and went back to Beijing in 1874, where he stayed until 1879, when he returned to Lamo Dechen once again. Beginning in 1882 he served as abbot of Kumbum Monastery and was an active builder and renovator. He finally returned to Lamo Dechen and passed away there in 1902.[92]

The Seventh Gyanakpa was Gendün Lungtok Nyima, born in 1904 in Trika. His education and experience followed the pattern established by his predecessors, as he traveled to Beijing in 1921. In the aftermath of the fall of the Qing dynasty, however, he was met with a different audience entirely. His visit was certainly more a matter of protocol than of imperial tutelage. Despite the Labrang Mongol Prince's negotiations with the Qinghai Muslim warlord Ma Qi, the Mongols were nevertheless subject to the disfavor of the Xining Muslims, who were antagonistic to the Qinghai Buddhist monasteries. Lamo Dechen and other monasteries, along with their local revenue-generating properties, were burdened with heavy taxation and harassed by the Muslims, a conflict that culminated in the 1931 murder and decapitation of the Seventh Gyanakpa lama.[93]

The eighth in the line of the Labrang Gyanakpas was Lozang Tenpé Gyeltsen (b. 1933), who, like his predecessor from Trika, hailed from and studied at both Lamo Dechen and Kumbum. In the 1950s he was examined in Beijing and met with Mao Zedong and Zhou Enlai. He returned to become abbot of Kumbum in 1955. He visited Moscow in 1957, and in the turbulent years that followed he was imprisoned in Xining, where he died in 1961. The ninth incarnate lama of the Gyanakpa lineage was born in 1968 and remains active at Kumbum and elsewhere in Qinghai.

This lineage of Gyanakpas were the holders of one of the wealthiest and most powerful estates at Labrang. The history of their political alliances included the close relationships the Second Gyanakpa—who was educated in Amdo, not Lhasa—maintained with the noted Monguor lamas Changkya and Tuken, and through them with the Manchu court. (The Monguors themselves, situated in eastern Qinghai, were historically subject to the Chinese and Manchus, and in earlier times, the Mongols.) The Gyanakpas consolidated their position through their rapports with the leading Monguor lamas and the Qing court. These factors together testify to a unique regional confluence of ethnicity, religion, and politics. The Gyanakpa estate at Labrang in some respects resembled an honorary consular office or center for cultural diplomacy. It was located in ethnographic Tibet, with a large Lhasa-educated (or at least Lhasa-oriented) constituency, and its role was to engage Labrang's Mongol, Monguor, Manchu, and Chinese neighbors.

The vital function played by the Gyanakpas of Labrang is further underscored by the existence of a second major Gyanakpa lineage situated there,[94] namely the Dükhor Gyanakpa lineage associated with Labrang's Kālacakra College (*dus 'khor grwa tshang*). The first in this line was Dükhor Gyanakpa Ngawang Püntsok (b. 1746, d. ca. 1805), the Seventh Throne-holder of the Kālacakra Temple at Labrang. He was born in a small village near Labrang to a family of laborers and was a disciple of the Second Jamyang Zhepa, Könchok Jikmé Wangpo (1728–1791). He held several offices before eventually being elevated to the Dükhor throne. Ngawang Püntsok was sent by the Second Jamyang Zhepa to serve as the chaplain to the Takten *beile* ("prince") of the Aru Horchen clan, where he was very active in his post, later even traveling to Mongolia.[95] He clearly enjoyed an influential position during this time at Labrang and in the Manchu and Mongol courts.

His rebirth was an enigmatic individual and prolific writer, Gyanakpa tsang Jamyang Tenpé Nyima (1806–1858). He was born among the Mongols in the community of Aru Horchen, and when he was seven he was ordained by the Third Detri rinpoché, Jamyang Tupten Nyima (1779–1862), who identified him as the reincarnation of Ngawang Püntsok.[96] He taught in the land of the Left-group Khalkha Mongols, where Hubei Qinwang (Tib. Hu be cung wang) became his sponsor, and he later went to China many times and taught extensively. The relationship between this Gyanakpa, his sponsor, and Labrang Monastery is illustrative of the *labrang* system's effectiveness to serve as a community building block. His palace, Demchok Lölangtargi Tsuklakhang, and his monastery, Demotang Ganden Chökhorling, were parts of his own *labrang*, though he himself held a post, the throne of the Kālacakra Temple, at Labrang Monastery,[97] which relied on the wealth of its constituents. His palace may be seen as a kind of sub-estate within the *labrang* system.

The third incarnation in this Gyanakpa lineage, Lozang Longdöl Chöki Nyima (1859–1934), was born in Dergé, in modern Sichuan Province.[98] While the exact details of his life are not well known, his education and activities seem to follow the pattern of his predecessors, and he and his followers were much involved in the greater Labrang monastery support community. He was educated at Labrang, traveled extensively in Mongolia and China, and was identified as a prodigy by the Fourth Jamyang Zhepa. It is suggested that he played an important role in the conflicts between the local Muslims, Chinese, and Tibetans during the tenure of the Fifth Jamyang Zhepa, as brief references to him note that he was a negotiator between the Muslim Ma Qi, the Alo/Huang clan, and the Chinese. Late in his life he is said to have moved to Inner Mongolia, where his current rebirth (the fourth in the line) is reported to be located at present. The precise details of Lozang Longdöl Chöki Nyima's work and status in the late 1920s remain, however, unclear.

Conclusion

The Gyanakpa estates at Labrang Monastery were among the wealthiest in the greater monastic community. In general, the Gyanakpa lamas from both lineages had strong connections to central Tibetan Gelukpa monasteries; some, though born and raised in Amdo in the vicinity of Labrang, were educated in Lhasa. But these lamas were also associated with the Mongol and Monguor lamas at Gönlung and Chuzang in Qinghai, and through these relationships, connections were formed with Mongolian monasteries and the Manchu court. Gyanakpas from both lineages became tutors in the Qing court, and in return the two Gyanakpa lines enjoyed endorsements from the Manchu imperial and Mongol princely courts.

In addition to their religious and diplomatic work in faraway places, the Gyanakpas played important roles in local Gansu-Qinghai Tibetan, Chinese, Mongol, and Monguor communities. They contributed to the establishment of Tibetan Buddhist institutions in the Sino-Tibetan borderlands, and had followings of educated lay people and pious commoners. In effect, these Tibetan lamas were engaging in missionary activity in Chinese regions, and this was represented by their title Gyanakpa, "Chinese." It may be significant that most of the prominent figures in this region were of local origin, whose activities in their home districts may have been undertaken simply out of the sense of commitment this entailed and who owed their more widely recognized high status to the institution of successive rebirth.

The Gyanakpa lamas acted as both missionaries and political emissaries, whose purpose at court and in rural China was to encourage conversion, garner support, and promote Labrang's political interests. To this end they taught both royalty and local populations. As for their converts, the Gyanakpas introduced them to the standard corpus of Gelukpa beliefs and practices, yet it also appears that the new Chinese and Manchu faithful continued to hold a wide spectrum of beliefs and commitments, quite apart from the elements of Tibetan Buddhism they adopted. This has sometimes led scholars to suppose that Buddhist and other ideological exchanges between Tibet and China were minimal, if not non-existent. However, the differences between Tibetan and Chinese religious milieux that are involved do not demonstrate a lack of exchange. Buddhism, after all, reveals a tendency to adapt itself to differing cultures and linguistic environments. In the final analysis, therefore, the forms in which Buddhism—including Tibetan Buddhism—appeared in China could not be anything but Chinese Buddhism.

The extent to which Kangxi, Yongzheng, Qianlong, and their successors believed or practiced Tibetan Buddhism is not always clear and they may have been involved in it at various times for different reasons. But the Labrang Tibetan "Chinese" were missionaries and diplomats in a dynamic and porous borderland environment and had the ability to adjust their teaching to the various types of disciple they encountered. Their adaptability allowed them to serve successfully as conduits for political and ideological communication and exchange between neighbors.

Notes

1 *Rgya nag pa* is Tibetan for "Chinese"; *tshang* may mean "dwelling-place," "family," "lineage," "seat," "palace," or "residence." Here, the word *tshang* is used only as an honorific suffix (a *zhe tshig*). This understanding is based on interviews and on A mang ban zhi da 阿莽班智达 (Dbal mang paṇḍita), in Ma qin Nuo wu geng zhi 玛钦 诺 悟更志 and Dao Zhou 道周, *Labuleng si zhi* 拉卜楞寺志 (*Bla brang bkra shis 'khyil gyi gdan rabs lha'i rnga chen*) (Lanzhou: Gansu People's Publishing House, 1997). (This is a Chinese-language translation and commentary on Dbal mang paṇḍita dkon mchog rgyal mtshan, *Bla brang bkra shis 'khyil gyi gdan rabs lha'i rnga chen* [Lanzhou: Gansu People's Publishing House, 1987], which is itself the third section of [Brag dgon pa] Dkon mchog bstan pa rab rgyas, *Deb ther rgya mtsho*.) In this and other Chinese sources, the editors and authors render the Tibetan word Rgya nag pa in Chinese phonetics (for example, phoneticized as *jia na hua cang* on p. 296 and as *jia na ba* on p. 518) rather than using a translation (such as the Chinese expression *zhongguoren*). In this chapter I use the spelling Labrang for the name of the monastery, and *labrang* in lower case and italics for the word "inherited monastic estate," though both usages would technically be transliterated as *bla brang*. The Mongolian transliteration system used in this article is adapted from the charts at the back of *Mongolian Studies: Journal of the Mongolia Society* 21 (1998): 110–112,

and from Christopher P. Atwood, *Encyclopedia of Mongolia and the Mongol Empire* (New York: Facts on File, 2004).

2 This is summarized explicitly, with reference to the Qing "strategic unity of empire," in Nicola DiCosmo, "Qing Colonial Administration in Inner Asia," *The International History Review*, 20.2 (June 1998): 289.

3 See Huang Pei, *Autocracy at Work: A Study of the Yung-cheng Period, 1723–1735* (Bloomington: Indiana University Press, 1974), pp. 51–110.

4 See Laura Hostetler, *Qing Colonial Enterprise: Ethnography and Cartography in Early Modern China* (Chicago: The University of Chicago Press, 2001), esp. pp. 25–30.

5 C. Pat Giersch, "'A Motley Throng': Social Change on Southwest China's Early Modern Frontier, 1700–1880," *The Journal of Asian Studies*, 60.1 (February 2001): 68.

6 Kun mkhyen 'jigs med dbang po, *Kun mkhyen 'jam dbyangs bzhad pa'i rnam thar* (Lanzhou: Gansu People's Publishing House, 1991), pp. 110, 149.

7 Waley-Cohen, citing Grupper (Samuel M. Grupper, "Manchu Patronage and Tibetan Buddhism during the First Half of the Ch'ing Dynasty," in *Journal of the Tibet Society*, 4 [1984]: 47–75), writes that "in the end the emperors seem to have become true believers": Joanna Waley-Cohen, "Religion, War, and Empire-Building in Eighteenth-Century China," *The International History Review*, 20.2 (June 1998): 341, 337. See also Huang Pei, *Autocracy at Work*, pp. 45–50; for a careful consideration of Qianlong's religious beliefs, see Elisabeth Benard, "The Qianlong Emperor and Tibetan Buddhism," in James A. Millward et al, ed., *New Qing Imperial History: The Making of Inner Asian Empire at Qing Chengde* (London: Routledge Curzon, 2004), pp. 123–135; for a slightly different assessment, see Patricia Berger, *Empire of Emptiness: Buddhist Art and Political Authority in Qing China* (Honolulu: University of Hawai'i Press, 2003). For discussions of ritual in Qing court life, see Pamela Kyle Crossley, *A Translucent Mirror: History and Identity in Qing Imperial Ideology* (Berkeley: University of California Press, 1999); Evelyn S. Rawski, *The Last Emperors: A Social History of Qing Imperial Institutions* (Berkeley: University of California Press, 1998); David Farquhar, "Emperor as Bodhisattva in the Governance of the Ch'ing Empire," *Harvard Journal of Asiatic Studies*, 38 (1978): 5–34; and Pamela Kyle Crossley, *The Manchus* (Oxford: Blackwell, 1997). These scholars and many others point to the assignment of the familiar Indian royal title of *cakravartirāja* to the Chinese emperors, and to the practice of considering the ruler to be a bodhisattva, or a religious deity, or at least somehow a vicar or agent of such a being. This phenomenon is well known in India, Tibet, Cambodia, China, Myanmar, and elsewhere. A succinct description of the practice in India can be found in Hermann Kulke and Dietmar Rothermund, *A History of India*, revised ed. (London: Routledge, 1990), pp. 136 ff.; see also Waley-Cohen 1998: 345 n. 1. See, too, chapter 1 above.

8 See especially Mark C. Elliott, *The Manchu Way: The Eight Banners and Ethnic Identity in Late Imperial China* (Stanford: Stanford University Press, 2001), pp. 2–35, 39–88. See also Evelyn S. Rawski, "Presidential Address: Reenvisioning the Qing: The Significance of the Qing Period in Chinese History," *The Journal of Asian Studies* 55.4 (November 1996): 832–833; on the institution of classical Chinese educational models see Evelyn S. Rawski, *Education and Popular Literacy in Ch'ing China*

(Ann Arbor: The University of Michigan Press, 1979), pp. 1–53; see also Crossley, *The Manchus*, pp. 122–130.

9 [Brag dgon pa] Dkon mchog bstan pa rab rgyas, *Histoire du Bouddhisme dans L'Amdo (Deb ther rgya mtsho)* (Paris: L'École Pratique des Hautes Études, 1972), part 2, 2b2–3a1. This remarkable individual's political career was perhaps fated to begin when he met the Fifth Dalai Lama Ngag dbang blo bzang rgya mtsho (1617–1682) in 1653 while the Dalai Lama was en route to a meeting with the Chinese. Years later, in Lhasa, the Fifth Dalai Lama conferred full ordination on the twenty-seven-year-old 'Jam dbyangs bzhad pa.

10 Luciano Petech, *China and Tibet in the Early XVIIIth Century. T'oung Pao* Monographie 1 (Leiden: E.J. Brill, 1972), pp. 9–12.

11 Petech, p. 16.

12 Petech, pp. 18, 21.

13 Petech, pp. 17–18.

14 Petech p. 18.

15 In the same year, the Kokonor Mongols divided the territory east of Kokonor into "two wings," the left one being placed under the command of Cagan Danjin, Lobjang Danjin (b. 1692), Dasi Batur's son and successor, and Dayan (a grandson of Gushri Khan's sixth son, d. 1718). See the detailed list of left and right members in Ho-chin Yang, *The Annals of Kokonor*, p. 53.

16 I have summarized the political situation at Labrang in the beginning of the eighteenth century at the Eighth Seminar of the International Association of Tibetan Studies. This section uses data from that paper.

17 See Farquhar, "Emperor as Bodhisattva," pp. 5–34.

18 Many Chinese were killed as well, not just Mongols: *bod du yod pa'i rgya mi phal cher mtshon gyis bsad nas lnga drug tsam las ma lus zer* (Dbal mang dkon mchog rgyal mtshan, *Rgya bod hor sog gyi lo rgyus nyung brjod pa byis pa 'jug pa'i 'bab stegs [deb ther]*, reproduced by Gyaltan Gelek Namgyal [New Delhi: Laxmi Printers, 1974], p. 654).

19 For a detailed description of Lubsangdanjin's 1723–1724 rebellion, see Louis M. Schram, *The Monguors of the Kansu-Tibetan Frontier*, Part I–III, vols. 44, 47, 51 (Philadelphia: The American Philosophical Society Transactions, 1954, 1957, 1961), part III, p. 58; Kato Naoto, "Lobsang Danjin's Rebellion of 1723: With a Focus on the Eve of the Rebellion," *Acta Asiatica: Bulletin of the Institute of Eastern Culture 64 (1993)*: 57–80; Kato Naoto, "The 1723 Rebellion of Lobjang Danjin," in Ch'en Chieh-hsien, ed., *Proceedings of the Fifth East Asian Altaistic Conference* (Taipei: National Taiwan University, 1980), pp. 182–191; Kato Naoto, "The Accession to the Throne of Yung-cheng and Lobdzang Danjin's Rebellion," in Ch'en Chieh-hsien, ed., *Proceedings of the 35th Permanent International Altaistic Conference* (Taipei: Center for Chinese Studies Materials, 1993), pp. 189–192; Ishihama Yumiko, "New Light on the 'Chinese Conquest of Tibet' in 1720 (Based on New Manchu Sources)," in Helmut Krasser et al, ed., *Tibetan Studies: Proceedings of the 7th Seminar of the Internaitonal Association of Tibetan Studies, Graz 1995*, Volume I (Vienna: Verlag der Osterreichischen Akademie der Wissenschaften, 1997), pp. 419–426; and passim.

20 See Arthur W. Hummel, *Eminent Chinese of the Ch'ing Period (1644–1912)*, vol. 1 (Washington: United States Government Printing Office, 1943), pp. 587–590.

21 Oddly, he eventually returned to China and was not persecuted.

22 *gong ma'i zhabs su bsdus.* Dbal mang, *Rgya bod hor sog*, p. 655.

23 Dbal mang, *Rgya bod hor sog*, pp. 653–655.

24 Josef Kolmaš, *Tibet and Imperial China: A Survey of Sino-Tibetan Relations up to the End of the Manchu Dynasty in 1912* (Canberra: The Australian National University, 1967), pp. 1, 33; see also Tsering Wangdu Shakya, *The Dragon in the Land of Snows: A History of Modern Tibet since 1947* (London: Pimlico Press, 1999), pp. 136 ff.

25 See references to the "Qing's New Dominion" in James A. Millward, *Beyond the Pass: Economy, Ethnicity, and Empire in Qing Central Asia, 1759–1864* (Stanford: Stanford University Press, 1998). Matthew Kapstein writes: "The Manchu rulers of China's Qing Dynasty (1644–1911) become directly involved in the events in Tibet and during the 1720s consolidate direct rule over large parts of the eastern Tibetan provinces of Amdo and Kham," *The Tibetan Assimilation of Buddhism: Conversion, Contestation, and Memory* (New York: Oxford University Press, 2000), p. xx. It seems rather that, at least in the Labrang region, the Qing was only indirectly involved and did not consolidate direct rule. The Mgo log group, for example, who initially refused to support the new monastery or even to grant safe passage to the First 'Jam dbyangs bzhad pa in 1709, remained fiercely independent down to the modern period. See Dbal mang, *Rgya bod hor sog*, p. 547. They were hardly under Qing imperial control.

26 Joseph Fletcher, "Ch'ing Inner Asia c. 1800," in Dennis Twitchett and John K. Fairbank, eds., *The Cambridge History of China*, vol. 10, Late Ch'ing, 1800–1911, Part I (London: Cambridge University Press), p. 105; for a discussion of Chinese presence in the region and the low level of their influence in Ming times, see Elliot Sperling, "The Ho Clan of Ho-chou: A Tibetan Family in Service to the Yuan and Ming Dynasties," in Paolo Daffina, ed., *Indo-Sino-Tibetica: Studi in Onore di Luciano Petech*, Studi Orientali 9 (1990), p. 368.

27 Petech writes of "the establishment of Manchu suzerainty over the Koke-nor Qošot," Luciano Petech, "Notes on Tibetan History of the 18th Century," *T'oung Pao* 52/4.5 (1966): 269.

28 Sum pa ye shes dpal 'byor, *Mtsho sngon gyi lo rgyus sogs bkod pa'i tshangs glu gsar snyan zhes bya bzhugs so* (Xining: Qinghai People's Publishing House, 1982). English translation in Yang Ho-chin, *The Annals of Kokonor* (Bloomington: Indiana University Press, 1969), p. 43. Sum pa explains the sequence of events leading up to and after this period, and writes that Kangxi gave titles and eventually gained influence in Qinghai: *mtsho sngon pa dbang du bsdus te rgya sog 'brel bzang gser thag gis bcings* (p. 19). Sum pa's view of things is important and not to be dismissed. However, Sum pa left Amdo in 1723 and returned only in 1732, and was therefore absent during a crucial period in Labrang's history.

29 Writing about Lcang skya and his biographer Thu'u bkwan, two lamas from the Monguor center of Dgon lung in Qinghai, Gene Smith advises that the "biography can be used as a primary source only with extreme caution," as both individuals "served as willing agents of Chinese imperial policy," and the text has a "strong pro-Chinese bias." This caution applies equally to Sum pa and his work, and to varying degrees to the Rgya nag pas. See E. Gene Smith, *Among Tibetan Texts: History and Literature of the Himalayan Plateau* (Boston: Wisdom Publications, 2001), pp. 133–134.

30 See Gaubatz, *Beyond the Great Wall*, pp. 24–26; Cohen, *Symbolic Construction*; and Anthony Smith, *Ethnic Origins*, pp. 1–5; cf. Millward, *Beyond the Pass*, pp. 2–19.

31 Fletcher, "Ch'ing Inner Asia," p. 106.

32 W.D. Shakabpa, *Tibet: A Political History* (New Haven: Yale University Press, 1967), p. 173. Central Tibet had some secular administrative authority in Amdo, whose agent was "till about the middle of the 19th century, a commissioner called *sgar dpon*, whose functions concerned above all trade and the control of local monasteries."

33 Rawski, *The Last Emperors*, p. 250.

34 The minimal extent of actual Qing control of the Labrang territories is made clear in Yu Xiangwen 俞湘文, *Xibei youmu zangqu zhi shehui diaocha* 西北游牧藏区之社会调查 (undated, ca. 1932), in Zhongguo Xibei Wenxian Congshu Weiyuanhui, eds., *Zhongguo xibei wenxian congshu* 中国西北文献丛书 (1991), pp. 320–327.

35 Rawski, *The Last Emperors*, p. 254.

36 Rawski, *The Last Emperors*, p. 256; Ishihama Yumiko, "New Light on the Chinese Conquest of Tibet," pp. 419–426.

37 See the map following p. 144 in Jacques Legrand, *L'Administration dans la domination sino-mandchoue Qalq-a* (Paris: Collège de France, 1976), which shows the number of Tibetan Buddhist monasteries founded in Mongolia between 1692 and 1820, some 132. Barfield argues that the proliferation of Tibetan Buddhist monasteries came as a result of—and in response to—unrestrained piety, gradual disintegration of central Mongol authority, and the increase of Manchu power. The Manchus did not attempt to change social structures or religious beliefs and practices; they sought only to control territorial boundaries, to increase trade and communications, and to secure even further boundaries against enemies in Ili, Zungaria, and Siberia. See Barfield, *The Perilous Frontier*, p. 301 and Rawski, *The Last Emperors*, p. 253.

38 Barfield, *The Perilous Frontier*, p. 286. See Stevan Harrell, ed., *Cultural Encounters on China's Ethnic Frontiers* (Seattle: University of Washington Press, 1995), pp. 27–36.

39 On Tibetan Buddhist, religiously based alliances in general, refer to D. Seyfort Ruegg, "*Mchod yon, yon mchod* and *mchod gnas/yon gnas*: On the Historiography and Semantics of a Tibetan Religio-Social and Religio-Political Concept," in Ernst Steinkellner, ed., *Tibetan History and Language: Studies Dedicated to Géza Uray on his Seventieth Birthday* (Wien, Austria, 1991), pp. 441–454.

40 Legrand, *L'Administration*, pp. 25, 44; see also Barfield, *The Perilous Frontier*, pp. 297–302. For a relevant analysis of inter-ethnic relations, see White, 1991, pp. x–xi; 50–93; Owen Lattimore, "Introduction," in Schram, *The Monguors of the Kansu-Tibetan Frontier*, Part I, pp. 4–17; and Rawski, *The Last Emperors*, pp. 6–8.

41 Lattimore, "Introduction," in Schram, I, p. 11.

42 Lattimore, "Introduction," in Schram, I, pp. 9–12.

43 Giersch, 2001, p. 71.

44 Rawski, *The Last Emperors*, p. 254, in the section titled "Qing administration of Tibetan Buddhism."

45 Fletcher writes that "[R]eligious affiliations had political significance and it should be remembered that religion in Tibetan eyes was not clearly distinguishable from political allegiances." And again, "[R]eligious affiliation . . . had underlying political significance, as [for example] with the local chiefs of Amdo and eastern Kham." Still again, "The Ch'ing and the Tibetans saw the relationship between the emperor

and the Dalai Lama from two very different perspectives. From the Ch'ing point
of view, the Dalai Lama was a mighty ecclesiastic and a holy being, but nonetheless
the emperor's protege. From the Tibetan point of view, the emperor was merely the
Lama's secular patron. This meant that in Tibetan eyes the Dalai Lama's position
was superior to that of the Ch'ing emperor." Joseph Fletcher, "Ch'ing Inner Asia"
p. 92–94, 101; see also Rawski, *The Last Emperors*, pp. 255–257. This combination
of "religious and secular leadership" was known in nearby Qinghai; see Jonathan
Lipman, "Ethnicity and Politics in Republican China: The Ma Family Warlords of
Gansu," *Modern China* 10.3 (1984): 290, n. 4. For descriptions of monastery life and
regional monastic bureaucratic infrastructures, see Schram, II, pp. 37–73.

46 The Qing was a colonial power, and has been described as an imperialist nation. See
Elliot Sperling, "Awe and Submission: A Tibetan Aristocrat at the Court of Quin-
long," *International History Review* 20.2 (1998): 325. Giersch, citing many related
studies, writes that "Qing China was a colonial empire because it ruled a variety of
territories and peoples using a multiplicity of institutions and techniques." Giersch,
"A Motley Throng," p. 71; see p. 72. In the case of Labrang the word "ruled" is misleading. I find Giersch's use of and rationale for the expressions "Qing imperialism"
(p. 70) and the Qing "colonial empire" (p. 71) ironic in the controversial case of
Tibetan and Chinese policies, for as he points out in the context of the southwestern Chinese borders, Qing policies helped to build the foundation of contemporary
political boundaries (p. 71) and to build the myth that "indigenous communities
simply became part of China." Similarly, again in the context of Yunnan, Elleman
describes the Qing's foreign policy: "Beijing's military actions in Yunnan clearly supported an imperialistic policy." Bruce A. Elleman, *Modern Chinese Warfare, 1795–
1989* (New York: Routledge, 2001), p. 63. The irony is that given this approach, the
eventual assertion of Chinese control over all of ethnic Tibet might be understood
as "imperialism" and the development of a Chinese "colonial" empire. See Hostetler,
Qing Colonial Enterprise. Another study useful for understanding the relationship
between the Qing and Labrang is Yang Hui, "The Dai *Tusi* System and Its History in
Dehong" (appendix), in Wang Zhusheng, *The Jingpo Kachin of the Yunnan Plateau*
(Tempe, Arizona: Program for Southeast Asian Studies Monograph Series, Arizona
State University, 1997), pp. 267–304. In comments that reinforce the present study,
Yang has written that the *tusi* system, operable in Qinghai, Sichuan, and Gansu—areas all around Labrang—but not, as far as I have seen, within the Labrang territories,
was inconsistent and often inefficient. (See also Schram.) Yang notes that the institutionalized system of *tusi* started in the Ming Dynasty, but that its roots go back as
far as the early Han Dynasty (ca. 109 BCE): "As an official instituion, *tusi* refers to
the appointing of native minority chieftains by the central authority as local hereditary officials. Unlike those of non-*tusi* regions, the polity of the *tusi* was quite autonomous. The *tusi* official had complete power [but cf. Schram] over the legislative,
administrative, and military systems within his domain. This power, however, was
predicated on the condition that orders and commands would be obeyed, and that
tributes, taxes, and corvée to the court would be paid. Different *tusi* regions varied
in rank and size, and each functioned as an independent administrative unit in dealing with its own internal affairs and with the court" (p. 280). These comments show
the variability of Qing control in *tusi*-governed regions, let alone in non-*tusi* regions

such as Labrang, where Tibetan Buddhist monastic officials had control of legislative, administrative, and military systems. Moreover, Yang (pp. 296–302) points out that the presence of a *tusi* was not an indication of Qing or Republican central control; the Qing and Republican governments often removed local *tusis* and replaced them with Han officials. For a comprehensive description and catalogue of the *tusis*, see Gong Yin 龚荫, *Zhongguo tu si zhi du* 中国土司制度 (Kunming: Yunnan People's Publishing House, 1992). This is a voluminous study with detailed historical data; information on *tusi* in Gansu on pp. 1282–1319, followed by information on Qinghai, including the Mgo logs, pp. 1358–1363. See also Yu Yize 余贻泽, *Zhongguo tu si zhi du* 中国土司制度 (Beijing: China Frontiers Study Association, 1945).

47 Firsthand accounts of the primacy of Labrang's regional authority are found in a number of Republican-era sources. See the Republican-period document by Yu Xiangwen, *Xibei youmu zangqu zhi shehui diaocha*, reprinted in Zhongguo Xibei Wenxian Congshu Weiyuanhui, eds., *Zhongguo Xibei Wenxian Congshu*, pp. 320–327. This document includes detailed information about the leadership structures of several different Tibetan and Mongol tribes in the Labrang region. Political control was uncertain in many cases in which groups were "religiously under Labrang Monastery and politically independent" (p. 327), and was subject to change.

48 For a list of some of the Qing and Chinese gifts to Labrang see manuscript, *Labuleng she zhi ju gu wu diaocha biao* 拉卜楞设志局古物调查表 (*A Local Government Record of Ancient Donations to Labrang Monastery*, undated, ca. 1925).

49 For a study of this phenomenon and how it evolved in Tibet, see Kapstein, *The Tibetan Assimilation*, pp. 38–65.

50 A very useful and relevant analysis of the ancient Chinese religious orientation that contributed to fundamental Chinese ideologies is found in Poo Mu-chou, *In Search of Personal Welfare: A View of Ancient Chinese Religion* (Albany: SUNY Press, 1998).

51 See Grupper, "Manchu Patronage", pp. 47–75; Grupper argues that the Chinese court officials were pious adherents of Tibetan Buddhism.

52 One example, the tradition of the immortal Lu Dongbin, a deity-like figure visualized in different aspects through history, is studied in Paul R. Katz, *Images of the Immortal: The Cult of Lu Dongbin at the Palace of Eternal Joy* (Honolulu: University of Hawai'i Press, 1999); see also Anne Birrell, *Chinese Myths* (Austin: University of Texas Press, 2000); and the very interesting illustrated dictionary of Chinese spirits/deities (and the two volumes of stories by the same author entitled *Zhongguo shen hua chuanshuo*): Yuan Ke 袁珂, ed., *Zhongguo shen hua chuanshuo cidian* 中国神话传说词典 (Shanghai: Cishu Chubanshe, 1985).

53 The preceding quotations are from Edward Slingerhand, "Effortless Action: The Chinese Spiritual Ideal of Wu-wei," *Journal of the American Academy of Religion*, 68.2 (June 2000): 294–298.

54 Tu Wei-ming. *Way, Learning, and Politics: Essays on the Confucian Intellectual* (Albany: SUNY Press, 1993), p. x.

55 See F.W. Mote's Foreword to Tu, pp. xiv–xviii.

56 Tu, *Way, Learning, and Politics*, p. 1.

57 The quotations in this paragraph are from Tu, *Way, Learning, and Politics*, pp. 1–3.

58 Tu, pp. 9, 23, 29, 32, 139.

59 Tu, p. 118.

60 Tu, p. 120.

61 Tu, p. 126. For the relationship between Chinese concepts of humanity, the pursuit of human perfectability, and the goal of attaining to heaven in the afterlife, see Li Shenzhi, "Reflections on the Concept of the Unity of Heaven and Man (*"tian ren he yi"*), in Karl-Heinz Pohl, ed., *Chinese Thought in a Global Context: A Dialogue Between Chinese and Western Philosophical Approaches* (Leiden: Brill Publishers, 1999), pp. 115–128.

62 Toni Huber, *The Cult of Pure Crystal Mountain: Popular Pilgrimage and Visionary Landscape in Southeast Tibet* (New York: Oxford University Press, 1999), p. 57.

63 I will not elaborate further on the well-known goals of Tibetan Buddhism, including the ultimate aim of attaining liberation from the cycle of births and deaths. For more on this, see again Kapstein, *The Tibetan Assimilation*, pp. 38–65.

64 See the summary of the corpus of Chinese ritual practices in Rawski, *The Last Emperors*, pp. 197–230, 264 ff. Angela Zito comments that "religious" ritual was an important part of everyday life. See Angela Zito, *Of Body and Brush: Grand Sacrifice as Text/Performance in Eighteenth-Century China* (Chicago: University of Chicago Press, 1997), p. xvi. See Pamela Crossley, *A Translucent Mirror* (Berkeley: University of California Press, 1999), pp. 223–246.

65 For a description of the imperial Chinese involvement with Tibetan Buddhism, see Rawski, *The Last Emperors*, pp. 244–263.

66 See especially Kapstein, *The Tibetan Assimilation*, chapter 5. In the same volume Kapstein also notes that there were likely influences on Tibetan religion from other non-Indian sources, not only the Chinese.

67 The Manchus and Chinese surely recognized that the Tibetan lamas, in addition to their expertise in Tibetan Buddhism, were very well-educated and were knowledgeable in fields of scholarship that rivaled the Chinese in depth and breadth. For example, one of the Rgya nag pa lamas, 'Jam dbyangs bstan pa'i nyi ma, wrote extensively on poetics, drawing from many Indian and Tibetan sources. The Tibetan scholars' command of the arts and literature was at least equal to that of the Chinese. See Lhun grub rdo rje, "Rgya nag pa 'Jam dbyangs bstan pa'i nyi ma'i 'sprin gyi bzhon pa'i rtogs brjod' la rags tsam dpyad" ("On the Book 'Yuncheng Prince,' written by 'Jam dbyangs bstan pa'i nyi ma"), in *Bod ljongs zhib 'jug* 1 (1999), pp. 83–94, esp. 89–90.

68 See Grupper, "Manchu Patronage," for example.

69 There are many descriptions of Chinese involvement with Tibetan Buddhist lamas, including Chinese monks and Tibetan lamas in residence at Wutai shan. See for example Gung thang bstan pa'i sgron me, *Kun mkhyen 'jam dbyangs bzhad pa sku 'phreng gnyis pa rje 'jigs med dbang po'i rnam thar* (Lanzhou: Gansu People's Publishing House, 1990), p. 189.

70 Wang Hengtong 王亨通 and Hua Pingning 花平宁, *Binglingsi shiku shangsi* 炳灵寺石窟上寺 *(The Bingling Grottoes Upper Monastery)* (Chongqing, Sichuan: Chongqing Publishing House, 2001), pp. 16–17.

71 Rawski, *The Last Emperors*, presents this problem in several places, for example on pp. 260–262 and in her sections on Tibet, where she describes the use of Tibetan Buddhist ritual as a method for legitimizing imperial status and, doubtless, for establishing Chinese authority in Tibet. Rawski's interesting arguments overstate the extent of Chinese influence on Tibetan Buddhism in central Tibet and

at Labrang, and fail to recognize the relevance of the actual practice of Buddhist tantrism, in which every initiate, not just the emperor, becomes a deity. For Qianlong's Tibetan chapel in the Forbidden City, see Berger, *Empire of Emptiness*, pp. 3–4 ff.

72 Rawski, *The Last Emperors*, pp. 248–251, in part quoting Snellgrove and Richardson, describes the phenomenon of a person's being the recognized incarnation of (i.e., the same individual as) a previously living religiously advanced individual eventually becoming a widespread means for ensuring the continuity of religious and secular political leadership (pp. 260–263). The *trülku* system was, as Rawski herself notes, a critical factor in regional politics and social structures (p. 255). For a considerably more accurate summary of the theory of rebirth, with reference to its emergence as a political mechanism, see Kapstein, *The Tibetan Assimilation*, pp. 5, 38–50, and especially 205 n. 19.

73 Dbal mang, in *Rgya bod hor sog*, exemplifies the traditional attitude emphasizing the necessity of understanding the emptiness of all things and the importance of regarding one's *bla ma* as the buddha, *chos thams cad bden med du ma rtogs par stong nyid rtogs zer pa rdzun yin/ chos byed pa la gzhi dad pa gal che/ de la bla ma sangs rgyas su mthong* (p. 647).

74 Petech, *China and Tibet*, pp. 70–71.

75 Rawski, *The Last Emperors*, p. 255.

76 Rawski, *The Last Emperors*, p. 300.

77 Rawski, *The Last Emperors*, pp. 257–258.

78 Petech, *China and Tibet*, p. 24, and "Notes on Tibetan History," pp. 284–286; Ishihama Yumiko, "New Light on the Chinese Conquest."

79 Further proof of the Mongol attempt to make politically expedient use of Buddhism is their construction of at least three hundred Tibetan Buddhist monasteries in the later seventeenth and early eighteenth centuries; see Legrand, *L'Administration*.

80 See the summary of important ethnic Mongol Tibetan Buddhists in Qinghai, Gansu, etc. in Miao Zhou 妙舟, *Meng zang fo jiao shi* 蒙藏佛教史 (Yangzhou, Jiangsu: Jiangsu Guanglin Guji Ke Yinshi, 1993). For the important ethnic Mongol Buddhists at Labrang, see Chinese People's Political Consultative Committee 中国人民政治协商委员会, Xiahe Branch, Committee on Cultural and Historical Resources, eds., *Xiahe wen shi zi liao* 夏河文史资料, Volume I (Chinese) (Lanzhou University Silk Road Culture Center, 1993), pp. 19–33.

81 The title *Rgya nag pa* and the practice of awarding it continue to the present day. See the photo of Rgya nag pa Yon tan rgya mtsho, who resides in Klu chu, on the inside back cover of *Zla ser* 51.3/4 (1997).

82 For details see Sangs rgyas rin chen, "La mo bde chen," pp. 109–110.

83 "In 1686, 44th made an agreement (*chings mdzad*) between the Khalka and O rod. In 1687, 44th met the Chinese Emperor." Chatring Jansar Tenzin, ed., *The Collected Works (Gsung 'bum) of Cha har Dge bshes Blo bzang tshul khrims: Reproduced from a set of xylographic prints from the Peking blocks* (New Delhi: Sungrab Partun Khang, 1972), vol. 8, pp. 51–52. This episode is summarized in detail in Dbal mang, *Rgya bod hor sog*, pp. 616–618. Dbal mang gives precise dates and identifies the key individuals, but casts the episode in the context of Lhazang's negotiations with the Chinese, and does not include any information about Amdo, about Blo gros rgya mtsho's home

and monastic seat there, or about Labrang's Rgya nag pa estate. See the report of this episode in Sangs rgyas rin chen, "La mo bde chen."

84 This is according to Chahar dge bshes (relying on a *Rnam thar* written by Rgyal dbang mchog) and Dkon mchog bstan pa rab rgyas. See Dkon mchog bstan pa rab rgyas, *Histoire du Bouddhisme dans L'Amdo (Deb ther rgya mtsho)* (Paris: L'Ecole Pratique des Hautes Etudes, 1972), part 2, fol. 89a1 ff.

85 In 1716—the same year that the Seventh Dalai Lama was escorted to Amdo by a retinue that included Cagan Danjin—the Kokonor Mongols divided the territory east of Kokonor into "two wings", the left one being placed under the command of Cagan Danjin, Lobjang Danjin (b. 1692), Dasi Batur's son and successor, and Dayan (a grandson of Guhsri Khan's sixth son, d. 1718). (See the detailed list of left and right members in Ho-chin Yang, *The Annals of Kokonor*, p. 53.)

86 Ko zhul grags pa 'byung gnas and Rgyal ba blo bzang mkhas grub, *Gangs can mkhas grub rim byon ming mdzod* (Lanzhou: Gansu People's Publishing House, 1992), pp. 1163–1164. This Blo bzang bstan pa'i nyi ma should not be confused with the one mentioned in the *Bod rgya tshig mdzod chen mo* (1984), p. 3278, where it says that Blo bzang bstan pa'i nyi ma was born in 1762 (*chu rta*, 13th *rab byung* cycle): *khri sprul blo bzang bstan pa'i nyi ma 'khrungs*. With regard to the Rgya nag pas, Chahar dge bshes clearly writes that Blo bzang bstan pa'i nyi ma, was born "in 1689, in the twelfth cycle" (*rab byung bcu gnyis pa . . . sa mo sprul*, Chatring Jansar Tenzin, *The Collected Works of Cha har Dge bshes*, p. 52). There is also some confusion in the *Ming mdzod* (p. 1163) where Blo bzang bstan pa'i nyi ma is not identified as the incarnation of the First Rgya nag pa and where it is also recorded that he died in 1772 (*chu pho 'brug*), not in 1762 (*chu rta*). It nonetheless seems clear that the *Ming mdzod* is referring to the Blo bzang bstan pa'i nyi ma who was the second Rgya nag pa. This individual should also not be confused with Stag lung Blo bzang bstan pa'i nyi ma, 1782–1836; see Yonten Gyatso, *Mkhas grub 'bum sde'i rol mtsho mdo sngags bstan pa'i 'byung gnas dga' ldan bshad sgrub bkra shis 'khyil gyi skor bzhed gzhung dal 'bab mdzod yangs las nye bar sgrub pa sngon med legs bshad ngo mtshar bkra shis chos dung bzhad pa'i sgra dbyangs* (Paris: Unpublished manuscript, 1987), p. 167, and Dkon mchog bstan pa rab rgyas, II, 1972, fol. 165b4.

87 See Dkon mchog bstan pa rab rgyas, *Histoire du Bouddhism*, part 2, 1972, fol. 91a7 ff. At this point in the narrative in the *Deb ther rgya mtsho*, the story of Blo bzang bstan pa'i nyi ma's request to the First and then the Second 'Jam dbyangs bzhad pa for the Mitrayogin cycle of initiations occurs as prophecied, fol. 91b1. The story is repeated in Gung thang bstan pa'i sgron me, *Kun mkhyen 'jam dbyangs bzhad pa sku 'phreng gnyis pa rje 'jigs med dbang po'i rnam thar* (Lanzhou: Gansu People's Publishing House, 1990), pp. 140–141. Except where noted the information on the Rgya nag pa lineage here is taken from Dkon mchog bstan pa rab rgyas, *Histoire du Bouddhisme*, part 2, fol. 89a1 ff.

88 Dkon mchog bstan pa rab rgyas, *Histoire du Bouddhism*, part 2, fol. 52.

89 Gung thang bstan pa'i sgron me, *Kun mkhyen 'jam dbyangs bzhad pa*, pp. 140–141. See the account in Sangs rgyas rin chen. "La mo bde chen," pp. 111–112.

90 See Sangs rgyas rin chen, "La mo bde chen," p. 112.

91 Gung thang bstan pa'i sgron me, 1990, pp. 383; this person is also named in Dkon mchog bstan pa rab rgyas, *Histoire du Bouddhism*, part 3, fol. 281.

92 See Dkon mchog bstan pa rab rgyas, *Histoire du Bouddhisme*, fol. 89a1–92b4, and Sangs rgyas rin chen, "La mo bde chen," pp. 113–114.

93 See Sangs rgyas rin chen, "La mo bde chen," pp. 114–116.

94 Oral traditons at Labrang Monastery mention Rgya nag pa lamas at Zam tsha Monastery and at Lha mo Monastery, two of Labrang's affiliated monasteries. Morevoer, there is at present an approximately fifteen-year-old reincarnated Rgya nag pa lama at Labrang, from the Kālacakra lineage of Yon tan rgya mtsho, who unfortunately knows little of his heritage, beyond what is included here.

95 Dbal mang paṇḍita dkon mchog rgyal mtshan, *Bla brang bkra shis 'khyil gyi gdan rabs lha'i rnga chen* (Lanzhou: Gansu People's Publishing House, 1987), pp. 530–531. Referred to as Rgya nag pa in Dkon mchog bstan pa rab rgyas, *Histoire du Bouddhisme*, part 3, fol. 186a7.

96 The *Ming mdzod* and other works that may simply be following similar sources have incorrect data on Rgya nag pa 'Jam dbyangs bstan pa'i nyi ma. The *Ming mdzod* says that he lived from 1686 to 1738. This version, though close to the First Rgya nag pa's dates, has been rejected by Yonten Gyatso (unpublished manuscript, 1987, p. 161) in favor of the later ones used here, which are clearly more reasonable. The earlier dates would incur several problems. For example, if he were born in 1686 he could not have studied at Labrang Monastery at age eleven as is stated in his record. Moreover, he is known as the reincarnation of Ngag dbang phun tshogs, b. 1746. The error (including the statement that he was born in 1686 and studied at Labrang at age eleven) is repeated in two sources: in the biographical sketch in Lhag pa tshe ring and Ngag dbang Chos grags, *Zhva ser bstan pa'i sgron me rje tsong kha pa chen pos gtsos skyes chen dam pa rim byung gi gsung 'bum dkar chag phyogs gcig tu bsgrigs pa'i dri med zla shel gtsang ma'i me long (Gsung 'bum dkar chag*, Lhasa: Tibetan People's Publishing House, 1990), p. 315; and in the rather more detailed account in Slob bzang chos grags and Bsod nams rtse mo, eds., *Gangs ljongs mkhas dbang rim byon gyi rtsom yig gser gyi sbram bu*, 3 vols. (Qinghai: Qinghai People's Publishing House, 1989, 1994), pp. 939–947. These accounts do however explicitly identify this individual as a Rgya nag pa, because of his long stay at Wutai shan late in his life and because he was the recognized rebirth of Ngag dbang phun tshogs. The former of these two sources states that there is no extended biography of this person, but there is a brief sketch of his life at the beginning of his three volumes of collected works. The latter source includes a *Rnam thar*, which is not really a biography but rather an homage, written in verse, praising him for his studies and intellectual achievements. There is a brief account of his life, with the correct 1806–1858 dates, in Lhun grub rdo rje, "Rgya nag pa 'Jam dbyangs bstan pa'i nyi ma," vol. 1, pp. 89–90.

97 Yonten Gyatso, *Dge ldan chos 'byung*, p. 161; confirmed in A mang ban zhi da (Dbal mang paṇḍita), *Labuleng si zhi*, pp. 518–519.

98 A mang ban zhi da (Dbal mang paṇḍita), *Labuleng si zhi*, p. 519, renders the name of the third Rgya nag pa in this lineage as Klong rdol Yon tan rgya mtsho, but according to Zha Zha 扎扎 (Bkra Bkra), *Labuleng si huo fo shi xi* 拉卜楞寺活佛世系 (Lanzhou: Gansu Minorities' Publishing House, 2000), pp. 417–418, a brief biographical sketch of Rgya nag pa, he is identified as Blo bzang Klong rdol chos gyi nyi ma (1859–1934).

6: Gangkar Rinpoché between Tibet and China: A Tibetan Lama among Ethnic Chinese in the 1930s to 1950s*

Carmen Meinert

I N RECENT YEARS, ethnic Han Chinese have dramatically increased their involvement in Tibetan Buddhism. In particular, Chinese seekers now frequently visit the Sino-Tibetan border areas of Kham in contemporary Sichuan province, traveling to places where Tibetan lamas can interact with their lay disciples. Reviewing the history of the past century, however, we find that development in this area is not unprecedented. During the Republican era (1912–1949) and the early 1950s, the Kagyü lama Bo Gangkar Rinpoché (1893–1957) worked in this region (during its incorporation into Xikang province and later Sichuan) as well as in China proper.[1] In accord with the religious activities of a Tibetan *trülku*, he established a *shedra*, or Buddhist seminary, in his monastery at Minyak Gangkar (Ch. Gongga shan, Mt. Minya Konka in older Western sources) to the southwest of Dartsedo (Dajianlu, modern Kangding) where he educated Tibetans and Chinese disciples alike. Furthermore, in the 1930s to 1950s, he made three trips in eastern China in order to propagate Tibetan Buddhism—representing equally the Kagyü and Nyingma traditions—on a grand scale among Chinese adherents and especially the intelligentsia. Gangkar Rinpoché's relations with ethnic Chinese also parallel the changing political circumstances of his time: while he was a Tibetan trülku who benefited from the religious freedom he enjoyed during the Republican era in China, his later life also demonstrates how communist leaders, following their takeover in 1949, took advantage of his earlier fame and made him part of their "civilizing project" in cultural Tibet.[2]

This chapter aims to give an initial overview of the activities and teachings of Gangkar Rinpoché, with special attention to his work among ethnic

Chinese during the 1930s and 1940s, and to situate him in the broader historical and religious milieu of Tibetan and Chinese interrelationships.[3]

Gangkar Rinpoché in Tibet

Education and Early Teaching Activities

Karma Shedrup Chöki Senggé was the fifth incarnation of the trülku from Bo Gangkar Monastery in southern Kham.[4] He received most of his education at Pelpung Monastery in Dergé, the seat of the Situ Rinpoché and the most prominent center of the Karma Kagyü order in far eastern Tibet. During his childhood Gangkar Rinpoché already expressed a strong wish to go to Pelpung, for his former incarnation had lived there as a student of the Ninth Situ Rinpoché, Pema Nyinjé Wangpo (1774–1853). In 1910, at the age of eighteen, he finally set out to Pelpung to receive his ordination before Khenchen Karma Dechen Ngedön Tendzin Rabgyé and to begin a period of twelve years of study, lasting until 1922. On arriving at Pelpung, Gangkar met for the first time with the Eleventh Situ Rinpoché, Pema Wangchok Gyelpo (1886–1952). They immediately liked one another and Situ Rinpoché became a highly influential and supportive figure in Gangkar's student years.

At the time, the shedra at Pelpung was one of the major places of learning in Kham, where the most prominent teacher was Khenpo Zhenga (1871–1927), the trülku of the great Nyingma master Gyelsé Zhenpen Tayé (b. 1800), founder of the renowned Śrī Siṃha college at Dzogchen Monastery.[5] Zhenga Rinpoché was delighted by the erudition of Gangkar, so that the latter together with Zurmang Penam became renowned as the most learned students at the college. Gangkar's studies under Khenpo Zhenga included works of the Nyingma tradition and the *Thirteen Great Root Texts of Philosophy* (*Gzhung chen bcu gsum*), while in studies with Khenchen Tsewang Peljor, he focused on grammar, astrology, and poetry.

During his twelve years of study at Pelpung Monastery, Gangkar made one journey to central Tibet in order to receive the essential teachings of the Kagyü order from the Fifteenth Karmapa Khakhyap Dorjé (1871–1922) at his seat at Tsurpu. There, the Karmapa gave him instructions on the highest yoga tantras including Cakrasaṃvara (*'khor lo bde mchog*), Vajrayoginī (*rdo rje rnal 'byor ma*), the *Six yogas of Nāropa* (*Nāro chos drug*), and Mahāmudrā (*phyag chen*). Following his return to Pelpung, at the age of twenty-five, Gangkar's accomplishments as a practitioner and scholar led to his three-year appointment as retreat master of the monastery's meditation center (*sgrub grwa*). In

FIG. 1 Gangkar Rinpoché in Kham.
(Courtesy of an anonymous private collection.)

1922 Gangkar returned to his home monastery of Bo Gangkar to assume his religious duties as a trülku, and to begin restoring the monastery and teaching there. He soon went once more into retreat, this time for a period of two years in a mountain hermitage.

In 1925, Gangkar was invited by the trülku from the nearby Rikhü monastery, then the center of Sakya learning in southern Kham, to teach for three years at that monastery's shedra, an offer he accepted. Rikhü monastery was responsible for administering this small Sakya academy, which neighbored Gangkar's own monastery, and it was the responsibility of the Rikhü trülku to choose a *khenpo* (preceptor) to administer it every three years. While Gangkar held this appointment, he recognized the monk Künzang as a trülku of that monastery; the latter became his disciple as well, later teaching in China.[6]

Owing to the good reference of his early advocate Situ Rinpoché, Gangkar was appointed as junior tutor (*yongs 'dzin*) to the Sixteenth Karmapa Rangjung Rikpé Dorjé (1924–1981). He traveled for a second time to Tsurpu in 1930, where he instructed the young lineage-holder for one year in the essential teachings he had himself received from the former Karmapa. Following this appointment, Gangkar's reputation as a learned teacher became established throughout Tibet.

Despite the prominence he held among Tibetans, Gangkar Rinpoché turned toward China later in his life, where he became one of the most renowned Tibetan lamas of the Republican era. It was due to his friend Norlha's (1876–1936) earlier activities in China that Gangkar came to teach among the Chinese,[7] as Gangkar took over the training of those Chinese students who had studied under Norlha. A sketch of the political situation of Kham during the Republican years, and of Norlha's involvements therein, will provide the context in which to place Gangkar's first trip to mainland China in 1936.

Kham during the Republican Era: Between the Warlordism of Liu Wenhui and the Interests of the Guomindang

During the life of Gangkar Rinpoché, the situation in Kham was extremely fluid and complex. Even though Gangkar Rinpoché himself played only a minor part on the Khampa political stage, he nonetheless became indirectly involved in the agenda of the Chinese Nationalist Party, the Guomindang (GMD), after he began teaching Chinese disciples in China proper during the mid-1930s.

In order to understand Gangkar Rinpoché's position among the local Tibetans and in the national Chinese scene, we first need to understand something of the important role played by the region now known as the Ganzi Tibetan Autonomous Prefecture (*Ganzi zangzu zizhizhou*) in the Khampa struggle for regional autonomy in the 1930s and 1940s. The recent research of Peng Wenbing offers a convincing analysis of the manner in which this movement had to compete with various other agendas exerting pressure in the same area: Chinese imperial expansionism, nation-building projects undertaken by both Chinese and Tibetans, Liu Wenhui's provincial warlordism, and the Red Army's enforcement of their version of Tibetan autonomy.[8]

From the perspective of the GMD leader Chiang K'ai-shek (Jiang Jieshi, 1887–1975), the warlord and then governor of Sichuan, Liu Wenhui (1885–1976), was a thorn in his side upsetting plans for the unification of all of China. For his part, Liu Wenhui promised only token allegiance to the GMD Government in Nanjing, which had been installed in 1927, and remained intent on his own objective, namely to consolidate his power throughout southwest China. However, after a bloody defeat at the hands of his nephew Liu Xiang (1888–1938), another Sichuanese warlord, Liu Wenhui withdrew to Kham.[9] His plan was to use that region as the base for a renewed expansion of his influence, and it was this that led him to become involved in the establishment of Xikang province (1939–1955).[10] Although Liu Wenhui was not himself a fervent advocate of the short-lived Xikang project, he nevertheless became its head.

The Xikang province came into existence at the height of the Chinese war with Japan (1937–1945). In an effort to stabilize Southwest China, the GMD's headquarters were transferred to Chongqing, Sichuan, at the end of 1938. Liu Wenhui was in a distinctly disadvantageous position in the power struggle among the different parties in Kham, and found himself fighting simultaneously against local Tibetans striving for Khampa autonomy and against the advancing GMD—both groups were trying to contain Liu Wenhui's provincial warlordism, although their motives were different. Among his opponents on the local Tibetan side were a number of religious leaders, among whom Norlha was undoubtedly one of the most influential. Norlha was one of the central figures working as a liaison between the GMD in Nanjing and the Tibetans in Kham in the 1930s and, for obvious reasons, Liu Wenhui disliked him.[11]

The Nyingma lama Norlha was a native of Riwoché in the Chamdo area. In Tibet he was also known as Garra Lama, whereas in China he was usually referred to as Nuona Hutuketu after the Mongolian title Khutughtu was conferred on him by the late Qing Emperor.[12] During the Sino-Tibetan conflict of 1917 near Chamdo, Norlha assisted the Chinese garrison in Riwoché and was subsequently arrested by the Central Tibetan government and sentenced to life imprisonment for treason.[13] An assortment of legends have been spun about how he subsequently escaped, but in any event, he managed to enter China in 1924. In 1926 he arrived in Chongqing and, as he was not yet on a political mission, mainly attended to his religious duties.

Before his arrival, most of the Tibetan lamas at Chongqing had belonged to the Gelukpa order, the dominant sect that held reign over Tibet's religio-political affairs. When Norlha began teaching in the Nyingma tradition, the novelty was enthusiastically welcomed and ethnic Chinese came in flocks to take refuge with him. Among his most famous disciples was the warlord Liu Xiang, the arch-enemy of Liu Wenhui and ultimately the most powerful warlord in Sichuan.[14] Many years later Liu Xiang would supply Norlha with military support in an attempt to break Liu Wenhui's monopoly interest in the formation of Xikang province in 1935.[15]

The turning point in Norlha's political career came in 1927 when he was appointed commissioner of the newly established Commission for

Mongolian and Tibetan Affairs (*mengzang weiyuan hui*) in Nanjing. The head of the Tibetan section of this commission was another native of Kham named Kelzang Tsering, who also assumed a key role in the Khampa self-rule movement.[16] Norlha was given the position of commissioner in part due to the personal recommendation of Kelzang Tsering and in part owing to the fame he had enjoyed among GMD officers since his involvement in the 1917 Riwoché incident. His office in Nanjing, once established, was designated the "Nanjing office of Nuona Khutughtu from Xikang" (*Xikang Nuona Hutuketu zhu jing banshi chu*). In order to facilitate his political work in Tibetan areas as well, another branch was established in Kangding, the "Kangding office of Nuona Khutughtu" (*Nuona Hutuketu zhu Kangding banshi chu*). However, Norlha himself mostly stayed in Nanjing before being appointed "Xikang Pacification Commissioner" (*Xikang xuanwei shi*) in 1935 and then traveling to Kangding on what would be his final voyage.

As described by Gray Tuttle in chapter 7, Norlha became respected as a religious leader within the Chinese community during the years he spent in Nanjing, from 1927 to 1935. In an amusing yet possibly apocryphal anecdote from Minyak Gönpo, during the period just preceding the war, when Sino-Japanese relations were already severely strained, but Japan had not yet attacked, a Japanese navy ship sank close to the Chinese shore just off of Nanjing. The incident happened to coincide with Norlha's teaching activities in the Nanjing area, leading many to believe that the sinking of the ship was a result of Norlha's meditative accomplishment. As a result, it is said that numbers of military personel became his students. Thus, although his fame in China was less a product of his erudition than of his supposed power, it is clear that the Tibetan lama became a popular and charismatic figure.[17]

The early 1930s marked the beginning of Norlha's widespread celebrity as a Buddhist teacher among ethnic Chinese, as he was among the first Tibetan masters to take advantage of the increased religious freedom during the Republican years. Some of Norlha's teachings are still preserved in Chinese in the form of notes taken by his students. Several of these documents, which demonstrate the esteem with which Norlha was regarded as a teacher, have recently been compiled in the *Secret Scriptures of Tibetan Esoteric Dharma Practices* (*Zangmi xiufa midian*) by Lü Xiegang.[18] A preface to one of these texts states that an initiation into the practice of the bodhisattva Tārā, conferred by Norlha in Nanjing in 1934, was attended by more than 200 disciples.[19] Furthermore, the colophon to the same text says that an earlier Tārā initiation given in 1932 at Huanglong Monastery on Lu shan was attended by 130 disciples.[20]

In 1935 Norlha took a last trip to Kham as an appointed "Xikang Pacification Commissioner." He was meant to organize opposition to the Red Army on the Long March in Kham, but he also used the opportunity to undermine Liu Wenhui's power by coordinating a propaganda campaign. When Norlha's conflict with Liu escalated, he proclaimed Khampa self-rule, but after several beatings, he finally surrendered himself to the Red Army in Ganzi (Dkar mdzes). There, he died in May 1936 in a Red Army hospital.[21] Norlha was cremated in Ganzi and his remains were handed over to Gangkar Rinpoché.[22] Minyak Gönpo confirms that Norlha and Gangkar were on very friendly terms and regularly exchanged letters throughout the years, with Norlha inviting the latter many times to China.[23] Upon Norlha's death, Gangkar finally complied with Norlha's wish and set out for China proper.

Gangkar Rinpoché in China

Travels during the Republican Period

In 1936, at the age of forty-four, Gangkar Rinpoché first traveled to eastern China. His primary motive for undertaking the journey was to build a stūpa to house Norlha's relics at Lu shan in Jiangxi province, where Norlha had taught many times and where many of his Chinese students still gathered.[24] Gangkar's sojourn marked the beginning of his relationship with ethnic Chinese disciples, a connection that lasted until his death in 1957, bringing him back to China from 1946 to 1949, and again from 1953 to 1955.[25] As a result of this teaching activity, Gangkar established life-long ties with high-ranking officials and an indirect involvement in Chinese politics, first with the GMD and later with communist leaders. In light of the materials presently available, we can only speculate about whether Gangkar had been aware of the impact his first trip to China would have on his subsequent career, though his predecessor Norlha provided an apt example of a Tibetan lama whose engagement with ethnic Chinese had profoundly changed the course of his life. Whatever his view, Gangkar assumed the role of Norlha's successor in eastern China, accepting Norlha's several thousand disciples as his own.[26] Although Gangkar was not as political as Norlha had been, his relationship with the GMD was positive and he was able to put his attention first and foremost to religious obligations; hence, he did not seek to thwart Liu Wenhui's plans in Kham. Because of this reticence, although Liu Wenhui disliked Gangkar for the same reason he had disliked Norlha—namely his engagement with GMD leaders—he did not hinder Gangkar's journeys.[27]

When Gangkar set out for China in 1936, he was traveling in the company of his treasurer, his attendants Khyenrap and Chödrak, the Chinese monk and translator known as Dharma-master Mankong, and the monks Gyeltsen and Sonam Tsering.[28] It is not clear where Mankong met Gangkar Rinpoché, as the latter does not appear to have had any Chinese disciples before this first trip to China. Minyak Gönpo assumes that the two of them came across each other in 1936, either in Chengdu or Chongqing. Be this as it may, Mankong later went on to spend many years at Gangkar's monastery and served as Gangkar's main translator not only on his first trip to China, but also on his second in 1946.[29] Mankong also became renowned as the translator for other Tibetan lamas teaching among ethnic Chinese.[30]

The itinerary Gangkar followed starting in mid-1936 brought him, via Dartsedo, to Chengdu and then Chongqing. In the beginning of 1937, Gangkar and his entourage embarked on a boat traveling on the Chang Jiang (Yangtse River) as far as Nanjing and Shanghai, and finally to Lu shan in Jiangxi province, where he was welcomed by thousands of Chinese waiting on both shores of the river. His arrival in eastern China was a major event, valued equally by Norlha's lay disciples and the GMD officials he had befriended. They greeted Gangkar with a military parade in honor of Norlha, and even the later GMD leader Li Zongren (1891–1969) welcomed him personally, eventually becoming Gangkar's disciple.[31]

Li Zongren was a major force in the fluctuating history of the GMD. During the first years of the GMD's Nanjing decade (1927–1937), just after Chiang K'ai-shek's consolidation of power in the capital, Li Zongren headed the Guangxi faction in southern China which challenged Chiang's power. In 1938 he fought together with other provincial militarists and the GMD, winning a victory against the Japanese in northern Jiangsu. Just before the demise of the Nationalist Government in 1949, Li served as the Vice President, becoming Chiang's successor when he resigned the presidency in January of that year. Li was the last president of the GMD on the Chinese mainland and shortly after taking office had to flee to safety and go into exile in Taiwan.[32] When Li Zongren met Gangkar for the first time in 1937, he was already a renowned figure within the GMD.

Gangkar arrived at Lu shan to keep his commitment to build a stūpa in honor of Norlha, as his Chinese disciples desired. One document in the Nanjing historical archives suggests that the project was realized in cooperation with the "Commission of Mongolian and Tibetan Affairs" in Nanjing, where Norlha had at one time held office.[33] The construction of the stūpa, an imposing structure of approximately fifteen meters in height, was completed

FIG. 2 Gangkar Rinpoché (seated) with an attendant in China. (Courtesy of an anonymous private collection.)

in about six months.[34] Gangkar additionally built a small Padmasambhava temple to its side. After installing Norlha's remains in the stūpa, he inaugurated both the stūpa and the temple together.[35]

In the late summer of 1937, as Gangkar was completing the promised construction, war with Japan broke out. Although he had already assented to the request of Norlha's Chinese disciples that he stay for a few more years to teach, the perilous situation that was developing forced him to leave immediately. He could not return to Tibet by the most direct route and instead made a detour through Nanchang, Changsha in Hunan province, to Chongqing, and then back to Dartsedo, finally arriving at his monastery in 1939.

Gangkar's teaching activities among ethnic Chinese were halted during the years of the Sino-Japanese war, but in 1946, soon after the war's conclusion, he set out on a second trip to China. This time, his objective was to teach Chinese disciples, who already numbered in the thousands. He was accompanied on this occasion again by his treasurer and attendant

Khyenrap,[36] Dharma-master Mankong, and the monks Chödrak, Sonam Tsering, Minyak Gönpo, and Ngawang Chödrak. Gangkar's itinerary took him to Dartsedo, Chengdu, and Chongqing, before reaching Kunming in Yunnan province. Some three months later he returned to Chongqing by air and in early 1948 continued his route, going to Hankou, then Nanjing, as he made his way to Shanghai and Beijing.[37] Close to the time of the founding of the People's Republic of China in the autumn of 1949, Gangkar returned to Chengdu, and roughly a month later to his monastery in Kham.[38]

Minyak Gönpo relates that during his second trip Gangkar gave teachings to tens of thousands of Chinese disciples. On one occasion in Chongqing, it was necessary to make arrangements for him to teach in a sports stadium in order to accommodate the masses.[39] Among the students who received initiation from Gangkar were the warlord Pan Wenhua in Chengdu, Li Zongren and another member of the Guangxi clique, Li Jishen (1885–1959), in Chongqing,[40] and the warlord and governor of Yunnan, Long Yun (1884–1962), in Kunming. In particular, the wife of Long Yun, Quan Rixiang, was known to be a fervent Buddhist who later emigrated to the United States, and is still remembered around Dartsedo as "Madame Quan."[41]

In Chengdu and Kunming, Gangkar was invited to give lectures at the universities, where he presented general introductions to Tibetan Buddhism and to the five genres of doctrinal texts (*bka' pod lnga*): logic (*tshad ma*), Madhyamaka (*dbu ma*), Prajñāpāramitā (*phar phyin*), Abhidharmakośa (*mngon pa mdzod*), and Vinaya (*'dul ba*).[42] During his stay in Chongqing, Gangkar had a remarkable encounter with one of Norlha's main disciples, a GMD cadre named Wang Jiaqi. Apparently, Norlha had already authorized him to teach the local community in his absence. In late 1946 Gangkar gave teachings on the highly esoteric Great Perfection system of contemplation (*rdzogs chen*) to Wang Jiaqi, who thereupon asked for authorization to transmit the dzogchen instructions himself. In response, Gangkar formally appointed him as a successor to Norlha, and confirmed this by presenting Wang Jiaqi with a tall, pointed paṇḍita hat adorned with three golden threads symbolizing mastery over the Tripiṭaka.[43]

Early in 1947, the highest ranking GMD leaders in Chongqing arranged a celebration in Gangkar Rinpoché's honor over which Chen Lifu presided.[44] Chen was known in the GMD as the Party's chief organizer and had held the post of Minister of Education during most of the Sino-Japanese war (1938–1944).[45] On this occasion Gangkar was honored as a "teacher of the Chinese nation" (*rgyal khab kyi bla ma*)[46] by the Nationalist government and was declared to be an "omniscient meditation master, a benefactor spreading Buddhism" (*bstan pa spel ba'i bshes gnyen kun mkhyen bsam gtan gyi slob dpon*); as a token of this distinction, he was given a golden seal decorated with a lion.[47] In the same year, the GMD government asked Gangkar to come to Beiping (Beijing) to perform a protection ceremony for the Chinese nation.[48]

To honor a Tibetan lama with titles and seals is a long-standing practice in China, particularly recalled in connection with the visits of Tibetan lamas to the Chinese court: the most famous example is perhaps the Qing Emperor Shunzhi's reception of the Great Fifth Dalai Lama in Beijing in 1652. Such attributions were consistently used by the Chinese authorities as a means to strengthen ties between Tibet and China, and later—as we now know—to legitimize China's supremacy over Tibet. Given the scanty evidence available, however, it is now difficult to judge the degree to which the GMD sought to use Gangkar as a stabilizing factor in Sino-Tibetan relations. At the very least, a famous Tibetan lama such as Gangkar Rinpoché might have been seen as a strong ally in the GMD's efforts to win the support of local Tibetans in Xikang at the height of the party's struggle with the CCP.[49]

Gangkar's second stay in China proper was again cut short, this time also because of the changing political situation. When the communists came to power in 1949, the lives of some of the lama's most important advocates among the top GMD officers were at stake and a few among them, including Li Zongren, found it necessary to go into exile in Taiwan. The political shift in China once again left its mark on the course of Gangkar's life.

Chinese Students in Kham and a Third Trip to China

The communist takeover in 1949 had immediate repercussions for Gangkar Rinpoché, who had enjoyed a close connection with the GMD from the time of his first trip to China in 1936. Some of the highest GMD officials were among his disciples, including such prominent figures as Li Zongren, Li Jishen, and Long Yun. During the late forties he had emerged as one of the most famous Tibetan lamas teaching in China proper, and his reputation alone therefore made him part of the feudal system that the CCP was determined to eliminate. As a consequence, Gangkar was placed under house arrest in Dartsedo for about ten months, until those GMD leaders who had not fled the country were taken into custody. Moreover, all the Chinese disciples staying at his monastery at the time were also arrested.[50] Upon his release Gangkar was permitted to return to the monastery, but the political cleansing of the early fifties soon involved him once more with ethnic Chinese and Chinese politics. This time, however, Gangkar's dealings were with the CCP, and it is doubtful that he went on his third trip to China in 1953–1955 with the same enthusiasm and motivation he had enjoyed on his second trip.

During the Sino-Japanese war, between his first and second trips to China, Gangkar had spent most of his time at the monastery and worked to develop the non-sectarian (*ris med*) shedra Jamchen Chökhorling in 1940. Initially, the college hosted around forty Tibetan students belonging to the four major orders. In the years 1942–1945 one Khenpo Tupten from Pelpung Monastery was invited to teach alongside Gangkar. The traditional syllabus of the college included such subjects such as the five sciences (*rigs pa'i gnas lnga*), Tibetan grammar (*sum rtags*), and poetry (*snyan ngag*). Khenpo Tupten taught the *Thirteen Great Texts* (*Gzhung chen bcu gsum*) of Buddhist doctrine and philosophy, which formed the basis for the curriculum that had been established by Gangkar's own teacher Zhenga Rinpoché.[51] Among the first few Chinese who studied under Gangkar in his shedra was Zhang Chengji, later renowned as the English translator of Milarepa's *Hundred Thousand Songs* (*Mgur 'bum*) and better known in the West as Garma C.C. Chang. He arrived in 1946 and stayed for six years.[52]

Events in 1952, however, ushered in changes to the traditional curriculum of Gangkar's monastery, when a group of some eighty young Chinese students arrived at the shedra from either the newly established Central Nationalities Institute (*Zhongyang minzu xueyuan*) in Beijing or from the Southwest Nationalities Institute (*Xinan minzu xueyuan*) in Chengdu.[53] This group of students was led by Yu Daoquan, the first Chinese teacher of Tibetan at the Central Nationalities Institute, and included some who would later become prominent representatives of the up-and-coming generation of Central Institute Tibetologists: Wang Yao, Kelzang Gyurmé, Tong Jihua (d. 1989), and Hu Tan, as well as the future political leaders Geng Yufang and Li Bingquan.[54] Even though the students were sent by the CCP, Minyak Gönpo relates that he felt comfortable with them in what was an atmosphere of mutual respect.[55] In the early years of the PRC, some of the Chinese cadres who were being educated in Tibetan language and culture in order to be posted in Tibet appear to have demonstrated a sincere interest in the object of their studies.[56]

The stay of the eighty Chinese students at Gangkar Monastery was organized in cooperation with the local office of the CCP in Dartsedo. Thanks to the negotiations of the local Khampa leader Jagö Topden, the young Namkhai Norbu, now a well-known teacher based in Italy, was chosen as one of the instructors.[57] The classes for the Chinese students were meant to introduce them to Tibetan language and culture. To this end, Gangkar used both his own teaching materials, such as the *Commentary to the Hymn of Eminent Praise* (*Khyad par 'phags bstod 'grel*), and traditional texts, including the *Elegant Sayings* by Sakya Paṇḍita (*Sa skya legs bshad*).[58]

After the Chinese had completed their ten months' stay at Gangkar Monastery, Yu Daoquan delivered a report on their accomplishments to the communist government in Beijing, in which he recommended that Gangkar be invited to teach at the Central Nationalities Institute. The invitation was issued and, under the circumstances, Gangkar had no choice but to accept. Despite the number of Chinese disciples in Beijing at the time, it is unclear how eager he was to make this visit. In any case, he remained at the Institute for three years (1953–1955), teaching mainly Tibetan language, history, and philosophy.[59] During this period, Gangkar Rinpoché was also invited to serve as a translator for the National People's Congress (*quanguo renmin daibiao dahui*) in 1954, accompanied by Wang Yao as his assistant translator.[60]

When Gangkar returned to his monastery in 1955,[61] the political situation in Kham had changed yet again. Xikang province, earlier governed by Liu Wenhui, was now incorporated into Sichuan province and had been renamed the Ganzi Tibetan Autonomous Prefecture (*Ganzi zangzu zizhizhou*). There was no longer any trace of the religious freedom that had prevailed in the first years following the communist takeover. In the last year of his life, Gangkar served as an advisor to the Political Consultative Conference (*zhengxie*) of the CCP in Dartsedo, an apparently innocuous position in which his activities could be easily controlled.[62] In February 1957, he took a month-long vacation to return to his monastery. With no signs of disease, Gangkar Rinpoché passed away in March 1957, just before the Tibetan New Year, at the age of sixty-five.[63]

Teachings to Chinese Students

On leaving for his first trip to China in 1936, Gangkar Rinpoché was unable to speak even conversational Chinese. He was therefore accompanied by the Dharma-master Mankong, who acted as his main translator. While Mankong could get by in everyday conversational Tibetan and was familiar with elementary Buddhist vocabulary, he was not initially a brilliant translator. Gangkar was known to give teachings in Chinese, but he generally wrote down the mantras in Tibetan first, and then added the Chinese pronunciation underneath, a method also used by Norlha. On these occasions when he would give teachings in Tibetan, one of his disciples, usually Wu Runjiang, would make notes, give summaries in Chinese, and draw tables giving the correct pronunciation of mantras, or even of whole Tibetan texts.[64]

Gangkar offered a wide range of teachings to his Chinese students. To Norlha's former disciples he gave mostly Nyingma teachings, whereas to his own students he later preferred to teach in the Kagyü tradition. The scope of the Nyingma material he covered included such texts as Longchenpa's (1308–1364) *Trilogy of Natural Ease* (*Ngal gso skor gsum*) and *Seven Treasures* (*Mdzod bdun*), the *Heart Essence of the Ḍākinīs* together with Longchenpa's commentary entitled *Quintessence of the Ḍākinīs* (*Mkha' 'gro snying thig ma bu*), Jikmé Lingpa's (1729–1798) *Guide to Dzogchen Practice* (*Rdzogs chen khrid yig ye shes bla ma*), and the special dzogchen instructions of *trekchö* ("cutting thorough," *khregs chod*) and *tögel* ("passing over," *thod brgal*). Among the Kagyü teachings, particularly in the Kamtsang tradition of the Karmapas, he offered instructions on the development and perfection stages of the yidams Cakrasaṃvara (*bde mchog*) and Vajrayoginī (*rdo rje rnal 'byor ma*), on the *Six Yogas of Nāropa* (*Nāro chos drug*), Mahāmudrā (*phyag chen*), and on the *One That When Known Liberates All* (*Gcig shes kun grol*), a collection of empowerments by the Ninth Karmapa Wangchuk Dorjé (1556–1603).[65] Mankong, together with the other Chinese monks, translated some of these teachings into Chinese, either in the form of a free rendering or only a summary.[66] Additionally, on many occasions Gangkar gave instructions on the practice of "transference of consciousness" (*'pho ba*), an exercise that, if mastered, is said to enable the consciousness to escape via the fontanel at the moment of death and to travel directly to the pure realm of Amitābha. Many Chinese disciples were particularly keen on this practice because of the immediate physical results that could be seen: the formation of blood drops at the practitioner's fontanel opening.[67] Minyak Gönpo recounts that Gangkar would sometimes circulate among the disciples engaged in this practice, inserting a blade of *kuśa* grass into the fontanel opening of each one as a symbolic confirmation of the successful result.

Gangkar's teaching curriculum varied with his students' desires. His dzogchen instructions, the pinnacle of the nine progressive *yāna*s, or vehicles (*theg pa rim pa dgu*), of the Nyingma school, were particularly well received among Chinese Chan monks, apparently because they regarded them as extremely similar to the contemplative instructions of their own tradition, a much contested view that still seems to be current.[68] Only very few among Gangkar's Chinese disciples seem to have really understood and practiced the essential instructions of dzogchen, yet Gangkar continued to transmit them.[69]

One of the dzogchen teachings Gangkar transmitted to his Chinese disciples is the *Essential Teaching of the Dzogchen yang ti* (*Dayuanman zuisheng xinzhongxin yindao lueyao*),[70] written by Jamgön Kongtrül Lodrö Tayé (1813–1899), a founder of the non-sectarian movement (*ris med*) and the leading successor of the Ninth Situ Rinpoché Pema Nyinjé Wangpo (1774–1853) at Pelpung Monastery.[71] Generally, when Gangkar granted instruction on such a difficult text, he first gave a comprehensive explanation of the entire teaching; then, one of his monks would provide more detailed clarifications to smaller groups of students. In the 1980s, the Chinese transcription of Gangkar's teachings of this text was published by Wu Jialiang in Taiwan in the *Collection Summing up the Essence of the Dzogchen of Samantabhadra* (*Puxian wang rulai dayuanman xinyao zongji*), a compilation of dzogchen teachings translated into Chinese in the last century.[72] Although the colophon to the *Essential Teaching of the Dzogchen yang ti* unfortunately does not mention the translator, it states that Gangkar Rinpoché first gave this teaching in Changsha, and then again in Chongqing and Chengdu, while on his way back to Kham in 1938.[73] Moreover, we know from another Chinese translation that this same teaching was given in Chengdu, Chongqing, and Changsha by other Tibetan lamas, including Gangkar's own disciple Künzang.[74]

The *Essential Teaching of the Dzogchen yang ti* offers a comprehensive treatment of the practice of dzogchen and not merely an exposition of its view. It has two major parts, the first concerning the preliminary practices and the second including the main body of instruction in the dzogchen practices themselves. In the preliminaries, the adept is introduced to the anatomy of the subtle body, comprising the channels (*mai, rtsa*), energy (*qi, rlung*), and seminal essences (*mingdian, thig le*). Following a sequence of visualization exercises, he or she first becomes familiar with the channels and the energies that flow through them, and then cultivates the yoga of divinities who are understood to embody the seminal essences. Through a series of meditations on the mind, the practitioner learns to enter into the natural state (*benran, gnas lugs*), which is the uncontrived, innate state of the mind's primordial simplicity. When the movements of the mind are controlled by virtue of the practices devoted to energy, the non-duality of mind and energy comes to be realized. This union of energy and mind is the prerequisite for completely opening the central channel, so that energy may flow freely through it and later be transformed into luminosity during the main practices.

Only after cultivating a thorough understanding of these preliminaries is the practitioner able to engage in the two main sequential dzogchen practices of *trekchö* ("cutting thorough") and *tögel* ("passing over"). Trekchö is a means of realizing the unlimited nature of mind and cutting through the proliferations of conceptual activity (*fenbie, rnam rtog*). The unlimited nature of mind is pointed out to the adept by an accomplished master, whereupon the former gradually attains stability in this view by means of repeated practice. Trekchö is concerned with the aspect of mind that is known as its primordial purity (*benlai qingjing, ka dag*). Tögel, on the other hand, focuses on the spontaneously accomplished presence that is primordial wisdom (*renyun chengjiu zhihui xianqian, rang bzhin lhun grub kyi ye shes*). Once again, through a series of meditations—undertaken in the course of prolonged retreats, some in the dark, some in light—the knowing and luminous aspect of mind, that is to say its intrinsic awareness (*jinzhi, rig pa*), is realized and perfected step-by-step. In this way, the energy that is cultivated in the dzogchen preliminaries is gradually refined into light. When one has accomplished stability in both the emptiness and the luminosity of mind, it is described as complete liberation.

Although this is not the place for a more thorough analysis and translation of this elaborate text, this short summary nevertheless demonstrates the complexity and sophistication of some of the teachings that Gangkar Rinpoché conferred, even during his first trip to China.

* * * *

Among ethnic Chinese, Bo Gangkar Rinpoché became one of two especially renowned Tibetan trülkus in Republican China. Yet even though Gangkar enjoyed the support of some of the highest GMD leaders, the material available at present does not suggest that he used his influence to achieve specific political aims in Kham—as his predecessor Norlha had done and which he paid for with his life—but in the first place fulfilled his religious duties. His commitment to the transmission of dzogchen instructions to his Chinese disciples, summarized above, clearly demonstrates his willingness to share with them the full complexity of the most elevated Buddhist teachings. In the end, however, Gangkar could not separate his religious life from political entanglement, so that following the communist takeover in 1949 he was appointed to teach the first group of Chinese students chosen by the CCP to be future cadres in Tibetan affairs. In this regard, Gangkar appears to have been used as an early representative of the CCP's "civilizing project" in cultural Tibet.

Despite his conscription by the CCP, however, Gangkar Rinpoché's religious activities in China, especially during the 1930s and 1940s, can also be seen as a precursor to the growing interest in Tibetan Buddhism on the part of ethnic Chinese that has become so prevalent in the PRC since the mid-1990s.[75] A new kind of religiosity seems to be on the rise in China, but it is too soon to tell whether intercultural encounters of the type pioneered by Gangkar Rinpoché will have the opportunity to ripen more fully than they did during the tumultuous times in which he lived.

NOTES

* Concerning Gangs dkar Rin po che's activities in China, I am very grateful for the information given to me by Mi nyag Mgon po in an interview in July 2001 in Beijing. Mi nyag Mgon po lived as a monastic with his teacher Gangs dkar Rin po che for twenty-eight years until the latter's death in 1957. He also accompanied Gangs dkar on his second trip to China in 1946. Furthermore, I am indebted to Prof. Wang Yao of the Central Nationalities Institute (*Zhongyang minzu xueyuan*) in Beijing for the information he shared with me during a telephone call in January 2002. Wang Yao studied with Gangs dkar at his monastery in 1952 and later in Beijing. I would also like to thank Wang Xiaojun, who arranged an interview for me with the late Liu Liqian in July 2001 in Chengdu. Liu Liqian was one of the early Chinese translators of Tibetan Buddhist texts from the Republican era onward and studied in eastern Tibet in the 1930s with both lama Kun bzang and Gangs dkar Rin po che. Kun bzang was himself a disciple of Gangs dkar and headed the neighboring Sa skya monastery (see below). He also travelled in China proper as a Buddhist teacher. Finally, I would like to thank Serdok Rinpoché for drawing my attention to the text *Essential Teaching of the Rdzogs chen yang ti* (*Dayuanman zuisheng xinzhongxin yindao lueyao*).
  This chapter was originally written in the winter of 2001. Hence, when I talk about recent publications, I refer to those of the late nineties. An excerpt of this chapter was also presented as a paper on the occasion of the eleventh conference of the International Association of Tibetan Studies held at Königswinter, Germany, in August 2006.

1 In Chinese Gangs dkar Rin po che is usually referred to as Gongga jingang shangshi and sometimes also as Gongga Hutuketu. However, it is not clear whether the title Khutughtu (Ch. Hutuketu) was ever officially conferred on him.

2 I use the term "civilizing project" here as it was introduced by Stevan Harrell ("Introduction: Civilizing Projects and the Reaction to Them," in *Cultural Encounters on China's Ethnic Frontiers*, ed. by Stevan Harrell [Seattle/London: University of Washington Press, 1997], pp. 3–36) in his research on so-called "ethnic minorities" in Republican China and the PRC. It refers to the effort to transform peripheral peoples in order to adapt them to the culture of the dominant and "civilized" power. Gangs dkar Rin po che may be seen as part of China's "civilizing project" in Tibet in so far as he acted as a teacher of the first group of Chinese cadres in the early 1950s, students educated in Beijing's Central Minority Institute to be sent to Tibetan areas later on (see below). Goldstein, however, notes that the Tibetans had seen themselves during the Manchu period as agents of their own "civilizing project," over and against that of the Chinese. Melvyn C. Goldstein, *Buddhism in Contemporary Tibet:*

Religious Revival and Cultural Identity, ed. Melvyn C. Goldstein and Matthew T. Kapstein (Berkeley: University of California Press, 1998), p. 6. This observation may also help us to understand in part the activities of lamas like Gangs dkar in China. The main emphasis in this chapter, in any case, is on Gangs dkar Rin po che's teaching activities during the period of religious freedom in the 1930s and 1940s.

3 Hardly any research has been done on Gangs dkar Rin po che so far. The only recent publication is his biography by Mi nyag Mgon po: *'Bo Gangs dkar sprul sku'i rnam thar dad pa'i pad dkar bzhugs so* [*Biography of 'Bo Gangs dkar Tulku: The White Lotus of Faith*] (Beijing: Mi rigs dpe skrun khang, 1997). There is only very limited material available concerning Gangs dkar Rin po che's activities in China and for this chapter I was not able to consult the Chinese historical archives. Cultural and historical data (*wenshi ziliao*) on the Chinese localities where Gangs dkar Rin po che stayed might eventually yield more detailed information.

4 This account of Gangs dkar's education and early activities as a teacher is based on Mi nyag Mgon po, *'Bo Gangs dkar sprul sku'i rnam thar*, pp. 34–54, so far the only biographical source available.

5 This figure has recently been studied in Achim Bayer, "The Life and Works of mKhan-po gZhan-dga' (1871–1927)," (master's thesis at the Department of History and Culture of India and Tibet, Hamburg University).

6 The Chinese scholar Liu Liqian had studied with Lama Kun bzang and translated some of his teachings into Chinese. For a recent publication representing their collaboration, see *Dayuan shenghui benjue xinyao xiuzheng cidi* 大圓勝慧本覺心要修証次第, by Wugouguang 無垢光 (Dri med 'od zer = Klong chen pa) taught by Gensang Zecheng 根桑澤程 (Kun bzang tshe 'phrin), trans. by Liu Liqian 劉立千 (Beijing: Minzu chubanshe, 2000). In China Lama Kun bzang was known under the name Gensang Zecheng shangshi.

7 In Gangs dkar Rin po che's biography the author Mi nyag Mgon po gives different spellings for Nor lha. On the first occurrence he is named "bla ma Nor lha Rin po che," but later on Mi nyag Mgon po usually refers to him simply as "Nor bla" (Mi nyag Mgon po, *'Bo Gangs dkar sprul sku'i rnam thar*, p. 57). Moreover, though Nor lha was apparently not recognized as a *trülku* (but about this see n. 13 below), he was still renowned under the title Rin po che—at least in China (interview, Serdok Rinpoche).

8 Peng Wenbin, "Frontier Process, Provincial Politics and Movements for Khampa Autonomy During the Republican Period," in Lawrence Epstein, ed., *Khams pa Histories: Visions of People, Place and Authority*, Proceedings of the Ninth Seminar of the International Association for Tibetan Studies, Leiden 2000, vol. 4 (Leiden: Brill, 2002), pp. 57–84.

9 The war between Liu Wenhui and Liu Xiang in 1932/33 is described in Robert Kapp, *Szechwan and the Chinese Republic: Provincial Militarism and Central Power, 1911–1938* (New Haven: Yale University Press, 1973), pp. 111–115. Liu's successful war against Liu Xiang became well-known as the "war to stabilize Sichuan" (*an chuan zhan*) (loc. cit.: 200).

10 For a study of the lengthy process of the incorporation of Eastern Tibet (Khams) as Xikang province, see Peng Wenbin, "Frontier Process, Provincial Politics and Movements for Khampa Autonomy."

11 In Feng Youzhi's *Xikang shi shiyi*, Nor lha is described as a "lama with political ambi-tions" (Feng Youzhi 馮有志, ed., *Xikang shi shiyi* 西康史拾遺 [*Omissions of the History of Xikang*], 2 vols. [Kangding: Ganzi zangzu zizhi zhou zhengxie wenshi ziliao weiy-uanhui, 1993], p. 143).

12 Feng Youzhi, *Xikang shi shiyi*, p. 142, does not give the year when the title was bestowed on Nor lha. The Tibetan use of the name Mgar ra bla ma is reported by Mi nyag Mgon po, *'Bo Gangs dkar sprul sku'i rnam thar*, p. 57.

13 Nor lha's motive for supporting the Chinese troops is not yet very clear. However, we may assume that this incident was already part of Nor lha's vision of an autono-mous Khams, whose final aim was the rejection of both the Chinese as well as the Central Tibetan authorities. Elliot Sperling has, however, kindly communicated to me a possible solution to the question of Nor lha's stance against Lhasa. In a recent Tibetan account of Nor lha by Skal bzang bkra shis, it is stated that as an infant Nor lha was in fact first recognized by the Tibetan Cabinet, or Bka' shag, to be the Thir-teenth Dalai Lama, but that the recognition was then withdrawn. His later enmity toward Lhasa may have been due to this. See Skal bzang bkra shis, "Mgar ra bla mas Lu'u cun dmag khams khul 'byor skabs mnyam 'brel dang Go min tang skabs bod sog u yon lhan khang gi u yon sogs byas skor," in Bod rang skyong ljongs srid gros lo rgyus rig gnas dpyad gzhi'i rgyu cha u yon lhan khang, eds., *Bod kyi lo rgyus rig gnas dpyad gzhi'i rgyu cha bdams bsgrigs* 10/19 (Beijing: Mi rigs dpe skrun khang, n.d.): 113–122.

14 In his detailed study on warlordism in Sichuan, Kapp, *Szechwan and the Chinese Republic*, pp. 66–70, gives a detailed portrait of Liu Xiang's character, but does not mention his Buddhist interest. He describes him, though, as having "superstitious tendencies."

15 Feng, *Xikang shi shiyi*, pp. 143–44.

16 Feng, *Xikang shi shiyi*, p. 116. Peng Wenbin, "Frontier Process, Provincial Politics and Movements for Khampa Autonomy," analyses Skal bzang tshe ring's role in the movement for Khams pa autonomy in the early 1930s. In 1931 the GMD had sent Skal bzang tshe ring back to Khams in order to establish a provincial party branch. However, in the following year he used this opportunity to oppose Liu Wenhui and the GMD in an armed rebellion, but was forced to withdraw. Peng Wenbin evalu-ates Skal bzang tshe ring's engagement as the first of a series of rebellions whose aim was Khams pa self-rule.

17 Mi nyag Mgon po, interview.

18 For a more detailed account, see following chapter.

19 Lü Tiegang 呂鐵鋼 (ed.), *Zangmi xiufa midian* 藏密修法秘典 [*Secret Scriptures of Tibetan Esoteric Dharma Practices*], 5 vols. (Beijing: Huaxia chubanshe, 1995): vol. 3, p. 767.

20 Loc. cit.: 817. Mount Lu (Lu shan) is about 400 km up the Yangtse River from Nan-jing and north of lake Poyang (Poyang hu) in Jiangxi province.

21 For a detailed analysis of Nor lha's movements in Khams in 1935, see Feng, *Xikang shi shiyi*, p. 144–162. Peng Wenbin, "Frontier Process, Provincial Politics and Move-ments for Khampa Autonomy," gives a good summary of these events.

22 Huang Yingjie gives a slightly different account in his *Almanac of Tantric Buddhism in Republican China* (*Minguo mizong nianjian*). According to him, Nor lha's remains

were sent to Nanjing and officially inspected by members of the GMD government (Huang Yingjie 黃英傑, *Minguo mizong nianjian* 民國密宗年鑒 [*Almanac of Tantric Buddhism in Republican China*] [Taibei: Quanfo wenhua chubanshe, 1995]: p. 101, no. 360). Unfortunately, Huang Yingjie does not cite the source of his information. Nevertheless, given Nor lha's position within the GMD, it seems plausible that his remains were sent to the Nanjing leaders rather than to Gangs dkar directly.

23 Unfortunately, the correspondence between Nor lha and Gangs dkar was destroyed during the Cultural Revolution. Nevertheless, Gangs dkar Rin po che had allowed Mi nyag Mgon po to read many of those letters and he reports that Nor lha often propagated GMD ideas, disdaining the communists. Party members in Nanjing were afraid that local Tibetans might shift their loyalties to the communists (interview, Mi nyag Mgon po).

24 Nor lha's teaching activities at Mount Lu are exemplified in the account of his conferring the Tārā initiation, mentioned above.

25 Mi nyag Mgon po only counts Gangs dkar's first two trips as part of his activities as a *trülku*. The third trip to Beijing in the early years of the People's Republic was apparently not the result of his own independent decision (interview). Concerning the period of this third trip, Prof. Wang Yao provided somewhat different information, saying that Gangs dkar stayed in Beijing from 1954 to 1957. Although I have not yet been able to verify the precise chronology on the basis of archival materials, I follow here the indications provided in Mi nyag Mgon po's biography of his teacher Gangs dkar.

26 I could not locate the exact number of the students Gangs dkar took over from Nor lha. On a number of occasions during my interview of him, Mi nyag Mgon po mentioned that sometimes a few thousand Chinese students participated in the teaching sessions.

27 Liu Wenhui was also said to have been a fervent Buddhist believer. However, Mi nyag Mgon po is uncertain of the sincerity of his faith (interview).

28 Mi nyag Mgon po, *'Bo Gangs dkar sprul sku'i rnam thar*, p. 59. The late Bsod nams tshe ring was the cousin of Mi nyag Mgon po.

29 Mi nyag Mgon po, *'Bo Gangs dkar sprul sku'i rnam thar*, p. 60, and interview.

30 In the *Secret Scriptures of Tibetan Esoteric Dharma Practices* (*Zangmi xiufa midian*: vol. 4, p. 661) Mankong appears as the translator of a *rdzogs chen* text taught by a certain Ga ma (not identified, but perhaps equivalent to Tib. Karma). The translation was verified by Gangs dkar Rin po che.

31 Interview, Mi nyag Mgon po; Mi nyag Mgon po, *'Bo Gangs dkar sprul sku'i rnam thar*, p. 60.

32 Denis Twitchett and John F. Fairbank, *The Cambridge History of China. Volume 13: Republican China 1912–1949, Part 2* (Cambridge: Cambridge University Press, 1986), pp. 125–127, 555, 783–784.

33 Unfortunately I was not able to directly consult this one document (including four letters) concerning the construction of the stupa in honor of Nor lha, which is preserved in the Number Two Historical Archives of China (*di er lishi dang'an guan*) in Nanjing. However, in the catalogue of the archives (Zhongguo di er lishi dang'an guan 中國第二歷史檔案館/Zhongguo zangxue yanjiu zhongxin 中國藏學研究中心 ed., *Zhongguo di er lishi dang'an guan suocun xizang he zangshi dang'an mulu* 中國

第二歷史檔案館所存西藏和西事檔案目錄 [*Catalogue to Files about Tibet and Tibetan Affairs Preserved in the Number Two Historical Archives of China*] [Beijing: Zhongguo zangxue chubanshe, 2000], vol. 1, p. 721, no. 10914), it bears the title *Nuona Hutuketu Nanjing jinian banshi chu wei chengbao Nuona jian ta xu kuan ji yiwu chuzhi deng shi yu mengzang weiyuanhui laiwang han (gong si jian)* ("Correspondence Between the Memorial Office for Nor lha Khutughtu and the Commission of Mongolian and Tibetan Affairs Reporting the Handling of Funds for Building a Stupa for Nor lha and [his] Relics [altogether four letters]") and is listed as document no. 141–3838 in the archives. The four documents included there date between November 4, 1936, and September 7, 1937.

34 Mi nyag Mgon po relates that the stūpa was destroyed during the tumultuous years of the Cultural Revolution, but was later rebuild by the grand-disciples of Nor lha.

35 Refer to Mi nyag Mgon po, *'Bo Gangs dkar sprul sku'i rnam thar*, p. 61. Huang, *Minguo mizong nianjian*, p. 107, no. 387, only mentions that Gangs dkar inaugurated the stūpa and the temple, but not that he played a role in their construction.

36 Mkhyen rab, who had been with Gangs dkar for more than thirty years, died during the return journey to the monastery while in the vicinity of Ya'an in Sichuan province in 1949 (Mi nyag Mgon po, *'Bo Gangs dkar sprul sku'i rnam thar*, p. 69).

37 According to Huang, *Minguo mizong nianjian*, p. 138, no. 516, Gangs dkar went once more to Kunming on his way back to Khams. During his stay at Miaogao Monastery he gave *rdzogs chen* empowerments and instructions on Cakrasaṃvara, on which occasion notes on these teachings were taken by a disciple named Jian Fu.

38 Mi nyag Mgon po, *'Bo Gangs dkar sprul sku'i rnam thar*, pp. 63–69.

39 Even though we do not know the actual number of Chinese students who took refuge with Gangs dkar or received his teachings, still the impression I have from Mi nyag Mgon po's report of the events confirms that Gangs dkar was extremely popular among ethnic Chinese. At one point during this second trip Mi nyag Mgon po was responsible for writing down the names given to each disciple during a refuge ceremony. However, as people came in thousands, he got confused about those who had already received a refuge name and those who had not yet received one (interview).

40 Twitchett and Fairbank, *op. cit.*, p. 125.

41 Mi nyag Mgon po, *'Bo Gangs dkar sprul sku'i rnam thar*, pp. 64–65, and interview.

42 Mi nyag Mgon po, interview.

43 Mi nyag Mgon po, *'Bo Gangs dkar sprul sku'i rnam thar*, p. 65, and interview. There is another story of an apparent dharma-heir of Gangs dkar Rin po che, the scholar Wang Zhiping from Chengdu, who was apparently also authorized as a *vajra*-master (*rdo rje slob dpon*). The story was related to me by the son of Wang Zhiping, Wang Desheng, in Chengdu in September 2000. He wrote a biography about his father that unfortunately was not yet published at the time I wrote the present chapter. Wang Desheng regards himself thus as a grand-student of Gangs dkar Rin po che and was apparently authorized by his father Wang Zhiping as a *vajra*-master as well. Recently, he finished a three-year retreat in a hermitage close to Gangs dkar's monastery. However, during a visit to Mi nyag Gangs dkar in 1998, I got the impression that the locals were not entirely convinced of his authenticity.

44 Mi nyag Mgon po, *'Bo Gangs dkar sprul sku'i rnam thar*, p. 67.

45 Twitchett and Fairbank, *op. cit.*, pp. 410, 604. Moreover, Chen Lifu together with his

brother Chen Guofu founded in 1927, the first year of the GMD's Nanjing decade, a secret organization that functioned as one of Chiang K'ai-shek's two principal secret police forces. It was also known as the "CC clique" (*CC-xi*), meaning either "Central Club" or "Chen and Chen." Chen Lifu is reported to have been personally very close to Chiang K'ai-shek (loc. cit.: 142).

46 I could not find a document giving the exact Chinese title. Yet, it should probably be the term *guoshi*. During imperial times the Chinese emperors often conferred the title *dishi* "imperial teacher" on Tibetan lamas, following the precedent of its bestowal upon 'Phags pa Blo gros rgyal mtshan (1235–1280), the teacher of the Yuan Emperor (Wang Yao 王堯 and Chen Qingying 陳慶英, *Xizang lishi wenhua cidian* 西 藏歷史文化辭典 [*Dictionary of the Cultural History of Tibet*] [Hangzhou: Zhejiang renmin chubanshe, 1998], pp. 6, 66; see also chapter 4 above). In the Republican era the term *dishi* was accordingly abandoned in favor of the title *guoshi*, which had also been granted from the Yuan-period onward to esteemed Tibetan ecclesiastical figures. Gangs dkar and Nor lha were apparently the only lamas to hold this title in Republican China.

47 Mi nyag Mgon po, *'Bo Gangs dkar sprul sku'i rnam thar*, p. 67.

48 Gangs dkar had performed a similar ceremony for the GMD in 1945 immediately after the Japanese had been defeated (refer to Huang, *Minguo mizong nianjian*, p. 129, no. 478 and 131, no. 485).

49 In this regard, the actions of the GMD could be interpreted similarly to their appointment of Nor lha as a Pacification Commissioner to Khams in 1935 in order to organize the resistance of Tibetans to the Red Army. As noted earlier, the big difference between Nor lha and Gangs dkar was the obviously political motivation of the former, whereas the latter—if politically motivated at all—kept this well hidden.

50 Mi nyag Mgon po, *'Bo Gangs dkar sprul sku'i rnam thar*, p. 72, and interview.

51 Mi nyag Mgon po, *'Bo Gangs dkar sprul sku'i rnam thar*, pp. 46–47, and interview.

52 Mi nyag Mgon po, *'Bo Gangs dkar sprul sku'i rnam thar*, p. 48. According to Huang, *Minguo mizong nianjian*, p. 104, no. 370, Zhang Chengji arrived at Gangs dkar's monastery in 1937, studying Tantric Buddhism there for eight years.

53 The Central Nationalities Institute, founded in May 1951, became at that time the most important institution for Tibetan Studies in China, enhanced by the move there of Tibetan programs from some of the other universities (especially, Beijing University). (Wang Yao, interview.)

54 Mi nyag Mgon po, *'Bo Gangs dkar sprul sku'i rnam thar*, pp. 49, 72–73, and interview; Wang Yao, interview.

55 Melvyn C. Goldstein, *A History of Modern Tibet, 1913–1951: The Demise of the Lamaist State* (Berkeley: University of California Press, 1989), p. 641, also remarks that the Khams pas did not see the Chinese communists as bitter enemies in the years 1949–1951. While they did not emphatically support the Tibetan government, some did foresee the coming confrontation between Lhasa and China.

56 Mi nyag Mgon po, interview.

57 Minyak Gönpo, at that time working in the Office of Religious Affairs (*zongjiao ju*) and responsible for registering the names of all the students and teachers, reports that Namkhai Norbu was then enrolled under the name Loden Wangpo.

58 Mi nyag Mgon po, *'Bo Gangs dkar sprul sku'i rnam thar*, p. 73, and interview. This commentary, *Khyad par 'phags bstod 'grel*, is one of the few original works by Gangs dkar Rin po che that is still available, a blockprint of which was prepared at Dpal spungs Monastery. Mi nyag Mgon po had one copy himself which he presented to Dil mgo Mkhyen brtse Rin po che (1910–1991) as an offering. (Mi nyag Mgon po, interview).

59 Mi nyag Mgon po, interview, and Huang, *Minguo mizong nianjian*, p. 168, no. 38. So far, there is hardly any documentation available about the third trip of Gangs dkar Rin po che to Beijing. However, recently Prof. Wang Yao of the Central Nationalities Institute has written a biography of Yu Daoquan, though unfortunately this was not yet available to me when this article was written. Gangs dkar's stay at the Central Nationalities Institute in Beijing, which Yu Daoquan had arranged, is no doubt discussed therein.

60 Wang Yao, interview.

61 According to the information given by Huang, *Minguo mizong nianjian*, p. 170, no. 48, Gangs dkar returned to Khams in 1954.

62 There is no material currently available to me which details Gangs dkar's real functions during his stay in Dar rtse mdo.

63 Mi nyag Mgon po, interview.

64 An example of these notes is given in Lü 1995: vol. 2, p. 488.

65 Mi nyag Mgon po, *'Bo Gangs dkar sprul sku'i rnam thar*, pp. 59–60; Huang, *Minguo mizong nianjian*, p. 138, no. 515.

66 Mi nyag Mgon po, *'Bo Gangs dkar sprul sku'i rnam thar*, p. 65.

67 Herbert V. Guenther, *The Life and Teachings of Nāropa* (Oxford: Clarendon Press, 1963), p. 201; Matthew T. Kapstein, "A Pilgrimage of Rebirth Reborn: The 1992 Revival of the Drigung Powa Chenmo," in *Buddhism in Contemporary Tibet, op. cit.*, pp. 95–119.

68 Liu Liqian, interview. For a discussion of the historical sources concerning the connection between Chinese Chan Buddhism and Tibetan Rdzogs chen see my articles: "Chinese *Chan* and Tibetan *Rdzogs Chen*: Preliminary Remarks on Two Tibetan Dunhuang Manuscripts," in *Religion and Secular Culture in Tibet, Tibetan Studies II (PIATS 2000)*, H. Blezer, ed. (Brill: Leiden, 2002), pp. 289–307; "Structural Analysis of the *bSam gtan mig sgron*: A Comparison of the Fourfold Correct Practice in the *Āryāvikalpapraveśanāmadhāraṇī* and the Contents of the Four Main Chapters of the *bSam gtan mig sgron*," in *Journal of the International Association of Buddhist Studies* 26/1 (2003): 175–195; "Legend of *Cig car ba* Criticism in Tibet: A List of Six *Cig car ba* Titles in the *Chos 'byung me tog snying po* of Nyang Nyi ma 'od zer (12th century)," in *Tibetan Buddhist Literature and Praxis, Studies in its Formative Period 900–1400*, Ronald Davidson and Christian Wedemeyer, eds. (Leiden: Brill, 2006), pp. 31–54; "The Conjunction of Chinese Chan and Tibetan rDzogs chen Thought: Reflections on the Tibetan Dunhuang Manuscripts IOL Tib J 689-1 and PT 699," in *Contributions to the Cultural History of Early Tibet*, Matthew T. Kapstein and Brandon Dotson, eds. (Leiden/Boston: Brill, 2007), pp. 239–301.

69 Mi nyag Mgon po and Liu Liqian, interviews.

70 This text was published in a Chinese collection of teachings on *rdzogs chen* (Gongga jingang shangshi 貢噶金剛上師, "Dayuanman zuisheng xinzhongxin yindao lueyao"

大圓滿最勝心中心引導略要 [Essential Teaching of Rdzogs chen yang ti], in: *Puxian wang rulai dayuanman xinyao zongji* 普賢王如來大圓滿心要總集 [*Collection Summing up the Essence of Rdzogs chen of Samantabhadra*], ed. by Wu Jialiang 吳家樑 [Taibei: Da zhidu chubanshe, 1987], vol. 2, pp. 834–921). See below.

71 The name of 'Jam mgon Kong sprul is given in Chinese according to the lexical meaning of his name Padma gar dbang Blo gros mtha' yas as "Lianhua youxi zizai zhihui wubian dashi" (see Gongga 1987: 915). The work of Kong sprul on which Gangs dkar based his teaching—*Rdzogs pa chen po gsang ba snying thig ma bu'i bka' srol chu bo gnyis 'dus kyi khrid yig dri med zhal lung*—was published xylographically at Dpal spungs, where Gangs dkar Rin po che no doubt studied it, in vol. 5 of Kong sprul's *Rgya chen bka' mdzod* and vol. 1 of the *Gdams ngag mdzod*. It has been reprinted many times on the basis of these initial publications. On Kong sprul's life and contributions generally, see E. Gene Smith, *Among Tibetan Texts: History and Literature of the Himalayan Plateau* (Boston: Wisdom Publications, 2001), ch. 17; Dudjom Rinpoche, *The Nyingma School of Tibetan Buddhism: Its History and Fundamentals*, trans. Gyurme Dorje and Matthew Kapstein (Boston: Wisdom Publications, 1991), vol. 1, pp. 859–868; and Richard Barron, trans., *The Autobiography of Jamgon Kongtrul: A Gem of Many Colors* (Ithaca, NY: Snow Lion, 2003).

72 The text we are considering is given there in vol. 2, pp. 834–921. The same collection also includes other teachings given by Gangs dkar Rin po che, e.g., the *Record of Teachings and Explanations of Empowerment and Meditation Methods in Rdzogs chen* (*Dayuanman guanding ji xiuchi fang fa jiangjie jilu*) taught during his second trip in the 1940s in Kunming, Yunnan (Wu Jialiang 吳家樑 ed., *Puxian wang rulai dayuanman xinyao zongji* 普賢王如來大圓滿心要總集 [*Collection Summing up the Essence of Rdzogs chen of Samantabhadra*], 2 vols. [Taibei: Da zhidu chubanshe, 1987]: vol. 2, pp. 746–799).

73 This information is also confirmed by Huang, *Minguo mizong nianjian*, p. 108, no. 395.

74 Gongga, *op.cit.*, p. 921. I could not identify the other Tibetan lamas who are mentioned as having transmitted this teaching in China as well. Their names are given in Chinese as Mingjue (= Tib. Mi 'gyur) shangshi, Qinzeng (= Tib. Mkhyen brtse?) shangshi, and Seke shangshi.

75 Cf. M. Kapstein, "A Thorn in the Dragon's Side: Tibetan Buddhist Culture in China," in *Governing China's Multi-ethnic Frontier*, ed. Morris Rossabi (Seattle: University of Washington Press, 2004), pp. 230–269.

PART III
THE MODERN CHINESE DISCOVERY
OF TIBETAN BUDDHISM

❧

7: Translating Buddhism from Tibetan to Chinese in Early-Twentieth-Century China (1931–1951)*

Gray Tuttle

O F THE TEXTUAL sources currently available, accounts of the transmission of Buddhism between China and Tibet during the Republican period (1912–1949) are predominantly recorded in Chinese. This is because it was the Chinese who were seeking instruction on Buddhism from Tibetans, at times from fairly marginal figures in the Tibetan cultural world. Thus, while Tibetan language records of time spent in China were left by major lamas, such as the Ninth Panchen Lama, Lozang Tupten Chöki Nyima (1883–1937), the most copious archive of Buddhist exchange in this period, involving less prominent teachers, is preserved in Chinese. Two important Chinese language collections of Tibetan Buddhist materials, reprinting rare materials first published in the 1930s and 1940s in China, are the *Dharma Ocean of the Esoteric Vehicle (Micheng fahai)* and the *Secret Scriptures of Tibetan Esoteric Dharma Practices (Zangmi xiufa midian)*.[1] These works preserve compilations made in 1930 in Chongqing and from 1931 to 1951 in Beijing, respectively. From reprints of Nenghai's (1886–1967), Fazun's (1902–1980), and Norlha Khutughtu Sonam Rapten's (1865 or 1876–1936) works, we know that additional material was preserved in other locations, and it is clear that we do not yet have access to everything that was printed at local presses or circulated in manuscript. Further, whatever is still extant is merely what happened to survive the decades of mid-twentieth-century warfare and Communist suppression of religion. Nonetheless, given the breadth of publishing activity during the Republican period and evidence in both this chapter and others in this volume, we are aware that we are just beginning to ascertain the efflorescence of Chinese involvement with Tibetan Buddhism at that time.[2] The two collections under discussion here, however, demonstrate the scope of Tibetan Buddhist activity among Chinese Buddhist communities in mid-twentieth-century China as no other available materials do.

The *Dharma Ocean* and *Secret Scriptures* indicate that Tibetan Buddhism was understood and practiced by the Chinese to a much greater degree than previous research has suggested.[3] The texts demonstrate the interest and success of the Chinese in mastering the Tibetan language as a way to more fully access Tibetan Buddhist teachings and illuminate the critical role of the laity and lay institutions in sponsoring the translation and publication of Tibetan Buddhist teachings in China. While previously the laity of the imperial court may have engaged in such activities, to my knowledge the widespread participation of ordinary laypeople that we see at this time marks an historic development in Chinese and Tibetan Buddhism. These translations also acquaint us with many lesser-known Tibetan Buddhist teachers active in China in the Republican period. Finally, the rapid growth of interest in Tibetan Buddhism in early-twentieth-century China provides a useful counterpoint to the late-twentieth-century explosion of interest around the globe. The early translation of Walter Evans-Wentz's work into Chinese is only one of the more obvious signs of the underlying trends that had already begun to integrate Tibetan and Chinese Buddhists into what has become a routine process of global religious exchange.

These texts also help chart the growth of interest in Tibetan Buddhism among Chinese from parochial provincial communities to a broad domestic audience. This is well illustrated by the significant shift that can be seen in the method of phoneticizing Tibetan between the 1930 *Dharma Ocean* publication and some of the later publications collected in the *Secret Scriptures*. For the earlier publication, the intended audience was clearly a local one, as the editor indicates that the Sichuan dialect was the basis for the Chinese character transliterations.[4] But by the late 1930s, many of the translators were using roman letters (presumably based on English pronunciation) to help standardize pronunciation. This reflected the more diverse audience (from Beijing, Kaifeng, Shandong, and Shanghai) that would have had access to these later, east coast, publications. But why would the Chinese be so interested in Tibetan script in the first place? In 1934, the argument for using Tibetan was that it preserved old Sanskrit pronunciation better than any other contemporary script or language (such as those that survived in Nepal). Therefore, the Tibetan script was taken as the basis for approximating Sanskrit sounds. To transliterate these correctly, English phonetics (*zhuyin*), "which were already familiar to [educated] society," were used alongside Chinese characters. Because Chinese pronunciations differ depending on dialect, the editors of this text chose the Beiping (Beijing) pronunciation as the standard, even though the book was published in China's new capital, Nanjing (a prescient decision given Beijing's downgraded status at the time).[5] Elsewhere I have argued that throughout China an indigenization of Tibetan Buddhism occurred among the Chinese after the departure of the Paṇchen Lama and the Norlha Khutughtu in the late 1930s, and this attempt to make the Tibetan language accessible to Chinese Buddhist practitioners lends support to that argument.[6]

The role of lay societies and laymen as translators and shapers of the Tibetan Buddhist teachings that entered China in the twentieth century has also not been substantially examined. Previously, I and others have examined the important accomplishments of the Chinese monks Nenghai and Fazun in making Tibetan Buddhism accessible to the Chinese, especially through translation of critical works. These same monks, as well as their colleagues Guankong (1902–1989), Chaoyi, Yanding, and Mankong, also played a role in the translations under consideration here. But they only contributed to fifteen of the seventy-six titles collected in these volumes, roughly twenty percent. Accordingly, a surprising new picture emerges of the heretofore neglected role that Chinese Buddhist laymen played in the translation and dissemination of a broad range of Tibetan Buddhist teachings.

With the exception of the six Chinese monks named above and one Mongol Tibetan Buddhist teacher (who authored three of the titles), translation and explication of these Tibetan Buddhist texts (and the oral teachings upon which many were based) relied on Chinese Buddhist laymen, accounting for approximately eighty percent of the works included in the Chinese collections. All told, some ten laymen were responsible for realizing this project, but nearly half of the translations were penned by just two men: Sun Jingfeng (twenty-one texts) and Tang Xiangming (thirteen texts). Yet to my knowledge, no one—certainly no Western scholar—has ever mentioned these two figures. Had their works not been preserved and reprinted in the 1990s, we might have remained ignorant of their impressive contribution to the spread of Tibetan Buddhism in China, since unlike the monks, they lacked disciples willing to write their biographies. That their works and those of so many other lay Buddhists dedicated to the propagation of Tibetan Buddhism in China were reprinted in the last years of the twentieth century is testament to the fact that there is a revived interest in Tibetan Buddhism in both China and Taiwan.

Another important facet of the history of Tibetan Buddhism in China that can be discovered in these texts is the role played by several lesser-known Tibetan Buddhist teachers of the late 1930s and early 1940s. These are: (1)

上師多傑覺拔尊者像讚
一切法空　空中有相
不有不空　是秘密藏

十方共讚　金剛總持
重重光影　為天人師
弟子潘文華和南敬題

顯密法海像讚

尊者詳多傑覺拔西康人也託質川達染
衣藏衛暨年入道優遊法海博通經藏深
蘊智練出顯入密參數十載拉薩蚌寺
者法王之裔都聖哲之淵府僧徒億萬奉
為師表尊者大悲所懷狀貌遊化內
地隨機演教歷京滬津浙邪漢與夫閩粵
嘗古越雲所至上泊元首王公下達僧俗
楊德藐不稽首皈依飽飯乳光俱所化
徒眾無其神異卒蒼海內宗仰當合肥粟
政時錫以諧們罕尊號以襃揚之民國
以卯木葉有也今春受川人士之請杯渡
來渝啓建西南和平法會孟夏四月石黜
花飛若重慶佛學社中禹四眾授戒傳法
灌頂已畢請留影以誌景仰於是遠以一
相而攝無量福雖然果有相耶無相耶
在尊者自證甚深智慧德相固非凡愚所
得而窺而淑之私於此光影重重水月
鏡相三密相應竭塵嚩中不揭圓陁
敬為之頌云

仁壽潘文華撰

FIG. 1 A page of the *Dharma Ocean of the Esoteric Vehicle* (82), with a photograph
of Geshé Dorjé Chöpa.

the best known, Dorjé-chang Trashilhünpo Ngakchen Darpa Khutughtu
(Ch. Anqin shangshi, Anqin duokengjiang), Dewé Jungné Gyelten Rinpoché, Lozang Tendzin Jikmé Wangchuk Pelzangpo (1884–1947); (2) Geshé
Nomunqan Lama Dorjé Chöpa (Ch. Duojie jueba gexi, 1874–?); (3) Vajra-
lama Nomci Khenpo Dorampa Lozang Zangpo (Ch. Jingang shangshi nuomoqi kanbu daoranba Luobucang sangbu); (4) Vajra-lama Tupten Nyima
(Jingang shangshi Tudeng lima, called a *gexi*, Tib. *dge bshes* in one instance[7]);
and (5) the Mongol Gushri Könchok Dorjé (Guxili Gunque duoji).[8] The last
of these seems to have been the only teacher whose command of Chinese
allowed him to pen his own Chinese texts, as no translator is listed. Though
he wrote only three of the works considered here, they are three of the lon-

ger and earlier works and likely played a seminal role in shaping the practice of many Chinese disciples of Tibetan Buddhism. Aside from Dorjé Chöpa, who was active in the late 1920s and early 1930s, the other three Tibetan figures were most active in the late 1930s, especially in 1939, in which year alone at least sixteen Tibetan Buddhist works were published.[9]

We are hampered by the relative paucity of historical and biographical information on most of these figures, lay and monastic. With the exception of lengthy biographies of Fazun, Nenghai, and Norlha Khutughtu, as well as a few brief observations on Guankong, Geshé Dorjé Chöpa, and Ngakchen Khutughtu, I know of no account of these men save what we can extract from the two collections under review, which is precious little.[10] There is so much more we would like to know. Regarding the Tibetans: Where were they from? Where did they train? How did they end up in China? Regarding the Chinese: How did they become interested in Tibetan Buddhism and capable of translating Tibetan Buddhist texts? What were the historic forces that shaped their rise and later near disappearance from the historical record? And in general: What roles did the presence or absence of Nationalist Chinese and later the occupying Japanese governance play in the explosion of interest in Tibetan Buddhism in 1930s China? These questions, and a detailed analysis of the contents of the texts, will have to await further exploration. My more limited aim in this chapter is to sketch an overview of the collections in order to introduce them, and their authors, to the scholarly community.

Dorjé Chöpa, Zhang Xinruo, and the Dharma Ocean of the Esoteric Vehicle

Geshé Dorjé Chöpa, along with his Chinese disciple Zhang Xinruo, was responsible for the practice-oriented work *Dharma Ocean of the Esoteric Vehicle* (*Micheng fahai*, hereafter called *Dharma Ocean*). This master was the first fully trained Tibetan monk to teach the Chinese in the Republican period. Originally from Dartsedo (Ch. Dajianlu, later renamed Kangding), he spent twenty years at Loséling in Drepung, the largest monastery in Lhasa, earning an advanced degree in Buddhist philosophy, before undertaking three years of tantric studies at a monastic school dedicated to these practices. For years afterward he lived in Mongolia and must have become familiar with Chinese Buddhists on his five trips to Wutai shan in the first decades of the twentieth century. As early as 1925, he initiated Chinese disciples into ten different Tibetan Buddhist tantric cycles and translated over twenty different types of Tibetan esoteric texts into Chinese. Dorjé Chöpa also started the Tantrayāna Study Society (*Micheng xuehui*) in Wuchang.[11] His teaching took him into China's far northeast, and he performed rituals for warlords as far south as Canton. But he was most productive, in terms of recorded activities and publications, during the time he spent in his native Sichuan province. There he conducted the second and third Dharma-Assemblies for Peace, in Chongqing and Chengdu respectively (the first had been held in Shenyang). The last of these ritual assemblies, along with details about the teachings that followed the event, is recorded in a special issue of Chengdu's Southwestern Dharma-Assembly for Peace (*Chengdu Xi'nan heping fahui tekan*).[12] However, the *Dharma Ocean* was produced while Dorjé Chöpa was in Chongqing and records his teaching activities there.

In the eulogizing prologue to the *Dharma Ocean*, the compiler (and most likely main translator), Zhang Xinruo, compares Dorjé Chöpa to Padmasambhava, Atiśa, and other great figures in the Tibetan Buddhist tradition. He praises his teacher for opening and revealing (*kaishi*) the esoteric vehicle to the east. He gradually narrows his focus, from China initially, then to the southwest, and finally to the particular teachings the master gave in Chongqing in 1930.[13] Discussing his master's prior teaching in eastern China, including in Zhejiang, Beijing, Hankou, and Wuchang, Zhang notes that other manuscripts had been circulated and edited previously. Yet these earlier translations suffered from certain shortcomings, most notably the reliance on Japanese esoteric Buddhist terminology. This situation is reminiscent of the earliest days of the entry of Buddhism into China, when Daoist terminology was used to translate Indian or Central Asian Buddhist terms. But what Zhang found problematic in this case was that the two forms of Buddhism—Japanese and Tibetan—were sufficiently dissimilar to lead to misconceptions in the context of translation. Given this problem, it is not surprising that Zhang's prefatory remarks clearly indicate that Dorjé Chöpa's Chinese was inadequate to produce a proper translation himself. Here too there is a comparable situation in the nearly simultaneous efforts of Walter Evans-Wentz to assist with the translation of Tibetan Buddhist texts through an oral exchange with a Tibetan teacher of English in Darjeeling, Kazi Dawa Samdup. Like Evans-Wentz, Zhang and his colleagues who recorded the teachings never claim to be translators.[14] Possibly they, also like Evans-Wentz, served as "living dictionaries" for their lama. Evans-Wentz's theosophic terms, like those of the Chinese Buddhists accessing Tibetan esoterica through the medium of Japanese esoteric Buddhism, embedded within this context a distinct and not necessarily compatible discourse. One gets the impression that in both cases, the terms in the "target" language were chosen from a pre-existing lexicon (theosophy and Japanese esoteric Buddhism, respectively) that did not approximate the concepts of the "source" language. How were the twentieth century Chinese to resolve this problem?

Zhang remarks that this edition contains new translations of each teaching, but that the method of translation made use of earlier translations, while also attending to the master's scriptural comparison and reliance on thorough research (*kaozheng*). Without seeing the earlier editions that used Japanese esoteric Buddhist terms, we cannot evaluate the degree of improvement afforded by the new edition. However, it is likely that over time the linguistic skills of translators would have improved considerably. In the case of the monastic translators, we know how their education progressed, from initial studies in China to completion of their studies abroad, in Kham and Central Tibet. As for the laymen who translated for various lamas, we know only that some of them had initially joined the short-lived Beijing Buddhist College for the Study of Tibetan Language in 1924–1925 or had studied with individual monks at Yonghegong.[15] Yet their resources were meager, lacking both language textbooks and dictionaries until the mid-1930s.[16] Of course, long-term interaction and study with a native speaker of the language may have proved a more valuable tool than any number of reference works. In any case, while the extent of their training is a matter of speculation, their motivations are made clear by the kinds of materials they chose to translate, from which we can only conclude that the objectives of these prolific authors and translators were decidedly religious. Several of the early texts in particular were devised as comprehensive introductions to the practice of Tibetan Buddhism. And unlike some recent works on Tibetan Buddhism in America, which mix advocacy for Tibetan political interests with Buddhist teachings, propaganda on the political status of Tibet was absent from any of the works consulted.[17]

In order to provide a sense of what one of these works did contain, it is necessary to briefly outline the earliest comprehensive set of Tibetan Buddhist practice materials to be printed in Chinese, the 1930 *Dharma Ocean of the Esoteric Vehicle* by Dorjé Chöpa and his disciple Zhang Xinruo. Though Tibetan precedents for the organization of parts of this work may be found,[18] I suspect that the precise shape it took was the result of the interaction of Tibetan and Chinese expectations about what should be taught and learned. The book, over six hundred pages long, is divided into six major sections (*bu*), and an appendix. The first section, the longest, is devoted to the fundamentals of Tibetan Buddhist practice. The other five sections build on this foundation but are devoted

respectively to specific (1) tantric deities, (2) (male) buddhas, (3) female buddhas, (4) bodhisattvas, and (5) dharma-protectors. The inclusion of the final
appendix, called "extra-curricular (*kewai*)" practices, indicates that the first
six sections should be considered a curriculum for practitioners to study and
practice. Tibetan Buddhist monasteries often had particular curricula that
they expected their monks to adhere to, but this seems to be the first example of a curriculum created for Chinese Buddhist lay disciples of Tibetan
Buddhism. In this respect, it anticipates the often unpublished English translations of Tibetan Buddhist practice texts that dharma-centers around the
United States have produced for their own use. The *Dharma Ocean of the
Esoteric Vehicle* may be outlined as follows:

1) Fundamentals (nine divisions)
    1. Dorjé Chöpa's Teachings of Spring 1930
    2. Basic Practices (refuge, *bodhicitta*, four immeasurables,
       making offerings)
    3. Short biography and explanation of proper ritual setting
       (with illustrations), proper sitting and daily practice
    4. Visualization of Dorjé Chöpa as one's root lama
    5. Visualization of Tsongkhapa
    6. Visualization of Yamāntaka
    7. Visualization of the Ten-wheeled Vajra Lama
    8. Visualization of Green Tārā
    9. Recitation of *Miktsé* (a popular Gelukpa practice)
2) Tantric Deities
3) [Male] Buddhas
4) Female Buddhas
5) Bodhisattvas
6) Dharma-Protectors
7) Appendix: Extracurricular Practices
[Index of Mantras, Recitations, and Hymns. Added to the reprint edition.]

An examination of the contents of the various sections of the *Dharma
Ocean* yields insights into this critical exchange between Chinese and Tibetan
Buddhists. The fundamentals (Ch. *genben*) section has nine internal divi-
sions; as the initial three are more central than the latter six, I turn to them
first.[19] These three are collections (*ji*) of the teachings basic to the practice of
Tibetan Buddhism. The first collection records the teachings given by Dorjé
Chöpa in the spring of 1930 for the Buddhist Study Society (Foxueshe) at

Chang'an Temple in Chongqing. On the first day, some 160 men and women took the fivefold precepts as well as the bodhisattva precepts.[20] This first day's teaching also records the Tibetan language verses that were taught to the Chinese audience. The verses are first given in Tibetan script, then in (Sichuan) Chinese transliteration, and finally in Chinese translation. This method, which would allow the Chinese to see and pronounce the Tibetan words, is repeated throughout the book. Usually the Tibetan passages are quite short, either a stanza or a mantra, though sometimes these fill an entire folio. This work's bilingual presentation marks it as the first such Republican-era text (or at least the first to have survived), and possibly the first such text ever produced without imperial sponsorship. Probably this type of text had been produced earlier by Dorjé Chöpa and his students in eastern China and served as the model here.

Following the bestowal of exoteric precepts on the first day, on the second day the esoteric or tantrayāna (*micheng*) precepts were given to the same group of men and women.[21] By the third day the crowd had nearly doubled to over three hundred people, including the four types of disciples, presumably meaning monks, nuns, laymen, and laywomen. On the final two days several dozen more—probably attendees who had missed the first round of precepts—received the same sets of precepts previously bestowed.[22]

Dorjé Chöpa's teachings were marked by a distinctively Tibetan Buddhist, and especially Gelukpa, teaching style. After transmitting the precepts on the first two days, he opened the third day by teaching about the difficulty of attaining a human existence within the six realms of cyclic existence that comprise saṃsāra.[23] This teaching was meant to inspire the audience to seize the rare opportunity they had to learn Buddhism in their present existence as human beings. He opened the next day by discussing how extraordinary it is to even hear Buddhist teachings.[24] The third day, he discussed the life and thought of the progenitor of the Gelukpa tradition to which he belonged: Tsongkhapa. The record of these three days of teachings, and the two days of conferring precepts before and after, comprise the first division of the fundamentals section.

The second division is devoted to the basic practices of taking refuge, developing bodhicitta, the four immeasurable states of mind (*si wuliang xin*), making offerings, and so forth. Unlike the first division of this section, which recorded details such as the date and time of the teachings given, this division is presented as a practical guide for daily use. The same format of providing Tibetan script, Chinese transliteration, and Chinese translation is used throughout this division. Only occasionally are short additional notes provided, as guides to the manner in which some portion of the text should be recited (such as: "repeat three times"). After describing the practices outlined above, the bulk of this division of the text is devoted to the recitation of mantras, as well as to the proper way to make offerings and set up an altar.

The third division of the fundamental section appears to have existed as a separate work before its inclusion in this compilation. It opens with a frontispiece, showing a photograph of the master, and a short biography of him. This is followed by a preface and introductory notes on the use of the text (*liyan*).[25] The body of this division is devoted to explaining how to create the proper ritual setting for practice and begins by describing how to approach and clean the altar and set up offerings before the image of the Buddha. A diagram illustrating the proper arrangement is included.[26] A description of the proper way to sit and meditate follows. Developing the correct mental state (*faxin*) that takes all beings into consideration and the associated visualizations preparatory to taking refuge are also described.[27] The daily practice routine goes into great detail regarding the ritual offerings, presenting a diagram of the universe (according to Indo-Tibetan cosmology) and a detailed breakdown of the thirty-seven precious objects, which are to be visualized as an offering.[28] As with the previous division, this section concludes with a series of mantras but also includes an addendum from the master about coming to Chongqing to teach Buddhism. With regard to the esoteric school's characteristic feature of becoming a buddha in this very body (*ji sheng cheng fo*), the master says: "Indians, Tibetans, and Mongolians who have practiced this dharma successfully are without measure, without limit. Recently transmitted to this land (*ci tu*, meaning China) [to] those who have received initiation . . . a great host has attained this secret dharma."[29] Thus, the promise here is that the Chinese, like the Indians, Tibetans, and Mongolians before them, would now have the opportunity to attain buddhahood in this lifetime.

The fourth to eighth divisions of the fundamentals section are short "combined practices (*hexiu*)" that each open with taking refuge, generating the four immeasurable attitudes and bodhicitta, and then turn to visualizations of: Dorjé Chöpa as one's fundamental lama in the fourth division; Tsongkhapa in the fifth division; Yamāntaka (Ch. Daweide, Tib. Rdo rje 'jigs byed) in the sixth division; the Ten-wheeled Vajra Lama in the seventh division; and Green Tārā in the eighth division. The ninth and concluding division contains a recitation (*niantong*), which is known as the *Miktsé* in Tibetan and has been called "the Creed of the Gelukpa." Through this recitation, the speaker prays to three central bodhisattvas of Tibetan Buddhism (Avalokiteśvara,

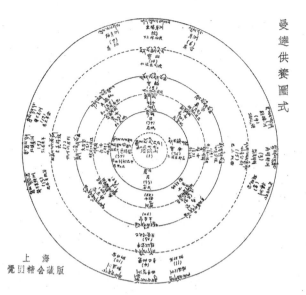

FIG. 2 The diagram of the universe according to Buddhist cosmology, as given in *Secret Scriptures of Tibetan Esoteric Dharma Practices* (1.748).

Mañjuśrī, and Vajrapāṇi), understanding them to be identical to the lineage master of the Gelukpa tradition, Tsongkhapa.[30] This short passage is so central to the Gelukpa tradition that both the Fifth Dalai Lama and his regent Desi Sanggyé Gyatso made reference to the first occasion on which Qing courtiers recited this verse in 1653.[31] Its recurrence here, among a lay Buddhist community in China, marks another significant advance of the Tibetan Buddhist missionary effort launched by the Gelukpa some three and half centuries before, among the Mongols on the eastern frontiers of Tibet.[32]

The transmission of the basic tenets of Tibetan Buddhist practice might seem unnecessary for a culture that had known of Buddhism for over 1500 years. However, there are several distinctive aspects to Tibetan Buddhism, differentiating it from Chinese Buddhism, that are made clear in these texts. Most important of these is the focus on the lama (Ch. *shangshi*) that is found in Tibetan Buddhism, a point also underscored in Ester Bianchi's study of Nenghai lama in chapter 9. Rather than taking refuge in only the standard Three Jewels—the Buddha, the Dharma, and the Sangha—Tibetan Buddhists introduce a fourth object of refuge at the head of the list: the lama. This unique formula for taking refuge is repeated throughout the texts of the *Dharma Ocean*, first appearing in the fundamentals section on proper

worship and thereafter at the start of nearly every one of the dozens of ritual texts devoted to a specific tantric deity, buddha, etc.[33] This attention and
devotion to the lama, who is elevated even above the other Three Jewels of
Buddhist refuge, is characteristic of late esoteric practice. Reliance on the
teacher over any other authority is seen as necessary for the disciple to be
guided through the tantric path. This introduces a second distinctive feature of these texts, namely that they involve tantric practice. Although many
of the short ritual texts are devoted to buddhas and bodhisattvas who are
also present in the (Mahāyāna) Chinese Buddhist world, many other texts
are dedicated to tantric deities and esoteric forms of various bodhisattvas
and dharma-protectors, beings who would not have been familiar to the
Chinese.

The next major section of the *Dharma Ocean* is devoted to these very esoteric deities. With the exception of the first text, these thirteen short works are
recitations (*niantong*) devoted to various tantric figures such as Yamāntaka,
the Kālacakra deity, and various versions of Hayagrīva (Tib. *rta mgrin*). Each
text opens with the fundamental practices of the four refuges, generating the
four immeasurables and bodhicitta, and then a threefold repetition of refuge.
The first text in this section, a completion stage (*chengjiu*) work, has the practitioner transforming him or herself into Heruka for the sake of all sentient
beings.[34] In each of these texts, the repetition of mantra(s) associated with the
particular deity is a central part of the ritual practice.

This pattern is followed throughout the rest of the work, for almost five
hundred pages, covering ninety-nine different Buddhist figures. Thus, on
average, these are short texts of some five pages (ten folios in their original
form, as two folios are copied on each page of the reprint). These include
roughly two hundred mantras, so many that a separate index of them has
been made for the reprint edition. This added index also lists nearly one hundred recitations (*niantong*) and over 120 hymns of praise (*jizan*) to the various figures, from Dorjé Chöpa to the White God of Wealth (Bai cai shen).

The section of the work focused on [male] Buddhas is the shortest, with
only nine texts. It is noteworthy that the section on the buddha-mothers
(*fomu*, or female buddha) is the second longest of the work, after the fundamentals section. Covering twenty-seven female figures in 125 pages, this section is extensive perhaps because it includes the female tantric deities, who
might otherwise have appeared in the Vajra section, such as the White Parasol Buddha-mother (Ch. Bai sangai fomu; Tib. Gdugs dkar can ma; Skt.
Sitātapatrā).[35] Moreover, the texts devoted to various forms of Tārā (Ch.
Dumu) are divided first by color (green, white, yellow) and then enumerate

each of twenty-one forms of Tārā separately. While I cannot offer a defini-
tive explanation for this attention to and segregation of the female figures,
it may be that Chinese Buddhists, well known for their transformation of
Avalokiteśvara into a female form and their attention to female salvific figures in various syncretic traditions, especially appreciated the diverse assortment of female forms of enlightened beings in the Tibetan Buddhist world
and chose to highlight them in this way.[36]

The section on bodhisattvas opens with four different texts devoted to
the various forms (colors) of Mañjuśrī, the bodhisattva most closely associated with China in the minds of Tibetans.[37] A favorite of Chinese Buddhists, Avalokiteśvara, including the esoteric eleven-headed and four-armed
versions of the deity, is the subject of ten texts.[38] Vajrapāṇi (Ch. Jingangshou;
Tib. Phyag na rdo rje), the third in the usual Tibetan trinity of bodhisattvas,
but foreign to the Chinese Buddhist world, is covered in six texts.[39] A Maitreya recitation ends this section.

The last regular section, on protectors of the Dharma (hufa), also includes
figures not typically found in the Chinese Buddhist world. Mahākāla, a
wrathful form of Avalokiteśvara, had long been venerated by Mongols and
Manchus who lived in or ruled over China from the Yuan to Qing dynasties.[40] But as far as I know, this is the first time that Chinese lay Buddhists
were granted access to texts devoted to this powerful protector. This may
be why this text is unusually long for the compilation, thirty-three pages
with roughly twelve pages of Tibetan script interspersed.[41] This section also
includes praises to the white and yellow gods of wealth and concludes with
a text dedicated to making offerings (gongyang) to the Four Heavenly Kings
(Si tian wang). The final, "extracurricular" section includes an assortment of
recitations and practice texts, such as one that promises Avalokiteśvara's aid
in curing eye ailments.[42]

For such a vast work, the Dharma Ocean is notably lacking the sorts of philosophical texts that Chinese monks such as Fazun were devoting themselves
to translating at this time, as will be seen in the following chapter. Although
this distinction cannot be made too rigidly (because there were monks, such
as Nenghai, who were also very interested in ritual and practice texts), I think
it is safe to say that lay interest in more directly efficacious forms of Buddhist
teaching and practice, namely mantras and merit-generating recitations and
hymns of praise, dictated the production of this work. What is remarkable
here is the abundance of short, focused texts, generally with very concrete
goals—salvation from particular dangers, such as the eight enumerated in an
Avalokiteśvara recitation;[43] the accumulation of wealth; or the curing of eye

problems. Moreover, the emphasis on attaining enlightenment in this very lifetime eschews the gradual approach of some of the philosophic works so central to the Gelukpa monastic tradition.

As for the distribution and popularity of the *Dharma Ocean*, presumably it would have enjoyed the same renown as did its editor, Dorjé Chöpa, whose reputation was widely known, especially in Chongqing, where the book was compiled. The mayor and other local notables were initiated into Tibetan esoteric practices and built an enduring monument, an enormous and expensive Tibetan-style stūpa set on a hill in the center of the city, to commemorate his visit and the forty-nine-day Southwestern Dharma-assembly for Peace held there early in 1930.[44] Early the next year, the second Southwestern Dharma-assembly for Peace was held in the nearby provincial capital, Chengdu, and was attended by leading warlords, dignitaries, and at least 4,500 individuals whose donations (totaling nearly 50,000 silver dollars) were individually recorded in a memorial volume. Such a following demonstrates that Dorjé Chöpa was a highly esteemed figure in Sichuan. We can be almost certain that by the middle of the twentieth century, his written work had spread as far as Beijing and Taiwan. A 112 page volume of what appears to be extracts from the larger work and dates to 1934 is found in a collection of esoteric texts from Beijing and seems to be a combination of various parts of the 1930 Sichuan work: a text dedicated to Amitāyus, the long-life Buddha, is here coupled with parts of the fundamentals section. To this, two letters from Dorjé Chöpa's disciples, one the principal editor of his works, were appended.[45] While Dorjé Chöpa had disappeared from the historical record by 1934, his work continued to be reproduced and dispersed throughout China and Taiwan.

Secret Scriptures of Tibetan Esoteric Dharma Practices (Zangmi xiufa midian)

The second major collection, *Secret Scriptures of Tibetan Esoteric Dharma Practices*, brings together esoteric materials collected from 1931 to 1951 in Beijing from a variety of printing presses on China's east coast. These materials were compiled by someone respectfully referred to as "forefather" Zhou Shujia, who in pointed understatement was said to have "attended to the esoteric tradition (*mizong*)." During the Cultural Revolution, when homes were being searched and books confiscated, these texts were preemptively bundled up and taken to a branch of the government's inspection stations by his son. At the end of the Cultural Revolution, the latter was able to recover the impounded materials and later donated his collection to China's Buddhist Library (Zhongguo Fojiao tushuguan). There, the layman Lü Tiegang catalogued them and published a booklist called the "Catalogue and Account of China's Buddhist Library's Manuscript Collection's Chinese Translations of Tibetan Buddhism." This list was published in the official Chinese Buddhist Association's journal *Fayin* (*Sound of the Dharma*) in 1988, just a year after Dorjé Chöpa's work was reprinted in Taiwan. The scholarly community in China apparently encouraged the reprinting of these rarely seen and important translations, for the benefit of Tibetologists, and as a result Lü had the collection published in this five-volume set.[46]

Rather than trying to summarize the contents of this vast and diverse body of work—five volumes containing seventy-five titles in 4,500 pages—it is perhaps more beneficial to highlight a few of the major institutions, teachers, and translators that seem to have played important roles in the Chinese and Tibetan Buddhist interactions recorded in its pages. The two major Beijing institutions involved in the initial publication of the individual texts were the Esoteric Treasury Institute (Ch. Mizang yuan, Tib. Gsang ngags chos mdzod gling; active 1931–1938) and the Bodhi Study Association (Puti xuehui, active 1938–1951).[47] The four most important teachers, already mentioned above, were the Mongol Könchok Dorjé, the Ngakchen Khutughtu, Lozang Zangpo, and Tupten Nyima. The translator Sun Jingfeng was active from 1936 to at least 1942, with most of his bilingual translations published in 1939 as part of the series of the *Collected Translations of Tibetan Esoterica* (*Zangmi congyi*) by the Tibetan Esoteric Practice and Study Association (Zangmi xuixuehui). Most of Tang Xiangming's numerous translations are not dated but his involvement with Esoteric Treasury Institute suggests he might have been active from as early as 1932. From his dated works, he was clearly active from at least 1939 to 1944. The only other figure that deserves special mention is Walter Evans-Wentz (1878–1965), whose English-language compilations of Tibetan texts served as the basis for five translations in the collection.

The Esoteric Treasury Institute and Könchok Dorjé

We know very little about Beijing's Esoteric Treasury Institute, but the books published at the institute during the mid-twentieth century hold important clues to the institute's activities. The key figures associated with this institute were the Mongol Könchok Dorjé, the Ninth Paṇchen Lama, the Ngakchen Khutughtu, and Tang Xiangming. Most informative is a short inscription written across a photograph in the opening pages of one of the institute's illustrated works, which reads: "Mizhou fazang si (The Dharma Treasury of Esoteric Dhāraṇī Monastery), named in brief: Mizang yuan; established in good order by the [Ninth] Paṇchen Lama."[48] The headboard inscription over the altar is too poorly reproduced to make out clearly, but from a later occurrence of the Tibetan name of the institute, it is clear that it reads "Sangngak Chödzöling," plainly a translation of Mizang yuan.[49] Despite the poor quality of the photograph, we can make out what may be the Lentsa script version of the Kālacakra Tantra's symbol decorating the hangings over the altar. If this identification is correct, this photograph would probably date from the 1932 Beijing Kālacakra ceremony led by the Paṇchen Lama, with the participation of the Ngakchen Khutughtu.[50] The presence of a photograph of the Ngakchen Khutughtu at the front of the book confirms this link with the Paṇchen Lama, though the Khutughtu also returned to Beijing just before the death of the Paṇchen Lama in 1937.[51]

Three of the four dated works we have from the institute were written by the Mongol translator Könchok Dorjé. Of him, we know only these writings, which include the earliest text in the *Secret Scriptures of Tibetan Esoteric Dharma Practices*: a 1931 work of over one hundred pages devoted to the eleven-headed form of Avalokiteśvara.[52] This text, like most of Könchok Dorjé's own compositions, contains no Tibetan script whatsoever. His next publication, a 1934 "essentials of daily recitations," included several translations as well as a text illustrating thirty-five buddhas. Alone among his writings, in this work a few syllables of Tibetan script are interspersed throughout the text.[53] The final, 1936 version that bears his name is a massive five-hundred-page work that opens with six pages of illustrations and a Yamāntaka text. The image of Tsongkhapa at the start of this publication confirms that Könchok Dorjé, like the Ninth Paṇchen Lama and the Ngakchen Khutughtu, adhered to the Gelukpa tradition.[54]

The appearance of the dated works at the Esoteric Treasury Institute from 1931 to 1938 provides the only indication of the time frame during which we know that the institute was active. We can therefore surmise that the other writings published by the institute, including four works consisting mostly of illustrations and their captions, were also produced during the same period. The terminal date of the only one of these illustrated works merits a detailed examination, in that the text either had no preface, or else the front matter was removed during the most recent editorial process. If the latter is the case,

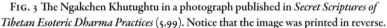

FIG. 3 The Ngakchen Khutughtu in a photograph published in *Secret Scriptures of Tibetan Esoteric Dharma Practices* (5.99). Notice that the image was printed in reverse.

the material may have been removed due to political sensitivity, as it may have reflected positively on the Japanese occupation of Beijing, or at least not been critical of the occupying force.

The Tibetan postscript, however, remains and includes a long series of phrases useful for dating the work, given in descending order as points of reference as the events approach the present, and interesting for what they tell us of the cultural and political concerns that were most relevant to the Tibetan author. Not surprisingly, the first reference is to the number of years since the Buddha's birth. Following this, the year is dated from the number of years that have elapsed since each of a series of major events: the Buddha teaching the Kālacakra root-tantra; his passing into nirvāṇa; the Muslims (*kla klo*) taking possession of Mecca—an interesting point of global reference; the appearance of the Kālacakra commentary; the birth of Tsongkhapa; and the ascension to the throne of the most recent ruler of Shambhala. At this point the method of dating changes and the reader is offered a significant anomaly—the reign date of the Qing Emperor—thereby extending the dynasty's "rule" of China some twenty-seven years beyond the dynastic abdication in 1911. The final chronometric references return to standard methods for dating in Tibetan texts, listing the years since the deaths of the thirteenth Dalai Lama and Ninth Paṇchen Lama, and finally noting the Tibetan year: Earth Male Tiger. All these points indicate that the year of publication was 1938.

For all their variety, the events noted share one common feature: not that they are all Buddhist, as they are not, but that none recognizes the end of the Qing dynasty or the foundation of any new state in China. Instead, the reference to the Qing Emperor's reign date is shocking: "the thirtieth year of the Mañjughoṣa Great Emperor Xuantong" ('jam dbang gong ma chen po shon thong gyal sar bzhug gnas lo sum cu).[55] Even the Japanese, when they installed Puyi, previously known as the Xuantong Emperor, as the "Chief Executive" of the puppet state Manchukuo in February of 1932, described him as the former Xuantong Emperor.[56] Useful as it might have been to their plans for the occupation of China, they no longer recognized his claim to the throne of the Qing empire. Yet this is exactly what the Tibetan strategy of dating his reign as continuous since 1908 succeeds in doing; the Tibetan author still acknowledges Puyi as the Qing Emperor. With the death of the Paṇchen Lama in 1937, did such lamas as the Ngakchen Khutughtu feel some fragile hope for a future alliance of Buddhist Tibet and Buddhist Japan under the banner of the Mañjughoṣa Emperor? It is this that leads me to suspect that there may have formerly been a politically offensive, Chinese-language preface that was omitted by the modern editors who failed to take note of the implications of the Tibetan-language postscript. In any event, certainly no alliance of the sort alluded to ever materialized, but the Japanese did have plans (and spies on the ground) for working with Tibetan Buddhists who might have been persuaded to envision a future within Japan's Asian empire.[57]

This speculative excursus aside, I turn now to consider the contents of the four largely pictorial texts printed by the Esoteric Treasury Institute, presumably between 1931 and 1939. The first two, which are the longest and very similar, consist mainly of single, mostly tantric, figures on the front side of the folio (measuring roughly five by nine inches), with bilingual captions including a number, and the name and color of the figure (as they were printed in black and white).[58] On the reverse of each is, again in both Tibetan and Chinese, information on the figure as well as the associated mantra. According to the postscript to the second text, five hundred and forty Chinese, Tibetan, and Mongolian monks and laity attended events at the Esoteric Treasury Institute in 1938 to receive initiations into the tantric cycles described in the book.[59] The third text, dedicated to Yamāntaka, is printed in Tibetan pecha format (unbound narrow horizontal leaves) with five figures illustrated on each page and bilingual captions below. On the reverse, behind each figure in a vertical line are the syllables "Oṃ āḥ hūng swā hā." The end of the text includes illustrations of ritual paraphernalia, symbols, and circular dhāraṇī (*zhou*).

The final illustrated text returns to the vertical orientation typical of Chinese works and has only Chinese captions describing the figure depicted and no other textual content. The opening image is again Yamāntaka and the final figures likewise depict paraphernalia and dhāraṇī similar to those found at the end of the third book. However, in this fourth text almost all the intervening pages are densely filled with four or five detailed line drawings of Buddhist figures. As suggested by the lone postscript to the second text indicating how it was to be utilized, it seems that all of these works were meant to accompany other ritual or training manuals. They appear to be aids rather than stand-alone guides to the practice of esoteric Tibetan Buddhism. The other consistent characteristic is the appearance of Tsongkhapa in the early pages of each text, indicating that the authors and users of these texts were adherents of the Geluk tradition. This is hardly surprising given the close association between this institute and the Ninth Paṇchen Lama and his envoy, the Ngakchen Khutughtu. Moreover, the Geluk tradition was still in power in Tibet at the time of these early Chinese publications, and it had had a long institutional presence in China proper, especially in Beijing.

Interlude: Nyingma and Kagyü Translations, 1932–1936

Given the tradition of imperial support for the Gelukpa tradition, there was a relatively strong showing of interest in other Tibetan Buddhist traditions over the next several years, especially in the Nyingma and the Kagyü. The most prominent figure from the non-Geluk traditions was the exiled Khampa lama, the Norlha Khutughtu (Ch. Nuona huofo), a Nyingmapa who, as we have seen in the preceding chapter, had been imprisoned by Tibet's Gelukpa government for cooperating with late Qing efforts to extend Chinese administrative control deep into Tibetan territory. Having escaped prison and arrived in China in 1925, it took some years for the lama to become well-established in China, gaining renown first in Sichuan province (by 1927) and in Nanjing by 1929. His teaching career in China peaked in the early 1930s, and the works he authored that are translated in the *Secret Scriptures* collection date from this time.[60] The first set of his translated texts to appear in the collection is dedicated to Sitātapatrā (Tib. Gdugs dkar, Ch. Da bai san'gai fomu), the female Buddhist deity associated with a protective white parasol, illustrated in this case with three faces and six arms. As described by Ishihama Yumiko, this deity had been worshipped by the rulers of China in the Yuan and Qing dynasties, and the Norlha Khutughtu used at least one of the previously translated practice texts as the basis for his teachings.[61]

The origins of the *Secret Scripture*'s set of Sitātapatrā texts can be found in the Nanjing Buddhist Lay Group (*Fojiao jushilin*), which invited the Norlha Khutughtu to transmit esoteric dhāraṇī (*mizhou*) in 1931. In the preface, the translator Wu Runjiang states that the goal of the teachings was to make the Sitātapatrā dhāraṇī widely available so that beings in this age of the decline of the dharma might escape saṃsāric suffering. Thus he translated the dhāraṇī into the national (vernacular) speech (*guoyin*).[62] As for the Tibetan portion of the text, the Norlha Khutughtu did not provide the Tibetan script of the dhāraṇī that is included in these texts. Instead, Zhong kanbu (Tib. *mkhan po*) of the Panchen Lama's Nanjing representative's office was asked to undertake this.[63] The second short text devoted to Sitātapatrā in this collection recommends that dharma-assemblies be held to eliminate disaster and protect the country (*xiaozai huguo*). At the end of the text, the Norlha Khutughtu is recorded to have said that if good men and women would practice reciting this dhāraṇī with the correct mindset, in dharma-assemblies, whether conducted by a single person or many people, and lasting for one, seven, twenty-one or forty-nine days, then the country would be shielded from disaster.[64] This was a powerful promise, especially given the threats that China was then facing from Japan.

The second set of collected texts associated with the Norlha Khutughtu was published in 1935, but includes texts from 1932 and 1934, all oriented around the same themes as the first set: female Buddhist figures who had the ability to save the Chinese from catastrophe. In this case, the female figures were the various forms of Tārā. The Norlha Khutughtu first gave teachings on Tārā in the winter of 1932 in Nanjing.[65] The audience for the event initially numbered only six people, but by spring of 1934 they had persuaded the master to teach a larger audience. Over the summer, the lama went to Lu shan, the nearest mountain retreat where one could hope for cool breezes and escape Nanjing's sweltering summers. There a Chinese monk and a layman invited him to give the same teaching to 130 people. Laymen wrote out the text and the lama corrected it somehow, though no source indicates that he knew Chinese. As before, a member of the Panchen Lama's office staff, Zhong kanpo, wrote the Tibetan text. Presumably, the printed text could then be distributed at other teaching events. In one instance, in Nanjing in 1934, the Nor-

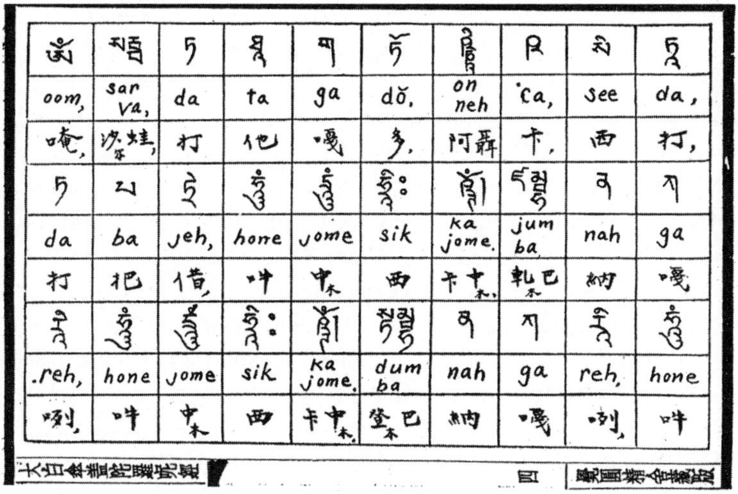

ལྗཱ	སཪྦ	ད	ཏ	ག	ད	༄	ཨ	ས	ད
oom,	sar va,	da	ta	ga	dŏ,	on neh	'ca,	see	da ,
ཌ	ཟ	ཇ	ཧོ	ཇོ	སིཀ	ཀ ཇོ	ཇུཾ བ	ན	ག
da	ba	jeh,	hone	jome	sik	ka jome.	jum ba	nah	ga
ཪེ	ཧོ	ཇོ	སི	ཀ ཇོ	དུཾ བ	ན	ག	ཪེ	ཧོ
.reh,	hone	jome	sik	ka jome.	dum ba	nah	ga	reh,	hone

FIG. 4 The phonetic scheme adopted to transcribe Tibetan in connection with Norlha Khutughtu's teachings. From *Secret Scriptures of Tibetan Esoteric Dharma Practices* (2.385).

lha Khutughtu's teachings on the Tārā practice were occasioned by a dharma assembly convened to avert disaster and benefit the people of Guangdong.[66] To lend an air of secrecy and importance to this revealed "esoteric" text, it was said that in Kham and Central Tibet (*Kang Zang*) this text had not yet been transmitted, while in China (*Zhongtu*) a broad transmission of this dharma had also never before occurred.[67]

The first distinctively Nyingma teaching, devoted to the tradition's progenitor, Padmasambhava, was also introduced in this second set of texts. In the introduction to this practice, readers are promised that making offerings to the image of Padmasambhava will generate unimaginable merit, which will clear away all future calamities and difficulties, and produce boundless fruits of virtue and the like.[68] A short biography of Padmasambhava included in this set is his earliest introduction to the Chinese in the history and culture of Sino-Tibetan Buddhist exchange that I have seen.[69] The Norlha Khutughtu left for the borderlands in 1935 to campaign against the Communist Red Army's Long March through Kham. He was captured and died in the custody of the Communists in 1936, putting to an abrupt end his short but promising teaching and publishing career in China.

Among these collected volumes, the only Tibetan Buddhist texts that are obviously from the Kagyü tradition came to be translated into Chinese via a circuitous route; these texts were not translated directly from the Tibetan, nor did they originate in China. Instead, two texts devoted to principal practices of the Kagyü school, the Six Yogas (*Ming xing dao liu chengjiu fa*) and the Great Symbol practices (*Da shou yin fa yao*), as well as two shorter texts, were translated from English language translations made by Kazi Dawa Samdub (Ka zi Zla ba bsam sgrub, 1868–1922) and edited by Walter Evans-Wentz, which were then published as *Tibetan Yoga and Secret Doctrines* in 1935. In all, five of this work's seven "Books of Wisdom of the Great Path"—the second, third, fourth, sixth, and seventh—are preserved here, but it appears that they were all translated and issued together as part of a series at the time. These five were "The Nirvanic Path: The Yoga of the Great Symbol," "The Path of Knowledge: The Yoga of the Six Doctrines," "The Path of Transference: The Yoga of Consciousness-Transference," "The Path of the Five Wisdoms: The Yoga of the Long Hûm," and "The Path of the Transcendental Wisdom: The Yoga of the Voidness."[70]

Although the impetus for translating Tibetan Buddhist texts into Chinese was clearly connected to modern ideas about Buddhism as a world religion, this is a dramatic instance of Chinese Buddhist involvement in the transnational circulation of Tibetan Buddhist works.[71] Previously, it had been Chinese Buddhist works that were translated into English. At that point, Chinese had been the "source" language, but now the positions were being switched and Chinese became the "target" language. And the original Tibetan source then had to be approached indirectly through the unique translations of a Himalayan school-teacher of English and an American student of yoga and theosophy.[72] The Chinese translation was accomplished by a Chinese student of Tibetan esoterica, Zhang Miaoding, just a year after the texts were first made available in English. He correctly credits the first text to Pema Karpo (Ch. Poma jia'erpo), whom he calls the twenty-fourth master of Tibet's Kagyü (Ch. Jiaju'er) tradition. But in what appears to be a misunderstanding of the English transliteration of the Tibetan translator's name, Lama Kazi Dawa Samdup is described as Tibet's Dawa Sangdu Gexi Lama. In Chinese, *gexi* typically transliterates Tibetan *dge bshes*, which is apparently how Zhang thought he should describe the translator.[73] This misconstrual transforms the lay boys-school teacher into a monastic lama trained in Central Tibet's highest institutions of Gelukpa learning.[74]

Another work is attributed to a certain American, Mrs. Evans (Meiguo Aiwensi furen), and listed as the co-author with the Chinese layman, Wang Yantao. This illustrated text, variously titled the (Ch. *Study of*) *Five Hundred Buddha-images of the* (Tib. *Four Classes of the*) *Esoteric Tradition* (Ch. *Mizong wubai fo xiang kao*; Tib. *Gsang chen rgyud sde bzhi'i sku brnyan lnga brgya*), is also included in the *Secret Scriptures*. Five hundred images are set twelve to the

FIG. 5 A sheet depicting twelve divinities, from the *Five Hundred Buddha-Images of the Esoteric Tradition.*

page with a Chinese caption added under the Tibetan name of each figure. On the reverse is a corresponding prayer or the mantra(s) associated with each figure written horizontally in Tibetan around a vertical string of Lentsa script letters reading "Oṃ āḥ hūṅ swā hā." The Chinese seals and Tibetan and Mongolian inscriptions of two prominent Gelukpa lamas (the Ngakchen/Anqin Khutughtu and the Changkya/Zhangjia guoshi) grace the front matter, and the inscriptions and opening images of Tsongkhapa with his two main disciples indicate that this text is of Gelukpa provenance. These are almost certainly reproductions of Qing-period block carvings.[75] As for the date of this text, I suspect it was around 1939, when the Ngakchen Khutughtu was actively publishing in China.

Layman Sun Jingfeng and the Collected Translations of Tibetan Esoterica Series

Sun Jingfeng was the most prolific Chinese Buddhist translator of Tibetan texts. Sun's twenty-one translations, though generally short, are notable for their frequent inclusion of complete Tibetan language texts as appendices. Fifteen of his translations include or incorporate a Tibetan text, five others use Tibetan script for the mantras, and only one is completely devoid of Tibetan letters. Sixteen of Sun's works were part of the *Collected Translations of Tibetan Esoterica (Zangmi congshu)* issued by the Tibetan Esoteric Practice and Study Association Printery (Zangmi xuixue hui shiyin). As for the dates of his translation activity, his earliest work is from 1936, and his last was published in 1942. He seems to have been attracted to Tibetan Buddhism by 1931, when the Paṇchen Lama was in Nanjing, as indicated by his awareness of the Paṇchen Lama's teaching on the six-syllable mantra (*Oṃ maṇi padme hūṃ*) there.[76] Another influence may have been the Mongol Vajra-Guru (*Jingang shangshi*) Bao Kanbu (Tib. Dkon mchog mkhan po, i.e. Gu shri Dkon mchog rdo rje), who was invited to Shanghai to teach in 1934. Also present in Shanghai at that time was Tupten Nyima, the Tibetan Buddhist teacher who transmitted nearly a third of the texts Sun translated.[77] On the basis of this rather limited evidence, we may tentatively conclude that Sun was introduced to Tibetan Buddhism in Nanjing and Shanghai, after which he probably studied Tibetan language for some years before he was sufficiently proficient to translate texts.[78] The learned Lozang Zangpo was another of Sun's major teachers, transmitting almost one quarter (five) of the texts that Sun translated.[79] Sun seems to have traveled widely in central and north China to attend teachings and find publishers for his materials, ranging from Beijing, where the Yonghegong's Jasagh Lama taught, to Shandong, Kaifeng, and Shanghai.

In assessing his work, it is necessary to consider both his early translations and the later ones found in the *Collected Translations of Tibetan Esoterica* series. His early work is distinguished by his attention to the importance of the Tibetan script and its pronunciation and his careful explication of these. Otherwise, it deals with the same fundamental practices of Tibetan Buddhism described by Dorjé Chöpa and Zhang Xinruo. His first two texts date to 1936, with the longer of the two, the *Precious Treasury of Esoterica* (Ch. *Micheng bao zang*; Tib. *Bsang sngag* [sic, *Gsang sngags*] *ren* [sic, *rin*] *chen gter bzang*) opening with a summary explanation of the Tibetan alphabet, with Chinese transliteration to assist the reader's pronunciation. Endnotes explain the consonants, vowels, as well as which letters can serve as prefixes, postfixes, and so forth, covering the variant spellings and pronunciations of Tibetan syllables. This is followed by prayers for blessings, taking refuge, and making maṇḍala-offerings (with an illustration of the world according to Indo-Tibetan Buddhist conceptions), dhāraṇī, and other ritual texts associated with Avalokiteśvara, including one taught by the fourth Paṇchen Lama.[80]

FIG. 6 A talisman with *dhāraṇī*s in Sanskrit and Tibetan scripts, together with Chinese transcription. From the works of Sun Jinfeng in *Secret Scriptures* (4.508).

Another text dated 1936, *Tibetan Esoteric Essentials of Worship and Praise* (*Zangmi lizan fayao*), was clearly used to introduce novices to basic Gelukpa practice.[81] Each Tibetan passage and its Chinese transliteration is followed by a second transliteration into Roman script, to clarify the proper pronunciation of the Tibetan text. Sometimes this format is extended to include a short Chinese explanation of the translation. For instance, the previously described Gelukpa "Creed" (*dmigs brtse*) here is called Tsongkhapa's heart dhāraṇī (*xinzhou*), and the text explains that Tsongkhapa is a manifestation (*huashen*) of Avalokiteśvara, Mañjuśrī, and Vajrapāṇi's compassion, wisdom, and strength, respectively.[82]

Like other translators, Sun was concerned with the correct pronunciation of mantras and was troubled by the difficulty of transliterating these into Chinese, with its many local dialects. This is apparent, for example, in Sun's third and much longer translated work, *Collected Tibetan Esoteric Dharma* (*Zangmi fa hui*), where the use of Tibetan script is limited to writing mantras, with Chinese transcriptions added to clarify the pronunciation.[83] In this text, however, Tibetan letters are introduced for their value in reproducing Sanskrit sounds, and a guide to the relevant letter combinations is included.[84] Sun's strategy was to use Tibetan letters to indicate the original Sanskrit, and then students could check with their Tibetan teacher for the correct pronunciation.[85]

Sun himself relied on the Vajra-guru Tupten Nyima for this third work. Tupten Nyima taught the material at Kaifeng's Henan Buddhist Study Society (Henan Foxue she) sometime before its June 1937 publication in Chinese translation.[86] Although few specifics of this event are described in the text, the preface and back matter reveal some noteworthy details, especially interesting given that our knowledge of Tibetan Buddhism in Kaifeng is extremely limited. First, the preface was written by a Chinese monk who briefly recounts the history of the transmission of Tibetan Buddhism to China, noting the role of Pakpa in the Yuan dynasty, and the imperial court's reception of Tibetan Buddhist teachings and initiations in the Ming and Qing dynasties. He also recognizes that the common people (*ping min*) had no access to these treasures until the present time, when Chinese could study abroad in Tibet and return to their ancestral country to transmit the results of their learning (*liuxueyu Xizang; xue cheng, fan chuan zuguo*). Finally, he celebrates the presence in China of the Panchen Lama, as well as other great and virtuous Tibetans and Mongols who were actively teaching and holding rituals in China.[87] The back matter reveals that this Chinese master was not alone in his support for Tibetan Buddhism in Kaifeng, although he was the only monk involved. The final page lists his donations and those of some forty individuals who sponsored the printing of the teachings in translation, namely, as the book examined here, the *Collected Tibetan Esoteric Dharma*.[88] The amounts collected were modest, from as much as five *yuan* from the master to as little as a single *jiao* from a lay Buddhist, but together they amassed around one hundred *yuan*. To put this into perspective, ten *yuan* was sufficient for basic living expenses for a month at this time, and one hundred *yuan* a month was considered a very generous salary.[89] The back-matter also mentions a second book to follow in the series, but it has not been preserved in the *Secret Scriptures*, if indeed it was ever published.

Sun's greatest publication success was the *Collected Translations of Tibetan Esoterica* (*Zangmi congyi*), a series that included at least thirty volumes. Only sixteen of these are preserved in the recent assemblage of reprints under the *Secret Scriptures*, but these suffice to give us some idea of the scope of this corpus. The earliest extant text, the third in the series, dates to 1937, and the latest, the twenty-eighth, dates to the fall of 1942; for some reason the thirtieth was printed out of order in 1941. Nine of the extant texts were published in a single year, 1939, while another four are undated. This series consistently incorporates Tibetan script, usually at length. Twelve of these works have complete Tibetan language texts, often with subscribed transliteration or translation in Chinese (and sometimes Roman letters). Four of the works use Tibetan script only for the mantras and dhāraṇī, which are then followed by Chinese transliteration. Most of these translations are based on teachings transmitted from Sun's Tibetan Buddhist teachers, but some are based on earlier translations from the Tang dynasty, with the addition of mantras written in Tibetan script, probably as correctives to the earlier translations.[90] By examining Sun's efforts we realize that, as was true for the Chinese monk who wrote the preface to his earlier translation, the central concern was esoteric Buddhism. Tibetan Buddhism, especially because of its ability to preserve the original Sanskrit sounds, was considered crucial for linking past Indian and Chinese Buddhist practice to modern Chinese Buddhist practice.

Master Guankong: Lamrim *Teachings and Activities at the Bodhi Study Association*

Shortly after Sun started publishing his translations, the Chinese monk Guankong, who had studied abroad in Kham and Central Tibet, began to publish numerous texts that have since been reprinted in the *Secret Scriptures* collection. Guankong graduated from Taixu's short-lived Wuchang Academy, probably by 1925. Thus, like Fazun, he was introduced in his formative years to Taixu's aspiration to unite Chinese and Tibetan Buddhism. Given his close association with Fazun, who published a Chinese translation of Tsongkhapa's *Great Sequential Path to Enlightenment* (*Byang chub lam rim chen mo*, Ch. *Puti dao cidi guang lun*), it is no surprise that Guankong's first recorded lecture after returning from Tibet was dedicated to this central teaching of the Gelukpa school. The preface to his 1937 *Notes on "The Practice of the Sequential Path to Enlightenment"* (*Puti dao cidi xiufa biji*) describes the origins and spread of these teachings in modern China. The preface first sketches the story of how his teacher Dayong founded the Beijing Tibetan language school, the school's relocation to Ganzi (Tib. Dkar mdzes), and Dayong's efforts to gain access to Central Tibet. Dayong apparently sent a letter to the Dalai Lama requesting permission to enter Tibetan territory (*qing ru jing*). However, according to the preface, because at the end of the Qing dynasty "the court had not been courteous to the Dalai Lama and the

Sichuan army resident in Tibet had acted harshly and unreasonably, therefore the Tibetan people had lost confidence [in the court and the Chinese, as represented by the Sichuan army]."[91] Permission to enter was not granted. As a result, the Chinese monks were stuck in Kham, where Fazun began to study the *Lamrim* genre of texts. The preface celebrates this circumstance as the moment when China proper gained access to these teachings.[92] For his notes on the *Lamrim* teachings, Guankong used Fazun's translation of *The Practice of the Sequential Path to Enlightenment* by Geshé Tendzin Pelgyé (Ch. Shanhui Chijiao zengguang) as the basis for his lectures to the North China Lay Group (Ch. Hua bei jushilin) in the winter of 1937.[93] This work, like Guankong's other translations, was printed in 1939 at the Beijing Central Institute for the Carving of Scriptures (Ch. Zhongyang kejing yuan).

Guankong's remaining translations were also published in the watershed year of 1939, all by the center most actively involved with Tibetan Buddhism in Beijing from 1938 to 1951: the Bodhi Study Association (Puti xuehui). These works were all translations of the Ngakchen Khutughtu's teachings, which had presumably taken place in Beijing.[94] It may even be that the North China Lay Group was renamed the Bodhi Study Association sometime in 1939. I suggest this because the description of the North China Lay Group's long-term interest in the *Lamrim* teachings in the above-mentioned preface would provide a logical connection between Guankong and the Ngakchen Khutughtu's presence, first at the North China Lay Group and later at the Bodhi Study Association. Moreover, the preface's narrative recounts that the elder Hu Zihu, a layman who had, since 1923, consistently funded Tibetan Buddhist activities in and around Beijing and supported the monks studying abroad in Tibet, invited one of the returned monks, Master Nenghai, to teach the *Lamrim* to the North China Lay Group in 1935.[95] The Lay Group was later happy to receive the Ngakchen Khutughtu, who was living in Beijing in 1938, and hear his teachings on the importance of developing bodhicitta. Guankong seems to have been following in the Ngakchen Khutughtu's footsteps when he too gave teachings on the *Sequential Path to Enlightenment*.[96]

We can further pursue the narrative of Guankong and the Ngakchen Khutughtu's activities by piecing together their collaborative work, all published in 1939. For instance, Guankong translated the Ngakchen Khutughtu's brief commentary on Tsongkhapa's *Praise for the Sequential Path to Enlightenment* (*Puti dao cidi she song luejie*), a commentary that elaborated on Fazun's Chinese translation of the root text, which the audience could follow while the Ngakchen Khutughtu's explanation was translated by Guankong.[97] The Ngakchen Khutughtu and Guankong also collaborated on practice oriented-texts dedicated to Green Tārā, the eleven-headed manifestation of Avalokiteśvara, the Medicine Buddha, White Mañjuśrī, and the six-armed Mahākāla, to name a few.[98] These texts may also serve as an indicator of some of the concerns of the laity affiliated with the Bodhi Study Association, the publisher of these texts.

Tang Xiangming: From Esoteric Treasury Institute to the Bodhi Study Association

Tang Xiangming was the other prolific lay Buddhist translator of this period, and he worked with both of Beijing's esoteric centers, though most of his translations seem to have been published by the Bodhi Study Association. As with Guankong, many of his works are devoted to particular bodhisattvas, such as Mañjuśrī, Avalokiteśvara, and Tārā. Presumably, in these later texts, he was building on the basic knowledge of Tibetan Buddhist practice already introduced by Dorjé Chöpa, Sun Jingfeng, and the Esoteric Treasury Institute. With the exception of one short undated text on taking refuge, his works do not describe basic practices. This text is also unusual for Tang's work, as it is a bilingual edition in Tibetan-formatted (narrow horizontal) pages, with Chinese transcriptions below the Tibetan text.[99] For the most part, Tang's translations either have no Tibetan at all, or use Tibetan only for the mantras associated with the texts.

Tang also collaborated with the Ngakchen Khutughtu in producing two undated translations that were published by the Esoteric Treasury Institute, probably during the last years during which it was still most active, 1932 or 1934, when the Ngakchen Khutughtu was in China.[100] We can surmise that these translations pre-date Guankong's 1937 arrival in Beijing, because after that time the Ngakchen Khutughtu would have been able to rely on this well-trained monastic translator, as their publication record shows he did. Once the Ngakchen Khutughtu ceased to need Tang, the latter was free to work with the seventh Changkya/Zhangjia Khutughtu, Lozang Pelden Tenpé Drönmé (1890–1957), and together they completed at least two translations.[101] Tang's datable works commence in 1939 and continue until 1944, with almost one translation a year.[102] Many of his translations deal with a typical assortment of Buddhist figures: Avalokiteśvara, Mañjuśrī, and Yamāntaka,[103] and more unusual, he translated two texts dealing with Kurukullā (Ch. Gulugule/Guluguli, Tib. Ku ru ku lu), goddess of wealth, said to be associated with Red Tārā.[104] His last dated work is a 1944 text praising the twenty one Tārās, originally written by the first Dalai Lama.[105] Earlier I argued that making Tibetan script accessible to the Chinese marked an indigenization of Tibetan Buddhism in China, but I think that the complete absence of Tibetan in these later texts may indicate a further stage of development and a new and more deep-rooted level of indigenization. It is possible that translators such as Tang felt that they and their readers had such a thorough understanding of Tibetan Buddhism that they had gone beyond the simple need to reproduce Tibetan script and phonetics.

Conclusion

Lay support for Tibetan Buddhism did not immediately disappear from China's cities with the rise of Communist control, but within two decades Chinese translations of Tibetan Buddhist texts had been supplanted by Tibetan translations of Chinese state policy documents.[106] I have no evidence that the lay translators I have discussed continued to use their talents in service of the state, but some of the monks, both Chinese and Tibetan, who had been involved in teaching and translating in Republican China did so. Fazun, Nenghai, and one of his disciples, Longguo, as well as the lama that the Norlha Khutughtu introduced to China, Gangkar Trülku, filled important roles in state institutions, though only Longguo was actually employed as a translator for the People's Liberation Army. In addition to figures such as Gangkar, Fazun, and Nenghai, who are discussed elsewhere in this volume, discovering what happened to the lay translators and the less well known lamas with whom they worked presents an important future research project.

Although many questions remain unanswered, this chapter has shed new light on several unheralded Chinese Buddhist translators, especially laymen, and the Tibetan Buddhist teachers and institutions that supported their work. In the early years, translations were typically the product of a special kind of team—a teacher and his devoted disciple, such as Dorjé Chöpa and Zhang Xinruo or the Norlha Khutughtu and Wu Runjiang. Once these teachers faded from the scene so too did their translators. Over time though, a more substantial base of translators and institutions that could support them developed. Based on current records, though this may simply be an artifact of where the collector of the texts lived, Beijing seems to have been the principal center for this activity, with important work also occurring in Chongqing, Shanghai, and Kaifeng. The three main translators I have highlighted here—Sun Jingfeng, Guankong, and Tang Xiangming—all worked with a variety of teachers, texts, and institutions in their efforts to expand Chinese access to Tibetan Buddhist teachings. The role of Mongols, such as Gushri Könchok Dorjé and the Changkya Khutughtu should also not be overlooked. The very relationship between Tibetan Buddhism and Beijing was set in place during the Qing dynasty, when Mongol monks filled the imperial capital's monasteries, and they remind us that the customary association of Mongols as teachers of Tibetan Buddhism to outsiders remained in force well into the twentieth century.

Notes

* I am grateful both to Yale University's Council on East Asian Studies for the post-doctoral year that funded me to do this research and to Valerie Hansen for her support and advice. Browsing Yale's wonderful Sterling Library shelves, I was fortunate enough to stumble across the first of the texts considered here.

1 Duojue jueda gexi 多覺覺達格西 [Duojie jueba 多傑覺拔], *Micheng fahai* 密乘法海 (*Dharma Ocean of the Esoteric Vehicle*) (Taipei [Chongqing]: Xinwenfeng chuban she gongci, 1987 [1930]), hereafter referred to as *Dharma Ocean*. This book is cat-alogued under the title *Misheng fahai* at Yale University, where I first located the text. There are several variants in the spelling of the Tibetan author's name. First, his name is given as Duojue jueda gexi, a pinyin transliteration of the incorrect char-acters used in the reprint edition, under which this book is catalogued. The second and third spellings are romanizations of the Chinese and Tibetan versions of his name—Duojie jueba and Rdo rje bcod pa, respectively—as found in the reprint of the original edition. The correct spelling of his Tibetan name is Rdo rje gcod pa. However, the true author of the *Dharma Ocean* was probably his Chinese dis-ciple, Zhang Xinruo, as the author of the preface notes that though the master had lived many years in China, he was "still not very highly skilled in the Chinese spo-ken language" (*bu shen xian hanyu*). Assuming this is true, it is likely that Rdo rje gcod pa's Chinese literary skills were not much better. This text was reprinted again in 1995. The other collection is Zhou Shao-liang 周紹良, Lü Tiegang 呂鐵剛, eds., *Zangmi xiufa midian* 藏密修法秘典 (*Secret Scriptures of Tibetan Esoteric Dharma Practices*), 5 vols. (Beijing: Huaxia chubanshe, 1996 [1931–1951]), hereafter referred to as *Secret Scriptures*. (This text was reprinted again in 2002.) Lü Tiegang first published a catalogue and account of these collected materials in the Chinese Bud-dhist Association's journal *Fayin* (*Sound of the Dharma*) in 1988. The first mention of either of these texts that I am aware of, in any language, is Huang Hao's four-page review of the latter collection: Huang Hao 黃顥, "Sanshi niandai Zhongguo Zangmi yanjiu—*Zangmi xiufa midian* ping jie" 三十年代中國藏密研究—藏密修法秘典評介 ("Chinese research on Tibetan esoterica in the 1930s—critique and intro-duction to *Secret Scriptures of Tibetan Esoteric Dharma Practices*"), *Minzu yanjiu hui xun* 民族研究會訊 [*Newsletter on Ethnic Studies*] n. 17 (March, 1997): 52–56. One more recent on-line article by Shunzo Onoda, "A Pending Task for the New

Century—The Pioneering works of Tai-xu Ta-shi (太虛大師): Han-Tibetan Inter-change of Buddhist Studies (漢藏佛學交流)" (http://www.bukkyo-u.ac.jp/mmc01/onoda/works/paper/0201taipei_e.html) refers to another collection: Zeyi 則一, ed. *Zhongguo Zangmi bao dian* 中國藏密宝典, 6 vols. (Beijing Shi: Min zu chu ban she, 2001).

2 Additional materials may be found in the following collections, which I have not examined closely: Ji Xianlin 季羨林 and Xu Lihua 徐麗華, eds., *Zhongguo shao-shu minzu guji ji cheng*: Hanwen ban中國少數民族古籍集成: 漢文版, vols. 99–100 (Chengdu Shi: Sichuan min zu chu ban she, 2002); Zhongguo zong jiao li shi wen xian ji cheng bian zuan wei yuan hui 中國宗教歷史文獻集成編纂委員會, *Zang wai fo jing* 藏外佛經, vol. 1–7 (Hefei Shi: Huang shan shu she, 2005).

3 Mei Jingshun 梅靜軒, "Minguo yilai de Han Zang Fojiao guanxi (1912–1949): Yi Han Zang jiaoli yuan wei zhongxin de tantao" 民國以來的漢藏佛教關系 (1912–1949): 以漢藏教理院為中心的探討 ("Sino-Tibetan relations during the Republi-can period [1912–1949]: Probing into the Sino-Tibetan Buddhist Institute at the center of relations"), *Zhonghua Foxue yanjiu* 中華佛學研究 (*Chung-hwa Institute of Buddhist Studies, Taipei*) 2 (1998): 251–288; and "Minguo zaoqi xianmi Fojiao chongtu de tantao 民國早期顯密佛教沖突的探討" ("Probing into the conflicts of exo-teric and esoteric Buddhism in the early Republic"), *Zhonghua Foxue yanjiu* 中華佛學研究 (*Chung-hwa Institute of Buddhist Studies, Taipei*) 3 (1999): 251–270; Fran-çoise Wang-Toutain, "Quand les maîtres chinois s'éveillent au bouddhisme tibétain: Fazun, le Xuanzang des temps moderns," *Bulletin de l'école française d'extrême-orient* 87 (2000): 707–727; Ester Bianchi, *The Iron Statue Monastery "Tiexiangsi": A Bud-dhist Nunnery of Tibetan Tradition in Contemporary China* (Firenze: L.S. Olschki, 2001); Monica Esposito, "Una tradizione rDzogs-chen in Cina: Una nota sul mon-astero delle Montagne dell'Occhio Celeste," *Asiatica Venetiana* 2 (1997): 221–224; Fabienne Jagou, *Le 9e Panchen Lama (1883–1937): Enjeu des relations Sino-Tibé-taines*, Monographies 191 (Paris: École française d'Extrême-Orient, 2004); Gray Tuttle, *Tibetan Buddhists in the Making of Modern China* (New York: Columbia University Press, 2005).

4 *Dharma Ocean*, p. 6.

5 *Secret Scriptures*, vol. 2, p. 377.

6 Tuttle, *Tibetan Buddhists*, pp. 212–220.

7 *Secret Scriptures*, vol. 1, p. 777.

8 Part of the spelling of the Sngags chen Khutughtu's name differs in contemporary and recent accounts. His religious name is given in two places in the *Secret Scriptures*: vol. 5, pp. 99, 351. For a contemporary biography of the Sngags chen Khutughtu, which translates the Chinese of Anjin Duokengjiang as Dazhou Jingangzhi, mean-ing "Great Mantra Vajra-holding [One] (from Tib. Sngags chen rdo rje 'chang)," see Miaozhou 妙舟, *Meng Zang Fojiao shi* 蒙藏佛教史 [*Rgyal bstan bod sog gyi yul du ji ldar dar ba'i lo rgyus/Mongol-Tibetan Buddhist History*], *Xizangxue Hanwen wen-xian congshu*, 2 (Beijing: Quanguo tushuguan wenxian zhongxin, 1993 [1934]), 214–218. For a later biography, see Bkras dgon lo rgyus rtsom sgrig tshogs chung, Sngags chen bdar pa Ho thog thu Blo bzang bstan 'dzin 'jigs med dbang phyug gi rnam thar rags bsdus (Short biography of the Sngags chen bdar pa Khutughtu, Blo bzang bstan 'dzin 'jigs med dbang phyug), in *Bod kyi rig gnas lo rgyus dpyad gzhi'i rgyu cha bdams*

bsgrigs, 'don thengs bzhi pa (*Materials on the culture and history of Tibet*, vol. 4), ed.
Bod rang skyong ljongs chab gros rig gnas lo rgyus dpyad gzhi'i rgyu cha u yon lhan
khang (Lhasa: Bod ljongs mi dmangs dpe skrun khang, 1985), pp. 80–91. Zhashi-
lunbu si lishi bianxie xiaozu 扎什论布寺编写小组, "Angqin daba kanbu shilüe 昂钦大
巴堪布事略" ("Brief Biography of Sngags chen bdar pa mkhan po"), in *Xizang wenshi ziliao xuanji* 西藏文史资料选辑, no. 4, ed. Xizang zizhiqu zhengjie wenshi ziliao
yanjiu weiyuanhui (Beijing: Renmin chubanshe, 1985), pp. 39–44. For a photo, see
Zhang Bozhen 張伯楨, *Canghai cong shu* 滄海叢書, 4 vols., vol. 4 (Shanghai: Shanghai shudian, 1934), illustration 5. Rdo rje gcod pa's full title, given on the original
cover page of *Dharma Ocean of the Esoteric Vehicle* (*Micheng fahai*) has several spelling errors: Bod pa 'bral sbongs ['bras spungs] blo gsal gling dge bshes no mon han
(from Mongol: *nom un qan*, originally from Tib. *chos rgyal*) bla ma Rdo rje bcod
[gcod] pa; Xizang Biebang si gexi nuomenhan da lama duojie jeuba zunzhe. The use
of "Bod pa," generally meaning "(Central) Tibetan," is interesting here as the lama
hailed from Khams, but the Chinese translation suggests it was used as a geographic
name, possibly to indicate the location of 'Bras spungs, rather than as an ethnic designation. The Mongol term *nomci* means "one learned in the law, dharma."

9 Four other texts in a particular series by Sun may have also been published in this
year, but no dates are recorded in those texts.

10 For Guankong's biography, see Lü Tiegang 吕铁刚, "Xiandai fanyijia—Guankong
Fashi 现代翻译家—观空法师" ("A Modern-day Translator—Master Guankong"), in
"Fayin" wenku-Fojiao renwu gujin tan <<法音>>文库—佛教人物古今谈, vol. 2 (Beijing: Zhongguo Fojiao xiehui chubanshe, 1996), pp. 648–652. On Sngags chen, see
n. 8 above. For Fazun, refer to *Fazun wenji* 法尊文集 (*Collected Works of Fazun*), ed.,
Hong Jisong and Huang Jilin (Taipei: Wenshu chubanshe, Wenshu Fojiao wenhua
zhongxin, 1988), and Zhihua Yao's chapter in the present work. On Nenghai, see
Dingzhi 定智, *Nenghai shangshi zhuan* 能海上師傳 (*Biography of Guru Nenghai*), vol.
6 of *Nenghai shangshi quanji* 能海上師全集 (*The Complete Works of Guru Nenghai*),
7 vols. (Taipei: Fangguang wenhua shiye youxian gongci, 1995) and Ester Bianchi's
contribution to this volume. On Nor lha Khutughtu, see especially Han Dazai 韓大
載, *Kang Zang Fojiao yu Xikang Nouna hutuketu yinghua shilüe* 康藏佛教與西康諾那
呼圖克圖應化事略 (*Khams-Tibetan Buddhism and a Brief Biography of the Manifestation of Nor lha Khutughtu of Khams*) (Shanghai: Zangbanchu yujia jingshe. 1937).
For more details on this figure, see Tuttle, *Tibetan Buddhists*, pp. 55–56, 93–97, 133–
· 134, 165–166. Chapter 6 above, by Carmen Meinert, includes selected additional references to Nor lha, as well.

11 Fafang 法肪, "Zhongguo Fojiao xianzhuang 中國佛教現狀" ["The current state of
Chinese Buddhism"], *Haichao yin* 海潮音 15, no. 10 (1934): 24; Mei, "Minguo yilai
de Han Zang Fojiao guanxi," 275, n. 20.

12 Chengdu Xi'nan heping fahui banshichu 成都西南和平法會辦事處, *Chengdu Xi'nan
heping fahui tekan* 成都西南和平法會特刊 [*Special issue of Chengdu's Southwestern
Dharma-Assembly for Peace*] (Chengdu: Chengdu Xi'nan heping fahui banshichu,
1932), p. 148. For further details on this event see Tuttle, *Tibetan Buddhists*, pp.
114–118.

13 *Dharma Ocean*, p. 2.

14 See Don Lopez, "Tibetology in the United States of America: A Brief History," in

Images of Tibet in the 19th and 20th Centuries, Monica Esposito, ed. (Paris: École Française d'Êxtrême-Orient, forthcoming).

15 For more information on this school see Tuttle, *Tibetan Buddhists*, pp. 74, 82, 89, 104. For a Chinese Tibetologist who studied at Yonghegong, see my "Modern Tibetan Historiography in China," *Papers on Chinese History* 7 (1998): pp. 85–108.

16 For development of these language training tools, see Tuttle, *Tibetan Buddhists*, pp. 203–205.

17 Somewhat politicized language does appear in one preface, however it seems only to reflexively signal the ambivalent status of Tibet as both a part of China and separate from it, and does not didactically argue either viewpoint. This preface opens with the explanation that esoteric teachings have come into "our country" (*wo guo*) through two different routes: 1) to China Proper (*neidi*) in the Tang dynasty through Bukong and others and 2) to Tibet through Padmasambhava and Atiśa; the inclusion of the latter route tacitly incorporates Tibet as part of China. Yet at the same time, this preface describes study in Tibet as "study-abroad" (*liuxue*) (*Secret Scriptures*, vol. 1, pp. 775–777). For a recent American translation that links Buddhist teachings with political activism, see His Holiness the Dalai Lama, *Advice on Dying and Living a Better Life*, trans. and ed. Jeffrey Hopkins (New York: Simon & Schuster, 2002).

18 I would like to thank Matthew Kapstein for noting that much of this text is a "pretty clear splice of a simplified work of the *chos spyod* genre (i.e. a collection of the most fundamental liturgical works of any given monastic order) together with the rudiments of a *sādhana* collection, though the progression of these latter is more often (but by no means exclusively): Buddhas, bodhisattvas, tantric deities, female Buddhas and deities, dharma-protectors." Personal communication, May 2007.

19 Chinese *genben* was also presumably used to translate Tibetan *rtsa ba*, as found in the Chinese phrase *genben lama*, corresponding to the Tibetan *rtsa ba'i bla ma*.

20 *Dharma Ocean*, p. 22.

21 *Dharma Ocean*, p. 28.

22 *Dharma Ocean*, pp. 33–35.

23 *Dharma Ocean*, p. 11.

24 *Dharma Ocean*, p. 16.

25 *Dharma Ocean*, pp. 82–86.

26 *Dharma Ocean*, p. 91.

27 *Dharma Ocean*, pp. 94–95.

28 *Dharma Ocean*, p. 105.

29 *Dharma Ocean*, p. 112.

30 *Dharma Ocean*, pp. 127–128.

31 The phrase "Creed of the Dge lugs pa" is drawn from Zahiruddin Ahmad's *Sino-Tibetan Relations in the Seventeenth Century*, Serie Orientale Roma 40 (Rome: Instituto Italiano per il Medio ed Estremo Oriente, 1970), p. 182, in his discussion of Sangs rgyas rgya mtsho's 1698 text *Vaiḍūrya ser po*, which repeats, almost verbatim, the description of this event from the fifth Dalai Lama's biography: Ngag dbang blo bzang rgya mtsho, *Ngag dbang blo bzang rgya mtsho'i rnam thar* (Lhasa: Bod ljong mi dmangs dpe skrun khang, 1989 [1681]), p. 400. For a Chinese translation see, Awang luosang jiacou 阿旺洛桑嘉措, *Wushi Dalai lama zhuan* 五世达赖喇嘛传,

trans. Chen Qingying 陈庆英 and Ma Lianlong 马连龙, *Zhongguo bianjiang shi di ziliao conggan-Xizang juan* (Beijing: Zhongguo Zangxue chubanshe, 1992), p. 333.

32 For more details on this missionary effort, see Gray Tuttle, "A Tibetan Buddhist Mission to the East: The Fifth Dalai Lama's Journey to Beijing, 1652–1653," in Bryan J. Cuevas and Kurtis R. Schaeffer, eds., *Power, Politics, and the Reinvention of Tradition: Tibet in the Seventeenth and Eighteenth Centuries* (Leiden: Brill, 2006), pp. 65–87.

33 *Dharma Ocean*, p. 99.

34 *Dharma Ocean*, p. 131.

35 *Dharma Ocean*, pp. 237–240.

36 See Chün-fang Yü, "Feminine Images of Kuan-yin in Post-T'ang China," *Journal of Chinese Religions* 18 (1990): 61–89, and *Kuan-yin (The Chinese Transformation of Avalokiteśvara)* (New York: Columbia University Press, 2001); and Daniel L. Overmeyer, *Folk Buddhist Religion: Dissenting Sects in Late Traditional China*, Harvard East Asian series 83 (Cambridge, Mass.: Harvard University Press, 1976).

37 *Dharma Ocean*, pp. 351–368.

38 *Dharma Ocean*, pp. 369–396.

39 *Dharma Ocean*, pp. 403–423.

40 Patricia Berger, *Empire of Emptiness: Buddhist Art and Political Authority in Qing China* (Honolulu: University of Hawai'i Press, 2003).

41 *Dharma Ocean*, pp. 435–468.

42 *Dharma Ocean*, pp. 582–584.

43 *Dharma Ocean*, pp. 388–390.

44 Gan Wenfeng, "Zangchuan Fojiao zai Chongqing 藏传佛教在重庆," in *Chongqing wenshi ziliao* 41 重庆文史资料 41 (Chongqing Historical and Cultural Materials, no. 41), ed. Zhongguo renmin zhengzhi xieshang huiyi and Chongqing shi weiyuahui wenshi ziliao weiyuanhui, pp. 170–171. The stūpa, known as the Bodhivajra Stūpa (*Putijingang ta*) was built under the direction of the mayor, the Public Security Bureau chief of Chongqing He Beiwei, and several others toward the end of 1930. The stūpa represented a substantial investment on the part of Chongqing's residents and officials. It stood about thirty feet tall, was filled with Tibetan scriptures, and inscribed with Buddhist scriptural passages and mantras in Chinese and Tibetan. The stūpa was said to have cost over 40,000 *yuan* (around US $13,000), a tremendous sum at the time.

45 *Secret Scriptures*, vol. 2, pp. 1–112.

46 Preface, *Zangmi xuifa midian*, vol. 1. Although the preface says that the list was published in *Fayin* 1988, issue 2, I could not find it there; Huang Hao, "Chinese research on Tibetan esoterica," p. 52 (refer to n. 1 above).

47 In my *Tibetan Buddhists in the Making of Modern China*, I followed Holmes Welch (*The Buddhist Revival in China*, Harvard East Asian series 33 [Cambridge: Harvard University Press, 1968]) in his translation of Shanghai's "Puti xuehui" as "Bodhi Society." In this article, I will use the more literal translation "Bodhi Study Association" to distinguish the Beijing center from the Shanghai organization, founded around the same time. The Beijing Bodhi Study Association was based in the Zhengjue Hall in the North Ocean Public Park (Beihai gongyuan, formerly part of the imperial grounds). For this association, see *Secret Scriptures*, vol. 1, p. 363.

48 *Secret Scriptures*, vol. 5, p. 101.

49 The Tibetan name of this institute is found in *Secret Scriptures*, vol. 5, p. 354.

50 On the Beijing Kālacakra see Tuttle, *Tibetan Buddhists*, pp. 169–172, and "Tibet as the Source of Messianic Teachings to Save Republican China: The Ninth Panchen Lama, Shambhala and the Kālacakra Tantra," in M. Esposito, ed., *Images of Tibet in the 19th and 20th Centuries*. For the Sngags chen Khutughtu's participation in the ritual, see the Panchen Lama's biography: Blo bzang thub bstan chos kyi nyi ma, Panchen Lama VI (IX), *Skyabs mgon thams cad mkhyen pa Blo bzang thub bstan chos kyi nyi ma dge legs rnam rgyal bzang po'i zhal snga nas kyi thun mong ba'i rnam bar thar pa rin chen dbang gi rgyal po'i 'phreng ba (The autobiography of the Sixth [Ninth] Panchen Lama Blo bzang thub bstan chos kyi nyi ma)*, in *Pan chen thams cad mkhyen pa rje btsun Blo bzang thub bstan chos kyi nyi ma dge legs rnam rgyal bzang po'i gsung 'bum (The collected works of the Sixth [Ninth] Panchen Lama Blo bzang thub bstan chos kyi nyi ma)* (Reproduced from the Bkra shis lhun po blocks, 1944), p. 637. For details on the travels of the Sngags chen Khutughtu in the service of the Panchen Lama, see Jagou, *Le 9e Panchen Lama (1883–1937)*, pp. 216–220, 241, 267–270; Bkras dgon lo rgyus rtsom sgrig tshogs chung, "Sngags chen bdar pa," pp. 80–91.

51 This photograph (*Secret Scriptures*, vol. 5, p. 99), though reversed, is an early source for the Sngags chen Quthughtu's full religious name, as listed above. See also, *Secret Scriptures*, vol. 5, p. 351.

52 *Secret Scriptures*, vol. 1, pp. 603–726.

53 *Secret Scriptures*, vol. 3, pp. 451–676.

54 *Secret Scriptures*, vol. 3, pp. 1–502. All of his works were first taught at a lay center for practice called Jilejingshe on Yangguan Lane (*hutong*), Beijing's Dongzhi Gate, see pp. 498–499, although he was also connected to the Mizang yuan during the same period.

55 *Secret Scriptures*, vol. 5, pp. 351–353.

56 Aisin-Gioro Pu Yi, *From Emperor to Citizen*, trans. W.J.F. Jenner (New York: Oxford University Press, 1988 [1964]), p. 253.

57 Hisao Kimura (as told to Scott Berry), *Japanese Agent in Tibet: My Ten Years of Travel in Disguise* (London: Serindia, 1990) and Scott Berry, *Monks, Spies and a Soldier of Fortune* (London: Athlone, 1995).

58 *Secret Scriptures*, vol. 5, pp. 95–372.

59 *Secret Scriptures*, vol. 5, p. 351.

60 Refer to n. 10 above.

61 *Secret Scriptures*, vol. 2, pp. 367–509. Ishihama Yumiko, "The Image of Ch'ienlung's Kingship as Seen from the World of Tibetan Buddhism," *Acta Asiatica: Bulletin of the Institute of Eastern Culture* 88: Ming-Ch'ing History Seen from East Asia (2005), 54–55. The text was the *Foshuo dabai san'gai zongchi tuoluoni jing*, Taishō no. 97.

62 *Secret Scriptures*, vol. 2, p. 375.

63 This must have been Li Jinzhong, who was made the director of the Panchen Lama's representative office in November of 1936. See Jagou, *Le 9e Panchen Lama*, p. 331.

64 *Secret Scriptures*, vol. 2, pp. 447–448. For similar language, see the postscript for the collected texts, vol. 2, p. 506.

65 *Secret Scriptures*, vol. 3, p. 817.

66 *Secret Scriptures*, vol. 3, p. 767.

67 *Secret Scriptures*, vol. 3, p. 768. For an earlier instance of the transmission of a Tārā mantra by the Ninth Paṇchen Lama in 1925, see Tuttle, *Tibetan Buddhists*, p. 91.

68 *Secret Scriptures*, vol. 3, p. 771.

69 *Secret Scriptures*, vol. 3, p. 785. A much more detailed biography of this figure also dates from around this time: Nuona Hutuketu 諾那呼圖克圖 (Nor lha Khutughtu), *Mizong Lianhuasheng dashi mifa* 密宗蓮華生大師秘法 (*The esoteric school's Padmasambhava's esoteric teachings*) (Taipei: Wulin, 1985 [1933–1936]).

70 Walter Y. Evans-Wentz, *Tibetan Yoga and Secret Doctrines* (New York: Oxford University Press, 1958). The Chinese translation of the series, called "Tibetan Esoterica, The Seven Great Essential Dharmas, nos. two, three, four, six, seven" (*Zangmi qi zhong fa er san si liu qi*) seems to indicate that the original books one and five were also translated and are just not preserved in this collection. *Secret Scriptures*, vol. 4, pp. 603–649, 509–586, 587–602, 650–652, 653–655, respectively.

71 Tuttle, *Tibetan Buddhists*, pp. 68–86.

72 For details on these figures, see D. Lopez, "Tibetology in the United States of America."

73 Chinese has an identical phonetic sound to reproduce the "ka" in "Kazi" if this had been Zhang's intent, but he clearly thought this was a term that he recognized, no doubt because of the predominance of Dge lugs monks in China proper. For evidence of the identification of these two phonemes, see *Secret Scriptures*, vol. 1, p. 684.

74 In reality, the first bona-fide Bka' brgyud master to come to Republican China was the Gangs dkar Sprul sku (1893–1957, Ch. Gongga hutuketu), on whom see Carmen Meinert's discussion in chapter 6 above. Shi Dongchu 釋東初, *Zhongguo fojiao jindai shi* 中國佛教近代史 (*Modern history of Chinese Buddhism*), 2 vols. (Taipei: Zhonghua fojiao wenhua guan, 1974), p. 401. See also Mi nyag Mgon po, *'Bo Gangs dkar sprul sku'i rnam thar dad pa'i pad dkar* (Beijing: Mi rigs dpe skrun khang, 1997), pp. 57–70.

75 See *Secret Scriptures*, vol. 1, pp. 749–764. For examples of such work circulating in America around the same time see, Walter Eugene Clark and A. Freiherr von Stael-Holstein, eds., *Two Lamaistic Pantheons*, Harvard-Yenching Institute monograph series 3–4 (Cambridge: Harvard-Yenching Institute, 1937). For the involvement of a previous incarnation of the Lcang skya Khutughtu with such illustrated works, see Patricia Berger, *Empire of Emptiness: Buddhist Art and Political Authority in Qing China*.

76 See *Secret Scriptures*, vol. 1, pp. 869–876; for a translation based on a text by the Paṇchen Lama, see pp. 715–724. These two texts are dated according to the Buddhist calendar (*Foli*), years 2963 and 2964, respectively, which I have converted to 1936 and 1937 based on similar dates found in other texts. However, it is possible that some minor variant in the understanding of the Buddhist calendar would place these texts in different years. On the 1931 event see Dai Jitao 戴季陶, *Banchan dashi shou liuzi daming zhenyan fa yao* 班禪大師說六字大明真言法要 (*Essentials of the Paṇchen Lama's teachings on the six syllable mantra*), vol. 3, *Dai Jitao xiansheng wencun* 戴季陶先生文存 (Taipei: Zhongguo guomindang zhongyang weiyuanhui, 1959 [1931]), pp. 1173–1174.

77 This date is arrived at by subtracting the "three years before" the lama was invited from the date of publication of the text, 1937. *Secret Scriptures*, vol. 1, p. 813.

78 From another text we know that the presence of Tibetan lamas in Shanghai continued into the late 1930s. The Guru Rongseng mkhan po of Central Tibet (Shangshi Xizang rongzeng kanbu) taught a text spoken by Rje btsun Blo bzang chos kyi rgyal mtshan (Zunzhe Luosang qiuji jiacang), presumably a reference to the fourth Paṇchen Lama (1570–1662). See *Secret Scriptures*, vol. 4, p. 415.

79 In the absence of any other indication, I have assumed that Thub bstan nyi ma and Blo bzang bzang po were ethnic Tibetans, as the Mongol teacher Gushri Dkon mchog rdo rje was singled out as a Mongol. However, the fact that one of these texts associated with Blo bzang bzang po was transmitted by the Mongol monk Bai Puren (1870–1927) casts some doubt on this assumption. (For more on Bai, see Tuttle, *Tibetan Buddhists in the Making of Modern China*, pp. 79–81 and *passim*; his biography and the memorial inscription from his stūpa can be found in Zhang Bozhen 張伯楨, *Canghai cong shu* 滄海叢書, 4 vols. [Shanghai: Shanghai shudian, 1934.]) It would be surprising for a Tibetan to seek such a text from a Mongol lama.

80 *Secret Scriptures*, vol. 1, pp. 677–772. For the Paṇchen Lama text, see pp. 715–732.

81 *Secret Scriptures*, vol. 1, pp. 255–270.

82 *Secret Scriptures*, vol. 1, p. 265.

83 *Secret Scriptures*, vol. 1, pp. 773–944.

84 *Secret Scriptures*, vol. 1, pp. 790–791.

85 *Secret Scriptures*, vol. 1, p. 781.

86 Another text published in 1939 was transmitted by Thub bstan nyi ma at Kaifeng's Henan Buddhist Study Society, possibly at the same time as this larger corpus. The later translation includes the Tibetan text with subscribed Chinese phonetics to assist with its recitation.

87 *Secret Scriptures*, vol. 1, pp. 775–777. This work also includes a translated work by the fourth Paṇchen Lama on Avalokiteśvara, vol. 1, pp. 877–878.

88 *Secret Scriptures*, vol. 1, p. 944.

89 Melvyn Goldstein, Dawei Sherap, and William Siebenschuh, *A Tibetan Revolutionary: The Political Life and Times of Bapa Phüntso Wangye* (Berkeley: University of California, 2004), pp. 29, 43.

90 *Secret Scriptures*, vol. 1, pp. 325–356.

91 Dayong, who had previously been an officer in the modern Sichuanese army during the early Republican period, had not served in Tibet.

92 *Secret Scriptures*, vol. 4, p. 227. He was mistaken in this, as the Qing period saw numerous instances of this genre being taught in China proper. To name just a few instances: according to their biographies, the fifth Dalai Lama taught a mixed ethnic audience at Sku 'bum on the way back to Central Tibet from Beijing, and Lcang skya Rol pa'i rdo rje taught at Xiangshan, outside Beijing; according to Dharmatala's *Hor Chos 'byung*, Erteni Nomon Han, Lcang skya's teacher and disciple, taught the *Lam rim* in China; moreover, the Qianlong Emperor studied an abbreviated version with Lcang skya Rol pa'i rdo rje in Beihai, Beijing, though the Qianlong Emperor was a Manchu.

93 *Secret Scriptures*, vol. 4, p. 231. I am assuming this society was based in Beijing.

94 According to Jagou (*Le 9e Paṇchen Lama*, p. 270) the Sngags chen Khutughtu returned to Beijing for three months in 1937.

95 In 1948, Nenghai was invited back to Beijing by the Bodhi Study Association; see Dingzhi, *Nenghai shangshi zhuan* [*Biography of Guru Nenghai*], *op. cit.*, p. 53. In 1951, the Bodhi Study Association would publish one of Nenghai's translations of a Yamāntaka text taught there in 1949. See *Secret Scriptures*, vol. 2, pp. 683–821.

96 *Secret Scriptures*, vol. 4, pp. 229–230.

97 *Secret Scriptures*, vol. 1, pp. 47–79. The root text proved so popular that in 1940, three different versions of Tsong kha pa's *Praise for the Sequential Path to Enlightenment* were published together, including the one used in Guankong's and the Sngags chen Khutughtu's collaborative efforts. See *Secret Scriptures*, vol. 1, pp. 31–45.

98 *Secret Scriptures*, vol. 2, pp. 113–156; vol. 4, pp. 7–34; vol. 3, pp. 885–912.

99 *Secret Scriptures*, vol. 1, pp. 1–8.

100 *Secret Scriptures*, vol. 2, pp. 821–970; vol. 1, pp. 357–451. See Jagou, *Le 9e Panchen Lama*, pp. 303, 218.

101 *Secret Scriptures*, vol. 2, pp. 565–574. The 1942 preface to another translation published by the Bodhi Study Association also mentions the Sngags chen Khutughtu, vol. 3, pp. 583–602.

102 Two of Tang's translations were published by the Esoteric Treasury Institute, but as they are not dated, we cannot know for certain whether they preceded his work with the Bodhi Study Association.

103 *Secret Scriptures*, vol. 3, pp. 583–602; vol. 2, pp. 565–574 and pp. 875–970.

104 *Secret Scriptures*, vol. 4, pp. 35–110. For this association, see Alice Getty, *The Gods of Northern Buddhism: Their History and Iconography*, 2nd ed. (New York: Dover, 1988 [1928]), p. 126. One of these texts opens with a bilingual section, in which the Tibetan script is subscribed with Chinese transliteration.

105 The preface to this work notes that the text was written by the first Dalai Lama and that Lama Yuwangbujiao wrote a commentary on it. See *Secret Scriptures*, vol. 3, pp. 729–731.

106 Lauran Hartley, "Contextually Speaking: Tibetan Literary Discourse and Social Change in the People's Republic of China (1980–2000)" (Ph.D. dissertation, Indiana University, 2003), pp. 56–87.

8: Tibetan Learning in the Contemporary Chinese Yogācāra School

Zhihua Yao

I N VERY GENERAL terms, contemporary scholars of Buddhism tend to divide the discipline according to its linguistic and geographic distribution into three fields: the Pali tradition in Southeast Asia, Chinese Buddhism in East Asia, and Tibetan Buddhism in Central Asia. This division is not entirely arbitrary, and is sometimes depicted as corresponding to the three vehicles of the Buddhist teaching, namely, the so-called Hīnayāna, Mahāyāna, and Vajrayāna. In terms of Buddhist philosophy, however, the Pali tradition descends from the Theravāda School, while the Tibetan commits itself above all to the Prāsaṅgika-Mādhyamika philosophy, ranking it as the highest truth. Chinese Buddhism, despite its complexity, is noteworthy for its heritage of Yogācāra, or hybrid Yogācāra-Tathāgatagarbha, thought.

Given this background, one may wonder what Chinese adherents of Yogācāra may learn from Tibetan Buddhism, with its emphasis on Mādhyamika philosophy. This chapter will consider why and how Chinese Buddhists engaged Tibetan Buddhist thought by introducing three representative figures of the contemporary Chinese Yogācāra school: Lü Cheng (1896–1989), Fazun (1902–1980), and Han Jingqing (1912–2003). Besides the common interest in Tibetan Buddhism, they shared a particular attraction to Indian Yogācāra texts preserved in Tibetan, especially the works of Sthiramati (active prior to the year 600), Dignāga (ca. 480–540), and Dharmakīrti (ca. 600–660). I will argue, too, that they were joined by a common hostility toward Sinicized Buddhism, and thus anticipated the "Critical Buddhism" that has developed in Japan in recent decades.

The Contemporary Chinese Yogācāra School

In referring to a "contemporary Chinese Yogācāra school," we look to the revival of *weishi xue*, the "learning of consciousness-only," in China since the beginning of the twentieth century. In Euro-American scholarship, familiarity with Chinese Buddhism during this period is primarily represented by Holmes Welch's well-known series *The Practice of Chinese Buddhism 1900– 1950* (1967), *The Buddhist Revival in China* (1968), and *Buddhism under Mao* (1972). These works detail the institutional and social changes to which Chinese Buddhist communities have been subject in modern times, yet have little to say about the intellectual life of contemporary Chinese Buddhists. Nevertheless, most scholars of Buddhism in China agree that this period bore significant intellectual fruit in the revival of Yogācāra Buddhism, a development that proved an ongoing resource for scholars inside and outside the Buddhist community. For instance, Xiong Shili (1885–1968), the founder of the contemporary movement known as New Confucianism, was educated in this school in his youth and named his own Confucian-Buddhist synthetic system the "new doctrine of consciousness-only."

During the Republican period (1911–1949), more than fifty scholars published research on Yogācāra.[1] Most were associated with three institutes, namely, the Chinese School of Buddhist Doctrine (*Zhina neixue yuan*) founded in 1921, the Society of the Third Time (*Sanshi xuehui*) founded in 1927, and Wuchang Buddhist College (*Wuchang foxue yuan*) founded in 1922. Among them, the first two, being called respectively the Southern and Northern School, were lay communities, while the third was a monastery. Each school was led by a famous teacher, respectively Ouyang Jian (1871– 1943), Han Qingjing (1884–1949), and Taixu (1889–1947), all of whom were active during the Republican period. These three schools were significant in the sense that they explored prospects for modernizing Chinese Buddhist communities, calling for lay Buddhism, or a Buddhist revolution within the monastic system. However, due to the linguistic limitations of their leaders, most scholars looked to Japan for authentic Yogācāra teachings. A printery associated with the Chinese School of Buddhist Doctrine, for instance, managed to recover two- to three-hundred fascicles of Buddhist texts unavailable in China but preserved in Japan.[2]

The next generation of scholars, however, included Lü Cheng of the Southern School, Han Jingqing of both the Northern and Southern Schools (but maintaining the lineage of the latter), and Fazun of the Wuchang Buddhist College. Lü Cheng and Fazun were active in both the Republican and

People's Republican periods, while Han Jingqing became active late in the eighties and nineties. Though representing different branches of the contemporary Chinese Yogācāra school, they shared a common interest in Tibetan Buddhism. Well trained in the Tibetan language—Lü Cheng was also good at Sanskrit and Pali—and Tibetan Buddhism, they engaged in translating or introducing Tibetan works with an emphasis on the Yogācāra, and contributed originally to the development of contemporary Chinese Yogācāra.

Learning from Tibetan Buddhism

Tibetan and Chinese Buddhism, though they are distinct traditions, have had a long history of intellectual and institutional exchange. The translation of Buddhist texts from Chinese sources into Tibetan can be traced back to the eighth century, the initial period in the history of Tibetan Buddhism. Many of them, including important works such as the *Mahāparinirvānasūtra*, the *Laṅkāvatārasūtra*, the *Suvarṇaprabhāsottamasūtra*, Kuiji's commentary on the *Lotus Sūtra* (P. 5518, T. 1723),[3] and Wŏn-ch'ŭk's commentary on the *Sandhinirmocanasūtra*[4] are still preserved in the Tibetan Tripiṭaka. From about the thirteenth century on, moreover, Chinese Buddhists started to translate large numbers of mainly esoteric Buddhist texts from Tibetan. Although, unfortunately, they are not all extant today, a few were included in the Chinese Tripiṭaka and some fragments have been also collected in the *Esoteric Collection of the Mahāyāna Path* (*Dacheng yaodao miji*).[5]

When we turn to the contemporary period, however, it appears that, for various reasons, Chinese Buddhists sought to learn more than they had previously from Tibetan Buddhism. Above all, they were dissatisfied with the established Tiantai, Huayan, Chan, and the Pure Land schools, and therefore took the initial step of evaluating what was lacking from the Chinese Tripiṭaka, and then accordingly began projects of translation. Their ideal goal was to translate from Tibetan everything that was missing in Chinese, despite the enormous work this would involve.

Lü Cheng took a particular interest in this enterprise. While he was initially a student of fine arts in Japan, upon returning to China he devoted himself to Buddhist studies, eventually becoming one of the country's most eminent Buddhist scholars. While virtually unknown in the West, he is renowned in China and Japan for his original contributions to the study of Yogācāra and historical studies of Indian and Chinese Buddhism. One of Lü Cheng's most important contributions to scholarship was a suggested list of works that should be translated into Chinese as a matter of priority. In enumerating these works, he adopted the fivefold division of the exoteric teaching of the Gelukpa school, as detailed below. At the same time, he also listed some works that should be translated from Chinese into Tibetan in order that the Tibetans might better understand Chinese Buddhism.[6] In sum, he conceived the program as follows:

1. Among the works of Buddhist logic or *tséma* (Skt. *pramāṇa*), the most important ones requiring translation into Chinese were thought to be Dharmakīrti's *Pramāṇavārttika* (P. 5709), his auto-commentary on the first chapter (P. 5717a), together with the commentary on the remaining three chapters by Devendrabuddhi (ca. 630–690) (P. 5717b). Although Dharmakīrti's seven major treatises—the *Pramāṇavārttika*, *Pramāṇaviniścaya* (P. 5710), *Nyāyabindu* (P. 5711), *Hetubindu* (P. 5712), *Vādanyāya* (P. 5715), *Sambandhaparīkṣā* (P. 5713), and *Santānāntarasiddhi* (P. 5716)—are treated as classics in Buddhist logic by the Tibetans, none of these works was known to the Chinese before the contemporary period. Chinese Buddhists have instead viewed Dignāga's *Nyāyamukha* (T. 1628, 1629), a work extant only in Chinese, as the most important source for their knowledge of Buddhist logic.[7] Lü Cheng also believed, therefore, that there should be a Tibetan translation of the *Nyāyamukha* in order for the Tibetans to better understand Buddhist logic through Dignāga, rather than his great commentator Dharmakīrti.

2. Among the works of the Yogācāra School, Maitreya's *Abhisamayālaṃkāra* (P. 5184), its commentary by Haribhadra (P. 5189), and Sthiramati's commentary on the *Triṃśikā* (P. 5565) were designated for translation into Chinese. For the Tibetans, the *Abhisamayālaṃkāra* is one of the five root treatises of Maitreya, but in China it is not contained in the list of the five essential texts ascribed to him. The fact that the great Chinese pilgrims Xuanzang (602–664) and Yijing (635–713) fail to mention it in their writings suggests that it is perhaps a later work, although commentator Hari bhadra (ca. 800) details an abundant prior commentarial tradition on it. Vasubandhu's *Triṃśikā* is by contrast one of the most important Yogācāra texts for traditional Chinese Buddhism, and numbers of commentaries on it circulated in India. The commentary by Sthiramati, however, though extant in Tibetan and in a Sanskrit original found in Nepal in the 1920s, was unknown in China. As a work judged especially helpful in the study of the *Vijñaptimātratāsiddhiśāstra* (T. 1585), the collection of ten commentaries to the *Triṃśikā* translated and edited by Xuanzang, Lü Cheng's opinion was that Sthiramati's commentary should be translated into Chinese, while Xuanzang's text would later be translated into Tibetan.

3. In connection with the Madhyamaka school, Candrakīrti's *Madhyamakāvatāra* (P. 5261, 5262) and his auto-commentary (P. 5263) were earmarked for translation into Chinese. The work is so far only available in Tibetan (though a unique Sanskrit manuscript is now known to be preserved in Tibet) and is considered to be the root text of the Prāsaṅgika-Madhyamaka school, the dominant philosophical tradition in Tibetan Buddhism. Nevertheless, Chinese Buddhists before the modern period knew neither of Candrakīrti (ca. 600–650), nor of the distinction between Prāsaṅgika- and Svātantrika-Madhyamaka. Chinese Madhyamaka, that is, the Sanlun school, instead takes Piṅgalanetra's commentary on the *Mūlamadhyamakakārikā* (T. 1564) as one of its core texts. For the most part, this commentary appears to be based on the *Akutobhaya* (P. 5229), an early commentary on the *Mūlamadhyamakakārikā* now extant only in Tibetan. It was ascribed to Nāgārjuna (ca. 150–250) himself by the Tibetans, though Tsongkhapa considered the attribution as doubtful. As a comparison of the *Akutobhaya* and Piṅgalanetra's commentary would contribute to understanding the development of the Madhyamaka School in its early period, Lü Cheng suggested that the commentary of Piṅgalanetra be translated into Tibetan.

4. The Vinaya: here, Guṇaprabha's *Vinayasūtra* (P. 5619) and its autocommentary (P. 5621) were to be translated into Chinese. This work concisely outlines the monastic rules of the Mūlasarvāstivāda order. Yijing highly praised this work when he was studying in India, but it does not count among the Sarvāstivāda Vinaya texts he translated. The most popular Vinaya text among Chinese Buddhists is the *Dharmaguptakavinaya*, which details the monastic rules of the Dharmaguptaka order, a work also known as the "fourfold division Vinaya." Lü Cheng wished to see it introduced to Tibet.

5. Finally, as far as the Abhidharma was concerned, Lü Cheng did not propose any work for translation from Tibetan into Chinese. However, he did suggest that two important Abhidharma works that are only extant in Chinese, the *Mahāvibhāṣā* (T. 1545) and the **Nyāyānusāra* (T. 1562), should be translated into Tibetan to help the Tibetans improve their study of Vasubandhu's *Abhidharmakośa*, a required work for students in the Tibetan monastic colleges. The two-hundred-fascicule *Mahāvibhāṣā* is an encyclopedic work that contains the most comprehensive and authoritative explanations on various issues in the Sarvāstivāda Abhidharma. The **Nyāyānusāra* by Saṅghabhadra (ca. fifth century) criticizes the *Abhidharmakośa* and records numerous debates between the Vaibhāṣika and Sautrāntika, two important Buddhist philosophical schools for the Tibetans.

Thus we see that an important dialogue had been conceived, in which

both Chinese and Tibetan scholars would be contributing work to the benefit of the other. With the plan outlined above in mind, let us now turn to the
accomplishments of Chinese Buddhist scholarship since Lü Cheng started
this translation project early in the 1920s.

The Yogācāra works of major significance that Lü Cheng himself translated
from Tibetan include parts of Sthiramati's *Triṃśikābhāṣya* (P. 5565), Dignāga's
Pramāṇasamuccaya (P. 5700, 5701, 5702), and the entire *Hetucakraḍamaru*
(P. 5708). Though the *Pramāṇasamuccaya* had been translated by Yijing
during the eighth century, it was lost shortly thereafter. This work and the
Triṃśikabhāṣya therefore became available, albeit partially, to Chinese readers for the first time thanks to Lü Cheng's efforts, and these and his other
translations contributed greatly to the revival of Yogācāra studies in contemporary China. Meanwhile, he partially retranslated some works that had
already been available in Chinese, including Asaṅga's *Mahāyānasaṃgraha* (P.
5549) and Dignāga's *Ālambanaparīkṣā* (P. 5703, 5704).[8] From 1927 to 1937,
he also edited a concise version of the Chinese Tripiṭaka, the *Zang yao*, which
contains seventy works in four hundred fascicules. One of the main features
of this new edition of the major canonical texts is its careful annotations with
references to the Tibetan, Sanskrit, and Pali sources. It has thereby served as
an excellent example of the role of other Buddhist traditions in improving
the understanding of Chinese Buddhism itself.

Fazun, a contemporary of Lü Cheng, was one of the few Chinese monk-
scholars to have entered the monastic colleges of Tibet. He went to study
there in the 1920s and 1930s, when he started to translate Tibetan works into
Chinese. Upon returning to Sichuan, he spent most of his time involved in his
translation projects. Early in his career, Fazun emphasized Vinaya texts and
the major works of Tsongkhapa, such as the *Great Sequential Path to Enlightenment* (*Byang chub lam rim chen mo*) (P. 5392) and his commentary on the
Madhyamakāvatāra (P. 5408). In this period, he also translated two Yogācāra
texts attributed by the Tibetans to Maitreya, the *Abhisamayālaṃkāra* (with
the commentary by Haribhadra) and the *Dharmadharmatāvibhāga* (P. 5524).
The publication of his Chinese translation of the latter provoked a debate
between Ouyang Jian and Fazun on the discontinuity of the treatise in relation to other works ascribed to Maitreya in China. Ouyang Jian suspected
that it was either because of a mistake in the translation by Fazun, or that the
Tibetans had significantly altered the text. Fazun, in turn, defended his position by pronouncing the work his "most careful translation."[9] He criticized
Ouyang Jian for not thoroughly understanding the fundamental ideas of the
Yogācāra as presented in the Chinese sources, and maintained that, although

differences might be noted between the *Dharmadharmatāvibhāga* and Chinese Yogācāra texts, these were not so great as to amount to "discontinuity." The debate marked a significant moment in that it highlighted Ouyang Jian's and Fazun's differing approaches to the study of Yogācāra traditions in Tibet and China.

Fazun continued his translation career after he moved to Beijing in 1950. Many of his translations during this period, however, were unfortunately left unpublished and were destroyed during the Cultural Revolution. He resumed his translation work in 1978 and during the last three years of his life translated Atiśa's *Bodhipathapradīpa* (P. 5343), Dignāga's *Pramāṇasamuccaya*, and Dharmakīrti's *Pramāṇavārttika* with its commentary by the first Dalai Lama Gendün Drupa.[10] It is difficult to imagine how he could finish translating these challenging texts while working independently in such a short span of time. His translation of the *Pramāṇavārttika*, in particular, is the only full modern translation in the world to date. He is also credited with introducing Chinese readers to Gendün Drupa's commentary on the *Pramāṇavārttika*, which illustrates the Tibetan reception of Yogācāra teaching. Fazun's translation of the *Pramāṇasamuccaya* not only is similarly complete, but also contains many insightful remarks. Unfortunately, it is often difficult for readers to discern these from Dignāga's original text, and may therefore be best considered a sort of exegetical translation.

Fazun was also the only scholar able to contribute to fulfilling the other facet of the project, namely, to introduce works conserved only in Chinese to the Tibetans. In the 1940s, he devoted four years to a Tibetan translation of the two-hundred-fascicule *Mahāvibhāṣā*. After completing the work in the summer of 1949, Fazun sent the manuscript to a lama in Dartsedo (modern Kangding), and in 1954 presented it to the Fourteenth Dalai Lama who was then visiting Beijing. However, despite the potential importance of the *Mahāvibhāṣā* for advancing Tibetan knowledge of the Abhidharma, it is a matter of regret that only the first fifteen pages of this vast translation are preserved today.[11]

Han Jingqing also studied for a short time in Tibet in the 1950s. In the early 90s, he founded the Maitreya Center in Beijing, which attracted a great number of young students including the present writer. In his teachings, Han Jingqing divided the Yogācāra doctrine into three main components—the doctrines of consciousness-only (*vijñaptimātratā*), perfection of wisdom (*prajñāpāramitā*), and the three self-natures (*trisvabhāva*). Following this division, one might say that Lü Cheng introduced contemporary scholars to the doctrine of consciousness-only by translating Sthiramati's

Triṃśikābhāṣya, while Fazun presented the doctrine of the perfection of wisdom in his translation of Maitreya's *Abhisamayālaṃkāra*. In contrast, Han Jingqing emphasized the doctrine of three self-natures in both his teachings and translations, and from 1993 to 2000 delivered 141 lectures on his new translation of the *Mahāyānasaṃgraha*, which, in his view, presents the best understanding of this doctrine.[12] He also published a translation of Vasubandhu's *Trisvabhāvanirdeśa* (P. 5559), a text unavailable in Chinese but extant in Tibetan and Sanskrit, and composed a lengthy commentary to this text. The other major translations that he published included Vasubandhu's commentary on the *Dharmadharmatāvibhāga* (P. 5529), Sthiramati's *Triṃśikābhāṣya*, Dharmakīrti's *Nyāyabindu*, Sāgaramegha's *Yogācārabhūmau Bodhisattvabhūmivyākhyā* (P. 5538), and Jñānagarbha's commentary on the Maitreya chapter of the *Sandhinirmocanasūtra* (P. 5535).[13] Compared to the two earlier translators, Han Jingqing in my view provides us with more reliable translations, all of which are complete and never overly-influenced by his own comments.

Though Han Jingqing started his translation career as early as the 1940s, he only began to publish his translations in recent years and many of them—more than fifty titles totaling about five thousand pages—are still left unpublished. Included among them are all the major works of Dignāga, Dharmakīrti, and Sthiramati. Most significantly, his production also embraces a long list of works by some comparatively late Indian commentators, whom Han Jingqing introduced to Chinese readers for the first time: Buddhaśrījñāna, Darmottara, Dharmakīrtiśrī, Dharmendra, Jñānacandra, Jinendrabuddhi, Kamalaśīla, Kumāraśrībhadra, Pṛthivibandhu, Prajñākaramati, Ratnākaraśānti, Ratnakīrti, Vimuktisena, and Vinītadeva are counted among them.[14] Another important work is his commentary on the *Vijñaptimātratāsiddiśāstra* entitled *Cheng weishi lun shuyi*.[15] Totaling 2.4 million words, this commentary is the first, among numerous commentaries on this important work, to make reference to the Tibetan sources and, at many points, takes a critical stance toward Xuanzang's translation and Kuiji's foundational commentary.

Besides the three scholars discussed here, there were also other individuals who translated Yogācāra texts from Tibetan into Chinese. For instance, the *Nyāyabindu* and the *Trisvabhāvanirdeśa* were translated by Yang Huaqun and Liu Xiaolan respectively prior to Han Jingqing.[16] Besides this, during the Republican and early People's Republican periods, some Tibetan lamas, collaborating with their Chinese disciples, translated various manuals of esoteric Buddhism from Tibetan into Chinese. Fazun was again one of the most productive translators in this field, though he himself was not overly interested in the tantric practice.[17]

Criticizing Sinicized Buddhism

I began to study Yogācāra Buddhism under Han Jingqing in the late eighties in Beijing at the Maitreya Center. Besides a long list of technical terms that I was required to master, I had the impression that many of the young scholars around him shared the following assumption: Chinese Buddhism is wrong, or, at least, there is something wrong with Chinese Buddhism. They wanted to search for a more authentic Buddhism, and so looked to Buddhism's Indian origins and its Tibetan transmissions in order to find this. Later, I discovered that this attitude had its root among Chinese Yogācāra scholars of the older generation.

From the very beginning, the different branches of the contemporary Chinese Yogācāra school shared hostility toward the traditional Chinese Buddhist schools, what I call "Sinicized Buddhism." For instance, Ouyang Jian criticized Sinicized Buddhism primarily with regard to intellectual issues, while Taixu's attitude was based on institutional grounds. Their critiques of Sinicized Buddhism anticipated in some respects the "Critical Buddhism" associated with figures such as Matsumoto Shirō and Hakamaya Noriaki in Japan in recent decades. In both cases, we find a common critical spirit directed against the same object—Tathāgatagarbha thought (specifically under the description of "Dhātuvāda"), a form of essentialism that, in their view, is a corruption of true Buddhism. The primary difference resides in the fact that the Japanese scholars adopt a Madhyamaka standpoint, while their Chinese counterparts were oriented to Yogācāra.[18]

Together with their promotion of the study of Yogācāra Buddhism, Ouyang Jian and his disciple Lü Cheng were severely critical of Sinicized Buddhism. They argued that its theoretical basis was to be found in apocryphal writings such as the *Awakening of Faith in the Mahāyāna* (*Dacheng qixin lun*), writings that, in their view, were composed by Chinese authors who misunderstood Indian Buddhist teachings. The only way to restore genuine Buddhism, they held, was to reintroduce Indian Buddhism to China. In the two major doctrinal systems of Indian Mahāyāna, i.e., Madhyamaka and Yogācāra, the latter, in their view, was the ultimate teaching of the Buddha as given in the third phase of his preaching. In this they were following an approach to doctrinal classification that indeed had an Indian origin, for in the *Sandhinirmocanasūtra* it states that the Buddha teaches in "three turns of the dharma wheel." The first turn contains the Hīnayāna teaching that there is no substantial self. This is superseded by a second teaching contained in the Perfection of Wisdom literature that discloses the emptiness of all things. The third and final teaching, which elucidates the hidden meaning of the Perfection of Wisdom, is taken to be the teaching of Yogācāra. In this context, Lü Cheng's debates with Xiong Shili, the founder of Contemporary New Confucianism, are interesting, in that what we really see here is a controversy between Indian Buddhism and Sinicized Buddhism, and not one between Buddhism and Confucianism. The focal point of Lü Cheng's critique of Xiong Shili is the idea of *benjue* or "original enlightenment," which is in turn one of the major issues for Japanese Critical Buddhism.

In directing his assessment of Sinicized Buddhism to institutional issues, Taixu was more sympathetic to traditional Chinese Buddhist Schools on intellectual matters. Among his disciples, Yinshun (1906–2004), a colleague of Fazun, was another leading intellectual and critic. Yinshun's thought was notable for its Madhyamaka orientation, which became very influential in Taiwan and overseas Chinese Buddhist communities. He created a unique, threefold system of doctrinal classification, using the categories of "empty-name-only" (*xingkong weiming*), "deluded-consciousness-only" (*xuwang weishi*), and "true-mind-only" (*zhenchang weixin*). In many of his writings he treated the three equally, but evidence shows that he favored the first.[19] In his view, only "empty-name-only" represented the true spirit of Buddhism, while the other two, especially the system of "true-mind-only," were not the original teachings of the Buddha. Sinicized Buddhism, under the influence of Tathāgatagarbha thought, did not reach the ultimate truth and so Chinese Buddhists should return to the Madhyamaka to recover the genuine teaching. Yinshun's doctrinal system of classification is almost unprecedented in the history of Chinese Buddhism, in that Madhyamaka was seldom treated as the pinnacle of Buddhist doctrine. It had usually been placed below Tathāgatagarbha thought or that of the Yogācāra School. Here Yinshun was obviously influenced by the Tibetan method of doctrinal classification, according to which four schools—Sarvāstivāda, Sautrāntika, Yogācāra, and Madhyamaka—are treated in ascending order. An explanation for this peculiarity may be that Yinshun and Fazun, both being disciples of Taixu, worked together closely from an early age. Yinshun learned from and formed his Prāsaṅgika position on the basis of Fazun's translations, and his criticism of Sinicized Buddhism also may reflect the influence of Fazun, who did not otherwise explicitly express his views on this matter.

Han Jingqing was also a critic of Sinicized Buddhism. He agreed with Lü Cheng in his skepticism about Chinese apocryphal writings and further identified the author of the *Awakening of Faith in the Mahāyāna* to be the Chinese monk Tanyan (516–588).[20] Following the convention of the Northern school of contemporary Chinese Yogācāra, he called Sinicized Buddhism *Huahua fojiao*, which suggests something like "playboy Buddhism."[21] He even went so far as to attack the traditional Chinese Yogācāra school, the Faxiang school represented by Xuanzang and Kuiji (632–682), which is usually considered by contemporary Chinese Yogācārins as the touchstone of authentic Buddhism. On many technical points in Yogācāra doctrine, Han Jingqing opposed the Dharmapāla-Xuanzang tradition by adopting Sthiramati's position, a move that had been fostered by his translation of Yogācāra works from Tibetan.

For these Chinese Buddhist scholars, the goal of their critical interrogation of Sinicized Buddhism was to present Chinese Buddhism with a new face. This became an urgent task when the Chinese Buddhist Association, an administrative bureau that oversees all the Buddhist communities in China, was founded in 1953. As Lü Cheng said about it: "Along with the founding of the Chinese Buddhist Association, the relationship between Han-Chinese and Tibetan Buddhism becomes closer, which demands more communication between Buddhist studies in the two places."[22] In the new era of the People's Republic, he believed, "Chinese Buddhism" (*Zhongguo fojiao*) should include both the Buddhism of Han-Chinese and that of the Tibetans. In this new context, "Chinese Buddhism," as commonly understood to refer to the traditional Chinese Buddhist schools, was now called *Hanchuan fojiao*, or Buddhism as transmitted among Han-Chinese adherents, in contradistinction to *Zhongguo fojiao*, which is Chinese Buddhism literally. Chinese Buddhism as *Zhongguo fojiao* has a political implication, and is taken to cover all kinds of Buddhism practiced in China, including the Theravāda communities of Yunnan province, and the Tibetan Buddhism that traditionally has predominated in Tibet and Inner Mongolia. Chinese Buddhism in this new sense thus refers broadly to all Buddhist schools that are present in the land of China. One may suspect that scholars like Lü Cheng, in making statements such as we see above, were tacitly acting in the service of ideological propaganda on behalf of the newly established communist regime. In my opinion, however, he was attempting to use ideology in order to justify his Tibetan-oriented approach to Buddhism, and striving to elevate it in the face of an unfriendly reception among the traditional Chinese Buddhist schools.

To conclude, the contemporary Chinese Yogācārins, due to their dissatisfaction with the traditional schools, attempted to search for authentic Buddhist teaching by translating the Yogācāra texts that were not available in Chinese but were preserved in Tibetan. This wave of translating and studying Yogācāra Buddhism in contemporary China is called "the third transmission of Yogācāra in China" by Han Jingqing, who considers that the first transmission began with Bodhiruci's arrival at China in 508 and ended with the death of Paramārtha (499–569) in 569, while the second was associated with the great translator Xuanzang. In the early 1990s, scholars in China came to debate whether the mainstream in pre-Qin (pre-221 BCE) thought was to be characterized as Confucianism or Taoism. Analogously, we may have to think about whether mainstream Buddhism in the post-Qing (1911– present) era is best represented by "Sinicized Buddhism" or the India- and Tibet-oriented contemporary Chinese Yogācāra school.

Notes

1 See Fori 佛日, "Faxiang weishi xue fuxing de huigu" 法相唯識學復興的回顧, *Fayin* 法 音 153 (1997): 10–16; 154 (1997): 5–8.

2 See H. Welch, *The Buddhist Revival in China* (Cambridge: Harvard University Press, 1968), pp. 5–6.

3 According to *The Tibetan Tripitaka Peking Edition: Catalogue and Index*, its author is Sa'i rtsa lag (*Pṛthivībandhu). All references to Tibetan texts in the present chapter are to the Peking edition (P.): *The Tibetan Tripiṭaka: Peking Edition, Kept in the Library of the Otani University, Kyoto*, ed. Daisetz T. Suzuki (Tokyo/Kyoto: Tibetan Tripiṭika Research Institute, 1961). Chinese Buddhist canonical works are referenced according to the Taishō edition (T.): *Taishō shinshū daizōkyō* 大正新修大藏經 ["The Buddhist Canon Newly Compiled during the Taishō Era"], ed. Takakusu Junjirō 高楠順次郎 and Watanabe Kaigyoku 渡边边海旭, 100 vols. (Tokyo: Taishō issaikyō kankōkai, 1924–1935).

4 The original Chinese text by Wŏn-ch'ŭk is collected in the *Zokuzōkyō*, no. 369.

5 See Lü Cheng 呂澂, ed., *Han Zang fojiao guanxi shiliao ji* 漢藏佛教關係史料集 (Chengdu: West China Union University, 1942), pp. 1–18.

6 See Lü Cheng, "Han zang fo xue gou tong de di yi bu," 漢藏佛學溝通的第一步, in *Lü Cheng foxue lunzhu xuanji* 呂澂佛學論著選集 (Jinan: Qi lu shu she, 1991), pp. 1407– 1410.

7 In the Tibetan Tripiṭaka, a work entitled *Tshad ma'i bstan bcos rigs pa la 'jug pa shes bya ba* (*Nyāyapraveśa-nāma-pramāṇaśāstra*, P. 5707) is ascribed to Dignāga. But this work is actually a translation of Śaṅkarasvāmin's *Nyāyapraveśa*, which was also translated into Chinese (T. 1630). Śaṅkarasvāmin (ca. 500–560) was a direct disciple of Dignāga. His *Nyāyapraveśa* was highly valued by Chinese Buddhists, but it cannot

be mistaken for Dignāga's *Nyāyamukha*. This mistake is still circulating today among some Buddhist scholars. See S.R. Bhatt and Anu Mehrotra, *Buddhist Epistemology*, with a preface by the Dalai Lama (Westport: Greenwood Press, 2000).

8   All these translations are collected in volume 9 of the *Da zang jing bu bian* 大藏經補編 (Taipei: Hua yü chu ban she, 1986) edited by Lan Jifu 藍吉富, except for the *Hetucakraḍamaru*, which is found in the *Neixue* 4 (1928): pp. 911–916. In 1947, Xu Fancheng translated the *Triṃśikābhāṣya* in its entirety from Sanskrit, but it was published only in late 1990. In 1980, Huo Taohui published his translation of this text from Sanskrit with annotations.

9   Lü Tiegang 呂鉄鋼 and Hu Heping 胡和平, ed., *Fazun fashi foxue lunwen ji* 法尊法師佛學論文集 (Beijing: Zhong guo fo jiao wen hua yan jiu suo, 1990), p. 286.

10   See Fazun 法尊, ed. and trans., *Ji liang lun lue jie* 集量論略解 (Beijing: Zhong guo she hui ke xue chu ban she, 1982), and Fazun, trans., *Shi liang lun* 釋量論 (Beijing: Zhong guo fo jiao xie hui, 1981).

11   See Lü Tiegang and Hu Heping, eds., *Fazun fashi foxue lunwen ji*, pp. 375–376. Thanks to Mr. Gene Smith for providing me the relevant information and to Dr. Li Shenghai for sending me the available pages of Fazun's manuscript.

12   Han Jingqing's new translation of the *Mahāyānasaṃgraha* and all his lectures on it are published on the web. See http://www.mldc.cn/x229.htm.

13   See Han Jingqing 韓鏡清, trans., *Cishi xue jiuzhong yizhu* 慈氏學九種譯著 (Hong Kong: Zhong guo fo jiao wen hua chu ban you xian gong si, 1998).

14   Among these unpublished works, more than thirty are translated for the first time into Chinese. They include five treatises of Dharmakīrti, i.e., *Pramāṇaviniścaya* (P. 5710), *Hetubindu* (P. 5712), *Sambandhaparīkṣā* (P. 5713), *Vādanyāya* (P. 5715), and *Santānāntarasiddhi* (P. 5716); three works of Sthiramati, i.e., *Sūtrālaṃkāravṛttibhāṣya* (P. 5531), *Madhyāntavibhāgaṭīkā* (P. 5534), and *Pañcaskandhaprakaraṇavaibhāṣā* (P. 5567); three works of Vinītadeva, i.e., *Triṃśikāṭīkā* (P. 5571), *Samayabhedoparacanacakre nikāyabhedopadeśasaṃgraha* (P. 5641), and *Ālambanaparīkṣāṭīkā* (P. 5739); three works of Ratnākaraśānti, i.e., *Abhisamayālaṃkārakārikāvṛttiśuddhamatī* (P. 5199), *Madhyamapratipadāsiddhi* (P. 5573), and *Prajñāpāramitopadeśa* (P. 5579); two works of Asaṅga, i.e., *Āryasaṃdhinirmocanabhāṣya* (P. 5481) and *Dhyānadīpopadeśa* (P. 5574); two works of Asvabhāva, i.e., *Mahāyānasūtrālaṃkāraṭīkā* (P. 5530) and *Ālokamālāṭīkāhṛdānandajananī* (P. 5869). The others are Bhavya's *Nikāyabhedavibhaṅgavyākhyāna* (P. 5640), Buddhaśrījñāna's *Abhisamayālaṃkārabhagavatī-prajñāpāramitopadeśaśāstravṛtti-prajñāpradīpāvalī* (P. 5198), Darmottara's *Nyāyabinduṭīkā* (P. 5730), Dharmakīrtiśrī's *Abhisamayālaṃkāra-nāma-prajñāpāramitopadeśaśāstravṛtti-durbodhāloka-nāma-ṭīkā* (P. 5192), Dharmendra's *Yogāvatāropadeśa* (P. 5576), Dignāga's *Trikālaparīkṣā* (P. 5705), Guṇaprabha's *Pañcaskandhavivaraṇa* (P. 5568), Haribhadra's *Abhisamayālaṃkāra-nāma-prajñāpāramitopadeśaśāstravṛtti* (P. 5191), Jñānacandra's *Kāyatrayavṛtti* (P. 5291), Jinendrabuddhi's *Pramāṇasamuccayaṭīkā* (P. 5766), Kamalaśīla's *Āryāvikalpapraveśadhāraṇīṭīkā* (P. 5501), Kumāraśrībhadra's *Prajñāpāramitāpiṇḍārtha* (P. 5195), Maitreyanātha's *Bhavasaṃkrāntiṭīkā* (P. 5241), Pṛthivībandhu's *Pañcaskandhabhāṣya* (P. 5569), Prajñākaramati's *Abhisamayālaṃkāravṛttipiṇḍārtha* (P. 5193), Ratnakīrti's *Abhisamayālaṃkāravṛttikīrtikalā* (P. 5197), and Vimuktisena's *Āryapañcaviṃśatisāhasrikā prajñāpāramitopadeśaśāstrābhisamayālaṃkāravṛtti* (P. 5185). Thanks to Mr.

Lü Xinguo for providing me the catalogue and some manuscripts of these unpublished works.

15   This work was published in Taiwan in 2002: Han Jingqing 韓鏡清, *Cheng weishi lun shuyi* 成唯識論疏翼 (Gaoxiong: Mile jiangtang, 2002).

16   Both translations are included in volume 9 of the *Dazangjing bubian*, which also contains a translation of the *Nyāyabindu* from Sanskrit by Wang Sen.

17   See Lü Jianfu 呂建福, *Zhongguo mijiao shi* 中國密教史 (Beijing: Zhong guo she hui ke xue chu ban she, 1995), p. 640. Refer also to E. Bianchi's chapter below.

18   Lin Chen-kuo has suggested similar points. See his "Metaphysics, Suffering, and Liberation: The Debate between Two Buddhisms," in Jamie Hubbard and Paul L. Swanson, eds., *Pruning the Bodhi Tree: The Storm over Critical Buddhism* (University of Hawai'i Press, 1997), pp. 298–313. I thank Prof. Lin, too, for his advice on the present chapter.

19   See, for instance, Yinshun 印順, *Wuzheng zhi bian* 無諍之辯 (Taipei: Zheng wen chu ban she, 1995), p. 137.

20   See Han Jingqing, "Wei shi xue de liang ci chuan yi" 唯識學的兩次傳譯, *Foxue yanjiu* 佛學研究 3 (1994): 59–69.

21   The usage of "huahua fojiao" can be traced back to Zhou Shujia, one of the early disciples of Han Qingjing. See Zhou Shujia 周叔迦, "Zhongguo fojiao shi" 中國佛教史, in *Zhou Shujia foxue lunzhu ji* 周叔迦佛學論著集 (Beijing: Zhong hua shu ju, 1991). This word sounds similar to the Chinese translation of "playboy", *huahua gongzi*.

22   Lü Cheng, "Han zang fo xue gou tong de di yi bu," in *Lü Cheng fo xue lun zhu xuan ji*, p. 1402.

9: The "Chinese Lama" Nenghai (1886–1967): Doctrinal Tradition and Teaching Strategies of a Gelukpa Master in Republican China*

Ester Bianchi

THE TWO PRINCIPAL Chinese masters within the "Movement of Tantric Rebirth" (Ch. *mijiao fuxing yundong*) in modern China were the monks Nenghai and Fazun, both representatives of the Gelukpa tradition and both authors of dozens of works and translations.[1] While Fazun's activities in China mainly focused on the teaching and translation of exoteric works,[2] Nenghai also devoted himself to tantric doctrines and believed it necessary to integrate them within the framework of monastic communities on the model of the great Tibetan monasteries. Nenghai was convinced that, in the period of the latter Dharma, only Chan Buddhism and the tantras offered possible ways to spiritual realization. Chan, he believed, was much too elitist to address the needs of his time,[3] and he thus decided to study Tibetan Vajrayāna teachings and spread them among Chinese people, ultimately translating and composing more than fifty works on various tantric subjects. Nenghai visited Tibet several times, initially staying in Kham (1926–1927) and then moving up to the Lhasa valley (1928–1932 and 1940–1941). At the Drepung monastery he studied under Khangsar (Ch. Kangsa) Rinpoché, who bestowed on him a tantric transmission belonging to the "Supreme Vajrayāna lineage of Yamāntaka-Vajrabhairava" (Ch. *Daweide wushang micheng fatong*). Afterward, once Nenghai had returned to Chinese territory, he founded seven monasteries in line with the Tibetan Buddhist tradition, some of which are still active in contemporary times. In these monasteries, his disciples could apply themselves to whatever teachings he transmitted to them.

Nenghai's disciples commonly addressed him as Shangshi (Tib. *bla-ma*) and as the Chinese lama (Ch. *Hanzu lama*). This identifies him with the Tibetan tradition of Buddhism (Ch. *Zangchuan Fojiao*), and, in fact, he is often described not only as the twenty-ninth master within Khangsar Rinpoché's lineage, but as a representative of the forty-fourth generation of the Linji branch of Chan Buddhism within the Chinese tradition (Ch. *Hanchuan Fojiao*).[4] Nenghai's works and teaching activities, in which Tibetan doctrines stand next to typically Chinese doctrines, reflect a clear intention to infuse the Chinese Buddhist environment with Tibetan Buddhist practice. The nun Longlian, for instance, one of Nenghai's closest disciples, describes the nature of her master's doctrine in these words:

> The Dharma has reached us in all its purity, because its transmission went uninterrupted. [...] Beginning with Buddha Śākyamuni, the Dharma has been transmitted from master to master without interruption so that its essence was unaltered. Thus, it reached Atiśa who brought it to Tibet. From Atiśa it reached Tsongkhapa, and from him it arrived at lama Kangsa Rinpoché. Twenty-eight generations of masters separate Śākyamuni from Kangsa Rinpoché. Master Nenghai received the Dharma from Kangsa Rinpoché and also from a forty-third generation master of the Linji school in China. [Nenghai], from whom we received the doctrine, *joined purely in one doctrine Tibetan and Chinese teachings*. He received merits and virtues from Śākyamuni, and his virtue is thus one and identical to the Buddha's.[5]

Nenghai legitimately belonged to a specific Tibetan doctrinal tradition, although he integrated it with methodological and doctrinal trends different from the ones he encountered in Tibet. With this in mind, the main objectives in this study are, first, to clarify the Tibetan influences characterizing his approach and to advance an interpretation of them. In order to understand Nenghai's innovative position both within the Chinese Buddhist environment of his time and within the Gelukpa school he aimed to represent, it is necessary to construct an in-depth portrait of Nenghai's doctrinal tradition (including notes on his Tibetan and tantric lineages, his personal biography, and his literary production). This will allow for a greater analysis of Nenghai's teaching strategies, comparing them with the works and activities of Fazun, while noting the Chinese influences that are recognizable in Nenghai's exoteric and tantric writings as well as in the organization of his monastic communities.

Nenghai's Doctrinal Tradition

Nenghai's Tibetan Lineage: Khangsar Rinpoché

Khangsar Rinpoché (1890–1941, fig. 1) was a Tibetan *lama* of the Drepung monastery in Lhasa.[6] Although his complete biography in Tibetan has not yet become available, a summary version is found in the posthumous work of the noted scholar Dungkar Lozang Trinlé. Nenghai's disciples, however, refer to only a few Chinese texts that discuss him, and even these contain curious anomalies and contradictions.

FIG. 1 Khangsar Rinpoché and lama Nenghai.
(Courtesy Duobaojiang Monastery.)

In order to better focus on the information regarding Khangsar's life and teachings that were available to his Chinese followers, let us first consider a partial translation of what is, to my knowledge, the only extant Chinese-language essay completely devoted to him. It was originally composed on the basis of Nenghai's recollection upon his return to China:

The doctrinal tradition of lama Tsongkhapa was transmitted to Kangsa[7] Rinpoché. Because that lama Tsongkhapa received the transmission of the "Gradual Path to bodhi"[8] directly from the

Buddha, Kangsa Rinpoché's teaching is nothing but the [orig-
inal] teaching of Śākyamuni Buddha, which has been transmitted without interruption to our times. [...] Kangsa Rinpoché was
thus bestowed the transmission of Śākyamuni's lineage. Beginning with the Buddha onward, [this teaching] has been sublime throughout all time. [Among those who received it,] there
is no one who did not achieve realization, there is no one who
could not attain supreme realization. According to historical documents, all teachings and practices belonging to this [specific]
group have been taught by Śākyamuni Buddha himself, and have
subsequently been passed down from master to master in an unin-
terrupted line of transmission. [Therefore,] Kangsa Rinpoché is
nobody else than lama Tsongkhapa; likewise, both of them have
the same "real aspect" (*zhen xiang*) as Śākyamuni Buddha. Those
who encountered [Kangsa] or who could listen to his words were
all granted a "fortunate karmic retribution and good roots" (*fubao
shan'gen*). [...]

Kangsa's name is Tibetan; *kang* refers to [the region of] Kham,
while *sa* means "place."[9] Lama Rinpoché[10] was so called because
his former incarnation was from the lands of Kham. This was
not a [real] name but a form of respect, in the same manner as
Tsongkhapa (Ch. Zongkapa) was called after the [river district]
of Tsong[-kha] (Ch. Zongshui). Lama Rinpoché's former incarnation was born in Litang, thirteen stations from Daxianghu
and a five or six day walk from Hekou. As a child he moved to
the Drepung monastery in Lhasa, which included four Monastic
Colleges (Ch. *zhacang*).[11] Most of the Chinese who went there [to
study] stayed at Loséling, but Lama Rinpoché resided at Gomang
College. Loséling College used to lodge more that three thousand
people and Gomang more than four thousand. The other two colleges were Deyang and Ngakpa, where a few hundred people lived.
The first two [colleges] were specialized in exoteric teachings (Ch.
xianjiao), while the other two particularly treated tantric teachings (Ch. *mijiao*).

Once he achieved the title of *geshé* (Ch. *gexi*), Lama Rinpoché
also obtained the title of *khenpo* (Ch. *kanbu*) at Gomang College;
mkhan means "good and sage in methods," while *po* is an honorific suffix. The two terms thus mean: "he who is extremely good
and sage in methods."[12] By the time he retired as "elder khenpo,"[13]

goods and treasures had been collected, buildings restored, and the whole monastic system reorganized [under his supervision] at Gomang. His successes were all noteworthy. Nowadays, Gomang College is still the most austere among all [the monastic colleges] belonging to the three great monasteries,[14] and this is completely due to Lama Rinpoché's activities. Since he had achieved great realization through the tantric practice of White Mañjuśrī, he was called Mañjuśrī lama (Wenshu lama).[15] After he passed away, a commemorative statue was prepared at Gomang College; the expression [on the face of this] *trülku* (Ch. *zhuanshi*) was in all [respects] a close resemblance.[16]

Kangsa Rinpoché [was recognized] as a *trülku* not in Kham but in Lhasa. His relatives had been merchants for generations, and had collected great amounts of wealth; they lived near the city walls and were all devout Buddhists. [...] [Kangsa] had two brothers. The elder one, who was born from a different mother, took the vows and [was recognized] as Ganden Rinpoché. [...] Afterward it was the time for Lama Rinpoché [to enter the Buddhist community]. Lastly, his younger brother was also recognized as a trülku (Ch. *hutuketu*) at Deyang College in Drepung Monastery. [...]

After Lama Rinpoché, at the age of four, was recognized as a trülku (Ch. *huashen*),[17] he entered the Buddhist community and devoted himself to Dharma studies. At eight, he had already finished reading all rituals[18] and could transmit the great initiations.[19] At thirteen, he had completed the study of the Yogācāra texts. He used to take part in doctrinal competitions with virtuous men,[20] where his qualities had no rivals. Nevertheless, since he was not old enough to be ordained as a monk, he could not yet take the geshé exams. Lama Rinpoché was born on the fifth month of *gen-gyin* year, in the sixteenth year of Guangxu era [1890]. As soon as he had received full ordination, during the second year of Xuan-tong era [1910], he attended the geshé exams and obtained the best points. In the preceding seven years, he had already completed the compulsory studies [of a geshé]; therefore, he [then] devoted himself to other scriptures and there was no text he did not read in depth. [...] In the third year of the Xuantong era [1911], at the age of twenty, soon after he was conferred the title of geshé, he took up a spiritual retreat in Juba,[21] and left it in the seventeenth year of the Republic [1928]. I [= Nenghai] arrived

in Lhasa in the eighteenth year [1929], right after Lama Rinpoché had abandoned his retreat. He passed away in the thirtieth
year [1941], and could thus only devote himself to the spreading
of the Dharma for thirteen years. In spite of this brief lapse of
time, he could transmit his teachings on many occasions. [For
instance,] he transmitted the Kālacakra[22] seven times and the
lung (Ch. *long*, i.e. the *Sūtrapiṭaka*) thirteen times.[23] The Tibetan
Sūtrapiṭaka is collected in 108 volumes, and he could completely transmit it in ten days. The Dalai Lama suggested that it
was probably too fast, and [told Kangsa] that he was afraid this
would arouse apprehension in the audience. [Kangsa] could not
but comply with him, and [from then on began] to transmit it in
thirty-odd days.[24] As for the *Mahāprajñāpāramitā* in 600 chapters, [he could] transmit it in only seven days every time. He used
to teach each day a hundred chapters, together with the explanation of all doctrinal implications. During the *wang* (Ch. *gang*,
i.e. Skt. *abhiṣeka*), Rinpoché used to simultaneously bestow both
che and *dujiche* enpowerments,[25] and could thus transmit more
than four hundred different [tantric] transmissions. [On the contrary,] other masters needed to gather together, not being able to
[endure such efforts] alone. Moreover, their tantric transmissions
lasted several months or one whole year, and it was quite exceptional that someone could fully receive them. Instead, [Kangsa]
lama only requested thirteen days and a half. In addition to the
[already mentioned] four hundred empowerments, in the case
that someone among his followers were more fit for the tantras
of the Kagyü or Nyingma traditions, he would also initiate them
[into those practices].

The doctrinal tradition of Yamāntaka includes more than ten
different categories [of scriptures]; the one of the *ḍākinīs* more
than twenty, while the *queba*[26] includes even more [scriptures]. His
"five flowers and eight doors"[27] were like a large well-stocked shop.
Even if people were [only] offering gifts, [Kangsa] *lama* requested
them to bow down for instructions. Every day, he used to practice
preliminaries in the morning, and to confer empowerments from
midday till seven or eight p.m. Together with empowerments he
also used to transmit *sādhanas* and, if requested, was ready to
explain similarities and differences among different groups [of
scriptures]. Once he had finished the transmission [period], he

used not to say a word for seven or eight days, probably because of exhaustion.

In brief, [Kangsa] lama preferred a rapid method to transmit tantras or to explain sūtras, probably because in the period of the latter Dharma all living beings' obstacles and karma increase; thus, if he had requested a longer lapse of time, many people [among his audience] would not have had the chance to complete their [spiritual] preparation. This is the reason why he was so rapid. Most of the people who received the Dharma [from him] could comprehend its subtleness, and [still] by studying and practicing it they could feel its benefits soon after it had been transmitted. This as an outline of [his] teaching strategy [...].[28]

Other sources from Nenghai's doctrinal tradition report that Khangsar Rinpoché was also the twenty-eighth representative of the specific "Supreme Vajrayāna lineage of Yamāntaka-Vajrabhairava," together with masters such as Lalitavajra, Amoghavajra, Atiśa, Tsongkhapa, and the first (or fourth) Paṇchen Lama.[29]

It seems notable that in Khangsar's Chinese biography, a detailed description of his trülku lineage is absent,[30] even if a former incarnation of a "Khamsa" Rinpoché is mentioned, a name which points to a place of origin. The Chinese text further states that Khangsar was recognized as his trülku at the age of four. Although some informants claim that a Khangsar Rinpoché belonging to a lineage connected with Drepung is nowadays living in Kham,[31] whether this master is actually a new manifestation of our Khangsar's trülku lineage remains unconfirmed. Nenghai's disciples themselves believe their master's lineage was extinguished since the "task" assigned to the spiritual influence he had embodied had been completed.[32]

In contrast to the Chinese account of Khangsar, the text by Dungkar Lozang Trinlé cited above states that Khangsar was recognized at age seven as the *trülku* of Gomang khenpo Lozang Namgyel and that he was given the title Khangsar ("new residence") because he was invited to take up permanent residence at Washül khangsar ("the Washül new residence").[33] Conforming to this, in Dorje Yudon's autobiography (1990) we find information about, and a photo of a Khangsar Rinpoché Ngawang Yangchen Chöki Wangchuk (1888–1941).[34] He is described there as being Lhasa-born to a middle class family. Educated at Drepung Gomang, and recognized by Gomang Khenpo Khyenrap Tenpa Chöpel as the reincarnation of Lozang Namgyel, a former Drepung abbot also known as the Drepung Tsokcha *trülku*, Khangsar served as guru to the Yuthok family. This work also derives the title Khangsar from the residence he took at Washül khangsar in Drepung Monastery, where he is reputed to have lived simply, emphasizing teachings rather than worldly affairs.[35]

The figure mentioned by Dorje Yudon is clearly the same as the figure discussed by Dungkar. In spite of the different birth dates (1890 versus 1888) and other points in the Chinese biography, which, as analyzed above, do not match the Tibetan account, it seems beyond doubt that this figure is the same as Nenghai's master. Matthew T. Kapstein suggests that they have similar names, were both associated with Gomang College, both achieved their geshé degrees at early ages and went to study in tantric colleges immediately afterward, that both were specialists in the *lung* of the Kanjur and in the Kālacakra, and finally that both had some connections with the Thirteenth Dalai Lama.[36] Regardless of the circumstances, Khangsar's activities as a Tibetan master to Chinese disciples are attested and his role within the Chinese movement of "Tantric Rebirth" are unquestionable.[37]

Nenghai's Life and Works

Lama Nenghai (1886–1967) was the principal Chinese disciple of Khangsar Rinpoché.[38] Born born in Mianzhu district, Sichuan province, his lay name was Gong Xueguang and his *zi* Jixi. Both parents died when he was very young, leaving him to be raised by his elder sister. Until the age of fourteen, Nenghai lived in his hometown where he attended a traditional school and left only in 1900, when he went to Chengdu to train as a workshop apprentice. Five years later he entered the local military school for officials and was nominated troop commander in 1907. In 1909, he was an instructor in a famous military school in Yunnan province. It was during this time that he first encountered Tibetan Buddhism, studying under a Yunnanese Tibetan lama. In 1910, the military academy was closed, and Nenghai returned to Chengdu, where he was promoted to regiment commander. During the following five years he came into contact with the major Buddhist monasteries and milieux of the city, accepted Buddhist refuge, and received the five vows of a layman. In 1915, military responsibilities sent Nenghai to Japan as a political and economic observer. Later, he recalled being greatly impressed by the widespread diffusion of Buddhism and its strong influence in every aspect of social life in Japan. When he returned to China, Nenghai was summoned to Beijing as representative of the Sichuanese army. In Beijing, he began attending Zhang Kecheng's lectures on Buddhist literature and philosophy at Beijing University.

In 1916, Nenghai informed his family of his intention to become a Buddhist monk, but his wife and his sister convinced him to wait until he produced a child so that his family would not be without successors. In the meantime, together with other lay Buddhists, he founded the Shaocheng Buddhist Studies Society (Ch. *Shaocheng foxue she*). This soon became one of the major Buddhist circles of Chengdu, a forum in which Chinese and Tibetan masters could interact. Finally, in 1924, at the age of thirty-nine, forty-one days after the birth of his son, Nenghai took the Buddhist vows. He was bestowed the precepts of novitiate by Foyuan, the Abbot of Tianbaosi in Fuling and a forty-third generation master in the Linji Chan tradition. A few months later, Nenghai received complete ordination in the Baoguangsi of Xindu.

It was while he was at the Yonghegong, the center of Tibetan Buddhism in Beijing,[39] that Nenghai read the catalogue of texts contained in the Tibetan canon and was surprised by the great number of tantric scriptures and other works not translated into Chinese, an experience that moved him to direct his efforts to learning the Buddhist tantras. Sometime later, Nenghai set off for Japan where he planned to study the Shingon form of esoteric Buddhism. On reaching Chongqing, however, he read a letter by Dayong, who was then returning from Japan and on his way to Tibet. This convinced Nenghai that that "Japanese Tantrism is not equally as deep and splendid as Tibetan Tantrism,"[40] whereupon he decided to change direction and travel to Tibet instead. In 1926 he entered Kham in order to learn Tibetan, and first stayed in Dartsedo[41] before meeting Dayong and Fazun in the Paoma mountains. There, supervised by geshé Jampa Gendün (Ch. Jiangba Gezun),[42] Nenghai began to read Tibetan Buddhist texts such as the *Stages of the Path* (*Lam rim*) and the tantric precepts. Nenghai also expanded his understanding of the monastic rules of the Vinaya and the bodhisattva precepts, and he studied the *Abhidharmakośaśāstra* by Vasubandhu, comparing the Chinese version with the Tibetan. Jampa Gendün also initiated him to the tantric practice of Tārā. Afterward, Nenghai spent a few months in the Namah monastery of Kangding, where he received tantric teachings—among them the *Gurupūjā*—from Jamyang (Ch. Jiangyang) Rinpoché, a Tibetan monk from Lhasa who had been on a ten-year pilgrimage to Wutai shan and other sacred Chinese sites.

In 1928, after a brief stay in Chengdu, Nenghai returned to Tibet with Yongguang and other monks.[43] The party reached Lhasa in November of the same year and remained there for four years, residing in Drepung Monastery. Nenghai first stayed in the Gyelrang Khangtsen of Loséling college, and later moved to Gomang,[44] where he became a disciple of Khangsar Rinpoché.

Among exoteric teachings, he particularly studied the *Abhisamayālaṃkāra*, but also devoted himself to the *Madhyamakāvatāra, Prajñāpāramitā* texts, the *Abhidharmakośa*, Buddhist logic, monastic discipline, and other important teachings of the Tibetan Buddhist tradition. As for tantras, Nenghai was granted the initiations of Yellow Mañjuśrī and Yamāntaka-Vajrabhairava, but he also studied other texts and tantric methods. In 1932, he returned to China, traveling via India, where he visited the Buddhist pilgrimage sites, finally reaching Chengdu in 1933.

Nenghai then moved to Wutai shan (1934–1937), where he began teaching Tibetan Buddhism to a Chinese audience. In 1936 the Paṇchen Lama founded a branch of the Bodhi Study Society on Wutai shan and appointed Nenghai chief-translator.[45] His translations included the *Experiential Song of the Sequential Path* (*Lam rim nyams mgur*, Ch. *Putidao cidi kesong*), the *Vajrabhairava Sādhana of the Thirteen Deities* (Ch. *Daweide shisanzun yigui*), and the *Abhisamayālaṃkāra*. In the same year he also wrote the "Five-syllable Mantra [of Yellow Mañjuśrī]" (Ch. *Wuzi zhenyan*), an important work to be discussed further below. Two years later, Nenghai founded in the Jincisi of Chengdu his first "tantric vajra monastery" (Ch. *micheng jingang daochang*),[46] and then translated a text on the generation stage of the *Anuttarayogatantra* and the *Gurupūjā* (Ch. *Shangshi gong*).

In 1939/1940, Nenghai and a group of disciples from the Jincisi began another journey to Tibet.[47] Nenghai first stayed at the Anjue monastery in Kangding, and later reached Lhasa for what would be his second and last visit. He passed a twelve-month period with Khangsar Rinpoché, who is said to have bestowed on Nenghai more than four hundred tantric transmissions. During this time, Nenghai also translated the *sādhanas* of Hayagrīva (Ch. Dangjiquejia), Mahākāla (Ch. Mahagana), Śrīdevī (Ch. Jixiangtian), and Vaiśravaṇa or Kubera (Ch. Pishamen).[48] Shortly before Nenghai departed from Lhasa, Khangsar gave him the three monastic robes, an alms bowl, sacred texts and images, shoes, clothing, and the "Dharma conch" (Ch. *faluo*, Tib. *chos kyi dung*), which, according to his biography, indicated that he had fully received his master's tradition.[49]

During the years that followed, Nenghai founded five more monasteries in line with Gelukpa tradition and devoted himself to translation and teaching activities, gathering hundreds of devotees. In 1942 he led the translation of the Kālacakra (Ch. *Dashilun shangshi xiangying fa*), in 1943 and 1950 he continued his translation work of the texts of the Yamāntaka-Vajrabhairava tantric cycle, and in 1946 he translated the *Vairocanatantra* (Ch. *Pilu yigui*). In 1943 Nenghai created his second *jingang daochang* at the Yunwu monas-

tery in the Xishan hills near Mianzhu. This monastery was intended to be a
"place for specialized practice" (Ch. *zhuan xiu zhi suo*) destined for his disciples who had already been initiated into the *Anuttarayogatantras*.[50] The following year, he founded the *jingang daochang* of Chongqing, situated in the
Zhenwu shan monastery.[51] The Cisheng'an, Nenghai's third monastery, was
established in 1947 on Emei shan within the monastic complex of Wannian.[52]
One year later, in the Tiexiangsi, a monastery situated in the neighborhood
of the Jincisi, Nenghai founded the first and only Gelukpa nunnery in Chinese Han territory.[53] In 1949 he founded the Shanghai *jingang daochang*, his
first monastery outside of Sichuan.[54]

In the 1950s, Nenghai devoted himself increasingly to public activities.
In 1952, he went to Vienna for the World Conference on Peace. He was a
member of the Permanent Committee and vice-president of the Chinese
Buddhist Association from its foundation in 1953 (the Association's activity
ended in 1966). In the same year he founded the Qingliangqiao Jixianglüyuan
(or Jixiangsi), his seventh and last *jingang daochang*, which was located on
Wutai shan and was to become his residence until the end of his life.[55] There,
he attended the first meeting of the People's National Congress (1954). The
following year, Nenghai also joined a Chinese delegation in Delhi for the
Conference of Asian Nations. In 1957 he was elected President of the newly
created Buddhist Association of Wutai shan and in 1959 participated in the
Second People's National Congress.

When the Cultural Revolution broke out in 1966, Nenghai was staying at
Wutai shan. He was repeatedly attacked and harassed, seriously weakening
his health. On the night of December 31 of that same year, Nenghai reached
the meditation hall of the monastery and, after dismissing a disciple with one
premonitory sentence, he began meditating. The next morning, New Year's
Day 1967, the religious community found him dead, his body still in the lotus
position. Today his relics are preserved on Wutai shan in a commemorative
stūpa that was built in 1981 in the Tibeto-Chinese style.[56]

Nenghai's works can be divided into two major groups: those belonging to the exoteric Buddhist teachings, and those dealing with the tantras.[57]
Among exoteric teachings, Nenghai strongly emphasized monastic discipline, following the tradition of Tsongkhapa. Of the Three Disciplines (*śīla*,
samādhi, and *prajñā*), he considered śīla to be the basis of the Buddhist Path,
which, he believed, should progress from the study of monastic discipline to
meditation, and from meditation to knowledge. In Nenghai's writings, the
term *jie* (Skt. śīla) refers to both the Vinaya (*xiaocheng jie*, lit. "Hīnayāna discipline") and the Mahāyāna discipline (*dacheng jie*) peculiar to bodhisattvas.

FIG. 2 The new memorial stūpa dedicated to Nenghai at Wutaishan.

In his translations and works dealing with this important theme,[58] the topics he treats range from the precepts for the layman to those for the novitiate, from complete ordination of bhikṣus and bhikṣuṇīs to the conferral of the bodhisattva vows. Some of his compositions also address meditation (*ding*) practices:[59] the preliminaries, *śamatha* and *vipaśyanā* (*zhiguan*),[60] and the four forms of *dhyāna* (*sichan*). Others concern the topic of *prajñā* (*hui*),[61] particularly the question of knowledge as it appears in both the Tibetan and Chinese canons, including the translations of Hīnayāna texts. His writings also include focused considerations of the *Avataṃsakasūtra* (the "Flower Garland Sūtra," *Huayan jing* in Chinese), and of the corpus of the *Prajñāpāramitā*, which Nenghai believed to contain the whole of Buddhist Truth.[62] Still other works address the *Āgamas*[63] and the *Abhisamayālaṃkāra*,[64] together with translations and commentaries on the *Lamrim* texts.[65]

Nenghai's vast literary production, however, consists mainly of tantric translations and commentaries: in this area, in all, he produced some fifty-five works (fourteen were compiled posthumously by his disciples, based on his teachings), most of which fall into nine basic groups.[66]

The first three groups address the lower tantric practices: First, the "Contemplation of the Three Refuges" (*Sanguiyi guan*) is a basic practice of Tibetan meditation concerning the "threefold refuge" (Ch. *sanguiyi*, Skt. *triśaraṇagamana*)—the Three Jewels of Buddha, Dharma, and Sangha—and particularly the "secret" refuge, one's own spiritual master.[67] The handbook describing it is understood to be a general introduction to the fundamental elements of Tibetan contemplation methods and provides a starting point for higher tantric practices.[68] Second, the *Gurupūjā* (Ch. *Shangshi gong*, Tib. *bla ma mchod pa*), or "Offering to the *guru*," is one of the main texts used for daily chanting services and other religious celebrations in Gelukpa monasteries.[69] Nenghai's text, which was written at the end of the 1930s, includes the translation of the root text, as well as other tantric practices absent in the original Tibetan work. This group also includes some commentaries written by both the master himself as well as his disciples.[70] The third group, which discusses the "Mañjuśrī sādhanas" (Ch. *Wenshu fa*, Tib. *'jam dpal sgrub thabs*), includes texts ranging from the practice of Yellow Mañjuśrī to that of White Mañjuśrī and also deals with the topic of the tantric vows (*mijie*). Of these texts, the most representative and important to Nenghai is the "Five-syllable mantra [of Yellow Mañjuśrī]," which was written in 1936 when the master, who was absorbed in meditation on Wutai shan, is said to have received the approval of Mañjuśrī himself. The result was a comprehensive work including the lower tantric practices and various exoteric topics, together with translations from the Tibetan and explanatory passages. These were clearly influenced by the Chinese Buddhist tradition in some cases. Nenghai believed this work to be the basis for the Yamāntaka-Vajrabhairava tantric practice.[71]

The fourth, fifth, and sixth groups concern the corpus of teachings on Yamāntaka as Vajrabhairava (*Daiweide fa*).[72] According to tradition, the *Yamāntaka-Vajrabhairava-tantra* was introduced to Tibet after having been revealed, in the land of Uḍḍiyāna, to Lalitavajra, a tenth-century scholar from Nālandā, by Vajravetala and the *ḍākinīs*.[73] The original work is said to have included three hundred chapters while the Tibetan version only has seven. It belongs to the highest *Yogatantra* and it is classified as Father Tantra.[74] All works dealing with the *Yamāntaka-Vajrabhairava-tantra* are extremely important to Nenghai because the image of Yamāntaka-Vajrabhairava is central in the tradition he received from Khangsar Rinpoché. In the fourth group, there are five works dealing with the "generation stage" (Skt. *utpattikrama*, Ch. *shengqi cidi*; Tib. *bskyed rim*) of this practice, in the fifth, three works referring to the "completion stage" (Skt. *utpannakrama*, Ch. *yuancheng cidi*; Tib. *rdzogs rim*),[75] and, in the sixth group, the majority of Nenghai's works are generic, dealing with such topics relating to Vajrabhairava as the root-tantra, *hōma* rites, self-generation practice, and other sādhanas.

The last three groups within Nenghai's tantric works are of minor importance: the seventh group contains works focusing on *abhiṣeka* (*guanding*), "consecration" or "empowerment," the eighth relates to the *dharmapālas*, and the last concerns tantric practice within the *Lamrim* tradition.

Nenghai's Teaching Strategy

Nenghai and Fazun

Nenghai and Fazun are often associated with one another because of the outstanding role each played in spreading Tibetan Buddhism's works and teachings throughout modern China. During the last two decades, their biographies and works have been repeatedly reprinted both in Taiwan and in the People's Republic of China,[76] probably owing to renewed interest in Tibetan Vajrayāna and the Tibetan Buddhist tradition in contemporary China.[77] In contrasting the activities and literary production of these two masters, I will seek to draw out their fundamental and undeniable differences.

Fazun and Nenghai met in 1926 on Paoma shan, where each began his work with Tibetan Buddhism. They stayed together for a few months, studied the same texts with the same Tibetan master, and received the same teachings from him. In the twenty years that followed, however, Fazun and Nenghai chose increasingly divergent paths. Fazun remained in Kham and Sichuan for a period, only afterward visiting Lhasa where he resided at Drepung between 1932 and 1933, and again between 1936 and 1937. Finally, he became a teacher at the Institute of Sino-Tibetan Studies in Chongqing. Nenghai also studied at Drepung, but from 1928 to 1932 and later from 1940 to 1941. Afterward, he devoted himself to teaching activities and to the organization of his own monasteries. Nevertheless, considering the relative proximity of the Jincisi of Chengdu and Chongqing Institute of Sino-Tibetan Studies as well as the fact that one of Nenghai's *jingang daochang* was founded right in the city where Fazun operated, it is probable that the two masters encountered one another during this lapse of time. They must have met again after 1949, and particularly beginning in the year 1953, when they were both chosen as members of the permanent committee of the newly founded Chinese Buddhist Association. Afterward, Nenghai and Fazun doubtlessly cooperated in the various public activities in which they both participated during the first fifteen years of the People's Republic of China.

Fazun and Nenghai were similarly motivated in their decisions to visit Tibet. In Nenghai's biography we read:

> In Chongqing [Nenghai] encountered a student from Nanjing, who told him: "The Tibetan Buddhist Dharma is extremely rich.

What has not been translated in Chinese territory is with no exception present in Tibet. [Those works] which were translated in China and are absent in Tibet are very few. Therefore, to study the Dharma one has necessarily to go to Tibet." The master was [thus] deeply attracted [by the idea to go to Tibet] [...].[78]

Turning to Fazun's autobiography, we find that his motivations were virtually identical:

It is true that, when it comes to difficulty, Tibet is difficult. [...] And in Tibet there was a perfect Buddhism, which one could study, translate, and promulgate. [...] I made a vow to study all the Buddhist texts existing in Tibet that one could not find in China, and to translate them so as to fill in the lacunae.[79]

Both masters shared the objective of making the vast *corpus* of Tibetan Buddhist scriptures available to Chinese Buddhists, whether through translations of original Indian works or through texts composed by Tibetan masters.[80] After their return in Chinese territory, both Fazun and Nenghai devoted themselves to the translation of the works they had collected in Tibet (Fazun in the Chongqing Institute of Sino-Tibetan Studies, and Nenghai mostly in the "Institute for the Translation of Scriptures" [*Yi jing yuan*] he had founded in the Jinci monastery). The literary output that the two produced consists mainly of translation from Tibetan into Chinese, but Fazun and Nenghai also translated from Chinese into Tibetan, in order to bridge gaps in both Tibetan and Chinese Buddhist canons. The exoteric works in which they were interested included some of the primary texts of the Gelukpa tradition:[81]

(1) *Lamrim* teachings. Fazun and Nenghai first discovered the short version of Tsongkhapa's *Lamrim* while they were together on Paoma shan. During their respective stays in Lhasa, both of them attached great importance to this doctrinal *corpus* within their teaching activities,[82] and translated part of it. Fazun devoted most of his efforts to translating Tsongkhapa's *opera omnia*, in which the *Lamrim* holds an outstanding position, ultimately making this teaching available in the Chinese Buddhist milieu.[83] He first edited and completed Dayong's short version of the *Lamrim*, and in 1930 translated a commentary on it. Finally, in the following year, Fazun undertook the translation of the *Great Sequence of the Path* (*Lam rim chen mo*), the longest version, which he completed in 1935.[84] This final translation is clearly a masterwork, and it is particularly notable from a philological point of view. Nenghai was

also interested himself in the *Lamrim*, producing eight works on this topic ranging from translations of the original texts and their commentaries to his own critical accounts.[85]

(2) Vinaya teachings. Because the Vinaya held a role of fundamental importance in Tsongkhapa's tradition, Nenghai studied and analyzed it, committing himself to strict observance of its rules in his own monastic life.[86] Both Nenghai and Fazun devoted much attention to this topic in their works and teachings. While they were together on Paoma shan, geshé Jampa Gendün provided lessons on the Vinaya rules for bhikṣus and on the Mahāyāna disciplinary rules of a bodhisattva.[87] During his stay in Lhasa between 1936 and 1937, Fazun deepened his understanding of the Vinaya and afterward wrote two works about it.[88] It was Nenghai, however, who showed most attention to monastic discipline. This is evident in the many works he devoted to this topic, as well as in its primary role within the study curricula of his disciples.[89] It is interesting to notice that Nenghai preferred to refer to the texts of the *Dharmaguptakavinaya*, the version followed in China, and not to the *Mūlasarvāstivādavinaya*, which is followed by Tibetan Buddhists.

(3) *Abhisamayālaṃkāra*. This work is one of the fundamental texts in the Gelukpa monastic college program leading to one's geshé degree, and as such it was studied by both Nenghai and Fazun while in Tibetan territory.[90] Fazun, for instance, received this teaching in the late 1920s in Ganzi (Tib. *dkar mdzes*). In 1932, he would study a commentary about it, penned by Tsongkhapa, the so-called "Golden Rosary" (*Jinman lun*).[91] Later, Fazun created a brief translation of the primary work.[92] Nenghai, on the other hand, devoted himself to this teaching with Khangsar Rinpoché during his first stay in Lhasa; he undertook its translation alone in 1936 and then together with a translation team in the Jinci monastery. Of the two masters, Nenghai took more interest in this scripture, dedicating four of his works to it, while his disciples composed three more on the basis of his teachings.[93] It is worth noting that Fazun and Nenghai translated the title of the *Abhisamayālaṃkāra* differently: Fazun employed the Chinese *Xianguan zhuangyan lun*, thus choosing to render the concept of "realization" as "vision" (*guan*). Nenghai, instead, translated the title as *Xianzheng zhuangyan lun*, using the Chinese term generally employed to express the Sanskrit *adhigama* (*zheng*), i.e. "experiential realization."[94]

(4) *Madhyamakāvatāra*.[95] This work, never translated into Chinese before the twentieth century, is one of the essential śāstras within the Gelukpa order. It was thus normal for Nenghai and Fazun to have studied it during their respective stays in Tibet. Nenghai studied *Madhyamakāvatāra*

with Khangsar Rinpoché, and afterward made it one of the most important works in the curriculum of study at his institute in the Jincisi. Nevertheless, it seems he never devoted any of his own writings to this text, while on the contrary, Fazun translated both the original work and some of its commentaries.[96]

In brief, Nenghai and Fazun both resolved to spread Tibetan Buddhism's teachings into China, devoted themselves to the translation of the texts they had collected in Tibet, and were faithful adherents of the Gelukpa tradition in their works and teachings. Nevertheless, they were in some respects also profoundly dissimilar. The most evident difference between them is seen in the contribution each made to the tantric teachings, a difference that became apparent even before their stay in Tibet. A passage from Nenghai's biography, mentioned above, makes this distinction quite clear:

> [Nenghai] read the Catalogue of the Tibetan Buddhist Scriptures in Beijing's Yonghegong, and realized they mostly included tantric texts. He thus made the vow to study tantric teachings. Once he received the monastic precepts, he went to Chongqing to transmit [Buddhist] teachings, planning to go to Japan to study the Buddhist Dharma. [. . .] He was already deeply attracted [by the idea to go to Tibet], when he read a statement by Dayong, who had just returned from Japan. It confirmed that the Japanese esoteric teachings were not as deep and splendid as the Tibetan ones. He thus decided to go to Tibet to study tantric teachings.[97]

Nenghai clearly decided to devote himself to the study of Tibetan Buddhism *primarily* because he was interested in tantric teachings. He can be connected with what contemporary scholars have defined as "tantric fever" (*mijiao re*).[98] In the years that followed, Nenghai continued to pursue his original interest: in Tibet he received numerous tantric initiations and transmissions; back in Chinese territory, he founded seven monasteries whose designation, *jingang daochang*, immediately identified them as places belonging to the Vajrayāna tradition; he pledged himself to perpetuate the "Supreme Vajrayāna lineage of Yamāntaka-Vajrabhairava," which he had received from Khangsar Rinpoché; and, finally, his literary production mainly consisted of tantric works.

In contrast, Fazun proved to be very cautious in regard to tantric teachings when he first met Dayong at the Institute of Buddhist Studies of Wuchang:

Everywhere, all the disciples, whether monks or laity, followed
the fashion of treating only tantrism as excellent. I too accompanied and served Master Dayong for some days, [...] and though I
did not receive the two great initiatory cycles that he had brought
from Japan, I found that the flavor of tantrism was already quite
strong. Only persons who have already studied it can understand
the true principles of tantrism and practice it. [...] My foundations
are feeble, I've not obtained an inkling of samādhi, nor received
the blessing; neither have I obtained the great and extraordinary
powers of spirit—it is for this reason that I am quite indifferent
to tantrism.[99]

It's possible that Fazun never really abandoned his originally detached attitude toward tantric teachings. His autobiography shows that he too was
bestowed many initiations and tantric teachings while he was studying in
Lhasa, yet, although some of his works are on tantric topics,[100] he seemed to
consider tantric practice as a strictly inner matter, so that, as Françoise Wang-
Toutain concludes, "his practice, following in this respect the traditional precepts, remained secret."[101]

Another difference between Nenghai and Fazun concerns their attitudes
regarding translation work. Fazun, as seen in the preceding chapter, was fundamentally a philologist, and his writings present a meticulousness that Nenghai's work does not display. In the preface to one of his works, for instance,
Fazun explains that he intends to be as accurate as possible in his translations
of Tibetan vocabulary, that wherever possible he will employ Xuanzang's
Buddhist terminology, and that in cases where a Chinese-attested translation
was not already available, he would try to literally translate the Tibetan technical terms into Chinese.[102] Fazun was renowned for both the prolific nature
of his works and the philological severity that informs them. One may readily affirm that the quality of his translations is far beyond those of his contemporaries, among them Nenghai, as the latter distinguished himself through
other activities which were only of secondary importance to Fazun. Nenghai's most notable contribution was the effort he invested in the foundation
of monastic communities where the study of Tibetan Buddhist teachings
could find a practical application. As a consequence, Nenghai's translations,
rather than being a philological exercise, were conceived as means to help
practitioners along their own spiritual paths. Although Nenghai's translations are not as meticulous as Fazun's are, Nenghai's stylistic and lexical
choices made them more accessible to Chinese readers. Both in his exoteric

and lower tantric works he often referred to teachings proper to the Chinese Buddhist tradition, which were likely more familiar to his Chinese disciples. Nenghai even innovated "new" Tibetan doctrines on the basis of the Chinese Buddhist thought. Moreover, in his literary production, Nenghai juxtaposed translations with explanatory works, some reporting oral teachings he himself had received in Tibet, and others offering his own interpretations of Tibetan doctrines. Among his works on the *Lamrim*, for instance, one finds writings which detail Nenghai's personal understanding of the "gradual path" to realization.[103]

In the light of these observations, it seems impossible to simply compare the two masters, as is commonly done in contemporary literature. I believe that they consciously chose quite distinct roles for themselves, as is evident if one considers their respective legacies in contemporary China. Fazun, the translator, wrote majestic works that appear within the academic curricula of the majority of contemporary monastic institutes of study, regardless of their relationship to the Chinese or Tibetan Buddhist traditions. Nenghai, the lama, amassed hundreds of devotees who have been able to perpetuate his doctrinal tradition and lineage into the twenty-first century.

Chinese Influence in Nenghai's Exoteric and Tantric Teachings

> Exoteric teachings are the manifest aspect of tantras; tantras are the secret aspect of exoteric teachings. They are both essential. If one does not have knowledge of the exoteric teachings, one cannot comprehend the nature of tantras; if one does not know the content of tantras, one cannot understand the scope of the exoteric teachings. Exoteric teachings are the fundamentals of tantras, and tantras are their skillful means.[104]

Nenghai deals with the relationship between the exoteric (or doctrinal) teachings of Buddhism and the secret ways of the tantras using an approach that is modeled on that of the Gelukpa school to which he belonged, and particularly on the *Lamrim* teachings. Yet Nenghai was convinced of both the fundamental identity of all Buddhist traditions in Asia regarding fundamental teachings and the necessity of integrating them with the methods derived from the tantras, which could only be found in Tibet. This position is characteristic of Nenghai, and it distinguishes his teachings from that of any other Chinese Buddhist master, Fazun included.

When Nenghai discussed "exoteric teachings," he was referring to "doctrinal"

Buddhism in general, regardless of different regional or linguistic traditions. While Fazun was primarily interested in the *Mūlasarvāstivādavinaya* and in the bodhisattva precepts included in the *Yogācārabhūmiśāstra*, the two main sources for the disciplinary rules followed by Tibetan Buddhists, Nenghai was also concerned with monastic discipline as it was traditionally seen in China. In his works about this, he referred mainly to the *Dharmaguptakavinaya* (*Sifen lü*, Taishō 1428),[105] whose precepts he himself had received when he was ordained as a monk and that he continued to bestow on his disciples during ordination ceremonies.[106] However, although his writings of the bodhisattva precepts refer primarily to the *Yogācārabhūmiśāstra*, particularly as understood in this context by Tsongkhapa,[107] nevertheless, according to his disciples, Nenghai employed the *Brahmajālasūtra* (*Fanwang jing*, Taishō 1484) during monastic ordinations,[108] as is still customary in his extant *jingang daochang*.

Within his works discussing meditation, Nenghai often referred to the four *dhyānas* as they are conceived in Chinese Buddhist texts, as for instance in the texts belonging to the *corpus* of the *Dharmaguptakavinaya*.[109] Other examples are the works he devoted to the meditation chapters within the *Śāriputrābhidharmaśāstra* (Taishō 1548).[110] As a matter of general practice, whenever a text was already available in the Chinese canon, Nenghai would employ that version, while he dealt with Tibetan texts only when no Chinese rendition existed. This is particularly true in his discussions of *prajñā*, especially when he turns to the *Prajñāpāramitā*, which Nenghai conceived as the ultimate essence of the Buddhadharma. At the same time, juxtaposed to texts clearly belonging to the Tibetan Buddhist tradition, such as the *Lamrim* or the *Abhisamayālaṃkāra*, one finds references to the *Avataṃsakasūtra* (Taishō 279),[111] and, as mentioned earlier, general works on the Chinese versions of the *Āgamas*. Moreover, in his teachings to his disciples, as well as in his personal study, he made use of the Chinese versions of some important works such as the *Abhidharmakośaśāstra* (Taishō 1821), and the *Mūlamadhyamakaśāstra* (Taishō 1564).

By contrast, when Nenghai discussed the tantras, he almost exclusively referred to Tibetan sources. Despite this, in Nenghai's esoteric works concerning the lower tantras, all of which are supposed to be translations from Tibetan texts or oral teachings, a certain degree of Chinese influence is still recognizable. For example, in the *Wuzi zhenyan* he made free use of Chinese terminology, Chinese style, and also some typical elements belonging to the Chinese tradition.[112] This text was the most important of his works dealing with lower tantric practices and is still chanted during daily services by the lower acolytes in monasteries such as the Duobaojiangsi, the Shijingsi, and the Tiexiangsi. The *Wuzi zhenyan* includes a tantric practice devoted to the Yellow Mañjuśrī, various exoteric teachings, and a revision of Tsongkhapa's *Lamrim*. While in many of Nenghai's esoteric works Chinese influences are marginal, the style and lexicon that he employed drew upon the tantric terminology already available in Chinese, which he clearly took from the many tantric works included in the Taishō.[113] Verse sections, the parts of the text to be chanted, are generally composed of five syllables each, a characteristic of traditional Chinese style, with only a few exceptional verses in seven or nine characters, the latter modeled on Tibetan Buddhist works. Chinese influence is even more evident in the contents of the text: most formulas, such as the "ode for the generation of the four immeasurables" (*faxin siwuliang song*),[114] the "*gāthā* of clouds of perfumed flowers" (*xianghua yun jie*),[115] the refuge formula (*guiyi jie*),[116] and the *gāthās* referring to the eight and five precepts for laypersons and novices (*shou bajie jie* and *wujie jie*),[117] for example, are taken from the Chinese Buddhist tradition. Moreover, in the section devoted to the "recitation of the precepts" (*song jie*),[118] there are clear references made to the *Dharmaguptaka* version of the *Prātimokṣa*, as there are too in Nenghai's exoteric works on the Vinaya.

Elsewhere, Nenghai's background as a Chinese monk produced new teachings in which the two Buddhist traditions could interact. A telling example is his concluding dedication formula (*jixiang yuan*),[119] which follows traditional dedications as given in Chinese Buddhist texts, but is addressed not only to the Three Jewels, but primarily to one's *guru*, as in Tibetan dedications. Moreover, Nenghai replaces the Tibetan expression "mother sentient beings" (Tib. *mar gyur sems can*) with the Chinese "mother and father sentient beings" (*fumu youqing*), referring to both parents in deference to Chinese cultural standards.[120] Similarly, of the two main Tibetan methods for the generation of the *bodhicitta*, Nenghai emphasized the "seven-point cause and effect method of Atiśa,"[121] according to his disciples, over the method of "exchanging oneself with others" (*zita xianghuan*), though the latter is discussed in some of his works.[122] His preference for the former was due to its reference to filial love, which seemed to him to be more suitable for his Chinese disciples. In light of such features, Nenghai probably conceived of the *Wuzi zhenyan* as an introduction to Buddhist doctrines and tantric practices, intended to serve as the basis for approaching the higher tantras, and in which some Chinese aspects were included so as to help Chinese devotees to better understand its teachings.

With regard to the tantras, analysis of the "*Sādhana* of the Solitary Deity

Yamāntaka" suggests that Nenghai was much more faithful to the Tibetan tradition in the context of the *Anuttarayoga*.[123] As in his writings on the lower tantras, however, he continued to use well-established Chinese terminology, for instance, for the names of some deities, or categories of beings.[124] Unfortunately, in some cases his terminological choices misleadingly suggested Chinese Buddhists ideas that did not quite suit the corresponding Tibetan concept.[125] Elsewhere, however, Nenghai created neologisms in order to render specific concepts and teachings, sometimes availing himself of transliteration[126] or, more often, of literal translation.[127] On occasion, too, he employed expressions that differed slightly from the Tibetan, but were more familiar and easily accessible to his Chinese audience.[128] Moreover, contrasted with his exoteric and lower tantric works, Nenghai's writings on the higher tantras exhibit sporadic examples of "censorship," as in the case of sexual or gruesome ritual prescriptions,[129] although such omissions did not substantially modify the deeper tantric core of the text. While the content of most sections to be chanted differs from that of the original Tibetan text (due to difficulties in the translation of verses), Nenghai faithfully translated all parts of the *sādhana* dealing with tantric meditation techniques. He even tried to stay close to the Tibetan in the transliteration of mantric syllables, giving Tibetan, instead of Sanskrit, phonetic readings of mantras and creating new characters to render some Tibetan sounds not found in Chinese.[130] The style of the *sādhana* exhibits no particular concession to Chinese tradition. For instance, verses are all composed of seven- or nine-syllable lines, in accord with Tibetan metrics, whereas in works on the lower tantras Nenghai often employed Chinese-style five syllable verses. Nenghai exhibits the same rigor in his translations of a commentary on the *sādhana*.[131]

Nenghai's "Tantric Vajra Monasteries"

Nenghai's works thus present us with a mixture of Chinese and Tibetan doctrinal and stylistic elements. This harmonization also becomes apparent upon entering any of the extant *jingang daochang*.[132] Chinese monks or nuns there are dressed in yellow robes, representing the Yellow Mañjuśrī, principal *yidam* of Nenghai's communities together with Mañjuśrī's wrathful aspect, Yamāntaka-Vajrabhairava.[133] In these monasteries, halls, statues, images, and religious objects in Tibetan style are juxtaposed with others in Chinese style. Buildings designed following Chinese conventions, the interiors of which are often structured like Tibetan Buddha halls, sit next to halls presenting Tibetan Buddhist architectural elements.[134] Life within these monasteries

FIG. 3 Entrance gate to Shijing Monastery (Longquan, Sichuan), the new site of Jincisi, Nenghai's first *vajra* monastery. On the roof it displays a pair of deer and the Dharma wheel, in accordance with Tibetan style.

presents the same unusual juxtaposition of Chinese and Tibetan elements, with the Chinese influence in the organization of activities, and a Tibetan influence in religious practice. Each of these monasteries follows the pattern of the seven *jingang daochang* founded by Nenghai between the late 1930s and the early 1950s, and among them Jinci Monastery, the first to have been established (1938), served as the foremost model.

Jincisi is located in the southern suburbs of Chengdu, in Sichuan.[135] Built in 1600, it became a branch monastery of the Wenshuyuan only in modern times.[136] In 1938, Faguang, then Wenshuyuan's abbot, donated Jincisi to Nenghai, who immediately inhabited it with his disciples and founded his first *jingang daochang*. Four years later, in 1942, the monastery accommodated a hundred monks, and this number continued to increase until finally about eighty novices and two hundred monks lived on the premises.[137] Nenghai abandoned Jincisi in 1953 when he moved to Wutai shan.

When Nenghai first entered Jincisi, he saw that the structure of the

monastic compound could be enlarged and modified so as to accommodate a community devoted to the kind of "joint exoteric and tantric practice"
(*xianmi shuangxiu*) he sought to promote. Behind the existing "Precious
Hall of the Great Hero" (*Daxiong bao dian*), the main hall of the monastery,
which was then and has remained in typical Chinese style, Nenghai erected a
"Yamāntaka Hall" (*Daweide dian*), a "Tsongkhapa Great Master Hall" (*Zongkaba dashi dian*), and a "Palace of the Scriptures" (*Zangjing lou*). Nenghai
also built new structures to house the five "departments" (or "halls," Ch. *tangkou*) in which the monastic community was to be organized.[138] Each structure had an independent management, was directed by a "head of the hall"
(*tangzhu*) and a number of "administrators" (*guantang*), and was attended
to by one of the three possible categories of disciples. The management and
the organization of offices within these departments was clearly taken from
the Chinese Buddhist tradition,[139] yet they were organized as a great monastic university intended to emulate the Tibetan monastic colleges that Nenghai himself had personally seen in Lhasa.[140] Like that of the Tibetan colleges,
Jincisi's curriculum required the study of the "five main subjects" (*wu dabu*):
Buddhist logic (*yinming*); *Prajñāpāramitā* teachings (*boluomiduo*), including *Lamrim* texts; Madhyamaka (*zhongguan*); Abhidharma (*jushe*); and
monastic discipline, or Vinaya (*jielü*).[141] Students not yet of age first entered
the Śramaṇa Hall, where as novices they studied the fundamental doctrines
of Buddhism. Then they devoted themselves to monastic discipline, and
only afterward could they begin learning the basics of tantric practice in the
next department. Finally, when the students entered the Vajra Institute, they
could study and practice the highest tantras. The specific programs of the five
departments were organized as follows:

(1) Śramaṇa Hall (*Shami tang*). This was designed for young novices,[142]
who were included in the category of the "lower acolytes" (*xiazuo*) among
the disciples. These were divided into three classes, and they devoted themselves primarily to the study of the monastic precepts for the novitiate and
the fundaments of Buddhist teaching. The students here were also supposed
to memorize a certain number of texts, such as the *Abhidharmakośaśāstra*,
Abhisamayālaṃkāra, *Mūlamadhyamakaśāstra*, minor *Lamrim* texts, and
works on Buddhist logic. Non-Buddhist lessons, including ancient Chinese,
general culture, mathematics, and Tibetan language, were also provided. The
classes were conducted by Nenghai himself, by "higher acolytes" (*shangzuo*),
and by external teachers.[143] At the age of twenty, novices were granted the
complete precepts of monastic ordination and were then eligible for promotion into the next department. Ritual practice in this department involved

FIG. 4 Monks studying in the Main Hall of Duobaojiangsi, Ningbo.
They wear a yellow robe, a characteristic of all Nenghai's monastic communities.
In the foreground, Tibetan musical instruments are displayed.

only the lower tantras: the morning ritual involved the chanting of the *Wuzi zhenyan*, the *Pishamen*, and the *Gurupūjā*; the evening chants centered on the *Wuzi zhenyan* and the *Mañjuśrīnāmasaṃgīti*.[144]

(2) The Hall for Ritual Studies (*Xueshi tang*). This was the department for those monks from all over China who decided to retire for some months (usually a semester or a whole year) in the Jincisi, regardless of their age or doctrinal background. They attended classes in the Novice Hall and if they were able to pass a special examination, they could also enter the Hall for Vinaya Studies. Long-standing older monks who only wished to attend Nenghai's teachings could apply for admission in the *Xueshi tang* without being required to take part in other classes. This department also lodged lay-men and external monks during the summer retreat.

(3) The Hall for Vinaya Studies (*Xuejie tang*). The monks of this depart-ment were also among the "lower acolytes" and devoted themselves to a five-year period of study, mainly mnemonic, of the *Prātimokṣa* texts. Classes

focused on the *Dharmaguptakavinaya* and on Nenghai's own works concerning the *vinaya*. A final examination preceded admission to the next department. Ritual practice in this hall was the same as in the Novice Hall. Senior students, however, could also be initiated into the basic practice of Yamāntaka-Vajrabhairava and were then expected to chant the corresponding *sādhanas* during the daily services.

(4) The Hall for Preliminary [Tantric] Practices (*Jiaxing tang*). This department was conceived as a basic introduction to higher tantric practices, and was thus "preliminary" (*jiaxing*)[145] to the Vajra Institute. Monks who entered it were raised to the higher rank of "intermediate acolytes" (*zhongzuo*). Doctrinal classes were similar to those in the Novice Hall, and students focused on the same topics so as to complete the curriculum in exoteric teachings. Monks were expected to memorize some tantric texts that were chanted during daily religious services. Most of these were *Anuttarayogatantra sādhanas* of the "generation stage": the *sādhanas* of the "five great Vajras" (*wu da jingang*),[146] and particularly the "*Sādhana* of the Solitary Hero Yamāntaka."

(5) "Vajra Institute" (*Jingang yuan*). This department was exclusively reserved for the "higher acolytes" (*shangzuo*), who were Nenghai's closest circle of disciples.[147] During an initial period, these monks stayed in the Jincisi and devoted themselves to the practice of the "Vajrabhairava *Sādhana* of the Thirteen Deities" and to the study of the *Anuttarayogatantra* "completion stage." Nenghai was the only master to hold the classes. As soon as he decided that disciples were ready to pursue their practice alone, he allowed them to move to Yunwu Monastery, founded in 1943 as a place for tantric practice destined for those who had already been initiated into the *Anuttarayogatantra*. There, they could devote themselves to individual study and meditation, meeting only for the two daily chanting services. It was also possible for a monk at this stage to choose solitary retreat, in which case the only common activities requiring his participation were the bi-monthly recitations of the *Prātimokṣa* precepts. According to a special schedule that Nenghai conceived, higher acolytes would meditate six times and chant the *sādhanas* four times daily. Following this routine, within a year they would master the "generation stage" and could enter the "completion stage."

In 1945 Nenghai founded an "Institute for the Translation of Scriptures" (*Yi jing yuan*), which paralleled the five departments and accepted about fifty monks, who were chosen from among Nenghai's disciples and had proven themselves to be particularly skilled in translation. At the beginning of the program, the chosen monks took Tibetan classes, focusing during a first semester on writing and phonetics, and afterward on the memorization of

FIG. 5 Master Zhimin during a tantric ritual
in Duobaojiang Monastery, Ningbo.

Tibetan texts. This lasted for two or three years, beginning with the memorization of short liturgical texts and concluding with entire works such as
the *Gurupūjā, Mañjuśrīnāmasaṃgīti, Abhisamayālaṃkāra, Kālacakra,* and
so on. Nenghai directed the translation work, usually operating in a team
with his disciples, although occasionally he would ask some of them to work
independently on certain texts.[148] The Institute for the Translation of Scriptures also published some translations into Western languages,[149] as well as a
few translations of Chinese works into Tibetan.

As for the daily routine within Jinci Monastery, the monks awoke at 3:00
a.m. every morning and gathered for the morning chanting services. They
then moved to the refectory for the first meal of the day, and afterward each
monk would devote himself to the scheduled activities of his own department, such as study in classes, translation works, or tantric practice. The
monks reunited at noon for the second and last meal of the day, and again in
the late afternoon for the evening chanting services. At 9:00 p.m. they retired
to their rooms and lights were turned off. Monastic life was strictly organized
according to the Vinaya. For instance, every morning resident monks were
supposed to recite the monastic precepts; whoever stayed within the monastic compound had to follow a vegetarian diet,[150] and could "not eat after noon"
(*guowu bu shi*),[151] in accordance with the Chinese Buddhist tradition. The
monastic community gathered twice a month for the complete recitation of

the *Prātimokṣasūtra*[152] and, in summer, it respected the *varṣa* retreat (*anju*).[153] The monastic compound was also the location for great monastic ordinations. As for tantric practices other than the daily services and individual meditation, long retreats were organized during which the teachings were expounded, initiations and empowerments were conferred, and the *homa* rites (*humo*) were performed during the first half of the month.[154]

Conclusion

The mixture of Tibetan and Chinese elements in Nenghai's works and discourses, as well as in the organization of even the physical plan of his monasteries clearly exemplifies the peculiarity of his doctrinal standpoint. This reflects the overall teaching strategy of this Chinese master, who was connected to a specific Tibetan lineage but was acting in a Chinese environment and addressing himself to Chinese devotees.

Nenghai's "eclectic" attitude places him within the general context of reflection and reformation of the Chinese Buddhist tradition that characterized the first half of the twentieth century. His determination to study Tibetan Buddhism and to spread its teachings in China was perpetuated uniquely within the Chinese Buddhist circles. Nenghai established translation teams in order to compare Buddhist scriptures in the Chinese and Tibetan canons, and he promoted the translation of Chinese works into Tibetan. He not only engaged in teaching Tibetan tantric practices, but also pledged himself to revitalize tantric methods and lineages that were part of the form of Buddhism practiced under the Tang. Whenever possible, Nenghai also resorted to tantric works in the Chinese canon to transmit teachings he had personally received in Tibet. Moreover, he referred to *Dhāraṇīsūtras*, or to Chinese translations of Tibetan texts realized under the Yuan and the Qing, as sources for his tantric terminology.[155] The Buddhist Reform meant to create a more complete form of Buddhism in China, and Nenghai responded to this need.

Nevertheless, as stated in comparing him with Fazun, Nenghai was above all the "Chinese lama," a Buddhist master who devoted his entire life in the Dharma to teaching activities within his vajra monasteries and who in doing so gathered hundreds of followers from all over China. He understood his works and teachings as means to aid practitioners to advance along their own spiritual paths. His lexical and stylistic choices, as well as those relating to the contents of his works, have to be seen in this light. They are attempts at making his teaching as comprehensible as possible to Chinese disciples.

FIG. 6 Monks presenting offerings to deities during a tantric ritual
in Duobaojiang Monastery, Ningbo.

We have seen that the presence of Chinese elements in Nenghai's engagements in the higher tantras decreases, relative to his works on less esoteric
subjects. Nenghai's teaching strategy can thus be understood as a gradual
method to introduce his disciples to Tibetan tantric doctrines. At the outset, Nenghai turns to the teachings available in the vast Chinese scriptural
corpus, referring to the concepts and images most easily acceptable to a Chinese mind, while avoiding nearly all intervention in the highest tantras. Later,
although sexual and excessively gruesome contents are carefully concealed in
Nenghai's translation of the "*Sādhana* of the Solitary Deity Yamāntaka," I am
inclined to believe that he nevertheless provided an understanding of their
symbolism through oral instruction. In so doing, he added a further phase to
the gradual path culminating in the tantras, a path which, in Nenghai's communities, was strictly structured both temporally and geographically. Nenghai's second monastery was thus explicitly created as a "place for advanced
practice," and it only welcomed those disciples who had been initiated into
the *Anuttarayogatantra*.

Notes

* This study is an English adaptation of a part of my Ph.D. dissertation: Ester Bianchi, "L'insegnamento tantrico del 'lama cinese' Nenghai (1886–1967): Inquadramento storico e analisi testuale del corpus di Yamāntaka-Vajrabhairava" (Ph.D. dissertation, Paris/Venice: Università Ca' Foscari di Venezia and École Pratique des Hautes Études [Sciences Religieuses], 2003), pp. 81–118 and 296–299; reference is also made to pp. 188–295.

1 On the so-called Movement of Tantric Rebirth, see, for instance, Bianchi, "L'insegnamento tantrico"; Chen Bing 陳兵 and Deng Zimei 鄧子美, eds., *Ershi shiji Zhongguo fojiao* 二十世紀中國佛教 (Beijing: Minzu, 2000), 347–381; Dongchu 東初, *Zhongguo fojiao jindai shi* 中國佛教近代史 (Taipei, Zhonghua Fojiao wenhua guan, 1974), 407–458 and 989–992; Monica Esposito, "Una tradizione rDzogs-chen in Cina: Una nota sul Monastero delle Montagne dell'Occhio Celeste," in *Asiatica Venetiana* 3 (1998): 221–224; Huang Yingjie 黃英傑, *Minguo mizong nianjian* 民國密宗年鑒 (Taipei: Chengfo wenhua, 1995); Fabienne Jagou, *Le 9e Panchen Lama (1883–1937), Enjeu des relations sino-tibétaines* (Paris: École Française d'Extrême-Orient, 2004), particularly pp. 117–135; Mei Jingxuan 梅靜軒, "Minguo yilai de Han-Zang Fojiao guanxi (1912–1949): Yi Han Zangjiaoliyuan wei zhongxin de tantao" 民國以來的漢藏佛教關係(1912–1949)。以漢藏教理院為中心的探討, in *Chung-Hwa Buddhist Studies* 2 (1998): 251–288; Mei Jingxuan 梅靜軒, "Minguo zaoqi xianmi Fojiao chongtu de tantao" 民國早期顯密佛教衝突的探討, in *Chung-Hwa Buddhist Studies* 3 (1999): 251–270; Gotelind Müller, *Buddhismus und Moderne. Ouyang Jingwu, Taixu und das Ringen um ein Zeitgemässes Selbstverständnis im chinesischen Buddhismus des frühen 20. Jahrhunderts* (Stuttgart: Franz Steiner Verlag, 1993), pp. 122–129; Onoda Shunzo 小野天俊藏, "A Pending Task for New Century: The Pioneer works by Tai-xu 太虛大師: Han-Tibetan Interchange of Buddhist Studies (漢藏佛學交流)," in *Fourth Chung-Hwa International Conference on Buddhism: The Role of Buddhism in the 21th Century*, Taipei, www.chibs.edu.tw/exchange/CONFERENCE/4cicob/fulltext/XIAO-IE-TIAN.htm (2002); Gray Tuttle, *Tibetan Buddhists in the Making of Modern China* (New York: Columbia University Press, 2005); Holmes Welch, *The Buddhist Revival in China* (Cambridge: Harvard University Press, 1968), pp. 173–179; and the articles and essays collected by Zhang Mantao 張曼濤: *Minguo fojiao pian* 民國佛教篇 (Taipei: Dacheng wenhua, 1978); and *Han zang fojiao guanxi yanjiu* 漢藏佛教關係研究 (Taipei: Dacheng wenhua, 1979). For collections of Chinese works and translations on Tibetan Buddhism published during the late 1920s to 1930s, see *Zhongguo Zangmi baodian* 中國藏密寶典, 6 vols. (Beijing: Minzu, 2001); and Zhou Shaoliang 周紹良 ed., *Zangmi xiufa midian* 藏密修法秘典, 5 vols. (Beijing: Huaxia, 1991). For different aspects of the same movement, see also Gray Tuttle's contribution to the present volume.

2 On Fazun (1902–1980), see in particular Martino Dibeltulo, "I testi della scuola dGe lugs pa nelle parole di Fazun fashi: Traduzione annotata e studio della sezione *Biepo Weishizong* nel *Ru Zhonglun Shanxian Miyi Shu* di Lama Tsongkhapa" (master's thesis, Venice: Università Ca' Foscari di Venezia, 2005); Tuttle, *Tibetan Buddhists*; and Françoise Wang-Toutain, "Quand les maîtres chinois s'éveillent au bouddhisme tibétain," in *Bulletin de l'Ecole française d'Extrême-Orient* 87/2 (2000): 707–727.

3 In the words of Nenghai, reported by John E.C. Blofeld, *The Wheel of Life: The Auto-*

biography of a Western Buddhist (Boston: Shambhala, 1972, 1988 [first ed.: 1959]), p. 137: "Now, a Zen adept [...] seeks to leap from the muddy whirlpools into the pure white, radiant stillness at the centre. This can be done and has been done, but it is an extraordinary feat of which few are capable."

4 The Linji school is one of the five schools of the Chan tradition. It was founded by Linji Yixuan (?–867) in the ninth century. In 1190 Eisai introduced it to Japan where it is known as Rinzai.

5 Longlian 隆蓮, *Sanguiyi guan chuxiu lüefa. Nenghai shangshi chuanshou* 三皈依觀初修略法。能海上師傳授 (Chengdu: Jincisi huguo jin'gang daochang, 1946), pp. 11–12, translated into English in Ester Bianchi, *The Iron Statue Monastery: "Tiexiangsi," a Buddhist Nunnery of Tibetan Tradition in Contemporary China* (Florence: Leo Olschki, 2001), pp. 42–43.

6 See Dung dkar Blo bzang 'phrin las, "Khang gsar Ngag dbang thub bstan chos kyi dbang phyug," in *Dung dkar tshig mdzod chen mo* (Beijing: Krung go'i bod rig pa dpe skrun khang, 2002), pp. 298–299. I owe a great debt of gratitude to Matthew T. Kapstein for acquainting me with this article, for helping me in comparing its contents with the Chinese biography of Khang gsar (Qingding 清定, *Qingding shang-shi kaishi lu. Qingding shangshi jianjie, Nenghai shangshi jianjie, Kangsaba renpoqing xingji chugao* 清定上師開示錄。清定上師簡介。能海上師簡介。康薩巴仁波卿行跡初稿 [Chengdu: Chengdushi xinwen, 1999]), and for all his other useful suggestions. I am grateful as well to Gray Tuttle (personal communication, May 2003), who first suggested identifying Nenghai's Tibetan master with the Khang gsar (full name: Ngag dbang dbyangs can chos kyi dbang phyug) mentioned in the memoirs of Dorje Yudon Yuthok, *House of the Turquoise Roof* (Ithaca, NY: Snow Lion, 1990), pp. 127–128; on this issue, see, too, Tuttle, *Tibetan Buddhists*, pp. 270–271. I am particularly grateful also to Ramon N. Prats, who kindly read the first draft of my translation of the Chinese biography, integrating it with the proper Tibetan terminology, and providing me with interesting suggestions and reflections about it.

7 The Chinese form Kangsa is used throughout this passage in preference to the Tibetan because, as will be seen below, the author's understanding of the name cannot be reconciled with the Tibetan form Khang gsar.

8 Ch. *Puti dao cidi*, Tib. *byang chub lam rim*. *Puti dao cidi* usually refers to the *Lam rim* teachings. However, in this context it seems to generally refer to the gradual transmission of the Buddhist Dharma that leads to spiritual realization.

9 As we shall see, on the basis of this etymology the Chinese biography refers to Kangsa's former incarnation as a Khams pa from the Li thang region. As a matter of fact, Khang gsar literally means "new house/residence." Though it is not possible to determine whether this misunderstanding was due to Nenghai himself or to the disciples in charge of recording his speech, it clearly appears that it was generated from the transliteration of the Tibetan name into Chinese: the phonetic reading of Khang gsar in fact is the same as Khams sa ("Khams-place"), and was thus rendered by the Chinese characters usually employed to transliterate the geographic term Khams and the Tibetan syllable *sa*.

10 Ch. *Lama Renboqing*. The Chinese text often employs this appellation, which literally means "the precious master," to refer to Khang gsar; sometimes, however, only lama (*bla ma*) or Rin po che are used.

11 The Tibetan term for these colleges is *grwa tshang*, lit. a "group of monks." The two

Chinese characters used to render it respectively mean "deposit" (*cang*) and "documents" (*zha*). Since they designate institutes of study where documents were collected, I believe that this is one of the particular cases where the transliteration of a foreign term is realized with Chinese characters intended to preserve, even if only partially, the original semantic value.

12   The Tibetan *mkhan po* means "qualified, expert," and refers to a spiritual preceptor (Skt. *upādhyāya*) and is commonly used to refer to an abbot.

13   As suggested by M.T. Kapstein, Ch. *lao kanbu* (lit. "elder *mkhan po*") probably refers to Tib. *mkhan zur* ("retired *mkhan po*"), i.e. someone who has retired from the formal administrative post of "abbot" in the Dge lugs pa monastic system (private communication, May 2007).

14   The three great Dge lugs pa monasteries in Central Tibet (*gdan sa chen po gsum*) were Dga' ldan, Se rwa, and 'Bras spungs.

15   This probably represents the Tibetan title *'jam dpal bla ma*.

16   In 2000 I joined Guoping, a nun from the Tiexiang monastery, in a pilgrimage she undertook to the Tibetan sites visited by Nenhai. While at 'Bras spungs, we were shown a statue of one of the former abbots and were told it was Khang gsar Rin po che; unfortunately, we were then unable to get more information about this same master.

17   It is notable that our text refers to a *sprul sku* indiscriminately employing the translation from the Tibetan (Ch. *zhuanshi*), the phonetic rendering of the Mongolian word *khutughtu* (Ch. *hutuketu*), and the usual Chinese term for the Sanskrit *nirmāṇakāya* (Ch. *huashen*), which are evidently considered as synonyms. On the contrary, it never uses the usual and somehow misleading common Chinese term for a recognized *sprul sku*, i.e. Ch. *huofo*, "living Buddha."

18   In Nenhai's texts, the term *yigui* ("ritual") usually refers to *sādhanas*, which can be translated as "realization rituals" and are tantric manuals for the evocation of a specific deity. See, for instance, Raniero Gnoli and Giacomella Orofino, *Nāropā, Iniziazione, Kālacakra* (Milan: Adelphi, 1994), p. 55.

19   Tibetan Buddhism distinguishes different types of initiations (Tib. *dbang*, Ch. *guanding*); the most common classification comprehends: 1) *kalaśābhiṣeka*, "vase initiation"; 2) *guhyābhiṣeka*, "secret initiation"; 3) *prajñājñānābhiṣeka*, "prajñā initiation"; and 4) *caturthābhiṣeka*, "fourth initiation." In addition to these, Tibetan masters also confer a number of empowerments which initiate disciples into specific tantric practices. See David Snellgrove, *Indo-Tibetan Buddhism: Indian Buddhists and Their Tibetan Successors*, 2 vols. (Boston: Shambhala, 1987), pp. 212–277; and Paṇchen Sonam Dragpa, *Overview of Buddhist Tantra: General Presentation of the Classes of Tantra, Captivating the Minds of the Fortunate Ones*, trans. M.J. Boord and Losang Norbu Tsonawa (Dharamsala: Library of Tibetan Works and Archives, 1996), pp. 66–84.

20   Most likely the term *jiren* ("virtuous men") translates *dge bshes*, i.e. "virtuous friend" (Skt. *kalyāṇamitra*). R.N. Prats, personal communication, October 2002.

21   According to M.T. Kapstein, "This is probably *rgyud smad*, the tantric college with which he was affiliated" (personal communication, May 2007).

22   On the *Kālacakra* texts (Tib. *dus kyi 'khor lo*, Ch. *Shilun jingang*), see Gnoli and Orofino, *Nāropā*.

23 *Lung* (Ch. *long*) is the Tibetan term for the Sanskrit *āgama* and usually refers to the formal reading of Buddhist scriptures, which are thus transmitted by a master to his disciples. Our text seams to identify the word *lung* with the Chinese *Jingzang*, i.e. with the *Sūtrapiṭaka*. As described in the following sentence, this "*Sūtrapiṭaka* in 108 volumes" is no doubt the *Kanjur* (Tib. *bka' 'gyur*), or "translation of the word," the first of the two Tibetan canonical collections of Buddhist works. Accordingly, the transmission referred to in our text is the transmission of the *lung* of the Kanjur.

24 According to M.T. Kapstein (private communication, May 2007), the Tibetan biography mentions that Khang gsar was famous for bestowing the *lung* of the Kanjur eleven and a half times, close to the thirteen mentioned in the Chinese biography. Professor Kapstein also suggested that it would be physically impossible to transmit this in ten days and that the figure of ten days given by the Chinese text ought to be increased ten times (though perhaps "thirty" should read 130).

25 I was not able to identify these two kinds of empowerment.

26 This term possibly refers to *gcod pa*, "those who practice *gcod*" (Tib. *gcod*, lit. "to cut"), a tantric offering ritual in which the practitioner visualizes one's own dismembered corpse. I thank Jean-Luc Achard (personal communication, January 2003) for this suggestion.

27 Prof. M.T. Kapstein suggests that this "possibly refers to the *gzhung chen lnga*—the five major categories of exoteric study—and the *khrid chen brgyad*—the 'eight great guides' (i.e. esoteric instructions)—of the Dge lugs pa school" (personal communication, May 2007).

28 See "Kangsaba renpoqing xingji chugao" ("First draft on Khang gsar Rin po che's tracks"), in Qingding, *Qingding shangshi kaishi lu*, pp. 47–57. For other information on Khang gsar, also see Nenghai's biography: Dingzhi 定智 et al. eds., *Nenghai shangshi zhuan* 能海上師傳 (Chengdu : Sichuan sheng Fojiao xiehui hongfa lisheng hui, 1995). In my translation, I skipped the first section of the text, where a general historical and doctrinal summary of Tibetan Buddhism is given, and the last three pages, where Nenghai describes the master's daily life and his personal experience at 'Bras spungs.

29 See for instance Nenghai's translation of the "*Sādhana* of the Solitary Hero Yamāntaka": *Wenshu Daweide jingang benzun xiuxing chengjiu fa* 文殊大威德金剛 本尊修行成就法 (Sanmen [Ningbo]: Duobaojiangsi, n.d.), pp. 221–305. For an Italian translation and a brief biography of each master, see Ester Bianchi, "*Sādhana della divinità solitaria Yamāntaka-Vajrabhairava*: Traduzione e glossario della versione cinese di Nenghai," in *Revue d'Etudes Tibétaines* 8 (2005): 4–39 and 10 (2006): 4–43. The list of the masters of the lineage is as follows: 1) Lalitavajra; 2) Amoghavajra; 3) Jñānākaragupta; 4) Padmavajra; 5) Atiśa Dīpaṃkara; 6) Rwa lo tsa ba Rdo rje grags pa); 7) Rwa chos rab; 8) Ye shes seng ge; 9) 'Bum seng; 10) Rga lo tsa ba Rnam rgyal rdo rje; 11) Rong pa Shes rab seng ge; 12) Ye shes dpal ba; 13) Don grub rin chen; 14) Tsong kha pa; 15) Mkhas grub dam pa; 16) Shes rab seng ge; 17) Dpal ldan bzang po; 18) Dge 'dun 'phel; 19) Bkra shis 'phags; 20) Bsam 'grub rgya mtsho; 21) Brtson 'grus 'phags; 22) Rdo rje bzang po; 23) Sangs rgyas rgya mtsho); 24) Blo bzang chos kyi rgyal mtshan; 25–27) three Tibetan masters whom I have not been able to identify; 28) Khang gsar Rin po che; 29) Nenghai lama. As for the Chinese

names of nos. 25–27, they are given alternative names in the *sādhana* (where the list of the masters occurs twice). With their variants, they are: 25) Jing chuan xianhui xianhui zizai yu 經傳賢惠賢惠自在語 / Shanqiao dache chengjiu zizai da xianhui yu zizai 善巧大車成就自在大賢惠語自在; 26) Jixiang yihu zhihui mingcheng 吉祥依怙智慧名稱 / Chi jingang shuofa zizai huihai xianyong 持金剛說法自在慧海賢勇; 27) Chi mi quanzai sengjia cheng zhongshi 持密權宰僧伽成眾事 / Chi jingang gengde youyi chengjiu shi 持金剛更得有義成就.

30 I am grateful to Prof. Ramon N. Prats for calling this to my attention.

31 I am very grateful to Dr. Pasang Yonten Arya for this precious information.

32 In a recent study, Fabian Sanders, "The Life and Lineage of the Ninth Khalkha Jetsun Dampa Khutukhtu of Urga," in *Central Asiatic Journal*, 45/2 (2001): 274–275, describes the process of the new manifestation of a *sprul sku* after the death of his predecessor: "When a *Sprul-sku* dies, the man will follow the usual path of the dead, which will be determined by his karmas, and after an intermediate period (Tib. *bar do*), take up a new place in a new world or whatever, according to the level of his knowledge. Yet the Divine influence he hosted, 'overwhelmed' with compassion, remains in this world and seeks out a new individual who will again possess the most suitable characteristics for the time and location where the action will take place." Yet, there are cases in which this process is interrupted: "[The *Sprul sku*] will be instructed on the Dharma and will have to venture into the practice of the meditative Sādhanas of the Buddhist Path that will finally enable him to willingly cooperate with the nature of the Principle he imbibes, and to bring his consciousness to a level of contact, if not identity, with the inspiring Principle"; in this case, "there will be no further transmigration; the identity with the divine is *rnam par thar pa*, enlightenment."

33 I am indebted to Prof. M.T. Kapstein for this information based on the Tibetan text that I personally could not consult.

34 I am grateful here to the personal communication received from Prof. Gray Tuttle, based on information in Yuthok, *House of the Turquoise Roof*, pp. 127, 171–172, 175, 180. On the Chinese biography of Khang gsar, Tuttle writes: "It may well be that the monks in China were able to find out some additional information about Kangsa Rin po che after Dingzhi had written Nenghai's biography. I wonder about this relatively new information. I also wonder about it as a place name. I know that Fazun referred to his teacher as Amdo *dge bshes*, but this kind of epithet I have heard frequently, even today. However, 'Khams sa' ('Khams place') is not attested in any of the dictionaries I have consulted. [. . .] It smacks a little of a 'folk etymology' to me. [. . .] The post-mortem construction of elaborate lineages tracing one back to elevated teachers is well attested in Tibetan literature. I think especially of the work that was done on the preexistence of the Lcang skya incarnation series by Everding. Even if the information in Qingding's text is not 'correct' it is a fascinating example of the Chinese adopting (or believing, if the source of this information was Tibetan) a practice that has heretofore been directed at Tibetan or Mongol Buddhists."

35 Gray Tuttle also adds: "One other piece of interesting connection is the photo in Yuthok, which though different from the one in Nenghai's biography matches the one in Qingding's biography, at least to my eye. Aside from this the only sugges-

tion I have that points me in this direction is that when I asked Shakabpa's younger brother, who was a young man at the time, who was Kangsa, he immediately said Khang gsar was his Tibetan title and that he was quite famous."

36 Prof. Kapstein further states: "Given the small number of scholar-monks at Sgo mang at any given time, it is not at all plausible that Nenghai was the disciple there of an otherwise unknown Khams sa, a term that is not in very good Tibetan, as Tuttle suggests" (personal communication, May 2007).

37 For instance, among Khang gsar's Chinese disciples there was also Guankong (1903–1989), who, like Fazun, first went to Khams in 1925 as a member of Dayong's delagation. He resided in Khams for ten years, moving then to Chongqing to teach at the Institute of Sino-Tibetan Buddhist Studies founded by Taixu and Fazun in 1930–1931. Afterward, he went to Lhasa, where he studied under Tibetan lamas, and among them Khang gsar Rin po che. In 1957 he was appointed professor at the Institute of Buddhist Studies of Beijing. See Chen and Deng, *Ershi shiji Zhongguo fojiao*, p. 361.

38 For Nenghai's biography, I have consulted the following materials: Qingding 清定, Longlian 隆蓮, Zhaotong 昭通, et al., *Nenghai shangshi yonghuai lu* 能海上師詠懷錄 (Shanghai: Xinwen, 1997); Qingding, *Qingding shangshi kaishi lu*; Zhimin 智敏 and Fu Jiaoshi 傅教石, "Nenghai fashi zhuan" 能海法師傳, in *Fayin* 法音 2 (1984): 23–28; and Dingzhi, *Nenghai shangshi zhuan*. Also see: Lü Jianfu 呂建福, *Zhongguo mijiao shi* 中国密教史 (Beijing: Zhongguo shehui kexue, 1995), pp. 643–648; and Yu Lingbo 于凌波, *Zhongguo jinxiandai fojiao renwu zhi* 中國近現代佛教人物指 (Beijing: Zongjiao, 1995), pp. 115–117. The biographical notes inserted in this paper are a revision of Nenghai's biography in my former study: Bianchi, *The Iron Statue Monastery*, pp. 43–50.

39 On the Yonghegong, see, for instance, Jean Bouchot, *Le Temple des Lamas* (Beijing: La Politique de Pékin, 1923); G. Bouillard, *Le temple des Lamas, Temple lamaïste de Yung Ho Kung à Péking: Description, Plans, Photos, Cérémonies* (Beijing: Albert Nachbaur Éditeur, 1931); Chang Shaoru 常少如, *Zangchuan fojiao gusi Yonghegong* 藏傳佛教古寺雍和宮 (Beijing : Beijing yanshan, 1996): Ferdinand Diederich Lessing, *Yung-ho-kung: An Iconography of the Lamaist Cathedral in Peking, With Notes on Lamaist Mythology and Cult* (Stockholm: Elanders boktryckeri aktiebolag, 1993 [1942]); and Niu Song 牛頌, ed., *Yonghe gong. Zhongguo Zangchuan Fojiao zhuming gusi* 雍和宮。中國藏傳佛教著名古寺 (Beijing: Dangdai Zhongguo, 2001).

40 Zhimin and Fu, "Nenghai fashi zhuan," p. 24.

41 In older sources, the name of this locality is given as Tatsienlu (Dajianlu). In the present work I will refer to it using its modern Chinese name, Kangding.

42 This same master is named differently by Fazun, who refers to him as Cigu or Ciyuan. See Wang-Toutain, "Quand les maîtres chinois s'éveillent," p. 715. He also gave Nenghai the Tibetan religious name Yon tan rgya mtsho. See Gray Tuttle, "Tibetan Buddhism at Ri bo rtse lnga/Wutai shan in Modern Times," in *Journal of the International Association of Tibetan Studies* 2 (2206): 9.

43 Yongguang (1901–1988) was one of Nenghai's closest disciples. He stayed in Tibet for nineteen years and was then appointed abbot of Shijing Monastery (Longquan, Sichuan) for the following ten years. The description of Nenghai's first journey into Tibet in the book by Dingzhi, *Nenghai shangshi zhuan*, pp. 8–14, is based on

Yongguang's narration of the events. The other two monks who followed Nenghai up to Lhasa were Yonglun and Yongyan.

44 See Gray Tuttle, "Tibetan Buddhism at Ri bo rtse lnga," p. 9.

45 The Bodhi Study Society (Ch. *Puti xuehui*) was first founded in 1934 in order to promote the translation of Tibetan Buddhist texts into Chinese. See Jagou, *Le 9e Panchen Lama*, p. 131. On Nenghai's activities in this period on Wutai shan, see Tuttle, "Tibetan Buddhism at Ri bo rtse lnga," pp. 10–11.

46 The Chinese term *daochang* (Skt. *bodhimaṇḍa*), here translated as "monastery," literally means "place of the *bodhi*." Originally it indicated the place where the Buddha attained spiritual realization, and was then employed to allude to the seat of a buddha or a bodhisattva while preaching the Dharma. In the Vajrayāna tradition, it often refers to the place where tantric rituals are performed. Therefore, the name chosen by Nenghai for his monasteries is of great significance, since it immediately identifies them as places where the tantras were studied and practiced. Moreover, the connection with the Vajrayāna tradition is indicated also by the terms *jingang*, which translates the Sanskrit *vajra*, and *micheng*, or "esoteric vehicle." Elsewhere, Nenghai refers to his monasteries as *mizong daochang*, "*bodhimaṇḍas* of the tantric school" or simply as *jingang daochang*, "*vajra bodhimaṇḍas*." The Jincisi will be discussed below, in the section on "Nenghai's Tantric Vajra Monasteries."

47 Among the monks who followed Nenghai on his second journey to Lhasa were Zhaotong, Rongtong, Puchao, Zhenglin, Renci, Qingquan, and Dengxin.

48 Together with Yamāntaka-Vajrabhairava, these four *dharmapālas* form the group of the "five great *vajras*" (Ch. *wu da jingang*), whose tantric scriptures, as we shall see, are of a certain importance in Nenghai's tradition. For a description of the hall devoted to these five *dharmapālas* in the Yonghegong, see Bouillard, *Le temple des Lamas*, pp. 89–94.

49 See Dingzhi, *Nenghai shangshi zhuan*, p. 27.

50 Built at the end of the Song dynasty, this monastery was restored and enlarged during the Jiaqing era (1796–1820) in Qing times. When Nenghai took it over, of the ancient complex only a *dharmapāla* hall, a patriarchs hall, and the main hall of the monastery subsisted. During the Cultural Revolution the Yunwusi was heavily damaged, and nowadays it only consists of the *dharmapāla* hall and of the main gate. On the Yunwusi, see Xingfa's essay, in Qingding, Longlian, Zhaotong, et al., *Nenghai shangshi yonghuai lu*, pp. 52–54.

51 In 1944 Nenghai was invited to give some lessons in Chongqing. Requested by some devotees, he agreed to found his third *jingang daochang* in that city. For the purpose he choose an ancient country-house, and then decided to entrust the monk Qingding to follow the building works. In 1947 the monastic complex was completed, and it was soon inaugurated by Nenghai himself, who decided to reside there during the summer retreat. For a description of the foundation of the Chongqing *jingang daochang*, see Qingding's essay in Qingding, Longlian, Zhaotong, et al., *Nenghai shangshi yonghuai lu*, p. 9, and Dingzhi, *Nenghai shangshi zhuan*, p. 32.

52 The foundation of this fourth *jingang daochang* is closely related to Nenghai's activities in the restoration of ancient temples. The Wanniansi is an important monastery located on the southwestern slope of Emei shan and dating back to the Eastern Jin dynasty. In 1946 it was heavily damaged by fire. In the same year Nenghai decided he

would help in restoring it and began gathering funds among his lay devotees living in Chongqing. Within two and a half years the complex is said to have regained its ancient features. Meanwhile, Nenghai also integrated it with new buildings, among which was the Cisheng'an. This was destined to lodge a new *jingang daochang*, whose abbot was chosen in the person of Zhishan, a disciple of Nenghai. On the *jingang daochang* on Emei shan, see Xu Borong's essay in Qingding, Longlian, Zhaotong, et al., *Nenghai shangshi yonghuai lu*, pp. 105–110.

53 The Tiexiangsi is a nunnery located in the southern suburbs of Chengdu, about two kilometers from Shiyangchang. In 1590 a statue of Śākyamuni Buddha was dug up in the place now occupied by the nunnery. In order to worship the holy image, a monastery was built to honor it and was named Tiexiangsi, the "Iron Statue Monastery." For more than three centuries the Tiexiangsi was a monks' monastery of the Chan tradition. During the Resistance War against Japan (1937–1945) the monastery became the property of the neighboring Jincisi. Many devotees gathered to listen to Nenghai preaching the Dharma, and among them there were several nuns. Since the Buddhist Vinaya states that nuns cannot live in the same buildings with monks, Nenghai decided that they should live in the Tiexiangsi. He put the nun Longlian in charge of the nunnery, and since then she has been its abbess. Nowadays, the Iron Statue Monastery lodges a community of more than sixty nuns who still devote themselves to the Dge lugs pa practice in the tradition of Nenghai. On the Tiexiangsi, see my earlier study: Bianchi, *The Iron Statue Monastery*.

54 In 1947 Nenghai sent Qingding to give some lessons on tantric teachings in Nanjing. Nenghai then told him that he should "stay in the southeast to spread the Dharma, without going back to Sichuan." At the end of the following year, Qingding went to Shanghai in order to officiate in tantric rituals for the purpose of promoting peace and averting calamities. On this occasion he was requested by a number of Buddhist monks to become their master. He thus invited some acolytes from Sichuan, so as to make up the quorum of twenty people which was necessary to open a new monastery. In 1949 Nenghai and Qingding inaugurated the new *jingang daochang*. The Shanghai *jingang daochang* was abandoned during the 1960s, but nowadays it is being reopened by lay devotees together with some monks from the Shijingsi. On the Shanghai *jingang daochang*, see Dingzhi, *Nenghai shangshi zhuan*, p. 33, and Qingding's essay in Qingding, Longlian, Zhaotong, et al., *Nenghai shangshi yonghuai lu*, p. 11.

55 It was here that the master retired during his last years of life. He is said to have always desired to live on the mountain devoted to Mañjuśrī; the politics of the period, too, which required the complete economic independence of Buddhist monasteries, favored this decision as well. The location he chose was the Jixiangsi, near Qingliang bridge (2440 m. above sea level). Founded during the Northern Wei dynasty, it became an important Buddhist site under the Tang dynasty, but later on was gradually abandoned. In 1953 Nenghai restored it, changed its name into Jixianglüyuan and moved there together with some of the Jincisi monks. The place was surrounded by fields to grow vegetables and to feed livestock, and could thus assure the survival of the monks' community. On the Jixiangsi, see Renjie, Qingding, and Zhimin's essays in Qingding, Longlian, Zhaotong, et al., *Nenghai shangshi yonghuai lu*, pp. 12,

42–47, and 68–69, respectively. On Nenghai's last thirteen years of life on Wutai shan, also see Tuttle, "Tibetan Buddhism at Ri bo rtse lnga," pp. 12–14. For a general outline of Wutai shan, see Hou Wenzheng 候文正 ed., *Wutaishan zhi* 五臺山誌 (Taiyuan: Shanxi Renmin, 2003).

56   The construction of this *stūpa* was sponsored by the Chinese Buddhist Association. The Chinese characters on the nearby stele were written by Zhao Puchu. Afterward, as I could personally see in August 2006, new *stūpas* were built on Wutai shan. See Tuttle, "Tibetan Buddhism at Ri bo rtse lnga," pp. 20–21.

57   See Bianchi, *The Iron Statue Monastery*, pp. 50–55. See also the list of Nenghai's works in Bianchi, *op. cit.*, pp. 169–173, and Dingzhi, *Nenghai shangshi zhuan*, pp. 98–106.

58   Among Nenghai's works dealing with monastic discipline, see Nenghai 能海, *Jiedinghui jibensanxue* 戒定慧基本三學, Nenghai shangshi quanji 1 (Shanghai: Xinwen, 1987), pp. 58–172; Nenghai, *Sanxue jianglu* 三學講錄, Nenghai shangshi quanji 2 (Shanghai: Xinwen, 1997); Nenghai, *Jiaoli chuji* 教理初基, Nenghai shangshi quanji 3 (Shanghai: Xinwen, 1998); and Nenghai, *Zai jia lü yao* 在家律要, Nenghai shangshi quanji 4 (Shanghai: Xinwen, 2000).

59   On Nenghai's teachings dealing with meditation, see for instance Nenghai, *Putidao cidi xinlun* 菩提道次第心論, Nenghai shangshi quanji 8 (Taipei: Fangguang wenhua, 1997), pp. 173–309, which gathers some texts on this topic.

60   *Śamatha* and *vipaśyanā*, "tranquility" and "insight," are two forms of Buddhist meditation which are fundamental in all Buddhist traditions, particularly in the Theravāda (see Mauro Bergonzi, "Osservazioni su *samatha* e *vipassanā* nel Buddhismo Theravāda," in *Rivista degli Studi Orientali* 54 [1980]: I–II, pp. 143–169, and II–III, pp. 327–357) and in Tibetan Buddhism. They make up the two main sections of Tsong kha pa's *Lam rim*; see, for instance, Alex Wayman, *Calming the Mind and Discerning the Real: Buddhist Meditation and the Middle View, From the* Lam rim chen mo *of Tson-kha-pa* (Delhi: Motilal Banarsidass, 1979), and the more recent translations by Georges Driessens, *Le grand Livre de la progression vers l'Eveil par Tsongkhapa Losang Drakpa* (Jujurieux: Éditions Dharma, 1990), vol. 2, and Joshua Cutler and Guy Newland, eds., *The Great Treatise on the Stages of the Path to Enlightenment: The Lam rim Chen mo by Tsongkhapa* (Ithaca NY: Snow Lion, 2002), vol. 3. Nenghai wrote a brief essay on this topic, "Zhiguan lüefa," explaining meaning and practice of *śamatha* and *vipaśyanā* according to Tsong kha pa's teachings. Interestingly enough, at the beginning of the text he refers to them employing phonetic transcriptions of the Sanskrit (*shemota* and *piposhena*), probably in order to distinguish his approach from the usual Chinese understanding of these two forms of meditation, which is closely linked to the Tiantai school. See Nenghai, *Jiedinghui jibensanxue*, pp. 197–213.

61   See the following among Nenghai's writings: *Jiedinghui jibensanxue*, pp. 311–332; *Banruo boluomiduo jiaoshou Xianzheng zhuangyan lun mingju songjie* 般若波羅蜜多教授現證莊嚴論名句頌解, Nenghai shangshi quanji 1 (Taipei, Fangguang wenhua, 1994); *Putidao cidi kesong* 菩提道次第頌—*Classifications and Verses on the Steps of the Way to Bodhi* (Chengdu: Xinwen, 1994); *Putidao cidi lun kesong jiangji* 菩提道次第論科頌講記, ed. Rending (Taipei: Fangguang wenhua, 1994); *Xianzheng zhuangyan lun qingliang ji* 現證莊嚴論清涼記 (Shanghai: Xinwen, 1994); *Xianzheng zhuangyan lun xianming yi qingliang ji* 現證莊嚴論顯明義清涼記 (Taipei: Fangguang

wenhua, 1996); *Putidao cidi xinlun*; and *Zongkaba dashi xianmi xiuxing cidi kesong* 宗喀巴大師顯密修行次第科頌 (Chengdu: Wenshuyuan, n.d.).

62 When asked about his doctrinal tradition, Nenghai would answer: "As long as our final objective is to study and understand the *Prajñāpāramitā*, we can say that we belong to the *Prajñāpāramitā* school" (Zhimin and Fu, "Nenghai fashi zhuan," p. 28). With this, Nenghai does not mean to refer to a specific school, but to show his special devotion to this group of Mahāyāna texts. Accordingly, the *Prajñāpāramitā* is fundamental and central in the teachings of the Dge lugs pa school. The "*Prajñāpāramitā* vehicle" (Skt. *prajñāpāramitāyāna*), or bodhisattva vehicle, is also defined in Tibetan texts as the "causal vehicle" (Tib. *rgyu'i theg pa*), so as to distinguish it from the Vajrayāna, or "fruitional vehicle." See Sonam Dragpa, *Overview of Buddhist Tantra*, pp. 2–3, and, for a general analysis of the *Prajñāpāramitā* in Tibetan Buddhism, Eugene Obermiller, *Prajñāpāramitā in Tibetan Buddhism*, reprint ed. (Kathmandu: Tiwari's Pilgrims Book House, 1990).

63 Nenghai dedicated four works written after 1960 to the *Āgamas*, or Hīnayāna teachings. He defines them as "the basic path to enter Buddhism" (*rumen yaodao*) because "they are the first words pronounced by the Buddha, and reveal the teaching in a clear and accessible manner" (Zhimin and Fu, "Nenghai fashi zhuan," p. 27). Only in the last years of his life did Nenghai study these scriptures in a systematic way. See Nenghai, *Sifenlü zang si Ahan ji song* 四分律藏四阿含集頌 (Shanghai: Xinwen, n.d.).

64 The *Abhisamayālaṃkāra* (Tib. *mngon rtogs rgyan*), or "Ornament of spiritual realization," is one of the five works attributed in Tibetan tradition to Maitreyanātha, and which, with the exception of just two (Taishō 1600 and 1604), are not included in the Chinese Buddhist canon. They are all fundamental works in the Dge lugs pa monastic curricula for the *dge bshes* degree. On the *Abhisamayālaṃkāra*, see Edward Conze, *Abhisamayālaṃkāra* (Roma: IsMEO, 1954), John Makransky, *Buddhahood Embodied: Sources of Controversy in India and Tibet* (Albany: State University of New York Press, 1997), and Obermiller, *Prajñāpāramitā in Tibetan Buddhism*.

65 The term *Lam rim*, "stages of the Path," is usually applied to a category of Tibetan doctrinal manuals outlining the various stages of the Path to spiritual realization. Tsong kha pa authored three works on *Lam rim*: the "Great exposition of the stages of the Path" (Tib. *lam rim chen mo*), the longest version, translated into Chinese by Fazun (*Putidao cidi guanglun* 菩提道次第廣論, Zongkaba dashi ji 1 [Beijing: Minzu, 2000]); an intermediate version (Tib. *byang chub lam rim chung ba*) which omits some sections and focuses on the union of the "two Truths"; and the "Verses on spiritual experience" (Tib. *lam rim nyams mgur*), a short verse epitome. On the origins of *Lam rim* works, see Tenzin Gyatso, *Path to Bliss: A Practical Guide to Stages of Meditation*, trans. Thubten Jinpa (Ithaca, NY: Snow Lion, 1991), pp. 20–22; for translations in Western languages, see n. 60 above, and Robert A.F. Thurman, *The Life and Teachings of Tsong Khapa* (Dharamsala: Library of Tibetan Works and Archives, 1992).

66 Refer to the outline of Nenghai's tantric works in Zhimin and Fu, "Nenghai fashi zhuan."

67 Tibetan Buddhism distinguishes three different types of refuge: 1. The outer refuge, which is common to all Buddhist traditions, and which consists of taking refuge in

the Three Jewels in the belief that Buddha, Dharma, and Sangha can protect one from potential dangers; 2. The inner refuge, which is uniquely taken by Mahāyāna practitioners, and which is based on compassion and on the determination to gain realization for the benefit of all sentient beings; 3. The secret refuge, which is typical of the tantric Path, and which involves the taking of refuge not only in the Three Jewels but also in one's *guru* and in the meditation deities. See Tenzin Gyatso, *The Union of Bliss and Emptiness*, trans. Thubten Jinpa (Ithaca, NY: Snow Lion, 1988), pp. 43, 221–222.

68 The teaching on the "threefold refuge" was passed on orally by Nenghai to his disciples beginning in the early 1930s, and was finally noted down by the nun Longlian in 1946 as the only written reference for its practitioners. See Longlian, *Sanguiyi guan chuxiu lüefa*, translated into English in Bianchi, *The Iron Statue Monastery*, pp. 136–165.

69 The *Gurupūjā* was composed by the fourth Paṇchen Lama (1570–1662); among the many variants of *guruyoga* texts belonging to the different schools of Tibetan Buddhism, it is the most popular among the Dge lugs pa. At the heart of this practice is the realization that one's own root *guru* is identical with the Buddha. It presents the main subjects of the sūtras and tantras, focusing on themes such as the *Lam rim* and the stages of generation and completion typical of the *Anuttarayogatantra*. Although *guruyoga* practice is said to have originated in India, it seems that manuals exclusively devoted to it may be found only in Tibet. For an English translation of the *Gurupūjā*, see Tenzin Gyatso, *The Union of Bliss and Emptiness*, and Tshering Gyatso, *The Guru Puja and The Hundred Deities of the Land of Joy* (Dharamsala: Library of Tibetan Works and Archives, 1995 [1979]).

70 Nenghai's version of the *Gurupūjā* is given in Nenghai, *Shangshi wushang gongyang guanxingfa* 上師無上供養觀行法 (Shanghai: Shanghaishi fojiao xiehui, 1990); see also Bianchi, *The Iron Statue Monastery*, pp. 122–132. Among its commentaries, see Longlian, *Shangshi wushang gongyang guanxingfa jiangji, Nenghai shangshi jiang* 上師無上供養觀行法講記。能海上師講 (Chengdu: Chengdushi xinwen, 1995). For other Chinese versions, see Liang Guimi 梁貴米, *Lama Chöpa—Shangshi gongyang jing* 上師供養經—*The Guru puja* (Taipei: Zhonghua geluba foxuehui, 1997), and Tang Xianming 湯薌銘, "Shangshi gongyang fa" 上師供養法, in Li Wuyang 李舞陽 ed., *Zangyuxi fojiao niansongji. Zanghan duizhao* 藏語系佛教念誦集。藏漢對照 (Beijing: Zongjiao wenhua, 1995), pp. 24–54.

71 The *yi dam* of the text is Arapacana-Mañjuśrī, whose name recalls the five-syllable mantra mentioned in the title. The tantric practice within the *Wuzi zhenyan* is a translation into Chinese of a *sādhana* on this deity belonging to the *Yogatantra* class, which is translated from the Tibetan as "Meditation on Yellow Mañjuśrī" in Glenn H. Mullin, *Meditation on the Lower Tantras, From the collected works of the previous Dalai Lamas* (Dharamsala: Library of Tibetan Works and Archives, 1983), pp. 87–89. Nenghai's version is shorter and slightly different in content. See Nenghai, *Wenshu wuzi genben zhenyan niansongfa* 文殊五字根本真言念誦法 (Chengdu: Zhaojuesi, 1995), and its commentary in Nenghai, *Wenshu wuzi genbenzhenyan niansongfa jianglu* 文殊五字根本真言念誦法講錄 (Chongqing: Jingang daochang, n.d.). Also see Bianchi, *The Iron Statue Monastery*, pp. 132–135, and Bianchi, "Arapacana-Mañjuśrī: Un esempio di sinizzazione tantrica all'interno della scuola *dGe lugs pa*

nella Cina contemporanea," in A. Cadonna and E. Bianchi, eds., *Facets of the Tibetan Religious Tradition and Contacts with Neighbouring Cultural Areas* (Firenze: Leo Olschki, 2002), pp. 225–254.

72 Nenghai's translations and works concerning the Yamāntaka-Vajrabhairava tantric cycle are central to my Ph.D. dissertation, Bianchi, "L'insegnamento tantrico del 'lama cinese' Nenghai," which focuses on his translation of the "Sādhana of the Solitary Hero Yamāntaka-Vajrabhairava" (*Daweide yizun chengjiu fa*): see Nenghai, *Wenshu Daweide jingang benzun xiuxing chengjiu fa* 文殊大威德金剛本尊修行成就法 (Sanmen, Ningbo: Duobaojiangsi, n.d.), and its commentary in Nenghai, "Daweide Wenshu chengjiu fangbian lüeyin" 大威德文殊成就方便略引, in Zhou Shaoliang 周紹良, ed., *Zangmi xiufa midian* 藏密修法秘典 (Beijing: Huaxia, 1991), pp. 683–820. For an annotated Italian translation of this text, see Bianchi, "*Sādhana della divinità solitaria Yamāntaka-Vajrabhairava.*" For other Chinese texts of this same tantric cycle authored by Nenghai and others, see my "La 'via del *vajra*' e il 'palazzo fiorito': Immagini sessuali in alcune traduzioni cinesi di testi tantrici tibetani," in M. Scarpari and T. Lippiello, eds., *Caro Maestro ... Scritti in onore di Lionello Lanciotti per l'ottantesimo compleanno* (Venezia: Cafoscarina, 2005), pp. 121–131; "The 'Sādhana of the Glorious Solitary Hero Yamāntaka-Vajrabhairava' in China," in G. Orofino and S. Vita, eds., *Buddhist Asia* 2 (Kyoto, forthcoming); and "Protecting Beijing: The Tibetan Image of Yamāntaka-Vajrabhairava in Late Imperial and Republican China," in M. Esposito, ed., *Images of Tibet in the 19th and 20th Centuries* (Paris: EFEO, forthcoming).

73 On the texts composing the Yamāntaka-Vajrabhairava tantric cycle, and for an English translation of the five tantras of the cycle, see Bulcsu Siklós, *The Vajrabhairava Tantras: Tibetan and Mongolian Versions* (Tring, UK: The Institute of Buddhist Studies, 1996). See also: Bianchi, "L'insegnamento tantrico del 'lama cinese' Nenghai," pp. 137–187; Daniel Cozort, *The Sand Mandala of Vajrabhairava* (Ithaca, NY: Snow Lion, 1995); Sharpa Tulku and Richard Guard, *Meditation on Vajrabhairava: The procedures for doing the serviceable retreat of the glorious solitary hero* Vajrabhairava *with the sadhana "Victory over Evil"* (Dharamsala/Delhi: Library of Tibetan Works and Archives, 1990); idem., *Self-initiation of Vajrabhairava* (Dharamsala/Delhi, Library of Tibetan Works and Archives, 1991); idem., *Instructions on the Generation and Completion Stages of the Solitary Hero Vajrabhairava—The Profound of the Great Secret—Cloud Offerings to Manjusri* (New Delhi: Tibet House, 1995); and Sonam Dragpa, *Overview of Buddhist Tantra*, pp. 47–49. On the texts devoted to Yamāntaka in the Chinese and Japanese Buddhist traditions, see Robert Duquenne, "Daiitoku Myōō" 大威德明王, in *Hōbōgirin: Dictionaire Encyclopédique du Bouddhisme d'après les Sources Chinoises et Japonaises* (Tōkyō/Paris: Maison Franco-Japonaise, 1983), vol. 6, pp. 652–670.

74 *Anuttarayogatantras* are distinguished into "Mother Tantras" (Tib. *ma rgyud*, an abbreviation for Skt. *yoginītantra*) and "Father Tantras" (Tib. *pha rgyud*, an abbreviation for Skt. *anuttarayogatantra*), according to their emphasis on knowledge or means, and also on the practice of "clear light" or the practice of the "illusory bodhi." See Daniel Cozort, *Highest Yoga Tantra* (Ithaca, NY: Snow Lion, 1986), pp. 179–180; and Sonam Dragpa, *Overview of Buddhist Tantra*, pp. 46–47. On other *Anuttarayogatantra* classifications according to the Dge lugs pa tradition, see Ferdinand

Diederich Lessing and Alex Wayman, *Introduction to the Buddhist Tantric Systems, Translated from Mkhas Grub Rje's* (Delhi: Motilal Banarsidass, 1978 [1968]), pp. 250–269; and Alex Wayman, *The Buddhist Tantras: Light on Indo-Tibetan Esotericism* (Delhi: Motilal Banarsidass, 1993 [1973]), pp. 133–236.

75 The highest *Yogatantra* practice comprises two stages: generation and completion. In both cases the practitioner is transformed into the meditation deity: in the generation stage, also called "emanation stage," the practitioner visualizes the transformation; and during the completion stage (or "realization stage"), according to traditional tantric literature, one actually does experience this same transformation. Generation involves the visualization of all the deities of a particular *maṇḍala*, and is associated with "relative truth." Completion, which must be preceded by generation, leads one to experience "clear light," and is representative of "absolute truth." It is characterized by particular *yogic* practices, as the *ṣaḍaṅgayoga* of Nāropā. On the latter, see, for instance, Raniero Gnoli and Giacomella Orofino, *Nāropā, Iniziazione, Kālacakra* (Milan: Adelphi, 1994), pp. 92–98. On the two stages, see Jean-Luc Achard, "La phase de perfection (rdzogs-rim)," in *Dictionnaire critique de l'esotérisme* (Paris: PUF, 1998), pp. 1026–1028; Cozort, *Highest Yoga Tantra*; and Yangchen Gawai Lodoe, *Paths and Grounds of Guhyasamaja, According to Arya Nagarjuna*, trans. Tenzin Dorjee and Jeremy Russell (Dharamsala: Library of Tibetan Works and Archives, 1995).

76 Beginning in the 1980s there have been many publications of collections of Fazun's works: Fazun wenji (Taipei, 1988); Fazun fashi foxue lunwen ji (Beijing, 1997); Fazun fashi lunwen ji (Taipei, 1997); and Zongkaba dashi ji (Beijing, 2000). (The latter is a collection of Fazun's works regarding Tsong kha pa's writings.) As for Nenghai, the most important collections are: Nenghai shangshi quanji (Shanghai: Xinwen, 1987; reprinted, 1997–1998); and Nenghai shangshi quanji (Taipei: Fangguang wenhua, 1994–1997). (It is notable that none of the works included in the latter is tantric.) Besides these collections, many of their writings have also been reprinted as independent volumes.

77 On the so-called second movement of Tantric Rebirth, which began in the 1980s and is particularly concerned with *qigong* practices and with Tibetan *Rdzogs chen* tradition, see Chen and Deng, *Ershi shiji Zhongguo fojiao*, pp. 362–363.

78 Dingzhi, *Nenghai shangshi zhuan*, p. 8.

79 Fazun, *Zhuzhe ru Zang de jingguo* 著者入藏的經過 (Chengdu: Dongfang shushe, 1943), pp. 127–129. After the French translation of Wang-Toutain, "Quand les maîtres chinois s'éveillent," p. 721: "C'est vrai que pour être difficile, le Tibet serait difficile. [. . .] Et il y avait au Tibet un bouddhisme parfait que l'on pouvait étudier, traduire et diffuser. [. . .] Tous ces textes bouddhiques qui existaient au Tibet mais que l'on ne trouvait pas en Chine, je fis vœux de les étudier, et de les traduire afin de combler ces lacunes."

80 The Buddhist Reform, to which the movement of "Tantric Reform" is closely linked, aimed at widening the horizon and creating a more complete form of Buddhism. Particularly, it aimed to investigate various Buddhist traditions aside from the Chinese and to revitalize the lineages and practices that had disappeared in China. In this sense, Nenghai's and Fazun's objectives are clearly connected to this general perspective. See my "The Tantric Rebirth Movement in Modern China: Esoteric Buddhism

revivified by the Japanese and Tibetan Traditions," in *Acta Orientalia Academiae Scientiarum Hungarica* 57/1 (2004): 31–54, and Zhihua Yao's contribution to the present volume.

81 The following texts can all be included in the five groups of teachings which form the curriculum within the Tibetan monastic colleges. The five are detailed in Zhihua Yao's chapter above.

82 Françoise Wang-Toutain, "Quand les maîtres chinois s'éveillent," p. 724, reports that the *Lam rim* was the first text taught by Fazun at the Institute of Sino-Tibetan Buddhist Studies in 1936, and that it was also the last text on which he gave lessons in 1949, shortly before leaving Chongqing. On the role of the *Lam rim* in the institutes of study at Nenghai's Jincisi, see below.

83 Although Tsong kha pa was known to the Chinese even during his own lifetime in Tibet, it seems that the *Lam rim* was never translated into Chinese, while a Mongol version was realized. Françoise Wang-Toutain, "Quand les maîtres chinois s'éveillent," p. 724, interprets this incredible lack—considering the position this text holds in the Dge lugs pa tradition—as clear evidence for the absence of a consistent interest toward Tibetan Buddhism in imperial China. Apart from Dayong's, Fazun's, and Nenghai's works, in modern and contemporary times other Chinese translations of the *Lam rim* and of related literature have been made; among them: Angwanglangji 昂旺朗吉, *Putidao cidi lüelunshi* 菩提道次第略論釋, 3 vols. (Chengdu: Chengdushi xinwen, 1995); Huizhuang 慧幢, *Xiu* Putidao cidi *chuxiu famen* 修菩提道次第初修法門 (Gaojian [Sanmen]: Duobaojiangs, 1995); *Putidao cidi jueyao* 菩提道次第訣要, Jingang cheng quanji 4 (Taipei: Jingang cheng xuehui, 1983); Rongzeng 榮增, *Puti zhengdao pusa jie lun* 菩提正道菩薩戒論 (Gaojian [Sanmen]: Duobaojiang, 1995); Tang Xiangming 湯薌銘, ed., *Puti zhengdao pusa jie lun* 菩提正道菩薩戒論 (Gaojian [Sanmen]: Duobaojiangsi, 1995). Also note the translations of Tsong kha pa's short work, the "Three Principles of the Path" (Tib. *lam gyi gtso bo rnam gsum*, Ch. *San zhuyao dao*): Renqin Quzha 仁欽曲扎, *San zhuyao dao, shenshen yindao biji, kai miaodao men* 三主要道,甚深引導筆記,開妙道門 (Taipei: Jingsu falin, 1997), and Tanying 譚影, *San zhuyao dao song jianshi. Zongkaba dashi zaosong. Kanbu Suodaji jiangshu* 三主要道頌簡釋。宗喀巴大師造頌。堪布索達吉講述 (Seda/Beijing: Wuming foxueyuan—Lingguangsi, 1997).

84 These three works are published, respectively, in Dayong and Fazun, *Putidao ciheng xiujiao shou* (cited in Wang-Toutain, "Quand les maîtres chinois s'éveillent," p. 723, and Fazun, *Putidao cidi guanglun* 菩提道次第廣論, Zongkaba dashi ji 1 (Beijing: Minzu, 2000), and *Putidao cidi lüelun* 菩提道次第略論 Zongkaba dashi ji 3 (Beijing: Minzu, 2000). Also note the article published in the Buddhist review *Buddhist Studies Today*: Fazun, "Zongkaba dashi de *Putidao cidi lun*" 宗喀巴大師的菩提道次第論, in *Xiandai foxue* 現代佛學 12 (1957): 4–10.

85 See, for instance, the following works: Nenghai, *Putidao cidi kesong*; *Putidao cidi lun kesong jiangji*; and *Putidao cidi xinlun*. On the other works that Nenghai devoted to the *Lam rim* teachings, see the list in Bianchi, *The Iron Statue Monastery*, pp. 172–173.

86 On the role of the Vinaya in Tsong kha pa's works and personal life, see Thurman (1992: 12), and Wang-Toutain, "Quand les maîtres chinois s'éveillent," p. 723.

87 Respectively: *Bichu jie shi* and *Pusa jie shi*. Françoise Wang-Toutain, "Quand les

maîtres chinois s'éveillent," p. 715, suggests that these texts could be the Tibetan *dge slong gi bslab bya gnam rtsed lding ma* and *byang chub sems dpa'i sdom pa byung nas tshul khrims kyi phung po yongs su dag par bya ba'i tshul rnam par bshad pa byang chub gzhung lam*, a text based on the chapter on ethics in the *Bodhisattvabhūmiśāstra*. The latter Tibetan text is the subject of a study and translation by Mark Tatz (1986); my thanks to M.T. Kapstein for acquainting me with this book.

88 In Lhasa he studied the extensive version of the *Bhikṣuprātimokṣa* (*Bichu jie guang-shi*). The two works he devoted to the monastic discipline are Fazun, *Bichu xue chu* 苾芻學處 and *Pusa jie pin shi* 菩薩戒品釋, both in Zongkaba dashi ji 5 (Beijing: Minzu, 2000).

89 On Nenghai's works on the Vinaya, see notes 58, 63, 106–7 and 109. Concerning the role of monastic discipline in Nenghai's teaching activities, it is notable that one of the institutes of study of the Jincisi was completely devoted to the Vinaya, as will be seen below.

90 On this work, see note 64 above.

91 Tib. *shes rab kyi pha rol tu phyin pa man ngag gi bstan bcos mngon par rtogs pa'i rgyan 'grel pa dang bcas pa'i rgya cher bshad pa legs bshad gser gyi phreng ba*. See Wang-Toutain, "Quand les maîtres chinois s'éveillent," p. 717.

92 Among Fazun's works on the *Abhisamayālaṃkāra*, refer to his *Xianguan zhuang-yan lun lüeyi* 現觀莊嚴論略譯 (Taipei, 1997), and the article "Banruo baqian song yu Xianguan zhuangyan lun duizhao kemu" 般若八千頌與現觀莊嚴論對照科目, in *Xiandai foxue* 現代佛學 3 (1958): 6–11.

93 See Nenghai, *Banruo boluomiduo jiaoshou Xianzheng zhuangyan lun mingju songjie*; *Xianzheng zhuangyan lun qingliang ji*; and *Xianzheng zhuangyan lun xianming yi qingliang ji*. On Nenghai's other works on the *Abhisamayālaṃkāra*, see Bianchi, *The Iron Statue Monastery*, pp. 170 and 173. Among the works on this topic written by Nenghai's disciples, there is a commentary by Longlian (see Bianchi, *The Iron Statue Monastery*, p. 39).

94 Both the Chinese terms *xianguan* and *xianzheng* are given as Chinese translations for the Sanskrit *abhisamaya* (see Ciyi 慈怡, ed., *Foguang dacidian* 佛光大辭典, 8 vols. (Taiwan: Shumu wenxian, 1989), p. 4731, and William Edward Soothill and Lewis Hodous, *A Dictionary of Chinese Buddhist Terms* (Delhi: Motilal Banarsidass, 1987 [1937], p. 359).

95 The *Madhyamakāvatāra* ("Introduction to the *Madhyamakaśāstra*," Ch. *Ru zhon-glun*), based on Nāgārjuna's *Madhyamakaśāstra* (Taishō 1564), was written in the seventh century by the Indian scholar Candrakīrti and presents the Madhyamaka teaching according to the ten stages of the Bodhisattva Path. Refer to Z. Yao's chapter above.

96 For Fazun's works on the *Madhyamakāvatāra*, see Fazun's translation of Tsong-khapa's commentary, *Ru zhonglun shan xian miyi shu* 入中論善顯密意疏 Zongkaba dashi ji 3 (Beijing: Minzu, 2000), and Longlian 隆蓮, *Ru zhonglun jiangji. Fazun fashi jiang* 入中論講記。法尊法師講 (Hangzhou: Zhejiangsheng fojiao xiehui, 1995 [1984]). The latter is a complete translation of the *Madhyamakāvatāra*, written by the author on the basis of the teachings she received from Fazun in 1943. On this work, also see Bianchi, *The Iron Statue Monastery*, p. 38. On Fazun's translation, see the master's thesis by Dibeltulo (2005). In the 1950s Fazun translated another com-

mentary, *Ru zhonglun lüeshi* (cited in Wang-Toutain, "Quand les maîtres chinois s'éveillent," p. 722). It should be noted that Fazun also translated other works by Tsong kha pa, notably the *Drang nges legs bshad snying po*: Fazun, *Bian liao bu liao yi shanshuo zanglun* 辯了不了義善說藏論, Zongkaba dashi ji 4 (Beijing: Minzu, 2000); for an English translation, see Robert A.F. Thurman, *The Central Philosophy of Tibet: A Study and Translation of Jey Tsong Khapa's* Essence of True Eloquence (Princeton: Princeton Library of Asian Translations, 1991 [1984]).

97 Dingzhi, *Nenghai shangshi zhuan*, p. 8.

98 See for instance Chen and Deng, *Ershi shiji Zhongguo fojiao*, pp. 347 et seq.

99 After Wang-Toutain, "Quand les maîtres chinois s'éveillent," p. 726, French translation of Fazun, *Zhuzhe ru Zang de jingguo*, p. 125: "Partout, tous les disciples, qu'ils soient religieux ou laïcs, suivaient la mode selon laquelle seul le tantrisme était excellent. Moi aussi j'ai accompagné et servi le maître Dayong pendant quelques jours, [...] et bien que je n'ai pas reçu les deux grands cycles d'initiations qu'il avait ramenés du Japon, je trouvais que la saveur du tantrisme était déjà très forte. Seules les personnes qui ont déjà étudié peuvent comprendre les principes véritables du tantrisme en le pratiquant. [...] Mes bases sont très faibles, je n'ai pas obtenu d'image de *samādhi*, ni reçu de bénédiction et je n'ai pas non plus obtenu les grands pouvoirs extraordinaires des esprits, c'est pourquoi je suis très indifférent au tantrisme."

100 Among Fazun's few works on tantric topics, one has to mention his translation of Tsong kha pa's "Progressive Path of the Mantras" (*sngags rim*): *Mizongdao cidi guanglun* 密宗道次第廣論, Zongkaba dashi ji 2 (Beijing: Minzu, 2000) and *Mizongdao cidi lun* 密宗道次論, Zongkaba dashi ji 5 (Beijing: Minzu, 2000). For English translations on the first two sections on *kriyā* and *caryā* tantra, see Jeffrey Hopkins, trans., *Tantra in Tibet* (Ithaca, NY: Snow Lion, 1987 [1977]), and *The Yoga of Tibet* (Ithaca, NY: Snow Lion, 1987 [1981]); my thanks to M.T. Kapstein for acquainting me with these books. Fazun is also credited with the *Wucidi lun*, a translation of Tsong kha pa's commentary on the *Guhyasamājatantra* (cited by Wang-Toutain, "Quand les maîtres chinois s'éveillent," p. 722).

101 Wang-Toutain, "Quand les maîtres chinois s'éveillent," p. 727: "sa pratique, suivant en cela les précepts de la tradition, demeura secrète." On the basis of such considerations, Wang-Toutain questions whether Fazun could be said to have belonged to the movement of "Tantric Rebirth," and concludes her argument in saying: "La tendance à classer le maître Fazun parmi les maîtres tantriques pourrait donc être totalement justifiée, mais à la condition qu'elle ne soit pas restrictive et que l'on prenne également en considération l'énorme activité qu'eut ce maître dans la diffusion de l'enseignement exotérique des traditions indiennes et tibétaines en Chine."

102 See Wang-Toutain, "Quand les maîtres chinois s'éveillent," p. 721.

103 On this issue, Françoise Wang-Toutain, "Quand les maîtres chinois s'éveillent," p. 724, informs us that Nenghai created a "tradition herméneutique chinoise du *Lam rim*, toujours vivante de nos jours." See, for instance, Nenghai, *Sanxue jianglu*, pp. 1–164; and *Jiaoli chuji*, pp. 305–364.

104 Dingzhi, *Nenghai shangshi zhuan*, p. 44.

105 Also see: Taishō 1429–1431, 1434, 1804–1808. The *Dharmagupta Prātimokṣa* includes 248 precepts for monks and 354 precepts for nuns, whereas the version belonging to the *Mūlasarvāstivāda* tradition has 250 precepts for monks and 348 for

nuns. On the *Prātimokṣa* in the *Dharmaguptakavinaya*, refer to Longlian, "Biejietuo jie" 別解脫戒, in *Zhongguo fojiao* 中國佛教 (Shanghai: Dongfang, 1996), vol. 4, pp. 405–411. On the monastic discipline according to the Tibetan tradition, see Fazun, *Bichu xue chu.*

106   For instance, references to the *Dharmaguptakavinaya* are to be found in the following among Nenghai's exoteric works: *Sanxue jianglu*, pp. 165–167; *Zai jia lü yao*, pp. 183–230 and 231–244; and *Sifenlü zang si Ahan ji song.* Further, in works belonging to the lower tantras, such as the *Wuzi zhenyan*, Nenghai referred to the most common Chinese version of the Vinaya: Nenghai, *Wenshu wuzi genben zhenyan niansongfa*, pp. 11–14; and *Wenshu wuzi genbenzhenyan niansongfa jianglu*, pp. 7–8.

107   See, for instance, Nenghai, *Jiedinghui jibensanxue*, pp. 101–171, and, for the *Wuzi zhenyan*, Nenghai, *Wenshu wuzi genben zhenyan niansongfa*, pp. 15–20; and *Wenshu wuzi genbenzhenyan niansongfa jianglu*, pp. 10–16. On the bodhisattva precepts in the Tibetan Buddhist tradition, see also Fazun, *Pusa jie pin shi.*

108   On the bodhisattva precepts of the *Brahmajālasūtra*, see Paul Demiéville, "Bosatsu-kai" 菩薩戒, in *Hōbōgirin: Dictionnaire encyclopédique du Bouddhisme d'après les sources chinoises et japonaises*, vol. 1 (Tōkyō: Maison Franco-Japonaise, 1930), pp. 142–147, and Longlian, "Pusa jieben" 菩薩戒本, in *Zhongguo fojiao* 中國佛教 (Shanghai: Dongfang, 1996), vol. 3, pp. 210–216. On modern Chinese monastic ordinations involving the conferral of the bodhisattva precepts, see Holmes Welch, *The Practice of Chinese Buddhism* (Cambridge: Harvard University Press, 1967), pp. 285–296, and Johannes Prip-Møller, *Chinese Buddhist Monasteries* (Hongkong: Hongkong University Press, 1973 [1937]), pp. 312, 324–326, 344 et seq.

109   See Nenghai, *Zai jia lü yao*, pp. 239–240, and Longlian's essay in the same work, pp. 209–215.

110   See Nenghai, *Jiedinghui jibensanxue*, pp. 217–309, and Longlian's notes based on the master's teachings in Nenghai, *Sanxue jianglu*, pp. 278–353.

111   See, for instance, Nenghai, *Jiaoli chuji*, pp. 229–268, on the chapter of Samantabhadra's vow, and pp. 269–303, on the twenty-second chapter of the *Avataṃsakasūtra.*

112   On the *Wuzi zhenyan* (Nenghai, *Wenshu wuzi genben zhenyan niansongfa*), see my earlier study: "Arapacana-Mañjuśrī."

113   Some examples are the following terms, which are well known among Chinese Buddhists: *jiachi* (Skt. *adhiṣṭhāna*, Tib. *byin rlabs*), *mantuluo* (Skt. *maṇḍala*, Tib. *dkyil 'khor*), *mingwang* (Skt. *vidyārāja*, Tib. *rig pa'i rgyal po*), together with most of the mantra syllables and the names of various deities (among which the different titles and names of Mañjuśrī, taken from the Chinese version of the *Mañjuśrīnāmasaṃgīti*, are particularly noteworthy).

114   Nenghai, *Wenshu wuzi genben zhenyan niansongfa*, pp. 1–2. The four immensurables (Ch. *si wuliang xin*, Skt. *catvāri apramāṇāni*, Tib. *tshad med bzhi*) are: 1) compassion (Ch. *ci*, Skt. *maitrī*, Tib. *byams pa*); 2) love (Ch. *bei*, Skt. *karuṇā*, Tib. *snying rje*); 3) joy (Ch. *xi*, Skt. *muditā*, Tib. *dga' ba*); 4) equanimity (Ch. *she*, Skt. *upekṣā*, Tib. *btang snyoms*). See, for instance, Étienne Lamotte, *Le Traité de la Grande Vertu de Sagesse de Nāgārjuna* (Louvain: Muséon, 1944), pp. 1239 et seq.

115   Nenghai, *Wenshu wuzi genben zhenyan niansongfa*, p. 9.

116   Nenghai, *Wenshu wuzi genben zhenyan niansongfa*, p. 11.

117   Nenghai, *Wenshu wuzi genben zhenyan niansongfa*, pp. 13–14.

118 Nenghai, *Wenshu wuzi genben zhenyan niansongfa*, pp. 11–22.

119 Nenghai, *Wenshu wuzi genben zhenyan niansongfa*, p. 62.

120 This expression often occurs in Tibetan texts in connection with the generation of *bodhicitta*. It refers to the reflection that all sentient beings have been our mothers in previous lives. With this, one generates a feeling of gratitude for each sentient being, whether they be friends, enemies, or unknown persons. Realizing that, like oneself, they all have the wish to achieve happiness and avoid suffering, one decides to achieve enlightenment for the benefit of all. The choice to translate the Tibetan expression as "our mother and father sentient beings" is generalized throughout Nenghai's work, as is found also in his Chinese version of the *Gurupūjā* (Nenghai, *Shangshi wushang gongyang guanxingfa* 上師無上供養觀行法 [Shanghai: Shanghaishi fojiao xiehui, 1990]); in Longlian, *Sanguiyi guan*; and in the "*Sādhana* of the Solitary Deity Yamāntaka" (Nenghai, *Wenshu Daweide jingang benzun xiuxing chengjiu fa*).

121 In Nenghai's text (*Wenshu wuzi genben zhenyan niansongfa*, pp. 24–27), the "seven-point cause and effect method of Atiśa" is divided into "six correct contemplations" and a conclusion: 1) Recognize others as mothers (*zhimu*, lit. "know mothers"); 2) "Recollect their kindness" (*nianen*); 3) "Repay their kindness" (*baoen*); 4) Love all sentient beings (*beixin*, lit. "love full mind"); 5) Generate compassion (*cixin*, lit. "compassionate mind"); 6) Generate the "unusual mind" (*zengshang xin*) to benefit them; and, in conclusion, 7) Generate the *bodhicitta* (*faxin*). See also Tenzin Gyatso, *Path to Bliss*, pp. 150–160.

122 For instance, this method is included in Nenghai's version of the *Gurupūjā*: Nenghai, *Shangshi wushang gongyang guanxingfa*, pp. 49–50.

123 See Nenghai, *Wenshu Daweide jingang benzun xiuxing chengjiu fa*. For an Italian translation and an analysis of this *sādhana*, see Bianchi, "The 'Sādhana of the Glorious Solitary Hero Yamāntaka-Vajrabhairava' in China." My thanks to Jean-Luc Achard for helping me with the comparison of the Chinese text with its Tibetan version.

124 Among many examples, I note here the names employed to refer to the five Jinas and to the bodhisattvas, as well as more specific cases such as the names for Brahmā (Ch. Fantian, Tib. Tshangs pa), Indra (Ch. Dishi, Tib. Dbang po), Rudra (Ch. Dazizaitian, Tib. Drag po), Sarasvatī (Ch. Miaoyin nü, Tib. Dbyangs can ma), and Viṣṇu (Ch. Bianrutian, Tib. Khyab 'jug). As for the categories of beings: *dharmapāla* (Tib. *chos skyong*) is translated as *hufa shen*; *rākṣasa* (Tib. *srin po*) as *luocha*; *vetāla* (Tib. *ro langs*) as *qishi gui*; *vidyādhara* (Tib. *rig pa* ['dzin pa]) as *chiming*; *yakṣa* (Tib. *gnod spyin*) as *yecha*; *yogin* (Tib. *rnal 'byor pa*) as *yujia zhe*; and *yoginī* (Tib. *rnal 'byor ma*) as *yujia mu*. Note that, here and below, the corresponding Tibetan terminology is taken from the Tibetan version of the same *sādhana*.

125 A noteworthy example is Nenghai's choice to render the Tibetan term for the directional protectors (Skt. *dikpāla*, Tib. *phyogs skyong*) with *hufa hufang* (lit. *dharmapāla* and *lokapāla*), or simply with *hufang* (*lokapāla*). Similarly, wherever the Tibetan text has the term *krodha* (Tib. *khro bo*), "wrathful," he alternatively employs the correct translation of it (*fennu*) or uses the Chinese term for *vidyārāja* (*mingwang*), which seems to be absent in the Tibetan version of the *sādhana*. It was probably chosen by Nenghai because it recalls particularly terrifying forms of divinity to a Chinese mind.

126 Transliterations of Tibetan names are: Gere nü (Tib. Gau rī ma) for the female deity Gaurī; Renpo xierao shizi shi (Tib. Rong pa Shes rab Seng ge) for the name of a Tibetan master of the lineage; *kangzhuma* (Tib. *mkha' 'gro ma*) for *ḍākinī*; *mamu* (Tib. *ma mo*) for *mātṛkā*, chthonic goddesses.

127 Nenghai in particular uses translation to render the names of the masters of the lineage; see Nenghai, *Wenshu Daweide jingang benzun xiuxing chengjiu fa*, pp. 2a1–3a5 and 16b4–18a6. Other examples (some are neologisms created by Nenghai, but others are translation conventions that were established earlier): *feixing zun* ("those who move by flying"), *kongxing nü* ("female [deities] moving in ether"), and *tianfei* ("those flying in the sky") for *ḍākinī*; *dachengdao* (Tib. *grub pa*) for *mahāsiddha*; *guandingfo* or, more correctly, *guanding sheng* for *abhiṣekadevatā*; *dizhu* or *shentong shouyu* (Tib. *zhing skyong*) for *kṣetrapāla*, "realm protector."

128 Thus, for instance, the expression "our mother and father sentient beings" also recurs in this *sādhana*.

129 Sometimes Nenghai employed metaphors or unintelligible transliterations from Tibetan to refer to concepts or images which, though explicit in the Tibetan text, he probably believed to be too "strong" for a Chinese mind. This particularly is seen with regard to sexual images; for instance, the erect phallus of a deity, which is explicitly described in the Tibetan text, is rendered by Nenghai with expressions such as "vigorous and imposing pestle" (*chushi wei zhuang*), "upright vigorous pestle" (*chushi xiangshang shuli*), or "stuck out belly" (*tingfu*). Elsewhere Nenghai refers to the phallus using the Chinese term *yuan*, probably to be understood in its meaning of "head." Similarly, while in the Tibetan text the vagina is indicated by the common metaphor of the lotus flower, Nenghai refers to it using the obscure expression *kunti*, "[the trigram] *kun*'s body," which in Taoist and Yijing traditions indicates the quintessence of feminine. In cases of gruesome contents, Nenghai chose to transliterate the Tibetan terms for the "inner offerings" (i.e., foul and macabre substances, such as urine, blood, human meat, and so on), no doubt because he wished to hide their meaning from beginners and the uninitiated.

130 As an example, in Nenghai's transliteration of part of the root mantra of Vajrabhairava (Ch. *Weng yama raza saduomaiya*; Sk. *Oṃ yama rāja sadomeya*, pronounced in Tib. *Oṃ yama rādza sadomeya*) the syllable *ra*, which is absent in Chinese language, was rendered by a composition formed of the two Chinese characters *ri* and *a*, following in this the traditional Chinese way of indicating pronunciation by joining initial of one character to final of another (Ch. *fanqie*). Note that Nenghai relied on the Sichuanese reading of Chinese characters.

131 See Nenghai, "Daweide Wenshu chengjiu fangbian lüeyin."

132 At the beginning of the twenty-first century, Nenghai's tradition is still alive in a number of monasteries which emulate the organization and activities of the monastic communities founded by the master, some of which I have been able to personally visit over the last decade. Three of the original *jingang daochang* are still active nowadays (Jixiangsi on Wutai shan, the Shanghai *jingang daochang*, and the Tiexiangsi), while the other four monasteries were definitely closed during the 1950s and 1960s. The Jincisi has recently been transferred to the Shijing monastery, in Longquan hills (Sichuan). Similarly, following the abandonment of the *jingang daochang* of Mianzhu, a new center of Dge lugs pa practice was established in the nearby monastery of

Xiangfusi. A nun from the Tiexiangsi informed me that, according to government regulation, monasteries in Nenghai's tradition cannot be more than seven monastic units. For this reason, in recent times only two other *jingang daochang* have been established: the tantric section within the Zhaojuesi of Chengdu, headed by Qingding until 1999, and the two compounds of the Duobaojiangsi (near Ningbo), whose abbot is Zhimin, one of Nenghai's direct disciples. It should be added that on Wutai shan, apart from the Jixiangsi, nowadays there are six other monasteries belonging to Nenghai's tradition, which are probably considered as a single unit; some are newly built while others were already connected with Nenghai during his lifetime. For a description of some of Nenghai's monasteries still active in contemporary times, see Bianchi, *The Iron Statue Monastery*, pp. 57–70; "L'insegnamento tantrico del 'lama cinese' Nenghai," pp. 116–136; and "Zhimin e il monastero Duobaojiang: Un ulteriore esempio di pratica *dGe lugs pa* nella Cina contemporanea," in A.M. Palermo, ed., *La Cina e l'Altro* (Naples: Università degli Studi di Napoli "L'Orientale"—Il Torcoliere, 2006), pp. 243–254.

133 The symbolic meaning of the yellow robes was explained to me by Zhimin, abbot of Duobaojiang Monastery. Another possible interpretation would connect Nenghai's choice of this color, which is uncommon not only in China but also in Tibet, with the Theravāda Buddhist tradition, whose monks often dress in saffron or ochre yellow.

134 It is noteworthy that a similar mixture of Chinese and Tibetan elements is shared by the monasteries belonging to the Tibetan Buddhist tradition founded in Chinese territory during the Qing dynasty, with precedents reaching back to the Ming (as seen in Karl Debreczeny's chapter above). Refer to Anne Chayet, *Les Temples de Jehol et leurs modèles tibétains*, Synthèse 19 (Paris: Editions Recherche sur les Civilisations, 1985), and Paola Mortari Vergara Caffarelli, *Architettura in "stile tibetano" dei Ch'ing: Diffusione di un linguaggio architettonico di tipo "occidentale" nell'Asia Centrale* (Rome: Istituto di Studi dell'India e dell'Asia Orientale Università di Roma, 1982); on the common structure of Chinese Buddhist monasteries, see Prip-Møller, *Chinese Buddhist Monasteries*, pp. 1–195. We can thus suppose that these monasteries, and particularly Beijing's Yonghegong and Huangsi, as well as some of the sites on Wutai shan, must have inspired Nenghai and later his disciples in the construction of their own monasteries. Despite this, I believe that the latter represent a unique style, typical of Nenghai's tradition. Among the outstanding features of Nenghai's *jingang daochang*: most of the buildings have red halls with golden roofs, on the top of which a "Dharma wheel" is placed, as in Tibetan monasteries; the halls are furnished with long wooden benches adorned with a lectern, so as to allow chanting in Tibetan style; long flags and banners hang from the ceiling, and, on the altars, offerings are laid out according to the Tibetan tradition; and Tibetan liturgical objects and musical instruments stand side by side with Chinese ones. Nearly all of these monasteries have a Great Master hall (*Dashidian*), devoted to the cult of Tsong kha pa. As for sacred images on the altars and walls, statues and paintings in Chinese style are mixed with others that are clearly Tibetan, and in most of the cases connected with the peculiar doctrinal tradition and tantric lineage of Nenghai: one finds, for instance, Khang gsar Rin po che, Nenghai and disciples, Lama Tsong kha pa, and other distinguished personalities within the Dge lugs

pa tradition, and, among other Tibetan deities, Yellow Mañjuśrī and Yamāntaka-Vajrabhairava.

135 On Jinci Monastery, see Chen Bing, *Xinbian fojiao cidian* 新編佛教辭典 (Beijing: Zhongguo shijieyu, 1994), p. 643; Dingzhi, *Nenghai shangshi zhuan*, pp. 17–20, 29–31, and 64–75; and Renjie's and Xingfa's essays in Qingding, Longlian, Zhaotong, et al., *Nenghai shangshi yonghuai lu*, pp. 70–82 and 52–54.

136 The Wenshuyuan is an important monastery of the Chan and Pure Land traditions situated in the center of Chengdu. See Chen Bing, *Xinbian fojiao cidian*, p. 642.

137 On the number of monks residing in the Jincisi, see Dingzhi, *Nenghai shangshi zhuan*, p. 20.

138 On Jincisi's five departments, and on everyday life within this monastery, see Dingzhi, *Nenghai shangshi zhuan*, pp. 65–70, and the essay by Renjie, in Qingding, Longlian, Zhaotong, et al., *Nenghai shangshi yonghuai lu*, pp. 52–54, 70–82. In 1940 Jincisi was visited by Rdo sbis dge bshes shes rab rgya mtsho (1884–1968), who is reported to have said: "Coming here makes me feel like I am actually in a Tibetan monastery!" (cited in Tuttle, *Tibetan Buddhists*, p. 214). According to Tuttle, *Tibetan Buddhists*, p. 296, note 115), in recent times it has reopened under the direction of a Khams pa lama.

139 The outer structure of the five departments, the organization of offices, and particularly the Chinese terms used to refer both to places and offices, were among the features derived from Chinese Buddhist conventions. For a comparison, see Welch, *The Practice of Chinese Buddhism*,.

140 On the organization of Tibetan monastic colleges, see, for instance: Georges Dreyfus, "Tibetan Scholastic Education and the Role of Soteriology," in *Journal of the International Association of Tibetan Studies* 20/1 (1997): 31–62; Melvyn C. Goldstein, "The Revival of Monastic Life in Drepung Monastery," in M.C. Goldstein and M.T. Kapstein eds. (1998), *Buddhism in Contemporary Tibet. Religious Revival and Cultural Identity* (Berkeley/Los Angeles/London: University of California Press, 1998), pp. 15–52, esp. 20–22; Li An-Che, "The Lamasery as an Educational Institution," in *Asiatic Review* 46 (1950): 915–922; and Giuseppe Tucci, *Le religioni del Tibet*, trans. S. Bonarelli (Milan: Mondadori, 1994 [1970]), p. 186. My thanks to M.T. Kapstein for acquainting me with these studies.

141 In Tibetan these five categories are as follows: (1) *tshad ma*; (2) *phar phyin*; (3) *dbu ma*; (4) *chos mngon pa*; and (5) *so sor thar pa* (Skt. *Prātimokṣa*). Refer, too, to Zhihua Yao's chapter above.

142 Since the Jincisi was a "large public monastery" (*shifang conglin*), it could not train unordained novices. The "Novice hall" was thus established by Nenghai in order to lodge and train those disciples between ages seven and twenty. On the large public monasteries in modern China, see Welch (1967: 3 *passim*).

143 For instance, the layman Song Limen held lessons on the *Gaoseng zhuan* (Biographies of Eminent Monks) and on the *Shiji*; master Longguo on Chan literature; master Bianneng on *Abhidharma*; lama Xingshan on Tibetan language.

144 The *Mañjuśrīnāmasaṃgīti* (Tib. *'jam dpal mtshan brjod* or, simply, *mtshan brjod*), which was translated into Chinese under the Song, is nowadays chanted during the daily services in many of Nenghai's extant monasteries. The text is periodically reprinted both by the Zhaojuesi and the Shijingsi. For English translations from the

Tibetan version, see Ronald M. Davidson, "The Litany of names of Mañjuśrī," in M. Strickmann, ed., *Tantric and Taoist Studies in Honor of R.A. Stein* (Brussels: Institut Belge des Hautes Études Chinoises, 1981), vol. 1, pp. 1–69, and Alex Wayman, *Chanting the names of Mañjuśrī: The Mañjuśrī-nāmā-saṃgīti* (London: Shambhala, 1985). On the importance of this work within the Tibetan Buddhist tradition, also see Gnoli and Orofino, *Nāropā*, pp. 53–55.

145 In Nenghai's texts the Chinese term *jiaxing* usually designates preliminary practices, as for instance in the *Wuzi zhenyan*: Nenghai, *Wenshu wuzi genben zhenyan niansongfa*, p. 1.

146 See above, note 48.

147 Among the "higher acolytes" we may mention Zhaotong, Xianxue, Rongkong, Qingfo, and Xingfa, among others.

148 Among Nenghai's disciples who worked in these translation teams were Renguang, Zongyuan, Tongyi, Changhao, and the already mentioned Longlian. As an example, see the list of Longlian's translations commissioned by Nenghai in Bianchi, *The Iron Statue Monastery*, pp. 40–41.

149 See, for instance, Nenghai, *Putidao cidi kesong*.

150 The prohibition to eat meat comes from the prohibition to kill any living being, which is clearly stated in the *pārājikas* (the first section of the *Prātimokṣa* containing unpardonable misdeeds; four for monks and eight for nuns), in the ten precepts of the novitiate and in the six precepts of the *śikṣamāṇa*. Originally, monks ate only what was offered to them in the begging bowl. Therefore meat was eaten only if offered and only if the animal had not been killed purposely for the monk. This principle underlies contemporary Theravāda Buddhism as well. On the contrary, in China the Buddhist diet is strictly vegetarian. The prohibition to kill any living being extends to the monks' dress code as well. In Chinese Buddhism, unlike the Theravāda tradition, silk robes and leather shoes are prohibited. Tibetan Buddhists in principle should also follow a vegetarian regimen, however, because of the particular climatic conditions and the scarcity of vegetables in Tibet, monks often eat non-vegetarian dishes. On the topic of meals and vegetarianism in Chinese Buddhist monasteries, see Welch, *The Practice of Chinese Buddhism*, pp. 111–113, and John Kieschnick, *The Eminent Monk: Buddhist Ideals in Medieval Chinese Hagiography* (Honolulu: University of Hawai'i Press, 1997), particularly pp. 23–27. On strict vegetarianism and more generally on the respect of Vinaya regulations in Nenghai's monasteries in comparison to Tibetan monasteries on Wutai shan, see John E.C. Blofeld, *The Wheel of Life: The Autobiography of a Western Buddhist* (Boston: Shambhala, 1988), pp. 139–140.

151 The Vinaya rule forbidding one from eating after noon was accepted by Chinese Buddhists in order not to upset the hungry ghosts haunting the earth in the afternoon and evening hours. However, this rule was never universally respected by the Chinese Sangha, owing to the colder weather of China as compared to India, and hence adherence to it relied more on individual choice. To honor this rule, in many Chinese monasteries the meal taken after noon is not considered formal, i.e., it does not require a ritual, and consists of a plain soup without any solid food. As for Nenghai's *jingang daochang*, speaking from my own experience in some of them (Tiexiangsi and Duobaojiangsi), it seems that the *guowu bu shi* rule is strictly applied, even if

light meals such as soups, sweetened tea, or hot water are admitted. For an analysis of the ritual of meals in one of the extant monasteries of Nenghai, see Bianchi, *The Iron Statue Monastery*, pp. 81–83. Refer also to Welch, *The Practice of Chinese Buddhism*, pp. 111–113.

152 The bimonthly recitation of the precepts (Skt. *uposadha*, Ch. *busa*), which involves the recitation of the complete version of the *Prātimoksa* (a short version is individually recited by monks or nuns as soon as they get up), is stipulated by a Vinaya rule and was originally conceived as a confessional ritual.

153 The summer retreat or *varsa*, which spans the period from the middle of the fourth to the middle of the seventh month, originated in India to avoid the movement of monks during the rainy season. Later it became a period of intensive religious practice and study, and this is the function it has maintained in China, where the concept of retreat was abandoned. During my visits to some of the extant monasteries of Nenghai's tradition, I could verify that they are trying to restore the original meaning of the retreat, as far as the monastic community is concerned (monks and nuns cannot thus leave the monastery at their will), but not with regard to lay people, who according to the Vinaya should have only a limited access to the monastic compound during this time. In Nenghai's monasteries, however, lay visits seem to be more numerous than ever during the summer. On the summer retreat in China and in Nenghai's monasteries, see respectively Welch, *The Practice of Chinese Buddhism*, pp. 109–110, and Bianchi, *The Iron Statue Monastery*, pp. 87–89. On the Tibetan tradition, see Tucci, *Le religioni del Tibet*, pp. 166–168.

154 On *homa* rites in the Tibetan Buddhist tradition, see Robert Beer, *The Encyclopedia of Tibetan Symbols and Motifs* (London: Serindia, 1999), pp. 335–341; Lessing, *Yung-ho-kung*, pp. 150–161; and Tadeusz Skorupski, "Tibetan homa rites," in F. Staal, ed., *Agni: The Vedic Ritual of the Fire Altar* (Berkeley: Asian Humanities Press, 1983), vol. 2, pp. 403–417. On these rituals within the tantric practice of Yamāntaka-Vajrabhairava, see Sharpa Tulku and Richard Perrott, *A Manual of Ritual Fire Offerings* (Dharamsala: Library of Tibetan Works and Archives, 1987), and Bianchi, "L'insegnamento tantrico del 'lama cinese' Nenghai," pp. 180–182. On the fire offering in the Chinese and Japanese Buddhist traditions, see Michel Strickmann, *Mantras et mandarins: Le bouddhisme tantrique en Chine* (Paris: Gallimard, 1996), pp. 337–368, and Michael Saso, *Homa Rites and Mandala Meditation in Tendai Buddhism* (Honolulu: University of Hawai'i, 1991).

155 A noteworthy example is his translation of the Vajrabhairava tantric corpus, which was clearly influenced both in style and lexicon by Qing-period translations, as for instance those sponsored by the Manchu Prince Xian Qinwang (1763). Yet, as showed in Bianchi, "The 'Sādhana of the Glorious Solitary Hero Yamāntaka-Vajrabhairava' in China," these influences were less evident in Nenghai than they were in other Republican translations of the same corpus of scriptures.

PART IV
CHINA AND THE DALAI LAMA
IN THE TWENTIETH CENTURY

∼

10: The Thirteenth Dalai Lama's Visit to Beijing in 1908: In Search of a New Kind of Chaplain-Donor Relationship*

Fabienne Jagou

On 30 June 1908, the United States' Minister to China, W.W. Rockhill, wrote to President Theodore Roosevelt, "The special interest to me is in that I have probably been a witness to the overthrow of the temporal power of the Dalai Lama..." And: "After the Dalai Lama's departure from China's capital, the correspondent of the London *Times* in Peking... writes... [that] the visit has coincided with the end of his temporal power, but he has been treated with the dignity befitting his spiritual office."[1]

THE THIRTEENTH DALAI LAMA (1876–1933), then 32 years old, arrived in Beijing on September 27, 1908. The only previously recorded visit of a Dalai Lama to the Manchu court had occurred two and a half centuries earlier, in 1652, after the accession of the Manchu dynasty to the throne of China (in 1644) and as the Fifth Dalai Lama (1617–1682) became the ruler of Tibet (in 1642).

When the Fifth Dalai Lama met the Shunzhi Emperor (r. 1644–1662) in 1652 he was received with great honor, as befitting his status as a central figure in the developing relations between China, Mongolia, and Tibet. The Fifth Dalai Lama and Gushri Khan (d. 1655), the chief of the Khoshot Mongols, were already in an established political-religious relationship: Gushri Khan had conquered a civil war-shaken Tibet and ceremonially offered it to the Fifth Dalai Lama, an event that marked the beginning of the Gelukpa school's governance. Though the Dalai Lama had at first only assumed spiritual power, turning actual administrative duties over to a regent (Sonam Chöpel, d. 1655) and military duties to Gushri Khan, his strong personality enabled him to become increasingly involved in politics, and indeed his visit to the Qing court could only heighten his prestige. The Qing Empire in China was still at odds with groups of Mongols who refused to submit and threatened the Manchus from the North. The Tibetans, because of their long relationship with the Mongols (we should remember that it was the Mongols who gave the Dalai Lama his title),[2] seemed to offer an avenue to secure Mongol submission. The Qing Emperor's wish was to make himself patron of the Tibetan Buddhist Gelukpa school, to which the Mongols also belonged.

Tibetan political conditions changed radically after the deaths of Gushri Khan in 1655 and the Fifth Dalai Lama in 1682. During the next century, the Qianlong Emperor (r. 1736–1795) became more interested in Tibetan Buddhism, patronizing monasteries, printing Buddhist scriptures, and promoting Buddhist monks. The Manchus exercised a de facto protectorate in Tibet from 1721 to 1793, and established an administrative office in Lhasa to serve as an intermediary between the Dalai Lama and the Manchu Emperor in the imperial capital at Beijing. The power of this office gradually decreased, however, so that by the end of the nineteenth century the amban (the Manchu residents in Lhasa) were impotent. Moreover, with the end of the Mongol threat and successive regencies with weak Dalai Lamas at the head of Tibet (until 1895, when the Thirteenth Dalai Lama was enthroned), "Tibet had become an uninteresting protectorate" for the Manchus.[3]

This began to change at the beginning of the twentieth century. The onset of the "great game" in Central Asia and the arrival of the British on the Tibetan political and military scene prompted the Qing court to renew its interest in Tibet: it was time to reestablish contacts with the spiritual and temporal head of the Gelukpa school, now the Thirteenth Dalai Lama.

Most Western authors who have briefly compared the visits of the two Dalai Lamas to Beijing note that the Thirteenth was not so well received as the Fifth had been.[4] This view derives from a comparison of Chinese and Tibetan records of the journeys of the two pontiffs to China. According to James Hevia, "the dimensions along which they [the account of the audiences] diverge involve ritual practice."[5] While Chinese sources are silent about the protocol adopted to receive the Fifth Dalai Lama in 1652, the Fifth Dalai Lama's own biography carefully details his reception as an honored visitor. Conversely, the Chinese archives and newspapers are prolix about the rituals adopted and adapted to the status of the political and religious leader of Tibet during his visit to Beijing in 1908, but the Thirteenth Dalai Lama's biography is silent about his treatment before the Qing court, mentioning only that he was well accommodated and entertained at the Yellow Temple

(Xihuangsi). The lack of information about protocol and ritual in his biography, however, suggests that the pontiff was not satisfied with the treatment he had received.

The main challenge during such meetings was to impose a hierarchical pattern that would suit both the circumstances and each party's hierarchical conception of itself. This challenge arose in every meeting between a Manchu Emperor and a Buddhist master (the Paṇchen Lama or the Mongol Khutughtu for example), but the situation became more sensitive when a Dalai Lama met a Manchu Emperor.[6] The hierarchical pattern was also complicated by the unusual form of governance of the Qing court when the two visits of the Tibetan pontiffs occurred. In 1653, the Shunzhi Emperor (r. 1644–1662) was 15 years old, while in 1908 the Guangxu Emperor (r. 1875–1908), who was then 38 years old, was inefficient and the Empress Dowager Cixi (1835–1908) was the dynastic head.[7]

Hierarchically, from the Manchu Emperor's perspective, he was to act as the sovereign, with the Dalai Lama as his subordinate. In the Tibetan cultural and religious concept of politics, however, the chaplain-donor relationship implied that the "patron"—the emperor of China—was subordinate to the chaplain.[8] This tension was subject to many interpretations and adaptations over the course of the relationship between the Dalai Lamas and the emperors. According to one point of view, both the Manchu Emperor and the Dalai Lama recognized one another as embodiments of bodhisattvas: the Dalai Lama was an emanation of Avalokiteśvara, the bodhisattva of compassion, while the Qing Emperor was Mañjuśrī, the embodiment of wisdom. In this sense, as beings partaking of an enlightened condition, both were equals. From another standpoint, however, only the Dalai Lama could serve as the spiritual ruler who recognized in the Qing Emperor a "universal king of the Buddhist Law" (Skt. Cakravartirāja, Tib. 'khor los sgyur ba'i rgyal po), just as was the case at the beginning of the reign of the Fifth Dalai Lama.[9] The Qing Emperor was thus expected to act as a protector of the Buddhist Law (dharma) by giving offerings to monasteries, editing Buddhist scriptures, or helping Tibet militarily. For his part, the Dalai Lama was then supposed to fulfill the function of the emperor's religious superior, giving him teachings or dedicating prayers to him.[10] The "universal king of the Buddhist Law" could therefore easily claim ascendancy over the Dalai Lama (especially during interregnum periods, when either there was no Dalai Lama or the claimant was still in his minority), who needed help to maintain his Buddhist order as the head of Tibet.

A third interpretation of their relationship considered the Dalai Lama as a temporal ruler, as the "king of the Law" (*dharmarāja, chos kyi rgyal po*) by definition,[11] the king who upholds the Buddhist Law within his estate. As such, the Dalai Lama was presumed to act as an independent ruler equal to the emperor of China. However, because the emperor of China had been recognized by the Tibetans as the universal king of the Buddhist Law, the Dalai Lama could also be seen as his subordinate.[12] He acted first as the temporal ruler of Tibet during his audiences with the empress dowager and Emperor Guangxu, then as the spiritual ruler of Tibet and the chaplain of the dowager at her birthday ceremony, and later of Emperor Xuantong (r. 1909–1912) at his enthronement.

In his recent study in Chinese, "A brief account of the Thirteenth Dalai Lama's visit to the Qing court,"[13] Chen Qiangyi focuses on the Dalai Lama's reception by the emperor and the empress dowager. He describes the Qing government's extensive preparations for the reception, the audiences themselves, and the gifts exchanged, but he passes over the Dalai Lama's religious activities in silence. This absence is best explained by the fact that the reports in the Chinese archives concentrate on state protocol and generally ignore the Thirteenth Dalai Lama's own activities between imperial audiences, and even his religious activities connected with the imperial family.

The Dalai Lama's visit to Beijing lasted eighty-four days. The first scheduled imperial audience was canceled because of a dispute over rituals, but after a period of debate, he met members of the imperial family on three separate occasions: on October 14, 1908, he was received in the Renshou Palace by Empress Dowager Cixi for five minutes, and then by the Guangxu Emperor for four minutes. Following this, on October 30, 1908, a banquet was organized in his honor at the Ziguang pavilion.

The Qing archives cite two major religious acts by the Thirteenth Dalai Lama. First, on November 2, 1908, he was invited to celebrate Cixi's birthday and to say long-life prayers. Eighteen days later, he performed the second religious act recorded in the archives: on November 20, 1908, the Dalai Lama recited prayers after the deaths of both Cixi and Guangxu. Yet many more religious activities are discussed in Tibetan sources, which are quite different in nature from the Qing archives. These Tibetan sources are mostly found in the official *Biography of the Thirteenth Dalai Lama*.[14] I also have consulted the original text of the long-life prayer he gave at the enthronement of Emperor Xuantong, located in the Fu Ssŭ-nien Library of the Institute of History and Philology, Academia Sinica, Taipei.[15] Altogether, the information found in these historical and religious archives allows an analysis of both the religious and the political aspects of the Dalai Lama's 1908 visit.

The Thirteenth Dalai Lama
as a Political Visitor to China

At the end of the nineteenth century and the beginning of the twentieth the situation in Tibet seemed calm and unthreatening. In 1895, the Dalai Lama was coming of age, ready to become the temporal and spiritual ruler of Tibet. However, the situation outside Tibet was different. The 1895 Qing defeat at the hands of the Japanese dealt a blow to the legitimacy of Qing rule and prompted a radical reform movement. As the Qing lost control over peripheral territories and foreign concessions, the reform movement was aborted. The Boxer Uprising and the ensuing invasion of the Eight Powers in 1901 shook the Throne, and a new reform program was consequently inaugurated that same year. The Throne promised that a constitution would be eventually promulgated and that the Han and Manchu subjects of the empire would be treated as equal citizens.

China was also threatened by the possibility of British penetration through Tibet from India. The British took a new interest in Tibet when the Tibetans ignored the trade treaties signed between England and China in 1886 and 1890.[16] Moreover, the British were suspicious of a Buriat monk, Agvan Dorjieff (1853–1938), who was close to the Thirteenth Dalai Lama, and who they thought was the Czar's envoy and thus proof of Russian interest in Tibet. This prompted a British mission, led by Colonel Younghusband (1863–1942) and Captain O'Connor (1870–1943), to push into Tibet in 1903: from the Indian-Tibetan border, the British attempted to obtain permission from Tibetan ministers to open roads and trading markets, but were unsuccessful, having been unable to communicate directly with the Thirteenth Dalai Lama.

A year later, in the spring of 1904, Colonel Younghusband led a successful raid into Tibet with five thousand soldiers. The British troops overthrew Gyantse, the first place where they met resistance in Tibetan territory, and then proceeded rapidly to Lhasa, determined to negotiate directly with the Dalai Lama.[17] Frightened, the Dalai Lama appointed Meru Lozang Gyeltsen, the Ganden Tri Rinpoché,[18] as regent and fled to Mongolia. The Thirteenth Dalai Lama became hostage to the conflicts surrounding the advancement of British trade interests and the negotiation of borders between the empires of British India and China, and was unwittingly involved in the events that led to the end of the Manchu dynasty and the emergence of a new political and economic map of Asia. The Dalai Lama's first departure from Tibet was thus the prelude to a long period of exile that started in Mongolia (1904), continued in China (1908), and finally led him to British India (1910).

During the Thirteenth Dalai Lama's exile in Mongolia, the British and the Ganden Tri Rinpoché negotiated the terms of the Tibetan surrender without Qing participation. At the end of the negotiations, on September 7, 1904, the Tibetans ratified the two treaties signed between England and China in 1886 and 1890 and were obliged to open two new trade markets: one in Gyantse, in Tsang Province, and the other in Gartok, in Ngari Province. The Tibetan government also agreed not to negotiate with other countries without the agreement of the British and, finally, to pay a war indemnity. In 1906, the Lhasa Convention of 1904 was amended so that the Qing could add their signature to it, also paying to the British the Tibetan war indemnity. In this way, the British kept their trade advantages, while the new text referred to Tibet as a Chinese region. The British thus committed themselves to avoiding direct negotiation with the Tibetan government.[19]

Tibet was at the heart of a changing world where alliances were being turned upside down. The Russians saw in the Lhasa Convention the establishment of a British protectorate over Tibet and decided to extend their own sphere of influence. Following its defeat in the Russo-Japanese war, Russia ceded parts of Manchuria and Korea to Japan in 1907, but at the same time they pushed their interests into Mongolia. Russia and Britain then signed a treaty demarcating each country's zone of influence over Persia, Afghanistan, and Tibet. This treaty included the bilateral agreement "to respect the integrity of Tibet and not intervene in Tibetan affairs." Both parties recognized Qing sovereignty over Tibet and agreed not to negotiate directly with the Tibetan government without first obtaining Qing permission to do so.[20] The Qing were thus able to reassert their control over the Tibetan government through the international recognition thus accorded and thanks to the exile of the Thirteenth Dalai Lama.

In Mongolia, however, the Dalai Lama began to contemplate returning to Tibet. After the Dalai Lama had spent one year in Urga, the Jebtsundampa Khutughtu (1870–1924)—the highest spiritual authority in Mongolia—began feeling encumbered by his presence, as this virtuous and highly respected guest drained religious offerings that were previously due to himself. At the same time, the Tibetan Ministerial Cabinet sent a delegation to Urga to urge the Dalai Lama to return to Tibet. Therefore, the latter left Urga in May 1906, traveling back to Tibet via Beijing. During this journey, he stopped for one year at the Kumbum monastery in Qinghai, within the Tibetan province of Amdo, and then stayed for a further few months at Wutai shan, in Shanxi Province.

During his sojourn in Mongolia, in Amdo, and in China, the Thirteenth

Dalai Lama remained well-informed of events in Tibet and on Tibet's borders, as he still controlled Tibetan policy, and still sent orders to the Ganden Tri Rinpoché, the regent.[21] Therefore, he knew that after his departure, both the Manchu and the British had, for the first time in history, tried to diminish his political and spiritual role in Tibet by using the Ninth Panchen Lama (1883–1937) as his substitute for the conduct of Tibetan affairs. Although such a substitution was not altogether unprecedented, in that a previous Panchen had served as regent in 1844–1845, it also reflected prior occasions during which the Manchu and British had relied on the Panchen instead of the Dalai Lama.[22]

In all events, the Manchu order depriving the Thirteenth Dalai Lama of his title was very brief and never effective: Cixi and Guangxu addressed him as "Dalai Lama" when they met him,[23] and the Qing court never issued an order reestablishing the Thirteenth Dalai Lama as the Dalai Lama, yet he clearly retained the temporal and political powers associated with the title.[24] The Qing had confused title and function by issuing the order to "deprive him of his title of Dalai Lama," understood to be the designation of the Tibetan spiritual and temporal ruler, and to have the Panchen Lama act temporarily in his place (*zhu jiang Dalai Lama minghao zanxing gequ, bing zhu Banchan E'erdeni zan she*).[25] This confusion reveals just how ignorant the Qing court was of the situation in Tibet at the beginning of the twentieth century. In any case, to enforce the court's orders the amban Youtai had the support of the British,[26] who were irritated by the Thirteenth Dalai Lama's constant refusal to respond to their letters and attempts to negotiate.[27] Youtai sent agents to look for the Panchen Lama and bring him back to Lhasa to take charge of Tibetan affairs, but the Panchen Lama refused to visit Lhasa on the pretext that he was required in Tsang because of the presence of British troops in Gyantse.[28]

Soon after, the Panchen Lama asked the amban for permission to visit the emperor and empress dowager in Beijing, an action that may have prompted the Dalai Lama's decision to visit the Chinese capital first.[29] The Ninth Panchen Lama knew that his January 1906 trip to British India had been misunderstood by the Qing, and the Panchen Lama wanted to explain his reasons directly to the court. Although the Tibetan reports of this trip contradicted themselves, the Chinese may have believed that the British forced the Ninth Panchen Lama to visit India.[30] The British used the conflicting visits to Beijing to highlight the disagreements between the Dalai Lama and the Panchen Lama, claiming that the return of the Dalai Lama to Tibet might disrupt the conduct of Tibetan affairs. Zhang Yintang (1864–1935), the new

Chinese vice-military governor (*fu dutong*) in Tibet, agreed, and he expressed this point of view to the court on November 9, 1906.[31]

The Ninth Panchen Lama was willing to visit Beijing (*bi jian*) to read longevity scriptures for the emperor and empress dowager, and he was ready to go there by the northern road through Nakchukha and China's Gansu province.[32] His request was initiated by Zhang Yintang, however, and not by the Panchen Lama himself, because Zhang did not want the Ninth Panchen Lama to change sides and support British views. The decision of the Thirteenth Dalai Lama, therefore, looks like a reaction to these events. The Qing government hesitated to receive either party in Beijing, waiting to see the reactions of the foreign powers. The British at the time were worried that the Dalai Lama might return to govern Tibet.[33] In the end, the Manchu postponed the possibility of either Tibetan Pontiff traveling to Beijing. The Dalai Lama was therefore ordered to stay at Wutai shan through the entire summer of 1908.

A Witness to the Tibetan Situation

The regent Ganden Tri Rinpoché suggested that another motive for the Dalai Lama's visit to Beijing may have been his desire to explain in person the Tibetan situation to the Qing court (*mian chen Xizang qingxing*).[34] The vagueness of this expression allows many interpretations. The Dalai Lama wanted China to recognize him as the independent spiritual and temporal ruler of Tibet, but he also knew that he had to find a protector for Tibet and renew the traditional chaplain-donor relationship between the Dalai Lama and the Qing Emperor, especially given that the Qing emperors had shown little interest in the Tibetan situation since the end of the eighteenth century. China's failure to help when Nepal invaded Tibet in 1855, or when the British arrived in Gyantse in 1904, signaled the end of the link between chaplain and donor.

On the other hand, the dismissal of Youtai and the appointment of Zhang Yintang suggested a new Manchu interest in Tibet. The Dalai Lama knew the Qing government had dismissed Youtai because he had neither participated in the negotiations between the Tibetans and British in 1904 nor protested against the signing of the Lhasa Convention (concluded without the agreement of Beijing). Zhang Yintang's appointment as vice military governor was the first example of a Han (and not a Manchu) being dispatched to Tibet. Zhang was born in Guangdong and had started his career as a secretary in the Grand Council, joining diplomatic missions to the United States in 1896 and Spain in 1897. He had also traveled to India in 1903 to negotiate with the British. After the treaty in Beijing was signed, Zhang Yintang was promoted to the fifth rank and appointed vice military governor of Tibet.

From exile, the Dalai Lama was able to communicate directly with the new vice military governor. In a correspondence from June of 1908, Zhang Yintang wrote both to affirm the Dalai Lama's request that he act benevolently toward the Tibetan people, and also to inform the Dalai Lama that he was preparing a reform project devoted to Tibetan welfare.[35] Zhang Yintang and the Thirteenth Dalai Lama had also met in Beijing, but there is no account of this meeting in the Chinese sources.[36] Meanwhile, because the Dalai Lama stayed at the Kumbum monastery in Amdo for a year and then at Wutai shan in Shanxi for six months, he could remain well informed of events in Kham province thanks to his many devotees in the area.

In October of the same year, Zhang informed Beijing that he was against the re-establishment of a "loose rein policy" (*jimi*) for the time being and would rather adopt a "quite strong policy" (*bu zhi you suo qianche*) at the beginning. Indeed, the exile of the Thirteenth Dalai Lama and the fact that Britain and Russia recognized Chinese suzerainty over Tibet gave the Qing the opportunity to reinforce their control over the Tibetan government. After the British invaded Lhasa, the Qing were conscious of the vulnerability of the southwest border, and attempted to take control of Kham. Zhao Erfeng (d. 1911), the dignitary in charge of the Chinese provinces of Sichuan and Yunnan (*Duban Chuan Dian bianwu dachen*), was given the responsibility to "pacify and collect the region" (*fuji difang*). Although the Tibetans resisted, Zhao and his troops forced Tibetan districts and towns under the Manchu administration.[37]

In telegrams justifying to the Qing court the Dalai Lama's trip to Beijing, Zhang Yintang cited arguments by the Ganden Tri Rinpoché that the Dalai Lama wished both to reaffirm his status as Tibet's only temporal and spiritual ruler and also to explain conditions in Tibet directly to the emperor. Although the sources do not directly reveal the key factors prompting the trip or the Qing's decision to issue a formal invitation, an analysis based on the imperial audiences can explain the purpose of the visit as it was seen by each party.

The Thirteenth Dalai Lama Received as the Supreme Ruler of Tibet

By rejecting imperial audiences obliging him to perform submissive rituals, the Thirteenth Dalai Lama posited himself as an autonomous ruler. The

Dalai Lama arrived at the Beijing train station on September 27, 1908, and was escorted to the Yellow Temple, which the Qing had renovated for him. The way from Wutai shan had been prepared by thousands of peasants. The road had been leveled, freed of every pebble, and raked; bridges had been built over the rivers. Camps were pitched in advance where everything was prepared: tents, aligned in perfect order, and proportioned to the rank of the personages of the suite; provisions, stores of fodder, etc.; together with a magnificent tent that was fully furnished, awaited the Dalai Lama. Vicompte d'Ollone noticed, however, that as he descended toward the plains the preparations glorified the Dalai Lama less and the monarch more. Generals, governors, and viceroys attended his passage, and a veritable army was assembled to do him honor. The imperial court had prepared a triumphal approach that was much more imposing than the actual entry into Beijing.[38]

At the time of the Dalai Lama's arrival in Beijing there was great discussion as to how he should enter the city. Although it was suggested that a temporary wooden pathway should be built, so that he might come in over the city wall in order to avoid having him go through the one of the chief gates reserved for the imperial family, the final decision was that the Dalai Lama would enter Beijing by train and pass through one of the ordinary gates preceded by mounted infantry with drawn swords accompanied by four mounted buglers. Twenty men carried the great yellow chair in which the Dalai Lama sat, carefully curtained from view. In front of the Yellow Temple stood rows of priests in long yellow robes to welcome the Thirteenth Dalai Lama. Thousands of followers arrived and were hosted in the Yellow Temple or in the Yonghegong. These crowds included Tibetan monks dressed in red and yellow robes, Tibetan lay people who wore animal skins and sold Tibetan ornaments to Chinese traders or bought Chinese commodities, Tibetan aristocrats with jewels, and Mongolians who cared for thousands of camels or sold horses. The latter were so numerous that they were initially mistaken for a Mongol army poised to north of the city, and preparing to force their entry into Beijing.[39]

Although the first imperial audience had been scheduled for October 6, it had to be postponed because of the *ketou* ritual: the Dalai Lama refused to perform the three genuflections and the nine prostrations (*san gui jiu kou li*) as required by the Manchu tradition. It is possible that several of the foreigners he met during his stay at Wutai shan may have influenced this decision, among them William W. Rockhill (1854–1914), the American Minister to China, who was well-versed in Tibetan language and ancient Buddhist scriptures, and the Japanese Buddhist priest Otani Sonya. As a result of his meeting with Otani, he later met the Japanese ambassador, Hayashe Gon-

FIG. 1 "A parade of the Manchu Emperor's army welcoming the Thirteenth Dalai Lama at his arrival to Beijing after his visit to Outer Mongolia." A mural realized in the Menri style at the Potala in 1934–1935. (After *A Mirror of the Murals in the Potala* [Beijing: Jiu zhou tushu chubanshe, 2000], p. 202.)

suke, in Beijing. While at Wutai shan, the Dalai Lama was also visited by the Japanese military attaché, Fufushima Masanoni, and Sir John Jordan (1852–1925), the British Ambassador to China.[40] A German official from Tianjin and a Russian high-ranking official sent by the Czar also visited the Dalai Lama.[41] While in Beijing, the Dalai Lama met Captain O'Connor, the British political officer in Sikkim, as well as the King of Sikkim.[42] Not only did the Westerners disapprove of the notion of genuflecting to the Qing, but the Qing court had come to accept Western forms of courteous greeting. Most fundamentally, however, the Dalai Lama rejected the political meaning of the *ketou* ritual: he did not want to position himself as a subordinate of the Qing Emperor or Empress Dowager.

In the end, the Dalai Lama reached an agreement with the court: he would be received by Emperor Guangxu and by the dowager separately, and he would kneel (*gui*) to greet each. On October 14, 1908, he went to the Summer Palace (*Yihe yuan*) where Cixi lived half of every year. He was received first by the dowager, then by Emperor Guangxu, in the Renshou Palace. The Dalai Lama, accompanied by the Tungsi Lama and two *khenbu* lamas,[43] knelt to their majesties and then offered greeting scarfs both to the empress dowager and the emperor. The emperor presented the Dalai Lama with a yellow greeting scarf. Both addressed the Tibetan pontiff through interpreters.[44]

The Qing court carefully noted every detail about the protocol, but no details are given in the *Zhengzhi guan bao* or in the Qing archives regarding the content of the discussions. Conversely, the biography of the Thirteenth Dalai Lama is silent about the rituals performed at the beginning and at the end of the interview. The biography mentions nothing about the protocol following the exchanges of gifts during the audience with Cixi, although in describing the interview with Guangxu, Purchok, the biographer, reveals that each in turn sat on his respective throne (*de nas so so'i bzhugs khrir rim gis 'khod 'phral*). The meaning of this, however, is not entirely clear. Subsequently, Purchok writes that the Thirteenth Dalai Lama left the palace and then returned to the Yellow Temple in his palanquin, which was of a yellow color like those of the imperial family, but he fails to record the rituals between the end of the interviews and the Dalai Lama's departure.

Purchok did, however, present a transcript of lively talk between the Dalai Lama and both Cixi and Guangxu, during which Cixi and Guangxu asked the Tibetan pontiff about his trip from Wutai shan to Beijing and about his acclimatization to the Chinese capital.[45] More interesting than the content of this talk is the direct manner in which each party addresses the other, a style not recorded in Chinese sources. According to the transcript, the Dalai Lama, Cixi, and Guangxu used secular rather than particularly religious terms: the Thirteenth Dalai Lama always addressed Cixi as *gyelyum chenmo* (Great Empress Dowager) and Guangxu as *gongma chenpo* (Great Emperor), while for their part they addressed him as Dalai Lama. That these talks occurred was significant politically, and the Qing court welcomed the Tibetan pontiff with the ceremonies used for the reception of European ambassadors.

Yet the degree of political content in these discussions is ambiguous: both Chinese and Tibetan sources confirm only that the Dalai Lama asked to be allowed to have a direct relationship with the emperor of China—that is, to have access to him without passing through the amban. In effect, the Tibetan leader expressed his disagreement with the present state of Qing policies,[46] an exchange that is noted in the Thirteenth Dalai Lama's biography as a conclusion to his visit to Beijing.

Zhang Yintang opposed such a change in policy. He argued that the Dalai Lama could be allowed to memorialize directly to the emperor on religious but not political issues, and, because the spiritual and temporal powers of the Dalai Lama were difficult to separate, the Dalai Lama should thus still ask permission from the amban to communicate with the Throne. Although Zhang admitted that the administration of Tibet had passed from the hands of the amban to those of the Thirteenth Dalai Lama since 1895, he claimed that Beijing should use the present opportunity to reassert its control over Tibet.[47] In fact, the power of the ambans had faded during the previous century because of their incompetence. They had not been able to turn to their advantage the longstanding absence of the Dalai Lamas from a genuine role in the Tibetan government.[48]

Moreover, the Thirteenth Dalai Lama revealed himself as a man who might possibly threaten Manchu power in Tibet. W.W. Rockhill, who became a close advisor to the Dalai Lama after both exchanged correspondence and met in Wutai shan and in Beijing, wrote that he was "a man of undoubted intelligence and ability, of quick understanding and of force of character. He was broad-minded, possibly as a result of his varied experiences during the last few years, and of great natural dignity." Rockhill added that the Dalai Lama "seemed deeply impressed with the great responsibilities of his office as supreme Pontiff of his faith, more so perhaps, than by those resulting from his temporal duties. He was quick tempered and impulsive, but cheerful and kindly."[49] Beijing's response, in all events, was that communications to the Throne still must be passed through the amban.[50]

Emperor Guangxu invited the Dalai Lama to a banquet in the Ziguang pavilion on October 30, 1908. On this occasion, the Ministry ruling the Outer Provinces (*Lifan bu*) asked the Grand Council what rituals should be followed and specifically whether the Dalai Lama should kneel before the emperor.[51] The rituals were modified to suit the "particular status" of the Dalai Lama, but the meaning of this status is not specified in the documents. According to the Chinese sources, during the event, the Dalai Lama was seated on a "little bed" to the left side of the emperor at the banquet. He made a genuflection to greet and bid farewell to the emperor from this place near him, while the other Buddhist masters performed their rituals in a row in front of the Throne.[52]

At the end of the audiences, the Dalai Lama performed a prostration to thank their majesties (*kou xie*), and at the banquet's conclusion he and the Buddhist masters made the three genuflections and nine prostrations to thank the emperor. This leads us to question why the Dalai Lama performed the prostrations when he had succeeded in convincing the Qing court to change the ritual. According to Chen Qiangyi, the genuflection represented a kind of compromise: the Dalai Lama was satisfied because the Qing court had arranged special rituals for him, while the emperor could be content that the changes in the rituals did not employ forms reserved for a sovereign, only those for ambassadors. Two murals painted on the walls of the Potala depict the reception of the Thirteenth Dalai Lama by the Qing court. In one of them, the Dalai Lama kneels before the empress and offers her the blessing of Amitāyus, the buddha of long-life. The other shows the empress dowager seated in the central position and the Dalai Lama (and the emperor) at her right side. Evelyn Rawski concludes that, considering the Chinese point of view, these murals firmly established the hierarchy of superior to inferior for all to see.[53] A Tibetan point of view, however, suggests that the first exposes the chaplain-donor relationship, while the second emphasizes not the centrality of the empress's seat, but the level of the seats: in the second mural, the seats are all of the same height, implying the empress dowager, the emperor, and the Dalai Lama to be equals.

What motivations could the emperor have had to extend himself so far in an effort to please the Dalai Lama? The most fundamental reason for the Qing's treatment of the Dalai Lama was probably the respect held by the empress dowager and the emperor for his spiritual powers. It does not seem that the Dalai Lama was a threat to Manchu power in Tibet at this time, but it is possible that the Qing may have suspected a need for the Dalai Lama in the future. It was clear that the foreign diplomats in Beijing were trying to meet the Dalai Lama and probably to advise him. Although they issued very strict rules to prevent foreigners from interfering in their relations with the Dalai Lama, the Qing did not want to upset the powers by snubbing the Dalai Lama, nor did they want to give the powers an opportunity to turn the Dalai Lama against the Qing. Indeed, according to Teichman, the manner in which the Dalai Lama could receive foreign Ministers and their Legation Staffs at Beijing gave rise to much discussion and conjecture in foreign diplomatic circles in the capital. The Qing allowed foreigners to meet the Thirteenth Dalai Lama in the Yellow Temple every day except Sunday, between the hours of noon and 3 o'clock. Indeed, foreign diplomats met the Thirteenth Dalai Lama accordingly, but only in the presence of Manchu officials.[54]

The Vicompte d'Ollone (1868–1945) met the Tibetan leader at Wutai shan. He described how the Dalai Lama was seated upon a throne which stood upon a raised platform while he himself had to sit in an armchair

FIG. 2 "The Thirteenth Dalai Lama met by the mother of the Emperor." A mural realized in the Menri style at the Potala in 1934–1935. (After *A Mirror of the Murals in the Potala* [Beijing: Jiu zhou tushu chubanshe, 2000], p. 203.)

placed in front and below the platform. The Vicompte noted that the Dalai Lama wore a short tunic of yellow silk, orange trousers, and boots of a bright yellow and a red scarf around his neck. According to Tibetan customs, the two exchanged white greeting scarves and gifts. The conversation, however, was quite labored, as the Vicompte d'Ollone spoke in French, his interpreter translated his words into Chinese, a monk repeated them in Mongolian, and another transmitted his words to the Dalai Lama in Tibetan, while the opposite series of translations brought him the Dalai Lama's reply in return.[55]

Because the Dalai Lama understood that the 1907 Anglo-Russian Convention barred the Russians from helping, he turned to the British, meeting unofficially with O'Connor. During a lengthy international tour, O'Connor and the Maharaja Kumar of Sikkim visited Beijing and met there with the Dalai Lama. The protocols that the Dalai Lama observed with the two were almost the same as for Vicompte d'Ollone except for the places of the seats: the Thirteenth Dalai Lama was at the center with his attendants on his right and O'Connor and the Maharaja Kumar on his left. Because the two could speak directly with the Dalai Lama and did not need interpreters, communication was also more efficient than it had been with Vicompte d'Ollone. The Dalai Lama asked O'Connor about the Mission to Lhasa, Great Britain's attitude toward Tibet and himself, and especially about the Ninth Panchen Lama's visit to India in 1905–1906.[56] This meeting and the positive reception the Panchen Lama had received in India seem to have assuaged the fears the Dalai Lama had of the British.[57]

Religious Activities in Beijing

One might expect that as the spiritual head of the Gelukpa school the Thirteenth Dalai Lama should have carried out many religious activities during the three months he spent in Beijing, but this was not the case. Obviously, he found the religious situation in China disastrous. The destruction caused by the Boxers was still easy to see. Many temples had not been repaired. Others were being transformed into schools under the new Qing reforms. Buddhist scriptures had been lost or were awaiting republication. The Qing had imposed restrictive rules to control the Buddhist clergy in China, regulating registration of the monks, the issuance of ordination certificates, and authorization to teach Buddhism. In any case, the Thirteenth Dalai Lama was supposed to be acting as the Buddhist Master of the Court, not to be performing religious functions elsewhere.

The religious activities of the Thirteenth Dalai Lama can be divided between official and non-official functions, of which the former are recorded in the Qing dynasty archives. These activities do not seem to have been originally planned into the Dalai Lama's trip to Beijing, but they are significant because they were occasions for reaffirming the chaplain-donor relationship that existed traditionally between the line of the Dalai Lamas and the Qing sovereigns. These official religious activities included the long-life ceremony dedicated to the Empress Dowager Cixi on her birthday (November 3) and the prayers of the Thirteenth Dalai Lama for the sake of Emperor Guangxu's and Cixi's souls after their deaths. The Thirteenth Dalai Lama's biography mentions various unofficial religious activities, as well, including visits and offerings made by the Tibetan pontiff to monasteries in Beijing and reforms that he tried to implement in the capital's Tibetan monasteries.

Cixi's Birthday Celebration: An Example of the Chaplain-Donor Relationship

The day before her birthday, the empress asked the Thirteenth Dalai Lama to come to the Qinzheng Palace (*Qinzheng dian*) to practice religious rituals in order to ensure her longevity:

> On the day appointed the Ministers of the Board of Dependen-
> cies shall escort the Dalai Lama and his suite to the apartment on
> the east of and outside of the Dechang Gate, where they shall await
> until Her Majesty has entered the Qinzheng Palace and the Minis-
> ters of the Presence and the Bodyguard have taken their positions.
> The Ministers of the Board of Dependencies shall then con-
> duct the Dalai Lama and his suite through the right gate of the
> Dechang Gate and into the Qinzheng Palace through the right
> entrance. The Dalai Lama shall then ascend the steps of the dais
> and make a genuflection in front of the Throne of Her Majesty,
> the lama interpreters doing likewise behind him. Then, holding
> in both hands a porcelain plate on which shall be placed a vase
> wrapped in yellow satin and containing clear water and known
> as a "longevity vase" (*changchou ping*), and also some "longevity
> pills" (*changchou dan*), and a yellow *khatak* under the plate, he
> shall chant the service. After this he shall make a genuflection and
> hand the Ministers of the Presence the plate and the objects on it
> to present to her Majesty.
>
> Her Majesty the Empress will then bestow on the Dalai Lama a
> rosary of pearls, a *khatak*, an Imperial yellow state umbrella, a hor-
> izontal scroll written by herself, a pair of perpendicular scrolls also
> written by herself, and a coral *ruyi* or sceptre.
>
> The Dalai Lama will make a genuflection on receiving these
> gifts, and will then perform the ceremony of three kneelings and
> nine head-knockings in thanks for the Imperial bounty.
>
> After this the Comptroller of the Imperial Household will offer
> tea to Her Majesty and the (chief of the) Bodyguard will pass it, in
> the name of Her Majesty, to the Dalai Lama. Then the Dalai Lama
> will make one kotow and will be escorted out of the Presence.[58]

This longevity ritual embodies the chaplain-donor relationship as conceived by the Tibetans in terms of their rapport with China. The chaplain,

in this case the Dalai Lama, performed rituals for the sake of his patron, the Empress Dowager Cixi. In return, the empress dowager gave him gifts as described above, and also gave him a new title and an annual salary. But it is still hard to assess the Dalai Lama's performance of the genuflections and prostrations in front of the empress. One explanation is that Qing archives wanted to emphasize the subordination of the Dalai Lama. Another explanation is that these practices were part of the traditional chaplain-donor rituals. Finally, it is also possible that the Dalai Lama recognized Cixi as a bodhisattva, although we have no evidence for that.[59]

Although there is no evidence that Cixi was a devout Buddhist, she seems to have envisioned herself as an incarnation of Guanyin.[60] She posed for photographs as a bodhisattva amid the lotuses at her new summer palace, had banners inscribed with the appellation "Holy Mother" (*shengmu*), and allowed herself to be addressed as "Venerable Buddha" (*foye*).[61] Sources do not reveal what the Thirteenth Dalai Lama thought of these appellations, or even how he, as an incarnation of Avalokiteśvara, felt in front of another such incarnation.[62] Perhaps the best explanation of the empress's interest in Buddhism was her age: at seventy-four, her health had been deteriorating since the mid-autumn festival on September 10, 1908.

The objects that the Dalai Lama and the empress dowager exchanged reveal a religious relationship. Every audience provided the opportunity to offer gifts: at the Imperial audiences with the Empress Dowager Cixi and the Guangxu Emperor, the Dalai Lama offered them religious tokens as well as products from Tibet: he presented images of Śākyamuni Buddha and the bodhisattva Vajrapāṇi to the empress, while to the emperor he gave two images of Śākyamuni, one an antique bronze statue, as well as a copy of the Kanjur. He also presented each with a rosary of 108 coral beads, as well as golden urns, precious wooden bowls, incense, together with gold dust, furs of lynx, fox, and bear, and Tibetan wool garments.[63] Cixi and Guangxu also offered religious artifacts to the Dalai Lama, including pearl rosaries, incense, monk's robes, ritual objects in jade and silk, a sedan chair, an imperial yellow state umbrella, and pictures of themselves.[64]

The chaplain-donor relationship is confirmed in the biography of the Thirteenth Dalai Lama, which adds that he touched the head of the Guangxu Emperor with his own head (*gong ma chen po dbu gdugs*), the highest benediction from a Tibetan Buddhist master to a disciple. But, according to the same source, the Dalai Lama also noticed during the ceremony that the face of the Guangxu Emperor was lifeless and that he seemed not at all to be handling the political affairs of the state,[65] a clear reference to the Guangxu

Emperor's deteriorating health. His condition in fact prevented the emperor from carrying out the rituals for the ceremony of the Empress Dowager Cixi's birthday.[66]

As hosts, the Qing court made repeated gestures expressing the willingness of the Guangxu emperor and the empress dowager to perform their roles as patrons of the Buddhist master. The court arranged for the Dalai Lama's visit by repairing the Yellow Temple and provided him with everything he needed during his stay.[67] The court even appointed an escort for the Dalai Lama's return to Tibet. Moreover, henceforth the Thirteenth Dalai Lama would receive an annual budget of ten thousand taels.[68] Although the Thirteenth Dalai Lama resented the fact that the guards appointed by the government prevented him from meeting Western diplomats directly, both parties tried to follow the traditional chaplain-donor relationship rituals between a Dalai Lama and the Qing Emperor. The empress dowager herself decided to give a new title to the Dalai Lama in order to follow the "traditional system" (*cunzhao congqian jiu zhi*): she modified the designation "Most Excellent, Self-Existent Buddha of the West" (*Xi tian da shan zizai fo*) received in 1653 by the Fifth Dalai Lama and bestowed it on the Thirteenth Dalai Lama in expanded form: "The Sincerely Obedient, Helpful Reincarnation, Most Benevolent, Self-Existent Buddha of the West" (*cheng shun zan hua xi tian da shan zizai fo*, Tib. *khrin hrun tsan wa nub phyogs snying rje chen po skyes bu sangs rgyas*).[69] The title revealed the polyvalence of the Dalai Lama's temporal as well as spiritual duties, and the empress dowager used this ambiguity: she thanked him with the gift of this title after he had performed religious rituals for her, but then asked him in return to perform certain political duties. Indeed, the new title made the intentions of the empress dowager obvious. Although she made some concessions to the imperial audience rituals by receiving the Dalai Lama as a foreign ambassador, she still marked him as a submissive ruler under Qing sovereignty by giving him a title—one that in fact emphasized his "obedience" to the throne—and an allowance. She expected the Dalai Lama to "be reverently submissive to the laws of the sovereign state and make known everywhere the sincere purposes of the Qing government." She also used the occasion to deny the Dalai Lama's request for direct communication between them, refusing to terminate the amban's role as intermediary. In the end, the Dalai Lama was ordered to leave China as soon as he formally received his title and to return to Tibet.

On November 14, 1908, the Guangxu Emperor died at the age of thirty-eight. The empress dowager followed him the next day, at seventy-four. Indeed, the death of the emperor was suspicious: as the empress dowager's illness worsened, she may have seen the emperor himself as an obstacle to the peaceful transmission of power she had planned.[70] Whether or not the Dalai Lama was aware of the suspicious nature of the death of the Emperor Guangxu, he performed religious rituals for both the emperor and the empress dowager in the Yonghegong, paid his last respects to their remains, and welcomed the new Xuantong Emperor, who ascended the throne on November 15, 1908.[71] As a last religious act, the Dalai Lama dedicated a long-life prayer to Xuantong. In this, he praised him as the embodiment of Mañjuśrī and recognized him as a powerful ruler of the world. He emphasized the emperor's political power as an opportunity to act for the welfare of the people. The colophon presented the Thirteenth Dalai Lama as the keeper of the powerful exoteric teachings and as the disciple of Śākyamuni, the holder of the Buddhist law, but failed to mention any political title. The prayer that the Dalai Lama performed sounds like a celebration of the chaplain-donor relationship: the Xuantong Emperor is described as a Cakravartin king while the Dalai Lama is mentioned as a chaplain.

Two other long-life prayers dedicated to Manchu emperors are held at the Fu Ssû-nien Library and merit comparison. The first, dedicated to Emperor Jiaqing (r. 1796–1820), and clearly referring to him as the Dharmarāja (*'jam dbyangs chos kyi rgyal po*), was composed by Siregetu Khutughtu Ngawang Tupten Wangchuk, the younger brother of the Changkya Khutughtu Rölpé Dorjé, in 1796. The second, dedicated to Emperor Guangxu, was composed by Ngukhor Khutughtu in 1875 in praise of the emperor's virtues.[72] The contents of these long-life prayers suggest that the decline in the relationship between Tibet and China during the nineteenth century led to the desire to create a new kind of chaplain-donor relationship.

During his stay in Beijing, when he was not participating in imperial audiences or performing official duties, the Dalai Lama visited and gave offerings to various temples, including the Yonghegong, which he visited several times, the Mahākāla Temple, the Songzhu Temple, and the Baita Temple.[73] These four temples, as well as the Yellow Temple where the Dalai Lama stayed, were connected with Tibetan Buddhism and linked to the chaplain-donor relationship. The Yonghegong, situated in the Inner City, was re-dedicated in 1744 by the Qianlong Emperor on the site of the princely palace of the former Yongzheng Emperor. It was mainly dedicated to the study of the scriptures of the Buddhist Gelukpa school headed by the Dalai Lama. This temple served as a preserve of the Dalai Lama, who appointed its abbot, but its activities depended on the subsidies of the Qing court. The Mahākāla Temple, built in 1638, symbolized the adhesion of the Qing Emperor to the cult of

Mahākāla, a wrathful deity known as a protector of the Buddhist Law. The Songzhu Temple, built for the first Changkya Khutughtu by the Emperor Kangxi, served as his residence during his visits to Beijing. (In the eighteenth century, the second Changkya Khutughtu would be the main Buddhist master of the Qianlong Emperor.) Finally, the Baita Temple had been built in honor of the Fifth Dalai Lama by Shunzhi in 1653.[74]

The biography of the Thirteenth Dalai Lama claims that he visited twenty-eight temples in Beijing in the company of Manchu dignitaries and of the Tongkhor Khutughtu.[75] The Dalai Lama apparently also visited other monasteries, but it remains unclear whether he tried to leave any permanent impression as a Buddhist master. He gave the Prajñāpāramitā, the White Tārā teachings, and delivered the chant of Kālacakra at the Yonghegong, and gave the "Hundred Divinities of Ganden" (*Dga' ldan lha brgya ma*) tantric initiation publicly to two hundred people.[76] But several questions still remain unanswered: Did the Dalai Lama give to or receive private teachings from any Chinese master? Did he develop an interest in Chinese Buddhism? Did he meet Tibetan and Chinese lay Buddhists? Did he learn about the emergent lay Buddhist movement for tantric textual research led by Yang Wenhui? Sources reveal only that the Thirteenth Dalai Lama met one Japanese Buddhist priest, Otani Sonya, with whom he exchanged Buddhist texts and discussed the possibility of a monastic student exchange between Tibet and Japan. This meeting took place in Wutai shan, however, not in Beijing, and it had political consequences in that the Dalai Lama later met the Japanese Ambassador, Gonsuke Hayashe, in Beijing.[77]

Overall, the Dalai Lama seems to have dedicated his time to the Qing court and to foreign diplomats, preparing himself for the world of international politics. Perhaps this is the reason for which his three months in Beijing so little influenced local Buddhist life. By contrast, the religious influence of the Dalai Lama was more obvious in the Tibetan areas he traversed on his return journey to Tibet.

Religious Activities at the Kumbum Monastery

After the deaths of Guangxu and Cixi, the Dalai Lama was ordered to the Kumbum monastery in Amdo, to stay there until he had received the title given to him by the Qing court.[78] The Dalai Lama left Beijing for Kumbum on December 21, 1908, and arrived at his destination to find the monastery in a turmoil of excitement: it had been well cleaned for his arrival, and a long and low building, built on the side of a steep hill overlooking the whole monastery had been arranged for him. When the Dalai Lama approached Xining, the roads were lined with Chinese soldiers and a Chinese band opened the march of the procession. Standard-bearers, mounted Tibetans in long yellow coats with hats made of gilded wood, followed. A crowd of Chinese looked at the procession without great respect, declining to offer prostrations, upset that it had been their task to provide supplies for the Dalai Lama's reception. Then, there arrived a group of horsemen who surrounded a large yellow cloth-covered chair carried by four horses and led by four mounted Tibetans. A great camp had been prepared outside of the monastery, with hundreds of tents, all pitched in a square, and a Mongol tent of rich yellow cloth, surrounded by a wall of the same material for the Dalai Lama's personal use. His followers made up a picturesque world of Mongol princes, Tibetan pilgrims, muleteers, and Chinese in gorgeous colored silks.[79]

On March 4, 1909, the Qing invested the Dalai Lama with his new title.[80] In the few months he spent at Kumbum the Dalai Lama made a number of reforms in the administration and rituals of the monastery.[81] But during this time, a disturbing incident occurred. In a letter addressed to the Qing throne and translated by the Xining amban, Qingshu (in office from 1905 to 1911), the Dalai Lama began by introducing himself as the spiritual head of the Gelukpa school, who, after many audiences with the Qing Emperor, had been invested with the duty to make the Gelukpa school prosper. He then asked that the Akya Rinpoché, a Tibetan Buddhist master of the Kumbum monastery, be dismissed on March 2, 1909. He judged that this master's behavior was not in accordance with Buddhist rules, adding that Akya Rinpoché drank, smoke, and quarrelled with everybody, and, finally, he accused him of holding the Qing Emperor and the Dalai Lama himself in contempt by declining to apply the new disciplinary rules decreed by his religious master. In conclusion, the Dalai Lama threatened to stay in the Kumbum monastery and not return to Tibet until the Akya Rinpoché was dismissed.

It was a strange coincidence, then, when the Akya Rinpoché died suddenly while the Dalai Lama was reciting mantras. But the monks of the Kumbum monastery who reported the incident to Qingshu accused the Dalai Lama of having chanted a special mantra to kill Akya. After inquiries, the Xining amban concluded that their report was unfounded; the Dalai Lama, for his part, said that he recited mantras for world peace. Clearly, the monks resented the Dalai Lama's attempts to implement a new discipline in their monastery.[82] While this shows how concerned the Dalai Lama was with protecting and respecting the Buddhist religion, and how he felt himself invested with the responsibility of restoring the glory of the Gelukpa, it also shows that the monks of the Kumbum dared to blame the Dalai Lama and even to accuse him of murder. The Thirteenth Dalai Lama left the Kumbum monastery on June 2, 1909.

Conclusion

The meetings between the Thirteenth Dalai Lama and the Qing Imperial family at the beginning of the twentieth century illustrate the difficulty each faced in establishing relationships in an environment of political transition. China was in the process of adjustment in the wake of the Boxer Rebellion, under which circumstances the Qing rulers were unsure how to treat traditional subordinate regimes, especially Tibet. They tried to adapt past traditions to deal with the new conditions, but the results were unsatisfactory for the Dalai Lama, who wished to be received as an independent ruler.

For his part, the Dalai Lama knew how to act according to circumstances: he acted as a statesman when the Qing court received him as an ambassador of an independent country (but not as the ruler of that country), and he took advantage of his trip to Beijing to meet diplomats who could help him to understand the world of politics and strengthen his conduct of Tibetan political affairs. But the Dalai Lama was also a spiritual master, performing rituals in the temples of Beijing and applying new rules in Tibetan monasteries in Outer Mongolia and Tibet. Finally, he acted as chaplain in a chaplain-donor relationship that defined his temporal and spiritual powers when he celebrated Cixi's birthday.

The Thirteenth Dalai Lama's long trip away from Lhasa began in 1904 and ended in 1909. During these five years, he used his temporal and spiritual powers to reaffirm himself as Tibet's ruler—both in terms of Tibetan domestic politics and internationally. He impressed people at the time through his conduct and his desire to lead Tibet to independence, a goal he ultimately attained with the fall of the Qing dynasty in 1911.

Notes

* I am grateful for the comments and improvements suggested to me by Susan Naquin, John Kieschnick, Pierre-Etienne Will, and Peter Zarrow.

1 Quoted by C. Bell, *Portrait of a Dalai Lama: The Life and Times of the Great Thirteenth* (London: Wisdom, 1987 [1946]), pp. 87, 89.

2   In 1578, Bsod nams Rgya mtsho (1543–1588), then abbot of the monastery of 'Bras spungs and the future Third Dalai Lama, went to the Mongol Tümet territory to meet Altan Khan (1502–1582), who had invited him to come. On this occasion, Altan Khan gave him the title of *Dalai Lama* (*Dalai* is a translation of the Tibetan word Rgya mtsho which means *ocean*) and the now Third Dalai Lama in turn gave to the Khan the title of "King of the Dharma" (*chos kyi rgyal po*).

3   L. Petech, "The Dalai Lamas and Regents of Tibet: A Chronological Study," *T'oung Pao* 47/3–5 (1959): 368.

4   Apparently, the Thirteenth Dalai Lama also complained about it. W.W. Rockhill, "The Dalaï-Lamas of Lhasa and their relations with the Manchu emperors of China 1644–1908," *T'oung Pao* 11 (1910): 77–89; C. Bell, *op. cit.*, p. 83.

5   J.L. Hevia, *Cherishing Men from Afar: Qing Guest Ritual and the Macartney Embassy of 1793* (Durham, NC: Duke University Press, 1995), p. 45.

6   J.L. Hevia, *op. cit.*, p. 43.

7   As an imperial concubine Cixi gave birth to the only son of the Xianfeng Emperor (r. 1850–1861), the future Tongzhi Emperor (r. 1861–1875), who established her status in the court. After two *coup d'état*, she succeeded in assuming power: first, in 1861, taking over from the eight high-ranking officials nominated by the Xianfeng Emperor before his death to help his son in the governance of the empire; then in 1898, from the Guangxu Emperor when he tried to implement reforms in the government and to release himself from her control.

8   D.S. Ruegg, "mChod-yon, Yon-mchod and mchod-gnas/yon-gnas: on the Historiography and Semantics of a Tibetan religio-social and religio-political concept," in *Tibetan History and Language: Studies Dedicated to Géza Uray on his Seventieth Birthday*, E. Steinkellner, ed. (Vienna: Universität Wien, 1991), pp. 441–453; idem, *Ordre spirituel et ordre temporel dans la pensée bouddhique de l'Inde et du Tibet* (Paris: Collège de France, Institut de Civilisation Indienne, 1995).

9   Khubilai also received the title "universal king of the Buddhist Law."

10 For example, the Qianlong Emperor received the tantric Saṃvara initiation from Lcang skya Rol pa'i rdo rje and the Mahākāla and Cakrasaṃvara initiations from the Sixth Paṇchen Lama (1738–1780) during his visit to Beijing in 1780.

11 This title used to refer to the kings of Tibet from Khri Srong lde btsan (r. 755–ca. 797) to Ral pa can (r. 815–841), as well as to the Mongol rulers Altan Khan and Gushri Khan.

12 For a detailed analysis of the chaplain-donor relationship during the Qing dynasty, see E.S. Rawski, *The Last Emperors: A Social History of Qing Imperial Institutions* (Berkeley: University of California Press, 1998), pp. 249–263.

13 Chen Qiangyi 陳鏘儀, "Jianshu shi sanshi Dalai Lama rujin" 簡述十三世達賴入覲, *Zhongguo Zangxue* 中國藏學 1 (1988): 82–92.

14 Phur lcog yongs 'dzin Thub bstan Byams pa tshul khrim bstan 'dzin, *Lhar bcas srid zhi'i gtsug rgyan gong sa rgyal ba bka' drin mtshungs med sku phreng bcu gsum pa chen po'i rnam thar rgya mtsho lta bu las mdo tsam brjod pa ngo mtshar rin po che'i phreng ba*, Śata-Piṭaka series, vols. 287–288 (New Delhi: International Academy of Indian Culture, 1981).

15 I am grateful to the librarians of the Institute of History and Philology for giving me access to this source.

16 The 1886 convention fixed the border between Tibet and Burma. The treaty of 1890 drew the border between Tibet and Sikkim and opened a trade market in Gro mo in Tibet. These two treaties had been signed between China and England without the participation of the Tibetans.

17 For British accounts of this campaign, see S. Chapman, *Lhasa the Holy City* (London: Readers Union Ltd, 1940); L.A. Waddell, *Lhasa and Its Mysteries* (Delhi: Cosmo, 1996 [1905]).

18 Rme ru Blo bzang rgyal mtshan, the eighty-sixth holder of Tsong kha pa's throne in the Dga' ldan monastery, in office from 1901 to 1908.

19 A. Lamb, *The McMahon Line: A Study in the Relations between India, China and Tibet, 1904 to 1914* (London: Routledge and Kegan Paul, 1966), pp. 36–51.

20 Article 1 of the Convention: cf. M.C. van Walt van Praag, *The Status of Tibet: History, Rights and Prospects in International Law* (London: Wisdom, 1987), appendix 12, p. 307.

21 The Thirteenth Dalai Lama, from his exile, appointed officers to his government: Bshad sgra dpal 'byor rdo rje, Zhol khang, and Chang khyim who became Prime ministers (*blon chen*).

22 The Qing considered that the Panchen Lama and the Dalai Lama had equal power in their own provinces. For them, "Outer Tibet" was divided into two areas: one, Dbus, the central region, was directed by the Dalai Lama, while the second, the western regions of Gtsang and Mnga' ris, were under the Panchen Lama. In cases of conflicts or in the absence of a Dalai Lama, the Qing asked for the Panchen Lama's advice. The Panchen Lamas, second spiritual authority in the Dge lugs pa school and *de facto* temporal head of Gtsang province, had special relations with the British in part because of the geographical situation of the Bkra shis lhun po monastery, the seat of the Panchen Lamas in Gzhis ka rtse. Visitors coming from India to go to Lhasa were obliged to go through Rgyal rtse, then to Gzhis ka rtse, and at the end of the eighteenth century, the British stopped at Gzhis ka rtse and were not allowed to go to Lhasa. They contacted the Sixth Panchen Lama after he acted successfully as an intermediary for the resolution of the conflict between Cooch Bihar, backed by the British from India, and Bhutan. From then on, the British tried to maintain their relation with the Panchen Lama hoping to open trade routes to Tibet, to make their position in the Himalayas more secure, and to get an access to China. (Refer to L. Petech, "The Missions of Bogle and Turner according to the Tibetan Texts," *T'oung Pao* 39/4–5 [1949]: 330–346; C.R. Markham, *Narratives of the Mission of Georges Bogle to Tibet and of the Journey of Thomas Manning to Lhasa* (New Delhi: Bibliotheca Himalayica, 1971 [1st ed. London: Trübner, 1876]). Some time after the visit to his monastery of G. Bogle, the emissary of the British East India Company, the Sixth Panchen Lama was invited by the Qianlong Emperor to attend the celebrations for his seventieth birthday, and went to China in 1780. The prelate was received with honors by Qianlong, who built for him the Xumi fushou miao in Jehol (today's Chengde), based on the architecture of the Bkra shis lhun po monastery, the temple of the Panchen Lama lineage. The Sixth Panchen Lama met the Manchu Emperor first in Jehol on August 20, 1780, then in Beijing on September 29, 1780. He died in Beijing on November 2, 1780.

23 Phur lcog, vol. 7, ff.108, 111.

24 The withdrawal of the Dalai Lama's titles that occurred a few years later, in 1910 after the Chinese troops of Zhao Erfeng had occupied Lhasa, was more severe and the Qing court on that occasion gave a long explanation for its decision.

25 著將達賴喇嘛名號暫行革去, 并著班禪額爾德尼暫攝. Telegram from the Grand Council to Youtai, Manchu commissioner in Tibet, July 16, 1904.

26 Youtai (1844–1910) was Manchu commissioner in Tibet from 1902 to 1906.

27 T.T. Li, *Tibet, Today and Yesterday* (New York: Bookman, 1960), p. 106.

28 Telegram of Youtai to the Foreign Ministry, July 11, 1904; telegram of the Grand Council to Youtai, July 16, 1904; Youtai's letter to the Dga' ldan khri pa, July 25, 1904; "Youtai zhu Zang riji" 有泰駐藏日記, in *Xizang xue hanwen wenxian huike* 西藏學漢文文獻匯刻, ed. Wu Fengpei 吳豐培 Beijing: Quan Guo tushuguan wenxian, 1991), *juan* 6, 32a (September 2, 1904) and 34a (September 8, 1904); Youtai's letter to the Ninth Panchen Lama, January 24, 1905.

29 W.W. Rockhill, *op. cit.*, p. 77.

30 Telegram of Zhang Yintang, who transmitted a report from the intendant of the Bkra shis lhun po monastery, October 9, 1906; report of Youtai, April 13, 1906.

31 Zhang Yintang was vice military governor in Tibet from 1906 to 1908.

32 Telegram from Zhang Yintang, February 6, 1907.

33 Telegrams of Zhang Yintang, November 9, 1906, August 5, 1907; telegram of the Foreign Ministry to Zhang Yintang, April 26, 1907; explanatory letter (*shuotie*) of Zhang Yintang to the Foreign Ministry, October 1908; P. Mehra, *Tibetan Polity, 1904–1937: The Conflict between the 13th Dalai Lama and the 9th Panchen Lama* (Wiesbaden: Otto Harrassowitz, 1976), p. 14.

34 Telegram from Zhang Yintang to the Grand Council, March 10, 1907. The request of the Thirteenth Dalai Lama is dated 1907, whereas the Tibetan pontiff left Tibet in 1904. Because the Dalai Lama could not write directly to the emperor, his communications still had to pass through the new vice-military governor.

35 This was the "reform process in nine steps" (*jiu ju shancheng*) initiated for Tibet by Zhang Yintang.

36 Phur lcog, vol. 7, f. 106.

37 As early as 1906, Zhao Erfeng controled 'Ba' thang and Li thang. In 1908, he controled Sde dge. In August 1908, 'Ba' thang and Dar rtse mdo became Chinese prefectures (*fu*) while Li thang and the San pa area became garrisons (*suo*) in the Chinese administrative framework. Refer to E. Sperling, "Chinese venture in K'am, 1904–1911 and the role of Zhao Erfeng," *The Tibet Journal*, 1/2 (1976): 10–36; J. Bacot, *Le Tibet révolté* (Paris: Peuples du Monde, 1988 [1912]); Huang Fengsheng 黃豐生, *Zangzu shilue* 藏族史略 (Beijing: Minority Press, 1989), pp. 313–317.

38 Vicompte D'Ollone, *In Forbidden China: The D'Ollone Mission, 1906–1910. China-Tibet-Mongolia*, trans. Bernard Miall (Boston: Small and Maynard, 1909), pp. 309–310.

39 T.H. Liddell, *China: Its Marvel and Mystery* (London: George Allen, 1909), pp. 154–155; 196–197.

40 T.W. Shakabpa, *Tibet: A Political History* (New York: Potala, 1988 [1967]), p. 221–222. The Japanese names are given as T.W. Shakabpa has written them.

41 Ya Hanzhang, *The Biographies of the Dalai Lamas* (Beijing: Foreign Languages Press, 1991), pp. 258–259.

42 C. Bell, *op. cit.*, p. 86; official document from Zhang Yintang to the Foreign Ministry, October 1908.

43 Phur lcog, vol. 7, f.109. These people are hard to identify. According to the biography, the interpreters working during the audiences were the Thung si, zhabs zhur 'Bras spungs 'dul li slob dpon, and the Beijing interpreter Ngag dbang dge 'dun. The Chinese sources seem confused about the identification of the Tibetans. Thung si bla ma simply means "monk interpreter" and sounds close to the Chinese word *tongshi*, meaning "interpreter."

44 *Zhengzhi guan bao* 政治官報, October 10, 1908, no. 356. pp. 8–9.

45 Phur lcog, vol. 7, f.108; 111.

46 Phur lcog, vol. 7, f.120.

47 Official document from Zhang Yintang to the Foreign Ministry, October 1908.

48 From the time of the Eighth, who ruled for three years in 1787–1790, to ascension of the Thirteenth Dalai Lama in 1895, only the Eleventh and Twelfth Dalai Lamas reached their majority, but together they were invested with (perhaps nominal) political authority for a total of only about two years in all.

49 W.W. Rockhill, *op. cit.*, p. 91. P. A. Varg, *Open Door Diplomat: The Life of W.W. Rockhill*, Illinois Studies in the Social Sciences, vol. 33, no. 4 (Westport: Greenwood Press, 1952), pp. 91–97. While in Urga, the Thirteenth Dalai Lama inquired of a Russian scientist about Western scholars who had studied the Tibetan language. The Russian referred to Rockhill and the Dalai Lama asked that Rockhill communicate with him. W.W. Rockhill became the Thirteenth Dalai Lama's advisor because of his knowledge of Tibetan language and culture, but also because his American nationality that made him neutral by comparison to the British or the Russians.

50 Imperial edict, October 10, 1908; Phur lcog, vol. 7, f. 120.

51 Opinion of the Ministry ruling the Outer Provinces to the Grand Council, October 22, 1908; *Zhengzhi guan bao*, October 28, 1908.

52 Rituals observed during the imperial banquet at the Ziguang Pavilion, October 30, 1908.

53 Liu Yi, "Cong lamajiao bihua kan Xizang yu Ming Qing zhongyang zhengfu de guanxi," *Lishi daguan yuan* 5 (1993): 8–11; cited by E. Rawski, *op. cit.*, p. 262.

54 E. Teichman, *Travels in Eastern Tibet* (London: Cambridge University Press, 1922), p. 14.

55 Vicompte D'Ollone, *op. cit.*, pp. 304–307.

56 W.F.T. O'Connor, *On the Frontier and Beyond: A Record of a Thirty Years Service* (London: John Murray, 1931), pp. 123–124.

57 A. McKay, *Tibet and the British Raj: The Frontier Cadre 1904–1947* (London: Curzon, 1997), p. 46.

58 W.W. Rockhill, *op. cit.*, pp. 83–84. This description of the ceremony was also published in the *Zhengzhi guan bao*, no. 371, dated thirteenth day of the tenth month.

59 It is perhaps worth noting here that, although it was not the practice in traditional China, the ritual submission of the head of the sangha to the ruler was not unknown in other Buddhist lands. However, such cases, intended to signify the political loyalty of the national Buddhist clergy as a whole, are not clearly analogous to the Dalai Lama's honoring of the Empress Cixi.

60 For a portrait of Cixi as the Goddess of Mercy, see the Princess Der Ling, *Two years in the Forbidden City* (San Francisco: Chinese materials center, 1977), p. 250.

61 S. Naquin, *Peking: Temples and City Life, 1400–1900* (Berkeley: University of California Press, 2000), pp. 347–348.

62 J. Hevia, *op. cit.*, p. 38, states that, in the Ming case, Tibetan sources add that the lama recognized the emperor and empress as the incarnations of the bodhisattvas Mañjuśrī and Tārā, but we do not know whether the Tibetan Buddhist masters qualified the empress dowager as a bodhisattva.

63 *Zhengzhi guan bao*, October 18, 1908. See also, W.W. Rockhill, *op. cit.*, p. 80, footnote 2; Chen Qiangyi, *op. cit.*, p. 87.

64 Some of these imperial presents to the Thirteenth Dalai Lama are reproduced in the Archives of the Tibet Autonomous Region, comp., *A Collection of Historical Archives of Tibet* (Beijing: Cultural Relics, 1995), documents 77–79.

65 Phur lcog, vol. 7, f. 115–116.

66 Chang Che-chia, "The Therapeutic Tug of War—The Imperial Physician-patient Relationship in the Era of Empress Dowager Cixi (1874–1908)" (Ph.D. dissertation, University of Pennsylvania, 1998), p. 225.

67 The Yellow Temple was originally built for the Fifth Dalai Lama when he came to Beijing in 1652. Danjiong Rannabanza 丹迥冉納班雜 and Li Decheng 李德成, comps., *Ming sha shuang Huang si, Qingdai Dalai he Banchan zai Jing zhuxi di* 名剎雙黃寺, 清代達賴和班禪在京駐錫地 (Beijing: Zongjiao wenhua chubanshe, 1997).

68 Order to the Grand Council, November 3, 1908.

69 Order to the Grand Council, November 3, 1908; Phur lcog, vol. 7, f.120. It is interesting to note that the Tibetan version of the title does not translate the four first characters, which were added to the previous title granted by Shunzhi to the Fifth Dalai Lama in 1653.

70 For a discussion about the deaths of the Guangxu Emperor and Cixi, see Chang Che-chia, *op. cit.*, pp. 205–237.

71 Communication from the Grand Council to the Court of Colonial Affairs, December 2, 1908; order of the Court of Colonial Affairs to the Dalai Lama, December 17, 1908. The Qing did not automatically select the eldest son of the empress as the heir apparent. The empress dowager had chosen Xuantong as the imperial heir in 1902. Xuantong was the eldest son of Zaifeng, the closest male relative of the emperor and of herself, and of the daughter of Ronglu, her most trustworthy minister. Before Xuantong, the empress dowager had also chosen the Guangxu Emperor, the Tongzhi Emperor's cousin as well as her sister's son.

72 I am grateful to the librarians of the Fu Ssû-nien Library for giving me access to this source. See F. Wang-Toutain, *Unpublished catalogue of some Tibetan texts preserved in the Fu Ssû-nien Library* (Taipei: Institute of History and Philology/Ecole française d'Extrême-Orient, 2002).

73 Chang Shaoru 常少如, comp., *Zang chuan fojiao gu si Yonghe gong* 藏傳佛教古寺雍和宮 (Beijing: Beijing yanshan, 1996).

74 Wang Yao, "The Cult of Mahakala and a Temple in Beijing," *Journal of Chinese Religions*, 22 (1994): 117–126; Pu Wencheng 蒲文成, *Gan Qing Zang chuan fojiao siyuan* 甘青藏傳佛教寺院 (Xining: Qinghai renmin chubanshe, 1990), pp. 155–158. E.S. Rawski, *op. cit.*, pp. 252, 257.

75 The Kangxi, Yongzheng, and Qianlong emperors renovated or built a total of thirty-two Tibetan Buddhist temples within Beijing. Refer to E. Rawski, *op. cit.*, p. 252. The Stong 'khor Khutughtu was the abbot of the Stong 'khor monastery in A mdo, situated halfway between Lhasa and Chahar in Inner Mongolia. Before the monastery was built at Stong 'khor in 1648, a diplomatic office was set up there as a link between the Dalai Lama and Altan Khan around 1580. The reincarnation line of the Stong 'khor Khutughtu became attached to Beijing from 1665. Phur lcog, vol. 7, f. 106. T.W. Shakabpa, *op. cit.*, pp. 96–97; E. Teichman, *op. cit.*, p. 3; 70; Pu Wencheng, *Gan Qing Zang zhuan fojiao siyuan* (Xining: Qinghai renmin chubanshe, 1990), pp. 155–158.

76 Phur lcog, vol. 7, f. 107; 113.

77 T.W. Shakabpa, *op. cit.*, p. 221.

78 Order from the Ministry ruling the Outer Provinces, December 22, 1908.

79 J.W. Brooke, chief of a British expedition into Tibet for geographical purposes, witnessed the arrival of the Thirteenth Dalai Lama at the Sku 'bum monastery and obtained an audience with him. W.N. Ferguson, *Adventure, Sport and Travel on the Tibetan Steppes* (London: Constable, 1911), pp. 1–6.

80 The rituals of this ceremony are described in the *Zhengzhi guan bao*, 17 January 1909, and the ceremony of investiture in a report written by Qingshu, Xining amban, to the emperor, dated March 4, 1908.

81 T.W. Shakabpa, *op. cit.*, p. 223.

82 Report from Qingshu, the Xining amban, to the emperor, June 5, 1909.

11: The Taiwanese Connection: Politics, Piety, and Patronage in Transnational Tibetan Buddhism*

Abraham Zablocki

The Dalai Lama's 1997 Trip to Taiwan

THE HISTORIC TRIP of the Dalai Lama to Taiwan in March of 1997 signaled a new phase in the long and tangled relationship between the Tibetan and Chinese peoples. To many observers, the implications of the trip were primarily political. The visit indicated a reorientation of strategic calculations in both Dharamsala and Taipei, and the rapprochement between the two formerly hostile governments infuriated the authorities in Beijing, altering the dynamics of both the Tibetan and the Taiwanese independence movements. From another perspective however, the Dalai Lama's visit also demonstrated the increasing importance of the religious connections between Tibetan exiles and Taiwanese followers of Tibetan Buddhism. These connections have transformed the religious landscape of both Taiwan and the Tibetan diaspora in South Asia. Indeed, the growing popularity of Tibetan Buddhism in Taiwan has generated substantial patronage for the Tibetan exiles, providing invaluable assistance in their efforts to reconstitute the Tibetan monastic system in India and Nepal.

Of course, as the foregoing chapters demonstrate, religion and politics have been thoroughly intertwined throughout the history of Sino-Tibetan relations. In this respect, the Dalai Lama's visit to Taiwan may be interpreted as simply one in a long sequence of visits to Chinese territory by Tibetan hierarchs, visits that have often combined Buddhist missionary activity with political theater. But the trip also reflected the newly transnational character of Tibetan society in exile, in which both the religious and political arenas, while remaining deeply intertwined, have been redefined along global lines.

This redefinition has been realized both through the creation of a global narrative around the Tibetan political struggle, and through the formation of new globalized Tibetan Buddhist identities by and for non-Tibetans. Thus, regarding the visit's political implications, the Dalai Lama's symbolic capital in Taiwan derived as much from his status as a figure of contemporary international acclaim as it did from recollection of the imperial-era priest-patron institution (Tib. *mchod yon*). Similarly, while the popularity of Tibetan Buddhism in Taiwan undoubtedly owes much to the longstanding Chinese fascination with esoteric Buddhism, it is also the consequence of new patterns of Tibetan transnational missionary activity that have emerged in response to the challenges—especially economic ones—of exile. Supporters of Taiwan's burgeoning independence movement lent further significance to the Dalai Lama's presence, using it to indirectly bolster their claim that Taiwan is separate from China. Therefore, while the Dalai Lama's 1997 visit to Taiwan certainly should be interpreted as opening a dramatic new chapter in the long history of Tibetan leaders conducting politics with the Chinese state while simultaneously providing religious teachings to Chinese people, it must also be understood in relation to much more recent historical transformations, including the global spread of Tibetan Buddhism, the internationalization of the Tibetan political struggle, and the growing aspirations of some Taiwanese to declare their island independent from China.

As noted above, most observers emphasized the visit's political implications, which were substantial in at least three areas of contention. First, following the stalled negotiations between the Dalai Lama and the People's Republic of China (PRC), the Tibetan leader seemed to hope that the visit would demonstrate to the leadership in Beijing the sincerity of his oft-stated willingness to accept autonomy, rather than independence, for Tibet. The stated policy of the government in Taiwan—officially, the Republic of China (ROC)—was that both Taiwan and Tibet are part of China, and thus, as the Dalai Lama pointed out to a gathering of reporters upon arrival, "If I were to seek Tibet's complete independence, my current visit to Taiwan would have been very difficult. Therefore, the fact that I can visit Taiwan without any problems can indirectly explain or imply that I am not pursuing Tibet's complete independence."[1] The authorities in Beijing clearly felt otherwise; according to Beijing's loud protests, the trip heralded the commencement of a new "splittist" alliance between what it regarded as the two principal opponents of a unified China—the Tibetan government-in-exile in Dharamsala and the Guomindang (GMD) government in Taipei.

Second, regarding the relationship between Taiwan and the PRC, the visit appeared to fan the flames of Taiwan's ongoing internal debate over whether the island should declare itself an independent state. Hundreds of pro-independence demonstrators greeted the Dalai Lama's arrival on the island in the southern city of Kaohsiung, with banners proclaiming their support for Taiwanese (and Tibetan) independence from China, while a smaller group of counter-demonstrators demanded Taiwan's reunification with China. Ostensibly, Taiwanese President Lee Teng-hui opposed independence for Taiwan, but the invitation to the Dalai Lama could also be interpreted as an implicit step toward independence, particularly since he was treated in many ways as a distinguished foreigner, rather than as a visitor from the provinces. (Ironically, this may have recapitulated an aspect of the Thirteenth Dalai Lama's reception by the Qing court, as recounted in the preceding chapter.) Despite pressure from Taiwan's pro-independence groups, the Dalai Lama was not received as a visiting head of state. He was, however, treated as an exalted guest in numerous ways, including the provision of a twenty-car motorcade. This treatment was publicly justified by his religious status—the Dalai Lama was a world-renowned Buddhist leader after all—rather than his political status, which was intentionally left unclear. The then-opposition party, the pro-independence Democratic Progressive Party (DPP), went the furthest in explicitly using the visit to express the idea that Taiwan and Tibet were separate from one another, yet even it left the question of which of them was separate from China deliberately murky. The DPP's tactics included flying the Tibetan flag over the city halls they controlled (including Taipei) and proposing the abolition of the government ministry charged with overseeing Tibetan affairs, the Mongolian and Tibetan Affairs Commission (MTAC, Tib. *bod sog las khungs*, Ch. *meng zang weiyuanhui*).

Third, regarding the relationship between Taiwan and the Tibetan exiles, the Dalai Lama's arrival signified an end to the long period of hostility and suspicion that had existed between them. The Tibetan exiles' mistrust of Taiwan was rooted in its history of meddling and shady dealings, which had threatened the reputation of any Tibetan who dared to travel there. For many years, relations between the Tibetan government-in-exile and the government in Taipei had been strained due to allegations of Taiwanese attempts to buy influence among the Tibetans in an effort to co-opt their struggle against the Communists and bring them under Taiwan's control. Yet many Tibetan exiles—especially those who were suspicious of Dharamsala's authority—found Taiwanese aid to be invaluable in establishing some degree of financial independence from the exile government. The result was a bitter division within the exile world, one that mirrored older sectarian and regional tensions in Tibet, and that led some Dharamsala loyalists to assert that Taiwan was as dangerous an enemy as the PRC. The arrival of the Tibetan leader in Taiwan signaled that this conflict was at an end; if even His Holiness the Dalai Lama was meeting with Taiwanese politicians and accepting donations from Taiwanese Buddhists, surely there could no longer be any objection to ordinary Tibetans doing the same.

However, side-stepping the political salience of the visit, both the Dalai Lama and the Taiwanese government were at pains to give another interpretation, one that highlighted its *religious* significance. Before the Dalai Lama's arrival in Taiwan, his office issued a statement emphasizing his interest in pursuing intra-Buddhist dialogue in Taiwan. In particular, the Dalai Lama expressed his desire to learn more about the lineage of full ordination for nuns, which occurs in Taiwan but not within Tibetan Buddhism. Indeed, in recent years the full ordination lineage has begun to take root within Tibetan Buddhism, largely through the joint efforts of Taiwanese and Western nuns, with the potential to significantly alter the gender dynamics of Tibetan religion.[2] Once in Taiwan, the Dalai Lama repeatedly asserted that he was visiting as a religious leader, rather than a political one, stating, "I make this visit from the point of view of religion and culture. I hope I can enhance the happiness of Tibetan and Taiwan people through prayer meetings."[3] And certainly these "prayer meetings" were immensely popular, with 80,000 free tickets to three events quickly snapped up.[4] Fortunately, for those who could not get tickets, television stations broadcast live coverage of the ceremonies throughout the six-day visit. As "Dalai Lama fever" swept the island, the prices of Tibetan religious articles, which had been in vogue for some time, surged, and photos of the Dalai Lama—in great demand as good luck charms—could be found selling for around $80 apiece.[5]

Taiwanese authorities likewise stressed that the Dalai Lama was visiting as a religious figure, not a political one. The first four days of his visit, they noted, were entirely devoted to religious events, and even the political meetings he attended in the final two days of the trip were cast in a religious light. To this end, they repeatedly sought to characterize the climax of his trip—a meeting with Taiwanese President Lee Teng-hui, himself a Presbyterian—as an "historic meeting between masters of philosophy" and a "philosophical encounter."[6] This formulation, of course, was a modern version of the characterizations typically given to imperial-era meetings between Tibetan lamas and Chinese rulers, in which political negotiations were subsumed and justified within a larger narrative of mutually accepted Buddhist legitimation.

However, notwithstanding the official Tibetan and Taiwanese pronouncements, the visit was, as discussed above, clearly an event of great political significance. Therefore it may be tempting to dismiss the religious rhetoric as a disingenuous tactic to mask the real purpose of the Dalai Lama's trip. Certainly, Beijing authorities saw it this way, insisting that the religious character of the visit was merely a cover story behind which Lee and the Dalai Lama were plotting "separatist activities." As one PRC government spokesperson put it, "On one side the Dalai Lama publicizes internationally the view that he does not want Tibetan independence. On the other side, he everywhere engages in activities to split the motherland. This makes clear he is basically not sincere and has certainly not put aside his stance for so-called Tibetan independence."[7] A year after the Dalai Lama's trip, at a press conference with U.S. President Bill Clinton, Chinese President Jiang Zemin introduced a new requirement for negotiations with the Dalai Lama to commence: now, in addition to Beijing's long-standing insistence that the Dalai Lama acknowledge that Tibet was a part of China, he also had to acknowledge that Taiwan was an inseparable part of China. This was clearly an effort to disrupt what the PRC perceived as a nascent alliance between the exiles and the Taiwanese, since any such statement by the Dalai Lama would infuriate the pro-independence faction in Taiwan; indeed, the Dalai Lama has responded to questions about this issue by insisting that "as far as the future of Taiwan is concerned, that mainly depends on the people of Taiwan."[8] Nevertheless, despite Beijing's rejection of the Dalai Lama's claim that his visit demonstrated his willingness to settle for less than full independence, after the Tibetan leader visited Taiwan a second time in 2001, the long-stalled talks between Beijing and Dharamsala appeared to regain some momentum. The Dalai Lama's envoy, Lodi Gyari, led a delegation to China and Tibet in 2002 and again in 2003; in order to avoid disrupting any progress in these negotiations, the Dalai Lama has since declined several invitations to visit Taiwan again.

The importance of the political dimensions of the 1997 trip, however, in no way detracts from its concomitant and immense religious significance. Tibetan Buddhism has been booming in Taiwan, and elsewhere in the Chinese world, as part of a larger craze for esoteric religion (Ch. *mi jiao*). The number of Tibetan religious centers has grown rapidly in Taiwan since the 1980s and large crowds routinely attend when important Tibetan lamas offer tantric initiations (Tib. *dbang*). Donations from these disciples have become an indispensable source of support, not only for many of the Tibetan exiles' monasteries in India and Nepal, but even for Tibetan Buddhist religious centers and practitioners in Western countries. Thus, when the Dalai Lama gave Buddhist teachings in a sports stadium in Kaohsiung, attended by 50,000 people and watched on television by countless more, he was participating in, and fuelling, a dramatic revival of interest in Tibetan Buddhism among Chinese people.[9]

How is this revival to be understood? Is it simply a renewal of Sino-Tibetan religious ties according to a pattern that has been followed since at least the thirteenth century, with a brief interruption by the Communist takeover of China? Or is it part of the emergence of a new globalized paradigm of Tibetan Buddhism, characterized by the growth of transnational religious networks, reliance on new uses of media, and complex interactions between Tibetan, Chinese, South Asian, and Western followers of the religion? As will be seen, the contemporary articulation of Tibetan Buddhism in Taiwan is a complex hybrid, encompassing diverse religious practices, institutions, and conceptions, and shaped by the combined influence of old imperial-era connections and new transnational ones.

Tibetan Buddhism in Taiwan

There are almost 240 Tibetan Buddhist centers registered with the Taiwanese authorities and, according to some estimates, half a million followers of Tibetan Buddhism on the island, though both of these figures should be treated cautiously—the former probably underestimates the number of Tibetan Buddhist groups, while the latter probably substantially overestimates the number of Tibetan Buddhist practitioners. Nevertheless, Tibetan Buddhism is undeniably flourishing in Taiwan and has attained a unique position in its public culture. According to some, this is largely a passing fad, but others I interviewed suggested that Tibetan Buddhism, and especially its perceived power to ensure long life, financial success, marital and family harmony, and other this-worldly benefits (as seen, too, in Paul Nietupski's chapter above), has struck a deep and enduring chord among many Taiwanese.

It is important to distinguish the reasons for Tibetan Buddhism's appeal in Taiwan from those that have popularized it in the West. Western followers of Tibetan Buddhism are rarely motivated, at least primarily, by the religion's presumed power to provide this-worldly benefits. Rather, Western involvement in Tibetan Buddhism is usually associated with the presumed superiority of its meditative methods and philosophical arguments, and with the charisma of its teachers. Although Taiwanese and other Chinese followers of Tibetan Buddhism are certainly motivated by the personalities of Tibetan lamas too, there is comparatively less interest in Tibetan meditation or philosophy, and more in the efficacy of Tibetan rituals. Several Taiwanese Buddhists explained to me that those interested in meditation or philosophy were more likely to investigate other schools of Buddhism available in Taiwan, such as Chan.

A very different perspective on the question of Tibetan Buddhism's popularity was offered to me by some of the most deeply engaged Taiwanese followers, who—though often contemptuous of what they regarded as their peers' superstitious fascination with Tibetan religion's supposed supernatural qualities—insisted that Tibetan Buddhism is in every respect superior to Chinese Buddhism. Various reasons were given for this claim, including especially the view that the richness of Buddhist literature is most fully preserved in the Tibetan canon. Others emphasized to me their belief that Tibetans had maintained an unbroken lineage of realization, passed from master to disciple, and contrasted this with the various schools of Chinese Buddhism, which they saw as having lost this transmission. Still others asserted that Tibetan meditation techniques, especially those of Dzogchen, were simply superior to anything that Chinese Buddhism had to offer.

While past background has no doubt contributed to the widespread interest in Tibetan Buddhism that currently occupies in Taiwan, the present boom is a recent phenomenon, beginning only in the 1980s. The history of this expansion can be divided into three phases: the Mainlander transmission following the arrival of the GMD forces on the island (1949–1979), the Tibetan exile transmission following the arrival of large numbers of visiting Tibetan lamas from the diaspora (1980–1997), and the Tibetan exile transmission following the Dalai Lama's first visit to the island (1997 to the present).[10]

The Mainlander Transmission (1949–1979)

The first period, often called the Mainlander transmission, is best understood as a continuation of the Chinese involvement in Tibetan Buddhism that had existed on the mainland during the Republican period. Chinese interest in Tibetan Buddhism during the Republican period has its own historical antecedents, of course, in the statecraft of the Yuan, Ming, and Qing dynasties. However, during the Republican period Tibetan Buddhism moved beyond its previous court constituencies to achieve a new level of popularity among ordinary Han. In the 1920s and 1930s, there were extensive religious interactions between Tibet and China, including Tibetan lamas coming to China, Chinese monks traveling to Tibet, and the formation of Tibetan Buddhist institutes in China. Much of the scholarship on these exchanges has focused on their political ramifications, and these were admittedly considerable, but as Tuttle, Bianchi, and others have shown, there were also many individual Chinese who were genuinely interested in Tibetan Buddhism as a religious discipline.[11]

When the GMD retreated to Taiwan in 1949, some mainland followers of Tibetan Buddhism established religious centers on the island. The lineages of two Tibetan lamas—Norlha and Gangkar—were of particular importance, although neither man ever visited Taiwan himself.[12] The Nyingma sect was established on the island by three of Norlha's followers—Qu Yingguang, Wu Runjiang, and Hantong—as well as Guru Lau, a disciple of Dudjom Rinpoché (1904–1987). Gangkar's followers, especially Shen Shuwen and Prof. Zhang Chengji, helped establish the Kagyü sect in Taiwan; Chen Jianmin was another important and influential Kagyü teacher during this early period. Three Geluk teachers also had some impact in Taiwan: Zhangjia Hutuketu, Kangyurwa, and Gelek Dorje. The only Sakya teacher active in Taiwan during this early period was the fifteenth Ming Zhu Rinpoché.[13]

Three main points are striking about the Mainlander transmission period. First, from the outset, the Kagyü and Nyingma sects were the most successful in Taiwan. This may have been a consequence of the greater emphasis those sects place on esoteric practices, or of the political gulf that estranged (some) Kagyü and Nyingma lamas from Lhasa (and later Dharamsala), or it may have been due to a combination of these factors, but both sects continue to this day to enjoy greater popularity in Taiwan than the Geluk and the Sakya.[14] Second, with the exception of a few Geluk and Sakya incarnations who went to Taiwan during this period, most of the early teachers of Tibetan Buddhism in Taiwan were themselves Chinese; this was a period in which Tibetan Buddhism in Taiwan was mainly conducted by and for Mainland Chinese. Third, the overall development of Tibetan Buddhism in Taiwan during this period was relatively small and cannot be regarded as representing any substantial reconfiguration or revitalization of Sino-Tibetan religious interaction. Rather, it is best understood as the re-institutionalization in Taiwan, following the GMD's retreat to the island, of some Mainlanders' interest in Tibetan Buddhism.

Indeed, the impact of Tibetan Buddhism on the overall religious life of the island was so small during this period that Hsing, describing Buddhism in Taiwan on the eve of Tibetan Buddhism's upsurge there, suggested that there was scarcely any esoteric Buddhism on the entire island. Describing the "reformation and renaissance" of Buddhism on the island in the period up to 1979, he wrote, "the only exception [to this renaissance] is the Tantric sect. I visited a monk who practiced Tantric Buddhism in Chu Ch'i Ssu at Tainan. He told me that there were no more than two monks practicing Tantric Buddhism in Taiwan at the present time."[15] While Hsing undoubtedly greatly underestimated the prevalence of Tibetan Buddhism in Taiwan during the Mainlander transmission period, it is clear that esoteric Buddhism had a very low profile in Taiwan at the time he wrote, in marked contrast to the considerable attention it has enjoyed since the 1980s.

The Tibetan Exile Transmission (1980–1997)

This situation changed quickly in the 1980s. During this period, seen as the first transmission from exiled Tibetans, visiting Tibetan lamas attracted widespread interest on the island. This "Tibet craze" ushered the rapid growth of Tibetan Buddhist centers in Taiwan, and a revitalization of Tibetan religion and art in Taiwan's public culture. This period began with visits to Taiwan by the Kagyü lamas Thrangu Rinpoche in 1980 and Kalu Rinpoche in 1982, and then accelerated in 1984, when the new chairman of the Mongolian and Tibetan Affairs Commission (MTAC) initiated a strong effort promoting Tibetan Buddhism in Taiwan, including facilitating the arrival of visiting lamas. Soon, many lamas, especially from the Kagyü and Nyingma sects, were traveling to Taiwan, first to teach and perform empowerments, and later to establish centers and communities of followers.[16]

What happened in the 1980s to cause this rapid transformation? From the Taiwanese perspective, Buddhist groups of all varieties were proliferating as the hegemony of state-sponsored Buddhism weakened, and the revival of Tibetan Buddhism was simply one manifestation of the Buddhist renaissance occurring.[17] Moreover, as the restrictions of martial law were eased, people in Taiwan had greater freedom to travel and some used the opportunity to cultivate relationships with Tibetan lamas living in exile in India and Nepal, and to invite them to visit the island. From this point of view, there had always been a latent demand for Tibetan Buddhism on the island, and as soon as the political situation relaxed, Taiwanese disciples took advantage of their new freedom to draw Tibetan religious teachers to Taiwan.

From the Tibetan perspective, by the 1980s the global networks of Tibetan Buddhism that had begun in the 1960s and 1970s were entering a new phase of rapid expansion. Senior lamas who had previously been preoccupied with reestablishing their monasteries in South Asia were now devoting more of their time and energy to establishing branch centers around the world, while a new cohort of younger lamas who had grown up in exile were increasingly establishing their own global followings. This transnational expansion was due both to the need of the exiles to find patrons to sponsor their reconstruction efforts in South Asia and to their recognition that there was a global demand for their religion that, in accordance with Buddhist doctrine, they ought to satisfy. Taiwanese Buddhists, enriched by the economic boom that had begun in Taiwan during the 1970s, proved to be particularly generous sponsors, and this helped make the island a frequent destination for many Tibetan Buddhist monastics and teachers. From this vantage, Taiwan was simply one site, albeit a very important one, in the emerging transnational networks of Tibetan Buddhism.

The question of how to understand the dramatic growth of Tibetan Buddhism in Taiwan depends substantially on which of these two perspectives we choose to emphasize. To the extent that we focus our attention on the ways in which—in the aftermath of the period of martial law—Buddhists in Taiwan reestablished religious ties with Tibetan lamas in the diaspora, the growth of Tibetan Buddhism in Taiwan will appear as a new chapter in an old story of Sino-Tibetan religious interaction. On the other hand, to the extent that we emphasize the emergence of new transnational networks of Tibetan Buddhism—networks which weave relationships between Tibetan monasteries in South Asia and branch centers in Taiwan, the United States, Europe, and elsewhere—the growth of Tibetan Buddhism in Taiwan will appear as one variant in a comparatively new story, the story of the globalization of Tibetan Buddhism.

Regardless of the reasons behind the sudden expansion of Tibetan Buddhism in the 1980s, by the time Keng surveyed 120 followers of Tibetan Buddhism in Taiwan in the mid-1990s, it was clearly no longer primarily a Mainlander subculture.[18] Twenty-eight percent of her respondents identified themselves as Mainlanders, while 63% were Fukienese and 8% Hakka, indicating that although Mainlanders still constituted an important constituency of Tibetan Buddhism in Taiwan, visiting Tibetan lamas enjoyed success across the spectrum of Taiwanese society. It should be noted here that Mainlanders (those inhabitants of Taiwan who came from the mainland with the GMD in 1949 and their descendants) make up only roughly 15% of Taiwan's population. Therefore, Keng's finding that 28% of Tibetan Buddhists in Taiwan are Mainlanders does indeed show the Mainlanders' disproportionate involvement, even as it also demonstrates that Tibetan Buddhism in

Taiwan is no longer solely of interest to them. In contrast to the view that it is primarily Mainlanders who are participating in Tibetan Buddhism—with the implication that the trend is mainly a carry-over from religious practices on the mainland, and hence only peripherally connected to the social and religious currents of Taiwanese society, I will argue that a major factor in the development of Tibetan Buddhism there has been the emergence of the Taiwanese independence movement, precisely because independence advocates have found in the issue of Tibetan autonomy a useful way to express their own desire to establish their own autonomy and fully break from the mainland.

In short, unlike the Mainlander transmission, the Tibetan exile transmission reflects a more complex interplay between longstanding Sino-Tibetan religious patterns and the recent globalization of Tibetan Buddhism. This transmission is also linked—on the Taiwanese side—to the religious boom that commenced following the liberalization of society in the 1980s and—on the Tibetan side—to the politics of infighting in the diaspora and the relationships between certain Tibetan exiles and the Taiwanese state, which will be discussed further below.

The Tibetan Exile Transmission (1997–present)

The Dalai Lama's arrival in Taiwan in 1997 began what I argue constitutes a third phase in the development of Tibetan Buddhism there. While it is still too soon to say definitively how the latest phase will differ from the ones that preceded it, three important transformations are already recognizable. First, the media sensation that the Dalai Lama created in a single week brought an entirely new level of public attention to Tibetan Buddhism in Taiwan. The treatment of the Dalai Lama as a cultural icon was not unlike the fusion of "exotic" spirituality and celebrity-worship present at his reception during his many visits to Western countries. This seems certain to further popularize not only Tibetan Buddhism itself—indeed, between 1996 and 2005 the number of Tibetan Buddhist centers in Taiwan more than doubled—but also to engender "orientalist" conceptions of Tibet and Tibetans in Taiwan, as it has elsewhere.

Second, as noted earlier, the Dalai Lama's visit effectively ended the debate within the Tibetan diaspora regarding the propriety of visiting or receiving funds from Taiwan. With the Dalai Lama himself now having done both, the path to Taiwan, and the patronage that it affords, is now open. Already there are indications that some of the Tibetan monastics who had previously maintained distance are beginning to establish religious contacts in Taiwan.

Third, following the Dalai Lama's visit, changes have taken place in the bureaucratic organization of Tibetan Buddhism in Taiwan. Most importantly, the MTAC, long the gatekeeper of Taiwan for Tibetans wishing to visit, and the bane of the Tibetan government-in-exile, has lost some of its power and budget, and may eventually be eliminated altogether if some of Taiwan's legislators have their way. In addition, the Tibetan diaspora now has a representative office in Taipei, the Tibet Religious Foundation, created in the wake of the Dalai Lama's 1997 visit, which is similar to the quasi-embassies that the Tibetan government-in-exile has established elsewhere. Another office, the Taiwan Tibet Exchange Foundation, opened in early 2003 and serves as a non-governmental channel for Taiwan to conduct affairs with Tibetan exiles without going through the MTAC.

In certain respects, the current, post–Dalai Lama period is similar to the phase of Tibetan exile transmission that preceded the Dalai Lama's visit. Charismatic Tibetan lamas continue to visit the island, attracting disciples, opening centers, and performing initiations and other tantric ceremonies that attract large crowds. Although the Dalai Lama and others strongly discourage Tibetan teachers from claiming magical powers, the supernormal qualities that Taiwanese are wont to attribute to Tibetan masters remain a powerful aspect of their appeal. In addition, donations from Taiwanese supporters continue to be a substantial source of revenue for Tibetan exiles.

In other respects, however, the post–Dalai Lama period has decisively diverged from the past. For Tibetans, the rapprochement between Taipei and Dharamsala has meant an end to questions about the loyalty of those Tibetans who travel there. Taiwan is no longer envisaged as the habitat of the "black Chinese," as hated and feared as the "red" variety; nor is it necessarily the special ally of those Tibetan exiles who have—for sectarian or regionalist reasons—found themselves in opposition to the authority of the Dharamsala government-in-exile.

For the Taiwanese, the rapprochement reflects a gradual and contested reorientation of identity, politics, and the state over the past several decades. Although the island's involvement with Tibetan exiles once constituted continuing evidence of Taiwan's vision of itself as the Republic of China, since the Dalai Lama's visit, this logic has been turned on its head. Tibetan lamas continue to visit Taiwan, and Tibetan Buddhism continues to thrive there, but increasingly these are markers not of Taiwan's participation in the logic of an imperial China, but rather of its emergence as a separate entity on the global stage.

Tibetan Buddhist Centers and Buddhists in Taiwan

In 1996, there were 101 Tibetan religious institutions registered with the Taiwanese government's Mongolian and Tibetan Affairs Commission. By 1998, that number had grown to 133. In 2005, the MTAC registry listed 238 centers, an increase of 140% over a ten-year period.[19] However, the actual number of centers where Tibetan Buddhism is practiced is clearly even greater than this, as many are overlooked and so not included in the MTAC's registry, a problem stemming mainly from the MTAC's former position as Taiwan's gatekeeper for visiting Tibetan lamas and monks, and in particular its role, now curtailed, in securing religious visas for these visitors. A number of these institutions, although Tibetan in form and lineage, have an entirely Chinese leadership structure and thus have never required the MTAC's assistance in procuring visas for Tibetan teachers. The Vajrayana Esoteric Society, for example, is not included in the MTAC's registry, even though its founder, Guru Lau Yui Che, was a disciple of the famous Tibetan master Dudjom Rinpoché, and its center in Taichung has an enormous image of the archetypal founding figure of Tibetan Buddhism, Padmasambhava, towering over its entrance. In addition, even centers that do extend invitations to Tibetan lamas do not always require the MTAC's help to bring them to Taiwan, especially if the visitors have North American or European travel documents. Although the situation has changed since the pro-independence DPP took power, at the time of the 1996 count, the many Tibetans from South Asia who wished to enter Taiwan could do so only under the auspices of the MTAC, which provided about 2,000 religious visas for Tibetan exiles each year. And finally, the MTAC requires institutions to meet minimum membership levels to be registered—thirty members for centers in Taipei, one hundred members elsewhere in the country—and therefore its registry does not include small or informal Tibetan Buddhist groups.

The number of Tibetan Buddhists in Taiwan is even more difficult to determine. During the Dalai Lama's 1997 visit, it was widely reported that there were some 500,000 Tibetan Buddhists on the island but it is safe to assume that this number is highly suspect. Its source appears to be an MTAC estimate, which one highly placed MTAC official admitted to me in 1996 was "rough."[20] It should be noted that the MTAC has every reason to overestimate, since some Taiwanese would like to see the commission abolished and the larger the constituency the MTAC can establish, the greater the justification it has for its own existence. For the MTAC's estimate to be correct, a substantial portion of the Buddhists in Taiwan would have to identify themselves as Tibetan Buddhists. This seems very unlikely, particularly given the fact that much of Tibetan Buddhism's appeal, in Taiwan as elsewhere, is a function of its otherness and its standing as an unusual alternative to normative forms of religious identity. One Taiwanese scholar of Tibetan Buddhism told me that she estimated the number of Tibetan Buddhists in Taiwan to be closer to 100,000.[21]

Of course, any estimate, whether 100,000 or 500,000, suffers from the difficulty of determining who is, and who is not, a "Tibetan Buddhist."[22] In Taiwan this distinction is often nebulous, encompassing both earnest devotees and followers of the latest religious fad. Tibetan religious symbols, artwork, and recorded chants can all be easily observed while making one's way around Taipei. Yet when I inquired into the reasons why a particular shop prominently displayed a Tibetan Kālacakra symbol, or a taxi driver had a set of Tibetan-style prayer beads, or several shopkeepers continuously played recordings of Tibetans chanting "Oṃ Maṇi Padme Hūṃ," I usually found that such presentations of Tibetan religious culture reflected little or no actual knowledge of, or participation in, traditional Tibetan religion. In this respect, the trajectory Tibetan Buddhism is following in contemporary Taiwan is similar to that it has followed elsewhere around the world, where serious interest is probably limited to a small core of avid participants, complemented by great popular appeal of a more superficial nature. Corroborating this contention, many interviewees revealed that although their centers have modest numbers of routinely active members, attendance surges when a *wang* ("empowerment") or other esoteric Buddhist ceremony is performed. Particularly charismatic or famous teachers routinely attract several thousand people to their events. In short, regardless of exactly how many people in Taiwan identify themselves as Tibetan Buddhists, it is undeniable that the religion resonates with the Taiwanese and that it is now an object of popular fascination, occupying a space in Taiwan's public culture that is dramatically different from the marginal status it had during the Mainlander transmission period.

Stories of Tibetan magic and mystery are common among Taiwanese followers of Tibetan Buddhism and can be understood as part of an old and continuing Chinese discourse about Tibet. In this respect, contemporary narratives about esoteric religion (Ch. *mi jiao*) in Taiwan echo records of imperial encounters with Tibetan holy men. But these narratives are also imbued with a new subtext that emphasizes the *traditionalism* of Tibetan culture, imagined as persisting more or less unchanged over the centuries, in marked distinction to the rapid transformations induced by Taiwanese *modernity*. Thus, Taiwanese engagement with Tibetan religion renders it doubly exotic, first by reinstating historical conceptualizations of Tibet as a "barbaric other" in contrast to Chinese civilization, and, second, by reflecting contemporary conceptualizations of Tibet as a "traditional other" in contrast to the (global) modernity found in Taiwan.

The mystique surrounding Tibetan Buddhism's capacity to bring good fortune has become so pervasive in Taiwan that the Dalai Lama felt it necessary, while meeting with Tibetans residing in Taiwan, to insist that anyone who actually has magical powers should immediately demonstrate them to him.[23] Nevertheless, the widespread perception among the Taiwanese that Tibetan Buddhist masters possess magical powers seems to have continued unabated. One high-ranking official in Taiwan's government told me that he had once enlisted the services of an important lama to ensure that a particular typhoon would miss the island. The lama had duly complied, commenting as an aside, the official told me, that it was much easier to control typhoons than it was to bring rain.[24] Belief in such possibilities is sufficiently prevalent so that, during a rainy press conference, reporters requested the Dalai Lama to "command the wind and the rain," but he demurred, insisting that it was "impossible."[25] Nonetheless, perhaps conceding to Taiwanese longings, on his second visit to the island, in 2001, the Dalai Lama sent eight monks to perform an earthquake prevention ritual in an area that had been devastated by an earthquake in 1999.

The Taiwanese Connection: The Politics of Patronage

I first began to take an interest in the relationship between Tibetan exiles and Taiwan while living in Kathmandu in the early 1990s. I lived in Boudhanath, a neighborhood that was a major center for Tibetans, and it was clearly prospering—new houses, new cars, new hotels, and, especially, large new monasteries were everywhere. There were a number of reasons for this economic success, but one major, and controversial, source of income was the island of Taiwan. In addition to the patronage of private individuals, state patronage from the ROC government has also provided significant financial support to Tibetan exiles. In the following sections, I examine the larger political context that has framed the relationship between Tibetans and Taiwan. Only by understanding this context can we understand how Tibetan Buddhism has developed in Taiwan, and why Taiwanese patronage has been of such consequence for some Tibetans in exile, who might otherwise have been marginalized within the larger diaspora community. By examining how Taiwan injected itself into ongoing regional and sectarian disputes within Tibetan society, we see how those same regional and sectarian distinctions have been replicated in the world of Taiwanese Tibetan Buddhism, and how the support of Taiwan enabled some Tibetan exiles to escape what they perceived as the hegemony of the Dharamsala government. The import of these developments must be understood if we are to recognize the revolutionary impact of the Dalai Lama's 1997 visit to Taiwan and the rapprochement that followed.

Taiwanese Claims of Sovereignty over Tibet

When the GMD retreated to Taiwan in 1949 after losing the civil war with the Communists, it continued to regard itself as the legitimate government of all of China. Taiwan's official name remains the "Republic of China," and in a variety of ways the structure of the state reflects this conception of itself. For example, until recently, the island had two parallel political structures, one of which existed for the governance of the province of Taiwan, within the larger Chinese state, and the other of which purported to be the government of all of China, even though it could exercise control only over Taiwan. Similarly, until the recent bureaucratic reorganization, the parliament of the national government had representatives from all of China's provinces, including Tibet. The inclusion of Tibetan representatives in this structure reflected the view, shared by both the ROC and the PRC, that Tibet was and is a part of China. That is, while the ROC and the PRC disagreed over which of them was the legitimate government of China, they were in agreement that Tibet was part of what they were fighting over. The ROC expressed its claims to sovereignty over Tibet in various ways, and in particular through the operations of the MTAC. This claim of sovereignty infuriated the Tibetan exiles, and it was this that led to serious conflict between the Taiwanese government and the Tibetan government-in-exile. Dharamsala's hostility toward the MTAC was provoked not only by the latter's rhetoric, but also by its disbursal of funds to Tibetans, which the Tibetan government viewed as a strategy to buy the loyalty of the Tibetan exiles and co-opt them to the ROC's side. This, more than anything, brought Dharamsala and Taipei into conflict. The MTAC, on the other hand, considers its provision of financial support a part of its fundamental mission: to attend to the needs of Tibetans and Mongolians, whom it sees as fellow citizens.

When I visited the MTAC in 1996, officials there told me that the Tibetan division had a budget of about US $2 million, of which about 60% was allocated for Tibetan exiles. The MTAC officials I spoke with explained the purpose and meaning of these funds using a rhetoric of Tibetan advancement, but in two distinct senses. From one perspective, articulated to me by Chen Yu-Hsin, the Chinese director of the MTAC's Tibetan section, their role is "to serve and help Tibetans."[26] He appeared to see the Tibetan exiles as unfortunate cousins, toward whom Taiwan had an obligation to render support because of the island's greater prosperity and their shared national identity. In this sense, Chen's justification for the MTAC's involvement with the Tibetan exiles portrayed the commission as a kind of *de facto* development agency, providing schools, scholarships, vocational training, and so forth to Tibetan exiles.

Alternatively, Cheuh-An Tsering, the MTAC's highest Tibetan official, told me that Tibetan engagement with Taiwan and China was a matter of political necessity. He argued that "Tibetans must engage with the Chinese in order to get Tibet back. It's no good remaining aloof from them. And engaging in politics in the Chinese world means personal relationships."[27] Thus, he suggested, his work at the MTAC was a means of furthering the Tibetan political struggle, since furthering the interest of Chinese people in matters Tibetan can only advance the Tibetan cause. Although he did not explicitly argue that Chinese practicing Tibetan Buddhism could be politically advantageous for the Tibetans, it is obvious that this is a potential consequence of the popularity Tibetan Buddhism is enjoying among Chinese in Taiwan and elsewhere.

Based on these justifications, the MTAC has for years pursued an active program of engagement with the Tibetan exiles. As of 1996, some of the programs the MTAC had funded or was then funding, included:

○ Between 1983 and 1996: vocational training in Taiwan for periods of six months was provided to 460 Tibetans from South Asia.
○ Between 1987 and 1996: year-long training programs in Mandarin language brought 50 Tibetan exiles to Taiwan.
○ Every year, fully-sponsored 5-year university educations in Taiwan are awarded to seven Tibetan students.
○ US $1000/year is provided to 10 Tibetan students for university studies in South Asia, and US $200/year to 30 students for secondary education in South Asia.
○ 400 Tibetan Muslims have been sponsored to study in Saudi Arabia, where the MTAC maintains a representative.[28]
○ In March 1996, a new program was created to provide vocational training to new arrivals from Tibet in Delhi and Kathmandu.

○ Although discontinued in 1990, there had been a program that brought small children from the age of six for long-term study in Taiwan.
○ Finally, grants are awarded to some Tibetan schools in India and Nepal for equipment and teachers' salaries.

Most of these programs have had the effect of strengthening ties between Taiwan and the exiles, through bringing Tibetan exiles to Taiwan, fostering Chinese language skills among Tibetans, and maintaining economic and educational aid programs in the Tibetan diaspora in South Asia. One of the MTAC's projects was even more successful than anticipated in furthering positive relations between Tibetans and Taiwan. As MTAC officials told me, the program for young Tibetan children in Taiwan was discontinued because the almost 100 students who participated between 1980 and 1990 had become so acculturated to Taiwan that they were largely unable to return and reintegrate into Tibetan exile society.

From the perspective of many Tibetan exiles, however, the MTAC is not engaged in benign efforts to "serve and help Tibetans." Rather, their programs are undertaken in order to buy influence and disrupt the unity of the Tibetan community, thereby furthering Taiwan's claim to sovereignty over Tibet and affording Taiwan some influence over the activities of Tibetans in exile. Internal divisions within the Tibetan diaspora, along regional and sectarian lines, moreover, exacerbated the friction between Taipei and Dharamsala. Some exiles, anxious to remain independent from the Tibetan government-in-exile, and especially from its perceived regional and sectarian biases, found the ROC to be a valuable ally. Their relations with Taiwan were conducted through the MTAC, making the commission anathema to those Tibetans who remained loyal to Dharamsala.

Tibetan hostility and suspicion toward Taiwan is certainly rooted in the long and tangled history between Tibet and China. In particular, the government in Taiwan is perceived as the direct descendant of the Nationalists who sought to meddle in Tibetan affairs throughout the first part of the twentieth century. Nevertheless, the antagonism has been reinvigorated by the ROC's interference, since 1949, in Tibetan political ambitions, including its alleged interference in the Tibetan resistance movement, both during the 1950s and later, during the Mustang phase of the operation. More recently, a pair of major scandals related to Taiwan, in 1989 and 1994, rocked the Tibetan diaspora community, exposing major regional and sectarian divisions among the exiles.

Taiwan and the Tibetan Resistance Forces

For Taiwan, its involvement with Tibetan exiles had propaganda value: in the early days, it was a morale booster for the defeated Nationalist armies to learn that, just as they too were prepared to fight on, other parts of China were also continuing to resist Communist hegemony, and doing it under GMD leadership. From the beginning of the Tibetan uprising against the Communists in 1956, the GMD claimed that the Tibetan forces were operating under their guidance. Indeed the first news of the uprising to appear in the American media came via Taiwan.[29] Some have suggested that the GMD's claims to have organized the Tibetan resistance were not merely propaganda, but reflected the GMD's real attempts to influence the resistance forces. According to Peissel, after Rapgya Pandatsang, a Khampa leader, failed to secure American support for the resistance he

> was obliged . . . to negotiate with Taiwan agents for Chinese Nationalist support. This was granted on the basis that the Chinese Nationalists still claimed Tibet to be theirs and also because it was known that in Amdo there were still in hiding some 12,000 Chinese Nationalist troops who had fled there after 1949. . . . It was a half-hearted involvement on both sides. The Khampas reluctantly having to seek support from their ancient enemies the Chinese Nationalists, the United States catering not so much to Tibetan interests as to those of Taiwan, and their own national fear of communism.[30]

D.T. Norbu, investigating Peissel's claims, asserted that "there is no denying that Khampas received aid from Taiwan in their pre-1959 operations." The initial U.S. assistance to the Tibetans was routed through Taiwan "which meant it was more a part of U.S. aid to the Nationalist Chinese than to the Tibetans." But later on the U.S. aid went directly to the Tibetans. "According to a Tibetan leader who was deeply involved in the hush-hush transactions, a State Dept authority told him in so many words: 'Why are you asking Taiwan for help? They are asking for everything from us. Why not contact us directly?'"[31]

These allegations created a furor in the exile community. For example, Norbu's article led to an angry rejoinder denying that Taiwan exerted any influence over the Tibetan resistance fighters:

We . . . wish to state that your accusation is an incredible lie that has needlessly and undeservedly cast an ugly blot on the names of our comrades who have fought and died for the cause of Tibetan freedom. You base your statement on the dubious words of a foreigner called Michel Peissel: an adventurer and a liar, who has written a cheap and sensational book that contains nothing but hearsay and generalizations. He pretends to be a friend of Tibet. But behind his mask of apparent friendship, there lurks the ugly, treacherous, buck-toothed face of a Taiwan agent. Our enemy is China! Whether it be the China of the Manchus, the Communists, or the KMT is of little difference. . . . [Unless you retract the statement and] publish an apology . . . we will be forced to regard you as a traitor.[32]

In a published interview, however, the Dalai Lama acknowledged that the Taiwanese had at least some role in the Tibetans' armed struggle:

Q: The Taiwanese also made an offer about arms?
Dalai Lama: I think even in 1957, 1958, 1959 up to 1963 some CIA involvement through Taiwan was there, but not at the time of [the] Uprising (of 1959).[33]

Despite—or perhaps because of—this acknowledgment, Taiwan's involvement with the Tibetan resistance movement continued to be a source of contention in the Tibetan exile community.

This tension deepened after a rift developed among the resistance forces in 1969. The Tibetan forces, which were by this time based in the Mustang region of Nepal, split into two factions, one led by Gyato Wangdu and the other led by Baba Yeshi. Yeshi's faction was supported by Khampa and Amdo partisans, particularly in the so-called "thirteen group" of settlements. These thirteen settlements in India and Nepal, mainly populated by Khampa and Amdowa Tibetans, resented what they perceived as the efforts of Dharamsala, and especially the Dalai Lama's elder brother Gyalo Thondup, to take control of the resistance forces. The rift reflected longstanding regionalist tensions within the Tibetan polity. Specifically, because the initial core of the Tibetan resistance in the 1950s had been Khampa and Amdo fighters, at a time when Central Tibetans were still attempting to accommodate the Chinese occupation forces, some Khampa and Amdowa were bitterly opposed to the apparent plan of the Tibetan government-in-exile—itself dominated by

Central Tibetans—to take control of the military force they had built with their own blood and sacrifice. For some Khampa and Amdowa, this was yet one more instance in the long history of the Central Tibetan efforts to dominate them.

Moreover, because the resistance forces were being funded and supplied by the CIA, this internecine contest had implications beyond questions of who had operational control over the troops. Dharamsala's efforts to displace Baba Yeshi's leadership can be read, in part, as a struggle over patronage. In response to the challenge, the thirteen group turned to Taiwan, which was more than willing to fund the resistance, as an alternative source of support. Thus the regionalist tensions that had so often afflicted Tibetan politics in the past were reinstated in exile. Moreover, although the regional and sectarian dynamics did not precisely correspond,[34] some of the most eminent non-Geluk lamas were Khampas who sympathized with the thirteen group. During this period, when the long-term survival of Tibetan culture, religion, and society was very much in doubt, Tibetans once again found themselves caught in the factionalism that had so often characterized the Tibetan political order. While they continued their struggle against the common Chinese foe, the exiles divided along regional and sectarian lines, and turned to outside patrons for support against their Tibetan rivals. Ironically, although this weakened the ability of the Tibetan government-in-exile to foster a nascent sense of nationalist loyalty among the exiles, it also contributed to the increasing globalization of Tibetan Buddhism, as individual communities (at least among the thirteen group), monastic institutions (at least among the non-Geluk sects), and Buddhist lamas, were forced to look beyond the Dharamsala government for support.

In sum, although much of the history of Taiwan's involvement with the Tibetan resistance remains murky, one point is clear: at some point Taiwan did establish links with some members of the exile community, at least some of whom had been active leaders in the Tibetan resistance struggle. Internal conflicts were behind this. Some Tibetan exiles were mistrustful of the policies of the Dharamsala government. There were sectarian fears that, under the guise of establishing an umbrella for Tibetan Buddhism in exile, all the orders would be brought under Geluk control. There were also regional fears that the Dharamsala government could not be relied on to look after the interests of Khampa and Amdowa. These concerns made some in the diaspora amenable to alternative sources of support, and they found a ready ally in Taiwan.

Conversely, this meant that Dharamsala loyalists came to hate and fear Taiwan. Already in the 1960s, some Tibetan exiles perceived Taiwan as an enemy that was—because of its surreptitious activities—as dangerous to the Tibetan cause as the PRC itself. A vivid expression of this perspective appeared in 1968:

> Instead [of stating their support for Tibetan independence] the Nationalist Government, or rather the Intelligence Department of the GMD, has been engaged in all kinds of dubious and insidious activities. Apart from making wildly imaginative claims of having close contacts with Tibetan resistance fighters and even more extravagant claims of directing their activities, the Department has been engaging in all sorts of intrigues sabotaging the unity of the Tibetan refugees. Large funds are spent on these nefarious activities and a number of individual Tibetans of doubtful character and record have been taken to Taiwan and paraded there as 'generals' and 'leaders' of the Tibetan resistance. The so-called 'Bureau of Tibetan and Mongolian Affairs' continues to function in Taipei and all the wishful thinking and pretence of Tibet being a part of China is kept. . . . [Officials are misleading] the Generalissimo and his son, the Defense Minister, describing the Tibetan national liberation movement as being instigated and led by foreigners. This would naturally mislead the Nationalist Government to conclude that Taipei should try and direct the "real" movement against the Chinese Communists in Tibet. . . . The time has come when Nationalist China should realize the nature of the Tibetan struggle and respect the demands of the Tibetan people.[35]

The 1989 Taiwan Scandal

The long simmering hostility of some Tibetan exiles toward Taiwan finally erupted in a major scandal in 1989. A leading member of the thirteen group of settlements, who had long been criticized by Dharamsala loyalists for taking Taiwanese funds, charged that Dharamsala was *also* secretly taking money from Taiwan and, moreover, that a high official of the exile government had pocketed a large quantity of these funds. In the ensuing uproar, the government's credibility was seriously compromised; this, in turn, led to the widespread suspicion that the entire affair had been engineered by Taiwan to sow dissension and mistrust in the exile community.

The scandal had its origins in the pro-independence demonstrations that occurred in Lhasa between 1987 and 1989. Shortly after the imposition of martial law in 1989, Yan Mingfu, the secretary of the CPC Central Secretariat in Beijing, accused Dharamsala of orchestrating the protests. Such accusations were not unusual, but this time there was a new twist: he alleged that this operation involved exiles smuggling arms into Tibet, using foreign tourists as agents, and, most inflammatory of all, that the Tibetan operatives had been trained in Japan by unspecified non-governmental organizations:

> [The Dalai Lama's] government-in-exile made use of the opening up of Tibet to send people across the border to plot a large-scale riot in Lhasa on 10 March. To prevent violence and to save the lives and properties of the Tibetan people, the central government decided to impose martial law in Lhasa, thus disrupting their plan of a large-scale riot. We confirmed that *they had shipped many weapons into Tibet; and that they had sent in some people who had undergone special training in Japan. These people were not trained by the Japanese Government, of course, but by different kinds of organizations that paid for the training.* Soon after we learned this, we sent a message to the Dalai Lama and requested that he stop doing this if he really intended to improve relations with us. Aware of our strict control, *the Dalai then turned to foreign tourists to infiltrate Tibet* through various channels, showing no sincerity in attempting to improve relations with us [italics mine].[36]

The implications of these allegations were enormous. If Tibetan operatives were being trained in Japan, it would have been the first time that a foreign power was involved in Tibetan efforts to resist China since the CIA had stopped its Tibetan operations in the 1960s. In addition, given that the Dalai Lama had recently made well-publicized proposals to China in an effort to open a pathway to a negotiated settlement,[37] if it were true that exiles were simultaneously smuggling arms to Tibet, it would suggest that the Dalai Lama's proposal had not been in good faith.

The Tibetan government-in-exile denied the Chinese accusations but later in 1989 new allegations surfaced, this time from within the Tibetan community, that there was indeed a Japanese link to the demonstrations in Tibet. It was further claimed that the financial backing for the operation had come from Taiwan and, perhaps most disconcerting, that some of these funds had been embezzled by an important member of the Tibetan government-in-exile, who was stationed in Japan. These allegations had an explosive impact on the Tibetan community. If they were true, it would mean that, contrary to Dharamsala's public stance, the Tibetan government-in-exile was *also* taking funds from the MTAC, but doing so secretly. The scandal surrounding these accusations was intense. It was widely believed that some members of the thirteen group of settlements were taking funds from Taiwan, and they were strongly criticized for this. So, when a leading member of the thirteen group charged that the Tibetan government-in-exile was also receiving funding from Taiwan, and moreover that the main conduit for these funds—a highly respected member of the Tibetan community—was suspected of pocketing hundreds of thousands of dollars, it produced an enormous uproar. The scandal was further intensified by allegations that the reason the Taiwanese had provided the funds was to help Dharamsala foment trouble inside Tibet, since this revived old suspicions from the days of the Mustang resistance that Taiwan sought to supplant Tibetan leadership of the independence struggle and bring the Tibetan political struggle under its wing. Dharamsala's oblique acknowledgment that it had used some Taiwanese funds for activities inside Tibet did not help matters.

The controversy also caused Taiwanese to question the purpose and role of the MTAC, which was seen as Taiwan's principal agent in the affair. At a committee meeting of Taiwan's Legislative Yuan on April 16, 1990, lawmakers proposed a variety of measures to limit the MTAC, including cutting its budget and even abolishing it outright.[38] Kao Tien-lai, a representative for Taiwanese aborigines pointed out the discrepancy that, although there were only 728 Mongolians and Tibetans in Taiwan, the commission had a budget of NT $180 million, whereas there were 340,000 aborigines in Taiwan, for whom only NT $66 million was allocated. Kao, with the support of three other lawmakers, proposed reallocating these budgets in proportion to the Tibetan, Mongolian, and aborigine populations. He also proposed changing the MTAC into an agency for all "Chinese minorities." Opposing this, a Tibetan member of Taiwan's Legislature pointed out that "there are 1.35 million [*sic*] Tibetans around the world," and yet, he claimed, the MTAC's budget was less than that which was allocated for Tibetan affairs by the United States, Japan, West Germany, or Britain. Therefore, he argued, Taiwan should actually increase its expenditure for the MTAC. Other lawmakers reportedly raised questions about whether the MTAC should exist at all, pointing out that (Outer) Mongolia was already independent and that the Tibetans were seeking independence.[39]

Although none of these proposals were enacted, the question of what to do about the MTAC has remained a thorny and complex issue in Tibet-

Taiwan relations. The debate reveals three main points of view within the Taiwanese polity regarding both the MTAC and the broader question of Taiwan's relations with Tibet. Advocates of the first point of view, who correlate closely with those Taiwanese who favor reunification with China, regard the MTAC as a positive and valuable arm of the government. Its funds should be expanded because Taiwan has an obligation to help Tibetans around the world as national compatriots. Those holding the second point of view, who correlate closely with Taiwanese who favor declaring Taiwan an independent state, separate from China, regard the MTAC as pointless or even detrimental. In their view, it should be abolished because it has nothing to do with Taiwan. Supporters of the third point of view, who correlate closely with those Taiwanese who favor independence from China in theory, but consider it impossible to achieve at the present, regard the MTAC's continued existence as necessary to demonstrate to China that Taiwan is not seeking to declare itself independent. In their view, abolishing the MTAC would indicate that the ROC no longer claims Tibet, either because Tibet is actually independent, or because Taiwan isn't really part of China. Thus, the MTAC is bureaucratically necessary to forestall Chinese hostility, but it can and should be emasculated by, for example, moving it to the government's bureau for aboriginal affairs. These three perspectives continue to motivate Taiwanese approaches to Tibetan affairs and were vividly apparent in the issues surrounding the Dalai Lama's 1997 visit to Taiwan.

The 1994 Taiwan Scandal

Just five years after the 1989 affair, a second major scandal regarding Taiwan erupted in the Tibetan exile community. On March 31, 1994, several of the leaders of Chuzhi Gangdruk (the "Four Rivers, Six Ranges" Tibetan guerrilla movement) met with MTAC officials in India and signed an agreement with them. Chuzhi Gangdruk had been the foremost Tibetan resistance force in the late 1950s, and its mainly Khampa leadership had long been admired throughout the Tibetan diaspora for their heroism in initiating the rebellion against the Chinese and ensuring the Dalai Lama's successful escape to India. Although Chuzhi Gangdruk was no longer a fighting force, its leaders continued to command respect among the exiles, particularly in the Khampa community. Thus, news that its leaders had undertaken to negotiation with the MTAC was a shock to the entire exile world, particularly since the pact seemed to implicitly affirm two highly contentious positions. According to the agreement, Taiwan would recognize Tibet "as a self-ruled region under united democratic China" and would support the Dalai Lama as the religious and political leader of Tibet. At first glance, this might not appear to be so scandalous. After all, by this point the Dalai Lama himself was insisting that he sought genuine autonomy rather than full independence for Tibet. But the Dalai Lama and the Tibetan government-in-exile looked upon the agreement with extreme disfavor. They emphatically objected to two implications of the accord. First, by suggesting that Taiwan had the power to authorize the Dalai Lama as the Tibetan leader, the accord obliquely recognized the ROC's ultimate authority over Tibetan politics and religion. Second, by presuming that Tibetans other than the government-in-exile had the authority to negotiate on behalf of the exiles, the leaders of Chuzhi Gangdruk had arrogated to themselves powers that the government in Dharamsala considered to be its alone. A huge uproar ensued.

Given the longstanding regional tensions, it was difficult for many exiles not to see this affair as a reprise of the long history of intermittent Khampa resistance to the authority of Lhasa (and Dharamsala). These regionalist concerns were further underscored when the leaders of Chuzhi Gangdruk offered to annul the agreement if the Tibetan government-in-exile would put in writing its commitment to refuse any settlement with China that did not include Kham and Amdo; Dharamsala refused to do so, further inflaming the suspicions of those Khampa and Amdowa who feared that the government was prepared to sacrifice their interests in return for concessions regarding Central Tibet.

Transforming Tibet-Taiwan Relations

How did these scandals affect the development of Tibetan Buddhism in Taiwan? On the one hand, all of my Tibetan interviewees emphasized the difference between going to Taiwan to help teach Tibetan Buddhism to interested individuals and going to Taiwan to support the state's political ambitions with regard to the Tibetan exiles. On the other hand, in practice this distinction was often blurred because the MTAC, in its capacity to grant religious visas, controlled access to the island for most Tibetans. Although this power has been curtailed, at present the MTAC continues to play a central role in organizing and facilitating Tibetan Buddhist affairs on the island. Because Dharamsala had proscribed contacts with the MTAC, it had been problematic for lamas to travel to Taiwan. Yet, the fundraising possibilities there were great, especially for those lamas who, for regional or sectarian reasons, felt that they could not rely on Dharamsala's assistance to reestablish themselves in exile. A pattern emerged in which, for the most part, the lamas at the center of Taiwan's booming interest in Tibetan Buddhism were relatively independent from Dharamsala. The Dalai Lama's trip in 1997 fundamentally altered this dynamic. Travel to Taiwan is no longer stigmatized within the Tibetan diaspora, and a wider assortment of the exiles, including lamas and monasteries that previously avoided the island, has begun to cultivate relationships there.

To understand the change in relations between the Tibetan government-in-exile and the ROC that allowed the Dalai Lama to make his historic 1997 trip, we have to examine the changes that had started to take place within the Taiwanese polity. During the martial law period (1949–1987), Mainlanders who had come to the island with Chiang K'ai-Shek ruled Taiwan. However, under post-martial law democracy, Taiwanese who emigrated from the mainland about 300 years ago (and who make up about 75% of the population) are increasingly dominant. For example, Lee Teng-hui, the first President to be directly elected, is a native Taiwanese, not a Mainlander. The ascendance of the Taiwanese has led to a burgeoning independence movement that seeks to establish Taiwan as an independent nation-state separate from China. As a result, questions of independence and national identity have become the central debates of contemporary Taiwanese society and, for increasing numbers of Taiwanese, the notion of claiming sovereignty over Tibet is, at best farcical, and at worst, harmful to the cause of Taiwanese independence.

The Dalai Lama's 1997 Trip: The View from Taiwan

In this light, the Dalai Lama's trip to Taiwan in 1997 involved high stakes for Tibetans, Taiwanese, and Chinese. For the Taiwanese, relations with the Tibetans had become a forum for playing out internal debates over the future political status of the island. Previously Taiwan's interactions with Tibetans were primarily motivated by the desire to legitimize its nationalist claims of sovereignty over China (including Tibet), and to gain control over one of the PRC's main opponents. But in the post-martial law context, relations between Taiwan and Tibet have taken on a new meaning. Taiwanese advocates of independence have no interest in claiming sovereignty over Tibet. On the contrary, they are likely to see the Tibetan exiles as potential allies in a common struggle against PRC domination. Moreover, Tibetan independence serves their own political cause, because it is a means of expressing Taiwan's own aspirations for independence without provoking China by directly proclaiming them. Despite the Dalai Lama's protestations that his trip was purely for religious purposes, from the outset it carried heavy symbolic weight for both advocates and opponents of independence in Taiwan.

The key measure that allowed the trip to go forward was the exclusion of the MTAC from any part of the arrangements. The Dalai Lama's visit was to be a private one (much as Lee's trip to the U.S. in 1995 had been private), and was arranged by a private organization, the Chinese Buddhist Association. Plans for the Dalai Lama to meet with Lee and other top political figures were not revealed until the last minute, and even then were couched in the language of spiritual dialogue, rather than political negotiation.

The protocol of the visit was also hotly debated. Independence advocates argued that the Dalai Lama should be received as a state visitor, with the protocol appropriate to a foreign head of state, since this would reinforce the view that Taiwan and Tibet are sovereign powers, separate both from one another, and China. On the eve of the Dalai Lama's visit, the DPP, the main pro-independence party, issued a statement: "To even consider His Holiness Dalai Lama a 'local citizen of the Republic of China' is ludicrous and highly inappropriate." In case the point was not clear, the statement added that, "On the map, Dharamsala appears far away from Taiwan, but we share a similar destiny." Evidently, adopting this stance and according the Dalai Lama the privileges of a head of state was deemed too provocative toward China, and ultimately there were no politicians, of any stripe, to greet him at the airport. There were however crowds of demonstrators, who used his arrival as a pretext for asserting their competing claims that Taiwan should either be independent or reunified with China.

The Dalai Lama commented on the significance of his visit in a way that indicated that he was well aware of the changing political currents in both Taiwan and China.

> My recent visit to Taiwan illustrates this growing understanding and concern by Chinese speaking people for the culture of Tibet. I believe that in the long run this will help establish mutual understanding and respect between the Chinese and Tibetan people. During my visit I was greatly impressed by the openness and frankness with which the Taiwanese people were able to discuss issues which concerned them. The democratic developments in Taiwan can certainly become a model for China where the people continue to be denied a role in the political decision making process.[40]

The DPP also pushed for the abolition of the MTAC—one of the Tibetan exiles' main demands—on the grounds that Tibet-Taiwan relations are essentially *diplomatic* ones which should be handled through diplomatic channels, not a special agency. Just prior to the Dalai Lama's 1997 visit, the DPP asserted that the MTAC continued to exist for only three reasons, none of which were still valid:

1. "To prop up the old myth that the GMD's sovereignty rule extended to China." Yet, "the mythical territorial claims are unrealistic, preposterous, and a joke to the international community."
2. "As a remnant of the outdated government bureaucracy." But since the "National Development Conference consensus is to eliminate the province and downsize government bureaucracy, there is no reason for the MTAC to continue to exist."
3. "To aid the Tibetan and Mongolian people." But, "the MTAC has not only failed to aid the Tibetans, it has created misunderstanding and turmoil."
   "The DPP therefore calls for the immediate abolishment of the MTAC."[41]

Ironically, the MTAC appears likely to continue, in one form or another, even under DPP rule, since its very existence is a visible sign to Beijing that, despite the independence movement, the Taipei government continues to regard itself as part of China.

Taiwan and Transnational Tibetan Buddhism

Finally, I return to the question of the relationship between the popularity of Tibetan Buddhism in Taiwan and its recent global expansion. As I have described, Taiwanese patronage has played a critical role in the reestablishment of Tibetan Buddhist institutions in exile. However, this support has not only flowed from Taiwan to the Tibetan diaspora, but has also facilitated the growth of Tibetan Buddhism in the West and elsewhere around the world. In this way, contemporary Taiwanese patronage has modified the traditional patron-priest relationship, transforming it into a globalized model of sponsorship in which the dispensation of money, ideas, and identities transcends ethnic and cultural boundaries.

One American practitioner of Tibetan Buddhism, whom I'll call Frank, told me about the moral and financial support he received from a group of

Taiwanese nuns as he made the challenging decision to ordain as a Tibetan Buddhist monk:

> I was living in Seattle as a layperson. I was organizing dharma teachings for Thubten Chodron [an American nun and teacher in the Tibetan tradition] and through that, I got to know some Taiwanese nuns who had a small nunnery in the area.[42]

The nuns had left Taiwan in order to pursue graduate studies at the University of Washington. They were, it seems, participants in the current nuns' movement in Taiwan, which has witnessed a tremendous growth in the number of Buddhist nuns (they now outnumber Buddhist monks, a first for any Buddhist society), and which has entailed a concerted effort to raise the educational standards for nuns. As part of this effort, many Taiwanese nuns have enrolled in graduate schools in the United States. One of my informant's friends was pursuing a Ph.D. in education; another had completed a master's degree in administration. Thus, just when Frank was developing an ever stronger interest in Buddhism—an interest that would culminate in the renunciation of his American lifestyle for a new identity as a Tibetan Buddhist monk—he was interacting with a group of Taiwanese Buddhist nuns who were likewise seeking to deepen their own understanding—not to mention raise the status of Buddhist nuns in general—through participation in the discursive and institutional realities of American universities, and thereby transforming the religious norms of Taiwan:

> Although they were from the Pure Land school, they had some interest in Tibetan Buddhism. . . . They would often ask me if I was interested in becoming a monk. I was organizing dharma students, studying intensely, selling my possessions. . . . They knew this. [After a year studying Tibetan Buddhism in India] I was thinking about ordination. . . . They were very supportive, but they never pressured me. When I decided to ordain, they offered me a set of robes.

These interactions would be unremarkable, even customary, within any existing Buddhist culture. A group of monastics giving financial, emotional, and moral support to a new recruit is a routine occurrence in Buddhist societies. Yet, in this instance, the interaction is remarkable for two reasons. First, the support was extended across ethnic and cultural boundaries, which appear to have been irrelevant to all concerned. Frank and the nuns were friends; they were supportive of his unfolding religious exploration; and this support took concrete form in the highly symbolic act of offering him a set of robes. Second, the nuns' support had nothing to do with Frank's recruitment into *their* order. They seem to have been quite happy to assist him in his spiritual life, without regard to issues of sectarian competition.

Once Frank had become a Buddhist monk, he had to deal with the financial challenge of monasticism in the West. For many Western nuns and monks financial support is a major issue. Strict adherence to their vows precludes paid employment. Without the established systems of financial support for Buddhist practice that one finds in Asian countries, Western Buddhist monastics are forced to support themselves in an ad hoc manner; many rely on sponsors or personal savings.

> I was very concerned about how I would live as a monk in the West since there's no institutional support. One of the nuns reminded me that every country where Buddhism has come, there wasn't institutional support at the beginning, so [this difficulty is] not just in America.... Although I hadn't asked for it, the nuns offered to sponsor my room and board.

Frank's story illustrates the complex character of globalized Tibetan Buddhism, in which it is not surprising to encounter an American from the metropolis who participates in Tibetan religion with the aid of Taiwanese nuns who are themselves engaged in American academic projects. Yet, it is important to recognize that the parties to these transnational relationships are well aware of the hybridity of their circumstances, and untroubled by it. As Frank put it,

> I'm from Seattle, but I'm sponsored by nuns from Taiwan, and I was ordained by Tibetans in India, and here we are in Ithaca, New York, talking about all of this. It's remarkable.

Moreover, this transnational dynamic also flows in the other direction. According to its author, the Chinese language edition of *The Tibetan Book of Living and Dying*—a popular account of Tibetan Buddhist teachings originally written in English—sold 100,000 copies in Taiwan in its first three months of publication.[43] Books by the American nuns Thubten Chodron and Sangye Khadro have also been translated from English into Chinese.[44] These books are part of a notable trend in the global spread of Buddhism:

the transmission of Buddhist ideas, not only by translating Asian texts or oral teachings into European languages, but also by generating *new* texts that consciously seek to present Buddhism to the West in culturally appropriate ways. The subsequent translation of these vernacular texts into Chinese is a striking reversal, perhaps best explained by Thubten Chodron herself:

> It shows that practical methods and easy language appeal to people there.... One of my [Chinese] friends ... says that young Chinese need books [written] in easy to understand language that deal with practical topics. Also, being American helps in this way—it sure did when I taught in Singapore. The young people want to be modern like the West, and it's tempting for them to abandon their culture. So it's helpful when "modern" and "American" happens to coincide with "Buddhist."[45]

There has recently been a dramatic increase in the appeal of Tibetan Buddhism for Chinese people. In Taiwan, this trend is governed by a combination of historical and contemporary influences. The cultural meaning of Buddhist practice in Taiwan draws upon centuries of Chinese imaginings about Tibetan spiritual potency. But it also taps the new interpretations that are being produced in the encounter between modernity and diasporic Tibetan culture, and that circulate through the transnational dissemination of Buddhist material, in which the Taiwanese fully participate. Similarly, the social organization of Tibetan Buddhist institutions in Taiwan has deep historical roots in the development of Tibetan Buddhism in Tibet and China. Yet, it is also the product of the recent reorganization of Tibetan religious networks into international communities that depend on faxes, email, and leaders who spend much of their time jetting from one country to another. Thus, while diplomats continue to seek a political formula for improved relations between Tibetans and Chinese, another process has been unfolding which also deserves our attention: once again, Tibetan lamas are establishing themselves as the gurus of Chinese disciples. It is unclear how this will affect Tibetan aspirations for independence or autonomy, but it seems certain to affect the relationship between the Tibetan and Chinese peoples.

NOTES

* Funding for research in Taiwan in 1996 and 1998 was provided in the form of two Hu Shih Awards from Cornell University's East Asia Program. Additional research in Taiwan in 2005 was supported by a Rappaport Faculty Development Grant from Hampshire College. An earlier version of this chapter appeared in Abraham Zablocki, "The Global Mandala: The Transnational Transformation of Tibetan Buddhism" (Ph.D. dissertation, Cornell University, 2005), chapter 4.

1 Lin Chun-tee, Wang Chiong-hua, and Liang Yu-li, "Dalai Lama's Press Conference," *Chung Yang Jih Pao* (Taipei), March 25, 1997, p. 1.

2 Yuchen Li, "Ordination, Legitimacy, and Sisterhood: The International Full Ordination Ceremony in Bodhgaya," in *Innovative Buddhist Women*, ed. Karma Lekshe Tsomo (Richmond, Surrey: Curzon Press, 2000), pp. 168–198.

3 "Dalai Lama Visits Taiwan to 'Enhance Happiness,'" Deutsche Presse-Agentur, March 22, 1997.

4 Yang Hsin-hsin, "Taiwanese Believe Tibetan Masters Have Supernatural Powers," *Agence France-Press*, March 23, 1997.

5 Anna Wang and Marlene Chen, "The Dalai Lama Sparks a Fever for Tibetan Buddhism," *Sinorama* (Taipei), 22.5 (May 1997), pp. 78–80.

6 Wang and Chen, "The Dalai Lama Sparks."

7 "China Slams Dalai Lama for Insincerity in Taiwan," Reuters, March 25, 1997.

8 Dalai Lama, interview by Zhang Jing, *Chinese/Mandarin Service*, Voice of America, September 11, 2003, <http://www.tibet.com/NewsRoom/hhinterview1.htm>.

9 I use the expression "Chinese people" here in its broadest sense, including not only those Chinese who live in the PRC, but also overseas Chinese who live in Singapore, Malaysia, the United States, and elsewhere around the world. I also include the inhabitants of Taiwan, although I realize that the debate over "Taiwanese" vs. "Chinese" identity is a central issue in contemporary Taiwan. My intention is not to take sides in this dispute, but to suggest that the followers of Tibetan Buddhism in Taiwan, whether they are Mainlanders or Taiwanese, and whether they are advocates of independence or reunification, are participating in a religious movement that also attracts other people with historical roots—cultural, ethnic, or political—in China.

10 This periodization is a modification of the two-period scheme used by both Keng and Cheng to describe the history of Tibetan Buddhism in Taiwan, although the choice of period names is my own and my dates differ slightly. I regard the Dalai Lama's 1997 visit as beginning a new, third, period. Both Keng and Cheng wrote their accounts of Tibetan Buddhism in Taiwan before the Dalai Lama's visit, and therefore it is not clear whether they would agree with my view that it constituted the beginning of a new period, or would argue that it was merely a continuation of the boom that began in the 1980s; see Cheng, Yu-jiao, "Tai Wan De Xi Zang Fo Jiao [Tibetan Buddhism in Taiwan]" in *A Collection of Essays in Tibetan Studies* (Taipei: Committee on Tibetan Studies, Chengchi University, 1990), pp. 105–117; Keng Chen-Hua, "Zang Chuan Mi Zong Zai Tai Wan Di Qu De Fa Zhang Ji Qi She Hui Gong Neng De Tan Tao [Discussions on the Development and its Social Function of Tibetan Tantric Buddhism in Taiwan]" (master's thesis, Taiwan: Normal University, 1996); and Chung Yang Jih Pao, "Dalai Lama Press Conference." Yao, writing

in 2000, suggested that the Dalai Lama's visit was more significant in political terms than religious ones, and that it did not herald a new period; see Yao Li-hsiang, "Zang Quan Fo Jiao Zai Taiwanfa Zheng De Qu Bu Yan Jiu [The Development of Tibetan Buddhism in Taiwan]," *Fo Xue Yen Qiu Zhong Xin Xue Bao* [*Journal of the Center for Buddhist Studies*] (Taipei) 5 (2000). However, the rapid growth of Tibetan Buddhist centers following the Dalai Lama's first visit suggests that Tibetan Buddhism in Taiwan has indeed entered another phase in its development.

11 Gray Tuttle, *Tibetan Buddhists in the Making of Modern China* (New York: Columbia University Press, 2005). See also chapters 7 and 9 above.

12 See Carmen Meinert's contribution to this volume for further discussion of Gangs dkar Rin po che.

13 Qu Yingguang Guru established an important center in Hsien Tien, Wu Feng Shan; after his death, he was succeeded by Fasiling Xianghuang. In 1958, Wu Runjiang Guru made the first of seven trips from Hong Kong to Taiwan for the purpose of teaching esoteric Buddhism; in the 1970s, his students established Nor lha lineage centers in Taipei and Taichung and, after his death in 1979, he was succeeded by Qiangzhi Minshao. Lau Yui Che started the Vajrayana Institute in Hong Kong in 1953 and became a disciple of Bdud 'joms Rin po che in Kalimpong in 1959; he was very active in both Hong Kong and Taiwan, and established centers in Taipei, Taichung, and Kaohsiung in the 1970s. Prof. Zhang Chengji (a.k.a. Garma C.C. Chang) studied in Tibet before taking an academic position in the United States; although he had relatively few students in Taiwan, his translations of the texts of Tibet's famous yogi, Mi la ras pa, into Chinese were very influential, as were his English renditions as well. Zhangjia (Lcang skya) Hutuketu was already famous on the mainland, but, because he passed away in 1957, his impact on the development of Tibetan Buddhism in Taiwan was relatively limited. These details about the Mainlander transmission are mainly drawn from Cheng Yu-jiao, "Taiwan de Xizang Fojiao [Tibetan Buddhism in Taiwan]."

14 It is also possible that the Bka' brgyud and Rnying ma sects had more Chinese adherents on the mainland, and that this preference was simply transmitted to Taiwan. Further research is needed regarding the role that these early Tibetan Buddhist centers played in facilitating the arrival of the first Tibetan missionaries during the later Tibetan exile transmission periods. To the extent that the early Mainlander centers helped generate the Tibet craze that began in the 1980s, it is possible that the contemporary bias toward the Rnying ma and the Bka' brgyud on the island simply reflects this earlier phase of Tibetan Buddhism in Taiwan. Whether this is true or not, it is clear that Tibetan Buddhism in Taiwan derives much of its appeal from its esoteric aspects, which have historically been a strength of both the Rnying ma and Bka' brgyud sects.

15 Lawrence Fu-ch'üan Hsing, *Taiwanese Buddhism and Buddhist Temples* (Taipei: Pacific Cultural Foundation, 1983).

16 Cheng, "Taiwan de Xizang Fojiao."

17 Charles Brewer Jones, *Buddhism in Taiwan: Religion and the State, 1660–1990* (Honolulu: University of Hawai'i Press, 1999).

18 Keng, "Zang Chuan Mi Zong Zai."

19 It should be noted that although some of these institutions own or rent dedicated

practice space, have regular meetings, and may have one or more resident teachers, others exist more casually, only gathering when their Tibetan teachers visit from India or Nepal. An academic survey conducted in 1996 listed 52 Tibetan Buddhist centers in Taiwan; see Keng, "Zang Chuan Mi Zong Zai." The reason for the discrepancy between this count and the MTAC's larger numbers is not clear. Coleman's handbook of Tibetan institutions around the world listed only eight Tibetan Buddhist centers in Taiwan, but this is clearly incorrect. Graham Coleman, ed., *A Handbook of Tibetan Culture: A Guide to Tibetan Centres and Resources Throughout the World* (Boston: Shambhala, 1994).

20 Cheuh-An Tsering, interview by author, Taipei, August 3, 1996.

21 Keng Chen-hua, interview by author, Taipei, August 17, 1996.

22 Such questions of religious identity are notoriously difficult to quantify, and census numbers often reveal more about the biases of the studies that produce them than they do about actual religious demographics. See, for example, Tweed's discussion of Buddhism in the United States. Thomas A. Tweed, "Who Is a Buddhist? Night-Stand Buddhists and Other Creatures," in *Westward Dharma: Buddhism Beyond Asia*, ed. Charles S. Prebish and Martin Baumann (Berkeley: University of California Press, 2002), pp. 17–33.

23 Tenzin Gelek, interview by author, Kathmandu, 2000.

24 Anon., interview by author, Taipei, August 20, 1996.

25 Lin Chun-tee et. al., "Dalai Lama's Press Conference."

26 Interview by author, Taipei, August 3, 1996.

27 Interview by author, Taipei, August 20, 1996.

28 The existence of this program deserves further research since it indicates fascinating transnational linkages between Tibet, Taiwan, and Saudi Arabia.

29 "Tibet Revolt Reported; Formosa Says 40,000 Farmers Took Part In Uprising," New York Times, August 24, 1954, p. 7.

30 Michel Peissel, *Cavaliers of Kham: The Secret War in Tibet* (London: Heinemann, 1972), pp. 61–62.

31 Dawa T. Norbu, "Who Aided the Khampas and Why?" *Tibetan Review* (July/August 1974), p. 21.

32 Jamyang Norbu, Lhasang Tsering, and Tsering Gyalpo, "Letters," *Tibetan Review* (October/November 1974), p. 27.

33 Dalai Lama XIV Bstan 'dzin rgya mtsho and A.A. Shiromany, *The Political Philosophy of His Holiness the 14th Dalai Lama: Selected Speeches and Writings*, ed. A.A. Shiromany (New Delhi: Tibetan Parliamentary and Policy Research Centre, 1998), p. 238.

34 There were many important Dge lugs figures who were not Central Tibetans, including, of course, the Dalai Lama and his influential elder brothers who acted as important liaisons between the Tibetan exiles and the CIA. Conversely, the non-Dge lugs sects had well-established institutional ties to Central Tibet, including the Sa skya sect's seat at Sa skya Monastery or the Karma Bka' brgyud's seat at Mtshur-phu.

35 Tenzin Namdhak Taklha, "Taiwan and Tibet," *Tibetan Review* 1.4 (1968), pp. 7–8.

36 "Yan Mingfu Talks About the Tibet Issue in Detail," *Zhongguo Xinwen She* (Beijing), March 21, 1989, in FBIS-CHI (Foreign Broadcast Information Service—China) 89-054, March 22, 1989, pp. 22–23.

37 In particular, the Dalai Lama enunciated his Five Point Peace Plan in 1987 and his Strasbourg Proposal in 1988.

38 It is unclear to me whether this meeting was called in response to the furor which the 1989 scandal had produced, or for some other reason.

39 "Taiwan Lawmakers Urge End to MTAC," *Tibetan Review*, 25.6 (June, 1990), p. 10.

40 Dalai Lama, *The Political Philosophy*, p. 152.

41 Hsin-liang, Hsu, "Let Us Learn from the Dalai Lama," *Tibetan Review*, 32.5 (May 1997), pp. 16–17.

42 Interview by author, Ithaca, NY, July 7, 1996.

43 Sogyal Rinpoche, public lecture, Malla Hotel, Kathmandu, February 22, 1997, discussing his *The Tibetan Book of Living and Dying*, ed. Patrick Gaffney and Andrew Harvey (San Francisco: Harper, 1992).

44 Ven. Thubten Chodron, interview by author, Bodhgaya, February 20, 1998.

45 Ibid.

Tibetan Spelling List

Achak-dri *a lcags 'bri*

Akya *a skya*

Amdo *a mdo*

Aru Horchen *a ru hor chen*

Ba Sangshi *sba sang shi*

Batang *'ba' thang*

Bo Gangkar Rinpoché *'bo gangs dkar rin po che*

Bön(po) *bon (po)*

Bönri shingpa Kunga Tupten Gyeltsen Senggé *bon ri shing pa kun dga' thub bstan rgyal mtshan seng ge*

Bumling *'bum gling*

Chamdo *chab mdo*

Changkya *lcang skya*

Changkya Ngawang Chöden *lcang skya ngag dbang chos ldan*

Chenrézi *spyan ras gzigs*

Chimé Lhawang *'chi med lha dbang*

Chödrak *chos grags*

Chögyel Pakpa Rinpoché *chos rgyal 'phags pa rin po che*

Chöjé *chos rje*

Chöjé Gön *chos rje dgon*

Chöki Lodrö *chos kyi blo gros*

Chörin *chos rin*

Chöying Dorjé *chos dbyings rdo rje*

Chöying Gyeltsen *chos dbyings rgyal mtshan*

Chuktsam *phyug tsams*

Chuzang *chu bzang*

Dalai Lama *tā la'i bla ma*

Dampa Kungadrak *dam pa kun dga' grags*

Dartsedo *dar rtse mdo*

Dechen *bde chen*

Dega Yutsel *de ga g.yu tshal*

delön *bde blon*

Demchok Lölangtargi Tsuklakhang *bde mchog blos bslang ltar gyi gtsug lag khang*

Demotang Ganden Chökhorling *bde mo thang dga' ldan chos 'khor gling*

Dergé *sde dge*

Desi Sanggyé Gyatso *sde srid sangs rgyas rgya mtsho*

Detri *sde khri*

Dewé Jungné Gyelten *bde ba'i 'byung gnas rgyal bstan*

Deyang *bde dbyangs*

Dokham *Mdo khams*

Domé *mdo smad*

Dorjé Chöpa *Dge bshes Rdo rje gcod pa*

Drepung *'bras spungs*

Drepung Tsokcha *'bras spungs tshogs cha*

Drom Pékhongma *'brom dpe khong ma*

Drotsang Dorjé-chang *gro tshang rdo rje 'chang*

Drotsang lhakhang *gro tshang lha khang*

Drungpa Rinchen-pel *drung pa rin chen dpal*

Dudjom *bdud 'joms*

Dükhor *dus 'khor*

Dungkar Lozang Trinlé *dung dkar blo bzang phrin las*

Dzamtang *'dzam thang*

Dzebo Dargyeling *rdze bo dar rgyas gling*

Dzika *'dzi ska*

Dziké Lhamo Dartang *'dzi ka'i lha mo dar thang*

Dziké Nyiang Shöda *'dzi ska'i myi nag shos mda'*

Dzogchen *rdzogs chen*

Ganden *dga' ldan*

Ganden Jangtsé *dga' ldan byang rtse*

Ganden Jinling *dga' ldan byin gling*

Ganden Tri Rinpoché *dga' ldan khri rin po che*

gang *sgang*

Ganzi *dkar mdzes*

Garra Lama *mgar ra bla ma*

Gartok *sgar thog*

Garwang Chöki Wangchuk *gar dbang chos kyi dbang phug*

Gelukpa *dge lugs pa*

Gendün Drupa *dge 'dun grub pa*

Gendün Lungtok Nyima *dge 'dun lung rtogs nyi ma*

Golok *mgo log*

Gomang *sgo mang*

Gongbu Maru *gong/gung bu/gu (r)ma/(r)me ru*

gongma chenpo *gong ma chen po*

Gönkar *dgon dkar*

Gönlung *dgon lung*

Gushri Könchok Dorjé *gu shri dkon mchog rdo rje*

Gyaja *rgya bya*

Gyanakpa tsang *rgya nag pa tshang*

Gyantsé *rgyal rtse*

Gyelmo Tsawerong *rgyal mo tsha ba'i rong*

Gyelrang Khangtsen *rgyal rang khang mtshan*

Gyelsé Zhenpen Tayé *rgyal sras gzhan phan mtha' yas*

Gyeltsap *rgyal tshab*

Gyeltsen *rgyal mtshan*

Gyelwa Mipam Gönpo *rgyal ba mi pham mgon po*

Gyelwa riknga *rgyal ba rigs lnga*

Gyelwa Senggé *rgyal ba seng ge*

Gyelwa Senggé Peljor Zangpo *rgyal ba seng ge dpal 'byor bzang po*

Gyelwa Zangpo *rgyal ba bzang po*

gyelyum chenmo *rgyal yum chen mo*

Gyümé *rgyud smad*

Hé Lama Sanggyé Trashi *he bla ma sangs rgyas bkra shis*

Jagö Topden *bya rgod stobs ldan*

Jamchen Chökhorling *byams chen chos 'khor gling*

Jamgön Kongtrül Lodrö Tayé *'jam mgon kong sprul blo gros mtha' yas*

Jampa Gendün *byams pa dge 'dun*

Jampa khawoche *byams pa kha bo che*

Jampaling *byams pa gling*

Jamyang *'jam dbyangs*

Jamyang Gyatso *'jam dbyangs rgya mtsho*

Jamyang Lodrö *'jam dbyangs blos gros*

Jamyang Tendzin Trinlé Gyatso *'jam dbyangs bstan 'dzin 'phrin las rgya mtsho*

Jamyang Tenpé Nyima *'jam dbyangs bstan pa'i nyi ma*

Jamyang Tupten Nyima *'jam dbyangs thub bstan nyi ma*

Jamyang Zhepa *'jam dbyangs bzhad pa*

Jang *'jang/ljang*

Jang Satam *'jang sa tham/dam*

Jangri Makpo Gön *'jang ri smag po dgon*

Jangshepa *byang bshes pa*

jasa *ja' sa*

Jebtsundampa *rje btsun dam pa*

Jikmé Lingpa *'jigs med gling pa*

Jikmé Trinlé Gyatso *'jigs med 'phrin las rgya mtsho*

Jonangpa *jo nang pa*

Kagyü(pa) *bka' brgyud (pa)*

Kalu *ka lu*

Kamtsang *kaṃ tshang*

Karma Garchen *karma sgar chen*

Karma Gardri *karma sgar bris*

Karma Kagyü *karma bka' brgyud*

Karma Mipam Tsewang Sonam Rabten *karma mi pham tshe dbang bsod nams rab brtan*

Karma Pakshi *karma pakshi*

Karma Shedrup Chöki Senggé *karma bshad sgrub chos kyi seng ge*

Karmapa *karma pa*

Katok Situ *kaḥ thog si tu*

Kelzang Gyatso *skal bzang rgya mtsho*

Kelzang Gyurmé *skal bzang 'gyur med*

Kelzang Tsering *skal bzang tshe ring*

Khakhyap Dorjé *mkha' khyab rdo rje*

Kham *khams*

"Khamsa" **Khams sa*, err. for *Khang gsar*

Khangsar *khang gsar*

Khartsen *mkhar btsan*

khatak *kha btags*

khenbu lama *mkhan bu bla ma*

Khenchen Karma Dechen Ngedön Tendzin Rabgyé *mkhan chen karma bde chen nges don bstan 'dzin rab rgyas*

Khenchen Tsewang Peljor *mkhan chen tshe dbang dpal 'byor*

khenpo *mkhan po*

Khenpo Dorampa Lozang Zangpo *mkhan po rdo rams pa blo bzang bzang po*

Khenpo Jikpün *mkhan po 'jigs phun*

Khenpo Tupten *mkhan po thub bstan*

Khenpo Zhenga *mkhan po gzhan dga'*

Khyenrap *mkhyen rab*

Khyenrap Tenpa Chöpel *mkhyen rab bstan pa chos 'phel*

Könchok Jikmé Wangpo *dkon mchog 'jigs med dbang po*

Könchok-kyap *dkon mchog skyabs*

Könchok Tenpa Rabgyé *dkon mchog bstan pa rab rgyas*

Künkhyen Dölpopa *kun mkhyen dol po pa*

Küntu Zangpo *kun tu bzang po*

Künzang *kun bzang*

Kumbum *sku 'bum*

Kyangtsang Lama Sönam Zangpo *skyang tshang bla ma bsod nams bzang po*

Kyangtsang Püntsok Dargyé Ling *skyang tshang phun tshogs dar rgyas gling*

Labrang Trashikyi *bla brang bkra shis dkyil*

Lamo Dechen *la mo bde chen*

Lamrim *lam rim*

Langkarpa *glang dkar pa*

Lentsa *lan tsha*

Lhamo *lha mo*

Lhasa *lha sa*

Lhashi Gön *lha shis dgon*

Lhodrak Drowolung *lho brag gro bo lung*

Litang *li thang*

Loden Wangpo *blo ldan dbang po*

Longchenpa *klong chen pa*

Loséling *blo gsal gling*

Lotsawa chenpo *lo tsā ba chen po*

Lozang Longdöl Chöki Nyima *blo bzang klong rdol chos kyi nyi ma*

Lozang Namgyel *blo bzang rnam rgyal*

Lozang Pelden Tenpé Drönmé *blo bzang dpal ldan bstan pa'i sgron me*

Lozang Tendzin Jikmé Wangchuk Pelzangpo *blo bzang bstan 'dzin 'jigs med dbang phyug dpal bzang po*

Lozang Tenpé Gyeltsen *blo bzang bstan pa'i rgyal mtshan*

Lozang Tenpé Nyima *blo bzang bstan pa'i nyi ma*

Lozang Tupten Chöki Nyima *blo bzang thub bstan chos kyi nyi ma*

Lozang Tupten Gyatso *blo bzang thub bstan rgya mtsho*

Lozang Yeshé *blo bzang ye shes*

Lubum (Ngawang) Lodrö Gyatso *klu 'bum (ngag dbang) blo gros rgya mtsho*

Luchu *klu chu*

Machik Labdrön *ma cig lab sgron*

Marpa Lotsawa *mar pa lo tsā ba*

Menri *sman ris*

Meru Lozang Gyeltsen *rme ru blo bzang rgyal mtshan*

Miktsé *dmigs brtse*

Mikyö Dorjé *mi bskyod rdo rje*

Milarepa *mi las ras pa*

Mingyur Gön *mi 'gyur dgon*

Minyak *mi nyag*

Minyak Gangkar *mi nyag gangs dkar*

Minyak Gönpo *mi nyag mgon po*

Minyak Tsowa Rading *mi nyag tsho ba ra lding*

Mipam Chögyel Trinlé Rabten *mi pham chos rgyal 'phrin las rab brtan*

Mönpa Pekar Dzinpa *mon pa pad dkar 'dzin pa*

Mugé Samten *dmu dge bsam gtan*

Muli *smi/mu li*

Nakchukha *nag chu kha*

Naktar *nag thar*

Namkhai Norbu *nam mkha'i nor bu*

Nechung *gnas chung*

Ngakchen Darpa *sngags chen 'dar/bdar pa*

Ngakpa *sngags pa*

Ngari *mnga' ris*

Ngawang Chödrak *ngag dbang chos grags*

Ngawang Lodrö Drakpa *ngag dbang blo gros grags pa*

Ngawang Püntsok *ngag dbang phun tshogs*

Ngawang Tupten Tenpé Nyima *ngag dbang thub bstan bstan pa'i nyi ma*

Ngawang Tupten Wangchuk Pelden Trinlé Gyatso *ngag dbang thub bstan dbang phyug dpal ldan 'phrin las rgya mtsho*

Ngawang Yangchen Chöki Wangchuk *ngag dbang dbyangs can chos kyi dbang phyug*

Ngawang Yeshé Gyatso *ngag dbang ye shes rgya mtsho*

Ngoring lake *ngo ring mtsho*

Ngukhor *ngu 'khor*

Norbu Zangpo *nor bu bzang po*

Norlha *nor lha*

Norlha Khutughtu Sonam Rapten *nor lha hu thog thu bsod nams rab brtan*

Nyen Gön *gnyan dgon*

Nyingma *rnying ma*

Padampa Gyagar *pha dam pa rgya gar*

Pakpa Lodrö Gyeltsen *'phags pa blo gros rgyal mtshan*

Panchen Lama *pan chen bla ma*

Pawo *dpa' bo*

pecha *dpe cha*

Pelchenpo *dpal chen po*

Pelden Yeshé *dpal ldan ye shes*

Pelpung *dpal spungs*

Pema Karpo *padma dkar po*

Pema Nyinjé Wangpo *padma nyin byed dbang po*

Pema Wangchok Gyelpo *padma dbang mchog rgyal po*

Pemabum *padma 'bum*

Püntsok Ling *phun tshogs gling*

Püntsok Namgyel *phun tshogs rnam rgyal*

Purchok *phur lcog*

Rangjung Rikpé Dorjé *rang byung rig pa'i rdo rje*

Rechungpa *ras chung pa*

Relpachen *ral pa can*

Rikhü *ri khud*

Rinchenkyap *rin chen skyabs*

Rinpoché *rin po che*

Riwoché *ri bo che*

Rölpé Dorjé *rol pa'i rdo rje*

Sakya *sa skya*

Sanggyé Gyatso *sangs rgyas rgya mtsho*

Sangngak Chödzöling *gsang sngags chos mdzod gling*

Sazang Mati Paṇchen *sa bzang ma ti paṇ chen*

Serkhog *gser khog*

Shaktup Ling *shāk thub gling*

Sharkhog *shar khog*

shedra *bshad grwa*

Shigatse *Gzhis ka rtse*

Siregetu Khutughtu Ngawang Tupten Wangchuk *si re ge thu hu thog tu ngag dbang thub bstan dbang phyug*

Situ *si tu*

Sonam Chöpel *bsod nams chos 'phel*

Sonam Tsering *bsod nams tshe ring*

Songtsen Gampo *srong btsan sgam po*

Sumpa Khenpo *sum pa mkhan po*

Takten *rtag brtan*

Tendzin Pelgyé *bstan 'dzin 'phel rgyas*

thangka *thang ka*

Thrangu *khra 'gu*

Tipupa *ti pu pa*

Tongkhor *stong 'khor*

Trabur Gön *khra 'bur dgon*

Trashi Chöpel Ling *bkra shis chos 'phel gling*

Trashilhünpo *bkra shis lhun po*

Trenka Pelgi Yönten *bran ka dpal gyi yon tan*

Tri Desongtsen *khri lde srong btsan*

Tri Detsukten *khri lde gtsug brtan*

Tri Songdetsen *khri srong lde'u btsan*

Tri Tsukdetsen *khri gtsug lde b(r)tsan*

Trika *khri ka*

Trimön *khri smon*

Trinlé Gyatso *'phrin las rgya mtsho*

trülku *sprul sku*

Tsang *gtsang*

Tsangpa desi *gtsang pa sde srid*

Tsangyang Gyatso *tshangs dbyangs rgya mtsho*

Tsarong *tsha rong*

tsema *tshad ma*

tsenpo *btsan po*

Tsering Samdrub *tshe ring bsam grub*

Tsishak *tsi shag*

Tso'ngön *mtsho sngon*

Tsongkha *tsong kha*

Tsongkhapa *tsong kha pa*

Tsonying *mtsho snying*

Tsurpu *mtshur phu*

Tuken *thu'u bkwan*

Tungsi Lama *thung si bla ma*

Tupten Nyima *thub bstan nyi ma*

Ü *dbus*

wang *dbang*

Wangchuk Dorjé *dbang phyug rdo rje*

Washül khangsar *wa shul khang gsar*

Welmang Könchok Gyeltsen *dbal mang dkon mchog rgyal mtshan*

Wokmin Ling *'og min gling*

yabyum *yab yum*

Yarmotang *dbyar/g.yar/g.yer mo thang*

yidam *yi dam*

yombokshing *yo(m) 'bog shing*

yomboktang *yo 'bog thang*

yutsel *g.yu tshal*

Zamtsa *zam tsha*

Zhamar *zhwa dmar*

Zhang Lhazang *zhang lha bzang*
Zhang Trisumjé *zhang khri sum rje*
Zhangpa *zhang pa*
Zhangpa Gön *zhang pa dgon*
Zhangpa Lodrö Gyeltsen *zhang pa blo gros rgyal mtshan*

Zhijepa *Zhi byed pa*
Zungchu(-kha) *zung chu kha*
Zurmang Penam *Zur mang Pad rnam*

Chinese Glossary

Ahan 阿含
an chuan zhan 安川戰
anju 安居
Anjue (si) 安覺寺
An Lushan 安祿山
Anqin duokengjiang 安欽多鏗鏘
Anqin s'hangshi 安欽上師
Anxi 安西

Bai cai shen 白財神
Bai san'gai fomu 白傘蓋佛母
Baishacun 白沙村
Baitasi 白塔寺
Bao 保
Bao kanbu 寶堪布
baoen 報恩
Baoningsi 寶寧寺
Basalawarmi 把匝剌瓦爾密
Batang 巴塘
bei 悲
Beiding 北定
Beihai 北海
Beihai gongyuan 北海公園
Beijing 北京
Beiping 北平

Beiting 北庭
beixin 悲心
Beiyu miao 北獄廟
benjue 本覺
benlai qingjing 本來清淨
benran 本然
Benzilan 奔子蘭
Bi jian 陛見
bian'e 匾額
Bianneng 遍能
Bianru tian 遍入天
Bichu jie shi 芯芻戒釋
bingbu 兵部
Binglingsi 炳灵寺
boluomiduo 波羅蜜多
bu 部
bu shen xian hanyu 不甚嫻漢語
bu zhi you suo qianche 不至有所
　牽扯
Buh He 布哈河
busa 布薩

caibi 綵幣
Cao 曹
Cao Yangong 曹延恭

423

Cao Yanjing 曹延敬
Cao Yuanzhong 曹元忠
CC-xi CC 系
Chan 禪
chanshi 禪師
Chang'an Temple 長安寺
changchou dan 長壽丹
changchou ping 長壽瓶
Changhao 常浩
Changjiang 長江
Changsha 長沙
chanhui 懺悔
chanshi 禪師
Chaoyi 超一
che 扯
chen 臣
Chen Guofu 陳果夫
Chen Lifu 陳立夫
cheng shun zan hua xi tian da shan zizai fo 誠順讚化西天大善自在佛
Cheng weishi lun shuyi 成唯識論疏翼
Chengdu 成都
Chengdu Xi'nan heping fahui tekan 成都西南和平法會特刊
Chenghua 成化
Chenghuang miao 城隍廟
chengjiu 成就
chiming 持明
Chongqing 重慶
Chujing zhanzang 初敬占藏
Chuoling 綽領
chushi wei zhuang 杵勢偉壯
chushi xiangshang shuli 杵勢向上豎立

ci 慈
ci tu 此土
Cigu 慈顧
Cisheng'an 慈聖庵
Cixi 慈禧
cixin 慈心
Ciyuan 慈願
Cunzhao congqian jiu zhi 循照從前旧制
Cuona xian 錯那縣

Da bai san'gai fomu 大白傘蓋佛母
Da shou yin fa yao 大手印法要
dabao 大寶
Dabao fawang 大寶法王
Dabaojigong 大寶積宮
Dabaosi 大寶寺
dacheng jie 大乘戒
Dacheng qixin lun 大乘起信論
Dacheng yaodao miji 大乘要道秘集
dachengdao 大成道
Dadingge 大定閣
Daheitian shen 大黑天神
Dahuisi 大慧寺
Dai Jin 戴进
Dajianlu 打箭鑪
Dajielin 達結林
Dajuegong 大覺宮
Dajuesi 大覺寺
Dali guo 大理國
Damosi 達摩寺
Danba 丹巴
Dangjiquejia 當己卻甲
Danpeilin 丹培林
Dao 道

dashan fawang 大善法王

Dashidian 大師殿

Dashilun shangshi xiangying fa 大時輪上師相應法

Datong fangguang jing 大通方廣經

Dawa Sangdu Gexi Lama 達瓦桑杜格西喇嘛

Dawangchu shenmiao 達王初神廟

Daweide 大威德

Daweide dian 大威德殿

Daweide fa 大威德法

Daweide shisanzun yigui 大威德十三尊儀軌

Daweide wushang micheng fatong 大威德無上密乘法統

Daweide yizun chengjiu fa 大威德一尊成就法

Daxia 大夏

Daxiong bao dian 大雄寶殿

Dayanzhen 大研鎮

Dayong 大勇

Dayuanman zuisheng xinzhongxin yindao lueyao 大圓滿最勝心中心引導略要

Dazhou Jingangzhi 大咒金剛持

Dazizai tian 大自在天

Dechang men 德昌門

Dege 德格

Dengke 鄧柯

Dengxin 澄心

Deqin 德欽

dijun 帝君

ding 定

Ding Yu 丁玉

Dishi 帝釋

dishi 帝師

dizhu 地主

Dongbao fawang 東寶法王

Dongzhi Gate 東直門

Duban Chuan Dian bianwu dachen 督辦川滇邊務大臣

dudu 都督

dugang 都綱

dujiche 獨吉扎

Dumu 度母

Dunhuang 敦煌

Dunhuang Yanjiu Suo 敦煌研究所

Duobaojiangsi 多寶講寺

Duojiejueba gexi 多傑覺拔格西

Edunpincuolin 額敦品措林

Emeishan 峨嵋山

Emingnangzhulin 俄命囊珠林

Erbao fawang 二寶法王

Faguang 法光

Fahaisi 法海寺

faluo 法螺

Famensi 法門寺

Fang Guoyu 方國瑜

fanqie 反切

Fantian 梵天

Fanwang jing 梵網經

Faxiang 法相

faxin 發心

faxin siwuliang song 發心四無量頌

Fayin 法音

Fayun'ge 法雲閣

Fazun 法尊

Feilaifeng 飛來峰

feixing zun 飛行尊

fenbie 分別

fennu 忿怒

Fo xue she 佛學社

Fojiao jushilin 佛教居士林

Foli 佛曆

fomu 佛母

Fomu dajing yao kongque mingwang jing 佛母大經耀孔雀明王經

Foshuo dabai san'gai zongchi tuoluoni jing 佛說大白傘蓋總持陀羅尼經

foye 佛爺

Foyuan 佛源

Fu 府

fubao shan'gen 福報善根

Fudi difang 福地地方

Fudoutong 副都統

Fuguosi 福國寺

gang 綱

Gannan 甘南

Gansu 甘肅

Gansu shiku yishu bihua bian 甘肅石窟藝術壁畫編

Ganzhou 甘州

Ganzi 甘孜

Ganzi zangzu zizhizhou 甘孜藏族自治州

Gaoseng zhuan 高僧傳

Gecanlin 噶參林

genben 根本

Geng Yufang 耿域芳

Gensang Zecheng shangshi 根桑澤程上師

Gere nü 各熱女

gexi 格西

Gong Xueguang 龔學光

Gongga hutuketu 貢噶呼圖克圖

Gongga jingang shangshi 貢噶金剛上師

Gongga shan 貢噶山

Gongshan 貢山

gongyang 供養

guan 觀

Guan Yu 關羽

Guan Xuexuan 管學宣

guanding 灌頂

guanding fo 灌頂佛

guanding sheng 灌頂聖

Guangdong 廣東

Guangshengsi 廣膡寺

Guangxi 廣西

Guangxu 光緒

Guangzhaisi 光宅寺

Guankong 觀空

guantang 管堂

Guanyin Pumen 觀音普門

Guanyin'ge 觀音閣

Guanyintang 觀音堂

Guazhou 瓜州

Gui 跪

Guihua 歸化

guiyi jie 歸依戒

Guiyitang 皈依堂

Gulugule/Guluguli 沽嚕沽勒/姑嚕姑力

Guo Dalie 郭大烈

Guo Ziyi 郭子儀

Guomindang 國民黨

Guoping 果平

guoshi 國師

guowu bu shi 過午不食

guoyin 國音

Guxili Gunque duoji 古冼里袞卻多吉

guzong 古宗

Guzong Guchang 古宗古昌

hada 哈達

hai 海

Han 漢

Han Jingqing 韓鏡清

Han Qingjing 韓清淨

Hanchuan Fojiao 漢傳佛教

Handong 罕東

Hangzhou 杭州

Hankou 漢口

Hanzu lama 漢族喇嘛

He Beiheng 何北衡

He Suonanpu 何鎖南普

He Zairui 和在瑞

Henan Foxue she 河南佛學社

Heqing 鶴慶

heshang 和尚

Hexi 河西

hexiu 合修

Hezhou 河州

hong jiao chanshi 弘教禪師

Honglusi 鴻臚寺

Hu Tan 胡坦

Hu Zihu 胡子笏

Hua bei jushilin 華北居士林

huagong guzong Gu Chang 畫工古宗古昌

Huahua Fojiao 華化佛教

huahua gongzi 花花公子

Huang Yongquan 黃湧泉

Huanglong si 黃龍寺

Huangsi 黃寺

huangtu ceng 黃土層

huashen 化身

Huayan 華嚴

Huayan jing 華嚴經

Huayansi 華嚴寺

hubu 户部

hufa 護法

hufa hufang 護法護方

Hufa qielan 護法伽籃

hufa shen 護法神

hufang 護方

Hufatang 護法堂

hui 慧

humo 護摩

Hunan 湖南

Huo Taohui 霍韜晦

Huofatang 獲法堂

huofo 活佛

hutuketu 呼圖克圖

Huyan Jingfu 虎嚴淨伏

ji 集

ji sheng cheng fo 即生成佛

Jia na ba 嘉那巴

Jia na hua 加那华

jiachen 甲辰

jiachi 加持

Jiajing 嘉靖

Jiaju'er 迦居爾

jian 間

Jian Fu 劍夫

Jian Mushi xunci ziji 建木氏勛祠自記

Jianchuan 劍川

Jianchuan shiku 劍川石窟

Jiang Jieshi 蔣介石

Jiangba Gezun 降巴格尊

Jiangxi 江西

Jiangyang 降陽

jiao ("extirpiration") 剿

jiao ("ten cents") 角

Jiaxiasi 嘉夏寺

jiaxing 加行

Jiaxing tang 加行堂

jie 戒

jielü 戒律

Jietoulin 解脫林

Jilejingshe 極樂精舍

Jimi 羈縻

Jincheng (princess) 金城公主

Jincisi 金慈寺

jingang daochang 金剛道場

Jingang shangshi nuomoqi kanbu daoranba Luobucang sangbu 金剛上師諸姆啟堪布道然巴羅布倉桑步

Jingang shangshi Tudeng lima 金剛上師吐登利嘛

Jingang shangshi 金剛上師

Jingang yuan 金剛院

Jingangdian 金剛殿

Jingangshou 金剛手

jingjie hongci guoshi 淨戒弘慈國師

Jingzang 經藏

Jinman lun 金鬘論

Jinsha jiang 金沙江

jinzhi 進詣

jiren 吉人

jishizhong 給事中

Jiu ju shancheng 九局善程

Jiu Tang shu 舊唐書

Jiuhe shenmiao 九河神廟

Jiuhuashan 九華山

Jixi 輯熙

jixiang yuan 吉祥願

Jixiangsi 吉祥寺

Jixiangtian 吉祥天

jizan 偈讚

Jizushan 雞足山

Jizushan zhi 雞足山志

Judian 巨甸

jushe 俱舍

Jushengsi 具聖寺

ka 喀

Kadasi 卡達寺

kaibiao 開示

Kaifeng 開封

Kan Lin 闞琳

kanbu 堪布

Kangding 康定

Kangsa 康薩

Kangsisi 康司寺

kangzhuma 康竹馬

kaozheng 考證

ketou 磕頭

kewai 課外

Kongque mingwang 孔雀明王

Kongque mingwang fahui tu 孔雀明王法會圖

kongxing nü 空行女

Kou xie 叩謝

Kuiji 窺基

Kunming 昆明

kunti 坤體

Laijingsi 來景寺

Laiyuansi 來遠寺

Lama Renboqing 喇嘛仁波卿

Langqu 滇藻

lao kanbu 老堪布

Lasa 拉萨

Leiyinsi 雷音寺

Li 礼

Li An 李安

Li Bingquan 李冰詮

Li Jiang 李絳

Li Jishen 李濟深

Li Kunsheng 李昆聲

Li Weiqing 李偉卿

Li Xu 李旭

Li Zai 李在

Li Zongren 李宗仁

Liangzhou 涼州

Lianhua youxi zizai zhihui wubian dashi 蓮花遊戲自在智慧無邊大師

Liba 離叭 / 黎巴

Liba Lama 離叭剌麻

Lijiang 麗江

Lijiang tusi 麗江土司

Lijiang xian Naxi Dongba wenhua bowuguan 麗江納西東巴文化博物館

Lijiang xian Wenhua Guan 麗江縣文化官

Lijiang zhifu 麗江知府

lin 林

Lin'an 臨安

Lingwu 靈武

Lingyin si 靈隱寺

Lingzhou 靈州

Linji 臨濟

Linji Yixuan 臨濟義玄

Linxia 臨夏

Linzhaosi 林昭寺

Litang 理塘

Litangsi 理塘寺

Liu Liqian 劉立千

Liu Wenhui 劉文輝

Liu Xiang 劉湘

Liu Xiaolan 劉孝蘭

Liu Yuanding 劉元鼎

Liulidian 琉璃殿

liuxue 留學

liuxue yu Xizang; xue cheng, fan chuan zuguo 留學於西藏; 學成, 返傳祖國

liyan 例言

long 礱

Long Yun 龍雲

Longguo 隆果

Longlian 隆蓮

Lü 律

Lü Cheng 呂澂

Lu shan 盧山

Lü Tiegang 呂鐵剛

luocha 羅剎

Luosuo 邏娑

Luozhi'er jianzang 羅只兒監藏

Lushan 盧山

Ma Xiaoxian 馬尚仙

Mahagana 馬哈嘎拿 / 瑪哈嘎那

Mahākāla 瑪哈噶拉 / 瑪哈嘎拉

mahuiceng 抹灰層

mai 脈

mamu 麻母

Manchukuo [Manzhouguo] 滿洲國

Mangkong (fashi) 滿空 (法師)

mantuluo 曼荼羅

manyi 蠻夷

Mao 茂

Mengzang weiyuan hui 蒙藏委員會

Mian chen Xizang qingxing 面陳西
藏情形

Mian zou le Xizang qingxing 面奏了
西藏情形

Miaogao si 妙高寺

Miaoyin nü 妙音女

miaozhi tongwu guoshi 妙智通悟國
師

micheng 密乘

Micheng bao zang 密乘寶藏

Micheng fahai 密乘法海

micheng jingang daochang 密乘金剛
道場

mijiao 密教

mijiao fuxing yundong 密教復興運動

mijiao re 密教熱

mijie 密戒

ming 名

Ming 明

Ming Chengzu 明成祖

Ming shilu 明實錄

Ming Shizong 明世宗

Ming Taizu 明太祖

Ming Wanli Mu tusi 明萬曆木土司

Ming Wuzong 明武宗

Ming Xianzong 明憲宗

Ming xing dao liu cheng jiu fa 明行道
六成就法

Ming Yingzong 明英宗

Mingdai Lijiang bihua 明代麗江壁
畫

mingdian 明點

Mingjue shangshi 明覺上師

mingwang 明王

Minjiang 岷江

Mizang yuan 密藏院

mizhou 密咒

Mizhou fazang si 密咒法藏寺

mizong daochang 密宗道場

Mizong wubai foxiang kao 密宗五百
佛像考

Mogao 莫高

Mosuo 摩梭

Mu 木

Mu Chang 木昌

Mu Chu 木初

Mu Ding 木定

Mu Gao 木高

Mu Gong 木公

Mu Guanyin shenmiao 木觀音神廟

Mu Qin 木嶔

Mu Sheng 沐晟

mu shui yang nian liu yue chu san ji
xiang ruyi 母水羊年六月初三吉
祥如意

Mu taishou ci 木太守祠

Mu Wang 木旺

Mu Yi 木懿

Mu Ying 沐英

Mu Zeng 木增

Mu Zhong 木仲

Muli 木里

Mulian 目連

Mushi tusi 木氏土司

Mushi xunci 木氏勛祠

Mutai shouci 木太守祠

Nanchang 南昌

Nangri Lingzhan xing 囊日領占省

Nanjing 南京

Nanwu amitafo hui 南無阿彌陀佛會

Nanwu daoshi rulai haihui 南無道師
如來海會

Nanwu daweide haihui 南無大威德
海會

Nanzhao (guo) 南詔 (國)

Naxi 納西

neidi 內地

Nenghai 能海

Nian Gengyao 年羹堯

nianen 念恩

niantong 念通

Ningbo 寧波

Ningbo tongzhi 寧波統志

Niseluo 尼色落

Nuona huofo 諾那活佛

Nuona Hutuketu 諾那呼圖克圖

*Nuona Hutuketu Nanjing jinian ban-
shi chu wei chengbao Nuona jian
ta xu kuan ji yiwu chuzhi deng shi
yu mengzang weiyuanhui laiwang
han (gong si jian)* 諾那呼圖克圖南
京紀年辦事處為呈報諾那建塔需款及
遺物處置等事與藏委員會來往函（共
四件）

Nuona Hutuketu zhu jing banshi
chu 諾那呼圖克圖駐京辦事處

Nuona Hutuketu zhu Kangding
banshi chu 諾那呼圖克圖駐康定
辦事處

Ouyang Jian 歐陽漸

Pan Wenhua 潘文華

Panbo yan 盼波彥

Pilu yigui 毗盧儀軌

Pilusi 毘盧寺

ping Qiang jiangjun 平羌將軍

pingmin 平民

piposhena 毗婆舍那

Pishamen 毗沙門

Poma jia'erpo 珀瑪迦爾波

Poyang hu 鄱陽湖

Puchao 普超

Puhuasi 普化寺

Pujiang 浦江

Pujisi 普濟寺

Pumi 普米

Pusa jie shi 菩薩戒釋

Puti dao cidi 菩提道次第

Puti dao cidi guang lun 普提道次第
廣論

Puti dao cidi kesong 菩提道次第科頌

Puti dao cidi she song luejie 普提道次
第攝頌略解

Puti dao cidi xiufa biji 普提道次第修
法筆記

Puti xuehui 菩提學會

Putijingang ta 普提金剛塔

Putuoshan 普陀山

*Puxian wang rulai dayuanman xin-
yao zongji* 普賢王如來大圓滿心
要總集

Puyi 溥儀

qi 氣
Qi 祁
Qi Quan 祁全
qian duyushi 僉都御史
Qiang 羌
Qianlong 乾隆
Qiming 祁命 /祈命
Qin 秦
Qin wang 亲王
Qing 清
qing ru jing 請入境
Qingding 清定
Qingfo 請佛
Qinghai 青海
Qingliangqiao Jixianglüyuan 清涼橋
吉祥律院
Qingquan 清泉
Qingshu 慶恕
Qingshui 清水
qingxiu guanghui guoshi 清修廣惠
國師
Qinzeng shangshi 親增上師
Qinzheng dian 勤政殿
qishi gui 起屍鬼
Quan Rixiang 全日香
Quanguo renmin daibiao dahui 全國
人民代表大會
queba 卻巴
Qutansi 瞿曇寺

Ranna xiri 然那西日
Raojielin 饒介林
Renci 仁慈
Renguang 仁光
Renpo xierao shizi shi 仁波寫饒獅
子師

Renshou dian 仁壽殿
renyun chengjiu zhihui xianqian 任運
成就智慧現前
Rong 戎
Rongkong 融空
Rongtong 融通
Ru Zhonglun 入中論
rumen yaodao 入門要道
ruyi 如意

San guan 三官
San gui jiu kou li 三跪九叩禮
San zhuyao dao 三主要道
sanbao 三寶
sanguiyi 三歸依
Sanguiyi guan 三歸依觀
Sangzhudajielin 桑珠達結林
Sanla 三剌
Sanlun 三論
Sanqing 三清
Sanshi xuehui 三時學會
Seke shangshi 色喀上師
Shami tang 沙彌堂
Shanbasi 山巴寺
Shandong 山東
Shang Jiezan 尚結贊
Shang Tazang 尚塔藏
Shangba Luozhier jianzang 商巴羅
只兒監藏
Shangbasi 商巴寺
Shanghai 上海
Shanghai Jingang daochang 上海金
剛道場
shangshi 上師
Shangshi gong 上師供

Shangshi Xizang rongzeng kanbu 上師西藏榮增堪布

shangzuo 上座

Shanhui Chijiao zengguang 善慧持教增廣

shanwu guanding guoshi 善悟灌頂國師

Shaocheng foxue she 少城佛學社

she 舍

shemota 奢摩他

Shengmu 聖母

shengqi cidi 生起次第

shentong shouyu 神通守禦

Shenyang 沈陽

shifang conglin 十方叢林

Shigu 石鼓

Shiji 史記

Shijing (si) 石經 (寺)

shilu 石綠

Shilun jingang 時輪金剛

Shimen guan 石門關

shiqing 石清

Shizong 世宗

shou bajie jie 受八戒偈

Shouguosi 壽國寺

Shouxing 壽星

Shuhe 束河

shuilu 水陸

Shuotie 说帖

Si tian wang 四天王

si wuliang xin 四無量心

sibao 四寶

sibao fawang 四寶法王

sichan 四禪

Sichuan 四川

Sifen lü 四分律

simiao zhi huibian 寺廟志匯編

Song (dynasty) 宋

Song (region near Zung chu) 松

song jie 誦戒

Song Limen 宋禮門

Songpan 松潘

Songpan dengchu anfusi 松潘等處安撫司

Songpan you qianhusuo qianhu 松潘右千戶所千戶

Songpan zhenshou du zhihui tongzhi 松潘鎮守都指揮同知

Songzhou 松州

Songzhusi 嵩祝寺

Sun Jingfeng 孫景風

Suo 所

Suzong 肅宗

Tabailiezhenglin 塔白列爭林

Tacheng 塔城

Tagong 塔公

Taihe (princess) 太和公主

Taiji'an 太極庵

Taixu 太虛

Talaisi 他來寺

Tang 唐

Tang shu 唐書

Tang Xiangming 湯薌銘

tangkou 堂口

tangzhu 堂主

Tankuang 曇曠

Tanyan 曇延

Teqin dajie lin 特欽達結林

tian di shui sanguan 天地水三官

tianfei 天飛

Tiantai 天台

tianxia 天下

tieqiao 鐵橋

Tiexiangsi 鐵像寺

ting fu 挺腹

Tong Jinhua 童錦華

tongshi xuban 通事序班

Tongyi 通一

Tufan wenzi bei 土蕃文字碑

tusi 土司

Wandegong 萬德宮

Wang Ao 王翱

Wang Desheng 王德生

Wang Jiaqi 王家齊

Wang Sen 王森

Wang Xuance 王玄策

Wang Yantao 王岩濤

Wang Yao 王堯

Wang Zhiping 王治平

Wanli 萬曆

Wannian(si) 萬年寺

Wanshoudian 萬壽殿

wei 衛

Wei 威

weishi xue 唯識學

Weixi 維西

Wenchang 文昌

Wenchanggong 文昌宮

Wencheng (princess) 文城公主

Wenfengsi 文峰寺

Weng yama raza saduomaiya 嗡雅馬日*阿雜薩埵麥雅

wenshi ziliao 文史資料

Wenshu fa 文殊法

Wenshu lama 文殊喇嘛

Wenshuyuan 文殊院

wo guo 我國

wu da jingang 五大金剛

wu dabu 五大部

Wu Jialiang 吳家樑

Wu pusa 五菩薩

Wu Runjiang 吳潤江

Wu Shisi 吳世思

Wu Yue 吳越

Wuchang 武昌

Wuchang foxue yuan 武昌佛學院

Wugou jingguang fo 無垢淨光佛

wujie jie 五戒偈

Wuliexian shenci 吳烈仙神祠

Wutaishan 五台山

Wuzi zhenyan 五字真言

xi 喜

Xi tian da shan zizai fo 西天大善自在佛

Xi Xia 西夏

Xiahe 夏河

Xi'an 西安

Xiangfusi 祥符寺

xianghua tuguan fanseng 向化土官番僧

xianghua yun jie 香花雲偈

Xiangshan 香山

xianguan 現觀

Xianguan zhuangyan lun 現觀莊嚴論

xianjiao 顯教

xianmi shuangxiu 顯密雙修

Xianxue 先學

xianzheng 現證

Xianzheng zhuangyan lun 現證莊嚴論

Xianzong 憲宗

Xiao Hua 蕭華

Xiao Shangba 小商巴

xiaocheng jie 小乘戒

Xiaoxian 肖仙

xiaozai huguo 消災護國

xiazuo 下座

Xibei Minzu Yanjiu 西北民族研究

Xidaruo 悉答爇

Xifan 西蕃

Xihuangsi 西黃寺

Xihuasi 喜化寺

Xikang 西康

Xikang Nuona Hutuketu zhu jing banshi chu 西康諾那呼圖克圖駐京辦事處

Xikang xuanwei shi 西康宣慰使

Xin Tang shu 新唐書

Xinan minzu xueyuan 西南民族學院

xing 姓

Xingfa 興法

xingkong weiming 性空唯名

Xingshan 興善

xingxiu 星宿

Xining Senggangsi 西寧僧綱司

Xinjiang 新疆

Xintang 新塘

xinzhou 心咒

Xiong Shili 熊十力

Xitanshensi 悉檀神寺

Xitansi 悉檀寺

Xiyuan'an 西園庵

Xizang Biebang si gexi nuomenhan da lama duojie jueba zunzhe 西藏別蚌寺格西諾們罕大喇嘛多傑覺拔尊者

Xizong 熹宗

Xu Fancheng 徐梵澄

Xuan Zhengyuan 宣政院

Xuantong 宣統

Xuanzang 玄奘

Xuanzheng yuan 宣政院

Xuejie tang 學戒堂

Xueshi tang 學事堂

Xuesong'an 雪嵩庵

xunan yushi 巡按御史

xuwang weishi 虛妄唯識

Ya'an 雅安

Yanding 嚴定

Yang Huaqun 楊化群

Yang Lianzhenjia 楊璉真加

Yang Xuezheng 楊學政

Yang Zhou 楊周

Yangguan (Lane) 羊管胡同

Yangxi 漾西

yecha 夜叉

yema 野馬

Yema Nanshan 野馬南山

Yema Shan 野馬山

Yematan 野馬灘

Yemotang 耶摩塘

Yi jing yuan 譯經院

yigui 儀軌

Yihe yuan 頤和園

Yijing 義淨

Yijing 易經

Yingxianlou 迎仙樓

zhenchang weixin 真常唯心
zheng 證
Zhengde 正德
Zhengjue Hall (dian) 正覺殿
Zhenglin 正臨
Zhengtong 正統
zhengxie 政協
zhenshou du zhihui 鎮守都指揮
zhenshou Songpan du zhihui shi 鎮守松潘都指揮使
Zhenwu 真武
Zhenwuci 真武祠
Zhenwushan 真武山
Zhesun 者孫
zhifu 知府
zhiguan 止觀
Zhimeiba 支梅巴
Zhimin 智敏
zhimu 知母
Zhina neixue yuan 支那內學院
Zhishan 智山
Zhiyunsi 指雲寺
zhizhao 執照
Zhong kanbu 鍾堪布
Zhongdian 中甸
zhongguan 中觀

Zhongguo fojiao 中國佛教
Zhongguo Fojiao tushuguan 中國佛教圖書館
Zhongyang kejing yuan 中央刻經院
Zhongyang minzu xueyuan 中央民族學院
zhongzuo 中座
Zhou Shujia 周叔迦
zhuan xiu zhi suo 專修之所
zhuanshi 轉世
Zhuma Yingzhui 珠瑪英追
zhusha zhi zangwen jingdian 朱砂之藏文經典
zhuyin 註音
Ziguang ge 紫光閣
zita xianghuan 自他相換
Zixiasi 孜夏寺
Zizhaitan 子宅壇
zongbing guan dudu 總兵官都督
Zongjiao ju 宗教局
Zongkaba 宗喀巴
Zongkaba dashi dian 宗喀巴大師殿
Zongshui 宗水
Zongyuan 宗元
Zunzhe Luosang qiuji jiacang 尊者羅桑秋既嘉倉

Index

Clans and Tribes

Dalai Lama

Districts and Regions

**Divinities (Including Buddhas
and Bodhisattvas)**

Monasteries, Temples, and Other Religious Sites

Mountains

About Wisdom

WISDOM PUBLICATIONS is dedicated to making available authentic Buddhist works for the benefit of all. We publish translations of the sutras and tantras, commentaries and teachings of past and contemporary Buddhist masters, and original works by the world's leading Buddhist scholars. We publish our titles with the appreciation of Buddhism as a living philosophy and with the special commitment to preserve and transmit important works from all the major Buddhist traditions.

Wisdom Publications
199 Elm Street
Somerville, Massachusetts 02144 USA
Telephone: 617-776-7416
Fax: 617-776-7841
Email: info@wisdompubs.org
www.wisdompubs.org

Wisdom is a nonprofit, charitable 501(c)(3) organization affiliated with the Foundation for the Preservation of the Mahayana Tradition (FPMT)